Microsoft® Official Academic Course

Windows 7 Configuration, Exam 70-680

WILEY

Credits

EXECUTIVE EDITOR	John Kane
DIRECTOR OF SALES	Mitchell Beaton
EXECUTIVE MARKETING MANAGER	Chris Ruel
MICROSOFT SENIOR PRODUCT MANAGER	Merrick Van Dongen of Microsoft Learning
EDITORIAL PROGRAM ASSISTANT	Jennifer Lartz
PRODUCTION MANAGER	Micheline Frederick
PRODUCTION EDITOR	Kerry Weinstein
CREATIVE DIRECTOR	Harry Nolan
COVER DESIGNER	Jim O'Shea
TECHNOLOGY AND MEDIA	Tom Kulesa/Wendy Ashenberg

This book was set in Garamond by Aptara, Inc. and printed and bound by Bind Rite Graphics. The cover was printed by Phoenix Color.

Foreword from the Publisher

Wiley's publishing vision for the Microsoft Official Academic Course series is to provide students and instructors with the skills and knowledge they need to use Microsoft technology effectively in all aspects of their personal and professional lives. Quality instruction is required to help both educators and students get the most from Microsoft's software tools and to become more productive. Thus our mission is to make our instructional programs trusted educational companions for life.

To accomplish this mission, Wiley and Microsoft have partnered to develop the highest quality educational programs for Information Workers, IT Professionals, and Developers. Materials created by this partnership carry the brand name "Microsoft Official Academic Course," assuring instructors and students alike that the content of these textbooks is fully endorsed by Microsoft, and that they provide the highest quality information and instruction on Microsoft products. The Microsoft Official Academic Course textbooks are "Official" in still one more way—they are the officially sanctioned courseware for Microsoft IT Academy members.

The Microsoft Official Academic Course series focuses on *workforce development*. These programs are aimed at those students seeking to enter the workforce, change jobs, or embark on new careers as information workers, IT professionals, and developers. Microsoft Official Academic Course programs address their needs by emphasizing authentic workplace scenarios with an abundance of projects, exercises, cases, and assessments.

The Microsoft Official Academic Courses are mapped to Microsoft's extensive research and job-task analysis, the same research and analysis used to create the Microsoft Certified Technology Specialist (MCTS) exam. The textbooks focus on real skills for real jobs. As students work through the projects and exercises in the textbooks they enhance their level of knowledge and their ability to apply the latest Microsoft technology to everyday tasks. These students also gain resume-building credentials that can assist them in finding a job, keeping their current job, or in furthering their education.

The concept of lifelong learning is today an utmost necessity. Job roles, and even whole job categories, are changing so quickly that none of us can stay competitive and productive without continuously updating our skills and capabilities. The Microsoft Official Academic Course offerings, and their focus on Microsoft certification exam preparation, provide a means for people to acquire and effectively update their skills and knowledge. Wiley supports students in this endeavor through the development and distribution of these courses as Microsoft's official academic publisher.

Today educational publishing requires attention to providing quality print and robust electronic content. By integrating Microsoft Official Academic Course products and Microsoft certifications, we are better able to deliver efficient learning solutions for students and teachers alike.

Bonnie Lieberman

General Manager and Senior Vice President

Preface

Welcome to the Microsoft Official Academic Course (MOAC) program for Windows 7 Configuration. MOAC represents the collaboration between Microsoft Learning and John Wiley & Sons, Inc. publishing company. Microsoft and Wiley teamed up to produce a series of text-books that deliver compelling and innovative teaching solutions to instructors and superior learning experiences for students. Infused and informed by in-depth knowledge from the creators of Windows 7 and crafted by a publisher known worldwide for the pedagogical quality of its products, these textbooks maximize skills transfer in minimum time. Students are challenged to reach their potential by using their new technical skills as highly productive members of the workforce.

Because this knowledgebase comes directly from Microsoft, architect of Windows 7 and creator of the Microsoft Certified Technology Specialist exams (www.microsoft.com/learning/mcp/mcts), you are sure to receive the topical coverage that is most relevant to students' personal and professional success. Microsoft's direct participation not only assures you that MOAC textbook content is accurate and current; it also means that students will receive the best instruction possible to enable their success on certification exams and in the workplace.

■ The Microsoft Official Academic Course Program

The *Microsoft Official Academic Course* series is a complete program for instructors and institutions to prepare and deliver great courses on Microsoft software technologies. With MOAC, we recognize that, because of the rapid pace of change in the technology and curriculum developed by Microsoft, there is an ongoing set of needs beyond classroom instruction tools for an instructor to be ready to teach the course. The MOAC program endeavors to provide solutions for all these needs in a systematic manner in order to ensure a successful and rewarding course experience for both instructor and student—technical and curriculum training for instructor readiness with new software releases; the software itself for student use at home for building hands-on skills, assessment, and validation of skill development; and a great set of tools for delivering instruction in the classroom and lab. All are important to the smooth delivery of an interesting course on Microsoft software, and all are provided with the MOAC program. We think about the model below as a gauge for ensuring that we completely support you in your goal of teaching a great course. As you evaluate your instructional materials options, you may wish to use the model for comparison purposes with available products.

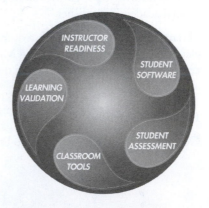

▪ Pedagogical Features

The MOAC textbook for Windows 7 Configuration is designed to cover all the learning objectives for that MCTS exam, which is referred to as its "objective domain." The Microsoft Certified Technology Specialist (MCTS) exam objectives are highlighted throughout the textbook. Many pedagogical features have been developed specifically for *Microsoft Official Academic Course* programs.

Presenting the extensive procedural information and technical concepts woven throughout the textbook raises challenges for the student and instructor alike. The Illustrated Book Tour that follows provides a guide to the rich features contributing to *Microsoft Official Academic Course* program's pedagogical plan. Following is a list of key features in each lesson designed to prepare students for success on the certification exams and in the workplace:

- Each lesson begins with an **Objective Domain Matrix**. More than a standard list of learning objectives, the Objective Domain Matrix correlates each software skill covered in the lesson to the specific MCTS exam objective domain.

- Concise and frequent Step-by-Step instructions teach students new features and provide an opportunity for hands-on practice. Numbered steps give detailed step-by-step instructions to help students learn software skills. The steps also show results and screen images to match what students should see on their computer screens.

- **Illustrations:** Screen images provide visual feedback as students work through the exercises. The images reinforce key concepts, provide visual clues about the steps, and allow students to check their progress.

- **Key Terms:** Important technical vocabulary is listed at the beginning of the lesson. When these terms are first used later in the lesson, they appear in bold italic type and are defined.

- Engaging point-of-use **Reader aids**, located throughout the lessons, tell students why this topic is relevant (*The Bottom Line*), provide students with helpful hints (*Take Note*), or show alternate ways to accomplish tasks (*Another Way*). Reader aids also provide additional relevant or background information that adds value to the lesson.

- **Certification Ready?** features throughout the text signal students where a specific certification objective is covered. They provide students with a chance to check their understanding of that particular MCTS exam objective and, if necessary, review the section of the lesson where it is covered.

- **Knowledge Assessments** provide progressively more challenging lesson-ending activities, including practice exercises and case scenarios.

- A **Lab Manual** accompanies this textbook package. The Lab Manual contains hands-on lab work corresponding to each of the lessons within the textbook. Numbered steps give detailed, step-by-step instructions to help students learn workplace skills associated with Windows 7. The labs are constructed using real-world scenarios to mimic the tasks students will see in the workplace.

■ Lesson Features

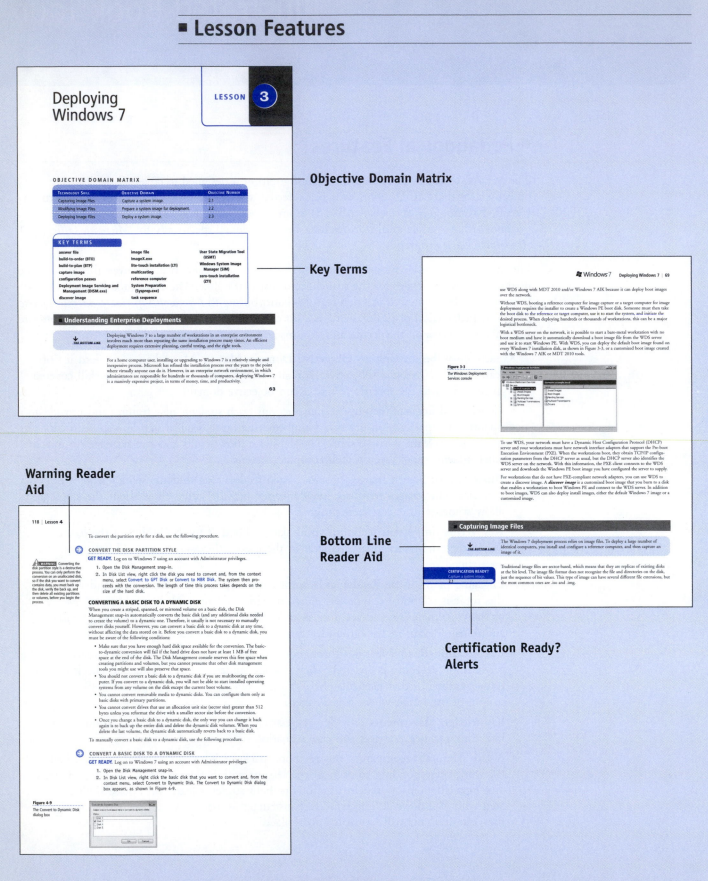

Objective Domain Matrix

Key Terms

Warning Reader Aid

Bottom Line Reader Aid

Certification Ready? Alerts

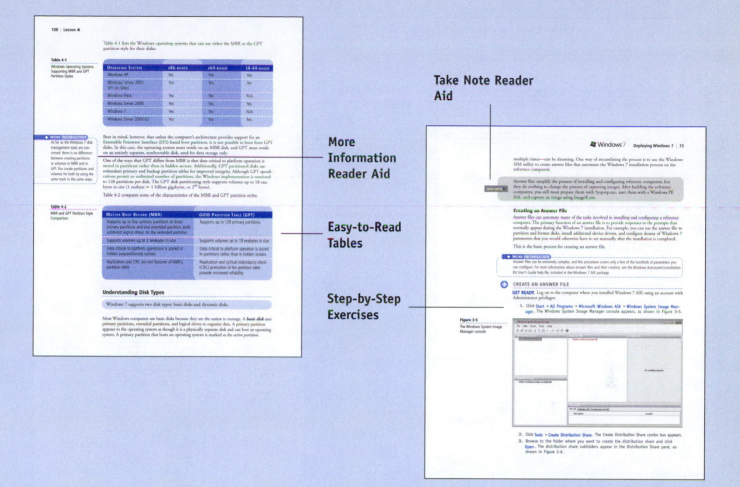

Take Note Reader Aid

More Information Reader Aid

Easy-to-Read Tables

Step-by-Step Exercises

Screen Images

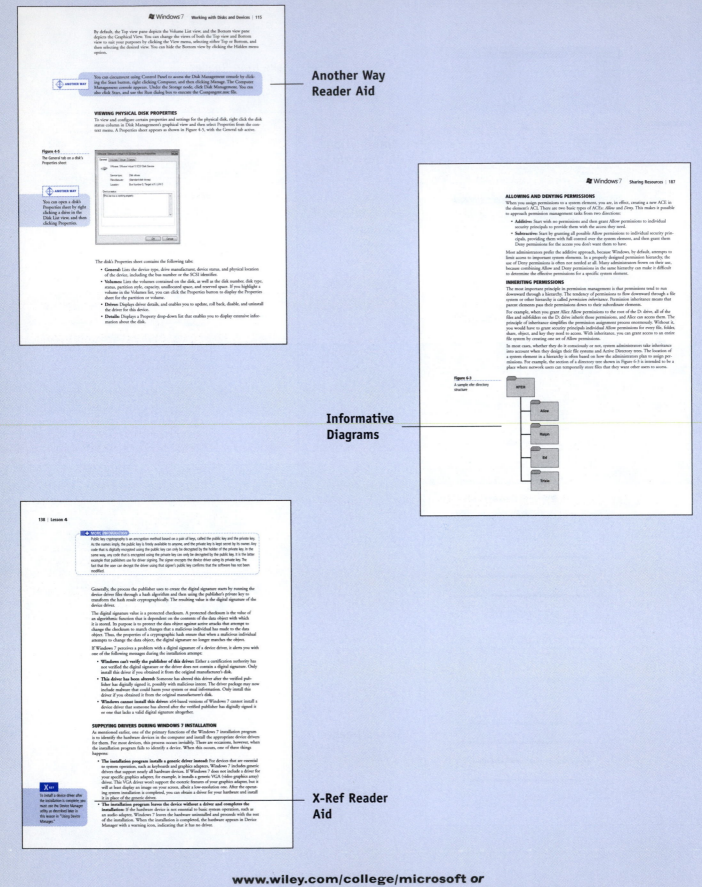

Another Way Reader Aid

Informative Diagrams

X-Ref Reader Aid

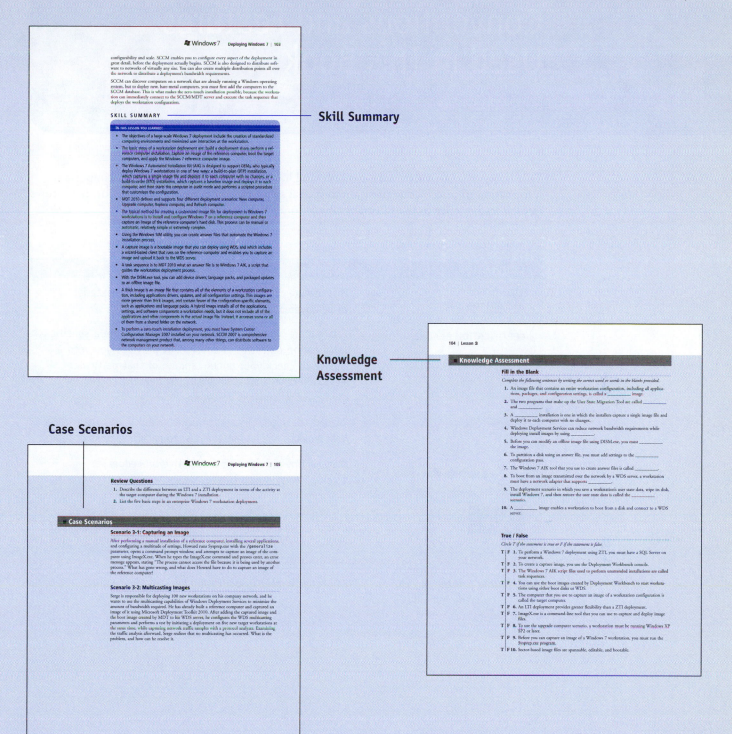

Skill Summary

Case Scenarios

Knowledge Assessment

Conventions and Features Used in This Book

This book uses particular fonts, symbols, and heading conventions to highlight important information or to call your attention to special steps. For more information about the features in each lesson, refer to the Illustrated Book Tour section.

CONVENTION	MEANING
↓ **THE BOTTOM LINE**	This feature provides a brief summary of the material to be covered in the section that follows.
CERTIFICATION READY?	This feature signals the point in the text where a specific certification objective is covered. It provides you with a chance to check your understanding of that particular MCTS objective and, if necessary, review the section of the lesson where it is covered.
TAKE NOTE *	Reader aids appear in shaded boxes found in your text. *Take Note* provides helpful hints related to particular tasks or topics.
⬥ **ANOTHER WAY**	*Another Way* provides an alternative procedure for accomplishing a particular task.
X REF	These notes provide pointers to information discussed elsewhere in the textbook or describe interesting features of Windows 7 that are not directly addressed in the current topic or exercise.
A *shared printer* can be used by many individuals on a network.	Key terms appear in bold italic on first appearance.

Instructor Support Program

The *Microsoft Official Academic Course* programs are accompanied by a rich array of resources that incorporate the extensive textbook visuals to form a pedagogically cohesive package. These resources provide all the materials instructors need to deploy and deliver their courses:

- Perhaps the most valuable resource for teaching this course is the software used in the course lab work. The **MSDN Academic Alliance (MSDN AA)** is designed to provide the easiest and most inexpensive developer tools, products, and technologies available to faculty and students in labs, classrooms, and on student PCs. A free 3-year membership to the MSDN AA is available to qualified MOAC adopters.

  Note: Windows 7 can be downloaded from MSDN AA for use by students in this course.

  Resources available online for download include:

- The **Instructor's Guide** contains solutions to all the textbook exercises as well as chapter summaries and lecture notes. The Instructor's Guide and Syllabi for various term lengths are available from the Book Companion site (www.wiley.com/college/microsoft).

- The **Test Bank** contains hundreds of questions organized by lesson in multiple-choice, true-false, short answer, and essay formats and is available to download from the Instructor's Book Companion site (www.wiley.com/college/microsoft). A complete answer key is provided.

- **PowerPoint Presentations and Images.** A complete set of PowerPoint presentations is available on the Instructor's Book Companion site (www.wiley.com/college/microsoft) to enhance classroom presentations. Tailored to the text's topical coverage and Skills Matrix, these presentations are designed to convey key Windows 7 concepts addressed in the text.

  All figures from the text are on the Instructor's Book Companion site (www.wiley.com/college/microsoft). You can incorporate them into your PowerPoint presentations or create your own overhead transparencies and handouts.

  By using these visuals in class discussions, you can help focus students' attention on key elements of the products being used and help them understand how to use them effectively in the workplace.

- When it comes to improving the classroom experience, there is no better source of ideas and inspiration than your fellow colleagues. The **Wiley Faculty Network** connects teachers with technology, facilitates the exchange of best practices, and helps to enhance instructional efficiency and effectiveness. Faculty Network activities include technology training and tutorials, virtual seminars, peer-to-peer exchanges of experiences and ideas, personal consulting, and sharing of resources. For details visit www.WhereFacultyConnect.com.

WileyPLUS

WileyPLUS is an innovative, research-based, online environment for effective teaching and learning.

What do Students Receive with *WileyPLUS*?

A Research-based Design. *WileyPLUS* provides an online environment that integrates relevant resources, including the entire digital textbook, in an easy-to-navigate framework that helps students study more effectively.

- *WileyPLUS* adds structure by organizing textbook content into smaller, more manageable "chunks".
- Related media, examples, and sample practice items reinforce the learning objectives.
- Innovative features such as calendars, visual progress tracking, and self-evaluation tools improve time management and strengthen areas of weakness.

One-on-one Engagement. With *WileyPLUS* for MOAC 70-680: Windows 7 Configuration, students receive 24/7 access to resources that promote positive learning outcomes. Students engage with related examples (in various media) and sample practice items specific to each lesson.

Measurable Outcomes. Throughout each study session, students can assess their progress and gain immediate feedback. *WileyPLUS* provides precise reporting of strengths and weaknesses, as well as individualized quizzes, so that students are confident they are spending their time on the right things. With *WileyPLUS*, students always know the exact outcome of their efforts.

What do Instructors Receive with *WileyPLUS*?

WileyPLUS provides reliable, customizable resources that reinforce course goals inside and outside of the classroom as well as visibility into individual student progress. Pre-created materials and activities help instructors optimize their time.

Customizable Course Plan: *WileyPLUS* comes with a pre-created Course Plan designed by a subject matter expert uniquely for this course. Simple drag-and-drop tools make it easy to assign the course plan as is or modify it to reflect your course syllabus.

Pre-created Activity Types Include:

- Questions
- Readings and resources
- Print Tests
- Projects

Course Materials and Assessment Content:

- Lecture Notes PowerPoint Slides
- Image Gallery
- Instructor's Guide
- Gradable Reading Assignment Questions (embedded with online text)
- Testbank

Gradebook: *WileyPLUS* provides instant access to reports on trends in class performance, student use of course materials, and progress toward learning objectives, helping inform decisions and drive classroom discussions.

***WileyPLUS*. Learn More. www.wileyplus.com.**

Powered by proven technology and built on a foundation of cognitive research, *WileyPLUS* has enriched the education of millions of students in over 20 countries around the world.

MSDN ACADEMIC ALLIANCE—FREE 3-YEAR MEMBERSHIP AVAILABLE TO QUALIFIED ADOPTERS!

The Microsoft Developer Network Academic Alliance (MSDN AA) is designed to provide the easiest and most inexpensive way for universities to make the latest Microsoft developer tools, products, and technologies available in labs, classrooms, and on student PCs. MSDN AA is an annual membership program for departments teaching Science, Technology, Engineering, and Mathematics (STEM) courses. The membership provides a complete solution to keep academic labs, faculty, and students on the leading edge of technology.

Software available in the MSDN AA program is provided at no charge to adopting departments through the Wiley and Microsoft publishing partnership.

As a bonus to this free offer, faculty will be introduced to Microsoft's Faculty Connection and Academic Resource Center. It takes time and preparation to keep students engaged while giving them a fundamental understanding of theory, and the Microsoft Faculty Connection is designed to help STEM professors with this preparation by providing articles, curriculum, and tools that professors can use to engage and inspire today's technology students.

Contact your Wiley rep for details.

For more information about the MSDN Academic Alliance program, go to:

msdn.microsoft.com/academic/

Note: Windows 7 can be downloaded from MSDN AA for use by students in this course.

Important Web Addresses and Phone Numbers

To locate the Wiley Higher Education Rep in your area, go to the following Web address and click on the "*Who's My Rep?*" link at the top of the page.

www.wiley.com/college

Or call the MOAC toll-free number: 1 + (888) 764-7001 (U.S. & Canada only).

To learn more about becoming a Microsoft Certified Professional and exam availability, visit www.microsoft.com/learning/mcp.

Student Support Program

Book Companion Web Site (www.wiley.com/college/microsoft)

The students' book companion site for the MOAC series includes any resources, exercise files, and Web links that will be used in conjunction with this course.

Wiley Desktop Editions

Wiley MOAC Desktop Editions are innovative, electronic versions of printed textbooks. Students buy the desktop version for 50% off the U.S. price of the printed text and get the added value of permanence and portability. Wiley Desktop Editions provide students with numerous additional benefits that are not available with other e-text solutions.

Wiley Desktop Editions are NOT subscriptions; students download the Wiley Desktop Edition to their computer desktops. Students own the content they buy to keep for as long as they want. Once a Wiley Desktop Edition is downloaded to the computer desktop, students have instant access to all of the content without being online. Students can also print the sections they prefer to read in hard copy. Students also have access to fully integrated resources within their Wiley Desktop Edition. From highlighting their e-text to taking and sharing notes, students can easily personalize their Wiley Desktop Edition as they are reading or following along in class.

Microsoft Visual Studio Software

As an adopter of a MOAC textbook, your school's department is eligible for a free three-year membership to the MSDN Academic Alliance (MSDN AA). Through MSDN AA, full versions of Windows 7 are available for your use with this course. See your Wiley rep for details.

Preparing to Take the Microsoft Certified Technology Specialist (MCTS) Exam

Microsoft Certified Technology Specialist

The new Microsoft Certified Technology Specialist (MCTS) credential highlights your skills using a specific Microsoft technology. You can demonstrate your abilities as an IT professional or developer with in-depth knowledge of the Microsoft technology that you use today or are planning to deploy.

The MCTS certifications enable professionals to target specific technologies and to distinguish themselves by demonstrating in-depth knowledge and expertise in their specialized technologies. Microsoft Certified Technology Specialists are consistently capable of implementing, building, troubleshooting, and debugging a particular Microsoft technology.

You can learn more about the MCTS program at www.microsoft.com/learning/mcp/mcts.

Preparing to Take an Exam

Unless you are a very experienced user, you will need to use a test preparation course to prepare to complete the test correctly and within the time allowed. The *Microsoft Official Academic Course* series is designed to prepare you with a strong knowledge of all exam topics, and with some additional review and practice on your own, you should feel confident in your ability to pass the appropriate exam.

After you decide which exam to take, review the list of objectives for the exam. You can easily identify tasks that are included in the objective list by locating the Lesson Skill Matrix at the start of each lesson and the Certification Ready sidebars in the margin of the lessons in this book.

To take an exam, visit www.microsoft.com/learning/mcp to locate your nearest testing center. Then call the testing center directly to schedule your test. The amount of advance notice you should provide will vary for different testing centers, and it typically depends on the number of computers available at the testing center, the number of other testers who have already been scheduled for the day on which you want to take the test, and the number of times per week that the testing center offers testing. In general, you should call to schedule your test at least two weeks prior to the date on which you want to take the test.

When you arrive at the testing center, you might be asked for proof of identity. A driver's license or passport is an acceptable form of identification. If you do not have either of these items of documentation, call your testing center and ask what alternative forms of identification will be accepted. If you are retaking a test, bring your identification number, which will have been given to you when you previously took the test. If you have not prepaid or if your organization has not already arranged to make payment for you, you will need to pay the test-taking fee when you arrive.

Acknowledgments

MOAC Instructor Advisory Board

We thank our Instructor Advisory Board, an elite group of educators who has assisted us every step of the way in building these products. Advisory Board members have acted as our sounding board on key pedagogical and design decisions leading to the development of these compelling and innovative textbooks for future Information Workers. Their dedication to technology education is truly appreciated.

Charles DeSassure, Tarrant County College

Charles DeSassure is Department Chair and Instructor of Computer Science & Information Technology at Tarrant County College Southeast Campus, Arlington, Texas. He has had experience as a MIS manager, system analyst, field technology analyst, LAN administrator, microcomputer specialist, and public school teacher in South Carolina. DeSassure has worked in higher education for more than ten years and received the Excellence Award in Teaching from the National Institute for Staff and Organizational Development (NISOD). He currently serves on the Educational Testing Service (ETS) iSkills National Advisory Committee and chaired the Tarrant County College District Student Assessment Committee. He has written proposals and makes presentations at major educational conferences nationwide. DeSassure has served as a textbook reviewer for John Wiley & Sons and Prentice Hall. He teaches courses in information security, networking, distance learning, and computer literacy. DeSassure holds a master's degree in Computer Resources & Information Management from Webster University.

Kim Ehlert, Waukesha County Technical College

Kim Ehlert is the Microsoft Program Coordinator and a Network Specialist instructor at Waukesha County Technical College, teaching the full range of MCSE and networking courses for the past nine years. Prior to joining WCTC, Kim was a professor at the Milwaukee School of Engineering for five years where she oversaw the Novell Academic Education and the Microsoft IT Academy programs. She has a wide variety of industry experience including network design and management for Johnson Controls, local city fire departments, police departments, large church congregations, health departments, and accounting firms. Kim holds many industry certifications including MCDST, MCSE, Security+, Network+, Server+, MCT, and CNE.

Kim has a bachelor's degree in Information Systems and a master's degree in Business Administration from the University of Wisconsin Milwaukee. When she is not busy teaching, she enjoys spending time with her husband Gregg and their two children—Alex and Courtney.

Penny Gudgeon, Corinthian Colleges, Inc.

Penny Gudgeon is the Program Manager for IT curriculum at Corinthian Colleges, Inc. Previously, she was responsible for computer programming and web curriculum for twenty-seven campuses in Corinthian's Canadian division, CDI College of Business, Technology and Health Care. Penny joined CDI College in 1997 as a computer programming instructor at one of the campuses outside of Toronto. Prior to joining CDI College, Penny taught productivity software at another Canadian college, the Academy of Learning, for four years. Penny has experience in helping students achieve their goals through various learning models from instructor-led to self-directed to online.

Before embarking on a career in education, Penny worked in the fields of advertising, marketing/sales, mechanical and electronic engineering technology, and computer programming. When not working from her home office or indulging her passion for lifelong learning, Penny likes to read mysteries, garden, and relax at home in Hamilton, Ontario, with her Shih-Tzu, Gracie.

Margaret Leary, Northern Virginia Community College

Margaret Leary is Professor of IST at Northern Virginia Community College, teaching Networking and Network Security Courses for the past ten years. She is the Co-Principal Investigator on the CyberWATCH initiative, an NSF-funded regional consortium of higher education institutions and businesses working together to increase the number of network security personnel in the workforce. She also serves as a Senior Security Policy Manager and Research Analyst at Nortel Government Solutions and holds a CISSP certification.

Margaret holds a B.S.B.A. and MBA/Technology Management from the University of Phoenix and is pursuing her Ph.D. in Organization and Management with an IT Specialization at Capella University. Her dissertation is titled "Quantifying the Discoverability of Identity Attributes in Internet-Based Public Records: Impact on Identity Theft and Knowledge-Based Authentication." She has several other published articles in various government and industry magazines, notably on identity management and network security.

Wen Liu, ITT Educational Services, Inc.

Wen Liu is Director of Corporate Curriculum Development at ITT Educational Services, Inc. He joined the ITT corporate headquarters in 1998 as a Senior Network Analyst to plan and deploy the corporate WAN infrastructure. A year later he assumed the position of Corporate Curriculum Manager supervising the curriculum development of all IT programs. After he was promoted to his current position three years ago, he continued to manage the curriculum research and development for all the programs offered in the School of Information Technology in addition to supervising the curriculum development in other areas (such as Schools of Drafting and Design and Schools of Electronics Technology). Prior to his employment with ITT Educational Services, Liu was a Telecommunications Analyst at the state government of Indiana working on the state backbone project that provided Internet and telecommunications services to the public users such as K-12 and higher education institutions, government agencies, libraries, and health-care facilities.

Wen Liu has an M.A. in Student Personnel Administration in Higher Education and an M.S. in Information and Communications Sciences from Ball State University, Indiana. He was formerly the director of special projects on the board of directors of the Indiana Telecommunications User Association, and used to serve on Course Technology's IT Advisory Board. He is currently a member of the IEEE and its Computer Society.

Jared Spencer, Westwood College Online

Jared Spencer has been the Lead Faculty for Networking at Westwood College Online since 2006. He began teaching in 2001 and has taught both on-ground and online for a variety of institutions, including Robert Morris University and Point Park University. In addition to his academic background, he has more than fifteen years of industry experience working for companies including the Thomson Corporation and IBM.

Jared has a master's degree in Internet Information Systems and is currently ABD and pursuing his doctorate in Information Systems at Nova Southeastern University. He has authored several papers that have been presented at conferences and appeared in publications such as the Journal of Internet Commerce and the Journal of Information Privacy and Security (JIPC). He holds a number of industry certifications, including AIX (UNIX), A+, Network+, Security+, MCSA on Windows 2000, and MCSA on Windows 2003 Server.

We thank Katherine James at Seneca College, Patrick Smith at Marshall Community and Technical College, Saraswathi Singh at National College, Ray Esparza at Glendale Community College, Gary Rollinson at Cabrillo College, Terry Williams at CDI College–Edmonton South Campus, Don Bowers at College of Western Idaho, Jason Eckert at triOS College, Ron Handlon at Remington College–Tampa, Derrell Harris at Okefenokee Technical College, and Jeff Riley for their diligent review and for providing invaluable feedback in the service of quality instructional materials.

Focus Group and Survey Participants

Finally, we thank the hundreds of instructors who participated in our focus groups and surveys to ensure that the Microsoft Official Academic Courses best met the needs of our customers.

Jean Aguilar, Mt. Hood Community College

Konrad Akens, Zane State College

Michael Albers, University of Memphis

Diana Anderson, Big Sandy Community & Technical College

Phyllis Anderson, Delaware County Community College

Judith Andrews, Feather River College

Damon Antos, American River College

Bridget Archer, Oakton Community College

Linda Arnold, Harrisburg Area Community College–Lebanon Campus

Neha Arya, Fullerton College

Mohammad Bajwa, Katharine Gibbs School–New York

Virginia Baker, University of Alaska Fairbanks

Carla Bannick, Pima Community College

Rita Barkley, Northeast Alabama Community College

Elsa Barr, Central Community College–Hastings

Ronald W. Barry, Ventura County Community College District

Elizabeth Bastedo, Central Carolina Technical College

Karen Baston, Waubonsee Community College

Karen Bean, Blinn College

Scott Beckstrand, Community College of Southern Nevada

Paulette Bell, Santa Rosa Junior College

Liz Bennett, Southeast Technical Institute

Nancy Bermea, Olympic College

Lucy Betz, Milwaukee Area Technical College

Meral Binbasioglu, Hofstra University

Catherine Binder, Strayer University & Katharine Gibbs School–Philadelphia

Terrel Blair, El Centro College

Ruth Blalock, Alamance Community College

Beverly Bohner, Reading Area Community College

Henry Bojack, Farmingdale State University

Matthew Bowie, Luna Community College

Julie Boyles, Portland Community College

Karen Brandt, College of the Albemarle

Stephen Brown, College of San Mateo

Jared Bruckner, Southern Adventist University

Pam Brune, Chattanooga State Technical Community College

Sue Buchholz, Georgia Perimeter College

Roberta Buczyna, Edison College

Angela Butler, Mississippi Gulf Coast Community College

Rebecca Byrd, Augusta Technical College

Kristen Callahan, Mercer County Community College

Judy Cameron, Spokane Community College

Dianne Campbell, Athens Technical College

Gena Casas, Florida Community College at Jacksonville

Jesus Castrejon, Latin Technologies

Gail Chambers, Southwest Tennessee Community College

Jacques Chansavang, Indiana University–Purdue University Fort Wayne

Nancy Chapko, Milwaukee Area Technical College

Rebecca Chavez, Yavapai College

Sanjiv Chopra, Thomas Nelson Community College

Greg Clements, Midland Lutheran College

Dayna Coker, Southwestern Oklahoma State University–Sayre Campus

Tamra Collins, Otero Junior College

Janet Conrey, Gavilan Community College

Carol Cornforth, West Virginia Northern Community College

Gary Cotton, American River College

Edie Cox, Chattahoochee Technical College

Rollie Cox, Madison Area Technical College

David Crawford, Northwestern Michigan College

J.K. Crowley, Victor Valley College

Rosalyn Culver, Washtenaw Community College

Sharon Custer, Huntington University

Sandra Daniels, New River Community College

Anila Das, Cedar Valley College

Brad Davis, Santa Rosa Junior College

Susan Davis, Green River Community College

Mark Dawdy, Lincoln Land Community College

Jennifer Day, Sinclair Community College

Carol Deane, Eastern Idaho Technical College

Julie DeBuhr, Lewis-Clark State College

Janis DeHaven, Central Community College

Drew Dekreon, University of Alaska–Anchorage

Joy DePover, Central Lakes College

Salli DiBartolo, Brevard Community College

Melissa Diegnau, Riverland Community College

Al Dillard, Lansdale School of Business

Marjorie Duffy, Cosumnes River College

Sarah Dunn, Southwest Tennessee Community College

Shahla Durany, Tarrant County College–South Campus

Kay Durden, University of Tennessee at Martin

Dineen Ebert, St. Louis Community College–Meramec

Donna Ehrhart, State University of New York–Brockport

Larry Elias, Montgomery County Community College

Glenda Elser, New Mexico State University at Alamogordo

Angela Evangelinos, Monroe County Community College

Angie Evans, Ivy Tech Community College of Indiana

Linda Farrington, Indian Hills Community College

Dana Fladhammer, Phoenix College

Richard Flores, Citrus College

Connie Fox, Community and Technical College at Institute of Technology West Virginia University

Wanda Freeman, Okefenokee Technical College

Brenda Freeman, Augusta Technical College

Susan Fry, Boise State University

Roger Fulk, Wright State University–Lake Campus

Sue Furnas, Collin County Community College District

Sandy Gabel, Vernon College

Laura Galvan, Fayetteville Technical Community College

Candace Garrod, Red Rocks Community College

Sherrie Geitgey, Northwest State Community College

Chris Gerig, Chattahoochee Technical College

Barb Gillespie, Cuyamaca College

Jessica Gilmore, Highline Community College

Pamela Gilmore, Reedley College

Debbie Glinert, Queensborough Community College

Steven Goldman, Polk Community College

Bettie Goodman, C.S. Mott Community College

Mike Grabill, Katharine Gibbs School–Philadelphia

Francis Green, Penn State University

Walter Griffin, Blinn College

Fillmore Guinn, Odessa College

Helen Haasch, Milwaukee Area Technical College

John Habal, Ventura College

Joy Haerens, Chaffey College

Norman Hahn, Thomas Nelson Community College

Kathy Hall, Alamance Community College

Teri Harbacheck, Boise State University

Linda Harper, Richland Community College

Maureen Harper, Indian Hills Community College

Steve Harris, Katharine Gibbs School–New York

Robyn Hart, Fresno City College

Darien Hartman, Boise State University

Gina Hatcher, Tacoma Community College

Winona T. Hatcher, Aiken Technical College

BJ Hathaway, Northeast Wisconsin Tech College

Cynthia Hauki, West Hills College–Coalinga

Mary L. Haynes, Wayne County Community College

Marcie Hawkins, Zane State College

Steve Hebrock, Ohio State University Agricultural Technical Institute

Sue Heistand, Iowa Central Community College

Heith Hennel, Valencia Community College

Donna Hendricks, South Arkansas Community College

Judy Hendrix, Dyersburg State Community College

Gloria Hensel, Matanuska-Susitna College University of Alaska Anchorage

Gwendolyn Hester, Richland College

Tammarra Holmes, Laramie County Community College

Dee Hobson, Richland College

Keith Hoell, Katharine Gibbs School–New York

Pashia Hogan, Northeast State Technical Community College

Susan Hoggard, Tulsa Community College

Kathleen Holliman, Wallace Community College Selma

Chastity Honchul, Brown Mackie College/Wright State University

Christie Hovey, Lincoln Land Community College

Peggy Hughes, Allegany College of Maryland

Sandra Hume, Chippewa Valley Technical College

John Hutson, Aims Community College

Celia Ing, Sacramento City College

Joan Ivey, Lanier Technical College

Barbara Jaffari, College of the Redwoods

Penny Jakes, University of Montana College of Technology

Eduardo Jaramillo, Peninsula College

Barbara Jauken, Southeast Community College

Susan Jennings, Stephen F. Austin State University

Leslie Jernberg, Eastern Idaho Technical College

Linda Johns, Georgia Perimeter College

Brent Johnson, Okefenokee Technical College

Mary Johnson, Mt. San Antonio College

Shirley Johnson, Trinidad State Junior College–Valley Campus

Sandra M. Jolley, Tarrant County College

Teresa Jolly, South Georgia Technical College

Dr. Deborah Jones, South Georgia Technical College

Margie Jones, Central Virginia Community College

Randall Jones, Marshall Community and Technical College

Diane Karlsbraaten, Lake Region State College

www.wiley.com/college/microsoft or
call the MOAC Toll-Free Number: 1+(888) 764-7001 (U.S. & Canada only)

Teresa Keller, Ivy Tech Community College of Indiana

Charles Kemnitz, Pennsylvania College of Technology

Sandra Kinghorn, Ventura College

Bill Klein, Katharine Gibbs School–Philadelphia

Bea Knaapen, Fresno City College

Kit Kofoed, Western Wyoming Community College

Maria Kolatis, County College of Morris

Barry Kolb, Ocean County College

Karen Kuralt, University of Arkansas at Little Rock

Belva-Carole Lamb, Rogue Community College

Betty Lambert, Des Moines Area Community College

Anita Lande, Cabrillo College

Junnae Landry, Pratt Community College

Karen Lankisch, UC Clermont

David Lanzilla, Central Florida Community College

Nora Laredo, Cerritos Community College

Jennifer Larrabee, Chippewa Valley Technical College

Debra Larson, Idaho State University

Barb Lave, Portland Community College

Audrey Lawrence, Tidewater Community College

Deborah Layton, Eastern Oklahoma State College

Larry LeBlanc, Owen Graduate School–Vanderbilt University

Philip Lee, Nashville State Community College

Michael Lehrfeld, Brevard Community College

Vasant Limaye, Southwest Collegiate Institute for the Deaf – Howard College

Anne C. Lewis, Edgecombe Community College

Stephen Linkin, Houston Community College

Peggy Linston, Athens Technical College

Hugh Lofton, Moultrie Technical College

Donna Lohn, Lakeland Community College

Jackie Lou, Lake Tahoe Community College

Donna Love, Gaston College

Curt Lynch, Ozarks Technical Community College

Sheilah Lynn, Florida Community College–Jacksonville

Pat R. Lyon, Tomball College

Bill Madden, Bergen Community College

Heather Madden, Delaware Technical & Community College

Donna Madsen, Kirkwood Community College

Jane Maringer-Cantu, Gavilan College

Suzanne Marks, Bellevue Community College

Carol Martin, Louisiana State University–Alexandria

Cheryl Martucci, Diablo Valley College

Roberta Marvel, Eastern Wyoming College

Tom Mason, Brookdale Community College

Mindy Mass, Santa Barbara City College

Dixie Massaro, Irvine Valley College

Rebekah May, Ashland Community & Technical College

Emma Mays-Reynolds, Dyersburg State Community College

Timothy Mayes, Metropolitan State College of Denver

Reggie McCarthy, Central Lakes College

Matt McCaskill, Brevard Community College

Kevin McFarlane, Front Range Community College

Donna McGill, Yuba Community College

Terri McKeever, Ozarks Technical Community College

Patricia McMahon, South Suburban College

Sally McMillin, Katharine Gibbs School–Philadelphia

Charles McNerney, Bergen Community College

Lisa Mears, Palm Beach Community College

Imran Mehmood, ITT Technical Institute–King of Prussia Campus

Virginia Melvin, Southwest Tennessee Community College

Jeanne Mercer, Texas State Technical College

Denise Merrell, Jefferson Community & Technical College

Catherine Merrikin, Pearl River Community College

Diane D. Mickey, Northern Virginia Community College

Darrelyn Miller, Grays Harbor College

Sue Mitchell, Calhoun Community College

Jacquie Moldenhauer, Front Range Community College

Linda Motonaga, Los Angeles City College

Sam Mryyan, Allen County Community College

Cindy Murphy, Southeastern Community College

Ryan Murphy, Sinclair Community College

Sharon E. Nastav, Johnson County Community College

Christine Naylor, Kent State University Ashtabula

Haji Nazarian, Seattle Central Community College

Nancy Noe, Linn-Benton Community College

Jennie Noriega, San Joaquin Delta College

Linda Nutter, Peninsula College

Thomas Omerza, Middle Bucks Institute of Technology

Edith Orozco, St. Philip's College

Dona Orr, Boise State University

Joanne Osgood, Chaffey College

Janice Owens, Kishwaukee College

Tatyana Pashnyak, Bainbridge College

John Partacz, College of DuPage

Tim Paul, Montana State University–Great Falls

Joseph Perez, South Texas College

Mike Peterson, Chemeketa Community College

Dr. Karen R. Petitto, West Virginia Wesleyan College

Terry Pierce, Onandaga Community College

Ashlee Pieris, Raritan Valley Community College

Jamie Pinchot, Thiel College

Michelle Poertner, Northwestern Michigan College

Betty Posta, University of Toledo

Deborah Powell, West Central Technical College

Mark Pranger, Rogers State University

Carolyn Rainey, Southeast Missouri State University

Linda Raskovich, Hibbing Community College

Leslie Ratliff, Griffin Technical College

Mar-Sue Ratzke, Rio Hondo Community College

Roxy Reissen, Southeastern Community College

Silvio Reyes, Technical Career Institutes

Patricia Rishavy, Anoka Technical College

Jean Robbins, Southeast Technical Institute

Carol Roberts, Eastern Maine Community College and University of Maine

Teresa Roberts, Wilson Technical Community College

Vicki Robertson, Southwest Tennessee Community College

Betty Rogge, Ohio State Agricultural Technical Institute

Lynne Rusley, Missouri Southern State University

Claude Russo, Brevard Community College

Ginger Sabine, Northwestern Technical College

Steven Sachs, Los Angeles Valley College

Joanne Salas, Olympic College

Lloyd Sandmann, Pima Community College–Desert Vista Campus

Beverly Santillo, Georgia Perimeter College

Theresa Savarese, San Diego City College

Sharolyn Sayers, Milwaukee Area Technical College

Judith Scheeren, Westmoreland County Community College

Adolph Scheiwe, Joliet Junior College

Marilyn Schmid, Asheville-Buncombe Technical Community College

Janet Sebesy, Cuyahoga Community College

Phyllis T. Shafer, Brookdale Community College

Ralph Shafer, Truckee Meadows Community College

Anne Marie Shanley, County College of Morris

Shelia Shelton, Surry Community College

Merilyn Shepherd, Danville Area Community College

Susan Sinele, Aims Community College

Beth Sindt, Hawkeye Community College

Andrew Smith, Marian College

Brenda Smith, Southwest Tennessee Community College

Lynne Smith, State University of New York–Delhi

Rob Smith, Katharine Gibbs School–Philadelphia

Tonya Smith, Arkansas State University–Mountain Home

Del Spencer–Trinity Valley Community College

Jeri Spinner, Idaho State University

Eric Stadnik, Santa Rosa Junior College

Karen Stanton, Los Medanos College

Meg Stoner, Santa Rosa Junior College

Beverly Stowers, Ivy Tech Community College of Indiana

Marcia Stranix, Yuba College

Kim Styles, Tri-County Technical College

Sylvia Summers, Tacoma Community College

Beverly Swann, Delaware Technical & Community College

Ann Taff, Tulsa Community College

Mike Theiss, University of Wisconsin–Marathon Campus

Romy Thiele, Cañada College

Sharron Thompson, Portland Community College

Ingrid Thompson-Sellers, Georgia Perimeter College

Barbara Tietsort, University of Cincinnati–Raymond Walters College

Janine Tiffany, Reading Area Community College

Denise Tillery, University of Nevada Las Vegas

Susan Trebelhorn, Normandale Community College

Noel Trout, Santiago Canyon College

Cheryl Turgeon, Asnuntuck Community College

Steve Turner, Ventura College

Sylvia Unwin, Bellevue Community College

Lilly Vigil, Colorado Mountain College

Sabrina Vincent, College of the Mainland

Mary Vitrano, Palm Beach Community College

Brad Vogt, Northeast Community College

Cozell Wagner, Southeastern Community College

Carolyn Walker, Tri-County Technical College

Sherry Walker, Tulsa Community College

Qi Wang, Tacoma Community College

Betty Wanielista, Valencia Community College

Marge Warber, Lanier Technical College–Forsyth Campus

Marjorie Webster, Bergen Community College

Linda Wenn, Central Community College

Mark Westlund, Olympic College

Carolyn Whited, Roane State Community College

Winona Whited, Richland College

Jerry Wilkerson, Scott Community College

Joel Willenbring, Fullerton College

Barbara Williams, WITC Superior

Charlotte Williams, Jones County Junior College

Bonnie Willy, Ivy Tech Community College of Indiana

Diane Wilson, J. Sargeant Reynolds Community College

James Wolfe, Metropolitan Community College

Marjory Wooten, Lanier Technical College

Mark Yanko, Hocking College

Alexis Yusov, Pace University

Naeem Zaman, San Joaquin Delta College

Kathleen Zimmerman, Des Moines Area Community College

We also thank Lutz Ziob, Merrick Van Dongen, Jim LeValley, Bruce Curling, Joe Wilson, Rob Linsky, Jim Clark, Scott Serna, Ben Watson, and David Bramble at Microsoft for their encouragement and support in making the Microsoft Official Academic Course programs the finest instructional materials for mastering the newest Microsoft technologies for both students and instructors.

Brief Contents

Contents

Lesson 12: Using Mobile Computers   446

Introducing Windows 7

OBJECTIVE DOMAIN MATRIX

TECHNOLOGY SKILL	OBJECTIVE DOMAIN	OBJECTIVE NUMBER
Understanding Windows 7 System Requirements	Perform a clean installation.	1.1
Running Windows 7 Upgrade Advisor	Upgrade to Windows 7 from previous versions of Windows.	1.2

KEY TERMS

Action Center	**federated search**	**ReadyBoost**
Aero Peek	**jump list**	**Resource Monitor**
Aero Shake	**language-agnostic**	**starter GPOs**
Aero Snap	**Libraries**	**VPN Reconnect**
BranchCache	**MinWin**	**Wake on Wireless LAN**
DirectAccess	**Problem Steps Recorder**	**Windows PowerShell 2.0**

■ Understanding Course Requirements

THE BOTTOM LINE

Windows Vista was the first major revision of the Microsoft Windows desktop operating system since the initial release of Windows XP in 2001. Windows 7 is a refinement of Windows Vista that retains the same basic architecture but improves performance and adds many new features.

For new users, Windows 7 provides a sleek new interface that many will find intuitive and easy to use. For experienced Windows XP users, an upgrade to Windows 7 will require a period of adjustment as they learn new procedures to perform familiar tasks.

For IT support personnel accustomed to working with Windows Vista, Windows 7 will be a minor adjustment. For Windows XP technicians, Windows 7 represents not only a new interface and all of the support issues that accompany it, but also an entirely new operating system (OS) architecture. In other words, not only do XP users have to learn to drive a new type of vehicle, but XP mechanics have to learn to repair a new type of engine as well.

In this course, you learn to install, configure, and manage Windows 7, all tasks that differ significantly from their Windows XP counterparts. You study the Windows 7 installation process for individual computers, as well as the deployment of Windows 7 on an enterprise network. You also learn to configure many of Windows 7's hardware, security, and networking controls; install and deploy applications; and manage configuration settings for a large fleet of Windows 7 desktops.

The book you are currently reading is the course textbook, which contains background and explanatory material on Windows 7, along with a number of exercises and scenarios to test how much you have learned. Your other book is a lab manual, which guides you through a series of hands-on exercises corresponding to the material in the textbook.

If you diligently work your way through the textbook and the lab manual, and complete all of the assignments given to you by your instructor, you will come out of this course ready to provide technical support for Windows 7 users and computers.

■ What's New in Windows 7?

THE BOTTOM LINE

Compared to Windows Vista, and even more so to Windows XP, Windows 7 has a great many improvements. The user interface has been modified, and Windows 7 also includes a number of new and enhanced features and applications.

As a Windows 7 technical specialist, you might have experience with Windows Vista, or you might be coming right from Windows XP. For XP users, Windows 7 requires more of an adjustment, but even those familiar with Windows Vista will find a lot that is new in Windows 7. The following sections examine the interface enhancements, the new features, and the security modifications in Windows 7.

Using the Windows 7 Interface

The first changes that are apparent to the user or the technical specialist in Windows 7 are the modifications to the user interface.

Although the basic components of the interface are the same as those in Windows Vista, Windows 7 introduces some refinements. However, many of the interface modifications in Windows 7 are simply changes to default settings. In many cases, you can reconfigure the interface elements to appear as they did in Vista, or even as they did in earlier Windows versions.

WORKING THE DESKTOP

In Windows 7, the taskbar is taller than in Windows Vista and Windows XP because its default setting displays running applications as large icons without the application name, as shown in Figure 1-1. The Quick Launch toolbar is gone; instead, you can now right click an application in the Start menu and select Pin To Taskbar from the context menu. This creates a permanent icon on the taskbar for the application you selected, whether it is running or not.

When you mouse over the taskbar icon for a running application while Aero is enabled, Windows 7 displays a live taskbar preview, that is, live thumbnail images of all the documents you have open in that application. Mousing over one of the thumbnails displays a full-screen preview, and clicking a thumbnail opens the document.

Figure 1-1

The default Windows 7 desktop

Icons on the taskbar, and in the Start menu, also now have *jump lists*, context menus that display the application's most frequently used functions. For example, right clicking the Internet Explorer icon displays the sites you have visited most often, as well as other useful functions, as shown in Figure 1-2.

Figure 1-2

A Windows 7 jump list

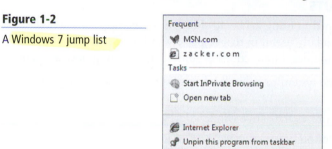

The notification area—known as the tray in Windows XP—is noticeably smaller as well. This is because Windows 7 displays only the Network and Action Center icons by default, as well as a few hardware-specific icons, such as a battery icon on mobile computers.

The Sidebar application from Windows Vista is also gone. However, the gadgets are still available when you right click the desktop and select Gadgets from the context menu, as shown in Figure 1-3. You can also now place gadgets anywhere on the Windows 7 desktop.

Figure 1-3

The Windows 7 gadget gallery

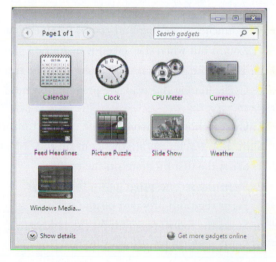

MANIPULATING WINDOWS

The fundamental paradigm that gives Windows its name is, of course, unchanged in Windows 7. You still open multiple windows on the desktop containing different applications, which you can manipulate as needed. However, Windows 7 adds some new methods for moving and resizing the windows on the desktop, including the following:

- **Aero Snap:** When you drag a window to the top of the screen, Windows 7 automatically maximizes it. When you drag a window to the left or right side of the screen, Windows 7 configures the window to exactly half of the screen size. When you drag a corner of a window to the top or bottom of the screen, Windows 7 extends the window vertically from the top of the screen to the bottom.

- **Aero Shake:** When you click the title bar of a window and shake it back and forth with the mouse, Windows 7 minimizes all of the windows except the one you shook. Shaking the active window again restores the other windows to their previous states.

- **Aero Peek:** Mousing over the right end of the taskbar with Aero enabled causes Windows 7 to render all of the windows on the desktop transparent, enabling you to see any gadgets on the desktop underneath. Clicking the right end of the taskbar minimizes all of the windows on the desktop.

- **Aero task switching:** When Aero is enabled, pressing Alt+Tab displays thumbnails of the open applications instead of the standard icons.

USING KEYSTROKE SHORTCUTS

Windows power users are accustomed to using keyboard shortcuts to manipulate the desktop, and the Windows key is particularly useful in that respect. Windows 7 adds some new Windows key shortcuts and also modifies the functions of some of the existing ones as follows:

- **Windows + Space:** Causes the system to enter "peek at desktop" mode, as long as you hold the keys down.
- **Windows + Up Arrow:** Maximizes the active window.
- **Windows + Down Arrow:** Restores the active window to its default size.
- **Windows + Left Arrow:** Snaps the active window to the left side of the screen.
- **Windows + Right Arrow:** Snaps the active window to the right side of the screen.
- **Windows + Shift + Left Arrow:** When using dual monitors, moves the active window to the left screen.
- **Windows + Shift + Right Arrow:** When using dual monitors, moves the active window to the right screen.
- **Windows + Home:** Toggles between minimizing and restoring all windows but the active one.
- **Windows + +:** Launches Magnifier and zooms in on the current cursor location.
- **Windows + −:** Zooms out when the screen is magnified.
- **Windows + G:** Brings the gadgets on the desktop to the front of the display.
- **Windows + P:** Cycles among the available presentation modes, such as single, clone, and extend.
- **Windows + T:** Cycles among the icons on the taskbar from right to left.
- **Windows + Shift + T:** Cycles among the icons on the taskbar from left to right.
- **Windows + 1:** Starts the first program on the taskbar.
- **Windows + 2:** Starts the second program on the taskbar.
- **Windows + 3:** Starts the third program on the taskbar.
- **Windows + 4:** Starts the fourth program on the taskbar.
- **Windows + 5:** Starts the fifth program on the taskbar.

Understanding Windows Feature Refinements

Windows Vista introduced many new features, and most of those features are still found in Windows 7. However, many of those features have been refined or enhanced.

Many of the feature refinements in Windows 7 are relatively subtle; technical specialists looking for big changes might overlook the small things. However, it is often the small things that cause problems for end users, and it is a good idea for technicians to familiarize themselves with the new aspects of the features discussed in the following sections.

USING EXPLORER LIBRARIES

The redesigned Windows Explorer interface from Windows Vista is retained in Windows 7, with a few refinements. When you open a Windows Explorer window in Windows 7, the most immediately identifiable new feature in the default view is the Libraries folder, as shown in Figure 1-4. *Libraries* enable users to aggregate files on multiple computers into a single folder that makes them appear as though they are all on a local drive.

Figure 1-4

A Windows Explorer window

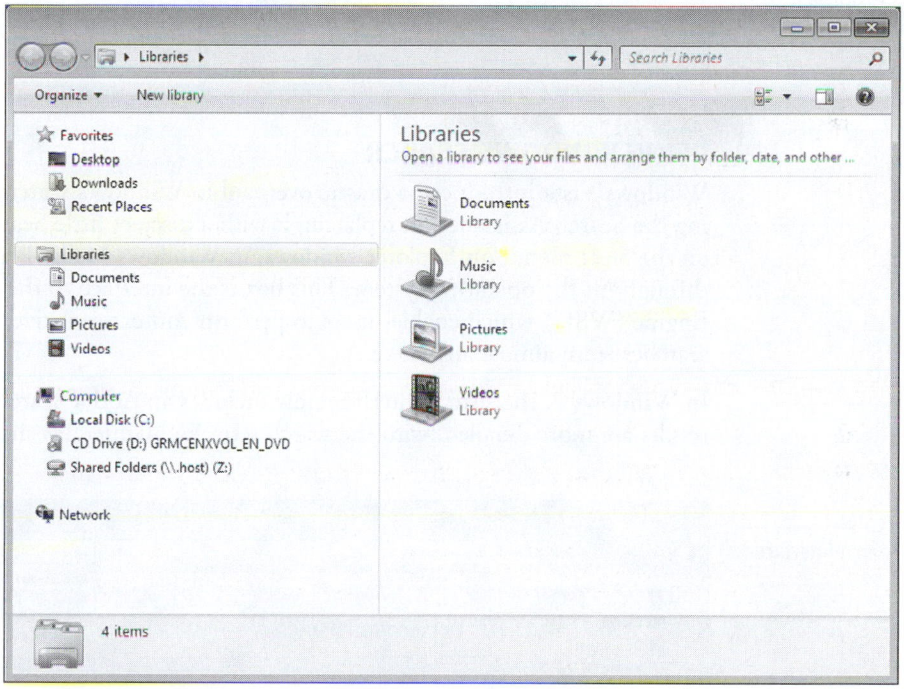

By default, Windows Explorer has four libraries, called Documents, Music, Pictures, and Video. Users can create as many additional libraries as they need. Each library consists of one or more locations, and each location is a folder on the local or a network computer. For example, the Documents library has two locations: the user's My Documents folder and the Public Documents folder. When you look at the Documents library, you see the files in both locations.

If you add more locations to the library, using the Properties sheet shown in Figure 1-5, the files in those locations appear in the library as well. In every library, one of the locations is designated as the save location, and this is where files go that the user saves to the library.

In addition to Windows Explorer windows, libraries also appear in Open and Save As combo boxes, and on the right side of the Start menu, where they replace the individual Documents, Pictures, and Music user profile folders.

Figure 1-5

A library's Properties sheet

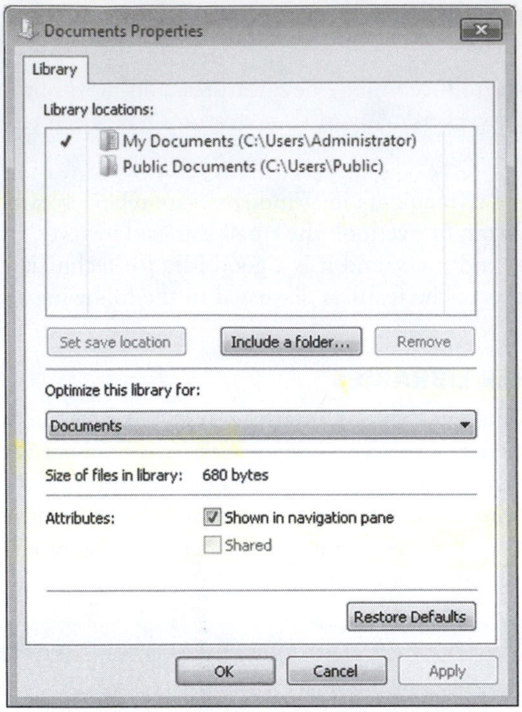

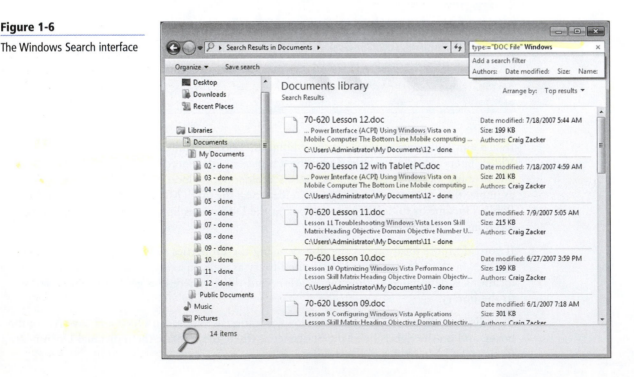

USING WINDOWS SEARCH

Windows Vista introduced a drastic overhaul in Window's search capabilities by eliminating the Search Assistant and replacing it with a discreet little Search box, which you can find on the Start menu, on Explorer windows, in Windows Media Player, and in other places throughout the operating system. This box is the interface to the new Windows Search Engine (WSE), which enables users to perform context-sensitive, metadata-based, as-you-type searches from almost anywhere.

In Windows 7, the search interface now includes an Add a Search Filter option, and search results are more detailed, with the search term highlighted, as shown in Figure 1-6.

Figure 1-6

The Windows Search interface

Windows 7 also enhances the behavior of the Start menu search. When you type a string in the Search box on the Start menu, the groups that the system searches are changed, as shown in Table 1-1.

Table 1-1

Start menu search groups in Windows 7 and Windows Vista

WINDOWS 7	WINDOWS VISTA
Programs	Programs
Control Panel	Favorites and History
Libraries	Communications
Indexed locations	Files

You can now locate Control Panel settings right from the Start menu and search entire libraries as well, as shown in Figure 1-7.

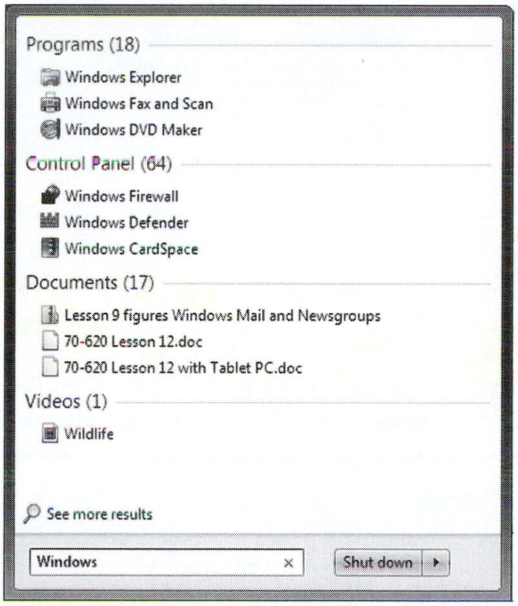

Figure 1-7

Windows 7 Start menu search results

Programs (18)
- Windows Explorer
- Windows Fax and Scan
- Windows DVD Maker

Control Panel (64)
- Windows Firewall
- Windows Defender
- Windows CardSpace

Documents (17)
- Lesson 9 figures Windows Mail and Newsgroups
- 70-620 Lesson 12.doc
- 70-620 Lesson 12 with Tablet PC.doc

Videos (1)
- Wildlife

See more results

Windows   ✕   Shut down ▶

Windows 7 also includes the ability to perform searches in shared folders on the network. To do this, the remote computer must be running the Windows Search service, and the shared folders must be indexed. Searching a remote share uses the Windows Search engine and the index on the remote computer, but Windows 7 displays only the results that the permissions on the remote system make accessible to it.

TAKE NOTE ✱

Windows 7 runs the Windows Search 4.0 service by default, but on servers running Windows Server 2008 R2 or Windows Server 2008, you must install the service manually using Server Manager by adding the File Services role and selecting the Windows Search role service. For older versions of Windows, it is recommended that you upgrade the service to Windows Search 4.0.

USING FEDERATED SEARCH

In addition to the refinements already described, Windows Search supports a new feature called federated search. *Federated search* enables users to perform searches on Windows SharePoint sites, intranets, and specific Internet sites, right from the Windows Explorer interface.

To use federated search, you must download or create search connectors, which are XML files for specific sites. When you install a search connector in Windows 7, a shortcut for the site appears under Favorites in the Windows Explorer window. Selecting the favorite and typing a string in the Search box performs a search on the site and displays the results in Explorer, as shown in Figure 1-8.

Figure 1-8

Windows 7 Federated Search results

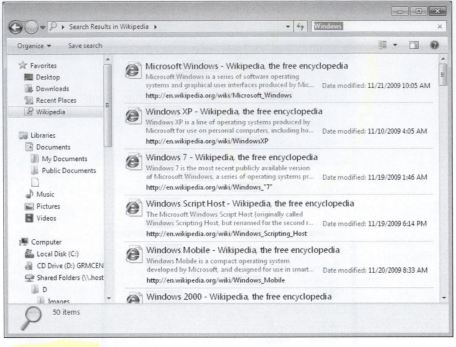

OFFLINE FILES

Offline files is a feature that enables users to automatically store copies of network files on a local drive, so that they can access the files even when the network is not available. In Windows 7, administrators can configure offline files to exclude specific file types from synchronization. For example, by setting the Exclude Files from Being Cached policy, as shown in Figure 1-9, with the extensions of video file formats, administrators can prevent users from overloading the network and their local drives with large video files.

Figure 1-9

The Exclude Files from Being Cached policy

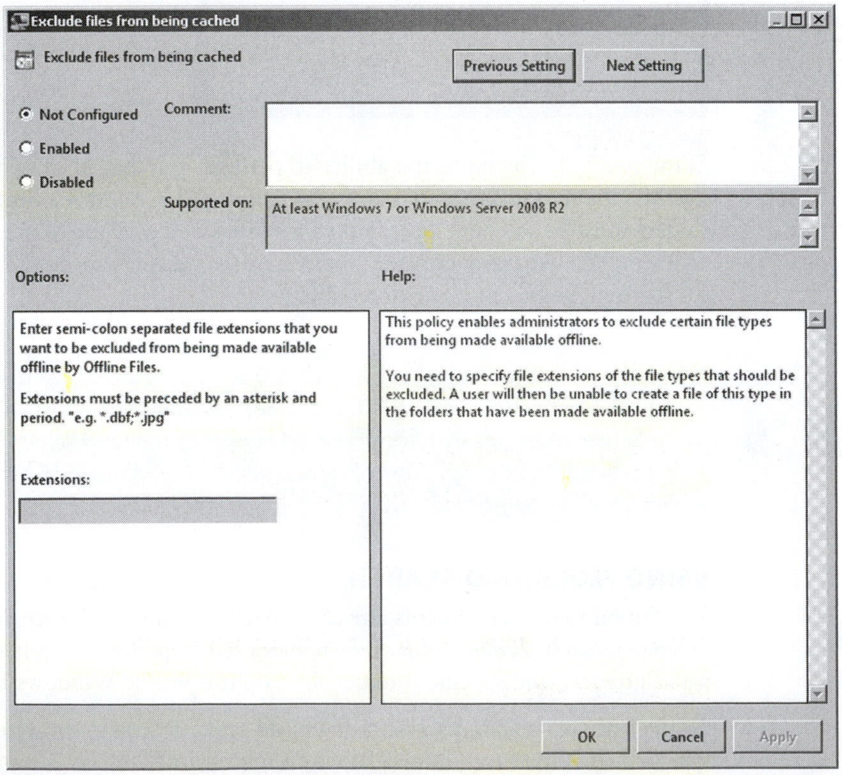

The most complicated aspect of offline files is the synchronization of the local copies with the originals on the network. When a user working offline modifies a file, the system must synchronize the file with the server copy once the workstation regains access to the network. In the previous version of Windows, synchronizations occurred when the user logged on or logged off. In Windows 7, synchronizations can now occur automatically, in the background, making the process invisible to users.

VPN RECONNECT

Mobile users have employed virtual private network (VPN) connections over the Internet to access resources on their enterprise networks for years, but it is only relatively recently that mobile connectivity has been largely wireless. Wireless Internet connections can often be intermittent, and one of the big problems this causes for remote network users is the loss of the VPN connection and the subsequent need to log on and authenticate all over again. This re-authentication process can often take several minutes, thereby reducing user productivity and increasing user frustration. Windows 7 now includes a feature called *VPN Reconnect* that enables a remote computer to automatically re-establish a connection to a VPN server running Windows Server 2008 R2.

X REF

For more information on virtual private networking, see Lesson 5, "Connecting to a Network."

GROUP POLICY

Group Policy has been a part of Windows since the introduction of Active Directory in Windows 2000. Administrators use Group Policy to automate the deployment of configuration settings to computers on the network. Each new Windows version, including Windows 7, has enhanced Group Policy by adding new settings and other features.

In Windows 7, the Group Policy preferences that were a downloadable feature in Windows Vista are included by default. Preferences are Group Policy settings that can configure Windows elements such as drive mappings and desktop shortcuts without locking them so that users can't modify them. Windows 7 also supports new preference settings that enable administrators to exercise greater control over power management and task scheduling.

Group Policy objects (GPOs) are the containers in which administrators select and configure Group Policy settings. On a complex Windows network, administrators might have to create and manage dozens of GPOs for various purposes. Windows 7 makes this process a bit easier by including a collection of starter GPOs. *Starter GPOs* are administrative templates with preconfigured settings that administrators can use as a baseline for creating new GPOs. It is also possible to create new starter GPOs to construct your own templates.

READYBOOST

X REF

For more information on ReadyBoost, see Lesson 8, "Managing and Monitoring Windows 7 Performance."

ReadyBoost is a feature first introduced in Windows Vista that enables a computer to utilize an external storage device, such as a universal serial bus (USB) flash drive or secure digital (SD) memory card, as a cache for data that would ordinarily be swapped to a (slower) hard disk. The Windows 7 version of ReadyBoost enhances the system's caching capability by supporting larger caches on as many as eight external devices simultaneously.

Introducing New Windows 7 Features

In addition to its modified interface and refinements of existing features, Windows 7 also includes a number of new features and applications.

Many of the new features in Windows 7 enhance the operating system's ability to communicate with other computers on the network safely and efficiently. The following sections discuss some of the most prominent of these new features.

ACTION CENTER

The Windows 7 *Action Center*, shown in Figure 1-10, is a replacement for the Security Center found in Windows Vista. The name change is due to the fact that, in addition to

Figure 1-10

The Windows 7 Action Center

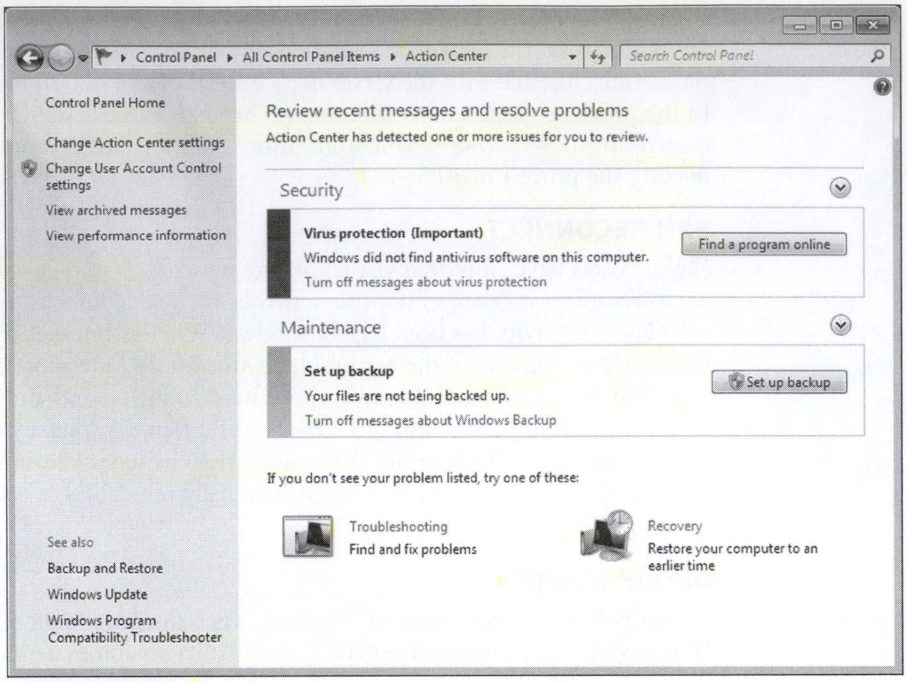

security notifications, Action Center also displays alerts generated by other Windows 7 applications and services, including backups and problem reports.

BRANCHCACHE

BranchCache is a new feature in Windows 7 and Windows Server 2008 R2 that is designed to reduce the wide area network (WAN) bandwidth utilized by branch office file sharing and provide branch office users with faster and more reliable access to the offsite files they need. Like all caching software, BranchCache is essentially a buffer that stores data accessed from a relatively slow medium on a faster medium. In this case, a computer on a branch network stores copies of the files that users access on remote servers, so that when other users need those files, they can access them locally.

X REF

For more information on how BranchCache works and how to configure it, see Lesson 8, "Managing and Monitoring Windows 7 Performance."

DIRECTACCESS

Even with the VPN Reconnect feature described earlier in this lesson, establishing remote VPN connections can be time consuming and can require a greater understanding of networking concepts than many users possess. *DirectAccess* is a new remote connection technology that is completely invisible to the end user. Whenever the remote computer has access to the Internet, it automatically establishes a connection with a DirectAccess server on the enterprise network. DirectAccess has other advantages as well, such as the ability to connect through firewalls that would block VPN connections; however, for administrators, it is more difficult to set up than a VPN and requires servers running Windows Server 2008 R2.

X REF

For more information on DirectAccess, see Lesson 5, "Connecting to a Network."

WINDOWS POWERSHELL 2.0

Microsoft is clearly positioning Windows PowerShell as the dominant scripting and command line language for all of its operating systems, replacing VB Script and the other languages supported by Windows Script Host. Windows 7 and Windows Server 2008 R2 both have *Windows PowerShell 2.0* installed by default, rather than requiring a separate download, as with previous Windows versions.

Windows 7 includes both a PowerShell command prompt and a graphical interface, the Windows PowerShell Integrated Scripting environment (ISE), as shown in Figure 1-11. Using its native commands and add-on modules, administrators can utilize Windows PowerShell to perform almost any task from a command prompt. PowerShell also functions as a rich scripting language, enabling administrators to automate tasks and create logon and startup scripts.

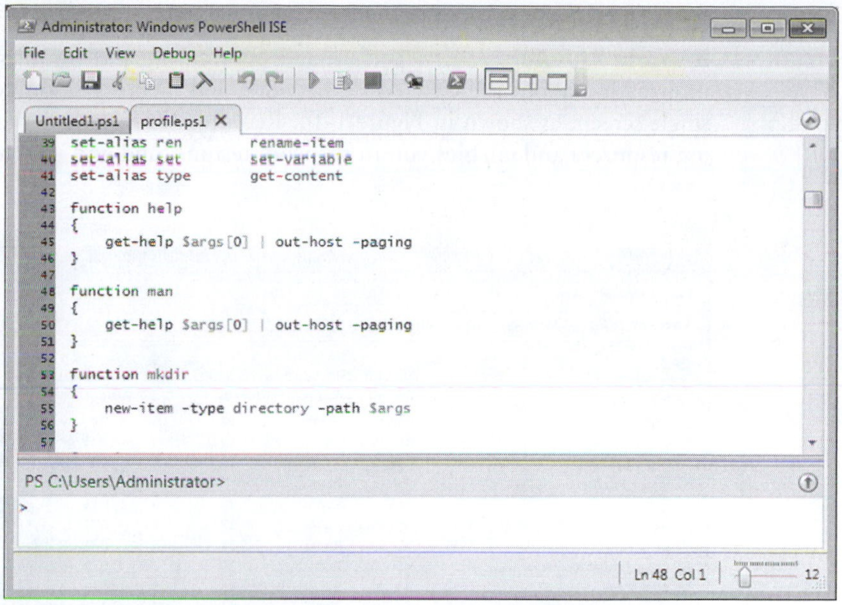

Figure 1-11

Windows PowerShell ISE

PROBLEM STEPS RECORDER

When computer users encounter a problem and call for help, one of the troublesome issues for the technical specialist is getting adequate information about what happened. The *Problem Steps Recorder*, shown in Figure 1-12, is a new Windows 7 tool that enables users and administrators to document the process that generated an error.

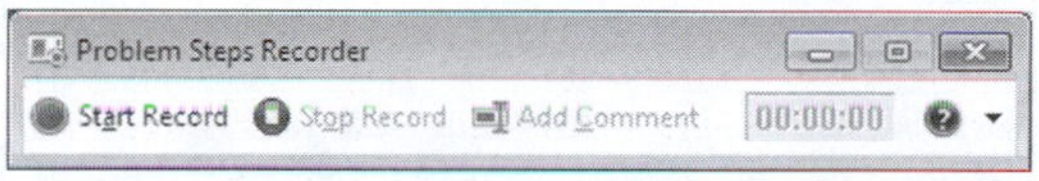

Figure 1-12

The Windows 7 Problem Steps Recorder

When you click Start Record in the Problem Steps Recorder, the program tracks your mouse movements and compiles a log of all the actions leading up to the error. You can add comments as you go, and when you click Stop Record, the program saves the log, with captured graphics of the screens you were working on, as shown in Figure 1-13. Users can provide this log to the help desk, and lower-level technicians can pass the information along to technical specialists when escalating an issue.

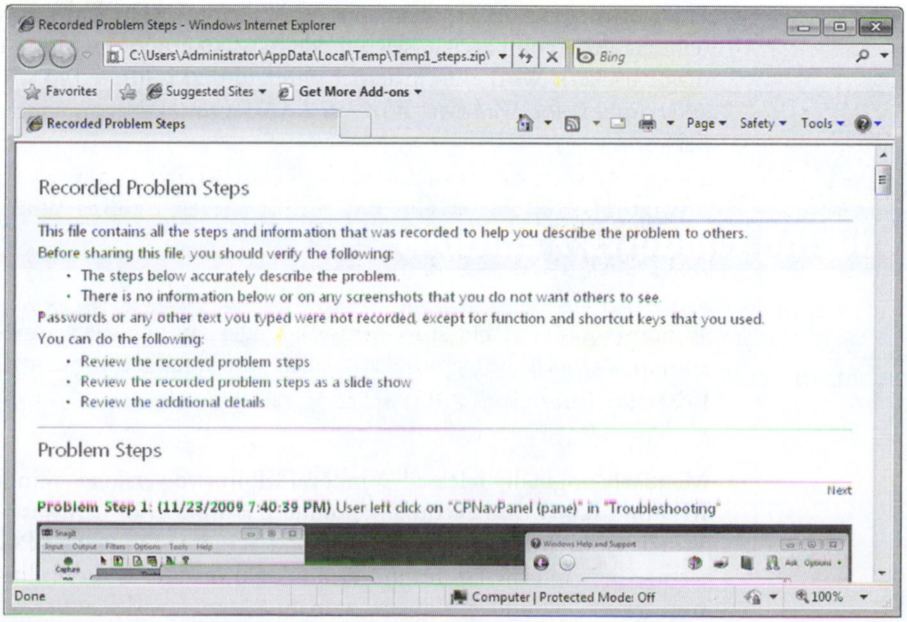

Figure 1-13

A log generated by the Problem Steps Recorder

X REF

For more information about Resource Monitor, see Lesson 8, "Managing and Monitoring Windows 7 Performance."

RESOURCE MONITOR

Resource Monitor is a new performance monitoring and troubleshooting tool that displays information about the CPU, disk, network, and memory resources used by Windows 7 on a single screen, as shown in Figure 1-14. Resource Monitor lists the processes that are consuming resources and enables you to suspend, resume, and end processes as needed.

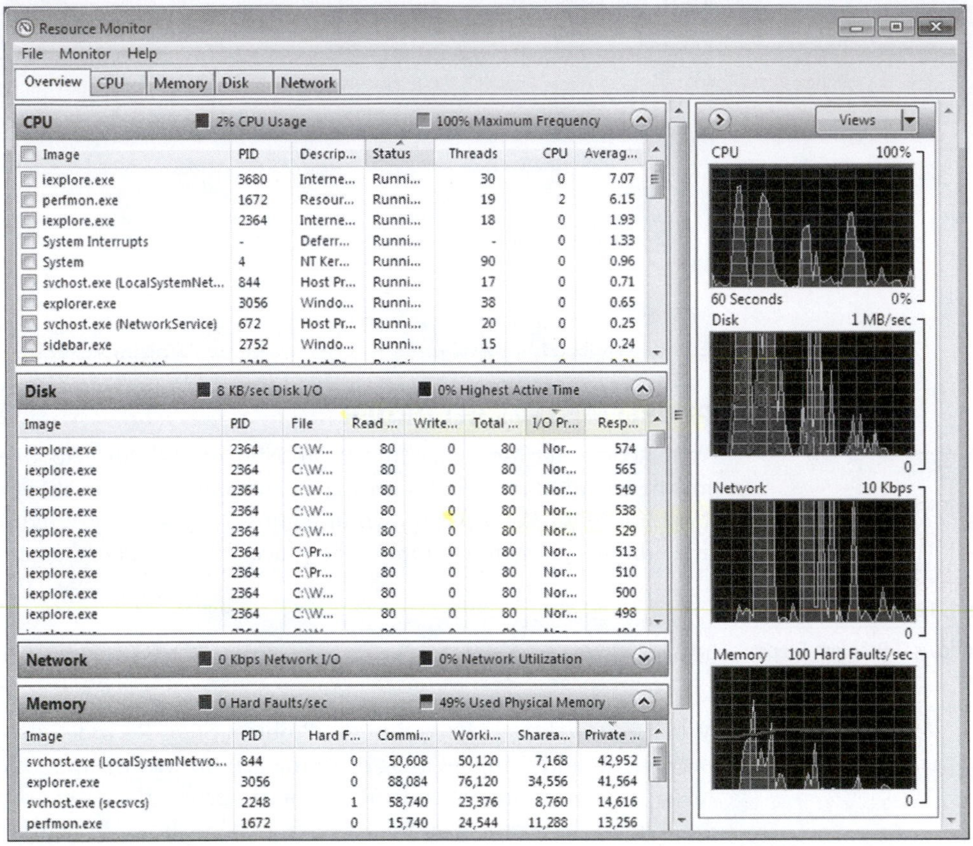

Figure 1-14

Windows 7 Resource Monitor

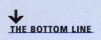

WAKE ON WIRELESS LAN

Previous versions of Windows support Wake on LAN (WoL), a type of network packet filter that enables a computer in sleep mode to wake up on receipt of a specific message (called a magic packet). WoL is an Ethernet standard that is limited to wired networks. Windows 7 adds support for *Wake on Wireless LAN* (WoWLAN), an equivalent standard for wireless networks.

■ Introducing Windows 7 Editions

THE BOTTOM LINE

Windows 7 is available in six editions. Understanding the features and capabilities of each edition is crucial for technical specialists who must recommend a specific product for their users.

Microsoft originally released Windows XP in two versions, Windows XP Home and Windows XP Professional, and eventually produced a number of hardware-specific editions, including Windows XP Media Center Edition and Windows XP Tablet PC Edition. The primary difference between the Home and Professional versions is the ability of the operating system to connect to a Windows network domain.

➕ MORE INFORMATION

The history of Microsoft Windows on desktop computers follows two parallel courses. Originally, Windows was a shell program that ran on top of the 16-bit MS-DOS operating system. Eventually, Microsoft combined MS-DOS and Windows into a single operating system product and developed it through several versions, including Windows 95, Windows 98, and Windows Me, which was the final product to use the MS-DOS kernel. At the same time, Microsoft was working on a completely new, 32-bit operating system that overcame most of the memory- and hardware-handling difficulties that were inherent in MS-DOS. Originally released as Windows NT 3.1 in 1993, the same basic NT kernel also formed the core of the Windows NT 4.0 and Windows 2000 operating system products. Intended primarily for servers at first, the NT kernel gradually gained popularity on the desktop, especially in business environments. With the release of Windows XP in 2001, Microsoft stopped using the MS-DOS kernel entirely; the NT kernel is now the basis of all new Windows operating systems, including Windows 7 and Windows Server 2008 R2. With Windows Vista, and now Windows 7, Microsoft has expanded its scope, making the operating system available in six versions.

The six versions of Windows 7 are as follows:

- **Windows 7 Starter:** Microsoft intends the Starter edition of Windows 7 to be a low-cost operating system alternative for original equipment manufacturers (OEMs) to use in netbook and low-end laptop products. Windows 7 Starter will be available worldwide, unlike Windows Vista Starter, but only on new computers sold through OEMs, and not through normal retail channels. The Starter edition has substantial limitations, such as no 64-bit version, no Windows Aero features, and limited processor support.

TAKE NOTE *

Aside from being available only in emerging markets, Windows Vista Starter edition was limited to running only three applications at a time. However, Microsoft has decided to remove this limitation from Windows 7 Starter edition.

- **Windows 7 Home Basic:** Microsoft intends Home Basic for emerging markets only, which means that it will not be an option available to most users and businesses. Home Basic lacks most Aero support, has limited networking capabilities, and does not include the Windows Media Center application.

TAKE NOTE *

In Windows 7, Microsoft has reversed the roles of the Starter and Home Basic editions. In Windows Vista, the Starter edition was distributed only in emerging markets and Home Basic was distributed through OEMs. In Windows 7, exactly the opposite is true.

- **Windows 7 Home Premium:** Home Premium is intended to be the primary retail and OEM version of Windows 7 for home users. This version includes full Aero support and multimedia capabilities, but it lacks business features, such as the ability to join an Active Directory Domain Services (AD DS) domain.
- **Windows 7 Professional:** Windows 7 Professional is intended to be the premium retail version for more advanced home users and small to medium-sized businesses. As a superset of Windows 7 Home Premium, Windows 7 Professional includes a basic array of management features, as well as the ability to join an AD DS domain, but it lacks some of the more advanced networking features, such as BranchCache and DirectAccess. Unlike Windows Vista Business, Windows 7 Professional includes the Windows Media Center application.
- **Windows 7 Enterprise:** Available only through the Microsoft Software Assurance and Enterprise Advantage volume licensing programs, the Enterprise edition includes the complete set of Windows 7 features, making it functionally identical to Windows 7 Ultimate, except for its licensing. The Windows 7 Enterprise license also includes support for all language packs and the right to run as many as four operating systems in virtual machines.

- **Windows 7 Ultimate:** Windows 7 Ultimate is the retail version of the complete Windows 7 operating system, with all of the same features as Windows 7 Enterprise, except those provided by the Enterprise license. Windows 7 Ultimate does not support volume licensing and includes only five years of product support, as opposed to ten years for Windows 7 Enterprise, which makes the latter preferable for business customers.

TAKE NOTE*

Unlike Windows Vista, which drew criticism for excluding in the Business edition certain features found in the Home Premium product, such as Windows Media Center, the Windows 7 editions are true supersets. As you move up from Starter to Ultimate, each higher edition includes all of the features of the next lower edition.

Table 1-2 lists the operating system features and applications that are included in each of the five main Windows 7 editions.

Table 1-2

Feature Support in Windows 7 Editions

	STARTER	HOME BASIC	HOME PREMIUM	PROFESSIONAL	ENTERPRISE	ULTIMATE
Licensing	OEM only	Emerging markets only	Retail/OEM	Retail/OEM/Volume	Volume only	Retail/OEM
AD DS domain support	No	No	No	Yes	Yes	Yes
Boot from VHD	No	No	No	No	Yes	Yes
Windows Aero	No	Partial	Yes	Yes	Yes	Yes
Create Homegroups	Join only	Join only	Yes	Yes	Yes	Yes
Remote desktop	Client only	Client only	Client only	Client and host	Client and host	Client and host
Folder redirection	No	No	No	Yes	Yes	Yes
Offline files	No	No	No	Yes	Yes	Yes
Encrypting file system (EFS)	No	No	No	Yes	Yes	Yes
Product support	5 years	5 years	5 years	10 years	10 years	5 years
Network-based backup	No	No	No	Yes	Yes	Yes
DirectAccess	No	No	No	No	Yes	Yes
BranchCache	No	No	No	No	Yes	Yes
BitLocker	No	No	No	No	Yes	Yes
AppLocker	No	No	No	No	Yes	Yes
Multiple User Interface (MUI) language packs	No	No	No	No	Yes	Yes
Windows Media Center	No	No	Yes	Yes	Yes	Yes
Mobility Center	No	No	No	Yes	Yes	Yes

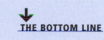

■ Understanding Windows 7 System Requirements

↓

THE BOTTOM LINE

Windows 7 has the same hardware requirements as Windows Vista, making the upgrade process relatively painless. However, an upgrade to Windows 7 from Windows XP is likely to require hardware upgrades, and a thorough understanding of the Windows 7 system requirements is essential for the technical specialist.

CERTIFICATION READY?
Perform a clean installation.
1.1

Because the various Windows 7 editions differ primarily in the number and type of applications included with each product, the basic minimum system requirements are the same for all (except Starter) editions. Table 1-3 shows the minimum hardware requirements for Windows 7.

Table 1-3

Minimum System Requirements for Windows 7

	32-BIT (x86)	**64-BIT (x64)**
Processor speed	1 GHz or faster	1 GHz or faster
System memory	1 GB	2 GB
Available hard disk space	16 GB	20 GB
Graphics adapter	DirectX 9 graphics adapter with WDDM 1.0 or higher driver	DirectX 9 graphics adapter with WDDM 1.0 or higher driver

Microsoft permits PCs conforming to these specifications to display an official logo such as the one shown in Figure 1-15. However, the appearance of the logo on a new computer does not necessarily mean that a license for the Windows 7 operating system is included in the computer's price. You might still have to pay for the operating system separately.

Figure 1-15

The "Compatible with Windows 7" logo

Apart from these minimum system requirements, there are also hardware limitations for each of the Windows 7 editions, as shown in Table 1-4.

Table 1-4

Hardware limitations for Windows 7 editions

	STARTER	**HOME BASIC**	**HOME PREMIUM**	**PROFESSIONAL**	**ENTERPRISE**	**ULTIMATE**
Processor architecture	32-bit only	32-bit or 64-bit	32-bit or 64-bit	32-bit or 64-bit	32-bit or 64-bit	32-bit or 64-bit
Maximum RAM (32-bit)	2 GB	4 GB	4 GB	4 GB	4 GB	4 GB
Maximum RAM (64-bit)	N/A	8 GB	16 GB	192 GB	192 GB	192 GB
Two-processor support	No	No	No	Yes	Yes	Yes
Peer network connections	0	5	10	10	10	10

While the official system requirements that Microsoft provides are a useful starting point, they do not provide the whole picture. Upgrading to Windows 7 is a subject that is sure to be on the minds of many Windows users, ranging from home users with a single computer to corporate executives responsible for thousands of workstations. For these users, simply falling within the system requirements is not enough. They want to be sure that Windows 7 will be an improvement over their previous OS, and that requires them to consider the individual system components carefully:

- **Processor:** Of the major computer components, the processor is likely to have the least effect on overall system performance. The 1 GHz processor called for in the Windows 7 system requirements is relatively outdated by today's desktop standards. Most of the PCs in use today have processors much faster than 1 GHz, and even computers that are four or five years old will most likely meet the required speeds. The benefits derived from a faster processor depend largely on the applications the computer is running. Hardcore gamers are the users most intent on wringing every last GHz from their systems, but for general computer use, the requirements are not so heavy. For the purposes of upgrading to Windows 7, it is probably not worthwhile to purchase a new computer just to get a faster processor.

- **System memory:** The memory requirements of the Windows operating systems have risen precipitously in recent years. The 512 megabyte (MB) minimum required for a Vista Capable PC was pushing the lower limit, and often resulted in disappointing performance levels. Microsoft now treats the 1 GB minimum previously cited for a Windows Vista Premium Ready PC as the minimum for Windows 7. Memory is easy and inexpensive to upgrade, however; no other hardware upgrade will yield a more immediately detectable performance increase. The Windows 7 one GB memory minimum is sufficient for a general-purpose workstation, but memory-intensive applications such as video and image editing, as well as high-end games, will benefit from more. Be sure to check the system documentation to determine what memory upgrades are possible for your computers.

- **Hard disk space:** Windows 7 requires much more hard disk space than earlier versions of Windows, but with the low prices and high capacities of today's hard disk drives, it is not difficult to meet or exceed the system requirements. For most users, the real disk space hog is not operating system files or even applications, but rather the collections of audio and video files that all users seem to accumulate. Another aspect to consider, however, is the performance level of the hard drive(s) in the computer. Older drives that spin at 5400 RPM can lead to palpably poorer performance than drives running at 7200 RPM or faster. In addition, if you plan to upgrade, you might consider using the newer Serial Advanced Technology Attachment (SATA) drives instead of the older Integrated Drive Electronics (IDE) models. If you do upgrade to SATA on older computers, remember that you will probably have to purchase SATA controller cards as well as the drives themselves.

- **Graphics adapter:** The system component that is causing the most upgrade worries for Windows XP users and administrators is the graphics adapter. Windows Vista was the first Windows operating system to require such specific graphics capabilities, compelling many users to take a crash course in graphics adapter specifications as a result. The operating system feature that requires these capabilities is Windows Aero, the interface element that gives the Windows 7 desktop its glass-like, translucent look. On a Windows 7 system with Aero enabled, the edges of the windows are translucent and contain a fuzzy image of the elements behind them. It is the rendering of those fuzzy images that is so graphic intensive, and that, incidentally, consumes significant system resources as well. The result is impressive; an Aero desktop has a slick, modern appearance that enhances the Windows user experience. However, if your existing graphics adapters have been serving you well, you can certainly wait to upgrade them. The Aero features are mostly cosmetic, and your workstations are likely to perform better using the similar but less graphic-intensive Windows 7 Basic interface instead.

For businesses running hundreds or thousands of workstations, the cost of hardware upgrades can be enormous, so you should carefully consider the current state of your computers and what new hardware your organization will need to make a Windows 7 upgrade practical and productive.

■ Running Windows 7 Upgrade Advisor

↓ THE BOTTOM LINE

All technical specialists should be familiar with the Windows 7 Upgrade Advisor application because it is the surest way of determining whether a computer is capable of running Windows 7.

CERTIFICATION READY?
Upgrade to Windows 7 from previous versions of Windows.
1.2

The easiest way to determine whether a computer is capable of running Windows 7 is to use Microsoft's Upgrade Advisor application, which replaces the Hardware Compatibility List (HCL) associated with earlier Windows versions. Upgrade Advisor is a Windows XP and Windows Vista application that scans an individual computer's hardware and software to determine whether it is capable of running Windows 7 at peak efficiency.

→ RUN UPGRADE ADVISOR

GET READY. Before you run Upgrade Advisor, be sure to plug in and turn on any USB devices or other devices such as printers, external hard drives, or scanners that you regularly use with the PC you are evaluating.

1. Insert the Windows 7 installation disc in the drive. The *Install Windows* page appears, as shown in Figure 1-16.

Figure 1-16

The Install Windows page

2. Click the Check compatibility online arrow. Internet Explorer launches and the *Windows 7 Upgrade Advisor* page appears, as shown in Figure 1-17.

TAKE NOTE*

If you do not have a Windows 7 installation disk, you can access the *Windows 7 Upgrade Advisor* page directly by entering the following URL into your browser: http://windows. microsoft.com/en-us/windows/downloads/upgrade-advisor.

Figure 1-17

The Windows 7 Upgrade
Advisor page

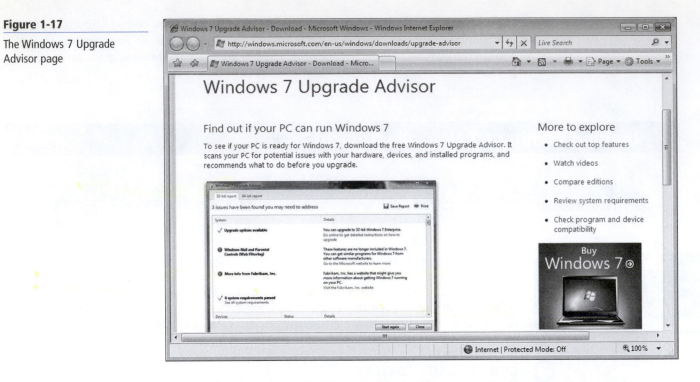

3. Click the Download the Windows 7 Upgrade Advisor hyperlink. The *Download Details Windows 7 Upgrade Advisor* page appears, as shown in Figure 1-18.

Figure 1-18

The Windows 7 Upgrade
Advisor Page

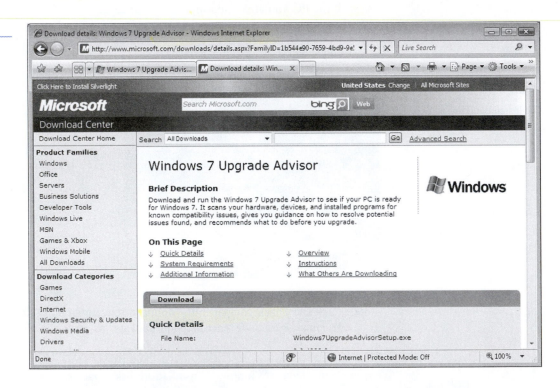

4. Click the Download button. A File Download—Security Warning message box appears.

5. Click the Run button. A progress indicator message box appears. Once the system has finished downloading the file, an Internet Explorer—Security Warning message box appears, asking if you want to run the software.

6. Click the Run button. The *Welcome to the Windows 7 Upgrade Advisor Setup Wizard* page appears, as shown in Figure 1-19.

Figure 1-19

The Welcome to the Windows 7 Upgrade Advisor Setup Wizard page

7. Select the *I Accept the License Terms* option and click Install. The wizard installs the program and the *Installation Complete* page appears, as shown in Figure 1-20.

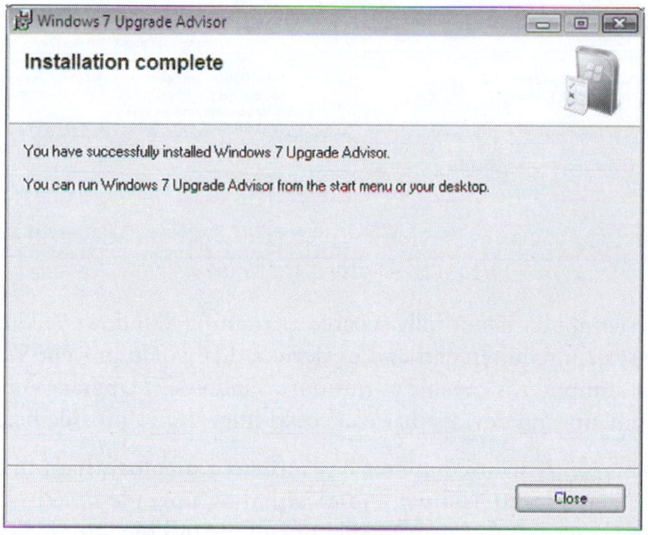

Figure 1-20

The Installation Complete page

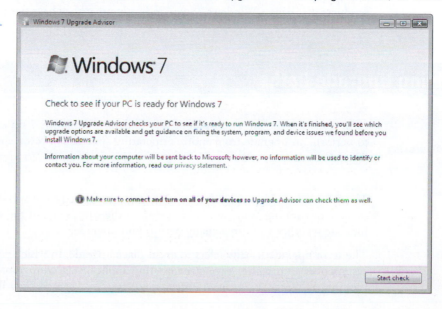

8. Click Close. The wizard closes.

9. On the Start menu, click All Programs > Windows 7 Upgrade Advisor. A User Account Control message box appears.

10. Click Continue. The Windows 7 Upgrade Advisor program loads, as shown in Figure 1-21.

Figure 1-21

The Windows 7 Upgrade Advisor program

11. Click the Start Check button. As it scans the hardware and the software on your computer, Upgrade Advisor displays information about Windows 7.

12. When the scan is completed, a report appears, as shown in Figure 1-22, specifying whether your computer is capable of running Windows 7 and, if so, recommending a specific edition.

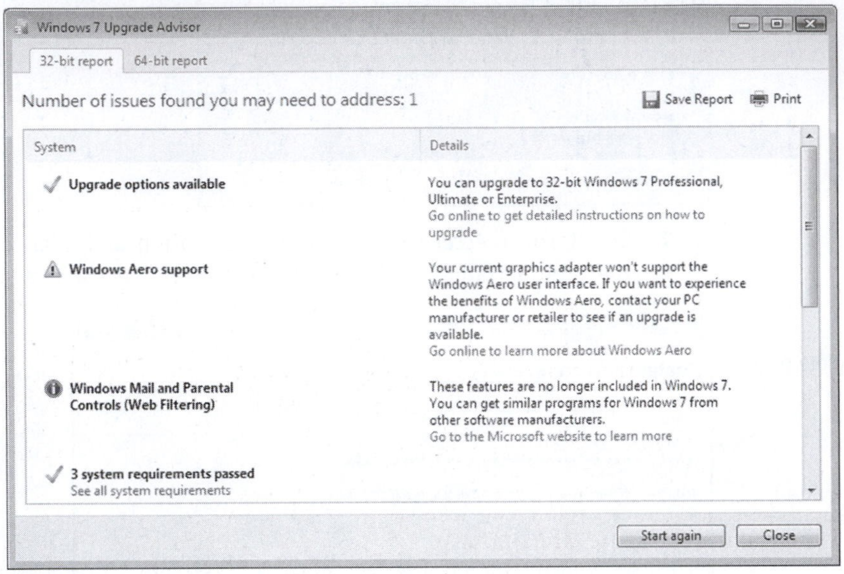

Figure 1-22

The Windows 7 Upgrade Advisor report

If your computer is not fully capable of running Windows 7, Upgrade Advisor displays a list of the system requirements and/or devices that would prevent Windows 7 from running. If your computer is capable of running Windows 7, Upgrade Advisor might display system requirements and devices that you could improve, to provide better performance.

For example, if your computer has sufficient memory, hard disk space, and processor speed, Upgrade Advisor will indicate that an upgrade to Windows 7 is possible, but if your graphics adapter is incapable of supporting the Windows Aero interface, the advisor will tell you so.

In addition to evaluating your hardware, Upgrade Advisor also scans the software on your computer and attempts to determine whether it will run with Windows 7. The Programs section lists applications with both major and minor compatibility issues, and also lists the software products that have a Windows 7 logo, indicating that they have been tested with Windows 7.

■ Identifying Upgrade Paths

THE BOTTOM LINE

In many cases, the most convenient way to deploy Windows 7 on existing computers is to perform an upgrade from another operating system. However, there are a multitude of Windows versions, and not all of them support upgrades to Windows 7.

The Windows 7 Upgrade Advisor utility scans computers and specifies whether they are capable of running Windows 7. However, in the strict sense of the word, the utility does not indicate whether you can actually perform an upgrade.

The term upgrade usually refers to an in-place upgrade, in which you install a new operating system over an old one, leaving the existing applications, configuration settings, and personal files intact. *Windows 7 actually only supports in-place upgrades from Windows Vista.*

TAKE NOTE* When discussing operating system upgrades, it is important to distinguish between the purchase of an upgraded operating system license and the actual installation of the upgraded operating system. The term *in-place upgrade* refers to an installation of Windows 7 on an existing computer, retaining all applications, files, and settings. Some users, however, might be eligible for an upgrade to Windows 7, but can't perform an in-place upgrade. For example, Microsoft allows all licensed Windows XP and Windows Vista users to purchase an upgrade version of Windows 7 at a reduced price, but this does not necessarily mean that they can install Windows 7 with Windows XP or Windows Vista in place. In fact, Windows XP systems always require a clean installation to run Windows 7.

Performing an in-place upgrade from Windows Vista to Windows 7 is a quick and convenient way to provide users with the new operating system without sacrificing the personal files and configuration settings that the users have built up over the years. If you choose to install Windows 7 to the partition that contains the old operating system, the Setup program renames the existing Windows folder to Windows.old, so that the old operating system is still recoverable.

For computers running Windows XP or earlier, you must wipe away the existing operating system and perform a clean Windows 7 installation.

Upgrading Windows 7 Editions

Windows Anytime Upgrade is a program that enables owners of the retail Windows 7 editions to upgrade to a higher Windows 7 edition simply and electronically.

TAKE NOTE*

Windows 7 Enterprise is excluded from Anytime Upgrade because it is only available through volume licensing, and because it already contains the entire set of Windows 7 features.

The idea of allowing users to upgrade their Windows computers to a higher-level edition of their current operating system is an excellent one. However, in Windows Vista, the execution of the idea was flawed. The upgrade paths between the Windows Vista editions were complex, and in many cases, users had to wait for delivery of an upgrade installation disk before they could proceed.

Windows 7 simplifies the Anytime Upgrade process in several ways. First, because each of the Windows 7 editions is a superset of its next lower edition, you can upgrade from any retail Windows 7 product to any higher-level retail product. The available Anytime Upgrade paths are shown in Table 1-5.

Table 1-5

Windows 7 Anytime Upgrade paths

	TO HOME PREMIUM	TO PROFESSIONAL	TO ULTIMATE
From Starter	Anytime Upgrade	Anytime Upgrade	Anytime Upgrade
From Home Premium	N/A	Anytime Upgrade	Anytime Upgrade
From Professional	N/A	N/A	Anytime Upgrade

The second way in which the Windows 7 Anytime Upgrade process is improved is that the entire process is electronic, and no installation disk is needed. Every Windows 7 installation, no matter what the edition, places the entire operating system on the computer's local drive. Therefore, an Anytime Upgrade is really not an upgrade at all, in the true sense of the word; it is just a matter of activating features that are already there.

In Windows 7, Windows Anytime Upgrade is a stand-alone program that you run from the start menu, instead of the Control Panel, as in Windows Vista. When you click Start and select All Programs > Windows Anytime Upgrade, the Windows Anytime Upgrade window appears, as shown in Figure 1-23. From this Window, you can go to the Internet and purchase a higher edition of Windows 7, or enter an upgrade key that you have already purchased.

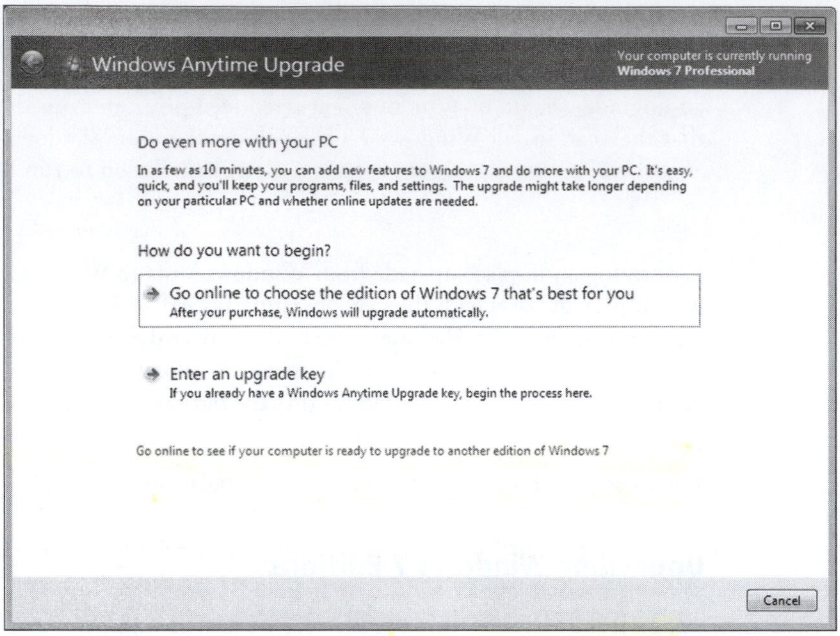

Figure 1-23

The Windows Anytime Upgrade program

Upgrading from Windows Vista

Windows Vista is the only operating system from which you can perform a true in-place upgrade to Windows 7.

TAKE NOTE *

Windows 7 does not support in-place upgrades of 32-bit to 64-bit operating systems under any circumstances, or vice versa.

To perform an in-place upgrade from Windows Vista to Windows 7, you run the Windows 7 Setup.exe program from within Vista and select the Upgrade option. The editions you can upgrade are limited, however. As a general rule, the allowed upgrade paths separate the home and the business versions of the operating systems, as shown in Table 1-6. The only exception is that you can upgrade any version of Windows Vista to Windows 7 Ultimate.

Table 1-6

Windows Vista to Windows 7 Upgrade paths

	WINDOWS 7 HOME PREMIUM	WINDOWS 7 PROFESSIONAL	WINDOWS 7 ULTIMATE
Windows Vista Home Basic	In-place upgrade	Migration only	In-place upgrade
Windows Vista Home Premium	In-place upgrade	Migration only	In-place upgrade
Windows Vista Business	Migration only	In-place upgrade	In-place upgrade
Windows Vista Ultimate	Migration only	Migration only	In-place upgrade

In theory, an in-place upgrade from Windows Vista to Windows 7 preserves everything you might want to retain on the system, substituting only the new operating system. However, in reality, this is not always the case. Not every application can run properly after an upgrade, and not every customized setting is retained. When planning an in-place upgrade, you should always run the Upgrade Advisor application, and pay particular attention to the compatibility report it provides.

For administrators in an enterprise environment, in-place upgrades take much more time to complete and are often unreliable in their results. Generally speaking, a migration of settings to a clean Windows 7 installation is a much better solution.

Upgrading from Earlier Windows Versions

Windows 7 does not support in-place upgrades from any Windows versions prior to Windows Vista. Instead, you can migrate the user profile data from the existing computer to a new, clean Windows 7 installation.

All Windows XP and Windows Vista owners qualify for the Windows 7 upgrades prices, but Windows 7 only supports the in-place upgrades listed in the previous section. To upgrade a Vista home version to a business version of Windows 7, or to upgrade any version of Windows XP to Windows 7, your only direct option is to perform an operating system migration. It is possible to upgrade Windows XP to Windows Vista and then upgrade Windows Vista to Windows 7, but few people are likely to find this path practical.

For computers running operating system versions prior to Windows XP, including Windows 2000, Windows Me, Windows 98, Windows 95, and Windows 3.1, there is no upgrade pricing available, so you must purchase the full version of Windows 7, and you can only perform a migration.

In an operating system migration, you copy the system configuration settings and personal files from the old operating system to the new one, using a program such as the User State Migration Tool. This process preserves many—but not all—of the existing user settings from the old system. Migration does not preserve third-party applications, so you must re-install and configure them after the Windows 7 installation is completed.

For more information on migrating older operating systems to Windows 7, see Lesson 2, "Installing Windows 7."

Migrations do not preserve as much of the existing system configuration as in-place upgrades, but they do result in a more uniform, and usually more stable, Windows 7 computer.

■ Understanding the Windows 7 Modular Architecture

↓ THE BOTTOM LINE

Microsoft has increased the number of operating system editions available from two in Windows XP to six in Windows Vista and Windows 7. However, when you begin working with the installation media, you will soon notice that working with six versions of the operating system does not mean working with six different sets of installation disks.

Microsoft has chosen to release Windows 7 only on DVD discs. The amount of code required to install Windows 7 is far too much to fit on one CD, so a single DVD was deemed preferable to a set of CDs.

TAKE NOTE*

There was a five-CD release of Windows Vista, but there is no equivalent for Windows 7. Virtually all new computers sold today come equipped with a DVD reader, and most users who already own computers have DVD support. For those who do not, aftermarket DVD-ROM drives are extremely inexpensive and easy to install. For enterprise administrators or corporate customers with fleets of computers lacking DVD drives, it is possible to install Windows 7 over a network connection by copying the installation files to a USB flash drive, or by creating CD sets using the createspannedshares.cdm script included with the Windows 7 Automated Installation Kit.

TAKE NOTE*

All of the Windows 7 editions except Starter support both 32-bit (x86) and 64-bit (x64) processor platforms. Because the platforms utilize totally different sets of instructions, the 32-bit and 64-bit versions of the operating system are supplied on different discs.

However, Microsoft is not distributing a different installation DVD for each Windows 7 edition. Technical specialists working with multiple editions will soon learn that all of the editions are included on a single disk. The operating system setup program determines which edition to install from the product key you enter during the installation process.

These innovations in the Windows 7 distribution method are possible, and practical, because of the modular architecture that Microsoft now uses for the operating system. All of the Windows 7 editions are based on a common core module that is sometimes called *MinWin*. The MinWin module contains approximately 95 percent of the operating system functionality. All Windows 7 setup procedures begin with the installation of the MinWin module; then the secondary module containing the functionality of the edition designated by the product key is installed.

The MinWin module, in addition to lacking all edition-specific code, also lacks all language-specific code. The module is therefore said to be *language-agnostic*. For this reason, Microsoft does not have to produce multiple versions of Windows 7 for different languages. The installer selects the appropriate language during installation, which results in the application of a language module that supplies all of the text the operating system displays. Figure 1-24 illustrates the installation process and the application of the edition-specific and language-specific modules.

Figure 1-24

The Windows 7 modular installation process

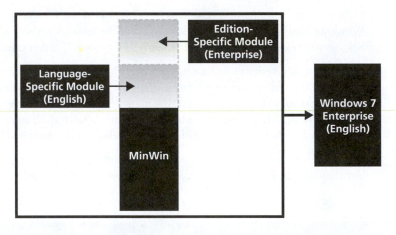

The single disc distribution medium also simplifies the process of upgrading Windows 7 to another edition or adding another language to the interface. The Windows Anytime Upgrade process consists of simply activating the appropriate edition in the operating system.

SKILL SUMMARY

IN THIS LESSON YOU LEARNED:

- Windows 7 includes a variety of interface refinements, as well as new and refined features, including BranchCache, DirectAccess, federated search, Explorer Libraries, and Windows PowerShell 2.0.

- Windows 7 is available in six editions: Starter, Home Basic, Home Premium, Professional, Enterprise, and Ultimate. Each successive edition is a superset of the next lower one.

- Upgrade Advisor is an application, capable of running on Windows XP or Windows Vista, that determines whether the computer's hardware and software is compatible with Windows 7.

- Windows 7 is based on a common core module called MinWin. The MinWin module contains approximately 95 percent of the operating system functionality. To create a full installation requires the addition of language-specific and edition-specific modules.

■ Knowledge Assessment

Fill in the Blank

Complete the following sentences by writing the correct word or words in the blanks provided.

1. The general public in the United States will be able to purchase all of the Windows 7 editions in retail stores except _____, _____, and _____.

2. The core module that provides all of the Windows 7 capability that isn't language- or edition-specific is called _____.

3. When you copy a file to a library, Windows Explorer writes the file to the folder designated as the _____.

4. To use federated search, you must download or create XML files for specific sites called _____.

5. The only operating system edition that you can upgrade in-place to Windows 7 Professional is _____.

6. Upgrading a computer running Windows 7 Starter to Windows 7 Ultimate using Windows Anytime Upgrade requires _____ megabytes of additional hard disk space.

7. To migrate a computer running Windows XP to Windows 7, you can use a utility called _____.

8. The new Windows 7 feature that renders all of the windows on the desktop transparent when you mouse over the right end of the taskbar is called _____.

9. The Windows 7 _____ edition is only available in a 32-bit version.

10. The maximum amount of system memory supported by Windows 7 Enterprise is _____.

True / False

Circle T if the statement is true or F if the statement is false.

T | **F**   1. Windows 7's ReadyBoost feature requires a USB flash drive.

T | **F**   2. 1 GB of system memory is sufficient to run any Windows 7 edition.

T | **F**   3. The Windows 7 Upgrade Advisor application only runs on Windows 7, Windows Vista, and Windows XP SP2.

T | **F**   4. Only the Professional and Ultimate editions of Windows 7 are capable of joining an AD DS domain.

T | **F**   5. DirectAccess, BranchCache, and BitLocker are only included with the Enterprise and Ultimate editions of Windows 7.

T | **F**   6. All of the Windows 7 editions can run on a 64-bit computing platform.

T | **F**   7. A computer with an inadequate graphics adapter is unlikely to be able to run Windows Aero.

T | **F**   8. All of the Windows 7 editions have full Homegroup networking support.

T | **F**   9. The Windows 7 Enterprise and Ultimate editions both contain the same features.

T | **F** 10. You can upgrade Windows 7 Starter edition to any other edition using Windows Anytime Upgrade.

Review Questions

1. Explain why it is not necessary for Microsoft to create separate installation media for each edition and each language supported by Windows 7.

2. Explain how Windows 7 can utilize a USB flash drive to enhance system performance.

■ Case Scenarios

Scenario 1-1: Selecting a Windows 7 Edition

You are a private computer consultant, and a new client has approached you about upgrading his small business network. The network currently consists of eight Windows XP workstations and a single server running Windows Server 2003. The server is functioning as a domain controller and the eight workstations are members of an Active Directory domain. The workstations each have 1 gigabyte of memory and a 1.8-gigahertz processor. The video cards support DirectX 9 and have WDDM drivers available from the manufacturer. Three of the workstations are located in a warehouse across town, while the other five in the main office run Microsoft Office applications almost exclusively. The server is also located in the main office. There have been problems with sluggish performance on the warehouse computers when they attempt to access server files. Which edition(s) of Windows 7 would you select for the workstations to provide the features and performance they require most economically? Explain your answers.

Scenario 1-2: Building a Workgroup Network

A business owner called Ortiz approaches you about the possibility of designing a network for deployment at his new branch office in Bolivia. He has already purchased twenty computers and shipped them to the site. Each computer has 1 gigabyte of memory, a 1-gigahertz processor, and an 80-gigabyte hard drive. He wants to connect the computers into a workgroup network that will be used primarily for accessing web-based applications. Because he will be operating the network in a South American country, Mr. Ortiz wants to use Windows 7 Home Basic for his workstations, as this is the most economical solution he can find. Will this be an adequate solution for his needs? Explain why or why not.

Installing
Windows 7

OBJECTIVE DOMAIN MATRIX

TECHNOLOGY SKILL	OBJECTIVE DOMAIN	OBJECTIVE NUMBER
Performing a Clean Installation	Perform a clean installation.	1.1
Upgrading to Windows 7	Upgrade to Windows 7 from previous versions of Windows.	1.2
Migrating to Windows 7	Migrate user profiles.	1.3

KEY TERMS

clean installation

dual boot

multilingual user interface (MUI)

side-by-side migration

Windows Preinstallation Environment (PE) 3.0

Windows Recovery Environment (RE)

wipe-and-load migration

■ Selecting Installation Options

THE BOTTOM LINE

Before installing Windows 7, or any operating system, whether on a single computer or a fleet of machines, you must first answer a number of questions to determine what type of installation to perform.

Every Windows 7 installation should begin with a planning phase, which varies depending on the complexity of the installation you are contemplating. For stand-alone home users, installing Windows 7 might mean thinking about what data to preserve, determining whether the existing hardware will work with the new operating system (OS), and finally, purchasing the right Windows 7 edition. For enterprise administrators responsible for hundreds or thousands of computers, an operating system deployment requires a huge amount of testing and preparation, and can represent a massive expense. However, the technicians supporting home users and enterprise technical specialists should ask themselves essentially the same questions, just on a different scale.

Will the Hardware Support the New Operating System?

In Lesson 1, "Introducing Windows 7," you learned about the various Windows 7 editions and their hardware requirements. The first question to ask yourself when contemplating an operating system upgrade is whether the computer's current hardware can run the new software effectively.

In many cases, this question is not just a matter of whether the computer meets the Windows 7 minimum hardware requirements. After all, the user expects the new operating system to run better than the old one, not worse. If the computer does not meet the Windows 7 hardware specifications, you should consider a hardware upgrade.

For the home user, a hardware upgrade might mean purchasing and installing a new memory module or two, or perhaps a graphics adapter. Experienced users might install the hardware themselves, while less savvy users might have a professional do it. Either way, the cost and the time involved are relatively small.

However, to perform hardware upgrades like these, enterprise administrators must multiply the cost and the installation time by hundreds or thousands of workstations, and factor in other elements such as lost productivity and overtime costs. Therefore, as with all aspects of a large-scale deployment, technical specialists in an enterprise environment must plan and test carefully before even considering an upgrade to Windows 7. For example, you might want to perform a series of test installations on differently configured computers to determine exactly which hardware upgrade provides the best performance at the lowest cost.

> **X REF**
>
> For more information on deploying Windows 7 in an enterprise environment, see Lesson 3, "Deploying Windows 7."

TAKE NOTE*

Some of Windows 7's hardware demands are unusual when compared with previous Windows versions. The Windows 7 specifications for graphics capabilities are necessary only to run the Windows Aero user experience. Windows Aero is a selling point for Windows 7, but it is essentially a cosmetic feature, and you should consider your user's needs carefully before recommending hardware upgrades. A home user is likely to want all of the "bells and whistles" that Windows 7 can provide, and replacing a graphics adapter is typically a small enough price to pay for that experience. However, for a corporation considering a mass upgrade to Windows 7, the time and cost of replacing hundreds of graphics adapters is far more substantial, especially when the only result is a cosmetic feature that business users could easily do without.

Will the New Operating System Support the Existing Applications?

The second major consideration for a client contemplating a Windows 7 installation is whether the applications the client already owns will run on the new operating system. The last thing clients want to hear after the successful installation of a new operating system is that they need to purchase additional new software.

As with hardware upgrades, the prospect of upgrading or changing applications is far more daunting in the enterprise environment than for the home user. Home users typically run commercial, off-the-shelf applications, and prices for upgrades supporting new operating systems typically fall soon after the release of the OS.

At the enterprise level, however, you are more likely to find special-purpose or customized applications; these present greater difficulties. It might take time for developers to produce updates for special-purpose applications; for customized applications, it might be necessary to commission additional work from a programmer. Commercial applications can be extremely costly to upgrade, especially when you have to purchase hundreds or thousands of licenses.

X REF

To aid in evaluating and testing applications in the Windows 7 environment, Microsoft provides a free Application Compatibility Toolkit. For more information on using this toolkit and deploying applications on Windows 7, see Lesson 7, "Working with Applications."

TAKE NOTE *

The Windows 7 Home Basic edition is left out of consideration unless you are located in an emerging market outside of North America, Europe, or Australia.

In enterprise environments, application testing is as important as hardware testing. Even if an updated version of an application is available, you must test it carefully with the new operating system to ensure that it functions properly. The alternative could be the failure of a mission-critical application across the entire enterprise, resulting in extended down time and lost productivity.

Which Windows 7 Edition Should I Install?

You should select a Windows 7 edition based on several factors, including the tasks the user will be performing and, of course, your budget.

For home users, the choice between Windows 7 Starter and Home Premium is primarily economic. If a client wants to burn DVDs and spends a lot of time working with audio and video files, then Home Premium is generally worth the additional investment. Home Premium provides the Windows Aero user experience; Starter does not. Many new computers ship with Starter installed, so there is likely to be a large number of users upgrading to Home Premium.

Most enterprise installations require their workstations to log on to an Active Directory Domain Services domain, which eliminates Starter and Home Premium as possible choices because they lack domain support. In most cases, the organization's relationship with Microsoft is the deciding factor in the choice between Windows 7 Professional and Enterprise. Windows 7 Professional is a retail product, available in stores everywhere, while Enterprise is only available directly from Microsoft as part of a volume license agreement.

Windows 7 Ultimate edition is a premium product intended for retail users who want all of the features of Windows 7 Enterprise without entering into a volume licensing agreement. Home users for whom price is not a major concern are likely to opt for the Ultimate edition, as are small business customers interested only in retail licensing.

Should I Perform an Upgrade or a Clean Installation?

The question of whether to install Windows 7 by performing an in-place upgrade or a *clean installation* depends on the amount and type of data stored on the computer, as well as the computer's current efficiency.

Obviously, new computers, or computers with new hard disk drives, require a clean installation in which you boot from the Windows 7 setup disk and create or select a blank partition where the operating system will reside. If the computer is currently running Windows Vista, you must consider whether it is preferable to wipe out the existing operating system and install Windows 7 from scratch or install Windows 7 over the previous operating system.

+ MORE INFORMATION

You can perform an in-place upgrade to Windows 7 only on computers running Windows Vista or another edition of Windows 7. It is not possible to perform an in-place upgrade to Windows 7 from Windows XP, Windows 2000, Windows Me, Windows 98, Windows 95, Windows NT, or Windows 3.1. For computers running these operating systems, you must perform a clean installation.

The primary advantage of performing a clean installation is that Windows 7 will achieve its best possible performance. Installing the operating system files on a blank disk means that they will be unfragmented, improving disk performance. A clean installation ensures that the user retains the maximum amount of disk space for applications and data. Of course, a clean installation also erases all existing data, so you must be careful to back up everything that the user wants to retain.

For home users, there is usually some data to preserve, such as image, audio, and video files, as well as data files for specific applications. Fortunately, writable CDs and DVDs, USB flash drives, and external hard drives make it relatively easy to back up a user's essential data. What can be more problematic in a case like this is the loss of important configuration settings, such as usernames, passwords, and customized application templates. Be sure to preserve this type of information before wiping out a partition to perform a clean installation.

Performing an in-place upgrade to Windows 7 means that whatever disk and registry clutter is present under the previous operating system will remain in place. Files might be extensively fragmented, even to the point of executing poorly, and outdated applications and data files could occupy significant amounts of disk space.

The advantage of performing an in-place upgrade is that all of the user's applications, data files, and configuration settings remain intact, but even this could be a problem. Upgrades can generate incompatibilities with drivers or applications that you must rectify before the computer can run properly.

In an enterprise environment, it is more typical for users to store their data files on servers, as opposed to local drives. Also, a properly maintained enterprise network should document all configuration settings and logon credentials. This minimizes the problem of potential data loss when performing a clean installation.

Clean installations are generally preferable in an enterprise environment because they ensure that all of the computers are running an identical system configuration. This eliminates many of the technical support problems that can occur when computers are running different configurations.

Should I Perform a Single or Dual Boot Installation?

One other solution to the problem of whether to perform an upgrade or a clean installation is to create a *dual boot* environment, in which you retain the old operating system installation on one disk partition and create a clean installation of Windows 7 on another.

Dual booting enables a user to run either operating system at any time. The original operating system installation retains all of its existing applications and settings, but you must configure the new Windows 7 installation from scratch and install all of your applications.

The disadvantages of dual booting include the following:

- You must have a separate disk partition available to install Windows 7.
- Two operating systems require twice as much disk space as one.
- Switching from one operating system to another to perform a specific task requires a computer restart, which can take several minutes.

Dual booting is not commonly found in enterprise computing environments, except as a makeshift compatibility solution, but some home users employ it to test new operating systems or maintain configurations to support different applications.

Do I Have to Install Multiple Languages?

Before Windows Vista, each language-specific version of a Windows operating system had to be developed, maintained, and distributed separately. Starting with Vista, however, and now with Windows 7, it is possible to install multiple language packs on a single computer so that individuals can work in multiple languages.

The main problems for multilingual users in the past have been the availability of the languages they need and the complex procedure for implementing multiple languages on a single computer. To use multiple languages on a Windows XP computer, you must begin with an installation of the English language Windows XP version. Then you install the *multilingual user interface (MUI)* pack and whatever additional language packs you need. Unfortunately, some of the language packs provide more complete support than others.

Windows 7 contains an MUI architecture that makes it easier to install multilingual support on a computer. In Windows 7, the binary code that makes up the operating system is entirely language neutral. During the operating system installation process, the Setup program installs the operating system and then applies a language pack containing the information needed to provide the localized user interface.

Because the language packs for Windows 7 contain no binary code, they are interchangeable. Therefore, it is no longer necessary for technicians to consider localization issues before installing the operating system. You can change a Windows 7 installation from one language to another at any time, or install multiple language packs that utilize the same binary code.

+ MORE INFORMATION

Because the Windows 7 binaries are language neutral there is no need for language-specific service packs or other updates. Microsoft is therefore able to release each update in one generic version suitable for all Windows 7 computers around the world, regardless of the language they use.

■ Understanding the Windows 7 Boot Environment

↓
THE BOTTOM LINE
Windows 7 eliminates DOS from the installation process and provides a new boot environment.

Those who have performed clean installations of stand-alone Windows XP systems should recall that the very beginning of the process, immediately after the system boots from the installation disk, consists of several character-based (that is, nongraphical) screens, like that shown in Figure 2-1. On these screens, you opt to perform the installation, agree to the terms of the End User License Agreement (EULA), select the drive partition on which you want to install Windows XP, and then watch as the program copies the installation files from the CD-ROM to a temporary folder on the hard disk.

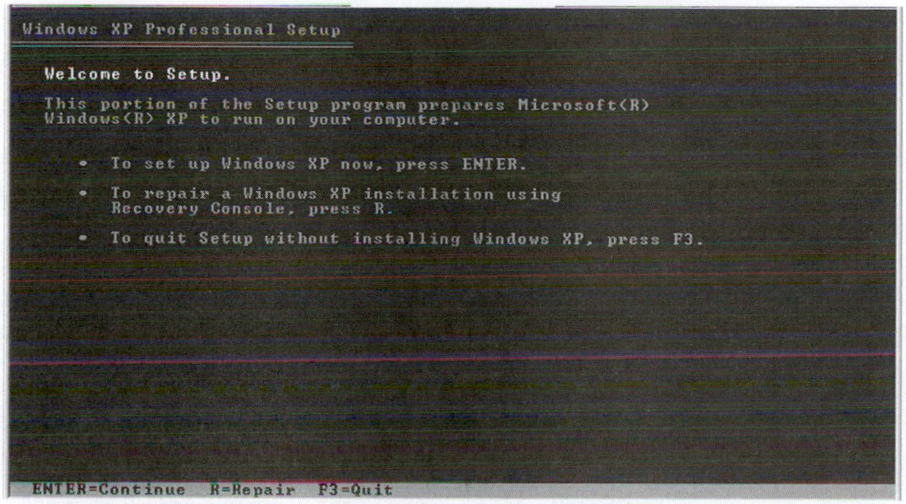

Figure 2-1

A character-based screen from the MS-DOS phase of a Windows XP installation

```
Windows XP Professional Setup

    Welcome to Setup.

    This portion of the Setup program prepares Microsoft(R)
    Windows(R) XP to run on your computer.

        •  To set up Windows XP now, press ENTER.

        •  To repair a Windows XP installation using
           Recovery Console, press R.

        •  To quit Setup without installing Windows XP, press F3.




    ENTER=Continue   R=Repair   F3=Quit
```

These screens are character-based because all of the Windows operating systems up to and including Windows XP required an MS-DOS boot at the beginning of the installation process. The MS-DOS boot was necessary because the computer required an operating system to run the installation program and to gain access to the disk drives.

For original equipment manufacturers (OEMs) and enterprise installations, deploying Windows on a large number of computers typically required a boot from an MS-DOS system disk to provide access to the computer's drives and to provide access to a network share where the Windows installation files or a disk image was located.

This need for an MS-DOS boot became increasingly problematic over the years for several reasons, including the following:

- **Limited disk support:** MS-DOS can provide access only to disk drives formatted using one of the File Allocation Table (FAT) formats. MS-DOS cannot provide access to the NTFS drives that most of today's Windows computers use.

- **No internal networking support:** MS-DOS has no internal networking support, and because it is a 16-bit operating system, administrators had to obtain and load 16-bit real mode network adapter drivers (as compared to the 32-bit drivers that current Windows versions use), as well as a TCP/IP client, before they can access a share containing Windows installation files.

- **Limited script support:** MS-DOS has no internal support for any scripting languages other than rudimentary batch files.

- **Boot device limitations:** Many computers today, especially those in corporate environments, do not have floppy disk drives, and creating bootable MS-DOS CD-ROMs can be problematic.

Introducing Windows PE

Ever since Windows Me was retired, Microsoft has eliminated the need for MS-DOS as an underlying operating system for Windows, but Windows 7 is only the second operating system (after Vista) to completely eliminate MS-DOS from the installation process. To replace the MS-DOS boot, Windows 7 includes Windows Preinstallation Environment 3.0 (Windows PE).

Windows PE 3.0 is a stripped-down operating system, based on the Windows 7 kernel, that enables system administrators to boot a computer that has no operating system installed and initiate the operating system setup process. When compared to MS-DOS, Windows PE has a number of distinct advantages, including the following:

- **Native 32-bit or 64-bit support:** Windows PE is a native 32-bit or 64-bit operating system that enables the computer to address memory just as the full Windows 7 operating system does. MS-DOS is a 16-bit OS and is relatively limited in its memory addressing capabilities.

- **Native 32-bit or 64-bit driver support:** Because Windows PE is a 32-bit or 64-bit OS, it can use the same drivers as a full Windows 7 installation. System administrators therefore do not have to search for antiquated 16-bit real mode network drivers as they did with MS-DOS.

- **Internal networking support:** Windows PE includes its own internal TCP/IP networking stack and is capable of functioning as a Windows file-sharing client. This means that after booting Windows PE, an administrator only has to supply a driver for the network adapter and the networking stack is complete.

- **Internal NTFS support:** Windows PE includes internal support for the NTFS file system used by Windows 7, as well as the FAT file systems that MS-DOS supports. This means that when you boot a system using Windows PE, you can read from and write to existing NTFS drives in the computer, as well as create and format new NTFS partitions. It is even possible to create and manage dynamic volumes using Windows PE.

- **Scripting language support:** Windows PE includes internal support for a subset of the Win32 application programming interface (API), meaning that it is possible to run some Windows programs in the preinstallation environment. Windows PE also includes support for Windows Management Instrumentation (WMI) and Windows Script Host that makes it possible for administrators to create scripts that are far more powerful than MS-DOS batch files.

- **Flexible boot options:** Windows PE can boot from a variety of media, including CD-ROMs, DVD-ROMs, USB devices, such as flash disks and floppy drives, or a Windows Deployment Services (WDS) server. The computer can then run the Windows PE operating system from a variety of media, including the DVD, a temporary folder on a hard disk, a USB flash drive, a RAM disk, or a network share.

➕ **MORE INFORMATION**

Windows PE 3.0 is available in both 32-bit and 64-bit versions. You must use the 32-bit version of Windows PE to install the 32-bit version of Windows 7 and the 64-bit version of Windows PE to install the 64-bit version of Windows 7.

What's New in Windows PE 3.0?

The latest version of Windows PE, version 3.0, is more readily available than previous versions and includes a variety of tools you can use to customize the Windows PE environment.

The most important new development in Windows PE 3.0 is that anyone can get it. Prior to Windows 7, Microsoft made Windows PE available only to customers with service agreements. Now, it's available for free in a stand-alone version as part of the Windows 7 Automated Installation Kit (AIK).

Some of the other new features of Windows PE 3.0 are as follows:

- **Windows Imaging format:** Windows 7 AIK provides Windows PE in the Windows Imaging (.wim) file-based image format. Unlike sector-based (iso) images, file-based images are editable.
- **Size reduction:** Windows PE 3.0 omits some of the optional components found in version 2.1, reducing the overall size of the image.
- **Customization:** Windows 7 AIK includes the Deployment Image Servicing and Management (DISM.exe) tool, which enables you to mount the Windows PE image file and customize it by adding device drivers and other components.
- **Hyper-V support:** Windows PE 3.0 includes all of the drivers needed to run in the hyper-V hypervisor environment.
- **Scratch space:** You can customize the Windows PE RAM scratch space to sizes ranging from 32 to 512 megabytes.

TAKE NOTE*   Windows 7 AIK, including Windows PE 3.0, is available free of charge from the Microsoft Download Center at http://www.microsoft.com/downloads/details.aspx?familyid=696DD665-9F76-4177-A811-39C26D3B3B34&displaylang=en.

Understanding Windows PE 3.0 Limitations

Microsoft intends Windows PE to be a reduced subset of the Windows 7 operating system, only providing sufficient capability to perform certain installation, diagnostic, and recovery functions while running from a minimized hardware environment, such as a RAM drive.

Because there was never any intention for Windows PE to function as a full-time operating system, and to facilitate its rapid deployment and execution, there are certain inherent limitations in the product, such as the following:

- Windows PE does not support the entire collection of Win32 APIs as a full installation of Windows 7 does. Microsoft limits the APIs in Windows PE primarily to those providing disk and network input/output functions, as well as certain APIs that make it possible to run basic programs. Reducing the API support enables Windows PE to run in a smaller memory space than Windows 7.

＋ MORE INFORMATION

Because Windows PE requires a relatively small memory space, the entire operating system can run from a RAM disk. A RAM disk is a driver that allocates a section of active memory for use as a virtual disk drive, complete with drive letter. Because the RAM disk is based in memory it is much faster than a hard disk drive, but it is also volatile; all of its contents are lost when the computer restarts. Running the Windows 7 Setup program from a RAM disk allows all the operating system file handles to remain open throughout the installation process, allowing you to remove the boot device, if necessary. By contrast, running the Setup program directly from a DVD makes it impossible to remove the disk (e.g., to load third-party drivers) without interrupting the installation procedure. In the same way, running the Setup program from a temporary folder on a hard disk interferes with partition creation and management functions that might be needed during the installation.

- Windows PE automatically stops and reboots the computer after 72 hours of continuous operation. This deliberate limitation prevents individuals from using the product as a permanent operating environment.
- Windows PE will not fit on a floppy disk, but it is possible to create bootable Windows PE CD-ROMs, DVD-ROMs, and USB flash drives.
- Windows PE networking support is limited to the TCP/IP and NetBIOS Over TCP/IP (NetBT) protocols. There is no support for IPX/SPX or any other network/transport layer protocols.
- You must use the 32-bit version of Windows PE to install the 32-bit version of Windows 7, and the 64-bit version of Windows PE to install the 64-bit Windows 7.
- While it is possible to modify the Windows PE registry when the operating system is running, all registry keys are reset to their default values each time the operating system restarts. It is possible to make permanent changes to the registry, but to do so you must make the changes offline by manually editing the registry while Windows PE is not running.
- You can create drive letter assignments in a Windows PE session, but these assignments are not persistent between sessions.
- Windows PE does not have file server or Terminal Server capabilities, nor does it support the Microsoft .NET Framework or the Common Language Runtime (CLR), Windows on Windows 32 (WOW32), Windows on Windows 64 (WOW64), Virtual DOS Machine (VDM), OS/2, or POSIX subsystems.
- Windows PE does not support the installation of Windows Installer package (.msi) files.
- Windows PE can access Distributed File System (DFS) folders, but only those in stand-alone DFS roots.

Using Windows PE

In addition to functioning as a platform for individual installations of Windows 7, Windows PE is useful for other scenarios that require a basic operating system with minimal resource usage.

Some of the other scenarios that can make use of Windows PE are as follows:

- **Custom deployments:** Windows 7 uses Windows PE during the default installation procedure, but it is possible for administrators to build their own unattended installation routines using Windows PE as a platform to run scripts and deploy customized disk images on fleets of workstations. You can even use Windows PE to deploy operating systems other than Windows 7.

- **System troubleshooting:** If a Windows 7 computer fails to start, or if it crashes repeatedly, a technician can launch the ***Windows Recovery Environment*** (Windows RE), which is simply another name given to Windows PE on a computer with Windows 7 already installed. In the Windows RE environment, the technician can use Windows' built-in troubleshooting utilities or run third-party or custom diagnostic tools.

- **System recovery:** OEMs who build their own computers typically supply their customers with a system recovery disk rather than an operating system installation disk. A system recovery disk contains image files that can restore the computer to its original state, just as it was when it left the factory. OEMs can use Windows PE to build recovery solutions that automate the process of setting up Windows 7, installing specific drivers, installing applications, and configuring the entire system to create a standardized environment.

■ Performing a Clean Installation

↓ THE BOTTOM LINE

A clean installation is the simplest way to deploy Windows 7 on a new computer or a computer with a partition that you are willing to reformat (losing all of the data on the partition in the process).

CERTIFICATION READY?
Perform a clean installation.
1.1

If a computer is brand new and has no operating system installed on it, then it cannot start until you supply a boot disk, such as the Windows 7 installation disk. During the installation you will select the disk partition on which you want to install Windows, and the Setup program will copy the operating system files there.

If the computer has an operating system installed on it, and you have already backed up all the data that you want to preserve, then you are ready to boot the computer from the Windows 7 installation disk. During the setup process you can erase a partition on the disk in preparation for installing Windows there.

TAKE NOTE *

The following procedure is for an installation of Windows 7 Professional edition. Although the installation procedure for the other editions is nearly identical, you might see minor differences in the procedure.

 PERFORM A CLEAN INSTALLATION

GET READY. Prepare the computer for the Windows 7 installation by making sure that all of its external peripheral devices are connected and powered on.

1. Turn on the computer and insert the Windows 7 installation disk into the DVD drive.
2. Press any key to boot from the DVD (if necessary). A progress indicator screen appears as Windows is loading files.

➕ MORE INFORMATION

The device that a PC uses to boot is specified in its system (or BIOS) settings. In some cases, you might have to modify these settings to enable the computer to boot from the Windows 7 DVD. If you are not familiar with the operation of a particular computer, watch the screen carefully as the system starts and look for an instruction specifying what key to press to access the system settings.

3. The computer switches to the Windows graphical interface and the *Install Windows* page appears, as shown in Figure 2-2.

Figure 2-2

The Install Windows page

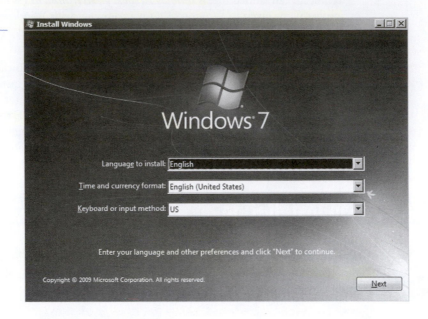

 TAKE NOTE *

At this point, the computer is running Windows PE as its operating system, providing it with the means to execute the Setup program and to load drivers providing access to the disk drives and other hardware resources.

4. Using the drop-down lists provided, select the appropriate Language to install, Time and currency format, and Keyboard or input method and then click Next. The *Windows 7 Install now* page appears, as shown in Figure 2-3.

Figure 2-3

The Windows 7 Install now page

5. Click the Install now button. The *Please read the license terms* page appears, as shown in Figure 2-4.

Figure 2-4

The Please read the license terms page

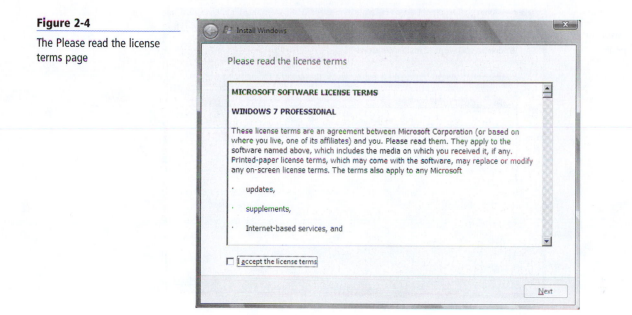

6. Select the I accept the license terms check box and click Next. The *Which type of installation do you want?* page appears, as shown in Figure 2-5.

Figure 2-5

The Which type of installation do you want? page

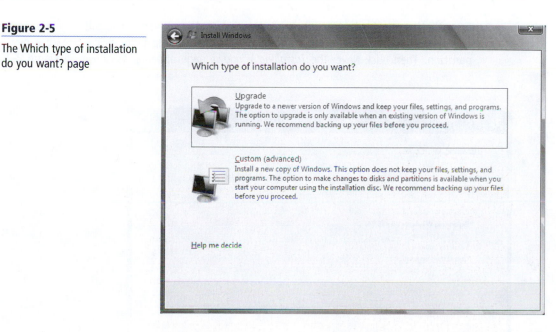

7. Click the Custom (advanced) option. The *Where do you want to install Windows?* page appears, as shown in Figure 2-6.

Figure 2-6

The Where do you want to install Windows? page

![Install Windows dialog showing the "Where do you want to install Windows?" page with Disk 0 Unallocated Space 24.0 GB total size and 24.0 GB free space]

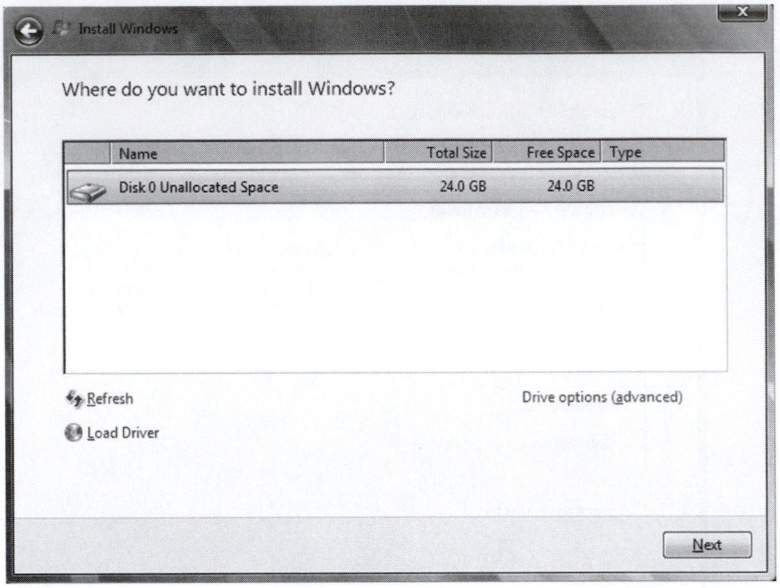

TAKE NOTE*

The Upgrade option is currently disabled because you booted the computer using the Windows 7 installation disk. For the Upgrade option to function, you must boot an existing Windows Vista operating system and start the Windows 7 installation program from there. See "Upgrading to Windows 7" later in this lesson for more information.

8. From the list provided, select the partition on which you want to install Windows 7, or select an area of unallocated disk space where the Setup program can create a new partition. Then click Next. The *Installing Windows* page appears, as shown in Figure 2-7.

Figure 2-7

The Installing Windows page

![Install Windows dialog showing the "Installing Windows..." page with progress steps: Copying Windows files (checked), Expanding Windows files (87%)..., Installing features, Installing updates, Completing installation]

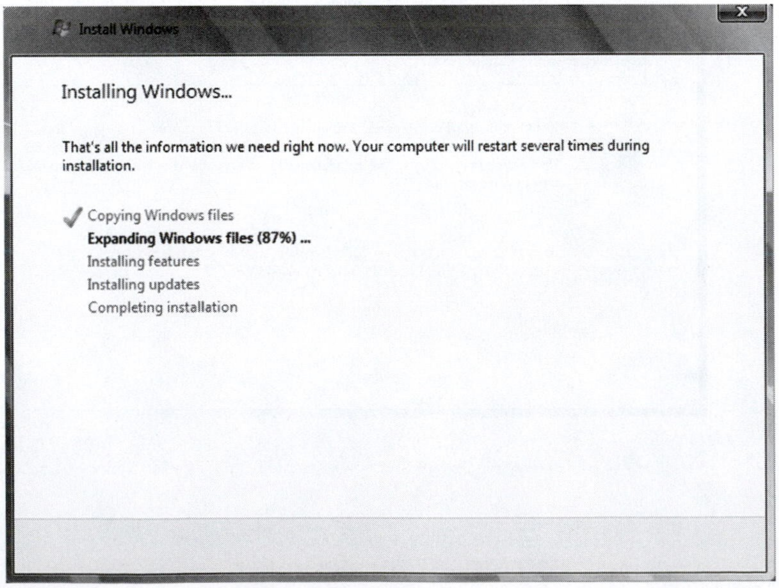

9. After several minutes, during which the Setup program installs Windows 7, the computer reboots twice and the *Set Up Windows* page appears, as shown in Figure 2-8.

Figure 2-8

The Set Up Windows page

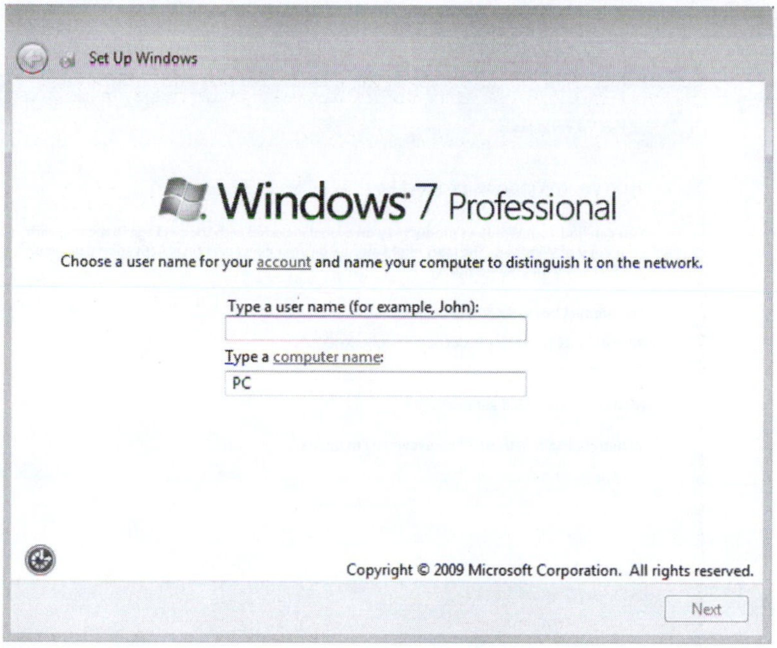

10. In the **Type a user name** text box, enter a name for the first user account on the system.

11. In the **Type a computer name** text box, enter a name, no more than fifteen characters long, by which the computer will be known on the network.

TAKE NOTE*

If the computer is connected to a Windows network, then the name you specify for the computer must be unique on that network.

12. Click **Next** to continue. The *Set a password for your account* page appears, as shown in Figure 2-9.

Figure 2-9

The Set a password for your account page

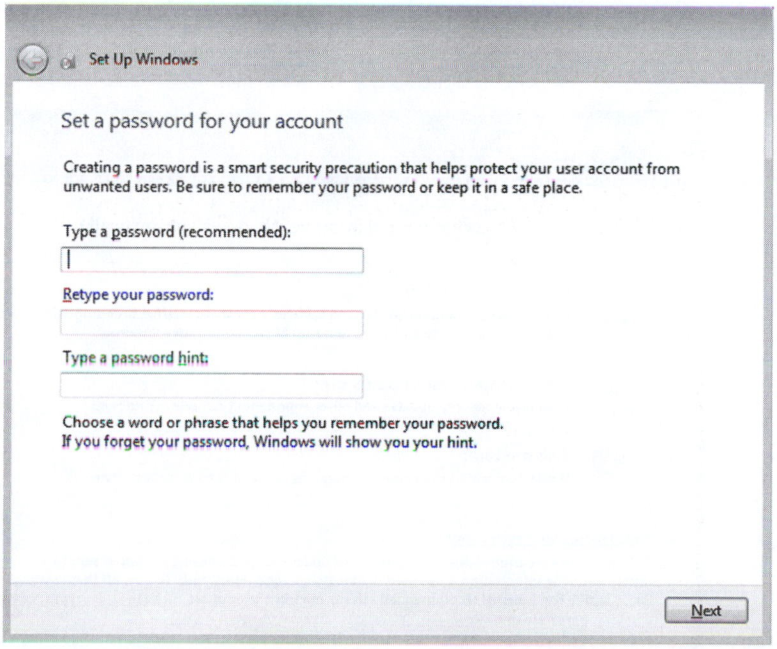

13. In the **Type a password** and **Retype your password** text boxes, enter a password for the user name you specified earlier.

14. In the Type a password hint text box, type a phrase to remind you of the password.

15. Click Next to continue. The *Type your Windows product key* page appears, as shown in Figure 2-10.

Figure 2-10

The Type your Windows
product key page

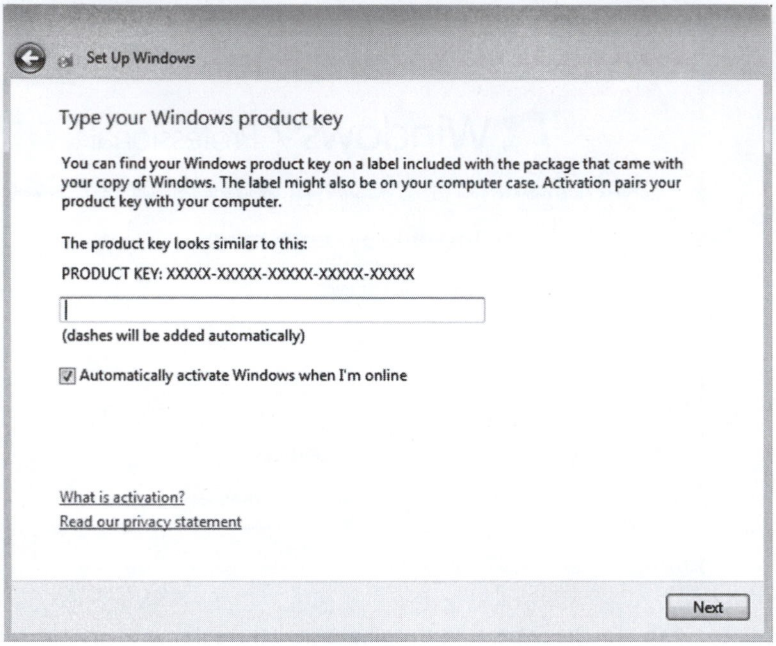

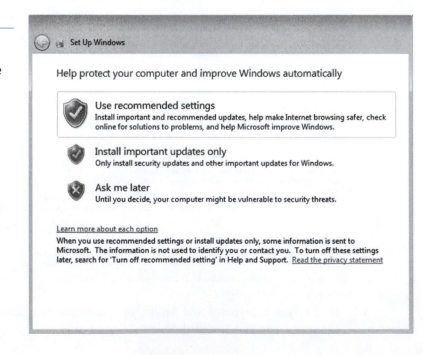

16. In the Product key text box, type the key code supplied with your copy of Windows 7. Leave the Automatically activate Windows when I'm online check box selected, unless you know you will have to activate your computer by telephone or some other means.

17. Click Next to continue. The *Help protect your computer and improve Windows automatically* page appears, as shown in Figure 2-11.

Figure 2-11

The Help protect your
computer and improve
Windows automatically page

18. Select one of the three options specifying what security settings you want the computer to use. The *Review your time and date settings* page appears, as shown in Figure 2-12.

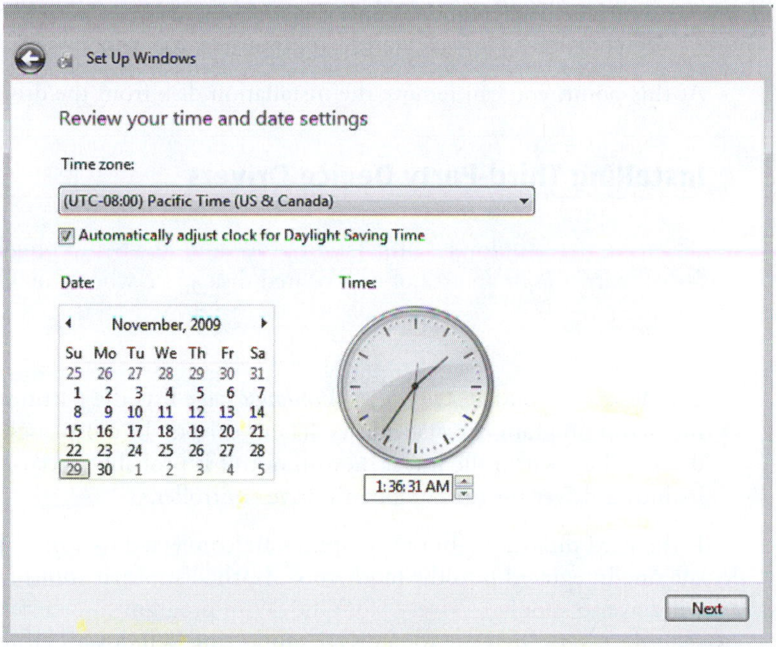

Figure 2-12

The Review your time and date settings page

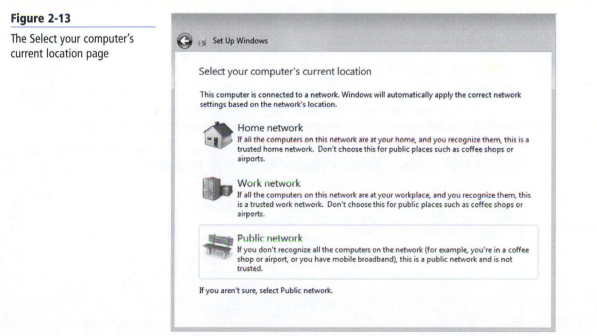

 TAKE NOTE *

As with most of the settings you configure during the Windows 7 installation, you can also select a different security option at a later time.

19. From the Time zone drop-down list, select the time zone in which the computer will be running. If the date and time specified in the calendar and clock are not accurate, or you want to prevent the computer from adjusting itself during Daylight Savings Time, correct the settings and click Next. The *Select your computer's current location* page appears, as shown in Figure 2-13.

Figure 2-13

The Select your computer's current location page

TAKE NOTE *

The *Select your computer's current location* page appears only when the Setup program success-fully detects and configures a network connection. Otherwise, the Setup program skips it.

20. Click the appropriate option specifying the computer's normal location. The system completes its new startup routine and the Windows desktop appears.

At this point, you can remove the installation disk from the drive.

Installing Third-Party Device Drivers

During the Windows 7 installation procedure, the Setup program enables you to select a disk partition or an area of unallocated disk space where you want to install the operating system.

The *Where do you want to install Windows?* page lists the partitions on all the hard disks that the Setup program detects with its default drivers. In most cases, all of the computer's hard disks will appear in the list; if they do not, it is probably because Windows PE does not include a driver for the computer's drive controller.

If the hard disk drives in the computer are connected to a third-party controller, rather than the one integrated into the motherboards, the list of partitions might appear empty, and you will have to supply a driver before the Setup program can see the disks. Check the controller manufacturer's Web site for a driver supporting Windows 7. If none is available, use the most recent Windows Vista driver.

+ MORE INFORMATION

There are several reasons why a computer might employ a third-party disk controller, rather than the one integrated into the motherboard. The computer might have a relatively old motherboard and more modern drives whose capa-bilities are not supported by the older controller. The computer might also be using SCSI (Small Computer Systems Interface) rather than SATA (Serial ATA) or IDE (Integrated Drive Electronics) hard drives, and a SCSI controller that is not supported by Windows PE. Finally, the computer might be using a specialized controller that provides advanced disk management technologies, such as RAID (Redundant Array of Independent Disks).

To install a driver, use the following procedure:

→ **INSTALL A THIRD-PARTY DISK DRIVER**

GET READY. If, during a Windows 7 installation, no disk partitions or unallocated space appear on the *Where do you want to install Windows?* page, you must install the appropriate driver for your disk controller using the following procedure before the installation can continue.

1. On the *Where do you want to install Windows?* page, click the Load Driver button. A Load Driver message box appears, as shown in Figure 2-14.

Figure 2-14

The Load Driver message box

Load Driver

To install the device driver needed to access your hard drive, insert the installation media containing the driver files, and then click OK.

Note: The installation media can be a floppy disk, CD, DVD, or USB flash drive.

[Browse] [OK] [Cancel]

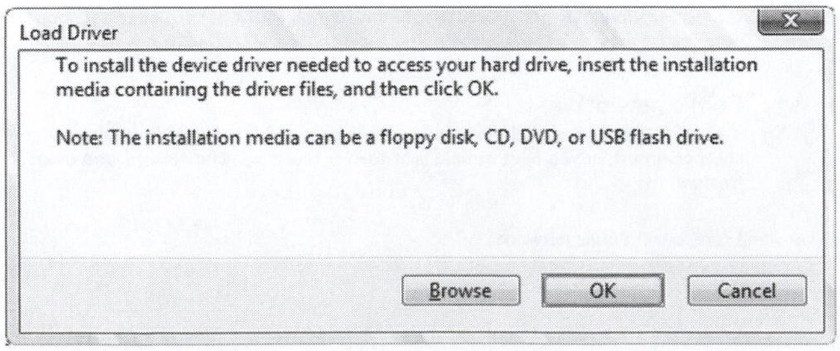

2. Insert the storage medium containing the driver into the computer. You can supply drivers on a CD, DVD, USB flash drive, or floppy disk.

TAKE NOTE*

Because Windows PE is running on a RAM drive, it is possible to remove the Windows 7 installation disk from the DVD drive and insert another disk containing drivers. You will later have to re-insert the Windows 7 disk to complete the installation.

3. Click OK if the driver is in the root directory of the storage medium, or Browse if it is necessary to locate the driver in the directory structure of the disk. When the driver loads, the partitions and unallocated space on the associated disks appear in the list on the *Where do you want to install Windows?* page.

4. Select the partition or area of unallocated space where you want to install Windows 7 and then continue with the rest of the installation procedure, as covered earlier in this lesson.

Working with Installation Partitions

In addition to installing disk drivers, the *Where do you want to install Windows?* page enables you to create, manage, and delete the partitions on your disks.

Clicking the Drive options (advanced) button on the page causes four additional buttons to appear, as shown in Figure 2-15. These buttons have the following functions:

- **Delete:** Removes an existing partition from a disk, permanently erasing all of its data. You might want to delete partitions to consolidate unallocated disk space, enabling you to create a new, larger partition.

- **Extend:** Enables you to make an existing partition larger, as long as there is unallocated space available immediately following the selected partition on the disk.

- **Format:** Enables you to format an existing partition on a disk, thereby erasing all of its data. There is no need to format any new partitions you create for the install, but you might want to format an existing partition to eliminate unwanted files prior to installing Windows 7 on it.

- **New:** Creates a new partition of a user-specified size in the selected area of unallocated space.

Figure 2-15

Additional buttons on the Where do you want to install Windows? page

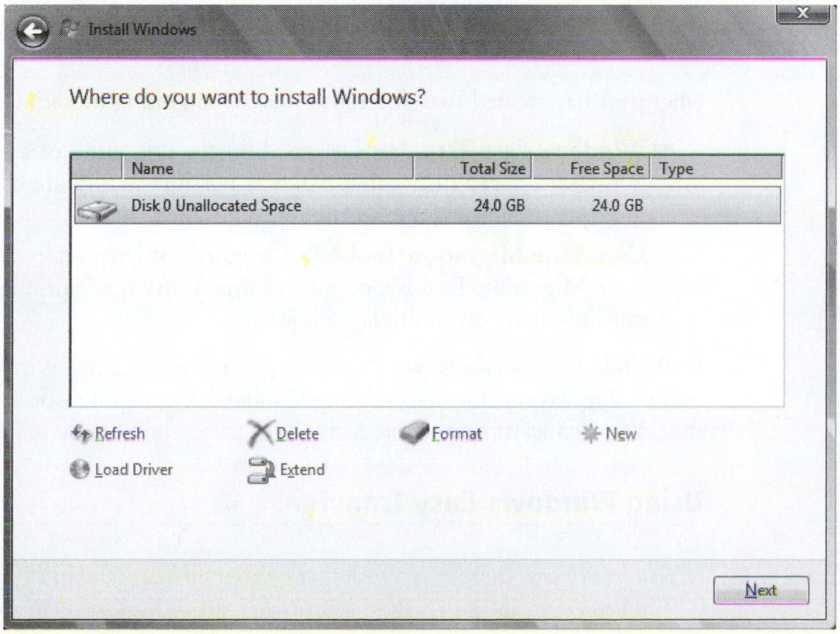

■ Migrating to Windows 7

↓ THE BOTTOM LINE

Performing a clean installation of Windows 7 on a user's workstation does not necessarily mean that the user has to lose his or her personal files and folders, operating system and application settings, and Internet favorites. Using tools supplied with Windows 7 or the Windows 7 AIK, you can migrate these elements from one operating system to another.

CERTIFICATION READY?
Migrate user profiles.
1.3

In some cases, performing a clean installation of Windows 7 is a perfectly adequate solution. You might be working with a brand new computer, or the user might not have any important data to carry over from the previous operating system. However, most experienced computer users have settings and data they want to keep, data that is typically stored in a Windows user profile.

A user profile is a series of folders, associated with a specific user account, that contain personal documents, user-specific registry settings, Internet favorites, and other personalized information—everything that provides a user's familiar working environment. On a standalone Windows XP workstation, user profiles are stored in the Documents and Settings folder, in subfolders named for the user accounts. On a Windows Vista or 7 workstation, the subfolders are found in the Users folder. On a workstation that is joined to an Active Directory Domain Services (AD DS) domain, the user profiles are also stored on a network server.

➕ MORE INFORMATION

User profiles consist of files, such as a user's personal documents and Internet favorites, stored in appropriate profile folders and settings stored in a registry file. The registry settings include basic display parameters, such as the colors, themes, and images you have designated for your Windows desktop, as well as configuration parameters for specific applications. Windows loads the profile information into memory each time that particular user logs on to Windows and saves any changes the user has made to the profile when that user logs off. User profiles make it possible for different users to maintain their own individual settings on one Windows computer.

There are two basic methods for deploying Windows 7 to a client while retaining the user profile settings: upgrade and migration. In an upgrade, you install Windows 7 on the computer running an earlier operating system. Windows 7 overwrites the old OS, but all of the user profiles already on the computer remain in place. In a migration, you copy the user profile information from the old operating system to some temporary medium and transfer it to a new, clean installation of Windows 7.

Microsoft has created two different tools for migrating files and settings to new computers:

- **Windows Easy Transfer:** Designed for the migration of a single computer, Easy Transfer is a wizard-based utility that makes it possible to migrate user profile information for multiple users from one computer to another.
- **User State Migration Tool 4.0:** Designed for large-scale enterprise deployments, User State Migration Tool is a command line utility that can migrate profile information for multiple users on multiple computers.

In the following sections, you learn the procedure for using Windows Easy Transfer to migrate user profile settings from an existing Windows Vista workstation to a new Windows 7 workstation. You also learn some basic facts about using the User State Migration Tool.

Using Windows Easy Transfer

Windows Easy Transfer is a tool that migrates user profile information from an existing Windows computer to a new computer with a clean installation of Windows 7.

Windows Easy Transfer migrates user profile data from one computer to another in a variety of scenarios. As long as you are working with the user accounts from one single computer, Windows Easy Transfer can function in virtually any hardware configuration. Some of the options you can select include:

- **Number of computers:** Windows Easy Transfer supports both side-by-side and wipe-and-load migrations. In a ***side-by-side migration***, you have two computers running simultaneously; one is the source computer containing the user profile information you want to transfer, and the other is the destination computer running Windows 7 to which you want to transfer the profile information. In a ***wipe-and-load migration***, you have only one computer, which initially contains the user profile settings you want to transfer. After saving the profile information to a removable storage medium, you perform a clean Windows 7 installation to wipe out all data on the computer's hard disk and then transfer the profile data from the removable medium back to the computer.

- **Direct or indirect:** When you are performing a side-by-side migration, you can use Windows Easy Transfer with the computers connected together directly, using a cable or a network, or connected indirectly, using a removable storage medium.

- **Storage medium:** Windows Easy Transfer can use virtually any storage medium to transfer profile data between computers, as long as it provides sufficient storage space and is accessible by both machines. You can use a writable CD or DVD, a USB flash drive, an external hard drive, or a network share. Floppy disks are not supported because they have insufficient capacity.

The procedure for migrating files consists of two basic elements: saving the user profile information on the existing computer and transferring the information to the new computer. Using the capabilities of Windows Easy Transfer, you should be able to satisfy the requirements of almost any stand-alone user that wants to move to Windows 7 without performing an upgrade. The most common scenarios are likely to be these:

- **Scenario 1:** A user purchases a new computer on which he wants to run Windows 7, but he also wants to retain the files and settings from his existing Windows Vista computer.

- **Scenario 2:** A user wants to install Windows 7 on her existing Windows Vista computer and retain all of her files and settings, but she wants to avoid performing an upgrade to maximize her Windows 7 performance.

The following sections describe the Windows Easy Transfer procedures for each of these scenarios.

Performing Migration Scenario 1

> Ed is a longtime Windows Vista user with a small network in his home. He has just purchased a new computer with Windows 7 preinstalled on it and wants to migrate his files and settings from his Vista computer to the Windows 7 computer. The new computer came with recovery disks, but no Windows 7 installation disk.

In this scenario, you perform a side-by-side migration with both computers connected to the user's home network. However, because you do not have access to a Windows 7 installation disk, you must add a third element to the procedure, in which you provide the Vista computer with access to the Windows Easy Transfer program.

PERFORM MIGRATION SCENARIO 1

GET READY. Both computers must be powered up and connected to the home network. Create a network share on one of the two computers and make sure that both systems can access it.

1. On the Windows 7 computer, click Start > All Programs > Accessories > System Tools and then select Windows Easy Transfer. The *Welcome to Windows Easy Transfer* page appears, as shown in Figure 2-16.

Figure 2-16

The Welcome to Windows Easy Transfer page

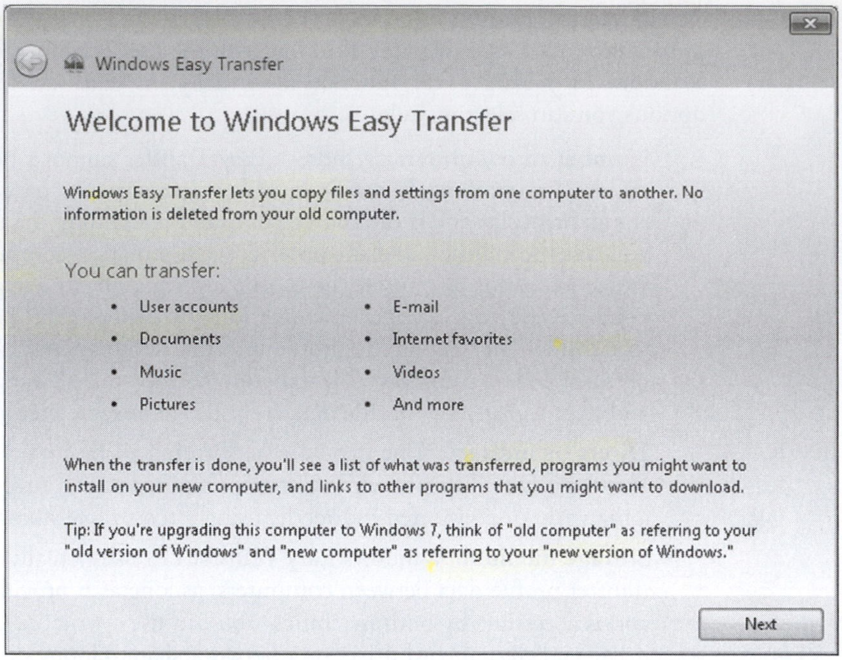

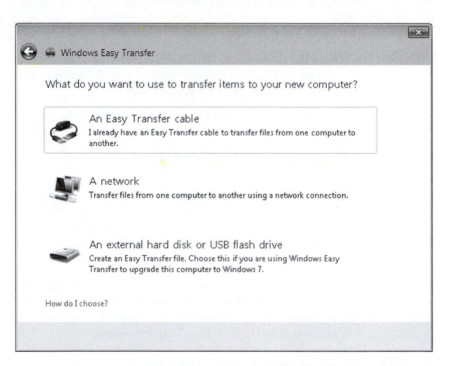

2. Click Next. The *What do you want to use to transfer items to your new computer?* page appears, as shown in Figure 2-17.

Figure 2-17

The What do you want to use to transfer items to your new computer? page

---

➕ **MORE INFORMATION**

An Easy Transfer cable is a special USB cable that you can use to connect two Windows computers together solely for the purpose of using the Windows Easy Transfer utility. In this particular scenario, the user has a network available, which performs the same function.

3. Click A network. The *Which computer are you using now?* page appears, as shown in Figure 2-18.

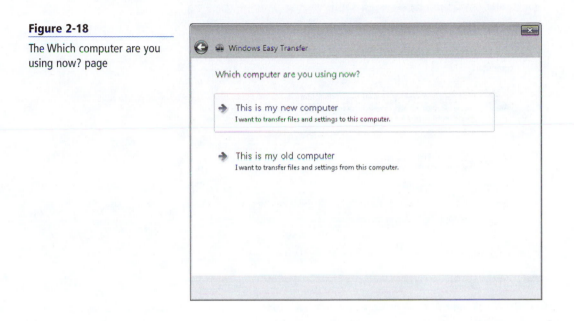

4. Click This is my new computer. The *Do you need to install Windows Easy Transfer on your old computer?* page appears, as shown in Figure 2-19.

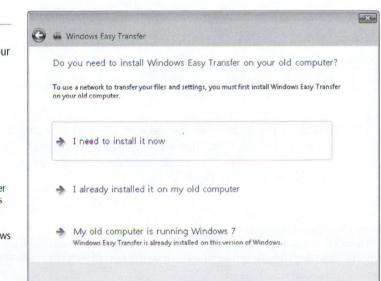

WARNING To transfer user profile information to a Windows 7 computer, you must use the Windows Easy Transfer program supplied with Windows 7. Windows Vista has its own version of Windows Easy Transfer, but this version is not compatible with Windows 7 user profiles.

5. Click I need to install it now. The *How do you want to install Windows Easy Transfer on your old computer?* page appears, as shown in Figure 2-20.

Figure 2-20

The How do you want to install Windows Easy Transfer on your old computer? page

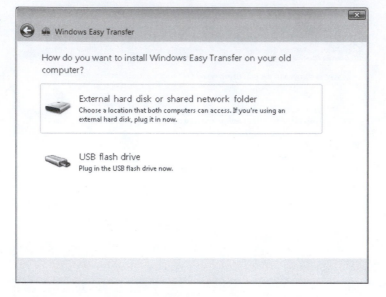

6. Click External hard disk or shared network folder. A *Browse for Folder* dialog box appears, as shown in Figure 2-21.

Figure 2-21

The Browse for Folder dialog box

7. Browse to the location of the network share you created before beginning the procedure and click OK. The wizard copies Windows Easy Transfer to the location you specified and the *Install Windows Easy Transfer on your old computer* page appears, as shown in Figure 2-22.

 TAKE NOTE * You can use any other storage medium to transfer the Windows Easy Transfer program to the Windows Vista computer, such as a writable CD or DVD or a USB flash drive, as long as the Vista computer is capable of reading it.

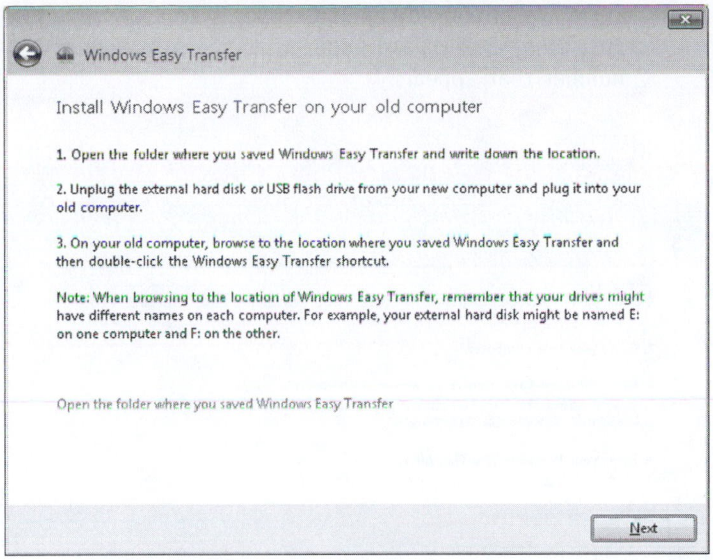

Figure 2-22

The Install Windows Easy Transfer on your old computer page

> **Windows Easy Transfer**
>
> Install Windows Easy Transfer on your old computer
>
> 1. Open the folder where you saved Windows Easy Transfer and write down the location.
>
> 2. Unplug the external hard disk or USB flash drive from your new computer and plug it into your old computer.
>
> 3. On your old computer, browse to the location where you saved Windows Easy Transfer and then double-click the Windows Easy Transfer shortcut.
>
> Note: When browsing to the location of Windows Easy Transfer, remember that your drives might have different names on each computer. For example, your external hard disk might be named E: on one computer and F: on the other.
>
> Open the folder where you saved Windows Easy Transfer
>
> Next

8. Switch to the Windows Vista computer, click Start > All Programs > Accessories, and then select Windows Explorer. A Windows Explorer window appears.

9. Browse to the location on the network you selected earlier and double click the Windows Easy Transfer shortcut. An Open File—Security Warning dialog box appears.

10. Click Open. A User Account Control message box appears.

11. Click Continue. The *Welcome to Windows Easy Transfer* page appears.

12. Click Next. The *What do you want to use to transfer items to your new computer?* page appears.

13. Click A network. The *Which computer are you using now?* page appears, as shown in Figure 2-23.

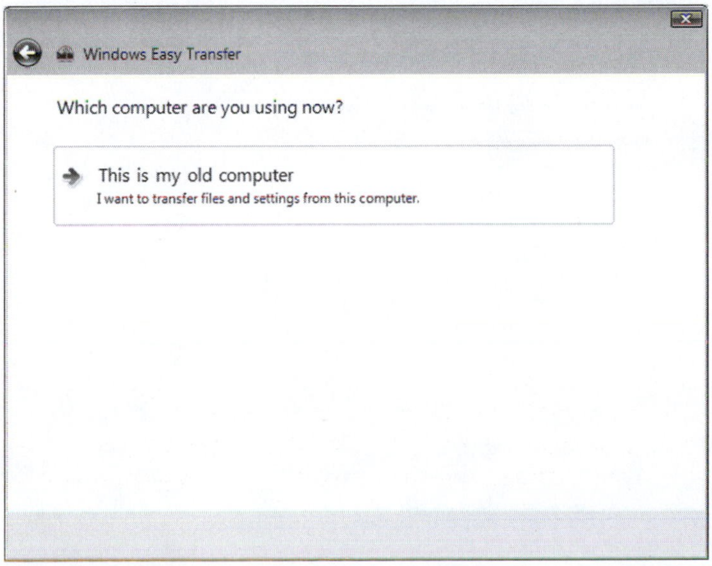

Figure 2-23

The Which computer are you using now? page

> **Windows Easy Transfer**
>
> Which computer are you using now?
>
> → This is my old computer
>   I want to transfer files and settings from this computer.

 TAKE NOTE* Now that you are running Windows Easy Transfer on Windows Vista, the program recognizes that this must be the old computer.

14. Click This is my old computer. The *Go to your new computer and enter your Windows Easy Transfer key* page appears, as shown in Figure 2-24. Take note of the key number that appears.

Figure 2-24

The Go to your new computer and enter your Windows Easy Transfer key page

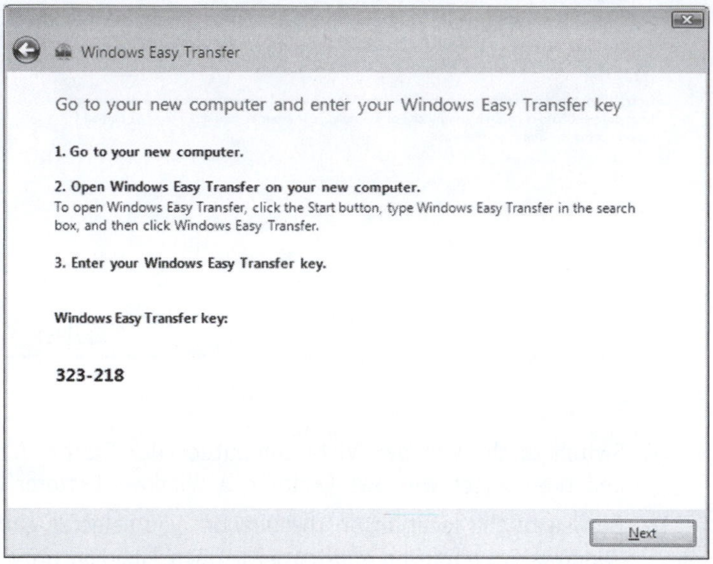

15. Switch back to the new computer and click Next. The *Enter your Windows Easy Transfer key* page appears, as shown in Figure 2-25.

Figure 2-25

The Enter your Windows Easy Transfer key page

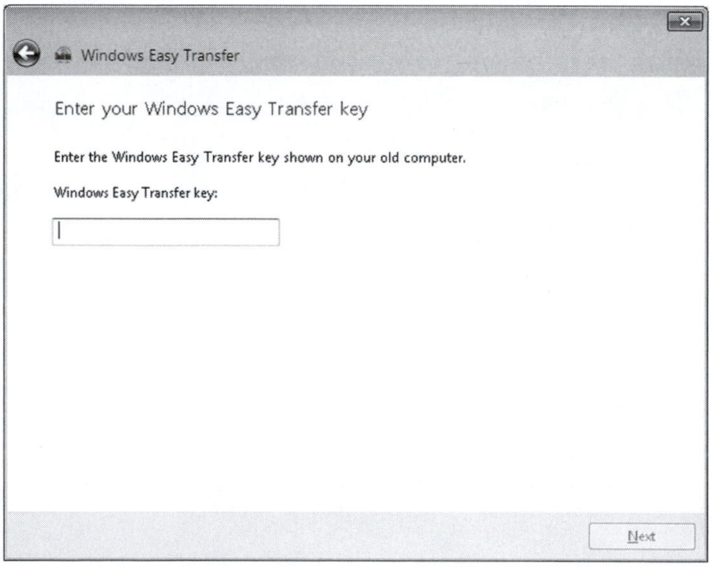

16. In the Windows Easy Transfer Key text box, type the key that appeared on your old computer and click Next. The new computer establishes a connection with the old computer, scans it for files and settings it can transfer, and displays the results in the *Choose what to transfer* page, as shown in Figure 2-26.

Figure 2-26

The Choose what to transfer page

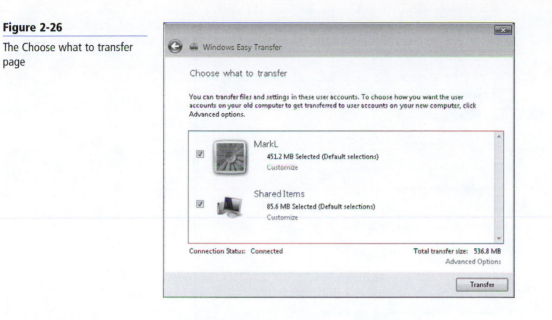

17. Select the items you want to copy to the new computer and click Transfer. The program transfers the selected items to the new computer, and then the *Your transfer is complete* page appears, as shown in Figure 2-27.

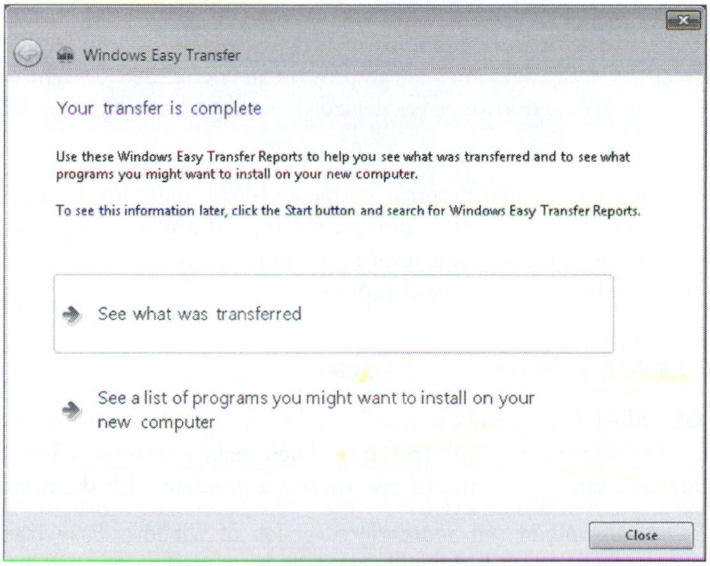

Figure 2-27

The Your transfer is complete page

18. Click See what was transferred. A Windows Easy Transfer Reports window appears, as shown in Figure 2-28.

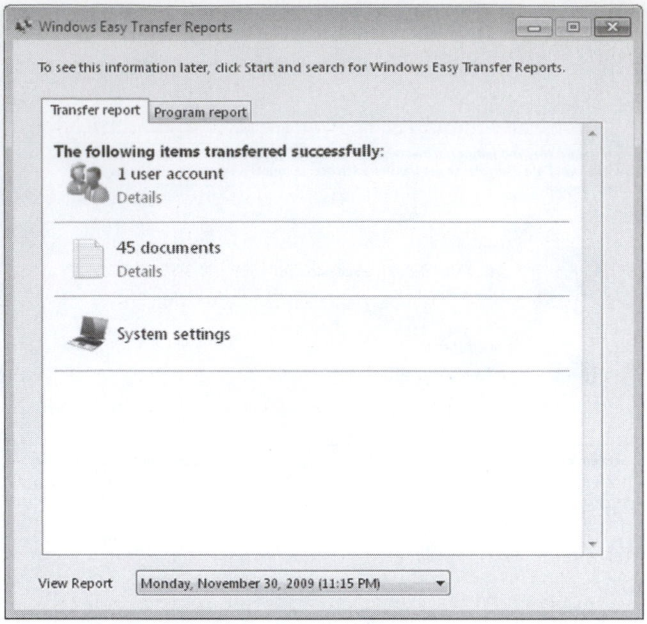

Figure 2-28

A Windows Easy Transfer Reports window

19. Close the Windows Easy Transfer Reports window and, on the *Your transfer is complete* page, click Close.

20. On the Windows Vista computer, on the *The transfer is complete* page, click Close.

Performing Migration Scenario 2

Alice has a Windows Vista computer that she has been sharing with her roommates for several years. She recently purchased the retail version of Windows 7, which came bundled with a free external hard drive. Alice wants to install Windows 7 on her existing computer, retaining the files and settings she has accrued and omitting the files and settings created by her roommates. However, she does not want to perform an upgrade, because she has recently noticed that the computer's performance has degraded, possibly due to file fragmentation and registry clutter.

In this scenario, you perform a wipe-and-load migration using the external hard drive to temporarily store the files and settings from the Windows Vista operating system. Then, after performing a clean installation of Windows 7, you transfer the files and settings from the external drive back to the computer.

➔ PERFORM MIGRATION SCENARIO 2

GET READY. Plug the external hard drive into a USB port on the computer and make sure that it is connected and operating. Then make a secondary backup of the client's important files as a safety measure, in case there is a problem with the migration procedure.

1. Download the appropriate version of Windows Easy Transfer from the Microsoft Download Center and install it by executing the Microsoft Update Standalone Installer (.msu) file.

TAKE NOTE*

Windows Easy Transfer is not accessible from the Windows 7 installation disk as it is from the Windows Vista disk. To perform a wipe-and-load migration without an existing computer running Windows 7, you have to download Windows Easy Transfer from the Microsoft Download Center Web site. The http://windows.microsoft.com/en-us/windows7/products/features/windows-easy-transfer page has links to versions for Windows Vista and Windows XP in 32-bit and 64-bit versions.

TAKE NOTE*

Windows Easy Transfer can migrate user profile information only from computers running Windows 7, Windows Vista, and Windows XP SP2.

2. Click Start > All Programs > Windows Easy Transfer 7. A User Account Control message box appears.
3. Click Continue. The *Welcome to Windows Easy Transfer* page appears.
4. Click Next. The *What do you want to use to transfer items to your new computer?* page appears.
5. Click An external hard disk or USB flash drive. The *Which computer are you using now?* page appears.
6. Click This is my old computer. The program scans the computer for files and settings it can transfer and displays the results in the *Choose what to transfer from this computer* page.
7. Select the items you want to copy to the new computer and click Next. The *Save your files and settings for transfer* page appears, as shown in Figure 2-29.

Figure 2-29

The Save your files and settings for transfer page

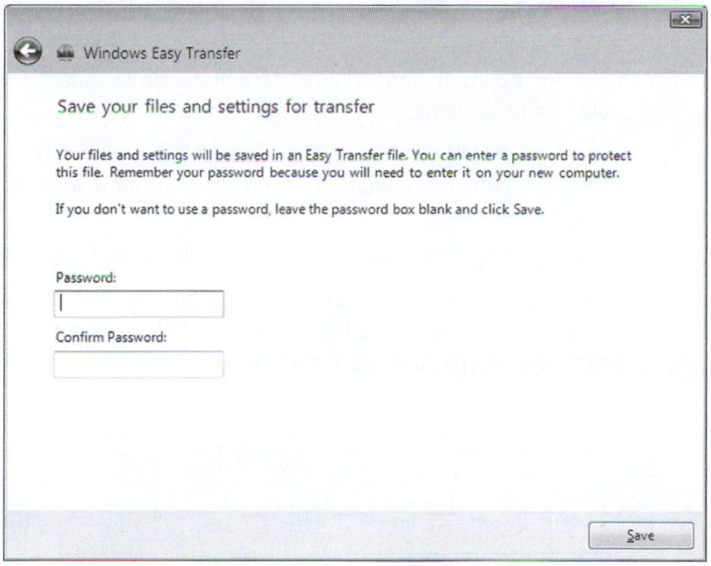

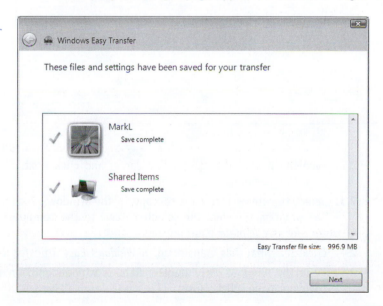

8. In the Password and Confirm Password text boxes, type a password to protect the data to be transferred and click Save. The *Save Your Easy Transfer File* combo box appears.
9. Browse to the external hard drive and click Save. The program transfers the selected items to the external drive and the *These files and settings have been saved for your transfer* page appears, as shown in Figure 2-30.

Figure 2-30

The These files and settings have been saved for your transfer page

10. Click Next. The *Your transfer file is complete* page appears, specifying the name and location of the file containing the transferred data.

11. Click Next. The *Windows Easy Transfer is complete on this computer* page appears.

12. Click Close.

13. Disconnect the external hard drive from the computer.

14. Perform a clean installation of Windows 7 on the computer, as detailed earlier in this Lesson, erasing the partition on which Windows Vista was installed.

15. Reconnect the external hard drive to the computer and make sure that it is functioning.

16. On the newly installed Windows 7 computer, click Start > All Programs > Accessories > System Tools and select Windows Easy Transfer. The *Welcome to Windows Easy Transfer* page appears.

17. Click Next. The *What do you want to use to transfer items to your new computer?* page appears.

18. Click An external hard disk or USB flash drive. The *Which computer are you using now?* page appears.

19. Click This is my new computer. The *Has Windows Easy Transfer already saved your files from your old computer to an external hard disk or USB flash drive?* page appears.

20. Click Yes. The Open an Easy Transfer File combo box appears.

21. Browse to the external hard drive, select the Windows Easy Transfer—Items From Old Computer file and click Open. The *Enter the password you used to help protect your transfer file and start the transfer* page appears, as shown in Figure 2-31.

Figure 2-31

The Enter the password you used to help protect your transfer file and start the transfer page

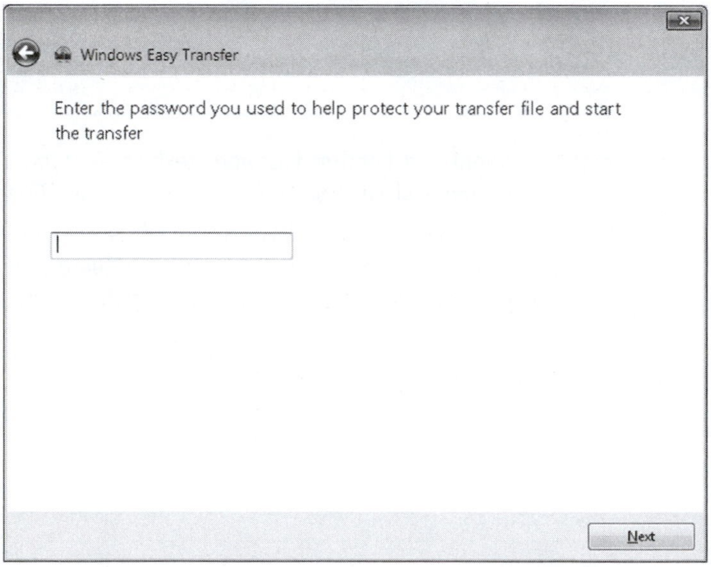

22. Type the password you specified earlier and click Next. The *Choose what to transfer from this computer* page appears.

23. Select the items you want to copy to the Windows 7 computer and click Transfer. The program transfers the selected items to the computer, and then the *Your transfer is complete* page appears.

24. Click See what was transferred. A *Windows Easy Transfer Reports* window appears.

25. Close the Windows Easy Transfer Reports window and, on the *Your transfer is complete* page, click Close.

Using User State Migration Tool

The User State Migration Tool (USMT) has the same basic capabilities as Windows Easy Transfer. The primary difference between the two is that USMT is a command line program that lacks a graphical interface.

USMT's command line interface is not a disadvantage, although individuals who prefer graphical utilities might perceive it as such. The command line interface enables administrators to incorporate USMT tasks into scripts, making it more suitable for large-scale deployments than Windows Easy Transfer.

For example, Microsoft Deployment Toolkit 2010 enables administrators to incorporate migration tasks into an installation script called a task sequence. A properly configured task sequence can save the user data on a workstation to a network share, perform a clean Windows 7 installation on the workstation, and then load the saved user data, all with little or no user interaction required.

USMT includes two separate command line programs: Scanstate.exe, which saves user profile data; and Loadstate.exe, which restores previously saved user profile data. Each program supports a variety of command line parameters that enable you to specify a storage location and control what data the programs save and restore.

In addition to the command line interface, the other big advantage to using USMT for large-scale deployments is the ability to customize the migration process. USMT uses XML (Extensible Markup Language) files to control the migration process. The default XML files supplied with the program enable it to migrate the most common user data sources, but it is also possible to create your own XML files to migrate specific application settings and data.

■ Upgrading to Windows 7

THE BOTTOM LINE

To the workstation user, performing an in-place upgrade to Windows 7 is a relatively simple procedure, but the activities the Setup program performs behind the scenes are highly complex.

CERTIFICATION READY?
Upgrade to Windows 7 from previous versions of Windows.
1.2

During the upgrade process, the Setup program creates a new Windows folder and installs the Windows 7 operating system files into it. This is only half of the process, however. The program must then migrate the applications, files, and settings from the old OS. This calls for a variety of procedures, such as importing the user profiles, copying all pertinent settings from the old registry to the new one, locating applications and data files, and updating device drivers with new versions.

While in-place upgrades often proceed smoothly, the complexity of the upgrade process and the large number of variables involved means that there are many things that can potentially go wrong. To minimize the risks involved, it is important for a technical specialist to take the upgrade process seriously, prepare the system beforehand, and have the ability to troubleshoot any problems that might arise. The following sections discuss these subjects in greater detail.

TAKE NOTE*

An in-place upgrade from Windows Vista to Windows 7 is much more complex than an upgrade from one Windows 7 edition to another. All of the Windows 7 editions use the same basic core files and architecture. Upgrades are primarily a matter of activating additional applications, which is not as invasive or dangerous.

X REF

For more information on Windows 7's hardware requirements, and on running the Upgrade Advisor program, see Lesson 1, "Introducing Windows 7."

Preparing to Upgrade

Before you begin an in-place upgrade to Windows 7, you should perform a number of preliminary procedures to ensure that the process goes smoothly and that the user data is protected.

Consider the following before you perform any upgrade to Windows 7:

- **Run Upgrade Advisor:** To be sure that the computer is capable of running the Windows 7 edition that you plan on installing, run Upgrade Advisor and take note of its advisories regarding the computer's hardware and software. If it is necessary to perform hardware upgrades, do so before installing Windows 7, making sure that the new hardware is operational before proceeding.

- **Check hardware compatibility:** The Upgrade Advisor program can point out hardware inadequacies in the computer, especially regarding Windows 7 system requirements. If it is necessary to upgrade hardware, make certain that the products you purchase are certified for use with Windows 7. The Upgrade Advisor program can also identify devices that might not function under Windows 7. However, it is sometimes possible to make such devices run properly with a driver or firmware upgrade. It is a good idea to perform an inventory of the computer's primary components and consider the age and capabilities of each one before you perform the upgrade. It is always best to locate potential hardware incompatibilities before you perform the upgrade procedure.

- **Search for updated drivers:** As part of your hardware inventory, be sure to consider the age of the device drivers installed on the computer. Check hardware manufacturers' Web sites for driver updates, especially those that are specifically intended to provide support for Windows 7. In some cases it might be preferable to install the new drivers while Vista is still running, but if the manufacturer provides separate Vista and Windows 7 drivers wait until you have installed Windows 7. Even if no updates are available, it is a good idea to gather all of the drivers for the computer's hardware together and copy them to a removable storage medium, such as a writable CD or flash drive. This way, if the Setup program requires a driver during the upgrade process, you have it available.

- **Check application compatibility:** Upgrade Advisor can point out possible application compatibility problems, but you can sometimes solve these problems by updating or upgrading the application. Create an inventory of the software products installed on the computer and check the manufacturers' Web sites for updates, availability of upgrades, and announcements regarding support for Windows 7. For example, if the computer is running Microsoft Office, use the Office Online Web site to download the latest updates. Check the applications' system requirements as well. Install any free updates that are available and consider the need for paid upgrades. In an enterprise environment, you should test all applications for Windows 7 compatibility, no matter what the manufacturer says, before you perform any operating system upgrades. However, for standalone clients, testing usually isn't practical. The best you can do is to inform the user that there might be problems with specific applications and warn them that there might be additional costs involved for new versions or different products.

- **Check disk space:** Make sure that there is at least 15 gigabytes of disk space free on the partition where the old operating system is installed. During the upgrade procedure, sufficient disk space is needed to hold both operating systems simultaneously. After the upgrade is complete, you can remove the old Vista files, freeing up some additional space.

- **Ensure computer functionality:** Make sure that Windows Vista is running properly on the computer before you begin the upgrade process. You must start an in-place upgrade from within Windows Vista, so you cannot count on Windows 7 to correct any problems that prevent the computer from starting or running the Setup program.

- **Perform a full backup:** Before you perform any upgrade procedure you should back up the entire system, or at the very least the essential user files. You can use Windows Easy

Transfer if no other tool is available. Removable hard drives make this a simple process, even if the client does not have a suitable backup device in the computer.

- **Purchase Windows 7:** Be sure to purchase the appropriate Windows 7 edition for the upgrade, and have the installation disk and product key handy.

Upgrading from Windows Vista

Once you complete the steps in the previous section, you are ready to perform an in-place upgrade from Windows Vista to Windows 7.

To upgrade a Windows Vista computer to Windows 7 while preserving all files and settings, use the following procedure.

→ UPGRADE WINDOWS VISTA TO WINDOWS 7

GET READY. Turn on the computer running Windows Vista and make sure you have the Windows 7 installation disk and product key ready.

1. Insert the Windows 7 installation disk into the DVD drive. An Autoplay dialog box appears.
2. Click Run setup.exe. A User Account Control message box appears.
3. Click Continue. The Install Windows screen appears.
4. Click Install now. The Get important updates for *installation* page appears.
5. Click Do not get the latest updates for installation. The *Please read the license terms* page appears.

> **TAKE NOTE** *
> If the computer is connected to the Internet, you might want to click *Go online to get the latest updates for installation* to ensure that the computer's drivers and other software are up to date.

6. Select the I accept the license terms check box and click Next. The *Which type of installation do you want?* page appears, as shown in Figure 2-32.

Figure 2-32

The Which type of installation do you want? page

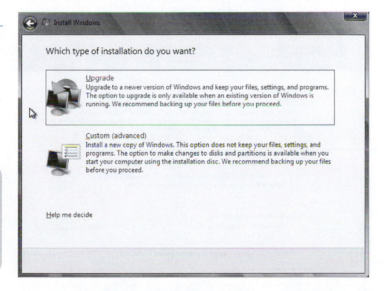

> **TAKE NOTE** *
> Note that unlike the previous Windows 7 installation procedures in this Lesson, the Upgrade option is activated.

7. Click Upgrade. The *Upgrading Windows* page appears.
8. After a delay, during which the Setup program installs Windows 7, the computer reboots and the *Type your Windows product key* page appears.

TAKE NOTE*

Depending on the applications installed and the complexity of the system configuration, an in-place upgrade can take anywhere from several minutes to several hours.

9. Type your product key in the text box provided and click Next. The *Help protect your computer and improve Windows automatically* page appears.

10. Select one of the three options specifying what security settings you want the computer to use. The *Review your time and date settings* page appears.

11. From the Time Zone drop-down list, select the time zone in which the computer will be running and then click Next. The *Select your computer's current location* page appears.

12. Click the appropriate option specifying the computer's normal location. A *Welcome* page appears as Windows 7 prepares and loads the desktop.

Upgrading Windows 7 Editions

> One of the main advantages of the new architecture that Microsoft devised for Windows 7 is that it makes upgrades to other editions incredibly simple.

There are three ways to upgrade a Windows 7 computer to another edition, as follows:

TAKE NOTE*

While it is possible to upgrade Windows 7 to a different edition, you cannot upgrade a 32-bit version of Windows 7 to a 64-bit version, or vice versa.

- **Purchase a retail version of a higher level Windows 7 edition:** When you purchase a full retail version of Windows 7 at a higher level, you can perform an in-place upgrade just as you would on a computer running Windows Vista.

- **Purchase a Windows 7 product upgrade package from a retailer:** The Windows 7 product upgrade package does not contain any software at all, just the upgrade key you need to activate the higher-level version of Windows 7.

- **Use the Windows Anytime Upgrade tool included with Windows 7:** The Windows Anytime Upgrade feature in Windows 7 enables you to select and purchase the upgrade key for a higher-level edition of Windows 7 in less than 10 minutes.

⊙ USE WINDOWS ANYTIME UPGRADE

GET READY. Log on to Windows 7, using an account with administrative privileges.

1. Click Start > Control Panel. The Control Panel window appears.

2. Click System and Security > Windows Anytime Upgrade. The Windows Anytime Upgrade Wizard appears, displaying the *How do you want to begin?* page, as shown in Figure 2-33.

Figure 2-33

The How do you want to begin? page

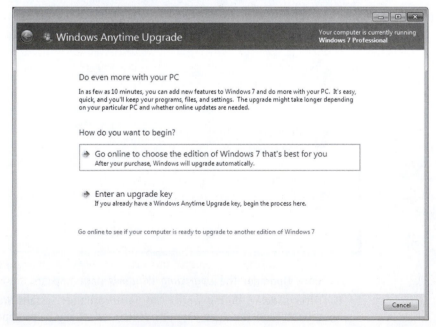

3. Click Go online to choose the edition of Windows 7 that's best for you. A *Compare* page appears showing the upgrades that are available to you, as shown in Figure 2-34.

Figure 2-34

The Compare page

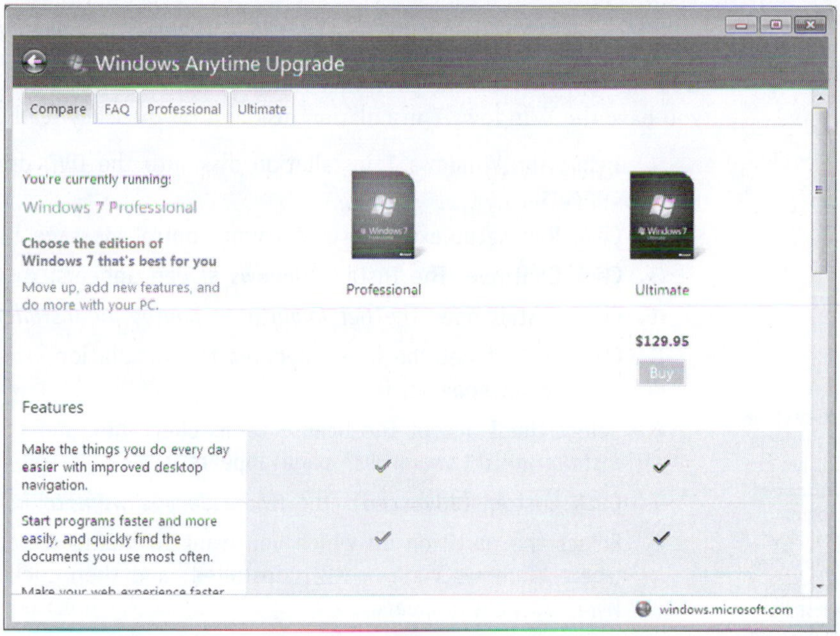

4. Click the Buy button for the upgrade that you want to purchase. A Microsoft Store Wizard appears to step you through the process of purchasing the upgrade.

5. Follow the instructions to purchase and install the upgrade.

Performing a Dual Boot Installation

↓ **THE BOTTOM LINE**

When a user wants to test Windows 7 without making a full commitment, or needs to maintain an older operating system for compatibility with specific applications, a dual boot environment can be ideal.

TAKE NOTE*

If you have sufficient disk space for a Windows 7 installation on your computer's only hard disk, but you have only one partition on that disk, there is no way to create a new primary partition out of that disk space using the tools in Windows Vista or XP without erasing the entire drive. You must use a third-party tool, such as Norton Partition Magic, to create the partition.

Although it has drawbacks, mainly in terms of disk space, many users rely on a dual boot environment to provide access to two independent operating system installations. In a dual boot environment, both operating systems are completely independent of each other, so restrictions regarding upgrade paths do not apply. You can dual boot any edition of Windows 7 with Windows Vista or Windows XP.

To create a dual boot environment, you must have all of the following:

- **Two disk partitions:** Windows does not support multiple operating systems on a single disk partition. Therefore, you must have two partitions to dual boot, one for the computer's original operating system, and one for the Windows 7 installation. In addition, be aware that Windows 7 must be installed on a primary partition, not on a logical disk in an extended partition. Make sure that the partition where you intend to install Windows 7 has sufficient disk space for a full installation.

- **Two full product licenses:** From a licensing standpoint, a dual boot environment is a full Windows 7 installation, not an upgrade. Do not purchase an upgrade license for Window 7, which requires Windows Vista or XP to be running to start the installation. As far as Windows 7 knows, it is the sole operating system on the computer.

- **A full system backup:** Dual booting is something of a hack, and not an officially supported environment. As a result, the behavior of the operating systems can sometimes be unpredictable. Be sure that you have a full backup of your existing installation before you attempt the following procedure.

⊙ INSTALL WINDOWS 7 IN A DUAL BOOT ENVIRONMENT

GET READY. Turn on the computer running Windows Vista or Windows XP and make sure you have the Windows 7 installation disk and product key ready.

1. Insert the Windows 7 installation disk into the DVD drive. An Autoplay dialog box appears.

2. Click Run setup.exe. A User Account Control message box appears.

3. Click Continue. The Install Windows screen appears.

4. Click Install now. The *Get important updates for installation* page appears.

5. Click Do not get the latest updates for installation. The *Please read the license terms* page appears.

6. Select the I accept the license terms check box and click Next. The *Which type of installation do you want?* page appears.

7. Click Custom (advanced). The *Where do you want to install Windows?* page appears.

8. Select the partition on which you want to install Windows 7 (not the partition where Windows Vista or XP is installed) and then click Next. The *Installing Windows* page appears.

9. After several minutes, during which the Setup program installs Windows 7, the computer reboots twice and the *Set Up Windows* page appears.

10. Complete the installation process by following the "Perform a Clean Installation" procedure described earlier in this lesson, starting at Step 10.

⚠ **WARNING** If you select the partition on which Windows Vista or XP is installed, you will not get a dual boot environment. Instead, the Windows 7 Setup program will rename the Windows folder to Windows.old and create a new Windows folder for the Windows 7 files. This is still a clean installation, however. The Setup program will not import the Vista or XP files and settings, and once the process is completed, you will no longer be able to boot to Windows Vista or XP.

Rebooting the system after completing the Windows 7 installation process causes the screen shown in Figure 2-35 to appear. From this menu, you select the operating system you want to start. "Earlier Version of Windows" refers to Windows Vista or XP. To switch between operating systems, you have to completely shut down the one that is running, and then restart the computer.

Figure 2-35

The Windows Boot Manager page

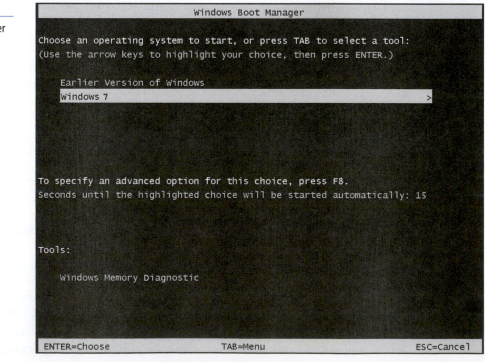

SKILL SUMMARY

IN THIS LESSON YOU LEARNED:

- Windows 7 includes a new preinstallation environment called Windows PE.

- In a clean installation, you boot from the Windows 7 Setup disk and create or select a blank partition where Windows 7 will reside.

- It is possible to migrate files and settings from an existing Windows installation to a newly installed Windows 7 installation using either Windows Easy Transfer or User State Migration Tool.

- Windows 7 supports in-place upgrades only from Windows Vista or another Windows 7 edition.

- To perform an in-place upgrade, you must launch the Windows 7 Setup program from within Windows Vista.

- To upgrade from one Windows 7 edition to another, you can use the Windows Anytime Upgrade tool found in the Windows 7 Control Panel.

- A dual boot installation is one in which two operating systems are installed on separate disk partitions, providing access to both at boot time.

■ Knowledge Assessment

Fill in the Blank

Complete the following sentences by writing the correct word or words in the blanks provided.

1. Windows Easy Transfer supports two types of migrations, called _____ and _____.

2. When a serious problem occurs with Windows 7, you might be able to repair it by starting the Windows PE operating system and running diagnostic tools. In this scenario, Windows PE is called by another name, which is _____.

3. To migrate user profile information from one computer to another, you can use either _____ or _____.

4. A computer running Windows PE will automatically reboot after _____.

5. Windows Easy Transfer supports migration using any removable storage medium common to the two computers except _____.

6. The Windows 7 component that enables the computer to support more than one language is called the _____.

7. The reason it is possible to remove the Windows 7 installation disk to supply the Setup program with drivers is that Windows PE runs on a _____.

8. To upgrade Windows XP to Windows 7, you must perform a _____.

9. The files and settings that Windows Easy Transfer can migrate to a Windows 7 computer are primarily stored in _____.

10. As a preinstallation environment, Windows PE is a vast improvement over MS-DOS because it includes internal support for _____ and _____.

True / False

Circle T if the statement is true or F if the statement is false.

T | F 1. Windows PE is the latest version of the MS-DOS operating system.

T | F 2. It is possible to perform an in-place upgrade from any 32-bit version of Windows Vista to the 32-bit version of Windows 7.

T | F 3. To create a dual boot environment with Windows 7, you must have two primary partitions on your computer.

T | F 4. Windows 7 Home Premium users can perform in-place upgrades to Windows 7 Professional without obtaining a new installation disk.

T | F 5. One way to perform an in-place upgrade from Windows Vista to Windows 7 is to boot from the Windows 7 installation disk, choose the Custom option, and then select the partition on which Windows Vista is installed.

T | F 6. To create a Windows 7 workstation that supports multiple languages, you must begin by installing the English language version.

T | F 7. It is not possible to "upgrade" a computer running the Windows 7 Ultimate edition to the Enterprise edition without performing a clean installation.

T | F 8. Windows XP users are eligible to purchase an upgrade version of Windows 7, but they cannot perform an in-place upgrade.

T | F 9. To migrate the user profiles of multiple user accounts located on the same computer, you must use the User State Migration Tool.

T | F 10. Any program that can run on Windows 7 can run on Windows PE.

Review Questions

1. Give two detailed reasons why Windows PE is a better installation environment for Windows 7 than MS-DOS.
2. Explain the difference between a side-by-side migration and a wipe-and-load migration, using Windows Easy Transfer.

■ Case Scenarios

Scenario 2-1: Upgrading Windows 7 Editions

You are working as a desktop support technician at a computer store, and a customer approaches you with a laptop computer he purchased three years ago. The computer came with Windows XP Home Basic installed on it, and the customer now wants to upgrade to Windows 7 and also use the computer to log on to the Active Directory Domain Services domain at his office. He knows he cannot do this with the Windows 7 Home Premium edition, so he wants you to upgrade the computer to Windows 7 Professional, without affecting his files and settings. Explain in detail the procedure you would have to use to fulfill the customer's request.

Scenario 2-2: Updating Graphics

When you run Windows Upgrade Advisor on a client's computer, the report's only recommendation is that you upgrade the graphics adapter after you upgrade the operating system to Windows 7. What is likely to be the result immediately after you install Windows 7 on the computer and before you upgrade the graphics adapter?

Deploying Windows 7

OBJECTIVE DOMAIN MATRIX

TECHNOLOGY SKILL	OBJECTIVE DOMAIN	OBJECTIVE NUMBER
Capturing Image Files	Capture a system image.	2.1
Modifying Image Files	Prepare a system image for deployment.	2.2
Deploying Image Files	Deploy a system image.	2.3

KEY TERMS

answer file

build-to-order (BTO)

build-to-plan (BTP)

capture image

configuration passes

Deployment Image Servicing and
  Management (DISM.exe)

discover image

image file

ImageX.exe

lite-touch installation (LTI)

multicasting

reference computer

System Preparation
  (Sysprep.exe)

task sequence

User State Migration Tool
  (USMT)

Windows System Image
  Manager (SIM)

zero-touch installation
  (ZTI)

■ Understanding Enterprise Deployments

↓ **THE BOTTOM LINE**

Deploying Windows 7 to a large number of workstations in an enterprise environment involves much more than repeating the same installation process many times. An efficient deployment requires extensive planning, careful testing, and the right tools.

For a home computer user, installing or upgrading to Windows 7 is a relatively simple and inexpensive process. Microsoft has refined the installation process over the years to the point where virtually anyone can do it. However, in an enterprise network environment, in which administrators are responsible for hundreds or thousands of computers, deploying Windows 7 is a massively expensive project, in terms of money, time, and productivity.

Technical specialists undertaking a large-scale Windows 7 deployment typically have to consider the following objectives:

- **Create standardized computing environments:** To facilitate the support of the workstations throughout their life cycle, enterprise administrators try to configure computers with the same applications and configuration settings, so that technicians servicing the computers know what to expect.

- **Minimize the amount of user interaction required at the workstation:** Depending on the size and nature of the deployment, enterprise administrators can automate some or all of the responses required during the Windows 7 installation process. This reduces the time and manpower required at each workstation.

- **Ensure continued functionality of all hardware and software resources:** Once the Windows 7 installation is completed, users must be able to perform all of the required tasks they could perform using the old operating system.

- **Minimize the interruption of user productivity:** Large-scale deployments can displace users and monopolize resources, causing a reduction in productivity. To minimize this effect, enterprise administrators must carefully plan the deployment process and take steps to prevent service interruptions.

To address these issues, Microsoft provides extensive documentation and several sets of tools designed specifically for administrators undertaking a mass deployment.

➕ MORE INFORMATION

Large-scale workstation deployments have complexities that reach well beyond the technical issues of operating system and application installation. A well-made deployment plan must also consider issues such as productivity, user training, workstation life cycles, and, of course, economy. In addition to the extensive documentation included with the Microsoft deployment tools, there is also another collection of documents, called the Microsoft Operations Framework (MOF), which defines the entire life cycle of an IT service. This life cycle begins with the initial recognition of a need, proceeds through the planning, building, and deployment processes, and culminates in the service's operation and finally its retirement. The Microsoft Operations Framework 4.0 package is available free from the Microsoft Download Center at http://www.microsoft.com/downloads/details.aspx?FamilyId=457ED61D-27B8-49D1-BACA-B175E8F54C0C&displaylang=en.

Understanding the Deployment Process

The Windows 7 deployment process in an enterprise environment does more than just install the operating system. A fully realized workstation deployment also configures the system and installs additional device drivers, updates, language packs, and applications, creating a working environment that is ready for the end user.

Performing a manual installation of a Windows 7 workstation is a lengthy process. First, you must install Windows 7 itself, along with any updates and other software modules it requires. Then, you must install the applications you want to run on the workstation, and finally, you must configure the operating system and applications to create the final working environment.

For a home user installing a single computer, this is not a terrible burden, but for technical specialists in an enterprise environment, who have to install hundreds of workstations, manual installations are completely impractical. Not only does a manual installation take a great deal of time and manpower, much of that valuable time is wasted as the technician sits around watching the various installation processes.

To deploy Windows 7 workstations more efficiently, Microsoft has created tools and procedures that enable enterprise administrators to automate all or part of the deployment process.

At the highest level, an enterprise workstation deployment consists of the following basic steps:

1. **Build a deployment share:** Rather than use individual disks to install software on the workstations, it is more efficient to create a share on a network server that contains the installation files, so that each workstation can download the software it needs.

2. **Perform a reference computer installation:** A *reference computer* is a template for a workstation configuration; a model containing all of the software the workstation requires; installed, configured, and ready to use.

3. **Capture an image of the reference computer:** An *image file* is a copy of the data stored on the reference computer's drives. By creating an image file, you can replicate the configuration on the reference computer to as many workstations as you need to deploy.

4. **Boot the target computers:** To start a bare-metal computer, you must boot it with Windows Preinstallation Environment (Windows PE), using either a removable boot disk or a boot image downloaded from a server.

5. **Apply the Windows 7 reference computer image:** By applying the image you made of the reference computer to the target computers, you create duplicate workstations, without the need for an elaborate interactive installation process.

This procedure greatly simplifies what can be an extraordinarily complicated process. A large-scale deployment requires a huge amount of planning and preparation, as described in the remainder of this lesson.

Introducing Windows Deployment Tools

While a Windows 7 installation disk provides everything you need to perform an individual workstation installation, Microsoft also provides additional tools that are designed specifically to aid in mass installations.

Microsoft's deployment tools are not unified applications as much as they are toolkits that technical specialists can mix and match to suit their needs. Mass Windows 7 deployments can take many different forms, from enterprise network rollouts to original equipment manufacturer (OEM) assembly lines, and Microsoft's intention was to create a collection of tools that technicians can combine and employ in a variety of ways.

The three main Windows 7 deployment products are described in the following sections.

WINDOWS 7 AUTOMATED INSTALLATION KIT

The Windows 7 Automated Installation Kit (AIK) is designed primarily for use by OEMs who have to install the operating system on large numbers of computers. However, the tools included in the Windows AIK are also prerequisites for Microsoft Deployment Toolkit (MDT) 2010.

OEMs typically deploy Windows 7 workstations in one of two ways:

- A *build-to-plan (BTP)* **installation:** The manufacturer deploys a large number of computers with identical operating system configurations. The installers capture a single image file and deploy it to each computer with no changes.

- A *build-to-order (BTO)* **installation:** Each computer has an individually customized configuration. The installers first capture a baseline image and deploy it to each computer, and then they start the computer in audit mode and perform a scripted procedure that customizes the configuration.

These are the primary tools in the Windows 7 AIK that enable installers to perform these tasks:

- **Windows System Image Manager (SIM):** A graphical utility, shown in Figure 3-1, that installers can use to create distribution shares and answer files that automate and customize Windows 7 installations. An **answer file** is an XML script that provides the Windows 7 Setup program with the information it needs to perform an unattended installation. After configuring specific settings in the Windows SIM interface, the program generates the correct XML code and creates the answer file.

Figure 3-1

The Windows System Image Manager interface

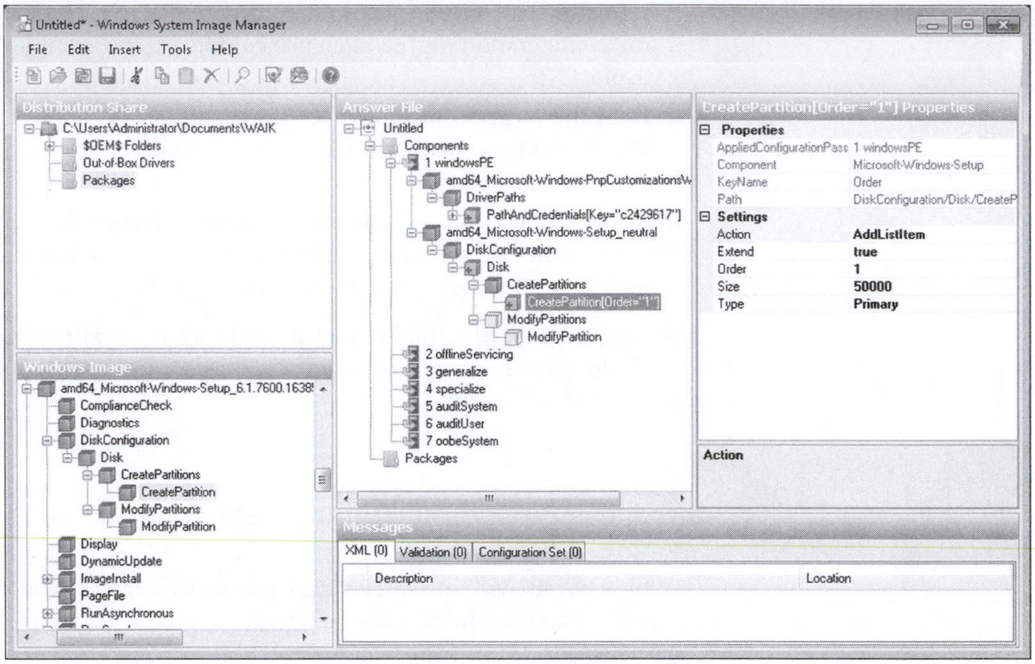

- **ImageX.exe:** A command-line tool that installers can use to capture, modify, and apply image files in the Windows Imaging format. In addition to running ImageX.exe manually from the Windows 7 or Windows PE command prompt, you can also incorporate commands into a script or an MDT 2010 task sequence.

- **Deployment Image Servicing and Management (DISM.exe):** A command line tool that installers can use to mount, edit, and upgrade image files in the Windows Imaging format. With DISM.exe, installers can maintain image files by adding updated files without having to perform another reference computer installation and capture. DISM.exe is new to Windows 7, and provides in one tool the same functionality as the Package Manager (Pkgmgr.exe), Peimg.exe, and Intlcfg.exe programs from earlier Windows AIK versions.

- **Windows Preinstallation Environment (PE):** A minimalized version of the Windows 7 operating system designed to provide an environment in which installers can prepare a computer for installation, capture reference computer images, and deploy existing image files. Unlike the DOS boot used in earlier Windows versions, Windows PE includes support for 32- and 64-bit device drivers, TCP/IP networking, the NTFS file system, and a limited subset of the Win32 application-programming interface (API). Using the tools and source files included in the Windows AIK, you can create Windows PE boot media in a variety of formats, including CD/DVD disks, flash drives, and Windows Imaging files.

- **System Preparation (Sysprep.exe):** A command-line program that installers can use to prepare Windows 7 computers for imaging, auditing, and deployment. You must use Sysprep.exe to prepare a reference computer by removing all of the individualized configuration information before you capture an image of it for distribution on multiple target workstations. Sysprep.exe is included with Windows 7, as well as with the Windows 7 AIK.

- *User State Migration Tool (USMT):* A set of two command-line programs, Scanstate. exe and Loadstate.exe, that installers can use to save user profile data from an existing workstation and restore that data to a newly-installed computer running Windows 7. USMT performs basically the same tasks as the wizard-based Windows Easy Transfer tool, but because it runs from the command line, it can be integrated into scripts and task sequences.

Windows 7 AIK is a free product available for download from the Microsoft Download Center at http://www.microsoft.com/downloads/details.aspx?familyid=696DD665-9F76-4177-A811-39C26D3B3B34&displaylang=en. The download takes the form of a sector-based image file with a .iso extension, which you must burn to a disk or mount to a drive letter using a third-party utility before you can install it.

Because the Windows 7 AIK is used to create answer files and manage images in preparation for Windows 7 deployments, it is not essential that the kit itself run on a Windows 7 computer. You can install Windows 7 AIK on any computer running Windows 7, Windows Vista SP1, Windows Server 2008 R2, Windows Server 2008, or Windows Server 2003 SP2.

MICROSOFT DEPLOYMENT TOOLKIT 2010

Microsoft Deployment Toolkit (MDT) 2010 is a tool designed specifically for enterprise network deployments. Essentially a superset of Windows 7 AIK, MDT 2010 provides a cohesive framework for the Windows 7 AIK tools that enables installers to perform two basic types of deployments: *lite-touch installation (LTI)* and *zero-touch installation (ZTI)*.

As the names imply, an LTI deployment requires some interaction at the target workstation site, usually a simple matter of selecting the configuration to install, while a ZTI deployment requires none. The primary difference between the two is that an LTI deployment only requires the tools supplied in MDT 2010 and the Windows 7 AIK, while a ZTI deployment requires Microsoft Systems Center Configuration Manager (SCCM) 2007 to be installed on the network. LTI deployments are also more flexible and easier to configure than ZTI deployments.

TAKE NOTE ✲

Systems Center Configuration Manager 2007 is a complex network management product that provides many features in addition to operating system deployment. The general rule of thumb for MDT 2010 users is that unless you already have SCCM 2007 deployed on your network, or were planning to obtain it anyway, you should stick to an LTI deployment. Do not plan on purchasing and installing SCCM 2007 solely for the purpose of performing a ZTI deployment.

OEMs always deploy Windows 7 on new, bare-metal computers, so Windows 7 AIK does not provide specific instructions for any other type of deployment. In a corporate enterprise environment, however, technical specialists are often faced with a variety of existing workstations on which they must deploy Windows 7. Therefore, MDT 2010 defines and supports four different deployment scenarios:

- **New computer:** An installation of Windows 7 on a new, bare-metal computer with a clean hard disk and no existing user data, applications, or configuration settings.
- **Upgrade computer:** An in-place installation of Windows 7 on a computer running Windows Vista SP1 or later, preserving all existing user data, applications, and configuration settings. The upgrade scenario requires no special workstation preparation, but it is limited only to systems running Windows Vista using the LTI deployment. In addition, an upgrade can require much more time than a clean installation and can conceivably result in an unstable operating system, depending on the computer's existing software.

- **Replace computer:** A migration of user state data from an existing workstation to a new computer with a clean Windows 7 installation. Also called a side-by-side migration, the deployment task sequence saves the existing user state data to a removable disk or network share with the User State Migration Tool (USMT) and then, after installing Windows 7 on a bare-metal computer, restores that user state data to the new computer. This scenario preserves only the user profile information from the old workstation; it does not migrate applications or files outside the user profile directory structure.

- **Refresh computer:** An in-place migration of user state data from an existing workstation to the same computer after a clean Windows 7 installation. Also called a wipe-and-load migration, the deployment task sequence saves the user state data to an alternate location, then erases the hard disk and installs Windows 7 on the same computer, after which it restores the user state data. As in the replace computer scenario, this scenario preserves only user profile information; it does not migrate applications or other files. In addition to deploying Windows 7 on an older workstation, installers can also use the refresh computer scenario to repair problems and implement standardized workstation configurations.

MDT 2010 is also a free download, which you can obtain from the Microsoft Download Center at http://www.microsoft.com/downloads/details.aspx?familyid=3bd8561f-77ac-4400-a0c1-fe871c461a89&displaylang=en. The download is a Microsoft Windows Installer package (with a .msi extension), but because MDT 2010 relies on the tools in the Windows 7 AIK to perform its actual tasks, you must install Windows 7 AIK before MDT 2010.

MDT 2010 is essentially a framework for the tools in Windows 7 AIK. The package includes a graphical application called Deployment Workbench, shown in Figure 3-2, and extensive documentation defining the procedures for the LTI and ZTI deployment processes.

Figure 3-2

The MDT 2010 Deployment Workbench interface

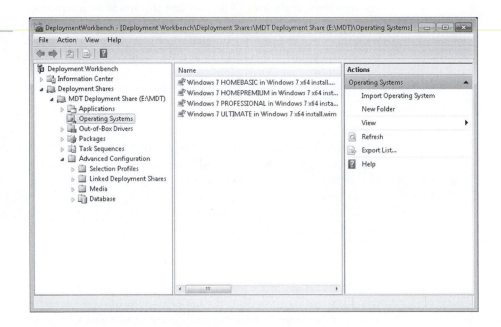

While the Windows SIM utility in the Windows 7 AIK package creates answer files that work with the Windows 7 Setup.exe program, Deployment Workbench creates *task sequences*, which can include answer files, but that can also perform additional tasks both before and after the Windows 7 installation. For example, you can implement an entire refresh computer scenario with a single task sequence that saves the computer's user state data and installs Windows 7.

WINDOWS DEPLOYMENT SERVICES

Windows Deployment Services (WDS) is a role included with Windows Server 2008 R2 and Windows Server 2008 that enables installers to deploy Windows Imaging files to workstations over the network. Not generally used on its own for large-scale deployments, many installers

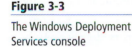

use WDS along with MDT 2010 and/or Windows 7 AIK because it can deploy boot images over the network.

Without WDS, booting a reference computer for image capture or a target computer for image deployment requires the installer to create a Windows PE boot disk. Someone must then take the boot disk to the reference or target computer, use it to start the system, and initiate the desired process. When deploying hundreds or thousands of workstations, this can be a major logistical bottleneck.

With a WDS server on the network, it is possible to start a bare-metal workstation with no boot medium and have it automatically download a boot image file from the WDS server and use it to start Windows PE. With WDS, you can deploy the default boot image found on every Windows 7 installation disk, as shown in Figure 3-3, or a customized boot image created with the Windows 7 AIK or MDT 2010 tools.

Figure 3-3

The Windows Deployment Services console

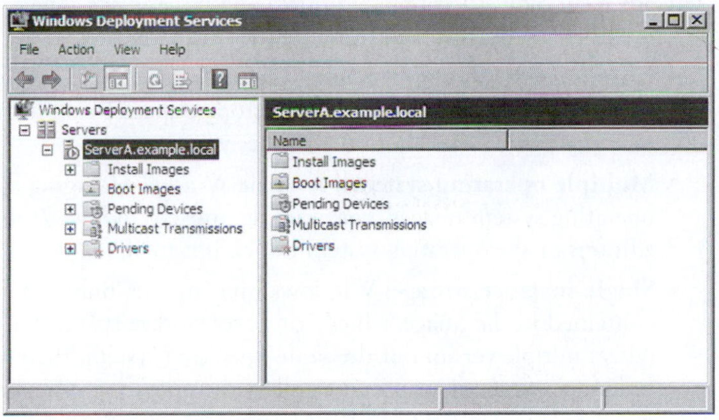

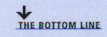

To use WDS, your network must have a Dynamic Host Configuration Protocol (DHCP) server and your workstations must have network interface adapters that support the Pre-boot Execution Environment (PXE). When the workstations boot, they obtain TCP/IP configuration parameters from the DHCP server as usual, but the DHCP server also identifies the WDS server on the network. With this information, the PXE client connects to the WDS server and downloads the Windows PE boot image you have configured the server to supply.

For workstations that do not have PXE-compliant network adapters, you can use WDS to create a discover image. A *discover image* is a customized boot image that you burn to a disk that enables a workstation to boot Windows PE and connect to the WDS server. In addition to boot images, WDS can also deploy install images, either the default Windows 7 image or a customized image.

■ Capturing Image Files

↓ **THE BOTTOM LINE**

The Windows 7 deployment process relies on image files. To deploy a large number of identical computers, you install and configure a reference computer, and then capture an image of it.

CERTIFICATION READY?
Capture a system image.
2.1

Traditional image files are sector-based, which means that they are replicas of existing disks at the bit level. The image file format does not recognize the file and directories on the disk, just the sequence of bit values. This type of image can have several different file extensions, but the most common ones are .iso and .img.

The image file format that Microsoft created for Windows deployment purposes is called Windows Imaging, which uses the .wim file extension. Windows Imaging files are not sector-based; rather, they are file-based, which means they are different from sector-based images in several important ways:

- **Bandwidth-efficient:** Transmitting a single large image file over a network is more efficient than transmitting hundreds of small files because the Server Message Blocks (SMB) protocol does not have to perform hundreds of separate file-open and file-close operations.

- **Nondestructive:** Deploying a Windows Imaging file does not overwrite the entire target disk as a sector-based image does. If the target disk contains data, an image deployment works just as if you copied the files in the image to the target; new files are added and existing files are overwritten.

- **Hardware-independent:** Windows Imaging files are completely independent of the storage technologies used by the source and target disks. The only requirement for the target is sufficient disk space to store the files in the image.

- **Compressed:** Windows Imaging files only contain actual file data; they do not contain empty space. You can also conserve storage space by omitting unnecessary files (such as memory paging files) from the images you capture.

- **Multiple operating systems:** A single Windows Imaging file can contain multiple operating system images. For example, most Windows 7 installation disks have multiple editions of the operating system in one image file.

- **Single-instance storage:** Windows Imaging files only contain one copy of every file contained in the image, which conserves storage space. If a Windows Imaging file contains multiple versions of the same operating system, there is only one copy of each unique file, even if it appears in all of the operating systems.

- **Spanable:** It is possible to divide a Windows Imaging file into multiple sections for easier downloading or burning onto multiple CD-ROMs.

- **Bootable:** Windows Imaging files can contain a bootable version of Windows PE.

- **Editable:** It is possible to mount a Windows Imaging file to a folder and modify its contents, enabling technical specialists to replace files, apply updates, and add software packages while the image is offline.

Capturing Images

To create an image file, you must capture an existing source and package it using the Windows Imaging format.

As noted earlier, the typical method for creating a customized image file for deployment to Windows 7 workstations is to install and configure Windows 7 on a reference computer and then capture an image of the reference computer's hard disk. This process can be manual or automatic, relatively simple or extremely complex.

Depending on the scope of your deployment project, you might have to build and capture only one reference computer, or dozens. This depends on how many workstation configurations you must deploy. If all of the workstations in your enterprise are identical in every way, then you only need to build one reference computer and capture one image, whether you are deploying ten workstations or ten thousand. In this case, manual procedures are usually preferable.

If, on the other hand, you have users with different needs, requiring you to deploy many different workstation configurations, you will have to build multiple reference computers and capture multiple images. The larger the number of images you have to create and maintain, the more you will benefit from automating some or all of the image creation process.

CAPTURING AN IMAGE MANUALLY USING IMAGEX.EXE

When you have only one image to capture, or a small number of images, it is usually not worth the trouble to automate the reference computer build process or the image capture process. Using the tools in the Windows 7 AIK, you can perform a manual image capture by completing the four tasks described in the following sections.

Installing the Reference Computer

The easiest way to create a single reference computer is to simply install Windows 7 using a standard installation DVD and then configure it to the exact specifications of your desired workstation configuration. To do this, you might have to do any or all of the following:

- Install applications.
- Apply updates.
- Add language packs.
- Configure workstation settings.

Preparing the Reference Computer

Once you have installed and configured the reference computer, you must prepare it for image capture by running the Sysprep.exe program from the command prompt. The Sysprep.exe program is included with Windows 7 and is located in the Windows\System32\Sysprep folder. When running Sysprep on the reference computer, use the following syntax:

```
sysprep /generalize /oobe
```

During the operating system installation, Windows 7 automatically generates certain values, such as the security ID, which must be unique on the network. Running Sysprep.exe with the `/generalize` parameter removes these unique values so that they are not captured in the image file and replicated to the target workstations.

The `/oobe` parameter configures Windows 7 to present the Windows Welcome interface the next time the computer starts. The alternative to the `/oobe` parameter is the `/audit` parameter, which causes the system to boot into a standard interface that the installer can use to customize the system by installing software components and altering configuration settings.

Creating a Windows PE Boot Disk

It is not possible to capture an image of a disk while the operating system located on that disk is running. Many critical files are locked open, preventing them from being copied. Therefore, before you can capture an image of the reference computer, you must start the computer with a boot disk (or boot image) running Windows PE.

To create a Windows PE boot disk, you run the Copype.cmd script included with Windows 7 AIK, using the following procedure:

CREATE A WINDOWS PE BOOT DISK

GET READY. Log on to the computer where you installed Windows 7 AIK using an account with Administrator privileges.

1. Click Start > All Programs > Microsoft Windows AIK. Then right click the Deployment Tools Command Prompt shortcut and, from the context menu, select Run as Administrator. An elevated command prompt window appears.
2. Run the Copype.cmd script using the following syntax, where *amd64* is the type of processor on the workstation, and *C:\winpe* is the location where you want to create the Windows PE build. The script creates a directory structure at the location you specify:

```
copype.cmd amd64 C:\winpe
```

TAKE NOTE*

To create a Windows PE boot disk for a workstation with an x86 processor, substitute x86 for amd64 wherever it appears in this procedure.

TAKE NOTE *

This reference to a sector-based image (with a .iso extension) is the only time in this lesson where the word "image" does not refer to a file-based image in the Windows Imaging format (with a .wim extension). Be sure not to confuse the two.

3. Copy the boot image file (Winpe.wim) to the C:\Winpe\ISO\Sources folder and rename it, using the following command:

```
copy c:\winpe\winpe.wim c:\winpe\ISO\sources\boot.wim
```

4. Copy the ImageX.exe file to the c:\winpe\ISO folder, using the following command:

```
copy "c:\Program files\Windows AIK\Tools\amd64\imagex.exe" c:\winpe\ISO
```

5. Package the Windows PE files into a sector-based image file (with a .iso extension) using the Oscdimg.exe program:

```
oscdimg.exe -n -bc:\winpe\etfsboot.com c:\winpe\ISO c:\winpe\winpe.iso
```

6. Burn the Winpe.iso image you created to a CD-ROM or DVD-ROM, using the software provided with your drive.

In addition to creating a boot disk, you can also burn the image to a USB flash drive or deploy the Winpe.wim image to a computer using WDS.

Capturing the Image File

Starting the reference computer with the Windows PE disk boots the system to a command prompt, as shown in Figure 3-4. From this prompt, you can use the ImageX.exe utility to capture an image of the system's hard disk.

Figure 3-4

The Windows PE command prompt

Windows PE creates a RAM disk out of workstation memory, and therefore does not utilize the computer's hard disk in any way. Because none of the files on the hard disk are in use, it is possible to capture them into a Windows Imaging file.

ImageX.exe is the primary tool for capturing and applying Windows Imaging files from the command line. With ImageX.exe, you can capture an image of your reference computer and save it to another disk in the system or to a shared folder on the network. To capture an image of the computer's C: drive and save it to a file called Win7.wim on the computer's D: drive, you would use the following command:

```
imagex.exe /capture c: d:\win7.wim "Win7" /verify
```

If the computer has only a single hard disk and you want to capture the image to a network share, you must first map a drive letter to the share using a command like the following:

```
net use z: \\server\share
```

USING WINDOWS SIM

When you undertake a deployment project that involves a number of workstation configurations, the prospect of building multiple reference computers—or of rebuilding the same one multiple times—can be daunting. One way of streamlining the process is to use the Windows SIM utility to create answer files that automate the Windows 7 installation process on the reference computers.

Answer files simplify the process of installing and configuring reference computers, but they do nothing to change the process of capturing images. After building the reference computers, you still must prepare them with Sysprep.exe, start them with a Windows PE disk, and capture an image using ImageX.exe.

Creating an Answer File

Answer files can automate many of the tasks involved in installing and configuring a reference computer. The primary function of an answer file is to provide responses to the prompts that normally appear during the Windows 7 installation. For example, you can use the answer file to partition and format disks, install additional device drivers, and configure dozens of Windows 7 parameters that you would otherwise have to set manually after the installation is completed.

This is the basic process for creating an answer file.

MORE INFORMATION

Answer files can be extremely complex, and this procedure covers only a few of the hundreds of parameters you can configure. For more information about answer files and their creation, see the Windows Automated Installation Kit User's Guide help file, included in the Windows 7 AIK package.

CREATE AN ANSWER FILE

GET READY. Log on to the computer where you installed Windows 7 AIK using an account with Administrator privileges:

1. Click **Start > All Programs > Microsoft Windows AIK > Windows System Image Manager.** The Windows System Image Manager console appears, as shown in Figure 3-5.

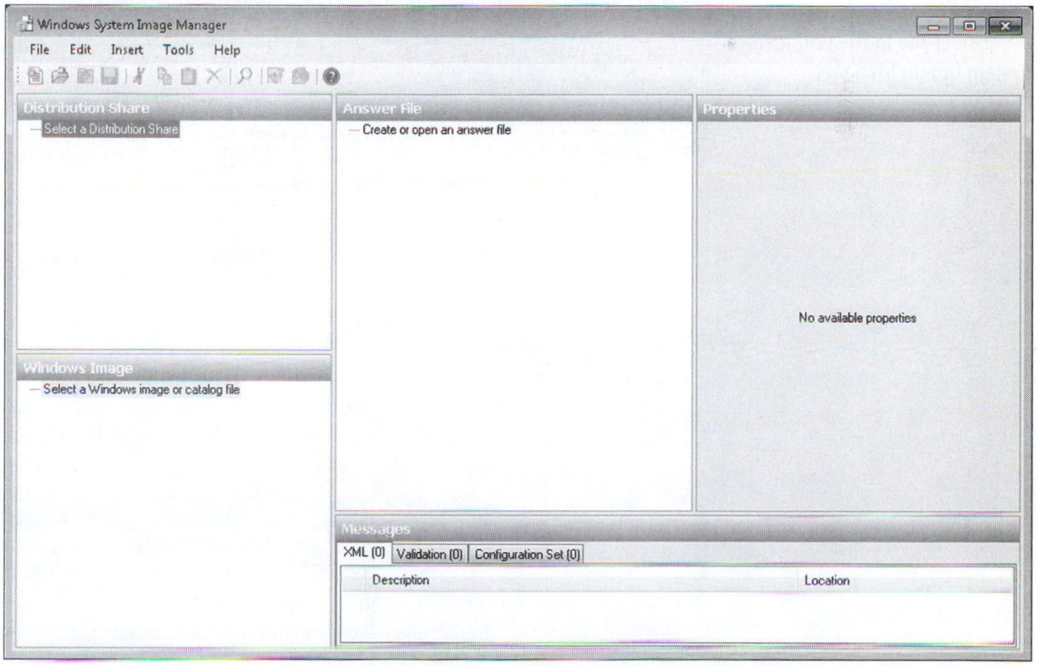

Figure 3-5

The Windows System Image Manager console

![Windows System Image Manager console screenshot showing menus File, Edit, Insert, Tools, Help; panes for Distribution Share ("Select a Distribution Share"), Windows Image ("Select a Windows image or catalog file"), Answer File ("Create or open an answer file"), Properties ("No available properties"), and Messages with tabs XML (0), Validation (0), Configuration Set (0)]

2. Click **Tools > Create Distribution Share.** The Create Distribution Share combo box appears.
3. Browse to the folder where you want to create the distribution share and click **Open.** The distribution share subfolders appear in the Distribution Share pane, as shown in Figure 3-6.

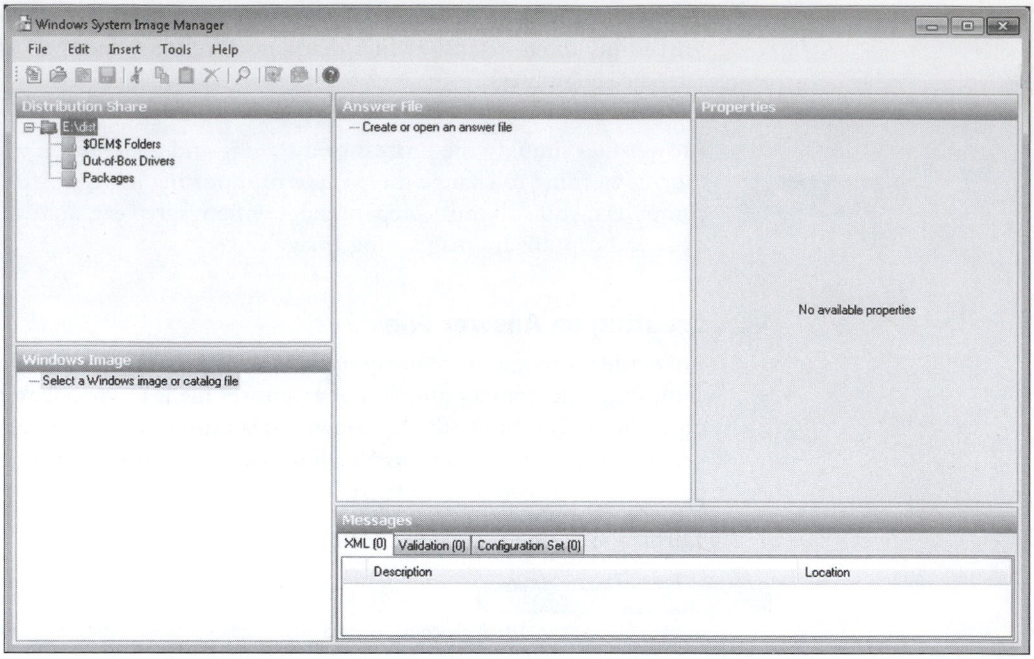

Figure 3-6

A distribution share in the Windows System Image Manager console

4. Insert a Windows 7 installation disk into the computer's DVD drive and click File > Select Windows Image. The Select a Windows Image combo box appears.

5. Browse to the Sources folder on the Windows 7 installation disk, select the Install.wim image file, and click Open. The image file appears in the Windows Image pane.

6. Click File > New Answer File. The answer file elements appear in the Answer File pane, as shown in Figure 3-7.

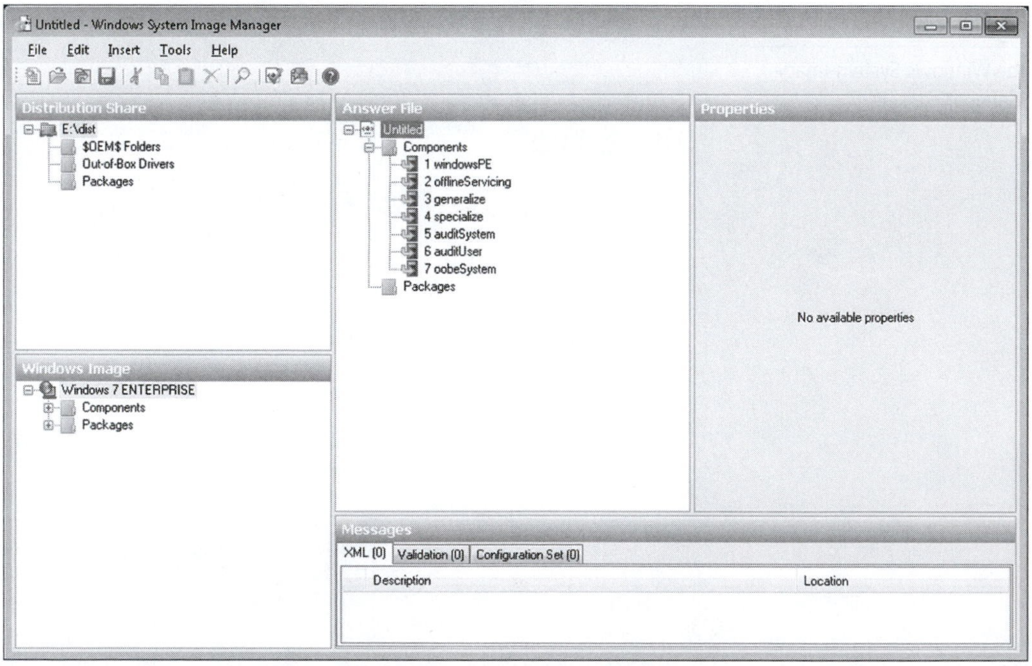

Figure 3-7

An answer file in the Windows System Image Manager console

Configuring Answer File Settings

At this point, you are ready to begin configuring the elements you want included in the answer file. You can populate the distribution share with device drivers, installation packages, or other files that you want to copy to the reference computer, and add them to the answer file to be installed with Windows 7. You can also browse for components and packages on the Windows Image pane and add selected configuration settings to the image file.

The Windows Setup program splits the Windows 7 installation process into seven phases, which it calls *configuration passes*. When you configure elements in an answer file, Windows SIM adds them to specific configuration passes, which dictate when in the installation process the setup program will configure that element. Sometimes Windows SIM gives you the choice of adding a particular element to several different configuration passes, while other elements can only exist in one configuration pass.

For example, the Microsoft-Windows-Setup\DiskConfiguration parameters enable you to partition and format the hard disks on the reference computer. Of course, you must do this before the setup program can begin copying the operating system files to their final destinations on the disk. Therefore, the only choice that Windows SIM provides when you configure these parameters is to add them to the windowsPE configuration pass, the very first one, which executes before Setup copies any files to the disk.

The seven configuration passes in an answer file are as follows:

- **windowsPE:** Configures settings specific to the Windows Preinstallation Environment and to the Windows 7 installation.
- **offlineServicing:** Applies settings to an offline image file using DISM.exe.
- **generalize:** Configures settings just before the removal of user- and computer-specific settings using the Sysprep.exe tool.
- **specialize:** Applies customized settings intended only for specific groups of computers after the generalize configuration pass.
- **auditSystem:** Applies settings when the computer boots into audit mode.
- **auditUser:** Applies settings when the computer boots into audit mode and after the auditSystem settings are applied.
- **oobeSystem:** Configures settings when the computer boots into Windows Welcome mode.

To add a configuration setting to the answer file, you browse through the available settings in the Windows Image pane, right click the setting you want to add and, from the context menu, select the configuration pass specifying when you want the setup program to configure the setting, as shown in Figure 3-8.

Figure 3-8

Selecting the configuration pass

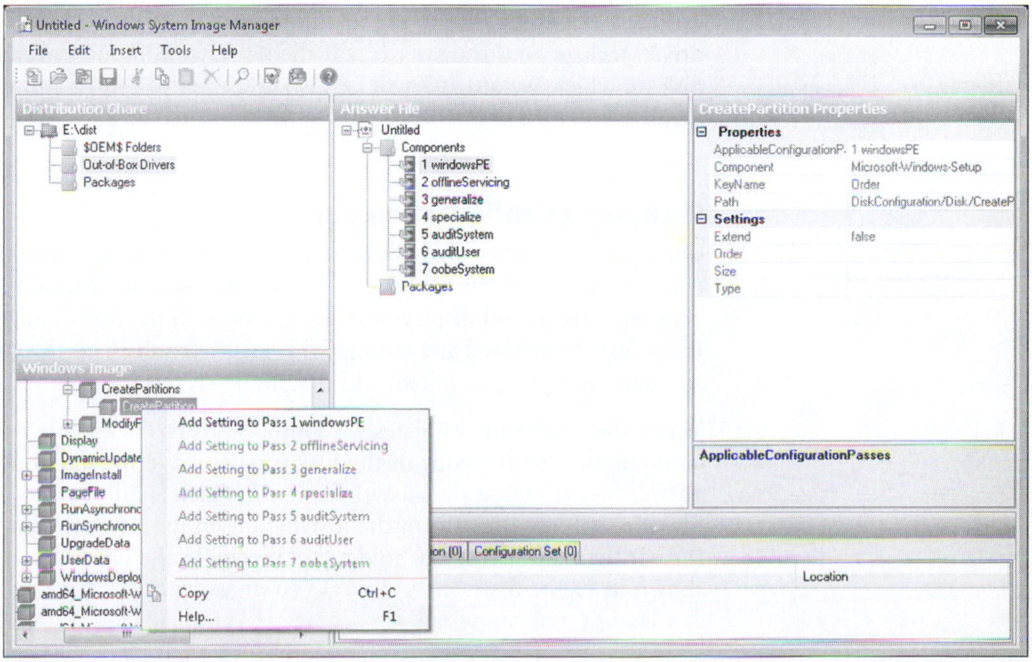

The setting then appears in the Answer File pane, and the properties specific to that setting in the adjacent Properties pane, as shown in Figure 3-9. You configure the values for the settings you want to apply in the Properties page of that setting.

Figure 3-9

Configuring setting properties

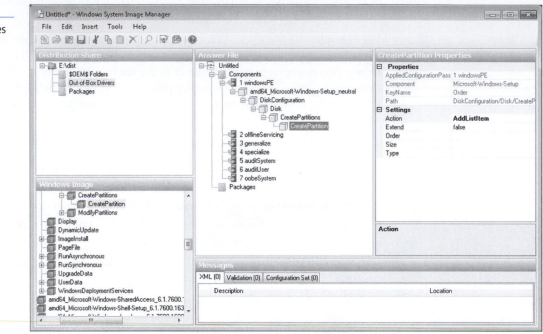

In addition to configuring Windows 7 settings in the answer file, you can also at this point populate the distribution share with device drivers and software packages you want to install on the reference computer during the setup process. If, for example, the reference computer has a host adapter for its hard disks that requires a driver not included with Windows 7, you can copy the driver files to the distribution share's Out-of-Box Drivers folder and add the driver package to the answer file. If the reference computer needs this driver to access the hard disk on which Windows 7 will be installed, then you must add the driver to the windowsPE configuration pass.

Creating a Configuration Set

Once you have configured all the settings you need in your answer file, click Tools > Validate Answer File. Windows SIM then checks your configuration values and the dependencies between settings and displays any discrepancies in the Messages pane, as shown in Figure 3-10. If you have configured any settings with incorrect values, correct them, and if you have omitted any settings that are required, add them.

When the answer file validates without any errors, click Tools > Create Configuration Set. A configuration set is a copy of the files you copied to the distribution share and added to the answer file, as well as the answer file itself, which is called Autounattend.xml. These are the files you will use to perform the installation on the reference computer. Windows SIM creates the configuration set in the folder you specify in the Create Configuration Set dialog box, as shown in Figure 3-11.

Figure 3-10

Validating an answer file

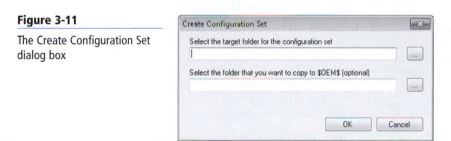

Figure 3-11

The Create Configuration Set
dialog box

Applying an Answer File

Once you have created the configuration set, copy the files to a removable medium, such as a CD-ROM, DVD-ROM, or USB flash drive. To perform an installation on the reference computer using the answer file, insert a Windows 7 installation disk into the computer and start it. Once the system has begun to boot from the disk, insert the removable medium containing the configuration set. The Windows Setup program automatically scans all of the removable drives on the computer for an answer file. When it finds one, it proceeds with the installation, using the answer file as a guide.

It is also possible to start the Windows Setup program from the Windows PE command prompt, specifying the location of the answer file on the command line. This makes it possible to access the configuration set from a network share, eliminating the need for a removable disk. To do this, you must run Setup.exe from the Windows 7 installation disk, using a command like the following:

```
setup.exe /unattend:\\server\share\configset
```

CAPTURING AN IMAGE USING WDS

You can always capture an image file of a reference computer by running ImageX.exe from a Windows PE command prompt, but there are also ways to automate the capture process. One of these ways is to use Windows Deployment Services to create a capture image.

A *capture image* is a bootable image that you can deploy using WDS, and which includes a wizard-based client that runs on the reference computer and enables you to capture an image and upload it back to the WDS server. To create a capture image, you add a boot image to your WDS server and then select Action > Create Capture Image. You can use the Boot.wim image file from any Windows 7 installation disk, or a customized Windows PE boot image file you have created yourself.

The Create Capture Image Wizard prompts you to specify a location for the new capture image file, as shown in Figure 3-12, and also enables you to add the capture image back to the WDS server, so that you can deploy it immediately.

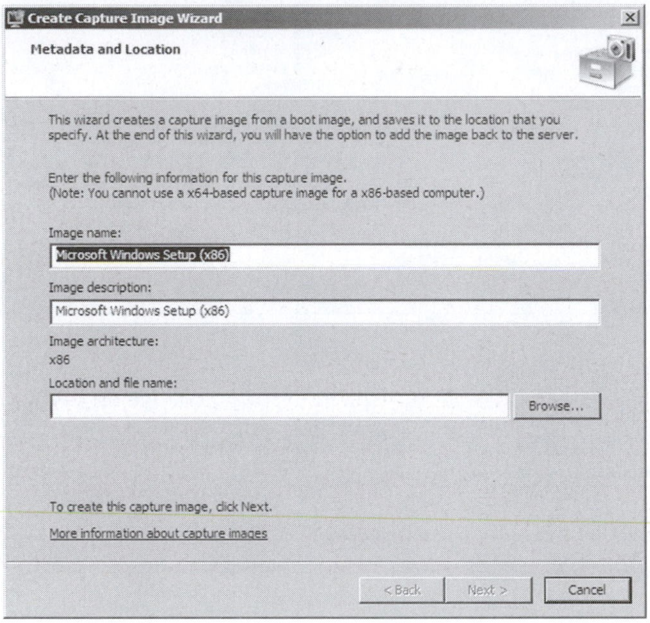

Figure 3-12

The Create Capture Image Wizard

To perform the capture on a bare-metal reference computer, use the following procedure.

➔ **CAPTURE AN IMAGE**

GET READY. Configure the boot order in your reference computer's BIOS to use its PXE-capable network adapter before its hard disk drive.

1. Turn on the reference computer. The system obtains TCP/IP settings from the DHCP server and connects to the WDS server on the network, as shown in Figure 3-13.

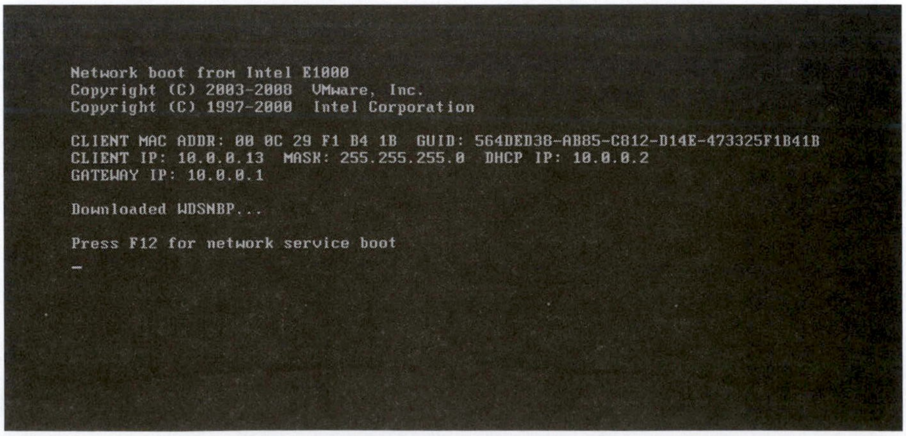

Figure 3-13

Booting from the network

2. If necessary, press F12 or another appropriate key to initiate a network service boot. The Windows Boot Manager screen appears, as shown in Figure 3-14.

Figure 3-14

Windows Boot Manager

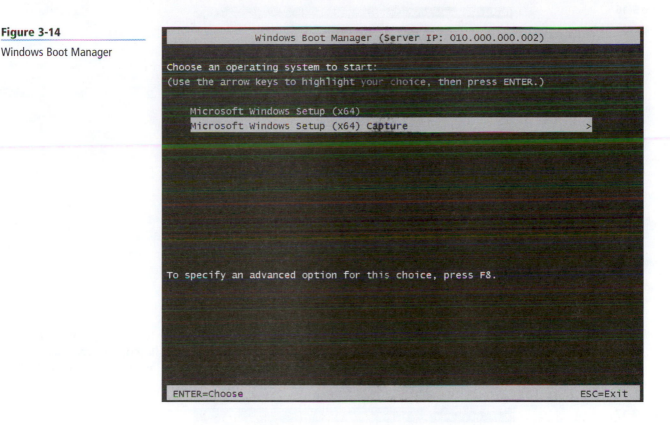

3. Select the capture image you created and press Enter. The Windows Deployment Services Image Capture Wizard appears, as shown in Figure 3-15.

Figure 3-15

The Windows Deployment Services Image Capture Wizard

4. Click Next to bypass the *Welcome* page. The *Directory to Capture* page appears, as shown in Figure 3-16.

Figure 3-16

The Directory to Capture page

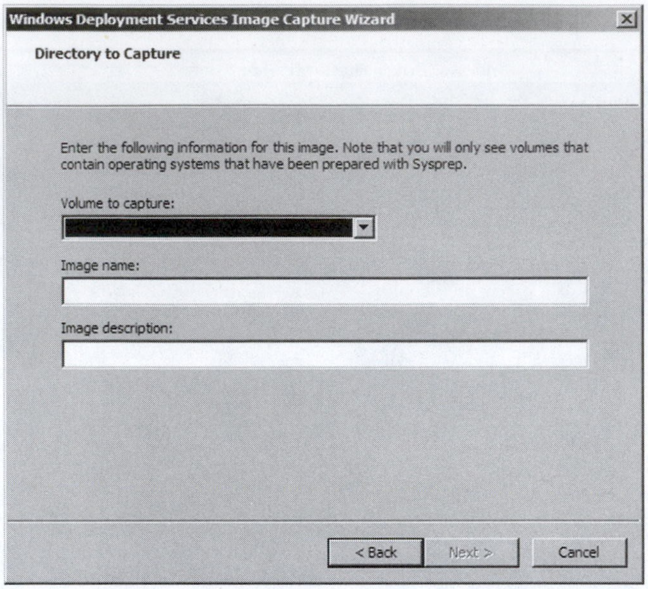

5. Select the volume containing Windows 7 in the Volume to Capture drop-down list, type appropriate values in the Image Name and Image Description text boxes, and then click Next. The *New Image Location* page appears, as shown in Figure 3-17.

Figure 3-17

The New Image Location page

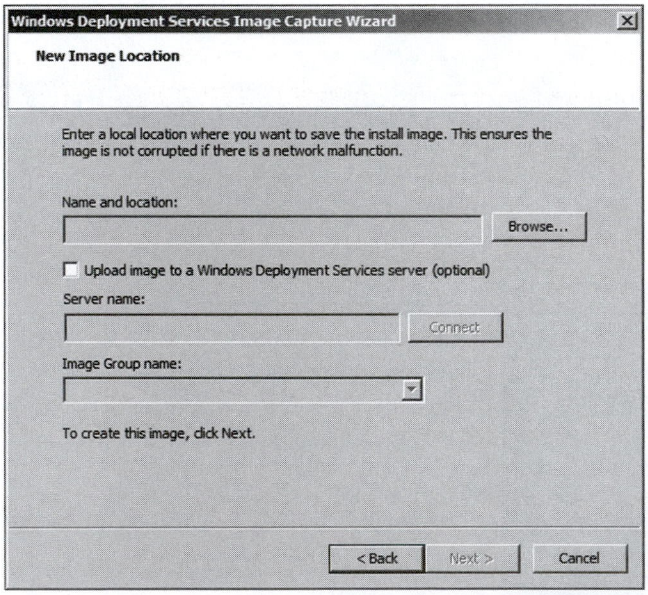

6. Click Browse and select a folder and filename for the new image file.
7. Select the Upload image to a Windows Deployment Services server check box.
8. Specify the name of your WDS server in the Server Name text box and click Connect. A Windows Security dialog box appears.
9. Supply administrative credentials in the User Name and Password fields and click OK.

10. Back on the New Image Location page, select a value from the Image Group Name drop-down list and click Next. The *Task Progress* page appears, as shown in Figure 3-18, as the wizard proceeds to capture the image.

Figure 3-18

The Task Progress page

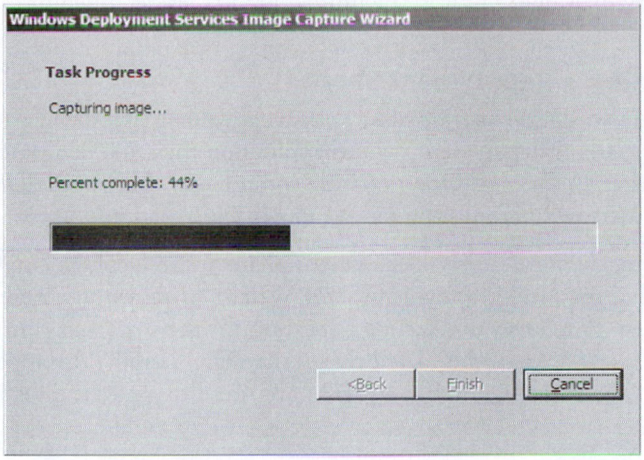

11. When the capture process is completed (which can take several minutes), click Finish. The computer restarts.

With the capture process complete, the new image appears in the Windows Deployment Services console, in the Install Images folder, in the group you selected in the wizard, as shown in Figure 3-19. This image is ready for deployment to target workstations.

Figure 3-19

A captured install image in the Windows Deployment Services console

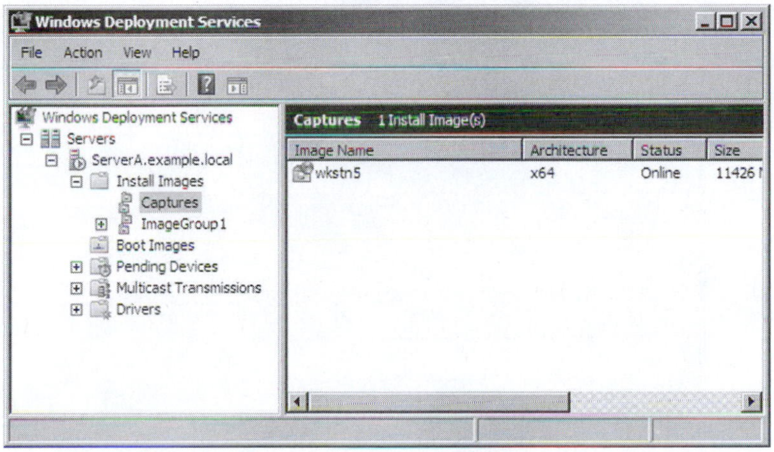

CAPTURING AN IMAGE USING MDT 2010

While Windows SIM can automate the process of installing reference computers, and WDS can automate the process of capturing reference computer images, neither one can do both. Microsoft Deployment Toolkit 2010 can, however. MDT 2010 is designed for large, complex deployment projects that might call for the creation of dozens of reference computer images and the deployment of hundreds or thousands of workstations. Not so much a collection of individual tools like Windows 7 AIK, MDT 2010 provides a comprehensive deployment solution, both in its tools and its documentation.

When you use Windows 7 AIK by itself, the computer on which you install it is essentially a platform where you create answer files and boot disks that you will use on other computers. The computer on which you install MDT 2010, however—also known as the build computer—functions as an actual distribution server on your network. Reference computers and target computers use a customized boot image to connect to the build computer and download the image files they use to install Windows 7.

With MDT 2010 and its Deployment Workbench, building the reference computer and capturing an image of it is one unified process, as described in the following sections.

Creating a Deployment Share

Before you can do anything else with Deployment Workbench, you have to create a deployment share. A deployment share is a folder on the build computer where you will store all of the install images and other software components that your reference computers and target computers will need during the Windows 7 installation process.

Selecting Action > New Deployment Share in the Deployment Workbench application launches the New Deployment Share Wizard, as shown in Figure 3-20. The wizard leads you through the process of selecting a location for the share and configuring various deployment options. By default, the wizard makes the share invisible (by appending a dollar sign to the end of the name) because users will never need to access it directly.

Figure 3-20

The New Deployment Share Wizard

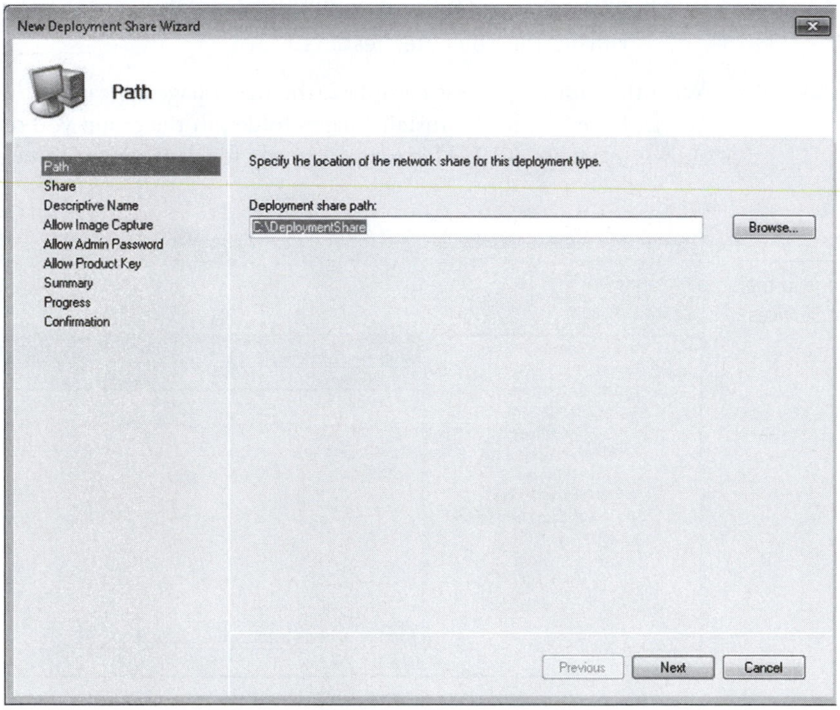

Once you have created the deployment share, you can begin to populate it with software. At the very least, you will need to add an operating system install image, such as the Install.wim file included in the Sources folder on every Windows 7 installation disk. To do this, you use the Import Operating System Wizard, as shown in Figure 3-21. Once you install your reference computers and capture images of them, you will add these new images to the share as well, so you can deploy them to your target computers.

In addition to operating systems, you can also add applications, device drivers, and Windows Installer packages to the deployment share, for installation on your reference computer. Deployment Workbench provides wizards that enable you to import each of these elements.

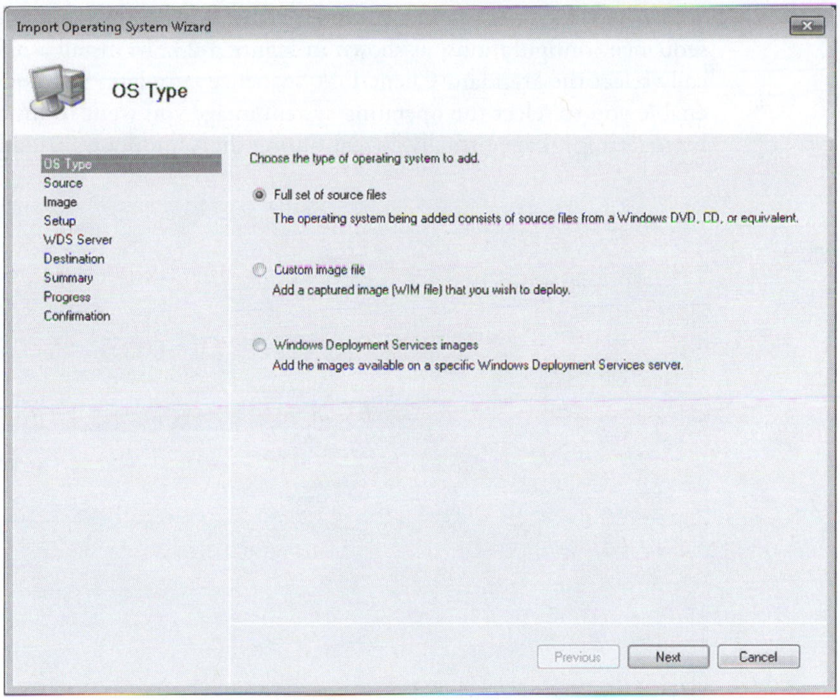

Figure 3-21

The Import Operating System
Wizard

Creating a Task Sequence

A task sequence is to MDT 2010 what an answer file is to Windows 7 AIK, a script that
guides the workstation deployment process. In fact, a task sequence includes an answer file,
which it creates automatically, but a task sequence can do much more than an answer file,
such as install applications and perform image captures.

When you select the Task Sequences container in Deployment Workbench and click Tools >
New Task Sequence, the New Task Sequence Wizard appears, as shown in Figure 3-22.

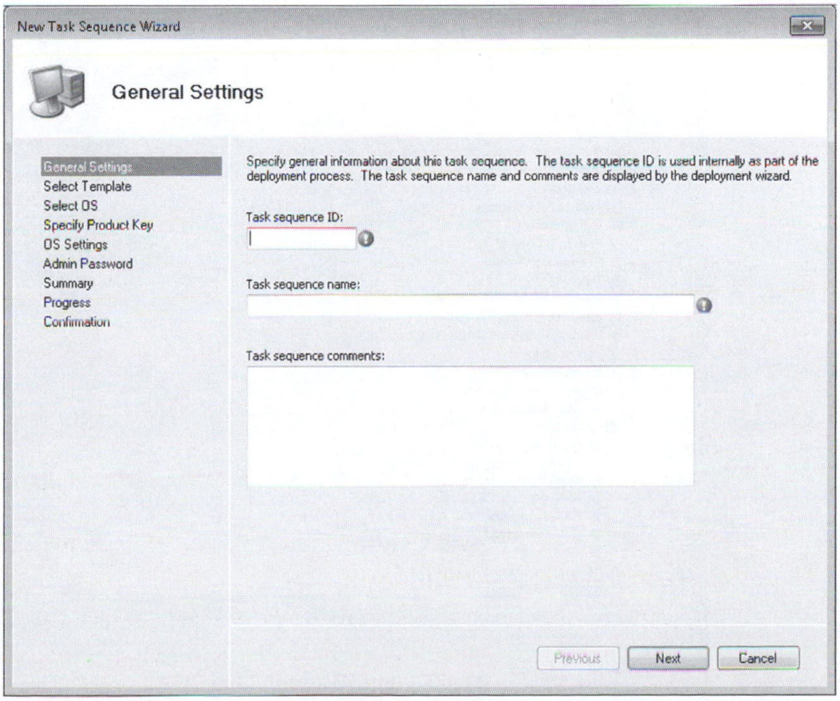

Figure 3-22

The New Task Sequence Wizard

The wizard includes a selection of templates that define some of the most common task sequence configurations, as shown in Figure 3-23. To install a reference computer, you typically select the Standard Client Task Sequence template. Subsequent pages of the wizard enable you to select the operating system image you want to install and configure some of the basic settings that normally appear during the Windows 7 installation.

Figure 3-23

Selecting a task sequence template

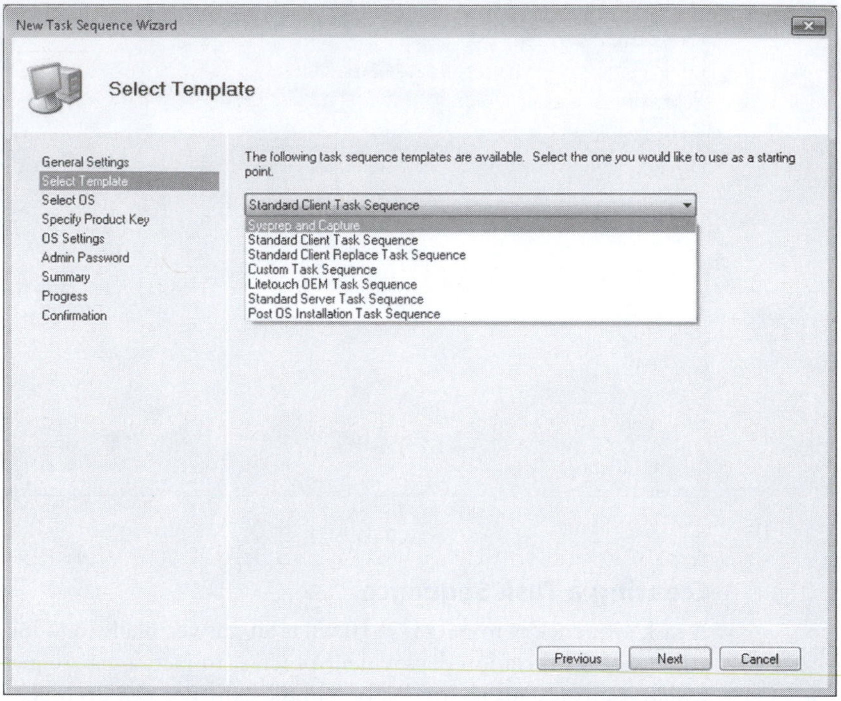

Once you have created a task sequence, you can modify it further using the interface shown in Figure 3-24. Using the many task sequence settings available, you can implement any of

Figure 3-24

Configuring task sequence properties

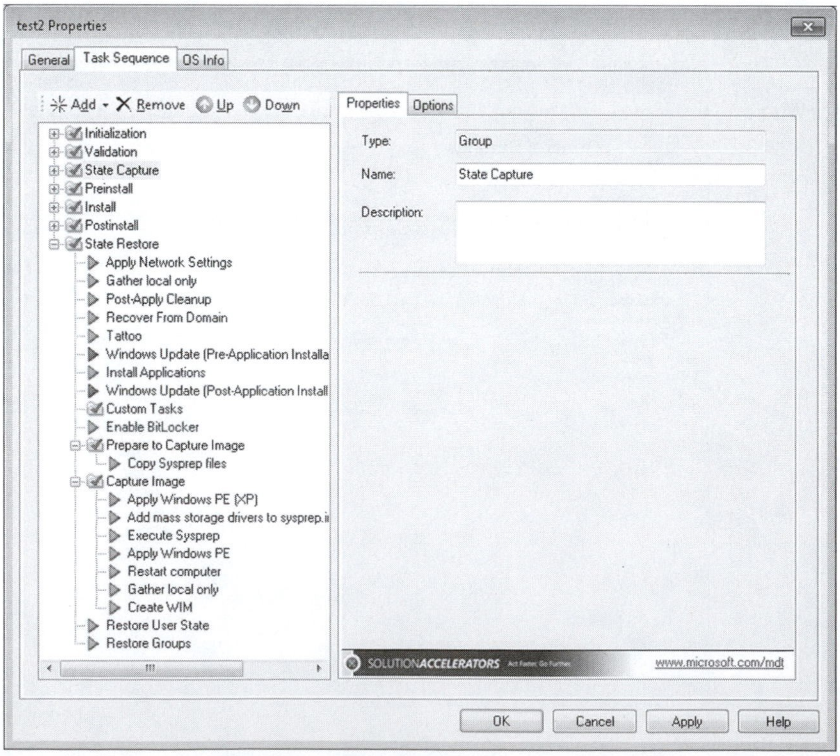

the four deployment scenarios described earlier in this lesson by using USMT to capture and restore system state data. You also use these options to configure the task sequence to generalize the reference computer and capture an image of it, all as part of a single deployment process.

Updating the Deployment Share

After creating the task sequence and configuring its settings, select your deployment share and click Action > Update Deployment Share, which launches the Update Deployment Share Wizard, as shown in Figure 3-25. Updating the share ensures that all of the MDT 2010 configuration files are up to date and creates a customized Windows PE boot image that enables the reference computer to start and connect to the deployment share.

Figure 3-25

The Update Deployment Share Wizard

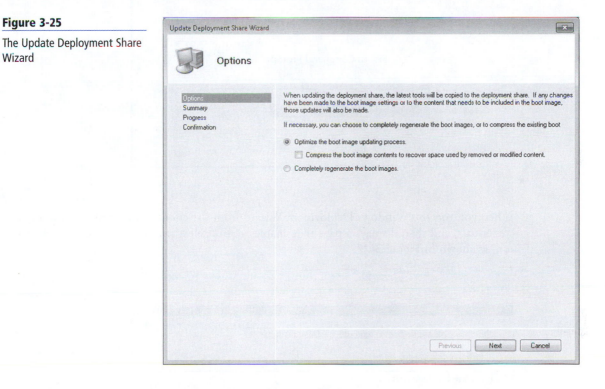

Deploying the Boot Image

The Update Deployment Share Wizard creates Windows PE boot images in both sector-based and file-based formats, in both x86 and x64 versions, using the following filenames:

- LiteTouchPE_x86.iso
- LiteTouchPE_x86.wim
- LiteTouchPE_x64.iso
- LiteTouchPE_x64.wim

This enables you to deploy the boot image to the reference computer in two ways. You can burn the .iso image file to a removable disk and boot the computer from it, or you can deploy the .wim file using WDS. Whichever method you choose, the reference computer boots and runs the MDT 2010 client, as shown in Figure 3-26.

Figure 3-26

The MDT 2010 client

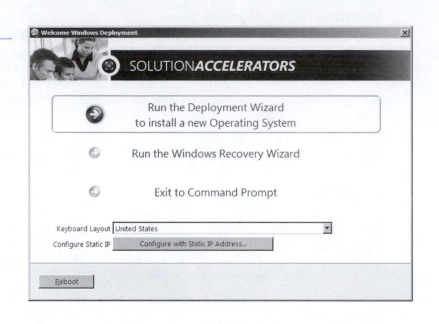

When you run the Windows Deployment Wizard from the client, it first prompts for logon credentials, and then displays a page that enables you to select the task sequence you want to run, as shown in Figure 3-27.

Figure 3-27

The Windows Deployment Wizard

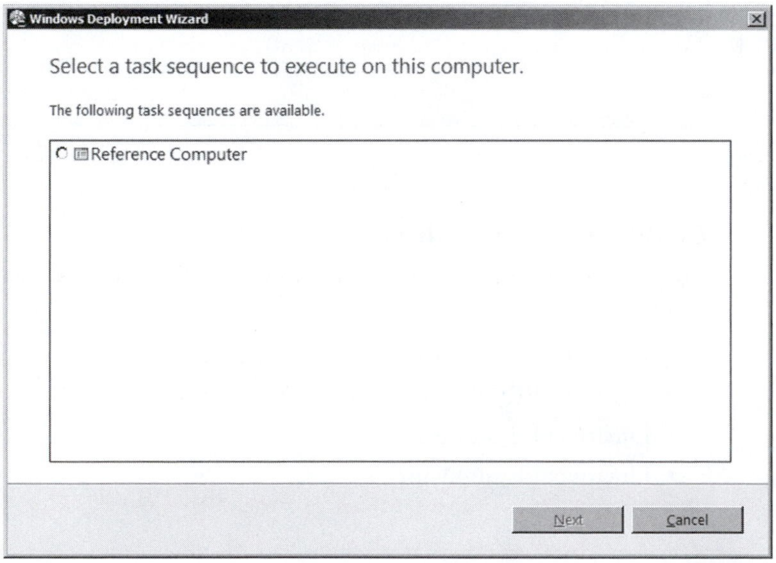

The following pages of the wizard gather responses to the standard configuration settings that appear during a Windows 7 installation. Pages then appear that enable you to restore user state data (which is not necessary on a reference computer), and capture an image, as shown in Figure 3-28, which is necessary.

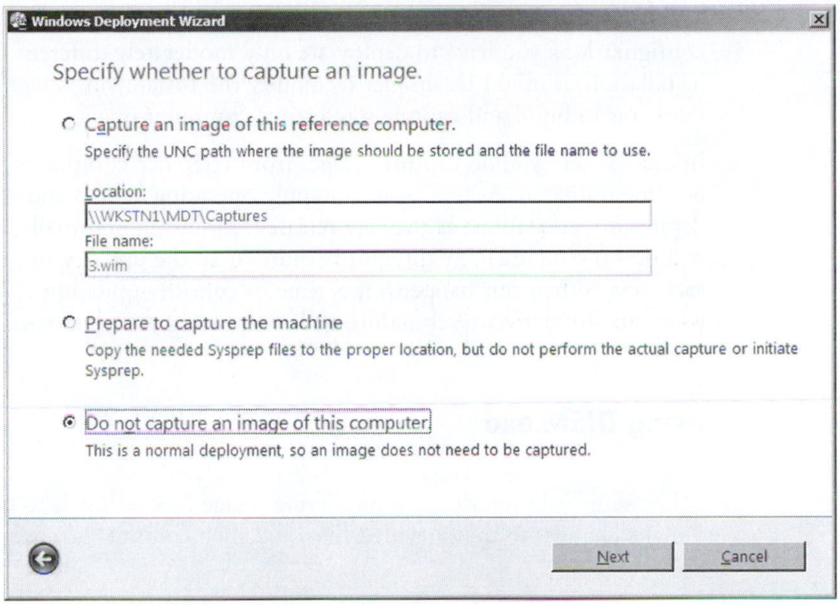

Figure 3-28

Configuring capture settings in the Windows Deployment Wizard

Specify whether to capture an image.

○ Capture an image of this reference computer.
Specify the UNC path where the image should be stored and the file name to use.

Location:
\\WKSTN1\MDT\Captures

File name:
3.wim

○ Prepare to capture the machine
Copy the needed Sysprep files to the proper location, but do not perform the actual capture or initiate Sysprep.

⦿ Do not capture an image of this computer.
This is a normal deployment, so an image does not need to be captured.

Next   Cancel

With all of the necessary settings configured, the wizard then proceeds to install Windows 7 unattended, configure all of the settings you specified in the task sequence, capture an image of the reference computer, and upload it back to the MDT 2010 build computer. The advantage of MDT 2010 is that while you still have to configure all of the same settings, you can complete all of the configuration at one time. Once the actual installation begins, no further interaction is needed at the reference computer.

Modifying Image Files

THE BOTTOM LINE

One of the advantages of the Windows Imaging file format is the ability to edit image files while they are offline.

CERTIFICATION READY?
Prepare a system image for deployment.
2.2

Building a reference computer and capturing an image of it is not a terribly difficult process, but as with all enterprise IT projects, it gets more difficult as you multiply it. If you are a technical specialist with dozens of workstation configurations to support, the prospect of building—or rebuilding—a large number of reference computers and capturing—or recapturing—new images of them is probably less than appealing.

Introducing Deployment Image Servicing and Management

Windows 7 AIK includes a new command-line tool called Deployment Image Servicing and Management (DISM.exe) that enables you to modify Windows Imaging files while they are offline.

With the DISM.exe tool, you can perform the following tasks:

- Add device drivers.
- Add language packs.
- Add packaged updates.
- Enable or disable operating system features.
- Append a volume image to a workstation image.
- Combine multiple images in a single Windows Imaging file.

Technical specialists can use this capability in several ways. In cases where the workstation configurations you have to deploy are only moderately different from a default Windows 7 installation, it might be simpler to modify the Install.wim image from a Windows 7 DVD than it is to build and capture a reference computer image.

In cases where you do capture images from reference computers, those images will eventually become outdated. At first, you can apply operating system and application updates to your deployed workstations as they are released. However, eventually, deploying new workstations will become increasingly difficult because of all the updates and changes you must apply to each one. When this happens, it is time to consider updating your image files, and this is when an alternative to rebuilding and recapturing your reference computers is welcome.

Using DISM.exe

The standard procedure for modifying image files offline is to mount an image to a folder, make changes to the expanded files, and then commit the changes back to the image file.

To modify an image file using DISM.exe, you must first mount it to a folder. This process creates copies of all the files in the image in their expanded form. You can then work with the copies, making any changes you need.

MOUNTING AN IMAGE

To mount an image, open an elevated command prompt and use the following syntax:

```
dism /mount-wim /wimfile:x:\filename.wim /index:1 /mountdir:c:\mounted
```

- **/mount-wim:** Specifies that the command should mount an image to a folder.
- **/wimfile:x:\filename.wim:** Specifies the name and location of the Windows Imaging file you want to mount.
- **/index:1:** Specifies the image within the Windows Imaging file that you want to mount.
- **/mountdir:c:\mounted:** Specifies the location where you want to mount the image.

The result of the command is as shown in Figure 3-29. Running DISM.exe with the /get-mountedwiminfo parameter displays information about the currently mounted image.

Figure 3-29

Mounting an image using DISM.exe

> **TAKE NOTE** *
>
> If you mount an image directly from a read-only source, such as a Windows 7 installation DVD, the DISM.exe program will mount the image in read-only mode. You will not be able to make any changes to the image, even though it is mounted to a folder on a read/write hard disk. To modify the image from a Windows 7 disk, you must first copy the Install.wim file from the DVD to a hard disk.

As noted earlier in this lesson, Windows Imaging files can contain multiple images, but you can only mount one of the images in the file at a time. This is the reason for the */index* parameter on the command line. To determine the index number for a specific image in a file containing more than one, you can use the following command:

```
dism /get-wiminfo /wimfile:x:\filename.wim
```

The result is a display like the one shown in Figure 3-30.

Figure 3-30

Displaying image information using DISM.exe

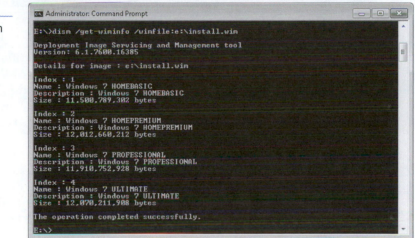

ADDING DRIVERS TO AN IMAGE FILE

For a workstation with a storage host adapter that Windows 7 does not support natively, a technical specialist might find it easier to add a device driver for the adapter to an existing image file rather than install a reference computer and capture a new image. This would be especially true if there were several workstation configurations with different drivers involved.

To add a driver to an image file that you have already mounted, use a command like the following:

```
dism /image:e:\mount /add-driver /driver:e:\drivers /recurse
```

- **/image:*e:\mount*:** Specifies the location of the image that you want to modify. Once you have mounted an image using DISM.exe, nearly all of the commands you use to work with the image begin with the */image* parameter, so that DISM knows what image it should access.
- **/add-driver:** Indicates that you want to add a driver to the image specified by the */image* parameter.
- **/driver:*e:\drivers*:** Specifies the location of the driver to be added to the image, either as a path to the driver file (with a .inf extension) or to the folder where the driver is located.

- **/recurse:** Causes the program to search for drivers in the subdirectories of the folder specified in the */driver* parameter.

The result of the command is as shown in Figure 3-31.

Figure 3-31

Adding a driver with DISM.exe

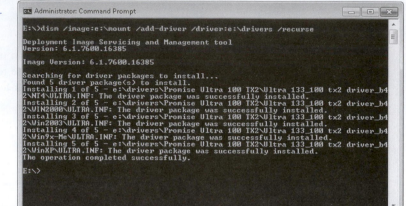

> **TAKE NOTE ***
>
> DISM.exe can only manage drivers that include a windows Information file (with a .inf extension). If you have drivers packaged as executable (.exe) files or Microsoft Windows Installer (.msi) packages, you cannot add them to an image using the */add-driver* parameter. You can however, use Windows SIM to create an answer file that installs these drivers and then apply the answer file to the image using the */apply-unattend* parameter.

During the driver addition process, DISM renames the driver files with consecutively numbered filenames, such as oem1.inf and oem2.inf. From that point on, you must use the new filenames when referring to the drivers on the command line. To display information about the drivers in an image, use the following command, as shown in Figure 3-32:

```
dism /image:e:\mount /get-drivers
```

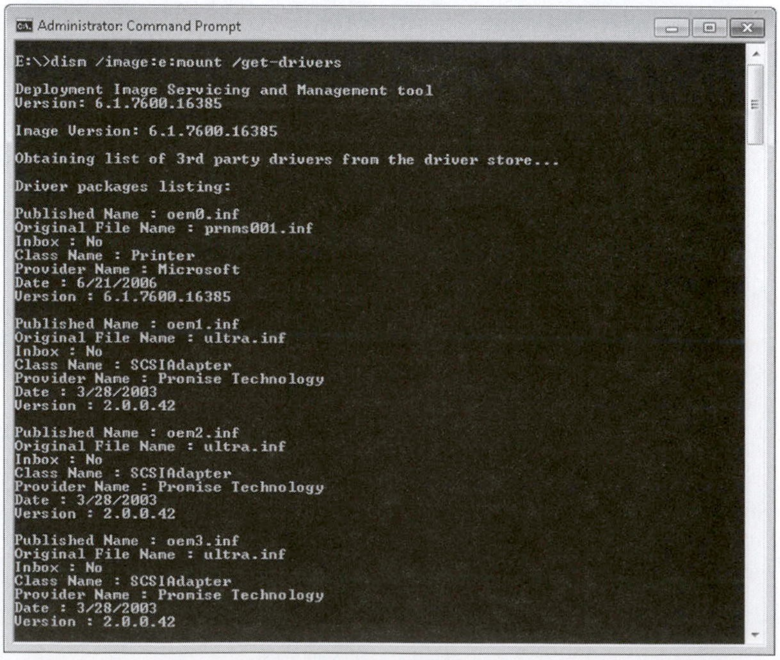

Figure 3-32

Displaying driver information with DISM.exe

ADDING UPDATES TO AN IMAGE FILE

In roughly the same way that you can add drivers to a mounted image, you can also add operating system updates, such as hotfixes, language packs, and service packs. To add an update to a mounted image, you use a command such as:

```
dism /image:e:\mount /add-package /packagepath:e:\updates\package.msu
```

- **/image:*e:**mount*:** Specifies the location of the image that you want to modify. Once you have mounted an image using DISM.exe, nearly all of the commands you use to work with the image begin with the */image* parameter, so that DISM knows what image it should access.
- **/add-package:** Indicates that you want to add a package to the image specified by the */image* parameter.
- **/packagepath:*e:**updates**package.msu*:** Specifies the location of the package to be added to the image.

DISM.exe can only add packages that take the form of cabinet (.cab) or Windows Update Stand-alone Installer (.msu) files.

ADDING APPLICATIONS TO AN IMAGE FILE

DISM.exe has similar command-line parameters for the various types of components the program supports. For example, when working with drivers, you can use the */add-drivers* parameter to add a driver to an offline image, as you have seen, the */remove-driver* parameter to remove a drive you have previously installed, the */get-drivers* parameter to list all of the drivers added to the image, and the */get-driverinfo* parameter to display information about a specific driver.

When working with packages, the */add-package*, */remove-package*, */get-packages*, and */get-packageinfo* parameters provide equivalent functions. When working with applications, however, there are */get-apps* and */get-appinfo* parameters, but no */get-app* or */remove-app*. This is because you cannot add an application to an image using DISM the way you can a driver or a package.

The only way to add an application to an offline image is to create an answer file that installs the application and apply the answer file to the image using DISM. The recommended practice is to create a separate answer file dedicated to this purpose using Windows SIM, adding the application to the offlineServicing configuration pass.

To apply the answer file to the offline image, use a command that specifies the name and location of the answer file, like the following:

```
dism /image:e:\mount /apply-unattend:e:\unattend.xml
```

An answer file is also the recommended way to add packages with dependencies to an image. Applying multiple packages using the */add-package* parameter does not guarantee that the computer to which you deploy the image will apply the packages in the same order you applied them to the image. If you have packages that are dependent on one another, adding them to an answer file ensures that the target computer will install them in the order you specify.

COMMITTING AND UNMOUNTING IMAGES

When you have made all of your modifications to the mounted image, you must commit the changes you made to the mounted copy back to the original Windows Imaging file and unmount the image, using a command like the following:

```
dism /unmount-wim /mountdir:e:\mount /commit
```

The result of the command is shown in Figure 3-33. The /commit parameter causes DISM to save the changes you made. To abandon the changes and unmount the image without saving, use the /discard parameter instead of /commit.

Figure 3-33

Unmounting an image with DISM.exe

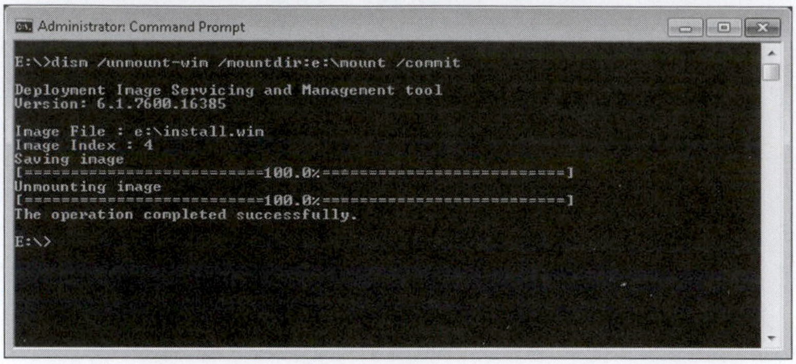

```
E:\>dism /unmount-wim /mountdir:e:\mount /commit

Deployment Image Servicing and Management tool
Version: 6.1.7600.16385

Image File : e:\install.wim
Image Index : 4
Saving image
[==========================100.0%==========================]
Unmounting image
[==========================100.0%==========================]
The operation completed successfully.

E:\>
```

■ Deploying Image Files

THE BOTTOM LINE

Once you have amassed the image files you need, it is time to consider the prospect of deploying them to your target computers, that is, the workstations for your end users.

CERTIFICATION READY?
Deploy a system image.
2.3

As with most other aspects of a workstation deployment, applying an image to a computer is a relatively simple task that can become quite complicated when you have dozens of images to deploy on hundreds or thousands of computers. As with the image capture process, the Microsoft deployment tools provide a number of solutions that range from manual to completely automatic.

Choosing a deployment solution is a matter of assessing the complexity of your project and deciding how much time and effort you want to spend on designing and implementing your deployment. The general rule is that the more automated your deployment is, the more complicated the process of planning it and setting it up.

For example, a deployment that uses the ZTI method in MDT 2010 has a long and difficult setup process, but once it's ready, the actual deployment is a pleasure. If you have hundreds of workstations to deploy, the extended setup might be worth the trouble. However, if you only have ten workstations to install, it would be faster and easier to deploy your images manually.

Of course, nearly all deployments fall somewhere between these two extremes, and prior planning is the key to determining which deployment method is most suitable to a particular situation. Microsoft provides a great deal of documentation with the Windows 7 AIK and MDT 2010 packages, much of which covers the overall deployment process, and not just the mechanics of using the deployment tools. Technical specialists should familiarize themselves with the ramifications of the entire deployment process and the capabilities of all the tools before selecting a solution.

Understanding Image Types

Determining how many images you will have to create and maintain is an important part of the deployment planning process, and the nature of the images you create dictates how you will deploy them.

The complexity of a large-scale workstation deployment process is dependent on how many workstation configurations you have to create. Deploying one thousand identically configured workstations with a single image is, after all, far easier than deploying twenty different configurations to fifty workstations each. When you are faced with the prospect of multiple workstation configurations, there are different ways to handle them, based on the types of images you choose to create.

USING THICK IMAGES

A thick image is an image file that contains all of the elements of a workstation configuration, including applications drivers, updates, and all configuration settings. You create a thick image by completely installing and configuring a reference computer to your workstation specifications and then capturing an image of it.

Thick images are preferable for deployments that require a relatively small number of workstation configurations. They are relatively quick to deploy to target computers because they are self-contained and don't require extensive scripting. However, thick images are also large in size and, if you have a lot of workstation configurations to deploy, capturing, storing, and maintaining the images can be labor intensive.

USING THIN IMAGES

Thin images are more generic than thick images and contain fewer configuration-specific elements, such as applications and language packs. If you have a large number of workstation configurations to deploy, you might find it preferable to create a few thin images and install some or all of the configuration-specific elements afterward. The ultimate thin image is the basic Install.wim image file on every Windows installation disk. You can deploy this image on all of your target computers and then customize specific workstation configurations using an external software distribution mechanism, such as SCCM 2007.

The advantages of thin images are that they are smaller and simpler to create and maintain. However, using thin images also complicates the deployment process because you have to do more extensive scripting and post-installation configuration.

USING HYBRID IMAGES

A hybrid image installs all of the applications, settings, and software components that a workstation needs, so in that sense, it is like a thick image. However, the hybrid image does not include all of the applications and other components in the actual image file. Instead, it accesses some or all of them from a shared folder on the network, which makes it similar to a thin image.

As with thin images, hybrid images require some scripting, and the actual deployment is more complex than that of a thick image, but the images are easier to create and maintain, and you do not need a complex software distribution platform such as SCCM 2007.

Deploying Images Manually

Just as you can use ImageX.exe to manually capture an image of a reference computer, you can also use the tool to apply an image to a target computer.

As in the capture process, you must create a Windows PE boot disk that contains the ImageX.exe utility and use it to start the workstation. There are also several preliminary steps you must perform before you can actually apply the image, as described in the following sections.

CREATING A DISK PARTITION

Unlike sector-based image files that define the entire file system of a disk, the Windows Imaging format defines only files. Therefore, you must prepare the hard disk on the target computer by creating and formatting a partition before you can actually apply the image.

Windows PE boot disks include the Diskpart.exe utility, which enables you to partition and format disks from the command prompt. Running the Diskpart.exe program opens a DISKPART > prompt from which you can execute commands that manipulate the disks on the computer. For example, on a computer with only one hard disk, you can use the following commands to create a single partition encompassing the whole disk, assign it the drive letter C, and format it using the NTFS file system:

```
create partition primary
format fs=NTFS label="New Partition" quick
assign letter=c
```

ACCESSING THE INSTALL IMAGE

With the workstation's hard disk prepared, you can now apply the image file, but first you must have access to the image file. There are several ways you can get the image file to the target computer manually, including the following:

- **Burn the install image file to your Windows PE boot disk:** As long as the boot disk is a DVD with enough space to hold the image file, you can add it to the disk during the creation process.
- **Burn the install image file to a separate disk:** You can place the image file on any DVD or USB flash drive with sufficient space to hold it. Because Windows PE creates a ram disk on the target computer by default, you can remove the boot disk from the drive once the system is running and insert another disk containing the install image.
- **Access the install image file from a network share:** You can place the install image on a shared network drive and map a drive letter to it from Windows PE on the target computer using the *net use* command.

APPLYING THE INSTALL IMAGE

To apply the install image to the partition you created on the target computer's hard disk, you use a command like the following:

```
imagex /apply z:\images\win7.wim 1 c:
```

- **/apply:** Indicates that you want to apply an image to a specified disk.
- **z:\images\win7.wim:** Specifies the name and location of the Windows Imaging file you want to apply.
- **1:** Specifies the number of the image inside the Windows Imaging file that you want to apply.
- **c::** Specifies the location where you want to apply the image.

APPLYING BOOT FILES

Once you have applied the image, the final step is to make the system disk on the target computer bootable. To do this, you use the Bcdboot.exe command-line tool, with a command like the following:

```
bcdboot c:\windows
```

Deploying Images Using WDS

Earlier in this lesson, you learned how you can deploy boot images using Windows Deployment Services. WDS can deploy install images as well.

The ability to deploy images over the network is what makes WDS unique among the Microsoft deployment tools. When deploying install images, you can use WDS as a self-contained deployment solution or as a means to deploy the images you have created with Windows 7 AIK or MDT 2010.

USING WDS AS A SELF-CONTAINED SOLUTION

When you capture an image of a workstation using a WDS capture image, you have the option of uploading the new image directly back to the WDS server. Once you have done this, you can add the captured image and deploy it using WDS.

Deploying a target computer using WDS requires you to have a boot image as well as your captured install image added to the WDS server. For the boot image, you can use the Boot.wim file from a Windows 7 installation disk, or a Windows PE image you have customized yourself.

With the images in place on the WDS server, use the following procedure to deploy Windows 7 on a bare-metal target computer.

DEPLOY AN INSTALL IMAGE USING WDS

GET READY. Configure the boot order in your reference computer's BIOS to use its PXE-capable network adapter before its hard disk drive:

1. Turn on the reference computer. The system obtains TCP/IP settings from the DHCP server and connects to the WDS server on the network. The Windows Boot Manager screen appears.

2. Select a standard boot image (not a capture image). The Install Windows Wizard appears, displaying the *Windows Deployment Services* page, as shown in Figure 3-34.

Figure 3-34

The Windows Deployment Services page of the Install Windows Wizard

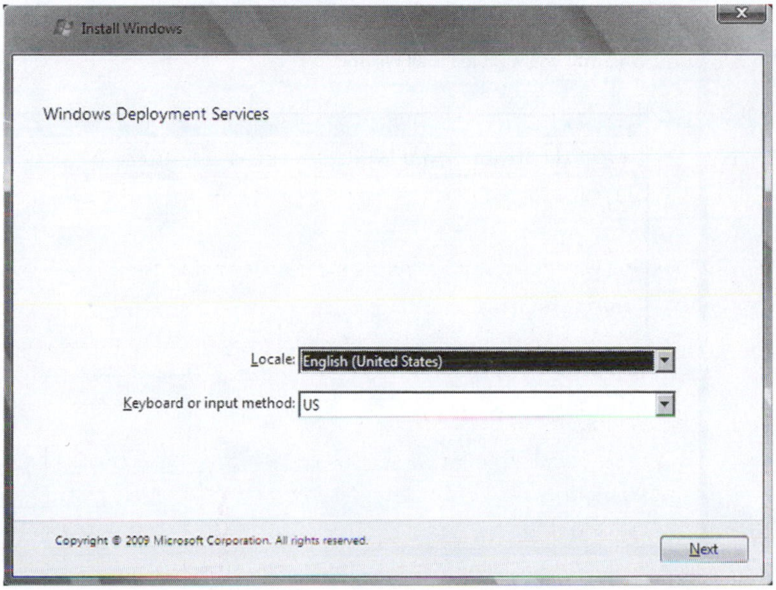

3. If necessary, select alternative values from the Local and Keyboard or input method drop-down lists and click Next. A Connect to dialog box appears.

4. Log on to the WDS server by supplying appropriate credentials. The *Select the operating system you want to install* page appears, as shown in Figure 3-35.

Figure 3-35

The Select the operating system you want to install page of the Install Windows Wizard

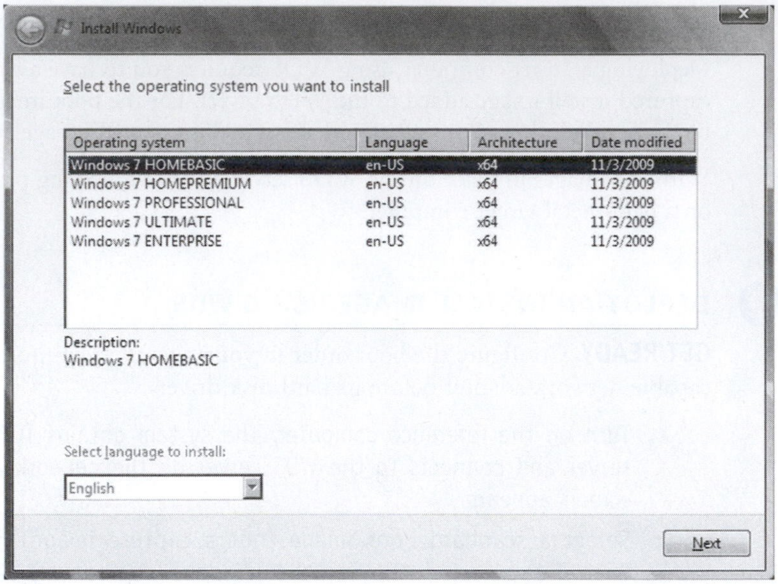

5. Select the image you want to deploy on the computer and click Next. The *Where do you want to install Windows?* page appears, as shown in Figure 3-36.

Figure 3-36

The Where do you want to install Windows? page of the Install Windows Wizard

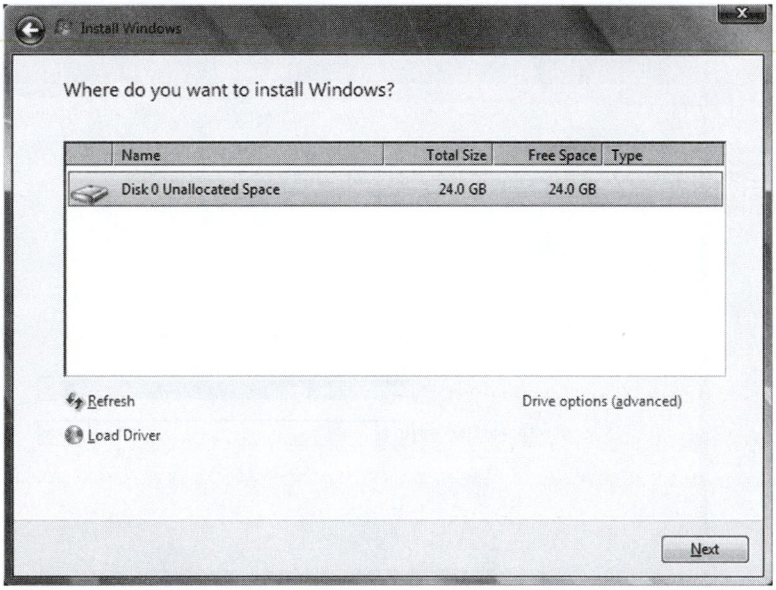

6. Select the volume on which you want to install Windows 7 and click Next. The computer accesses the selected image on the WDS server and the installation begins.

MULTICASTING WITH WDS

Another important advantage of deploying install images with WDS is its ability to transfer image files over the network using multicast transmissions. *Multicasting* is a TCP/IP methodology that enables a computer to transmit the same data to multiple destinations at the same time. Also called a *one-to-many* transmission, multicasting can conserve network bandwidth during a large-scale deployment by replacing the individual one-to-one unicast transmissions between the WDS server and the target workstations with a single transmission.

To configure WDS to use multicasts, you use the Create Multicast Transmission Wizard to select an image and specify when the transmission should occur, as shown in Figure 3-37. You can configure WDS multicasts to occur at a scheduled time (scheduled-cast), or to begin when a client requests access to the image (auto-cast).

Figure 3-37

The Create Multicast
Transmission Wizard

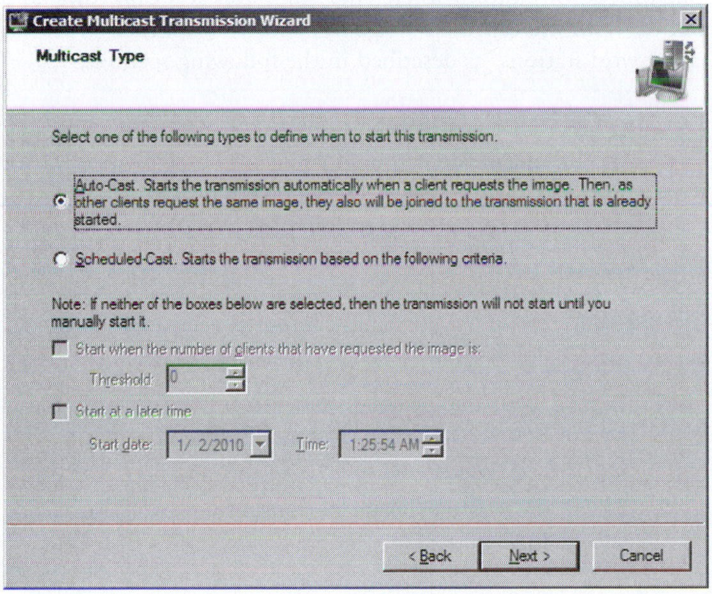

Deploying Images Using MDT 2010

The process for deploying images with MDT 2010 is similar to the process for capturing them. You add your image files to the MDT deployment share and create task sequences that apply the images to your target computers. If you have created thick images, the task sequences should be relatively simple, but thin or hybrid sequences are likely to require more extensive scripting.

As noted earlier in this lesson, MDT 2010 supports two types of deployments: LTI and ZTI. The basic procedures for these deployments are essentially the same; what differs is the tools that you use to implement the procedures.

The primary advantage of the ZTI deployment is the ability to simply turn on the target computer and have the entire workstation installation proceed automatically and with no interaction. For large deployments, this can save IT staff an enormous amount of time, money, and effort, because the end user can turn on the computer and initiate the installation. However, this advantage comes at a rather substantial price. ZTI requires an SCCM 2007 infrastructure and limits the flexibility of the deployment.

The advantages and disadvantages of these deployment types are discussed in the following sections.

PERFORMING AN LTI DEPLOYMENT

The lite-touch installation type is so named because it requires, at the very least, someone at the target workstation site to boot the computer, run the Deployment Wizard, and select the task sequence that will install Windows 7. The configuration of the task sequence then determines what other interaction is required before the installation begins.

With a carefully prepared task sequence, explicit instructions, and reasonably savvy users, the installation of each target computer could conceivably proceed without the presence of a technical specialist. If IT personnel will be present at each computer, the task sequence can be simpler and more generic, which reduces the amount of preparation required for the deployment. This is the same trade-off as described earlier: the more preparation you are willing to do beforehand, the less interaction required during the workstation installation.

The process of building a reference computer and capturing an image of it was described earlier. With the captured image in hand, you can then proceed to deploy that image to the target workstations, as described in the following sections.

Adding Captured Images

To deploy the image you captured using MDT 2010, you must add it to the deployment share you created earlier, using the following procedure.

ADD A CAPTURED IMAGE

GET READY. Log on to your build computer using an account with administrative privileges and launch the Deployment Workbench console.

1. Expand your deployment share, select the Operating Systems folder, and click Action > New Operating System. The New Operating System Wizard appears, displaying the *OS type* page.

2. Select the custom image file option and click Next. The *Image* page appears, as shown in Figure 3-38.

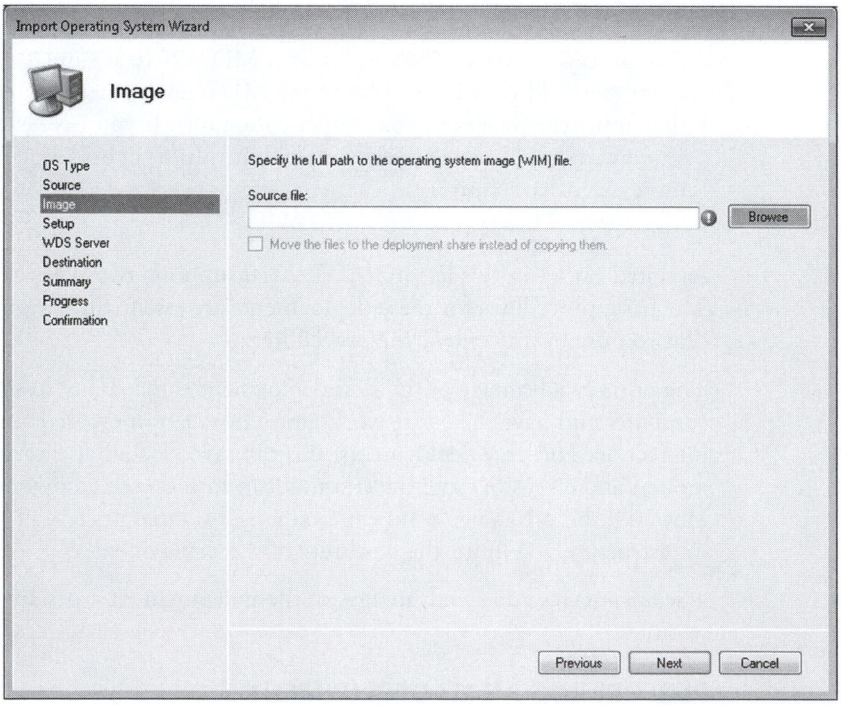

Figure 3-38

The Image page of the Import Operating System Wizard

3. Type or browse to the path and filename of the image you captured on your reference computer and click Next. The *Setup* page appears, as shown in Figure 3-39.

Figure 3-39

The Setup page of the Import Operating System Wizard

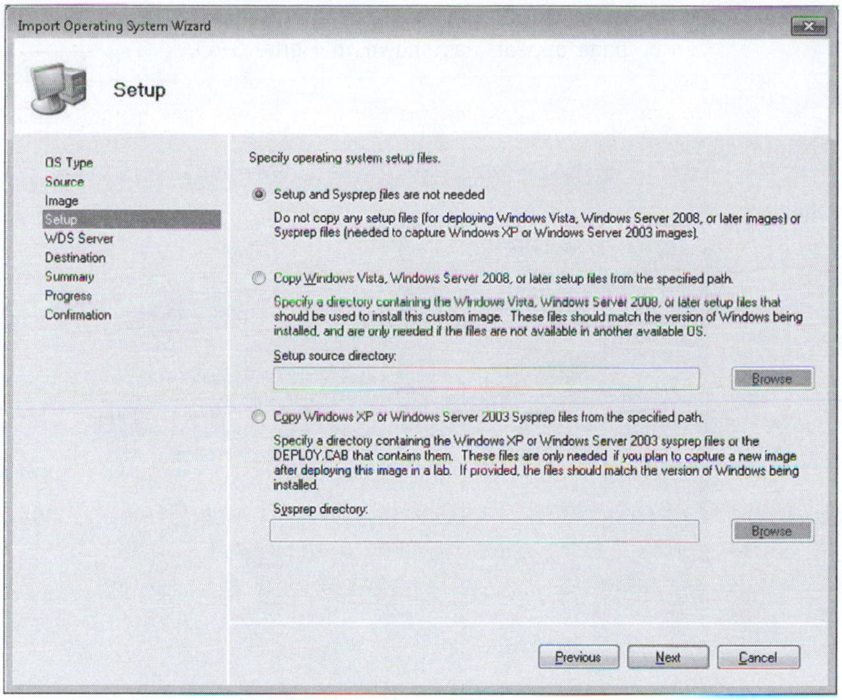

4. Click Next to accept the default Setup and Sysprep files are not needed option. The *Destination* page appears.
5. Click Next to accept the default folder name. The *Summary* page appears.
6. Click Next. The wizard adds the image to the deployment share.
7. Click Finish.

The captured image is now available from the deployment share.

Creating a Task Sequence

Just as you did when capturing an image with MDT 2010, you must create a task sequence to deploy a captured image to your target computers. The process is the same, using the New Task Sequence Wizard; the differences will be in the task sequence elements you choose to configure.

For a deployment using the new computer scenario, you create your task sequence using the following procedure.

CREATE A TASK SEQUENCE

GET READY. Log on to your build computer using an account with administrative privileges and launch the Deployment Workbench console.

1. Expand your deployment share, select the Task Sequences folder, and click Action > New Task Sequence. The New Task Sequence Wizard appears, displaying the *General Settings* page.
2. Supply appropriate values in the Task sequence ID and Task sequence name text boxes and click Next. The *Select Template* page appears.

3. Select the Standard Client Task Sequence template and click Next. The *Select OS* page appears, as shown in Figure 3-40.

Figure 3-40

The Select OS page of the New Task Sequence Wizard

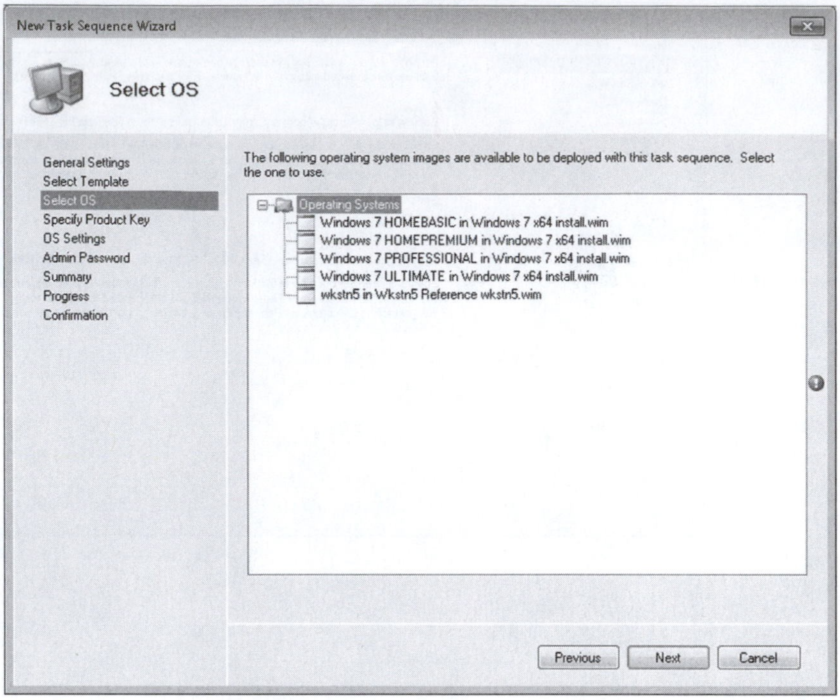

4. Select the custom image you added to the deployment share and click Next. The *Specify Product Key* page appears, as shown in Figure 3-41.

Figure 3-41

The Specify Product Key page of the New Task Sequence Wizard

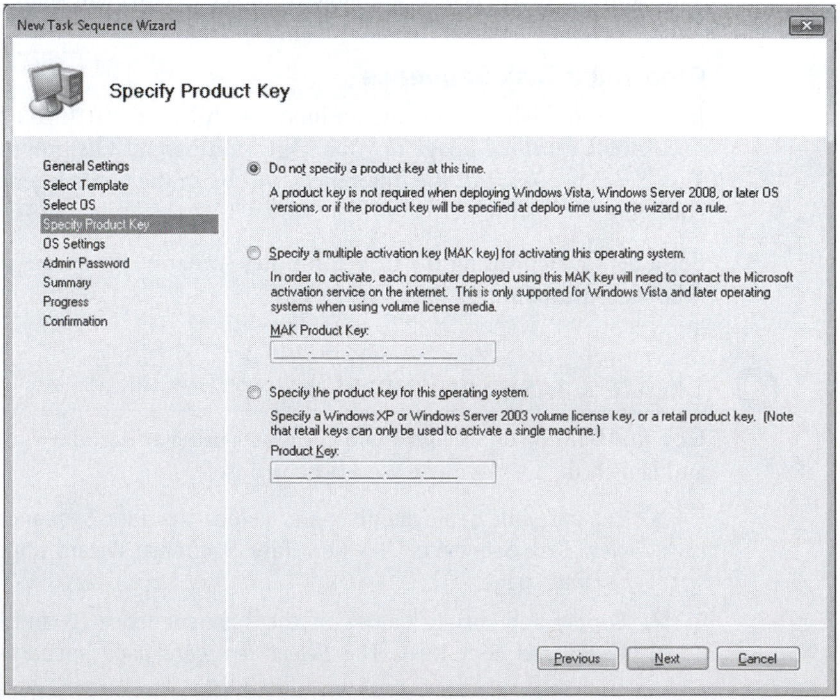

5. Select the Specify a multiple activation key (MAK key) for activating this operating system option and type your key in the MAK Product Key text box. Then click Next. The *OS Settings* page appears, as shown in Figure 3-42.

> **TAKE NOTE**＊ If you will be using individual retail Windows 7 licenses for your workstations, you do not want to specify a product key in a task sequence that you will be deploying on multiple computers. You must supply individual keys on each workstation during the installation.

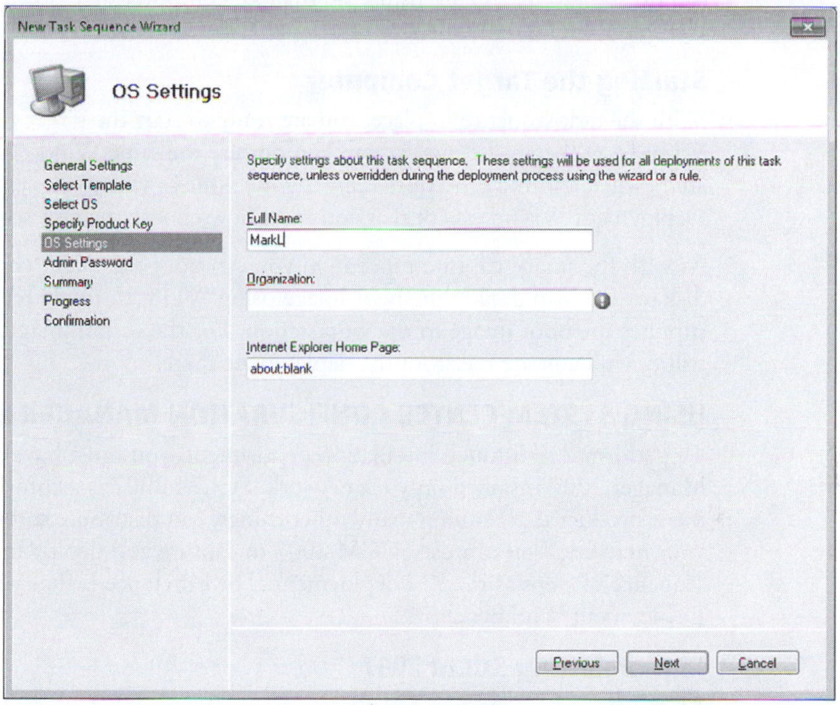

Figure 3-42

The OS Settings page of the New Task Sequence Wizard

6. Specify values in the Full Name, Organization, and Internet Explorer Home Page text boxes and click Next. The *Admin Password* page appears, as shown in Figure 3-43.

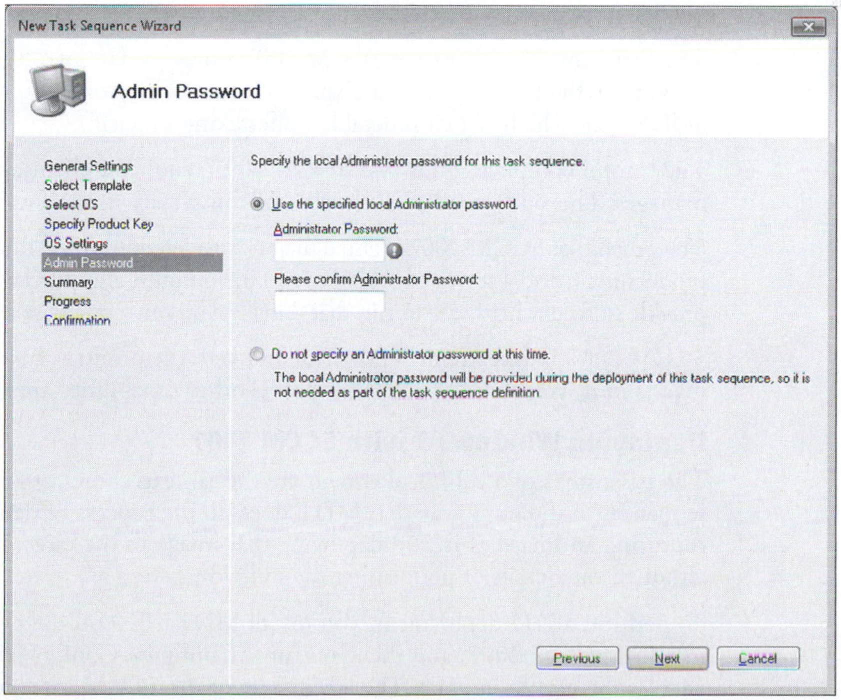

Figure 3-43

The Admin Password page of the New Task Sequence Wizard

TAKE NOTE *
If you do not want to assign the same Administrator password to all of your target computers, select the Do not specify an Administrator password at this time option.

7. Type a password in the Administrator Password and Please confirm Administrator Password text boxes and click Next. The *Summary* page appears.
8. Click Next. The wizard creates the task sequence.
9. Click Finish.

Your new task sequence now appears in the deployment share. Once you have created the task sequence, you can open its Properties sheet and customize it as much as you want. For example, if there are applications you want to install that are not in the captured image, you can do so here. If you are using the Replace computer or Refresh computer scenario, you can configure the task sequence to capture and/or restore the workstation's user state data.

Starting the Target Computer

With the task sequence in place, you are ready to start the target computer, run the Deployment Wizard, and begin the installation. You can use the same Windows PE boot image you created earlier, and the procedure is exactly the same as when you captured an image using the Deployment Wizard except that you must now choose the task sequence you just created.

As with the image capture procedure, you can boot the target computer using a Windows PE disk, or you can deploy the boot image using WDS. In the latter case, the WDS server only supplies the boot image to the workstation. For the install image, the Deployment Wizard still downloads the file from the deployment share.

USING SYSTEM CENTER CONFIGURATION MANAGER 2007

To perform a zero-touch installation deployment, you must have System Center Configuration Manager 2007 installed on your network. SCCM 2007 is a comprehensive network management product that, among many other things, can distribute software to the computers on your network. You can use SCCM 2007 to capture and deploy image files using the same basic sequence of steps as the LTI deployment. The difference is that you use SCCM tools instead of Deployment Workbench.

Implementing SCCM 2007

As mentioned earlier, it is usually not worth the time, effort, and expense to implement SCCM on your network solely for the purpose of deploying workstations using ZTI. SCCM is not a simple application that you install by inserting a disk into a drive and running the Setup program. It requires considerable planning in its own right because the application has many components and options.

The first complication is that SCCM 2007 stores its data in a SQL Server database, and it cannot use the free SQL Server Express Edition. Therefore, you must purchase and install SQL Server, which is a considerable undertaking in itself.

The second complication is that SCCM 2007 requires a client agent on each computer it manages. This adds another dimension of complexity to the implementation process.

The expense of SCCM 2007 is also a major consideration. Aside from purchasing the SCCM product itself, and a server on which to run it, you must also purchase the SQL Server software and provide sufficient hardware to run that. Finally, you must purchase a license for each client agent.

SCCM 2007 is an extremely powerful and versatile product, but before your organization invests in it, you should be certain that its other capabilities are useful to you as well.

Deploying Windows 7 with SCCM 2007

The basic steps of a ZTI deployment are the same as those for an LTI one. SCCM uses task sequences in the same way that MDT does, so the process of deploying a reference computer, capturing an image of it, and deploying that image to the target computers is the same, although the details of performing the individual steps are quite different.

To perform a ZTI deployment, you install MDT 2010 on the computer where you have installed SCCM 2007, and then you run a Configure ConfigMgr 2007 Integration script that enables the two to interact. The advantages of the SCCM integration are primarily those of configurability and scale. SCCM enables you to configure every aspect of the deployment in great detail, before the deployment actually begins. SCCM is also designed to distribute software to networks of virtually any size. You can also create multiple distribution points all over the network to distribute a deployment's bandwidth requirements.

SCCM can discover computers on a network that are already running a Windows operating system, but to deploy new, bare-metal computers, you must first add the computers to the SCCM database. This is what makes the zero-touch installation possible, because the workstation can immediately connect to the SCCM/MDT server and execute the task sequence that deploys the workstation configuration.

SKILL SUMMARY

IN THIS LESSON YOU LEARNED:

- The objectives of a large-scale Windows 7 deployment include the creation of standardized computing environments and minimized user interaction at the workstation.

- The basic steps of a workstation deployment are: build a deployment share, perform a reference computer installation, capture an image of the reference computer, boot the target computers, and apply the Windows 7 reference computer image.

- The Windows 7 Automated Installation Kit (AIK) is designed to support OEMs, who typically deploy Windows 7 workstations in one of two ways: a build-to-plan (BTP) installation, which captures a single image file and deploys it to each computer with no changes, or a build-to-order (BTO) installation, which captures a baseline image and deploys it to each computer, and then starts the computer in audit mode and performs a scripted procedure that customizes the configuration.

- MDT 2010 defines and supports four different deployment scenarios: New computer, Upgrade computer, Replace computer, and Refresh computer.

- The typical method for creating a customized image file for deployment to Windows 7 workstations is to install and configure Windows 7 on a reference computer and then capture an image of the reference computer's hard disk. This process can be manual or automatic, relatively simple or extremely complex.

- Using the Windows SIM utility, you can create answer files that automate the Windows 7 installation process.

- A capture image is a bootable image that you can deploy using WDS, and which includes a wizard-based client that runs on the reference computer and enables you to capture an image and upload it back to the WDS server.

- A task sequence is to MDT 2010 what an answer file is to Windows 7 AIK, a script that guides the workstation deployment process.

- With the DISM.exe tool, you can add device drivers, language packs, and packaged updates to an offline image file.

- A thick image is an image file that contains all of the elements of a workstation configuration, including applications drivers, updates, and all configuration settings. Thin images are more generic than thick images, and contain fewer of the configuration-specific elements, such as applications and language packs. A hybrid image installs all of the applications, settings, and software components a workstation needs, but it does not include all of the applications and other components in the actual image file. Instead, it accesses some or all of them from a shared folder on the network.

- To perform a zero-touch installation deployment, you must have System Center Configuration Manager 2007 installed on your network. SCCM 2007 is comprehensive network management product that, among many other things, can distribute software to the computers on your network.

■ Knowledge Assessment

Fill in the Blank

Complete the following sentences by writing the correct word or words in the blanks provided.

1. An image file that contains an entire workstation configuration, including all applications, packages, and configuration settings, is called a _____ image.

2. The two programs that make up the User State Migration Tool are called _____ and _____.

3. A _____ installation is one in which the installers capture a single image file and deploy it to each computer with no changes.

4. Windows Deployment Services can reduce network bandwidth requirements while deploying install images by using _____.

5. Before you can modify an offline image file using DISM.exe, you must _____ the image.

6. To partition a disk using an answer file, you must add settings to the _____ configuration pass.

7. The Windows 7 AIK tool that you use to create answer files is called _____.

8. To boot from an image transmitted over the network by a WDS server, a workstation must have a network adapter that supports _____.

9. The deployment scenario in which you save a workstation's user state data, wipe its disk, install Windows 7, and then restore the user state data is called the _____ scenario.

10. A _____ image enables a workstation to boot from a disk and connect to a WDS server.

True / False

Circle T if the statement is true or F if the statement is false.

T | F 1. To perform a Windows 7 deployment using ZTI, you must have a SQL Server on your network.

T | F 2. To create a capture image, you use the Deployment Workbench console.

T | F 3. The Windows 7 AIK script files used to perform unattended installations are called task sequences.

T | F 4. You can use the boot images created by Deployment Workbench to start workstations using either boot disks or WDS.

T | F 5. The computer that you use to capture an image of a workstation configuration is called the target computer.

T | F 6. An LTI deployment provides greater flexibility than a ZTI deployment.

T | F 7. ImageX.exe is a command-line tool that you can use to capture and deploy image files.

T | F 8. To use the upgrade computer scenario, a workstation must be running Windows XP SP2 or later.

T | F 9. Before you can capture an image of a Windows 7 workstation, you must run the Sysprep.exe program.

T | F 10. Sector-based image files are spannable, editable, and bootable.

Review Questions

1. Describe the difference between an LTI and a ZTI deployment in terms of the activity at the target computer during the Windows 7 installation.
2. List the five basic steps in an enterprise Windows 7 workstation deployment.

■ Case Scenarios

Scenario 3-1: Capturing an Image

After performing a manual installation of a reference computer, installing several applications, and configuring a multitude of settings, Howard runs Sysprep.exe with the `/generalize` parameter, opens a command prompt window, and attempts to capture an image of the computer using ImageX.exe. When he types the ImageX.exe command and presses enter, an error message appears, stating "The process cannot access the file because it is being used by another process." What has gone wrong, and what does Howard have to do to capture an image of the reference computer?

Scenario 3-2: Multicasting Images

Serge is responsible for deploying 100 new workstations on his company network, and he wants to use the multicasting capabilities of Windows Deployment Services to minimize the amount of bandwidth required. He has already built a reference computer and captured an image of it using Microsoft Deployment Toolkit 2010. After adding the captured image and the boot image created by MDT to his WDS server, he configures the WDS multicasting parameters and performs a test by initiating a deployment on five new target workstations at the same time, while capturing network traffic samples with a protocol analyzer. Examining the traffic analysis afterward, Serge realizes that no multicasting has occurred. What is the problem, and how can he resolve it.

4 LESSON

Working with Disks and Devices

OBJECTIVE DOMAIN MATRIX

TECHNOLOGY SKILL	OBJECTIVE DOMAIN	OBJECTIVE NUMBER
Working with VHDs	Configure a VHD.	2.4
Working with Devices and Drivers	Configure devices.	3.1
Working with Disks	Manage disks.	7.2

KEY TERMS

basic disk

Diskpart.exe

dynamic disk

exFAT

FAT (file allocation table)

FAT32

globally unique identifier (GUID)

GUID (globally unique identifier) partition table (GPT)

master boot record (MBR)

mirrored volume

native boot

NTFS

simple volume

spanned volume

striped volume

Virtual Hard Disk (VHD)

■ Working with Disks

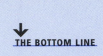
THE BOTTOM LINE

Hard disks are nearly always the primary storage medium in a computer running Windows 7, but in many cases, technician specialists must prepare a hard disk to store data by performing certain tasks before the computer can use it. Once you prepare the hard disk, you can keep the data stored on the disk secure with tools and features provided by Windows 7.

When you install Windows 7 on a computer, the setup program automatically performs all of the preparation tasks for the hard disks in the computer. However, adding another disk is a common upgrade, and after you install the hardware, you must perform the following tasks before the user can begin storing data on it:

- **Select a partitioning style:** In Windows 7, two hard disk partition styles are available for both x86- and x64-based computers. The ***master boot record (MBR)*** partition style has been around as long as Windows and is still the default partition style. ***GUID (globally unique identifier)*** partition table (GPT) has been around for a while also, but no x86 version of Windows prior to Vista supports it. (Windows XP Professional x64 edition does support GPT.) You must choose one of these partition styles for a drive; you cannot use both.

- **Select a disk type:** Two disk types are available in Windows 7—basic disks and dynamic disks. Both the MBR and the GPT partition styles support basic and dynamic disks. You cannot use both types on the same disk drive. You have to decide which is best for the computer.

- **Divide the disk into partitions or volumes:** Although many professionals use the terms partition and volume interchangeably, it is correct to refer to creating partitions on basic disks, and volumes on dynamic disks.

- **Format the volumes with a file system:** Because of the high capacities of the hard drives on the market today, NTFS is the preferred file system for Windows 7. However, the ***FAT (File Allocation Table)*** file system is also available, in the form of ***FAT32*** and ***exFAT***.

CERTIFICATION READY?
Manage disks.
7.2

Understanding Partition Styles

The term *partition style* refers to the method that Windows operating systems use to organize partitions on the disk.

There are two hard disk partition styles that you can use in Windows 7:

- **Master boot record (MBR):** This is the default partition style for x86-based and x64-based computers.
- **GUID (globally unique identifier) partition table (GPT):** First introduced in Windows Vista, you can now use the GPT partition style on x86-, as well as x64-based, Windows 7 computers.

Before Windows Vista, all x86-based computers used the MBR partition style only. Computers based on the x64 platform could use either the MBR or GPT partition style, as long as the GPT disk was not the boot disk.

MBR uses a partition table to point to the locations of the partitions on the disk. Windows selected this style automatically on x86-based workstation computers because, prior to Windows Vista, this was the only style available to them. The MBR disk partitioning style supports volumes up to 2 terabytes in size, and up to either four primary partitions or three primary partitions and one extended partition. Data critical to platform operations is stored in hidden (unpartitioned) sectors.

Table 4-1 lists the Windows operating systems that can use either the MBR or the GPT partition style for their disks:

Table 4-1

Windows Operating Systems Supporting MBR and GPT Partition Styles

OPERATING SYSTEM	x86-BASED	x64-BASED	IA-64-BASED
Windows XP	No	Yes	Yes
Windows Server 2003 SP1 (or later)	Yes	Yes	Yes
Windows Vista	Yes	Yes	N/A
Windows Server 2008	Yes	Yes	Yes
Windows 7	Yes	Yes	N/A
Windows Server 2008 R2	Yes	Yes	Yes

+ MORE INFORMATION

As far as the Windows 7 disk management tools are concerned, there is no difference between creating partitions or volumes in MBR and in GPT. You create partitions and volumes for both by using the same tools in the same ways.

Bear in mind, however, that unless the computer's architecture provides support for an Extensible Firmware Interface (EFI)-based boot partition, it is not possible to boot from GPT disks. In this case, the operating system must reside on an MBR disk, and GPT must reside on an entirely separate, nonbootable disk, used for data storage only.

One of the ways that GPT differs from MBR is that data critical to platform operation is stored in partitions rather than in hidden sectors. Additionally, GPT partitioned disks use redundant primary and backup partition tables for improved integrity. Although GPT specifications permit an unlimited number of partitions, the Windows implementation is restricted to 128 partitions per disk. The GPT disk partitioning style supports volumes up to 18 exabytes in size (1 exabyte = 1 billion gigabytes, or 2^{60} bytes).

Table 4-2 compares some of the characteristics of the MBR and GPT partition styles.

Table 4-2

MBR and GPT Partition Style Comparison

MASTER BOOT RECORD (MBR)	GUID PARTITION TABLE (GPT)
Supports up to four primary partitions or three primary partitions and one extended partition, with unlimited logical drives on the extended partition	Supports up to 128 primary partitions
Supports volumes up to 2 terabytes in size	Supports volumes up to 18 exabytes in size
Data critical to platform operations is stored in hidden (unpartitioned) sectors	Data critical to platform operation is stored in partitions rather than in hidden sectors
Replication and CRC are not features of MBR's partition table	Replication and cyclical redundancy check (CRC) protection of the partition table provide increased reliability

Understanding Disk Types

Windows 7 supports two disk types: basic disks and dynamic disks.

Most Windows computers use basic disks because they are the easiest to manage. A ***basic disk*** uses primary partitions, extended partitions, and logical drives to organize data. A primary partition appears to the operating system as though it is a physically separate disk and can host an operating system. A primary partition that hosts an operating system is marked as the *active partition*.

During the Windows 7 operating system installation, the setup program creates a *system partition* and a *boot partition*. The system partition contains hardware-related files that the computer uses to start. The boot partition contains the operating system files, which are stored in the Windows folder. In Windows 7, the system partition is the active partition, which the computer uses when starting.

When you use the Disk Management snap-in to work with basic disks using the MBR partition style, you can create up to three primary partitions. The fourth partition you create must be an extended partition, after which you can create as many logical drives as you need from the space in the extended partition. You can format and assign drive letters to logical drives, but they cannot host an operating system. Table 4-3 compares some of the characteristics of primary and extended partitions.

Table 4-3

Comparison of Primary and Extended Partitions

PRIMARY PARTITIONS	EXTENDED PARTITIONS
A primary partition functions as if it is a physically separate disk and can host an operating system.	Extended partitions cannot host an operating system.
A primary partition can be marked as an active partition. You can have only one active partition per hard disk. The system BIOS looks to the active partition for the boot files it uses to start the operating system.	You cannot mark an extended partition as an active partition.
You can create up to four primary partitions or three primary partitions and one extended partition.	A basic disk can contain only one extended partition, but an unlimited number of logical partitions.
You format each primary partition and assign a unique drive letter.	You do not format the extended partition itself, but the logical drives it contains. You assign a unique drive letter to each of the logical drives.

When you use DiskPart, a command-line utility included with Windows 7, to manage a basic disk, you can create up to four primary partitions or three primary partitions and one extended partition.

The DiskPart command-line utility contains a superset of the commands that the Disk Management snap-in supports. In other words, DiskPart can do everything Disk Management can do, and more. The Disk Management snap-in prohibits you from unintentionally performing actions that may result in data loss. DiskPart does not have the built-in protections that Disk Management possesses, and so does not prohibit you from performing such actions. For this reason, Microsoft recommends that only advanced personnel use DiskPart and that they use it infrequently and with due caution because, unlike Disk Management, DiskPart provides absolute control over partitions and volumes.

The alternative to using a basic disk is to convert it to a ***dynamic disk***. The process of converting a basic disk to a dynamic disk creates a single partition that occupies the entire disk. You can then create an unlimited number of volumes out of the space in that partition. The advantage of using dynamic disks is that they support several different types of volumes, as described in the next section.

Understanding Volume Types

Dynamic disks can support five types of volumes: simple, spanned, striped, mirrored, and RAID-5 (Redundant Array of Independent Disks, level 5). Windows 7 only supports four of these volume types, however: simple, spanned, striped, and mirrored.

A dynamic disk is able to contain an unlimited number of volumes that function like primary partitions on a basic disk. However, you cannot access a dynamic disk from any operating system instance other than the one that converted it from basic to dynamic, which means you cannot use dynamic disks on multiboot systems.

When you create a volume on a dynamic disk in Windows 7, you can choose from the following four volume types:

- *Simple volume:* Consists of space from a single disk. Once you have created a simple volume, you can later extend it to multiple disks to create a spanned or striped volume, as long as it is not a system volume or boot volume. Windows 7 supports simple volumes on both basic and dynamic disks.

- *Spanned volume:* Consists of space from at least 2, to a maximum of 32, physical disks, all of which must be dynamic disks. A spanned volume is essentially a method for combining the space from multiple dynamic disks into a single large volume. Windows 7 writes to the spanned volume by filling all of the space on the first disk, and then filling each of the additional disks in turn. You can extend a spanned volume at any time by adding additional disk space. Creating a spanned volume does not increase the read/write performance, nor does it provide fault tolerance. In fact, if a single physical disk in the spanned volume fails, all of the data in the entire volume is lost.

- *Striped volume:* Consists of space from at least 2, to a maximum of 32, physical disks, all of which must be dynamic disks. The difference between a striped volume and a spanned volume is that in a striped volume, the system writes data one stripe at a time to each successive disk in the volume. Striping provides improved performance because each disk drive in the array has time to seek the location of its next stripe while the other drives are writing. Striped volumes do not provide fault tolerance, and you cannot extend them after creation. If a single physical disk in the striped volume fails, all of the data in the entire volume is lost.

- *Mirrored volume:* Consists of an equal amount of space from 2 disks, both of which must be dynamic disks. In a mirrored volume, each disk holds an identical copy of the data written to the volume as a fault tolerance measure. If one disk fails, the data remains accessible from the second disk. Because of the data redundancy, a mirrored volume only provides half as much storage space as any of the other volume types.

TAKE NOTE*

The disk volume limitations described here are those of Windows 7 itself. It is also possible to implement these disk technologies using third-party hardware and software products that have their own capabilities and limitations. For example, while Windows 7 does not support RAID-5, there are many disk adapter products on the market that enable you to create RAID volumes of various types on computers running Windows 7.

Windows 7 does not support dynamic disks in the following environments:

- portable computers
- removable disks
- detachable disks that use the Universal Serial Bus (USB) or IEEE 1394 (FireWire) interface
- disks connected to shared Small Computer System Interface (SCSI) buses
- computers running Windows 7 Starter, Home Basic, or Home Premium

The type of disk configuration you choose for a Windows 7 computer depends on the user's needs. While stand-alone systems for home or small business users might benefit from striped, spanned, or mirrored volumes, for most Windows 7 workstations in an enterprise environment, basic disks are adequate. If the client's computer stores data that requires additional performance or protection against failure, dynamic disks can fill the bill.

Understanding File Systems

> To organize and store data or programs on a hard drive, you must install a file system. A file system is the underlying disk drive structure that enables you to store information on your computer. You install file systems by formatting a partition or volume on the hard disk.

In Windows 7, there are two basic file system options to choose from: NTFS and FAT. *NTFS* is the preferred file system for Windows 7; its main benefits being improved support for larger hard drives and better security in the form of encryption and permissions that restrict access by unauthorized users.

Because the FAT file systems lack the security that NTFS provides, any user who gains access to your computer can read any file without restriction. Additionally, most of the various FAT file systems have disk size limitations that render them impractical.

The FAT file systems that Windows 7 supports are as follows:

- *FAT:* The original 16-bit FAT file system for hard disks, also known as FAT16, is limited to partitions no larger than 4 GB, which makes it virtually useless for today's computers.

- *FAT32:* Using the 32-bit version of FAT, called FAT32, Windows 7 can create partitions up to 32 GB in size, with individual files up to 4 GB. Although these limits at one time seemed outlandishly large, they make FAT32 an impractical file system solution on computers today. The 32 GB maximum partition size is a deliberate restriction in Windows 7, not an inherent limitation of FAT32. In fact, Windows 7 can access FAT32 partitions up to 2 TB in size; it just can't create them. This limitation is intended to prevent Windows performance degradation caused by large FAT32 partitions.

- *exFAT:* Introduced in Windows Vista SP1, the Extended File Allocation Table (exFAT) file system, also known as FAT64, is a 64-bit FAT implementation that is intended primarily for large USB flash drives. The theoretical limitations of exFAT are partitions and files of up to 64 zettabytes in size. (1 zettabyte equals 1 billion terabytes or 10^{21} bytes.) The recommended maximum size for an exFAT partition in Windows 7 is 512 TB. The exFAT file system does not support the encryption and permission features found in NTFS, and is therefore not recommended for use on Windows 7 hard disks.

When you create or format a partition or volume using the Disk Management snap-in, the interface displays only the file system options that are available to you, based on the size of the partition or volume. Because of these size limitations, the only viable reason for using any of the FAT file systems on Windows 7 hard disks is the need to multiboot the computer with an operating system that does not support NTFS.

Using the Disk Management Snap-In

> Disk Management is the primary Windows 7 graphical utility for creating and manipulating hard disk partitions and volumes.

Disk Management is a Microsoft Management Console (MMC) snap-in that you use to perform disk-related tasks, such as:

- Initializing disks.
- Selecting a partition style.

TAKE NOTE*

You can also use command-line utilities, such as the DiskPart command, to perform Disk Management tasks.

- Converting basic disks to dynamic disks.
- Creating partitions and volumes.
- Extending, shrinking, and deleting volumes.
- Formatting partitions and volumes.
- Assigning and changing driver letters and paths.
- Examining and managing physical disk properties, such as disk quotas, folder sharing and error-checking.

Opening the Disk Management Snap-In

The Disk Management snap-in is a graphical tool you use to manage hard disks.

To access the Disk Management snap-in, use the following procedure:

OPEN THE DISK MANAGEMENT SNAP-IN

GET READY. Log on to Windows 7 using an account with Administrator privileges.

1. Click Start, then click Control Panel. The Control Panel window appears.
2. Click System and Security, and then, under Administrative Tools, click Create and Format Hard Disk Partitions. The Disk Management window appears, as shown in Figure 4-1.

Figure 4-1

The Disk Management window

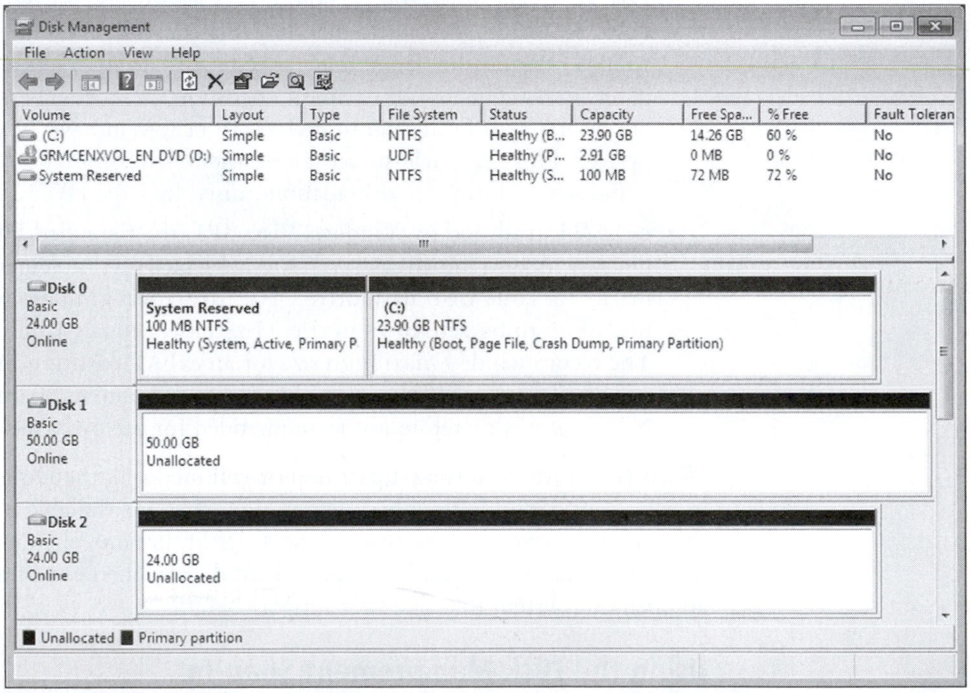

The Disk Management console is divided into two customizable panes: the Top view and the Bottom view, which display disk and volume information, respectively. Although Disk Management can display only two views at any one time, three views are available:

- **Disk List:** As shown in Figure 4-2, this view provides a summary about the physical drives in the computer. This information includes the disk number; disk type, such as basic or DVD; disk capacity; size of unallocated space; the status of the disk device, such as online, offline, or no media; the device interface, such as small computer system interface (SCSI) and integrated device electronics (IDE); and the partition style, such as MBR or GPT.

Figure 4-2

Disk Management's Disk List view

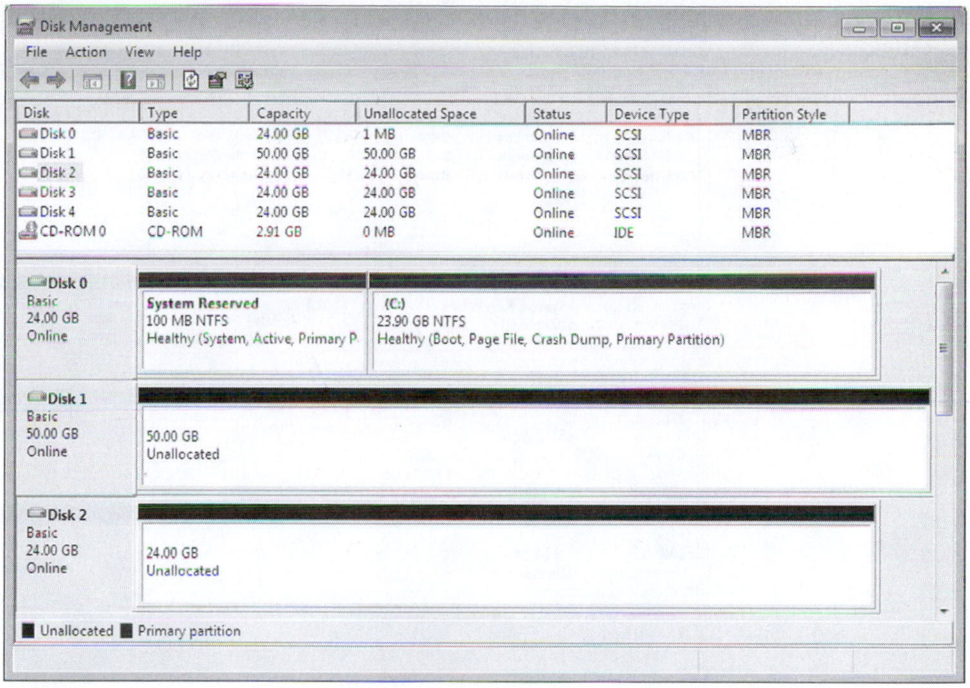

• **Volume List:** As shown in Figure 4-3, this view provides a more detailed summary of all the drives on the computer. This information includes the volume name; the volume layout, such as simple; the disk type, such as basic or dynamic; the file system in use, such as NTFS or CDFS; the hard disk status, such as healthy, failed, or formatting; the disk capacity and available free space; the percentage of the hard disk that is free; whether the hard disk is fault tolerant; and the disk overhead percentage.

Figure 4-3

Disk Management's Volume List view

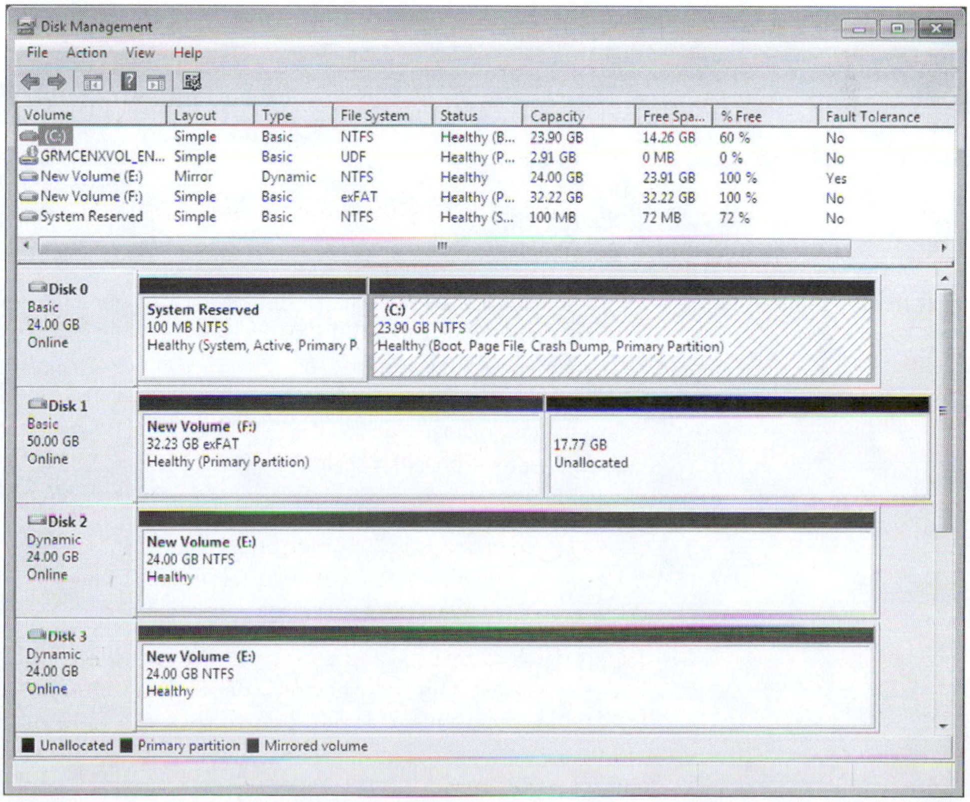

Figure 4-4

Disk Management's Graphical
View

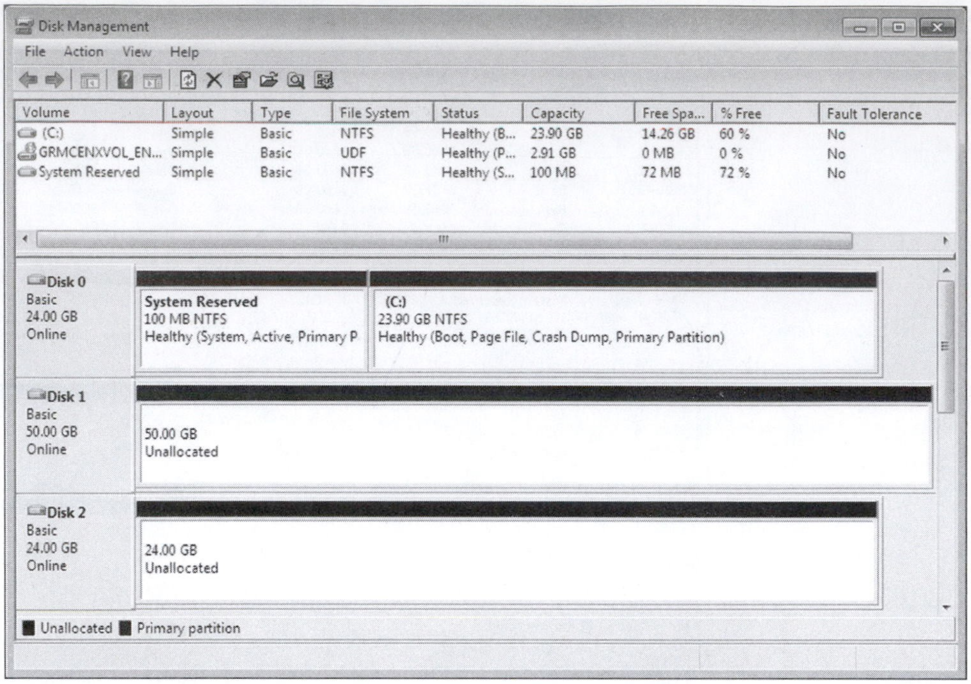

- **Graphical View:** As shown in Figure 4-4, this view displays a graphical representation
  of all the physical disks, partitions, volumes, and logical drives available on the computer.
  The graphical view is divided into two columns: the disk status column (located on the
  left) and the volume status column (located on the right). The information displayed in
  these columns and the commands available in the context menu produced by right clicking them, are shown in Table 4-4.

Table 4-4

Disk Management Graphical View Information

	DISK STATUS COLUMN	**VOLUME STATUS COLUMN**
Information displayed	Disk number Disk type Disk capacity Disk status	Volume name Volume size File system Volume status
Context menu commands	Convert a basic disk to a dynamic disk Convert an MBR disk to a GPT disk Create a new spanned, striped, or mirrored volume Take the disk offline Open the disk's Properties sheet	For a mounted partition or volume: • Mark a basic disk as active • Change the drive letter and paths • Format the partition or volume • Extend the volume • Shrink the volume • Add a mirror • Delete the volume • Open the volume's Properties sheet For unallocated space: • Create a new simple volume • Create a new spanned volume • Create a new striped volume • Create a new mirrored volume • Open the disk's Properties sheet

By default, the Top view pane depicts the Volume List view, and the Bottom view pane depicts the Graphical View. You can change the views of both the Top view and Bottom view to suit your purposes by clicking the View menu, selecting either Top or Bottom, and then selecting the desired view. You can hide the Bottom view by clicking the Hidden menu option.

ANOTHER WAY   You can circumvent using Control Panel to access the Disk Management console by clicking the Start button, right clicking Computer, and then clicking Manage. The Computer Management console appears. Under the Storage node, click Disk Management. You can also click Start, and use the Run dialog box to execute the Compmgmt.msc file.

VIEWING PHYSICAL DISK PROPERTIES

To view and configure certain properties and settings for the physical disk, right click the disk status column in Disk Management's graphical view and then select Properties from the context menu. A Properties sheet appears as shown in Figure 4-5, with the General tab active.

Figure 4-5

The General tab on a disk's Properties sheet

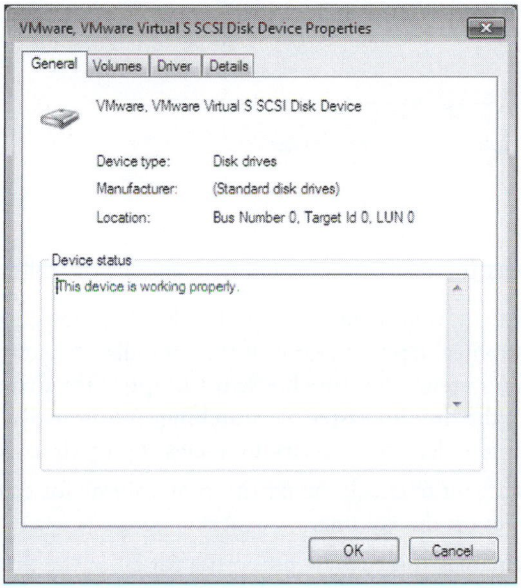

ANOTHER WAY

You can open a disk's Properties sheet by right clicking a drive in the Disk List view, and then clicking Properties.

> VMware, VMware Virtual S SCSI Disk Device Properties
>
> General | Volumes | Driver | Details
>
> VMware, VMware Virtual S SCSI Disk Device
>
> Device type: Disk drives
> Manufacturer: (Standard disk drives)
> Location: Bus Number 0, Target Id 0, LUN 0
>
> Device status
> This device is working properly.
>
> OK   Cancel

The disk's Properties sheet contains the following tabs:

- **General:** Lists the device type, drive manufacturer, device status, and physical location of the device, including the bus number or the SCSI identifier.
- **Volumes:** Lists the volumes contained on the disk, as well as the disk number, disk type, status, partition style, capacity, unallocated space, and reserved space. If you highlight a volume in the Volumes list, you can click the Properties button to display the Properties sheet for the partition or volume.
- **Driver:** Displays driver details, and enables you to update, roll back, disable, and uninstall the driver for this device.
- **Details:** Displays a Property drop-down list that enables you to display extensive information about the disk.

VIEWING PARTITION OR VOLUME PROPERTIES

To view or configure the properties of a partition or volume, right click the volume status column in Disk Management's Graphical View and then select Properties from the context menu. The volume's Properties sheet appears, as shown in Figure 4-6.

Figure 4-6

The General tab on a volume's Properties sheet

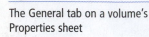

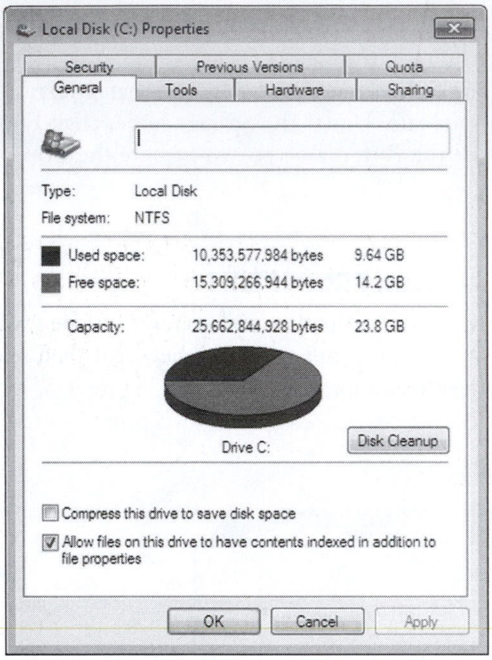

ANOTHER WAY

You can also open a volume's Properties sheet by right clicking a drive in the Volume List view and selecting Properties from the context menu.

The Properties sheet for a partition or volume contains the following tabs:

- **General:** Lists the volume label, type of disk, file system, used space, free space, and provides a graphical representation of the total disk capacity. For drives formatted with the NTFS file system, you can choose to compress the drive and to have the Indexing Service index the disk for faster file searching. Additionally, you can run the Disk Cleanup tool to delete unnecessary files, clearing up disk space.

- **Tools:** Enables you to check the partition or volume for errors and fragmentation, and to back up files on the volume.

- **Hardware:** Enables you to view properties for all of the disk drives on the computer, including their manufacturers, bus locations, and device status.

- **Sharing:** Enables you to share the drive or specific folder(s) on the drive, set permissions for the share, and specify the type of caching for the share.

- **Security:** Enables you to set NTFS permissions to secure files and folders by assigning permissions that allow or deny users or groups to perform specific actions on that object. (Appears only on NTFS drives and in the Windows 7 Professional, Enterprise, and Ultimate editions).

- **Previous Versions:** Displays shadow copies that Windows automatically saves to your computer's hard disk as part of a restore point. A restore point represents a specific point in time of your computer's system files. You can use these previous versions of files to restore files that users have accidentally deleted or modified.

- **Quota:** Enables you to configure disk quota management on the computer, which limits the amount of disk space a user can consume. You must format the disk with the NTFS file system in order for this tab to be available.

ADDING A NEW DISK

To add a new secondary disk, shut down your computer and install or attach the new physical disk per the manufacturer's instructions. Use the following procedure to initialize the new disk.

ADD A NEW DISK

GET READY. Log on to Windows 7 using an account with Administrator privileges.

1. Open the Disk Management snap-in.
2. If the disk does not have a disk signature, the console automatically displays the Initialize Disk dialog box, as shown in Figure 4-7.

Figure 4-7

The Initialize Disk dialog box

> **Initialize Disk**
>
> You must initialize a disk before Logical Disk Manager can access it.
>
> Select disks:
>
> ☑ Disk 1
>
> Use the following partition style for the selected disks:
>
> ⦿ MBR (Master Boot Record)
> ◯ GPT (GUID Partition Table)
>
> Note: The GPT partition style is not recognized by all previous versions of Windows. It is recommended for disks larger than 2TB, or disks used on Itanium-based computers.
>
> [OK] [Cancel]

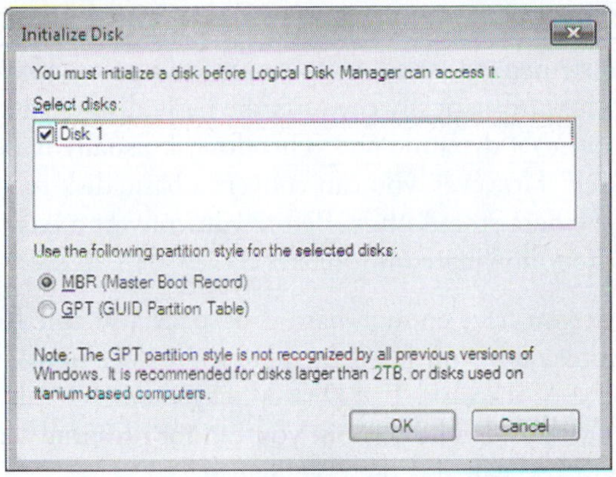

3. Select the partition style (MBR or GBT) that you want to use for the disk and click OK. The disk is ready to be partitioned.

CHANGING THE PARTITION STYLE

If you are running an x86-based computer, Disk Management has most likely selected the MBR partition style by default. You can quickly check which partition style the hard disk is assigned by right clicking the disk status column in the Graphical view. If the context menu contains the Convert to GPT Disk menu item, then the disk is using the MBR partition style.

You can also check the volume's information by opening the Properties sheet for disk and clicking the Volumes tab, as shown in Figure 4-8. This tab displays information such as disk type, disk status, and partition style.

Figure 4-8

The Volumes tab of a disk's Properties sheet

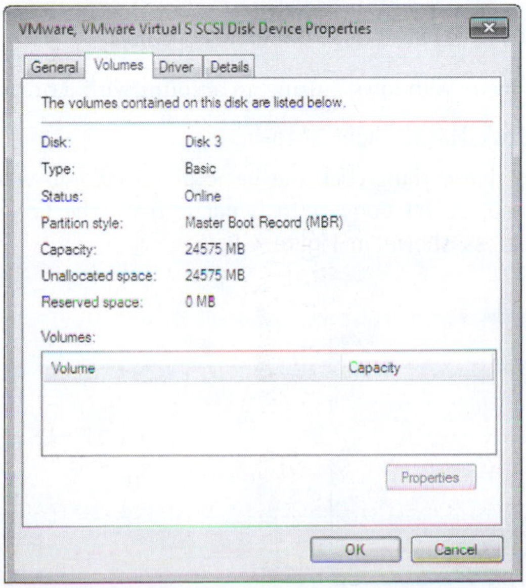

> **VMware, VMware Virtual S SCSI Disk Device Properties**
>
> | General | Volumes | Driver | Details |
>
> The volumes contained on this disk are listed below.
>
> Disk: Disk 3
> Type: Basic
> Status: Online
> Partition style: Master Boot Record (MBR)
> Capacity: 24575 MB
> Unallocated space: 24575 MB
> Reserved space: 0 MB
>
> Volumes:
>
> | Volume | Capacity |
> |--------|----------|
> | | |
>
> [Properties]
>
> [OK] [Cancel]

To convert the partition style for a disk, use the following procedure.

CONVERT THE DISK PARTITION STYLE

GET READY. Log on to Windows 7 using an account with Administrator privileges.

1. Open the Disk Management snap-in.
2. In Disk List view, right click the disk you need to convert and, from the context menu, select Convert to GPT Disk or Convert to MBR Disk. The system then proceeds with the conversion. The length of time this process takes depends on the size of the hard disk.

WARNING Converting the disk partition style is a destructive process. You can only perform the conversion on an unallocated disk, so if the disk you want to convert contains data, you must back up the disk, verify the back up, and then delete all existing partitions or volumes, before you begin the process.

CONVERTING A BASIC DISK TO A DYNAMIC DISK

When you create a striped, spanned, or mirrored volume on a basic disk, the Disk Management snap-in automatically converts the basic disk (and any additional disks needed to create the volume) to a dynamic one. Therefore, it usually is not necessary to manually convert disks yourself. However, you can convert a basic disk to a dynamic disk at any time, without affecting the data stored on it. Before you convert a basic disk to a dynamic disk, you must be aware of the following conditions:

- Make sure that you have enough hard disk space available for the conversion. The basic-to-dynamic conversion will fail if the hard drive does not have at least 1 MB of free space at the end of the disk. The Disk Management console reserves this free space when creating partitions and volumes, but you cannot presume that other disk management tools you might use will also preserve that space.

- You should not convert a basic disk to a dynamic disk if you are multibooting the computer. If you convert to a dynamic disk, you will not be able to start installed operating systems from any volume on the disk except the current boot volume.

- You cannot convert removable media to dynamic disks. You can configure them only as basic disks with primary partitions.

- You cannot convert drives that use an allocation unit size (sector size) greater than 512 bytes unless you reformat the drive with a smaller sector size before the conversion.

- Once you change a basic disk to a dynamic disk, the only way you can change it back again is to back up the entire disk and delete the dynamic disk volumes. When you delete the last volume, the dynamic disk automatically reverts back to a basic disk.

To manually convert a basic disk to a dynamic disk, use the following procedure.

CONVERT A BASIC DISK TO A DYNAMIC DISK

GET READY. Log on to Windows 7 using an account with Administrator privileges.

1. Open the Disk Management snap-in.
2. In Disk List view, right click the basic disk that you want to convert and, from the context menu, select Convert to Dynamic Disk. The Convert to Dynamic Disk dialog box appears, as shown in Figure 4-9.

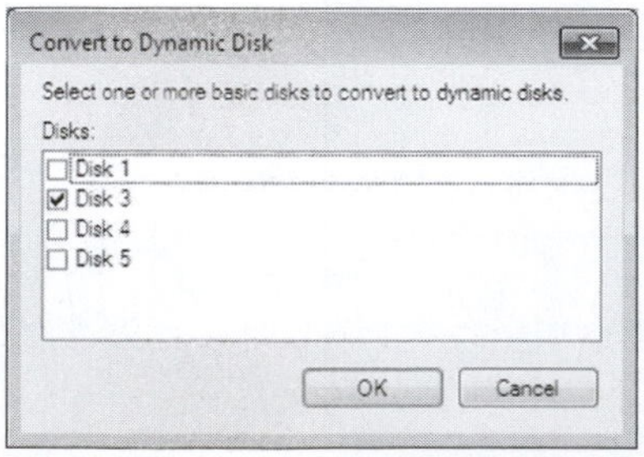

Figure 4-9

The Convert to Dynamic Disk dialog box

3. Select the check boxes for the disks you want to convert, and click OK. If the disks you selected do not contain formatted partitions, clicking OK immediately converts the disks, and you do not need to follow the remaining steps. If the disks you are converting to dynamic disks do have formatted partitions, clicking OK displays the Disks to Convert dialog box, as shown in Figure 4-10, which means that you need to follow the remaining steps to complete the disk conversion.

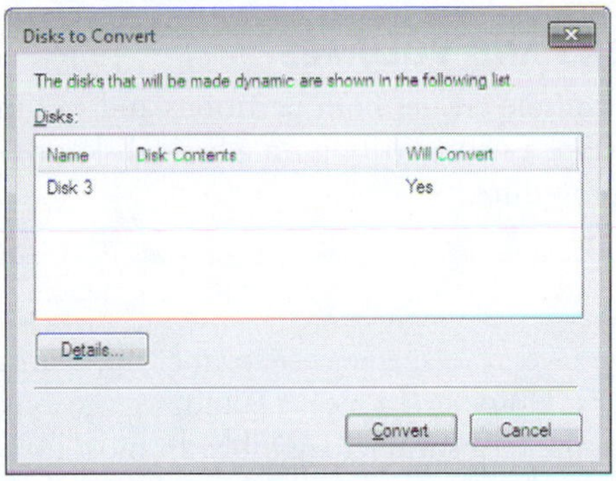

Figure 4-10

The Disks to Convert dialog box

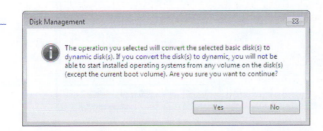

4. The Disks to Convert dialog box lists the disks you chose for conversion for your confirmation. Check the value in the Will Convert column. It should be set to Yes for each of the disks that you are converting. If any of the disks have the value No, then they may not meet Windows conversion criteria.

5. Click Details. The Convert Details dialog box appears, as shown in Figure 4-11. This dialog box lists the partitions on the selected drives that Disk Management will convert.

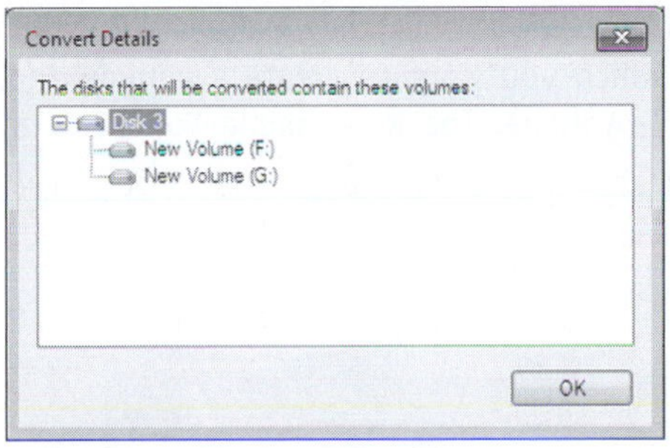

Figure 4-11

The Convert Details dialog box

6. Click OK when you are ready to continue with the conversion.

7. On the Disks to Convert dialog box, click Convert to start the conversion. A Disk Management information box appears, as shown in Figure 4-12, to warn you that once you convert the disks to dynamic disks, you will not be able to boot installed operating system from any volume other than the current boot volume.

Figure 4-12

A Disk Management information box

8. Click Yes to continue. Disk Management completes the conversion. If a selected drive contains the boot partition, the system partition, or a partition that is in use, Disk Management will prompt you to restart the computer.

When you convert from a basic disk to a dynamic disk, Disk Management performs the following tasks:

- Basic disk partitions are converted to dynamic disk volumes of equal size.
- Basic disk primary partitions and logical drives in the extended partition are converted to simple volumes.
- Any free space in a basic disk extended partition is marked as unallocated.

CREATING PARTITIONS AND VOLUMES

The Disk Management console creates both partitions and volumes with one set of dialog boxes and wizards. To create a new partition on a basic disk, or a new volume on a dynamic disk, use the following procedure.

TAKE NOTE *

Technically speaking, the Disk Management snap-in creates partitions on basic disks and volumes on dynamic disks. However, in recent Windows versions, including Windows 7, the interface tends to use the terms interchangeably. In most instances, the snap-in refers to volumes on both basic and dynamic disks, but it still uses the term *partition* when referring to formatting and making a partition active.

→ CREATE A VOLUME

GET READY. Log on to Windows 7 using an account with administrator privileges.

1. Open the Disk Management snap-in.
2. In the Graphical view, right click the unallocated area on the volume status column for the disk on which you want to create a volume and, from the context menu, select New Simple Volume. The New Simple Volume Wizard appears.
3. Click Next to bypass the Welcome page. The *Specify Volume Size* page appears, as shown in Figure 4-13.

Figure 4-13

The Specify Volume Size page

New Simple Volume Wizard	☒

Specify Volume Size
Choose a volume size that is between the maximum and minimum sizes.

Maximum disk space in MB:	51197
Minimum disk space in MB:	8
Simple volume size in MB:	51197

`< Back` `Next >` `Cancel`

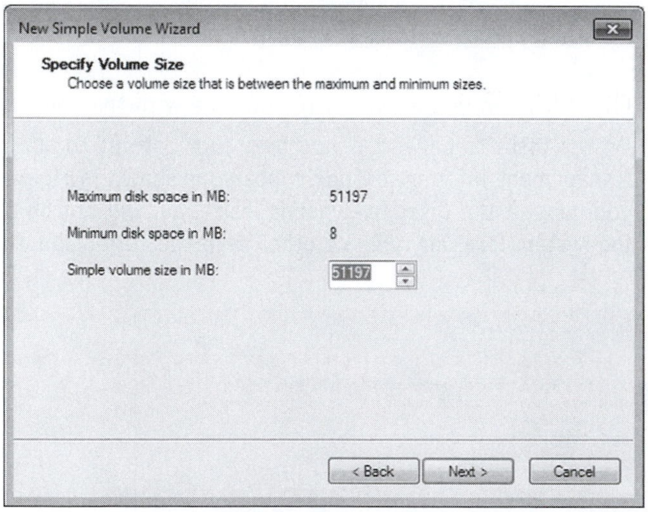

4. In the Simple Volume Size in MB spin box, specify the size for the new volume, within the maximum and minimum limits stated on the page, and then click Next. The *Assign Drive Letter or Path* page appears, as shown in Figure 4-14.

Figure 4-14

The Assign Drive Letter or Path page

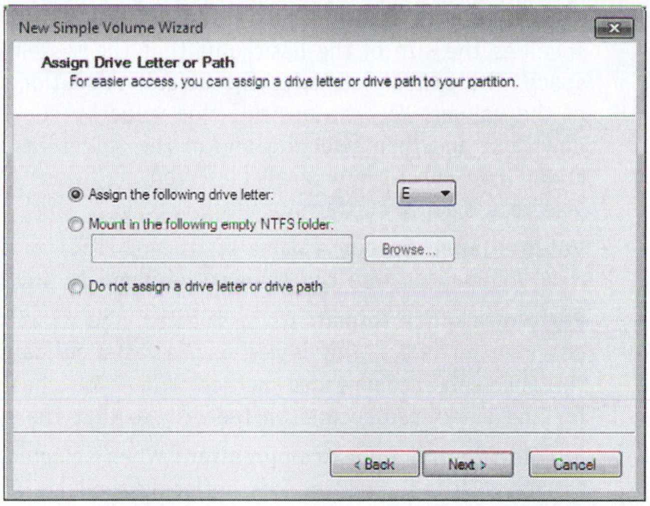

5. Configure one of the following three options, and then click Next. The *Format Partition* page appears, as shown in Figure 4-15:
   - **Assign the following drive letter:** If you select this option, click the associated drop-down list for a list of available drive letters, and then select the desired letter you want to assign to the drive.
   - **Mount in the following empty NTFS folder:** If you select this option, you are required to either type the path to an existing NTFS folder, or click Browse to search for or create a new folder. The entire contents of the new drive will appear in the folder you specify.
   - **Do not assign a drive letter or drive path:** Select this option if you want to create the partition, but are not ready to use it yet. When you do not assign a volume a drive letter or path, the drive is left unmounted and inaccessible. When you want to mount the drive for use, assign a drive letter or path to it.

Figure 4-15

The Format Partition page

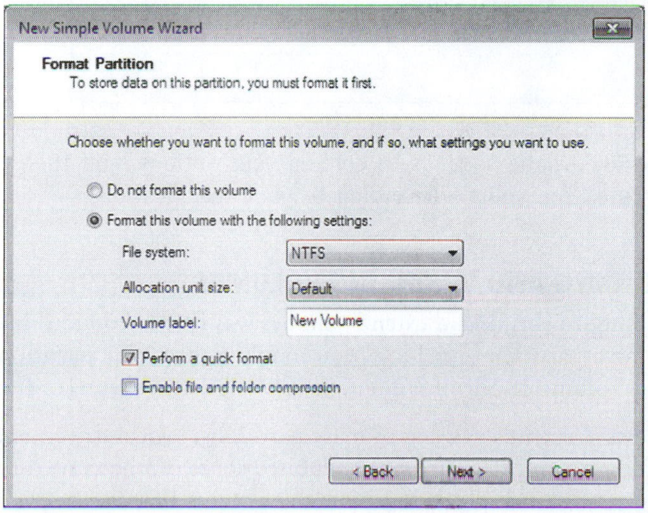

6. Specify whether and how the wizard should format the volume. If you do not want to format the volume at this time, select the *Do not format this volume* option. If you do want to format the volume, select the *Format this volume with the following settings* option, and then configure the associated options, which are as follows:
   - **File system:** Select the desired file system—NTFS, FAT, FAT32, or exFAT. The options that appear in the drop-down list are based on the size of the partition or volume you are creating.

- **Allocation unit size:** Specify the file system's cluster size. The cluster size specifies the size of the basic unit that the system will use to allocate disk space. The system calculates the default allocation unit size based on the size of the volume. You can override this value by clicking on the associated drop-down list and then selecting one of the values in the list. For example, if your client uses consistently small files, you may want to set the allocation unit size to a smaller cluster size.

- **Volume label:** Specify a name for the partition or volume. The default name is New Volume, but you can change the name to anything you want.

- **Perform a quick format:** When selected, the wizard formats the disk without checking for errors. This is certainly a faster formatting method, but it is not the Microsoft recommended method. When you check for errors, the system looks for and marks bad sectors on the disk so that the system will not use them.

- **Enable file and folder compression:** When selected, file and folder compression for the disk is turned on. This option is available for the NTFS file system only.

Then click Next. The Completing the *New Simple Volume Wizard* page appears, as shown in Figure 4-16.

Figure 4-16

The Completing the New Simple Volume Wizard page

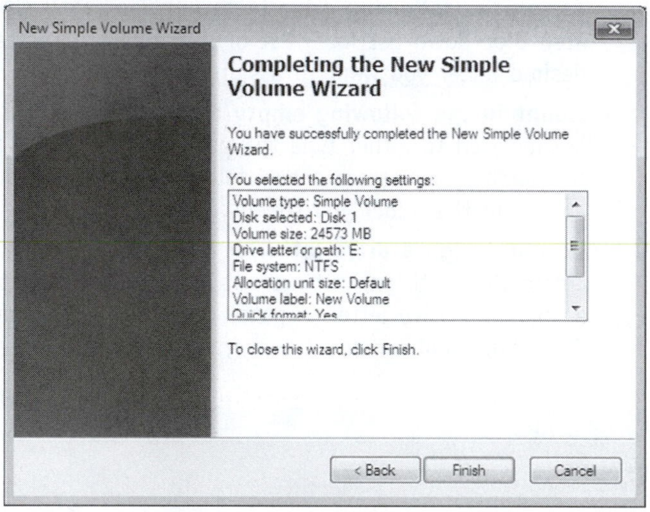

7. Review the settings to confirm your options, and then click Finish. The wizard creates the volume according to your specifications.

EXTENDING AND SHRINKING VOLUMES

The ability to shrink and extend volumes was first introduced in Windows Vista. To extend or shrink a partition or volume, you simply right click a partition or volume and select Extend Volume or Shrink Volume from the context menu, or from the Action menu.

Windows 7 extends existing primary partitions, logical drives, and simple volumes by expanding them into adjacent unallocated space on the same disk. When you extend a simple volume across multiple disks, the simple volume becomes a spanned volume. You cannot extend striped volumes.

To extend a partition on a basic disk, the system must meet the following requirements:

- A basic partition must be either unformatted or formatted with the NTFS file system.
- If you extend a logical drive, the console first consumes the contiguous free space remaining in the extended partition. If you attempt to extend the logical drive beyond the confines of its extended partition, the extended partition expands to any unallocated space left on the disk.

TAKE NOTE*

You must be a member of the Backup Operator or the Administrators group to extend or shrink any partition or volume.

- You can extend the partition of logical drives, boot volumes, or system volumes only into contiguous space, and only if the hard disk can be upgraded into a dynamic disk. The operating system will permit you to extend other types of basic volumes into non-contiguous space, but will prompt you to convert the basic disk to a dynamic disk.

To extend a simple or spanned volume on a dynamic disk, the system must meet these requirements:

- When extending a simple volume, you can only use the available space on the same disk, if the volume is to remain simple.
- You can extend a simple volume across additional disks if it is not a system volume or a boot volume. However, once you expand a simple volume to another disk, it is no longer a simple volume but becomes a spanned volume.
- You can extend a simple or spanned volume if it does not have a file system (a raw volume) or if you formatted it using the NTFS file system. (You cannot extend FAT volumes.)

When shrinking partitions or volumes, the Disk Management console frees up space at the end of the volume, relocating the existing volume's files, if necessary. The console then converts that free space to new unallocated space on the disk. To shrink a basic disk partition or any kind of dynamic disk volume except for a striped volume, the system must meet the following requirements:

- The existing partition or volume must not be full and must contain the specified amount of available free space for shrinking.
- The partition or volume must not be a raw partition (one without a file system). Shrinking a raw partition that contains data mighty destroy the data.
- You can shrink a partition or volume only if you formatted it using the NTFS file system. (You cannot shrink FAT volumes.)

CREATING SPANNED, STRIPED, AND MIRRORED VOLUMES

Spanned, striped, or mirrored volumes require dynamic disks. When you create a spanned, striped, or mirrored volume, you create a single dynamic volume that extends across multiple physical disks.

To create a spanned, striped, or mirrored volume, use the following procedure.

CREATE A SPANNED OR STRIPED VOLUME

GET READY. Log on to Windows 7 using an account with administrator privileges.

1. Open the Disk Management snap-in.
2. In the Graphical view, right click an unallocated area on a disk and, from the context menu, select New Spanned Volume, New Striped Volume, or New Mirrored Volume. A wizard appears, named for the volume type.
3. Click Next to bypass the *Welcome* page. The *Select Disks* page appears.
4. On the Select Disks page, under the Available standard list box, select each disk you want to use in the volume and then click Add. For a spanned or striped volume, you can add up to 31 additional disks; for a mirrored volume, you can add only 1.
5. Specify the space you want to use on each disk by selecting the disk in the Selected standard list box, and then, using the *Select the amount of space in MB* spin box, specify the amount of disk space that you want to include in the volume. For spanned or striped volumes, you can use different amounts of space on each drive. For mirrored volumes, you must use the same amount of space on both disks. Then click Next. The *Assign Drive Letter or Path* page appears.

6. Specify whether you want to assign a drive letter or path, and then click Next. The *Format Partition* page appears.

7. Specify whether or how you want to format the volume, and then click Next. The *Completing* page appears.

8. Review the settings to confirm your options, and then click Finish. If one or more of the disks you selected is a basic disk, a Disk Management message box appears, informing you that the wizard will convert the basic disk(s) to dynamic disk(s). Click Yes to continue. The wizard creates the volume according to your specifications.

Once the wizard has created the volume, it appears in the Graphical view with a single color on each of the disks contributing to the volume space, as shown in Figure 4-17.

Figure 4-17

A spanned volume in the Disk Management snap-in

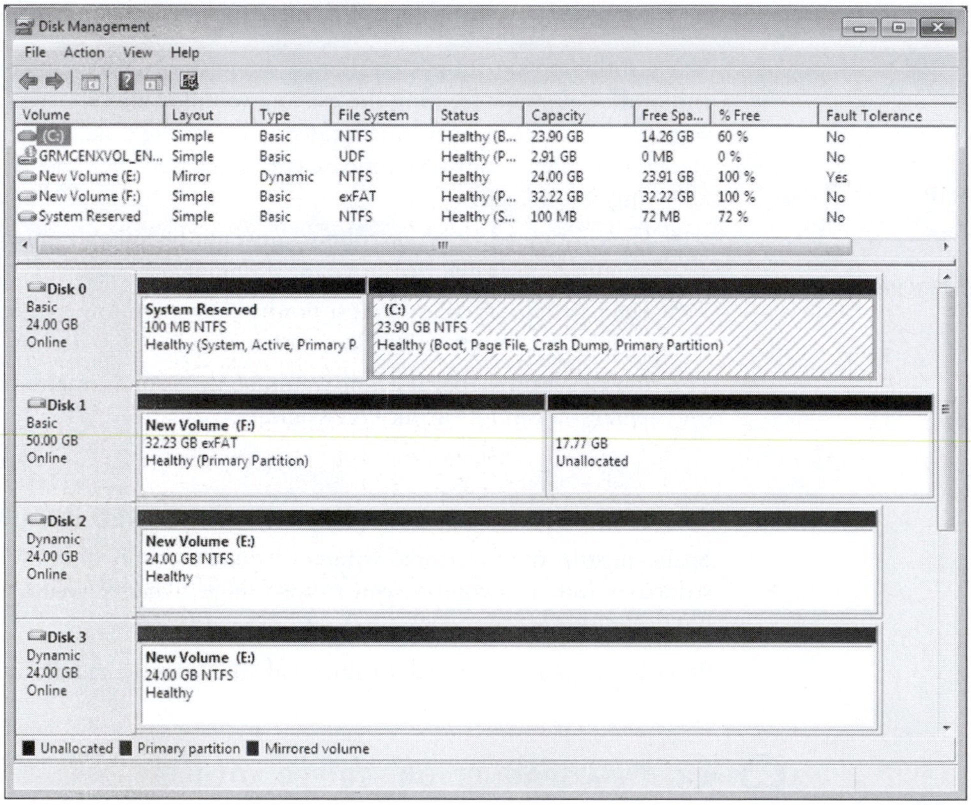

TAKE NOTE*

Windows Server 2008 R2, in addition to simple, spanned, striped, and mirrored volumes, also supports RAID-5 volumes. RAID-5 stripes data and parity blocks across three or more disks, making sure that a block and its parity information are never stored on the same disk. Parity is a bit-level fault tolerance mechanism that enables the system to reconstruct the data from any one of the disks in the array that fails. During the development process, Microsoft considered including support for RAID-5 volumes in Windows 7. However, in the final release, RAID-5 support is disabled under all conditions, despite its appearance in the Disk Management interface.

Using Diskpart.exe

In addition to the graphical interface in the Disk Management snap-in, Windows 7 also includes a command-line tool called *Diskpart.exe*, which you can use to manage disks.

Diskpart.exe is a powerful utility that can perform any task the Disk Management snap-in can and more. For example, Diskpart enables you to create a fourth primary partition on a basic disk, rather than an extended partition and a logical disk.

Diskpart.exe has two operational modes: a script mode and an interactive mode. If you choose to create Diskpart scripts, you can run them from the command prompt using the following syntax:

`Diskpart.exe /s scriptname`

When you run Diskpart.exe from the Windows 7 command prompt without any parameters, a DISKPART> prompt appears, from which you execute additional commands. The typical working method is to shift the focus of the program to the specific object you want to manage, and then execute commands on that object.

For example, the `list disk` command displays a list of the disk drives in the system, as shown in Figure 4-18. The `select disk 1` command then shifts the focus to Disk 1. The program will now apply any disk-specific commands that you execute to Disk 1. The `create partition primary size=10000` command therefore creates a new 10 GB primary partition on Disk 1.

Figure 4-18

Shifting object focus in Diskpart.exe

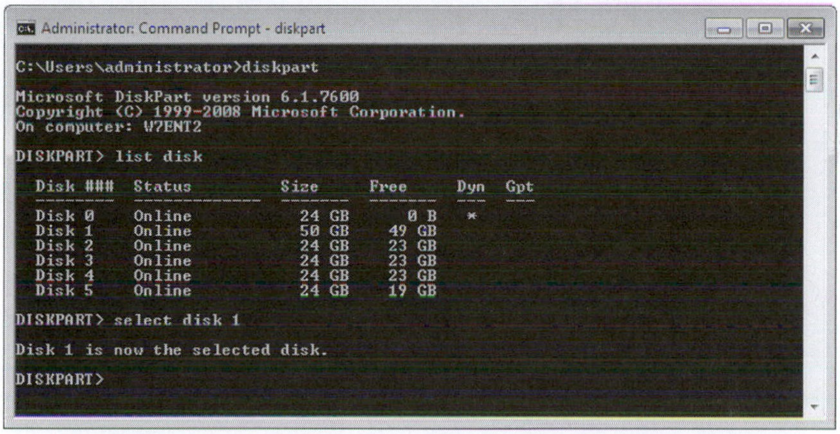

TAKE NOTE*

Unlike the Disk Management snap-in, the Diskpart.exe program is particular about disk terminology. When you are working with a basic disk, for example, you can only create partitions, not volumes, unless you convert the basic disk to a dynamic disk first.

Using Disk Tools

Windows 7 provides a selection of tools that you can use to free up disk space, defragment volumes, and check disks for errors. These tools are simple and safe enough for most end users and still powerful enough for technical specialists.

The Windows 7 disk tools are all accessible from each volume's Properties sheet. You can therefore access the tools from any Windows Explorer window or from the Disk Management snap-in.

USING DISK CLEANUP

When a disk starts to run low on storage space, it is often possible to reclaim space occupied by unnecessary files, such as temporary files, setup logs, and files in the Recycle Bin. Windows 7 refers to the process of deleting these files as cleaning up a disk.

To clean up a Windows 7 volume, use the following procedures.

CLEAN UP A VOLUME

GET READY. Log on to Windows 7 using an account with administrator privileges.

1. Open the Disk Management snap-in.

2. In the Graphical view, right click a volume and, from the context menu, select Properties. The Properties sheet for the volume appears.

3. On the General tab, click Disk Cleanup. After a scan of the volume, the Disk Cleanup dialog box appears, as shown in Figure 4-19. The dialog box lists the types of files that are available for cleanup and specifies the amount of disk space you can reclaim.

Figure 4-19

The Disk Cleanup dialog box

```
Disk Cleanup for (C:)                                    [_][□][X]

 Disk Cleanup | More Options |

      You can use Disk Cleanup to free up to 5.09 MB of disk
      space on (C:).

   Files to delete:
   [✓] 📁 Downloaded Program Files          0 bytes  ▲
   [✓] 📄 Temporary Internet Files          10.0 KB  ▤
   [ ] 🗑 Recycle Bin                        0 bytes
   [ ] 📄 Setup Log Files                   15.3 KB
   [ ] 📄 Temporary files                    0 bytes  ▼

   Total amount of disk space you gain:          5.01 MB
   ┌─ Description ─────────────────────────────────────┐
   │ Downloaded Program Files are ActiveX controls and Java applets │
   │ downloaded automatically from the Internet when you view certain │
   │ pages. They are temporarily stored in the Downloaded Program │
   │ Files folder on your hard disk.                    │
   │                                                     │
   │                                                     │
   │                            [ View Files ]           │
   └─────────────────────────────────────────────────┘
   How does Disk Cleanup work?

                              [ OK ]    [ Cancel ]
```

4. Select the check boxes for the files you want to delete, and then click OK. A Disk Cleanup message box appears.

5. Click Delete Files to confirm that you want to delete the selected files. Disk Cleanup deletes the selected files.

6. Click OK to close the volume's Properties sheet.

Once you delete files using the Disk Cleanup tool, you cannot reclaim them from the Recycle Bin.

DEFRAGMENTING DISKS

Hard disk drives write data in clusters, units of a standard size designated when you format the disk. Initially, when you save a file to a hard disk, the drive writes it to contiguous clusters, that is, a sequence of clusters that are next to each other. Over time, however, as files are written and rewritten to the disk, the contiguous spaces grow smaller, and the drive is forced to split files into clusters located at different places on the disk. This process is called *fragmentation*.

Fragmentation reduces the efficiency of the disk because it forces the drive to relocate its heads many times to read a single file. The effect is the same as if you were forced to read a book with pages not in numerical order. You would spend a lot of time looking for each page and less time actually reading.

Windows 7 includes a tool that enables you to defragment your volumes by recopying fragmented files to contiguous space on the disk. The Disk Defragmentation tool in Windows 7 is changed substantially from the one in Windows Vista.

 **WARNING** It is strongly recommended that you perform a full backup of your volumes before you defragment them. While the Windows 7 Disk Defragmenter is a reliable tool, defragmentation is a hardware-intensive process, and drive failures can conceivably occur.

To defragment a volume, use the following procedure.

➔ **DEFRAGMENT A VOLUME**

GET READY. Log on to Windows 7 using an account with administrator privileges.

1. Open the Disk Management snap-in.
2. In the Graphical view, right click a volume and, from the context menu, select Properties. The Properties sheet for the volume appears.
3. Select the Tools tab, as shown in Figure 4-20.

Figure 4-20

The Tools tab of a volume's Properties dialog box

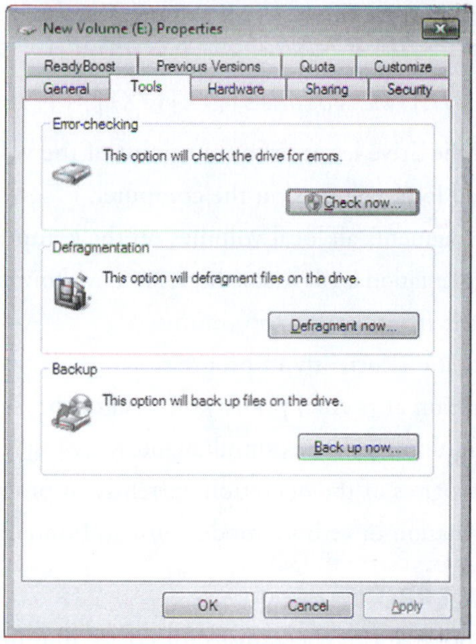

4. Click Defragment now. The Disk Defragmenter dialog box appears, as shown in Figure 4-21.

Figure 4-21

The Disk Defragmenter dialog box

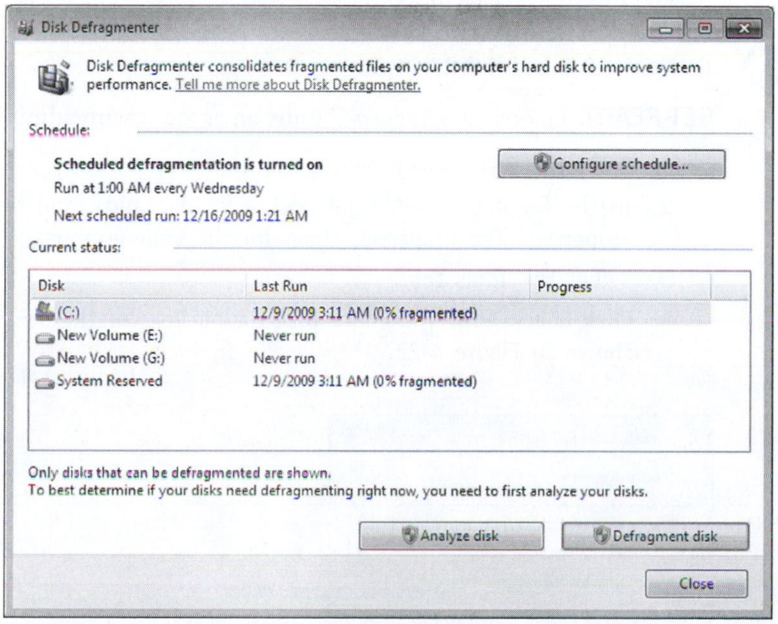

5. In the Current Status box, select the volume you want to work with and click Analyze Disk, The Current Status box displays the percent of the volume that is fragmented.

6. In the Current Status box, select the volume you want to work with and click Defragment Disk, The Disk Defragmenter manipulates the files on the volume to eliminate as much fragmentation as possible. When the process is completed, the Current Status box displays the new fragmentation percentage for the volume.

7. Click Close to close the Disk Defragmenter dialog box.

8. Click OK to close the volume's Properties dialog box.

The time required for the defragmentation process depends on the size of the volume, the number of files stored there, the amount of free space, and the degree to which the volume is fragmented. The process can easily take several hours. In addition to the graphical interface, it is also possible to defragment disks from the command prompt, using the Defrag.exe program. This enables you to incorporate defragmentation into scripts. The syntax for the command line interface is as follows:

```
Defrag.exe volume [/C][/E volumes][/A][/X][/T][/H][/M][/U][/V]
```

-   volume: Specifies the drive letter or mount point of the volume to defragment.
-   /C: Defragments all local volumes on the computer.
-   /E volumes: Defragments all local volumes on the computer except those you specify.
-   /A: Displays a fragmentation analysis for the volume without performing a defragmentation.
-   /X: Consolidates the free space on the volume.
-   /T: Tracks the operation currently in progress.
-   /H: Runs the operation at normal priority, instead of the default low priority.
-   /M: Defragments multiple volumes simultaneously.
-   /U: Displays the progress of the operation currently in progress.
-   /V: Displays information in verbose mode, with additional detail and statistics.

CHECKING FOR DISK ERRORS

Windows 7 includes a tool that can check disks for errors and, in many cases, repair them. If, for example, one of a system's volumes is unavailable for defragmentation, it could be due to errors that you must repair first.

To check a volume for errors, use the following procedure.

CHECK FOR DISK ERRORS

GET READY. Log on to Windows 7 using an account with administrator privileges.

1. Open the Disk Management snap-in.

2. In the Graphical view, right click a volume and, from the context menu, select Properties. The Properties sheet for the volume appears.

3. Select the Tools tab.

4. Click Check now. The Check Disk dialog box for the selected volume appears, as shown in Figure 4-22.

Figure 4-22

The Check Disk dialog box

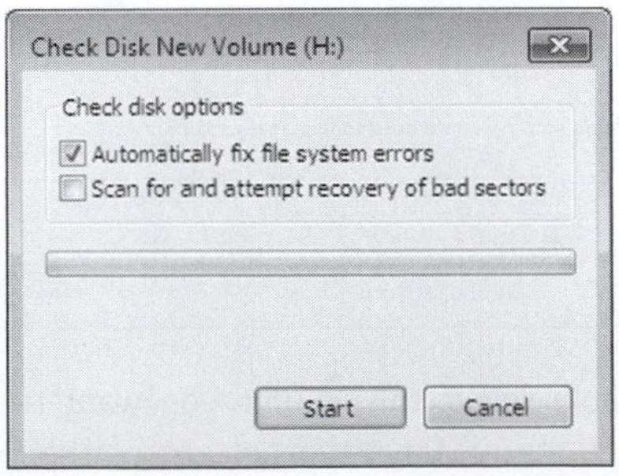

5. Configure the following options and click Start to begin scanning for errors:

   • **Automatically fix file system errors:** Selected by default, this option configures the program to repair any errors that it finds. Clearing this check box causes the program to scan for errors only.

   • **Scan for and attempt recovery of bad sectors:** Cleared by default, this option configures the program to scan the disk for bad sectors and mark any that it finds, to prevent the drive from using them. Depending on the size of the disk, this option can take from several minutes to several hours.

6. When the scan is completed, the *Your device or disk was successfully scanned* dialog box appears. Click the See Details down-arrow to display the verbose record of the scan, as shown in Figure 4-23.

Figure 4-23

The expanded Checking Disk dialog box

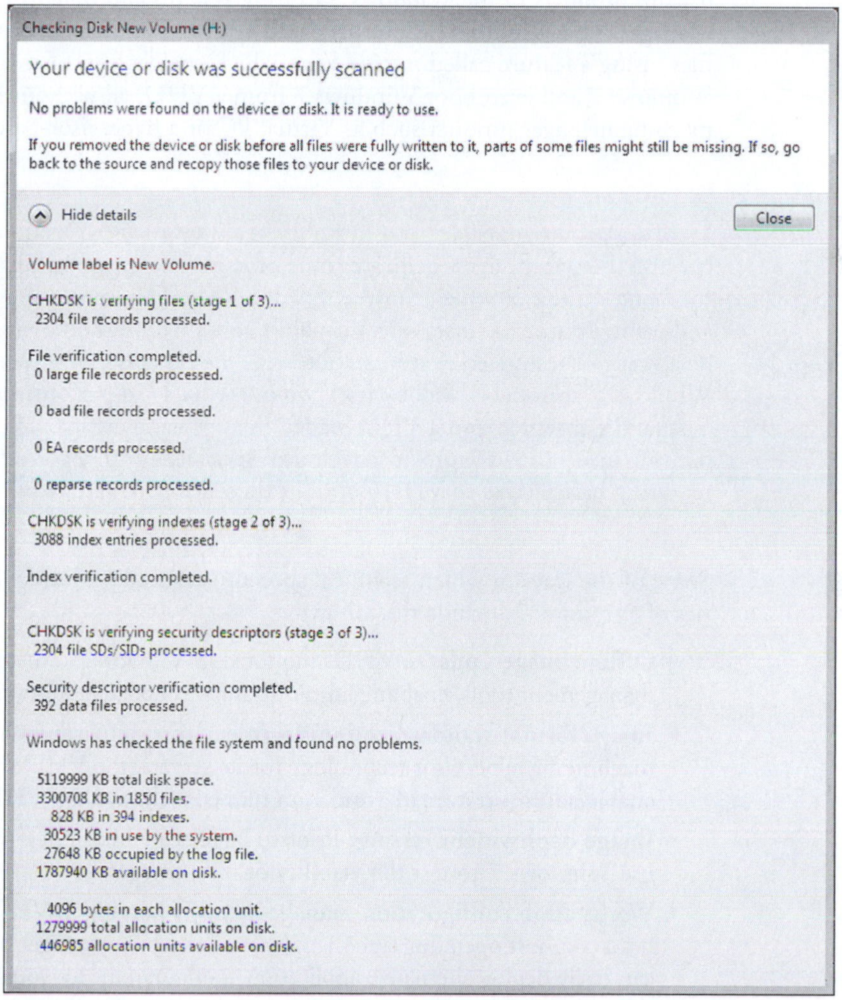

Checking Disk New Volume (H:)

Your device or disk was successfully scanned

No problems were found on the device or disk. It is ready to use.

If you removed the device or disk before all files were fully written to it, parts of some files might still be missing. If so, go back to the source and recopy those files to your device or disk.

⌃ Hide details   [Close]

Volume label is New Volume.

CHKDSK is verifying files (stage 1 of 3)...
 2304 file records processed.

File verification completed.
 0 large file records processed.

 0 bad file records processed.

 0 EA records processed.

 0 reparse records processed.

CHKDSK is verifying indexes (stage 2 of 3)...
 3088 index entries processed.

Index verification completed.

CHKDSK is verifying security descriptors (stage 3 of 3)...
 2304 file SDs/SIDs processed.

Security descriptor verification completed.
 392 data files processed.

Windows has checked the file system and found no problems.

 5119999 KB total disk space.
 3300708 KB in 1850 files.
  828 KB in 394 indexes.
 30523 KB in use by the system.
 27648 KB occupied by the log file.
 1787940 KB available on disk.

  4096 bytes in each allocation unit.
 1279999 total allocation units on disk.
 446985 allocation units available on disk.

7. Click Close.

8. Click OK to close the volume's Properties dialog box.

If you select the boot volume for error checking, the program defers the check until the next time you start the computer. This is because the program cannot check a disk with open files stored on it.

■ Working with VHDs

Windows 7 supports the native use of VHD files, which enables technical specialists to access their contents and even boot from them without installing a virtual machine manager or hypervisor.

Microsoft created the *Virtual Hard Disk (VHD)* format to support its Virtual PC, Virtual Server, and Hyper-V products. A VHD file contains the entire contents of a hard disk in a single, portable file that administrators can use to move entire virtual machines (VMs) from one host computer to another. In the logical environment of a virtual machine, a VHD functions exactly like a hard disk drive does in a physical machine.

Since its introduction, Microsoft has found other uses for the VHD file format, such as the backup products in the Windows operating systems and System Center Data Protection Manager. The Windows 7 Enterprise and Ultimate editions also include support for VHD files, using a feature called *native boot*, which enables you to create and modify VHDs in Windows 7 and even boot Windows 7 from a VHD, all without having to run a virtual machine manager product such as Virtual PC or a hypervisor-based product such as Hyper-V.

TAKE NOTE*

Virtual machine managers and hypervisors always incur a certain amount of overhead because the system must dedicate some of its resources to running the VM hosting environment, on top of which run the separate VMs. To access a single VHD for maintenance and testing purposes, installing Virtual PC on a workstation or Hyper-V on a server can be a waste of resources. A workstation with the processor and memory resources to run Windows 7 reasonably well by itself would be likely to perform relatively poorly with Virtual PC installed and a VHD loaded in a virtual machine. The ability to access VHDs natively in Windows 7 provides technical specialists with a convenient platform for tasks requiring basic access to VHDs without excessive hardware requirements.

Some of the ways in which technical specialists can take advantage of the native boot capabilities of Windows 7 include the following:

- **Offline image updates:** VHDs mounted in Windows 7 are accessible by all standard file management tools, enabling administrators to update and service the images stored in them.
- **Image format standardization:** In an enterprise environment that relies on virtual machine or hypervisor technology for its servers, the VHD capability in Windows 7 can enable administrators to avoid.wim files entirely and use VHDs for all of their image files.
- **Image deployment testing:** Prior to large-scale image deployments, administrators can use Windows 7 to test the viability of their images.
- **Workstation configuration management:** By booting to VHDs without incurring the overhead of a host operating system and virtual machine manager or hypervisor, administrators can easily deploy alternative application configurations to workstation computers as needed.

Creating a VHD

Windows 7 can create VHDs using the Disk Management snap-in.

To create a new VHD in Windows 7, you can use the Disk Partition snap-in, accessible from the Computer management console, or the Diskpart.exe command-line program.

To create a new VHD file, use the following procedure.

⊕ CREATE A VHD

GET READY. Log on to Windows 7, using an account with administrative privileges.

1. Click Start, and then click Control Panel > System and Security > Administrative Tools. The Administrative Tools control panel appears.
2. Double click Computer Management. The Computer Management console appears.
3. Select Disk Management. The Disk Management snap-in appears, as shown in Figure 4-24.

Figure 4-24

The Disk Management snap-in

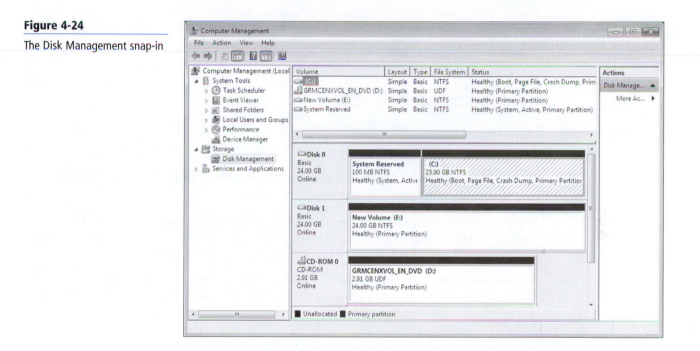

4. Right click Disk Management and, from the context menu, select Create VHD. The *Create and Attach Virtual Hard Disk* dialog box appears, as shown in Figure 4-25.

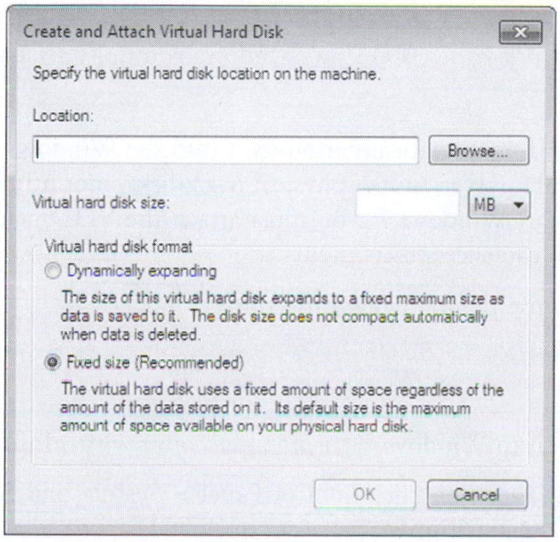

Figure 4-25

The Create and Attach Virtual Hard Disk dialog box

5. In the Location text box, type the path and filename of the VHD you want to create.
6. In the Virtual Hard Disk Size text box, specify the size of the VHD you want to create, in megabytes (MB), gigabytes (GB), or terabytes (TB).

7. Select the *Virtual hard disk format* option you want to use and click OK. The new VHD appears in the graphical view pane of the Disk Management snap-in.

8. Right click the new disk in the graphical view and, from the context menu, select Initialize Disk. The Initialize Disk dialog box appears, as shown in Figure 4-26.

Figure 4-26

The Initialize Disk dialog box

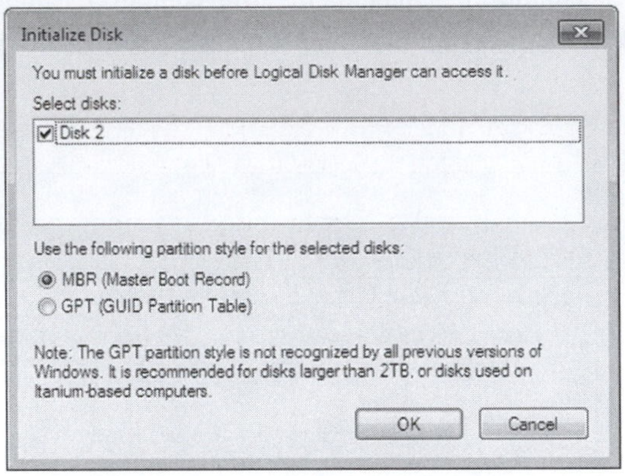

9. Click OK to accept the default MBR (master boot record) partition style. The VHD appears in the graphical view as a basic, online disk.

Once you have created and initialized the VHD, you can create a volume on it in the usual manner, format it, and assign it a drive letter, which makes it accessible through the Windows Explorer interface. Copying files to the drive adds them to the VHD.

You can also create a VHD using the Diskpart.exe utility from the command line. To perform the same tasks described in this procedure using Diskpart, use commands like the following:

```
diskpart
create vdisk file=e:\filename.vhd maximum=20000
select vdisk file=e:\filename.vhd
attach vdisk
```

Attaching and Detaching VHDs

Before you can work with a VHD in Windows you must attach it to the file system.

Creating a new VHD automatically mounts it into the Windows 7 file system, a process called attachment. However, unlike physical hard disks, mounting a VHD is not persistent. Each time you restart Windows 7, you must attach the VHD using the Disk Management snap-in before you can access its contents.

To attach a VHD, use the following procedure.

ATTACH A VHD

GET READY. Log on to Windows 7, using an account with administrative privileges.

1. Click Start, and then click Control Panel > System and Security > Administrative Tools. The Administrative Tools control panel appears.

2. Double click Computer Management. The Computer Management console appears.

3. Select Disk Management. The Disk Management snap-in appears.

4. Right click Disk Management and, from the context menu, select Attach VHD. The *Attach Virtual Hard Disk* dialog box appears, as shown in Figure 4-27.

Figure 4-27

The Attach Virtual Hard Disk
dialog box

5. Type the name or browse to the location of the VHD file you want to mount and
   click OK. The VHD is added to the Disk Management snap-in.

Once attached, the VHD is accessible from the Windows Explorer interface. To detach a
VHD, which you must do before you move it to another location, right click the disk in
the Disk Management snap-in and, from the context menu, select Detach VHD. A *Detach
Virtual Hard Disk* dialog box appears, as shown in Figure 4-28, which allows you to delete
the VHD file as well.

Figure 4-28

The Detach Virtual Hard Disk
dialog box

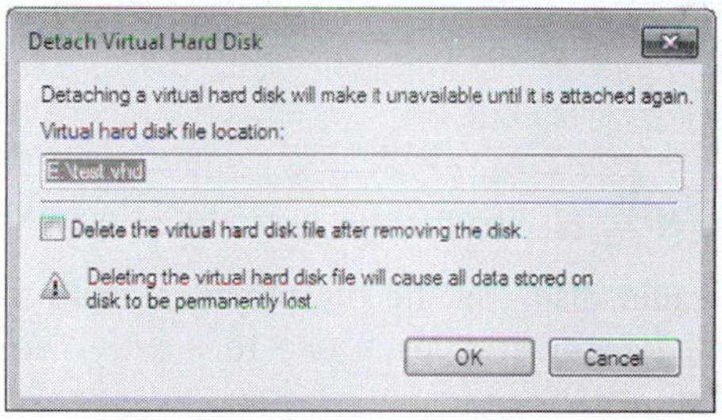

Booting from VHDs

The ability to boot from a VHD is a major new feature that enables administrators to
deploy virtual machines to Windows 7 computers without using a virtual machine manager or hypervisor. You can create a bootable VHD by deploying an image to a VHD file
you have created in the Disk Management snap-in and then adding the VHD to the boot
menu of the computer running Windows 7.

The process of deploying an image to a VHD is no different from deploying it to a physical disk. You can use the ImageX.exe utility from the command line, Windows Deployment
Services, or any of the other Windows deployment tools. Once you have deployed the image,
you must add it to the Windows 7 boot menu before you can select it when the system starts.
To do this, you use the BCDedit.exe utility from the command line.

ADD A VHD TO THE BOOT MENU

GET READY. Log on to Windows 7 using an account with administrative privileges. This
procedure assumes that you have already created or attached a VHD called filename.vhd, on
which you have deployed an image file.

1. Click Start, and then click All Programs > Accessories. Right click Command Prompt
   and, from the context menu, select Run as administrator. An Administrator:
   Command Prompt window appears.

2. From the command prompt, copy an existing boot entry and disclose its globally
   unique identifier (GUID) by typing the following command and pressing Enter, as
   shown in Figure 4-29:

   ```
   bcdedit /copy {default} /d "vhs boot (locate)"
   ```

TAKE NOTE *

If you are working on a
computer that is a mem-
ber of a workgroup, a
User Account Control
message box appears, in
which you must click
Yes to continue.

Figure 4-29

Copying a boot entry

 MORE INFORMATION

A *globally unique identifier (GUID)* is a 128-bit hexadecimal value that Windows uses to identify a particular operating system component. The value consists of five numerical groups, with 8, 4, 4, 4, and 12 hexadecimal digits, respectively, surrounded by curly brackets. When you use the GUID in subsequent commands, you must type the entire value precisely, including the brackets.

3. Using the GUID value displayed by the previous command, type the following two commands, pressing Enter after each one to modify the boot entry you just copied, as shown in Figure 4-30:

```
bcdedit /set {guid} device vhd=[locate]\filename.vhd
bcdedit /set {guid} osdevice vhd=[locate]\filename.vhd
```

Figure 4-30

Modifying a boot entry

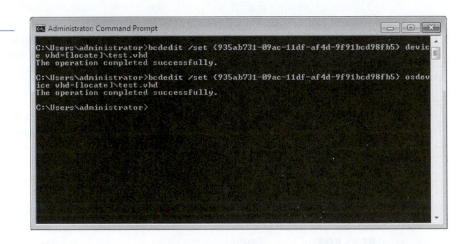

4. To configure the system to detect the computer's hardware abstraction layer automatically during startup, type the following command and press Enter:

```
bcdedit /vbcedit /set {guid} detecthal on
```

5. Close the Administrator: Command Prompt window.

Now when you restart the computer, a boot menu appears from which you can select whether you want to boot the system from the active hard disk partition or from the VHD. You can also view and configure the new boot menu entry from the Boot tab of the System Configuration tool (Msconfig.exe), as shown in Figure 4-31.

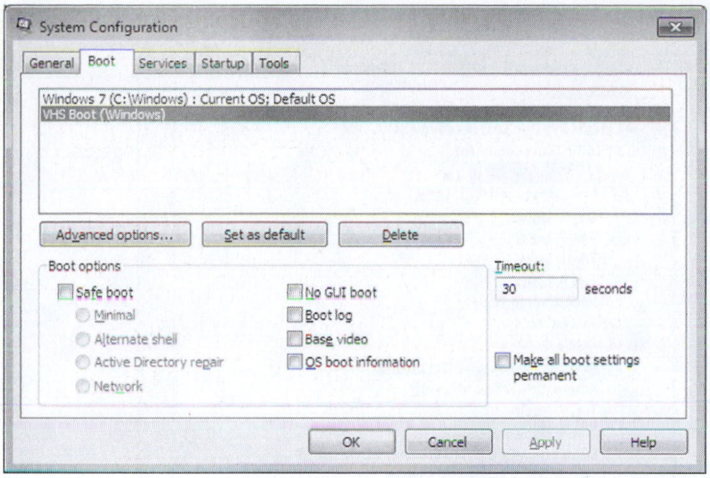

Figure 4-31

The new boot entry in the
System Configuration tool

■ Working with Devices and Drivers

THE BOTTOM LINE

A computer is a collection of hardware devices, each of which requires a piece of software called a device driver in order to function. Windows 7 includes a large library of device drivers, but it is still sometimes necessary to obtain them yourself.

CERTIFICATION READY?
Configure devices.
3.1

As most people know, a PC is a collection of hardware devices, all of which are connected together and installed in a single case. Disk drives, keyboards, mice, modems, and printers are all types of devices. To communicate with the operating system running on the computer, each device also requires a software element called a *device driver*. The device driver provides the operating system with information about a specific device.

For example, when you use a word processing application to save a file to a hard disk, the application issues a generic WriteFile function call to the operating system. The application knows nothing specific about the disk drive hardware; it just issues an instruction to store a particular file there. When the operating system processes the function call, it accesses the device driver for the hard disk drive, which provides detailed information about how to communicate with the drive. If the user selects a different target location for the file, the operating system accesses the device driver for that location, whether it's a hard drive, a floppy drive, or USB flash drive.

In most cases, the information the device driver provides is integrated into the Windows interface. For example, the Properties sheet for a printer includes generic system information, such as which port the printer is connected to and who is permitted to use it. Other tabs, and particularly the Device Settings tab, as shown in Figure 4-32, are based on hardware-specific information provided by the device driver.

In addition to providing information about a device, drivers also permit the operating system to modify the hardware configuration settings of the device. For example, when you configure a printer to print a document in landscape mode instead of portrait mode, the printer device driver generates the appropriate command and sends it to the hardware.

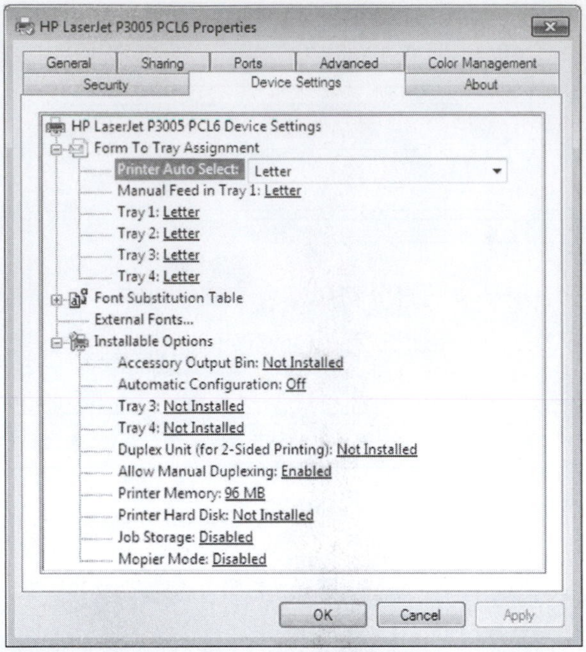

Figure 4-32

The Device Settings tab of a printer's Properties sheet

Understanding Device Drivers

The process of installing a hardware device consists primarily of identifying the device and installing a device driver for it. This process can occur during the operating system installation or at a later time, but the steps are fundamentally the same.

A major part of the Windows 7 installation process consists of identifying the devices in the computer and installing the appropriate drivers for them. The Windows 7 installation package includes hundreds of drivers for many different devices, which is why many installations finish without any user intervention. Sometimes, however, you might have to supply device drivers yourself.

UNDERSTANDING DRIVER COMPLEXITY

Virtually every component in a PC requires a device driver, but they can vary greatly in complexity. Many of the standard computer devices are so standardized that their drivers operate virtually invisibly. When was the last time you had a problem with a keyboard driver, for example? Nearly every computer has a keyboard and the generic keyboard driver included with Windows 7 functions properly in almost every case. If you have a keyboard with special features, you might need a special driver to access them, but the basic keyboard functions will still function even without it.

At the other end of the scale are more complex drivers, such as those for graphics adapters. Many of the graphics adapters on the market are really self-contained computers in themselves, with their own processors and memory. The drivers for these complex devices are equally complex, and are often much more problematic than simple keyboard drivers, for the following reasons:

- **The device driver is likely to be revised more often:** Drivers that are required to do more are more likely to have problems. Generic keyboard drivers can go for years without upgrades, because keyboards rarely change. Manufacturers often release new graphics adapters, however, and therefore require new drivers as well.

- **The device driver is less likely to be included with the operating system:** The Windows 7 installation disk includes hundreds of device drivers, but the older the operating system gets, the less likely it is to include the latest drivers for the newest devices. In these cases, you must obtain the drivers you need from the hardware manufacturer and install them yourself.

- **The device driver is more likely to cause compatibility or functionality problems:** New devices are often rushed to market, and as a result, the drivers that ship with them might not be fully debugged. This is particularly true, again, with graphics drivers. It is always a good idea to check the manufacturer's Web site for the latest drivers before installing new hardware.

CREATING A DRIVER UPDATE POLICY

As a technical specialist, you are likely to be working with many different computers, each containing many devices. Keeping up with the drivers for all of these devices can be difficult, and you also must consider whether installing each driver update is necessary and, above all, safe.

There are two basic schools of thought when it comes to updating drivers. The "latest is the greatest" school advocates downloading and installing every new driver that is released, while the "if it ain't broke, don't fix it" school prefers to leave things as they are until they experience a problem. Both of these philosophies have their advantages and disadvantages, and unfortunately, this is not likely to be a question that can be answered with a hard-and-fast rule or a company policy.

There are three main reasons why hardware manufacturers release new driver updates:

- To address problems with the previous driver release(s)
- To implement new features
- To enhance performance of the device

The question of whether to update a driver is most easily answered for the first of these reasons. If you are experiencing the problem that the update is designed to address, then you should install it. Otherwise, you probably should not. As to the other two reasons, new features and enhanced performance are certainly desirable, but you should be sure that the driver update does not introduce new problems at the same time.

As a general rule, it is a good idea to test all driver updates before deploying them, especially in an enterprise environment. Another good safety measure is to avoid installing driver updates as soon as they are released. Waiting at least a week or so gives the manufacturer time to address any major issues that arise.

Above all, the question of whether to install driver updates should depend on the hardware devices involved and the policies and reputation of the hardware manufacturer. Some manufacturers release driver updates frequently and haphazardly, while others are more careful. Examining the manufacturer's support Web site is a good way to ascertain how they deal with hardware problems and how often they release driver updates.

UNDERSTANDING DRIVER SIGNING

As with any other software, device drivers have the potential to damage a computer configuration. Unscrupulous programmers can conceivably alter device drivers by adding their own malware, and the average user, downloading the driver from the Internet, would never know the difference. For that reason, Microsoft has instituted the practice of digitally signing the device drivers they have tested and approved.

A signed driver is a device driver that includes a digital signature. The signer uses a cryptographic algorithm to compute the digital signature value and then appends that value to the device driver. A *signer* is an organization, or publisher, that uses a private key to create the digital signature for the device driver. This process ensures that the device driver does come from the authentic publisher and that someone has not maliciously altered it.

Public key cryptography is an encryption method based on a pair of keys, called the public key and the private key. As the names imply, the public key is freely available to anyone, and the private key is kept secret by its owner. Any code that is digitally encrypted using the public key can only be decrypted by the holder of the private key. In the same way, any code that is encrypted using the private key can only be decrypted by the public key. It is the latter example that publishers use for driver signing. The signer encrypts the device driver using its private key. The fact that the user can decrypt the driver using that signer's public key confirms that the software has not been modified.

Generally, the process the publisher uses to create the digital signature starts by running the device driver files through a hash algorithm and then using the publisher's private key to transform the hash result cryptographically. The resulting value is the digital signature of the device driver.

The digital signature value is a protected checksum. A protected checksum is the value of an algorithmic function that is dependent on the contents of the data object with which it is stored. Its purpose is to protect the data object against active attacks that attempt to change the checksum to match changes that a malicious individual has made to the data object. Thus, the properties of a cryptographic hash ensure that when a malicious individual attempts to change the data object, the digital signature no longer matches the object.

If Windows 7 perceives a problem with a digital signature of a device driver, it alerts you with one of the following messages during the installation attempt:

- **Windows can't verify the publisher of this driver:** Either a certification authority has not verified the digital signature or the driver does not contain a digital signature. Only install this driver if you obtained it from the original manufacturer's disk.

- **This driver has been altered:** Someone has altered this driver after the verified publisher has digitally signed it, possibly with malicious intent. The driver package may now include malware that could harm your system or steal information. Only install this driver if you obtained it from the original manufacturer's disk.

- **Windows cannot install this driver:** x64-based versions of Windows 7 cannot install a device driver that someone has altered after the verified publisher has digitally signed it or one that lacks a valid digital signature altogether.

SUPPLYING DRIVERS DURING WINDOWS 7 INSTALLATION

As mentioned earlier, one of the primary functions of the Windows 7 installation program is to identify the hardware devices in the computer and install the appropriate device drivers for them. For most devices, this process occurs invisibly. There are occasions, however, when the installation program fails to identify a device. When this occurs, one of three things happens:

- **The installation program installs a generic driver instead:** For devices that are essential to system operation, such as keyboards and graphics adapters, Windows 7 includes generic drivers that support nearly all hardware devices. If Windows 7 does not include a driver for your specific graphics adapter, for example, it installs a generic VGA (video graphics array) driver. This VGA driver won't support the esoteric features of your graphics adapter, but it will at least display an image on your screen, albeit a low-resolution one. After the operating system installation is completed, you can obtain a driver for your hardware and install it in place of the generic driver.

- **The installation program leaves the device without a driver and completes the installation:** If the hardware device is not essential to basic system operation, such as an audio adapter, Windows 7 leaves the hardware uninstalled and proceeds with the rest of the installation. When the installation is completed, the hardware appears in Device Manager with a warning icon, indicating that it has no driver.

X REF

To install a device driver after the installation is complete, you must use the Device Manager utility as described later in this lesson in "Using Device Manager."

- **The installation program permits you to supply an alternate driver or, failing that, halts:** The sole exception to the preceding condition is when the installation program cannot access a disk drive with sufficient free space to install Windows 7. When this happens, the setup program halts, unless you are able to supply the device driver for an unrecognized mass storage hardware device. For example, if your hard drives are connected to an interface card that Windows 7 does not recognize, you can click Load Driver on the installation program's *Where Do You Want to Install Windows?* page, and specify the location of a driver for the interface card.

UPDATING DRIVERS WITH WINDOWS UPDATE

The Windows Update Web site was originally designed to provide users with operating system updates, but it now includes a large library of device driver updates as well. The drivers distributed through Windows Update have all undergone Windows Hardware Quality Labs (WHQL) testing and have received the Windows logo.

When you access the Windows Update Web site manually, Windows 7 transmits a list of installed hardware and device version numbers to the site. If there are any updated drivers available for your hardware, the Web site makes them available, usually as an optional download.

If Windows 7 is configured to use automatic updating, the system will download device drivers only for hardware that does not have a driver installed. If you use Device Manager to search for updated drivers, Windows 7 examines the drivers that are available and only downloads a new driver if it is a better match for the device than the driver that is currently installed.

Using Device Manager

The primary Windows 7 tool for managing devices and their drivers is called Device Manager. You can use Device Manager to get information about the devices installed on the computer, as well as to install, update, and troubleshoot device drivers.

Although it is not immediately apparent, Device Manager is a snap-in for the Microsoft Management Console (MMC). This means that there are many ways that you can access Device Manager, including the following:

- Open the hardware and Sound control panel and click the Device Manager link.
- Open the Computer Management console from the Administrative Tools program group in the System and Security control panel and click Device Manager in the scope (left) pane.
- Run the Microsoft Management Console shell application (Mmc.exe), select File > Add/Remove Snap-in, and select Device Manager from the list of snap-ins provided.
- Open the Start menu, type the filename of the Device Manager snap-in (Devmgmt.msc) in the Search programs and files box, and then execute the resulting file.

Each of these procedures launches the Device Manager and displays a window with an interface like that shown in Figure 4-33.

Figure 4-33

The Windows 7 Device Manager

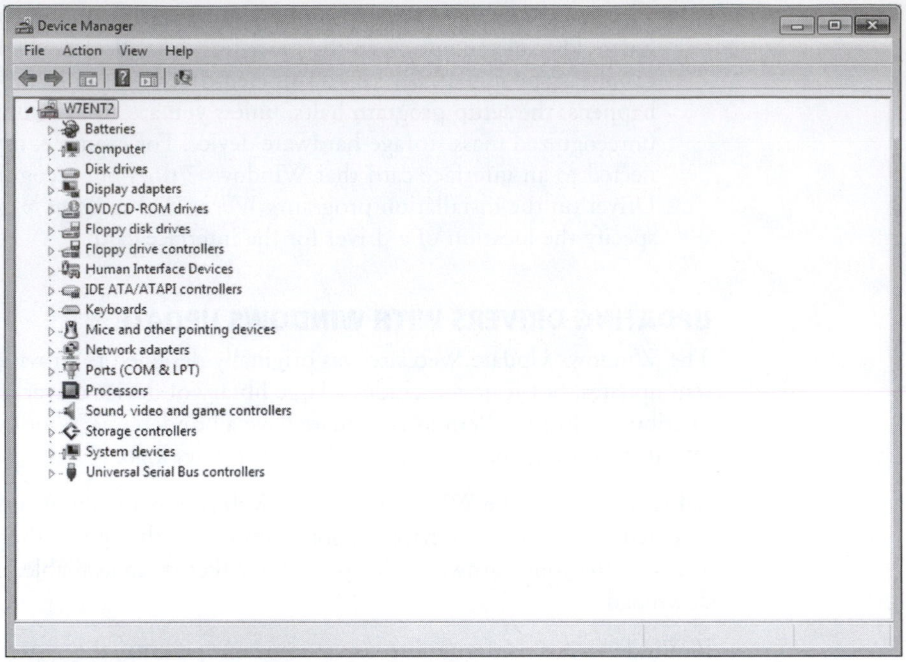

VIEWING DEVICE PROPERTIES

Device Manager is capable of displaying information in the following four modes:

- **Devices by type:** Displays a list of device categories, which you can expand to show the devices in each category. This is the default Device Manager view, as shown in Figure 4-34.

Figure 4-34

Device Manager's Devices by Type display, expanded

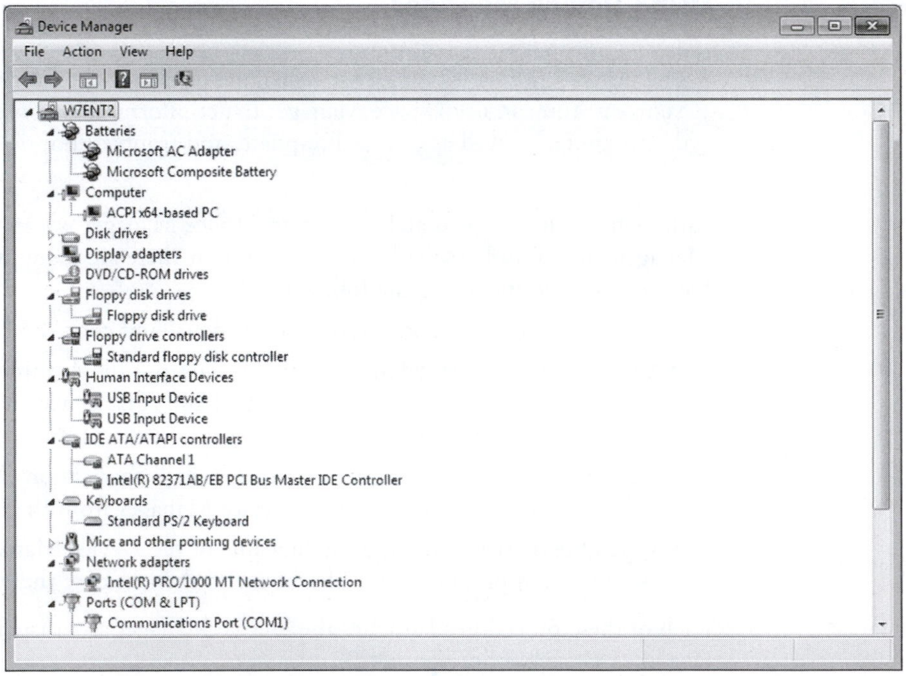

- **Devices by connection:** Displays a list of the interfaces that hardware devices use to communicate with the computer. Expanding a connection shows the devices using that connection.
- **Resources by type:** Displays a list of resource types, including Direct Memory Access (DMA), Input/Output (I/O), Interrupt Request (IRQ), and Memory, which you can expand to show the resources of each type and the devices that are using them.

- **Resources by connection:** Displays a list of resource types, including Direct Memory Access (DMA), Input/Output (I/O), Interrupt Request (IRQ), and Memory, which you can expand to show the connection associated with each individual resource and the device using each connection.

To examine the properties of a device, simply locate it in the tree display and double click it to open its Properties sheet, as shown in Figure 4-35.

Figure 4-35

A Device Manager Properties sheet

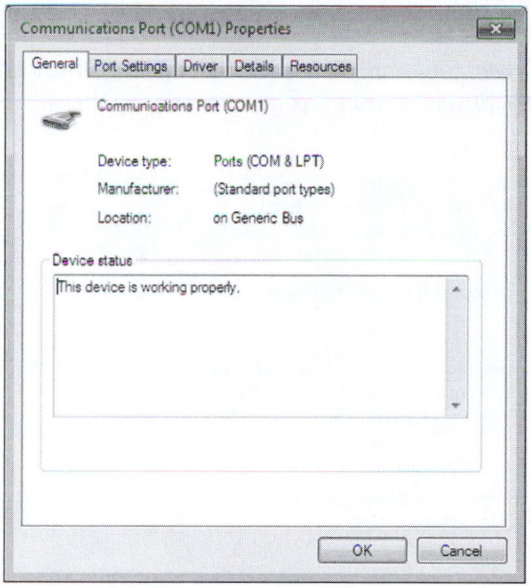

[Communications Port (COM1) Properties dialog box, General tab showing Device type: Ports (COM & LPT), Manufacturer: (Standard port types), Location: on Generic Bus, Device status: This device is working properly.]

The tabs on the Properties sheet vary depending on the nature of the device you select, but virtually all devices have the following four tabs:

- **General:** Displays the name of the device, its type, manufacturer, and location in the system. The Device Status box indicates whether the device is functioning and, if not, provides troubleshooting help.
- **Driver:** Displays the device driver's provider, date, version, and digital signer. The tab also provides buttons you can use to display driver details, update, roll back, or uninstall the driver, and enable or disable the device.
- **Detail:** Displays extensive information about the driver and its properties.
- **Resources:** Displays the hardware resources being used by the device and indicates whether there are any conflicts with other devices in the computer.

ENABLING AND DISABLING DEVICES

With Device Manager, you can disable any device in the computer, using any of the following procedures:

- Select the device and choose Disable from the Action menu.
- Right click the device and choose Disable from the context menu.
- Open the device's Properties sheet and click the Disable button on the Driver tab.

Disabling a device does not affect the hardware in any way or uninstall the device driver, it simply renders the device inoperative until you enable it again. Obviously, you cannot disable devices that are necessary for the system to function, such as the processor, and some devices that are in use require you to restart the system before they can be disabled.

TAKE NOTE*

Disabling a device releases the hardware resources it was using back to the operating system. If you restart the computer with the device disabled, Windows might reassign those hardware resources to other devices. If you re-enable the device, the computer might allocate different hardware resources to it than it had originally.

UPDATING DRIVERS

When you update a driver using Device Manager, you can point to a location on your computer where you have already saved the new driver, or you can run a search of your computer and the Internet. To update a device driver, use the following procedure.

UPDATE A DEVICE DRIVER

GET READY. Log on to Windows 7 using an account with administrator privileges.

1. Open Device Manager and locate the device that you want to update.
2. Double click the device you want to update, so that its Properties sheet appears.
3. Click the Driver tab, and then click the Update Driver button. The *How do you want to search for driver software?* page appears, as shown in Figure 4-36.

Figure 4-36

The How do you want to search for driver software? page

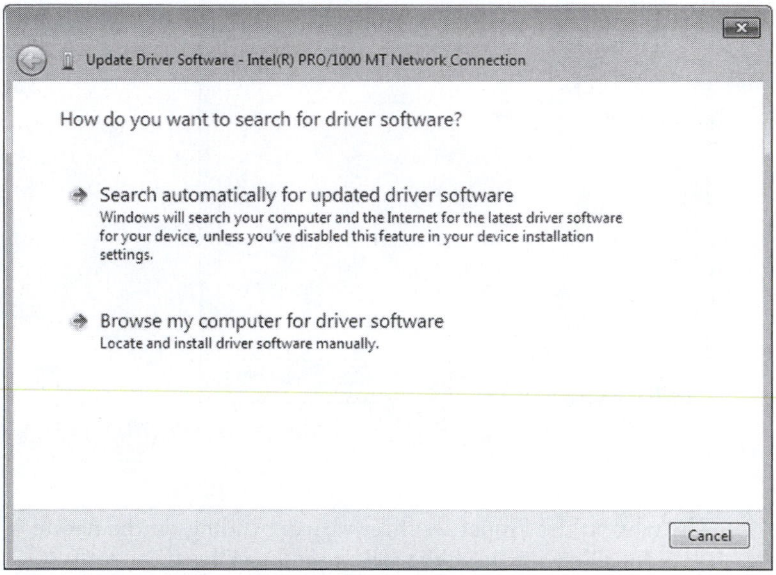

4. Click Browse my computer for driver software to specify a location for the driver or select from a list of installed drivers, as shown in Figure 4-37. Click Search automatically for updated driver software to initiate a search for a driver.

Figure 4-37

The Browse for driver software on your computer page

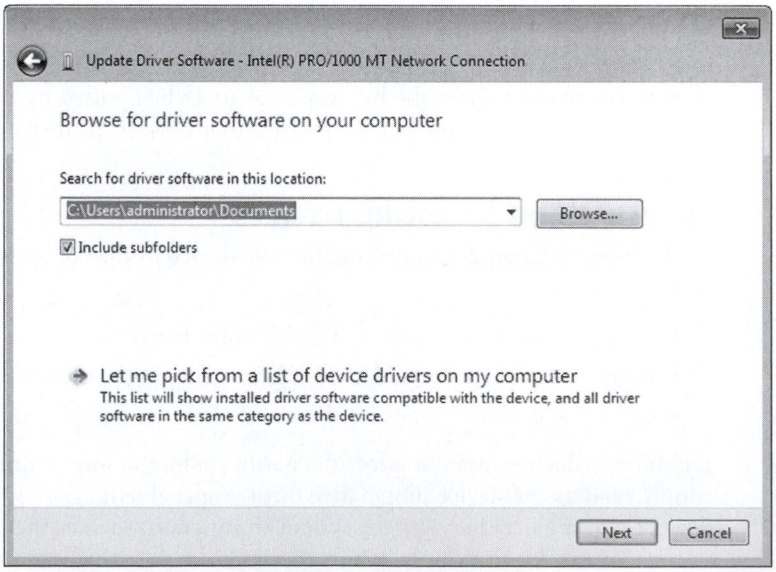

5. Click Next when you locate the driver you want to install. The *Windows Has Successfully Updated Your Driver Software* page appears.

6. Click Close.

7. Close the Device Manager window.

ROLLING BACK DRIVERS

When you update a device driver in Windows 7, the operating system does not discard the old driver completely. It is not uncommon for new drivers to cause more problems than they solve, and many users find that they would prefer to go back to the old version. Windows 7 makes this possible with the Roll Back feature, which you initiate by clicking the Roll Back Driver button on the Driver tab of the device's Properties sheet. This procedure uninstalls the current driver and reinstalls the previous version, returning the device to its state before you performed the most recent driver update.

TROUBLESHOOTING DRIVERS

Installing a new hardware device or a new device driver is a risky undertaking. There is always the possibility of a problem that, depending on the devices involved, could be trivial or catastrophic. For a peripheral device, such as a printer, a hardware misconfiguration or faulty driver would probably just cause the new device to malfunction. However, if the device involved is a graphics adapter, a bad driver could prevent the system from functioning.

To troubleshoot hardware or driver problems, consider some of the following techniques:

- Open the Properties sheet for the device and check the Device Status box on the General tab. If the device is malfunctioning, this tab informs you of its status and enables you to launch a troubleshooter.

- Open the Device Manager and delete the device entirely. Then restart the system and allow Windows 7 to detect and install the device over again. This process will cause Windows to re-allocate hardware resources to the device, which could resolve the problem if it was caused by a hardware resource conflict.

- If the device or driver malfunction prevents the system from running properly, as in the case of a bad graphics driver that prevents an image from appearing on the screen, you can start the computer in Safe Mode by pressing the F8 key as the system starts. Safe Mode loads the operating system with a minimal set of generic device drivers, bypassing the troublesome ones, so you can uninstall or troubleshoot them.

SKILL SUMMARY

IN THIS LESSON YOU LEARNED:

- There are two hard disk partition styles that you can use in Windows 7: MBR and GPT.

- Windows 7 supports two disk types: basic disks and dynamic disks.

- Basic disks can have up to four partitions: three primary partitions and the fourth usually being an extended partition, on which you can create multiple logical drives.

- Windows 7 supports four types of dynamic volumes: simple, spanned, striped, and mirrored.

- You use the Disk Management snap-in for MMC to manage disks.

- The Virtual Hard Disk (VHD) format defines a file that contains the entire contents of a hard disk in a single, portable file that administrators can use to move entire virtual machines (VMs) from one host computer to another.

(continued)

SKILL SUMMARY (*continued*)

- The Windows 7 Enterprise and Ultimate editions also include support for a feature called native boot, which enables you to create and modify VHDs and even boot Windows 7 from a VHD, all without having to run Virtual PC or Hyper-V.

- Device drivers are software components that enable applications and operating systems to communicate with specific hardware devices. Every hardware device you install in a computer must have a corresponding driver.

- Plug and Play (PnP) is a standard that enables computers to detect and identify hardware devices, and then install and configure drivers for those devices. PnP dynamically assigns hardware resources to each device, and can reconfigure devices at will to accommodate each component's special needs.

- The drivers included with Windows 7 have all been digitally signed to ensure that they have not been modified since they were published.

- Device Manager is an MMC snap-in that lists all hardware devices in the computer and indicates problems with hardware identification or driver configuration. Using Device Manager, you can enable and disable devices, update and roll back drivers, and manage devices and device driver properties.

■ Knowledge Assessment

Fill in the Blank

Complete the following sentences by writing the correct word or words in the blanks provided.

1. By default, Windows 7 standard users are permitted to install Plug and Play devices only if their drivers are _____.

2. The debilitating condition in which files are stored as clusters scattered all over a disk is called _____.

3. The file system included in Windows 7 that is specifically designed for use on flash drives is called _____.

4. Technically speaking, you create _____ on basic disks and _____ on dynamic disks.

5. In Windows 7, the _____ file system is limited to volumes no larger than 32 gigabytes.

6. The digital signature of a driver consists of a _____ that is appended to the driver itself before publication.

7. To create a fourth primary partition on a basic disk, you must use the _____ utility.

8. To extend or shrink a partition on a basic disk, you must be a member of the _____ or _____ group.

9. The default partition style used by Windows 7 on an x86 computer is _____.

10. All digitally signed drivers have undergone _____ testing.

True / False

Circle T if the statement is true or F if the statement is false.

T | F **1.** There is no way to create a fourth primary partition on a basic disk in Windows 7.

T | F **2.** Striped volumes provide greater fault tolerance than simple volumes.

T | F **3.** All dynamic disks have only one partition on them.

T | F **4.** By default, all device drivers must be digitally signed to be installed on a computer running Windows 7.

T | F **5.** Windows Update dynamically updates device drivers only when a hardware device has no driver installed.

T | F **6.** Disabling a device in Device Manager causes its device driver to be uninstalled.

T | F **7.** The x64-based versions of Windows 7 do not permit the installation of unsigned drivers under any circumstances.

T | F **8.** You cannot convert an MBR disk to a GPT disk without erasing all data on the disk.

T | F **9.** You cannot extend a striped volume unless it is on a dynamic disk.

T | F **10.** Windows 7 can access VHDs without the use of a hypervisor.

Review Questions

1. Explain the difference between a spanned volume and a striped volume, and specify which (if any) provides increased performance and/or fault tolerance.
2. List the three main reasons why manufacturers release driver updates.

■ Case Scenario

Scenario 4-1: Troubleshooting Graphics Drivers

A user asks you to troubleshoot his Windows 7 workstation, which is behaving erratically. He has recently purchased and installed a new graphics adapter, and since then, he sees occasional wavy lines in the display. You run Device Manager on the system and note the manufacturer, model, and version number of the device driver for the graphics adapter. Then, you check the adapter manufacturer's Web site and discover that there is a new driver available for the adapter. After downloading and installing the driver update, you restart the system. The system appears to start normally, except that the graphical interface has been replaced by incomprehensible noise. Because you can't see the display, you can't work with the system. What should you do to return the computer to an operational state?

Connecting to a Network

OBJECTIVE DOMAIN MATRIX

TECHNOLOGY SKILL	OBJECTIVE DOMAIN	OBJECTIVE NUMBER
Configuring IPv4 Settings	Configure IPv4 network settings.	4.1
Configuring IPv6 Settings	Configure IPv6 network settings.	4.2
Managing Network Connections	Configure networking settings.	4.3

KEY TERMS

classless inter-domain routing (CIDR)

connectionless protocol

connection-oriented protocol

data encapsulation

datagram

8P8C connectors

firewall

frame

Internet Protocol (IP)

IP address

Link Local Multicast Name Resolution (LLMNR)

media access control (MAC) addresses

network address translation (NAT)

open systems interconnection (OSI) reference model

packet-switching networks

ports

protocols

router

socket

stateless address autoconfiguration

subnet mask

Transmission Control Protocol (TCP)

unshielded twisted pair (UTP)

■ Networking Basics

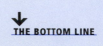

THE BOTTOM LINE

The networking modifications introduced in Windows Vista were the most significant changes to the Windows networking engine since it was first incorporated into the operating system in Windows 95. Windows 7 networking now includes a revamped TCP/IP stack and a variety of new tools that simplify the networking process, for both users and administrators.

Networking is one of the primary functions of Windows 7. Most Windows computers are connected to either a private local area network (LAN) or to the Internet, and many are connected to both. These connections provide users with access to remotely stored data, shared resources, network-attached hardware, and the virtually unlimited information and services available on the Internet.

Most Windows users are unaware of how computer networks function or even of when they are accessing a network resource, as opposed to a local one. Users expect Windows to provide a seamless network experience, wherever they happen to be located, and Windows 7 includes many new networking features that help to provide this experience.

To promote interoperability between hardware manufacturers' products, computer networks are, for the most part, based on independent standards. The networking capabilities built into Windows 7 are implementations of those standards. Before you work directly with the Windows 7 networking tools, it is helpful to have a firm grasp of the underlying principles on which they were designed.

Computer networking is a highly complex process, but most of the technology operates invisibly, both to the user and the administrator. Computers on a network communicate using *protocols*, which are nothing more than languages that all of the computers understand. These protocols operate on different levels, forming what is commonly known as a networking stack or protocol stack. The most common method for illustrating the operations of the networking stack is the *Open Systems Interconnection (OSI) reference model*, which consists of seven layers, as shown in Figure 5-1.

Figure 5-1

The OSI reference model

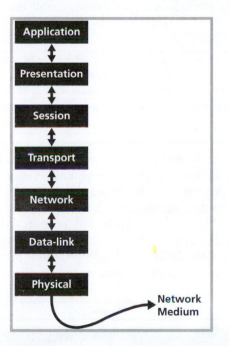

The Physical Layer

> At the bottom of the OSI model is the physical layer, which represents the hardware that forms the network.

The physical layer of the OSI model consists of the cable or the radio signals that carry data from one system to another and the network interface adapters, which are the hardware components in the computers that provide the connection to the physical network.

Most cabled networks use a type of cable called *unshielded twisted pair (UTP)*, which is similar to the cable used for telephone wiring. UTP cable consists of four pairs of wires, with

X REF

For more information on wireless networking, see Lesson 12, "Using Mobile Computers."

each pair twisted individually. At either end of each cable run are modular *8P8C connectors* (often incorrectly referred to as RJ45 connectors), which are similar to the RJ11 connectors used for telephones.

A network interface adapter is the component that provides the connection to the network. Most of the computers manufactured today have Ethernet network interface adapters integrated into their motherboards, but the adapter can also take the form of an expansion card that you install into the computer or an external device that connects to a Universal Serial Bus (USB) port. For wireless networking, the cables and cable connectors are replaced by radio transceivers that transmit the same data using a different kind of signal.

The Data-Link Layer

As you move up beyond the physical layer, the subsequent layers of the OSI model are realized in software, as protocols that provide different types of communications.

Most Windows networks use a protocol called Ethernet at the data-link layer. Local area networks are sometimes described as *packet-switching networks* because the messages generated by each computer are divided up into small pieces called packets, which the computer transmits individually over the network. A single file might be divided into hundreds or thousands of packets, each of which is transmitted separately. The packets might take different routes to the destination, and might even arrive there in a different order. The receiving computer is responsible for putting the pieces back together to reassemble the file.

✚ MORE INFORMATION

The cable on a packet-switching network, at any given moment, can be carrying packets generated by dozens of different computers. The alternative to a packet-switching network is called a circuit-switching network, in which two systems establish a dedicated connection that they use exclusively until their transaction is completed. The most common example of a circuit-switching network is the public switched telephone network (PSTN), the standard telephone system.

For the packets to reach their destination, they have to know where they are going; therefore, they need an address. Just like letters mailed in the post office, each packet needs an address identifying the computer that will be its destination. Ethernet is the protocol responsible for addressing the packets at the data-link layer, which it does by surrounding the data it receives from the network layer just above it with a header and footer, as shown in Figure 5-2. This header and footer and the data they contain are collectively called a *frame*, and the process of applying it is called *data encapsulation*. The header and footer perform the same functions as the envelope does for a letter, protecting the contents and displaying the address of the recipient.

Figure 5-2

Data-link layer data encapsulation

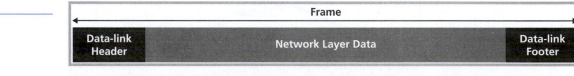

TAKE NOTE＊

There are other data-link layer protocols, such as Token Ring, but the vast majority of LANs today use Ethernet. Two computers must both be running the same data-link layer protocol to communicate.

The addresses computers use at the data-link layer are six-byte hexadecimal sequences, hard-coded into each network interface adapter by the manufacturer. These sequences are called hardware addresses or *media access control (MAC) addresses*. The first three bytes of a hardware address identify the manufacturer of the network interface adapter, and the last three bytes identify the adapter itself.

In addition to addresses, the Ethernet header contains other information that helps to direct and protect the data in the packet. Each Ethernet frame contains a code that identifies the network-layer protocol that generated the data in the packet and a checksum that the receiving system will use to confirm that the packet has not been altered in transit.

The Network Layer

The protocols that Windows uses by default at the network and transport layers are collectively called TCP/IP. TCP is the *Transmission Control Protocol* and IP is the *Internet Protocol*. Early versions of Windows used a different protocol called NetBIOS, but TCP/IP is the native protocol of the Internet, and the explosive growth in the Internet's popularity eventually led developers of all network operating systems to adopt TCP/IP as their default protocol.

IP is the network layer protocol that performs many important networking functions. These functions are described in the following sections.

 TAKE NOTE*

There are other network layer protocols that perform functions similar to those of IP, such as Internetwork Packet Exchange (IPX), a proprietary protocol developed by Novell for use with its NetWare operating system. However, the ubiquity of TCP/IP on the Internet has lead to the almost universal adoption of IP at the network layer.

IP ROUTING

The term internet (with a lowercase "i") literally means a network of networks. The Internet as we know it (with a capital "I") is a huge conglomeration of networks, all connected together by devices called routers. A *router* is simply a device that connects one network to another. When you install a LAN in a home or office, and connect it to the Internet, you are actually installing a router that connects your network with another network, that of your Internet service provider (ISP).

IP is the primary end-to-end protocol used on most data networks. Data-link layer protocols like Ethernet are actually LAN protocols; they are designed to send packets from one system to another system on the same local network. An *end-to-end protocol* like IP is responsible for the complete transmission of a packet from its source to its final destination on another network.

To get to that final destination, packets must be passed from router to router, through many different networks. A single packet might pass through dozens of routers before it reaches its destination network. The IP protocol is responsible for this routing process. Every TCP/IP system maintains a routing table that functions as the road map to other networks. By examining the destination address on each packet, and comparing it with the information in the routing table, IP decides which router to send the packet to next. The next router to receive the packet does the same thing, and step-by-step, the packet makes its way to the destination. Actually, each router the packet passes through is called a *hop*, so it is really a hop-by-hop process.

Of course, this process occurs much more quickly than this text can describe it. When you type a URL into your web browser and press the Enter key, in the time it takes for the web page to begin appearing on your screen, dozens of packets have traveled back and forth through dozens of routers to and from a destination that might be in another city or another country.

+ MORE INFORMATION

To see how many routers there are between your Windows 7 computer and a destination on the Internet, open a Command Prompt window and type **tracert** *destination*, where *destination* is the name of a server on the Internet, such as www.microsoft.com. The Tracert.exe program will gradually compile a list of the routers as they process the packets on the way to the destination.

IPv4 ADDRESSING

IP has its own addressing system, which it uses to identify all of the devices on a network. Every network interface in a computer, and every device that is directly connected to a TCP/IP network, must have an *IP address*. IP addresses are independent of the hardware addresses assigned to network interface adapters. A Windows 7 computer that is connected to a LAN has both a hardware address and an IP address.

As mentioned earlier, data-link layer protocols like Ethernet are LAN protocols; their addresses are only used to transmit packets to other systems on the same local network. The IP address in a given packet, on the other hand, always identifies the packet's final destination, even if it is on another network. This is why IP is called an end-to-end protocol. When you use your web browser to connect to a site on the Internet, the packets your computer generates contain the IP address of the destination site, but at the data-link layer, they carry the hardware address of a router on the local network that they can use to access the Internet. Thus, the data-link layer and the network layer both have their own addressing systems, and the two addresses do not have to point to the same destination.

The current standard for IP is version 4 (IPv4), which defines a 32-bit address space. Each address is split into two parts:

- **Network identifier:** As the name implies, specifies the network on which a particular system is located.
- **Host identifier:** Specifies a particular network interface (also called a *host*) on the network.

Unlike hardware addresses, however, which always use three bytes for the network and three bytes for the interface, IP addresses can have variable numbers of network bits and host bits. To locate the division between the network identifier and the host identifier, TCP/IP systems use a mechanism called a *subnet mask*.

+ MORE INFORMATION

The TCP/IP protocols are defined by public domain documents that are published by a body called the Internet Engineering Task Force (IETF). When they are first published, these documents are known as Requests For Comments (RFC). They then proceed through a lengthy ratification process before being declared Internet standards. The original IP standard, published as RFC 791, "Internet Protocol: DARPA Internet Program Protocol Specification" in September 1981, is a relatively short document that concentrates largely on IPv4 addressing. There are numerous other RFCs that define other aspects of the IP protocol, all of which are available from the IETF Web site at http://www.ietf.org.

Subnet Masking

IPv4 addresses are expressed in dotted decimal notation, that is, four eight-bit numbers, separated by dots (or periods), such as 192.168.3.64. An eight-bit binary number, when expressed in decimal form, can have any value from 0 to 255. A subnet mask is also a 32-bit number, expressed in dotted decimal notation, such as 255.255.255.0. The difference between a subnet mask and an IPv4 address is that a subnet mask consists, in binary form, of a series of consecutive 1s followed by a series of consecutive 0s. When you compare the binary values of the subnet mask to those of the IPv4 address, the 1 bits in the mask represent the network identifier, while the 0 bits represent the host identifier.

For example, a Windows 7 computer might be configured with the following IPv4 address and subnet mask:

- **IP address:** 192.168.3.64
- **Subnet mask:** 255.255.255.0

The whole concept of the subnet mask is easier to understand if you convert both values from decimal to binary, as follows:

- **IP address:** 11000000 10101000 00000011 100000000
- **Subnet mask:** 11111111 11111111 11111111 00000000

In binary form, you can see that the first 24 bits of the subnet mask are ones. Therefore, the first 24 bits of the IPv4 address form the network identifier. The last eight bits of the mask are zeroes, so the last eight bits of the address are the host identifier. As a result, in decimal form, the network identifier is 192.168.3 and the host identifier is 64.

The original IP standard defines three classes of IP addresses, based on the byte divisions of their subnet masks. These classes, and their characteristics, are shown in Table 5-1.

Table 5-1

IPv4 Address Classes

	CLASS A	CLASS B	CLASS C
Subnet mask	255.0.0.0	255.255.0.0	255.255.255.0
First bit values (binary)	0	10	110
First byte value (decimal)	0–127	128–191	192–223
Number of network identifier bits	8	16	24
Number of host identifier bits	24	16	8
Number of possible networks	126	16,384	2,097,152
Number of possible hosts	16,777,214	65,534	254

Classless Inter-Domain Routing (CIDR)

In practical use, the IP address classes proved to be wasteful, and when the Internet first experienced a massive period of growth in the 1990s, it was feared that there might at some time be a shortage of addresses. To avoid assigning entire addresses of a particular class to networks that didn't have that many hosts, the IETF eventually published a new standard for assigning IP addresses called *classless inter-domain routing (CIDR)*.

CIDR differs from traditional addressing (now called *classful addressing*) by allowing the division between the network identifier and the host identifier to fall anywhere in an IPv4 address; it does not have to fall on one of the eight-bit boundaries. For example, a subnet mask of 255.255.240.0 translates into a binary value of 11111111 11111111 11110000 00000000, meaning that the network identifier is 20 bits long and the host identifier is 12 bits. This falls between a Class B and a Class C address, and enables ISPs to assign clients only the number of addresses they need, which conserves the IP address space.

CIDR also introduced a new syntax for IP network address references. In classful notation, an address like 172.23.0.0 was assumed to be a Class B address and use the standard 255.255.0.0 Class B subnet mask.

In CIDR notation, the network address is followed by a slash and the number of bits is the network identifier. Therefore, 172.23.0.0/16 would be the CIDR equivalent of a Class B address. An address that used the 255.255.240.0 subnet mask described earlier would therefore look something like 172.23.0.0/20.

Private IP Addressing

Computers that are connected directly to the Internet must use IPv4 addresses that are registered with the Internet Assigned Numbers Authority (IANA). This is to prevent the duplication of IP addresses on the Internet. The IANA assigns blocks of network identifiers to ISPs, who assign them in turn to their customers. Once an organization is assigned a network identifier, it is up to the network administrators to assign a unique host identifier to each computer on the network.

Private LANs do not need registered addresses, so they can use network identifiers from three special ranges of private addresses that are reserved for that purpose. The three private address ranges are shown in Table 5-2.

Table 5-2

IPv4 Private Addresses

ADDRESS CLASS	IPv4 PRIVATE ADDRESS RANGE	SUBNET MASK
Class A	10.0.0.0 through 10.255.255.255	255.0.0.0
Class B	172.16.0.0 through 172.31.255.255	255.255.0.0
Class C	192.168.0.0 through 192.168.255.255	255.255.255.0

Internet routers do not forward these private addresses, so computers that use them are theoretically not accessible from the Internet. However, most networks today that use private IP addresses provide their computers with Internet access using a technology such as *network address translation (NAT)*.

NAT is a feature built into many routers that takes the packets destined for the Internet that are generated by the computers on a private network, substitutes a registered address for the computer's private address, and then forwards the packets to the Internet destinations. When the Internet servers send replies, the NAT router does the same thing in reverse. As a result, an entire private network can share a single registered address.

Assigning IP Addresses

Windows 7 computers can acquire IP addresses in the following three ways:

- **Manual configuration:** It is possible for administrators to manually assign IP addresses to hosts and configure each computer to use the address assigned to it. However, this method requires much more time and effort than the other alternatives and is prone to error.

- **Dynamic Host Configuration Protocol (DHCP):** DHCP is a client/server application and protocol that enables clients to obtain IP addresses from a pool provided by a server. It then returns the addresses to the pool when the clients no longer need them. Windows 7 includes a DHCP client, which it uses by default. The Windows server products all include a full-featured DHCP server, which you can configure to assign any range of addresses in a variety of ways. Windows 7 also includes a DHCP server, which is incorporated into the ICS feature, but it has only rudimentary capabilities and is not configurable.

- **Automatic Private IP Addressing (APIPA):** When a Windows 7 computer with no IP address starts, and it fails to locate a DHCP server on the network, the TCP/IP client automatically configures itself using an address in the 169.254.0.0/16 network. This enables computers on a small network with no DHCP server to communicate without the need for manual configuration.

DNS NAME RESOLUTION

All TCP/IP communication is based on IP addresses, and in TCP/IP parlance, each network interface in a computer is called a host. In addition to IP addresses, hosts can also have names, and the host names are grouped together in units called domains. When users access a Web site on the Internet, they do so by specifying or selecting a DNS name, which consists of a host name and two or more domain names (such as www.adatum.com), not an IP address. This is because names are far easier to remember and use than IP addresses.

For TCP/IP systems to use these friendly host names, they must have some way to discover the IP address associated with a specific name. This discovery process is called *name resolution*, and the application that resolves names into IP addresses is the Domain Name System (DNS).

DNS is a client/server application that is essentially a distributed database. Information about the names and addresses of Internet computers is distributed among thousands of DNS servers all over the world. Virtually all operating systems have a DNS client, called a resolver, that enables them to send a host name to a DNS server and receive the IP address associated with that name in return.

In its most basic form, the DNS name resolution process consists of a resolver submitting a name resolution request to the DNS server specified in its TCP/IP configuration settings. When the server does not possess information about the requested name, it forwards the request to another DNS server on the network. The second server generates a response containing the IP address of the requested name and returns it to the first server, which relays the information in turn to the resolver. In actual practice, the DNS name resolution process can be considerably more complex, but the basic message exchanges are essentially the same.

IPv6 ADDRESSING

When the IP protocol was first developed, in the late 1970s, the Internet was an experimental network used only by a few hundred engineers and scientists. At that time, the 32-bit address space defined in the IPv4 standard seemed enormous. No one could have foreseen the explosive growth of the Internet that began in the 1990s, and which soon threatened to deplete the existing IP address space.

To address this situation, work began in the 1990s on a new revision of the IP protocol, known as Internet Protocol Version 6, or IPv6. IPv6 expands the address space from 32 to 128 bits, which is large enough to provide more than 6.7×10^{23} addresses for each square meter of the Earth's surface.

Because this address space is so huge, IPv6 supports multiple subnet levels, not just one as in IPv4. Individual hosts can also have multiple IPv6 addresses for various purposes, with little chance of the address space being depleted in the near future. IPv6 supports automatic assignment of addresses, in both stateful and stateless configurations.

IPv6 also simplifies the packet header format by moving some of the IPv4 header information to optional fields. This reduces the size of routing tables and decreases the processing burden on routers throughout the IPv6 universe.

IPv6 Address Format

Unlike IPv4 addresses, which use decimal notation, IPv6 addresses use hexadecimal notation, in the form of eight two-byte values, separated by colons, as follows:

```
XX:XX:XX:XX:XX:XX:XX:XX
```

Each X is a hexadecimal value for one byte, resulting in a total of 16 bytes, or 128 bits. An example of an IPv6 address would be as follows:

```
FDC0:0000:0000:02BD:00FF:BECB:FEF4:961D
```

To simplify the address somewhat, you can remove the leading zeroes, leaving you with the following:

```
FDC0:0:0:02BD:FF:BECB:FEF4:961D
```

> In hexadecimal (or base 16) notation, each digit can have a value from 0 to 9 or A to F, for a total of 16 possible values. Remember, an eight-bit (one-byte) number can have 256 possible values. If each hexadecimal digit can have 16 values, two digits are required to express the 256 possible values for each byte of the address ($16^2 = 256$). This is why some of the two-byte values in the sample IPv6 address require four digits.

To simplify the notation further, you can eliminate the zero blocks from an address and replace them with a double colon, as follows:

```
FDC0::02BD:FF:BECB:FEF4:961D
```

Subnetting IPv6

To identify the network bits of an address, IPv6 uses the same type of notation as CIDR, a prefix followed by a slash, as in the following example:

```
FDC0::02BD/64
```

Subnet prefixes are the only way to identify subnets in IPv6; there are no subnet masks.

Understanding IPv6 Address Types

Much as IPv4 supports unicast, broadcast, and multicast addresses, IPv6 also has three address types:

- **Unicast:** Identifies a single network interface in a computer or other device. Packets addressed to a unicast address are delivered to one node only.
- **Anycast:** Identifies a set of network interfaces. Packets addressed to an anycast address are delivered only to the interface closest to the source (by number of hops).
- **Multicast:** Identifies a group of multiple network interfaces. Packets addressed to a multicast address are delivered to all of the interfaces designated as members of the group. One standard multicast address, known as the "all nodes" multicast group, performs the role of the IPv4 broadcast address, so there is no need for an explicit broadcast address type in IPv6.

IPv6 addresses each have a scope, which defines the area within which the address is unique. The scopes defined in the IPv6 standards are as follows:

- **Node-local:** Limited to an individual interface. This is the equivalent of the loopback address in IPv4.
- **Link-local:** Limited to systems on the directly attached network.
- **Site-local:** Limited to interfaces at a single site. Once intended to be the equivalent of private IPv4 addresses, this scope is now deprecated.
- **Organization-local:** Designed to span multiple sites belonging to an individual organization.
- **Global:** Unique throughout the IPv6 universe.

IPv6 Name Resolution

Name resolution for computers with global IPv6 addresses is provided by the Domain Name System (DNS), just as it is in IPv4. For computers with link-local addresses, which might not have access to a DNS server, the system uses the *Link Local Multicast Name Resolution (LLMNR)* protocol.

To use LLMNR, systems transmit name query request messages as multicasts to the local network. The request contains the name the computer is trying to resolve. The other computers on the local network, on receiving the messages, compare the requested name with their own names. The computer with the requested name then replies with a message containing its IP address, which it transmits as a unicast to the original requestor.

IPv6 Address Autoconfiguration

At the time IPv4 was conceived, there were some data-link layer implementations that required network administrators to manually assign addresses to the network interface hardware for media access control purposes. The designers of IPv4 therefore decided to design an addressing system that was completely independent from the underlying protocol at the data-link layer.

Today, all network interface adapters have factory-assigned hardware addresses, so IPv6 derives its host identifiers from those hardware addresses. There is therefore no need for APIPA or NAT or DHCP host address assignments.

IPv6 address assignment is much more of an automatic process than in IPv4. A technique called *stateless address autoconfiguration* enables computers to configure their own addresses after transmitting router solicitation multicasts to the routers on the network and receiving router advertisement messages in return. For situations where stateless autoconfiguration is not appropriate, Windows 7 workstations can use DHCP for stateful address autoconfiguration instead.

IPv6 Transition

More than ten years after the initial publication of the IPv6 standard, and despite its almost universal operating system and router support, the vast majority of the systems on the Internet still rely on IPv4. However, the inclusion of IPv6 support in Windows 7 and Windows Server 2008 R2 makes the operating systems ready for the transition when it occurs. Windows 7, by default, installs support for both IPv4 and IPv6 addressing when it detects a network interface adapter in the computer, as shown in Figure 5-3. Microsoft refers to this as Windows 7's *dual IP stack*.

Figure 5-3

Windows 7 support for IPv4 and IPv6

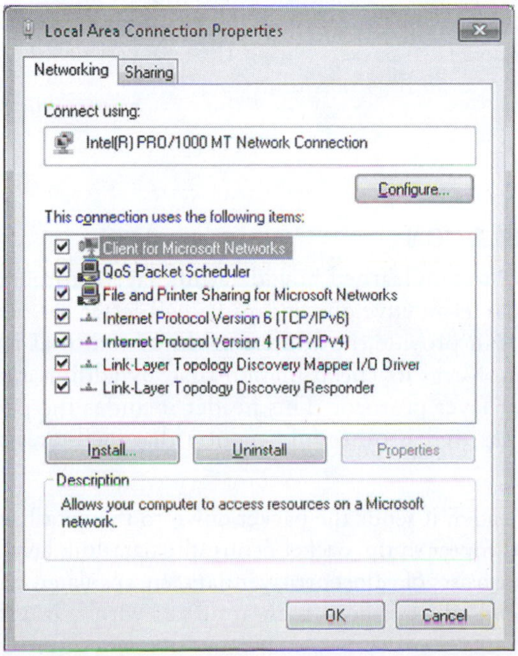

In addition, the DHCP server application in Windows Server 2008 R2 supports both addressing standards, so when a Windows 7 computer requests an IP address, the DHCP server supplies both IPv4 and IPv6 information. Windows 7 applications that are capable of using IPv6 do so by default; otherwise, applications revert to IPv4.

As the transition from IPv4 to IPv6 proceeds, there are times when it is necessary for computers running IPv6-only applications to exchange messages over an IPv4-only network. Windows 7 (and Windows Server 2008 R2) supports a number of transition mechanisms that make this possible, including the following:

- **IPv4-compatible addresses:** A hybrid IPv6/IPv4 address that enables an IPv6 system to communicate using an IPv4 infrastructure. The address format consists of 96 bits of zeroes, followed by an IPv4 address in its standard dotted decimal notation, as in the following example:
  ::192.168.1.99.

- **IPv4-mapped addresses:** A hybrid IPv6/IPv4 address that enables an IPv6 system to recognize an IPv4-only system. The address format consists of 80 bits of zeroes, followed by 16 bits of ones, followed by an IPv4 address in its standard dotted decimal notation, as in the following example:
  ::ffff:192.168.1.99.

- **6to4:** A tunneling technology that enables computers to transmit IPv6 packets over an IPv4 network. The 6to4 address that an IPv6 system uses when connecting to the IPv6 Internet through an intermediate IPv4 network takes the following format: 2002:<first 156 bits of the IPv4 address>:<second 16 bits of the IPv4 address>::/16. For example, the IPv4 address 192.168.1.99 would appear as follows:
  2002:C0A8:0163::/16.

- **Teredo:** A tunneling protocol that enables computers to transmit IPv6 packets through NAT routers that do not support IPv6. A Teredo address consists of a 32-bit prefix: 2001:0000, followed by the IPv4 address of the Teredo server, 16 flag bits, and the UDP port number and public IPv4 address of the NAT router. These last 48 bits are obfuscated by reversing their bit values.

TAKE NOTE*

Tunneling is a networking technique that enables systems to encapsulate packets within other packets, for security or compatibility purposes. In the case of 6to4, for example, a computer encapsulates IPv6 packets within IPv4 packets using UDP, so that the system can transmit them over an IPv4 network.

DATA ENCAPSULATION

Earlier in this lesson, you learned how data-link layer protocols encapsulate data for transmission, much as an envelope encapsulates a letter for mailing. IP encapsulates data as well, so that it can provide the address of the system that is the packet's final destination. In fact, IP performs its encapsulation first, by adding a header to the data it receives from the transport layer protocol. This header includes the packet's source and destination IP addresses, as well as other information that facilitates the transmission of the packet.

After IP adds its header, it sends the packet down to the data-link layer, where Ethernet adds its own header and footer to the packet. Thus, the data-link layer packet that gets transmitted over the network consists of transport layer data, encapsulated within an IP packet, which is called a *datagram*, which is in turn encapsulated within an Ethernet frame, as shown in Figure 5-4.

Figure 5-4

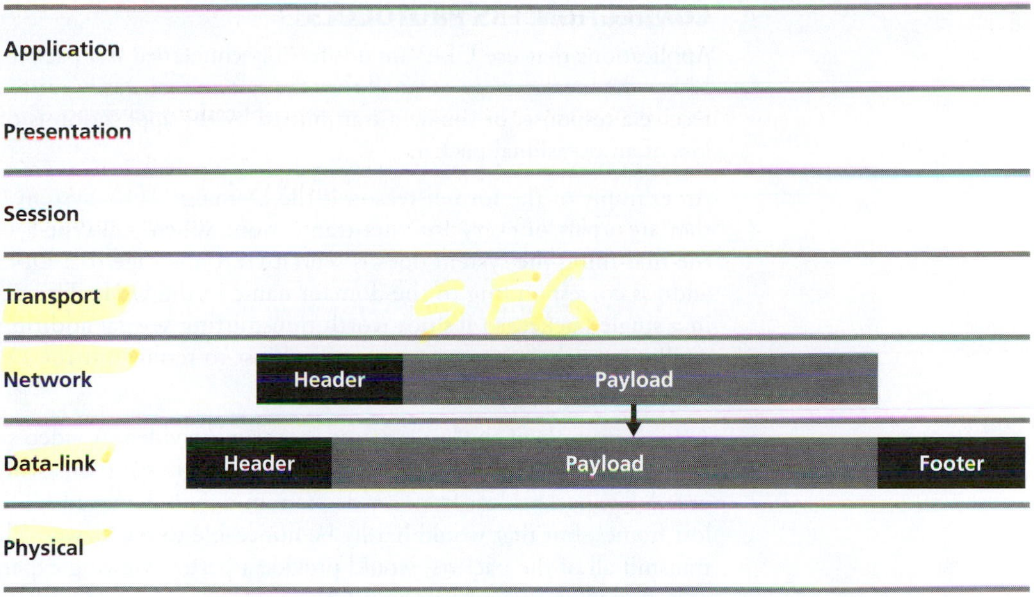

IP data encapsulation

| Application |
| Presentation |
| Session |
| Transport |
| Network |
| Data-link |
| Physical |

(Network layer: Header | Payload)

(Data-link layer: Header | Payload | Footer)

As with Ethernet, one of the functions of the IP header is to identify the protocol that generated the data in the datagram. The Protocol field in the IP header uses codes standardized by the IANA to specify the transport layer protocol that created the packet.

The Transport Layer

The OSI reference model calls for the network and transport layers to provide a flexible quality of service, so that applications can operate at peak efficiency.

There are two types of protocols that operate at the network and transport layers:

- A **connection-oriented protocol** is one in which two communicating systems establish a connection before they transmit any data. Once the connection is established, the computers exchange packets with complex headers designed to provide error detection and correction. A connection-oriented protocol ensures bit-perfect data transmissions, but at the price of greatly increased overhead.

- A **connectionless protocol** does not require the establishment of a connection, nor does it perform error detection or correction. Systems simply transmit their packets to the destination, without knowing if the destination system is ready to accept data, or if it even exists. Connectionless protocols do not guarantee delivery of their data, but they operate with a very low overhead that conserves network bandwidth.

IP, at the network layer, is a connectionless protocol, and there is no connection-oriented alternative at that layer. At the transport layer, TCP is the connection-oriented protocol, and the connectionless alternative is the User Datagram Protocol (UDP).

CONNECTION-ORIENTED PROTOCOLS

Applications that use TCP require every bit of data they transmit to be received properly at the destination. For example, if you download a service pack from the Microsoft Web site, a single garbled bit could render the package useless. Using the combination of TCP and IP guarantees that every packet arrives intact. If a packet is damaged or lost, the system retransmits it. However, to use TCP, the systems must exchange extra packets to establish a connection and append a 20-byte header to each packet. This adds up to a lot of extra data that has to be transmitted over the network.

CONNECTIONLESS PROTOCOLS

Applications that use UDP are not terribly concerned if a packet goes astray for two reasons. Either the messages are so small that the systems can easily retransmit them if they do not receive a response, or the data transmitted by the application is of a type that can tolerate the loss of an occasional packet.

An example of the former reason is the Domain Name System (DNS) communications that are a part of every Internet transaction. When you type a URL into your web browser, the first thing the system does is send a UDP message to a DNS server requesting the IP address corresponding to the domain name in the URL. This is a tiny message that fits in a single packet, so it's not worth transmitting several additional packets to establish a TCP connection. It's more economical just to retransmit the DNS request if no response is forthcoming.

A good example of the latter reason is streaming video. A video stream consists of large amounts of data, but unlike a file transfer, a few missing bits will not cause a catastrophic failure. A few packets lost from a video stream due to damaged UDP packets might mean a few lost frames, but that would hardly be noticeable to the viewer. The alternative, using TCP to transmit all of the packets, would provide a perfect viewing experience for the user, but at the cost of vastly increased bandwidth.

PORTS AND SOCKETS

Just like the network and data-link layers, transport layer protocols encapsulate the data they receive from the layer above by appending a header to each packet, as shown in Figure 5-5. Unlike the lower layers, however, transport layer protocols are not concerned with addressing packets to the correct system. IP and Ethernet performed the addressing, so there is no need for it here. However, transport layer protocols are concerned with identifying the applications that created the packet and to which the packet will ultimately be delivered.

Figure 5-5

Transport layer data encapsulation

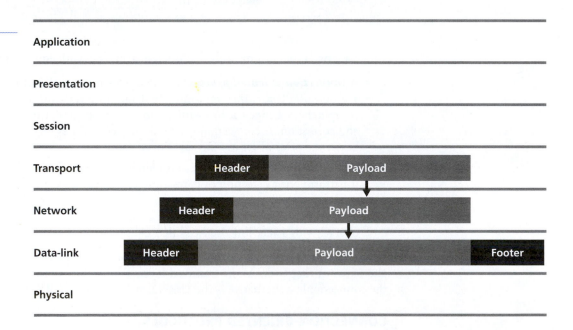

As with the protocol codes included in IP headers, the TCP and UDP headers both contain codes that identify specific applications running on the system. The codes, called *ports*, are again published by the IANA, and the combination of an IP address and a port number is called a *socket*. For example, the standard port number for the Hypertext Transfer Protocol (HTTP), the application layer protocol used for web communications, is 80. If your web browser is sending an HTTP request to a web server with the IP address

192.168.87.33, the web server application on that computer can be identified by the socket 192.168.87.33:80.

There are two basic types of port numbers: *well-known port numbers*, which are numbers permanently assigned to specific applications, and *ephemeral port numbers*, which are created automatically by client applications. In the previous example, the web browser is using the well-known HTTP port 80 as the destination for its packets, but the source port would be an ephemeral port number created by the system running the browser.

This system works because the client is initiating contact with the server. The client has to know the port number to use in its messages to the server, so it uses a well-known port. There is no need for the client to have a well-known port number because the server will be able to discover the client's ephemeral port number from its incoming messages.

Some of the most common well-known port numbers are listed in Table 5-3.

Table 5-3

Well-Known Port Numbers Used by TCP and UDP

SERVICE NAME	PORT NUMBER	PROTOCOL	FUNCTION
ftp-data	20	TCP	FTP data channel; used for transmitting files between systems
ftp	21	TCP	FTP control channel; used by FTP-connected systems for exchanging commands and responses
Ssh	22	TCP and UDP	SSH (Secure Shell) Remote Login Protocol; used to securely log on to a computer from another computer on the same network and execute commands
telnet	23	TCP	Telnet; used to execute commands on network-connected systems
Smtp	25	TCP	Simple Mail Transport Protocol (SMTP); used to send e-mail messages
Domain	53	TCP and UDP	DNS; used to receive host name resolution requests from clients
Bootps	67	TCP and UDP	Bootstrap Protocol (BOOTP) and DHCP servers; used to receive TCP/IP configuration requests from clients
Bootpc	68	TCP and UDP	BOOTP and DHCP clients; used to send TCP/IP configuration requests to servers
http	80	TCP	HTTP; used by web servers to receive requests from client browsers
pop3	110	TCP	Post Office Protocol 3 (POP3); used to retrieve e-mail requests from clients
nntp	119	TCP and UDP	Network News Transfer Protocol; used to post and distribute messages to, and retrieve them from, Usenet servers on the Internet
ntp	123	TCP and UDP	Network Time Protocol; used to exchange time signals for the purpose of synchronizing the clocks in network computers
imap	143	TCP and UDP	Internet Message Access Protocol version 4; used by e-mail client programs to retrieve messages from a mail server
snmp	161	TCP and UDP	Simple Network Management Protocol (SNMP); used by SNMP agents to transmit status information to a network management console
https	443	TCP and UDP	Hypertext Transfer Protocol over TLS/SSL; used by web servers to receive encrypted requests from client browsers

DATA ENCAPSULATION

The headers that the TCP and UDP protocols add to the data they receive from the application layer are vastly different in size and complexity. The headers for both protocols contain source and destination port numbers. The UDP header includes little else, except for a checksum used to check for errors in the header. The TCP header, on the other hand, includes a multitude of fields that implement additional services, including the following:

- **Packet acknowledgment:** Informs the sender which packets have been delivered successfully.
- **Error correction:** Informs the sender which packets must be retransmitted.
- **Flow control:** Regulates the rate at which the sending system transmits its data.

The Upper Layers

The application layer is the top of the networking stack, and as such, it provides the entrance point for programs running on a computer.

TAKE NOTE*

The session and presentation layers typically do not have individual protocols dedicated to them. In most cases, application layer protocols include functions attributed to all three top layers.

Windows applications themselves have no networking capabilities. They simply make function calls to application layer protocols, which in turn initiate the entire network communications process.

For example, a mail client is a program that enables you to send messages to users on other computers, but the mail program knows nothing about the nature of your network. When you send an e-mail message to someone, the client takes the message and the address of the intended recipient and packages it using an application layer protocol called Simple Mail Transfer Protocol (SMTP). SMTP creates a properly formatted e-mail message and passes it down to the proper protocol at the next lower layer in the networking stack, the transport layer, which for this application is TCP.

TCP then adds its header, passes the packet down to IP at the network layer, which encapsulates it and passes it down to Ethernet at the data-link layer, which adds its frame and transmits it over the network. Thus, by the time the e-mail message reaches the network, it has been encapsulated four times by SMTP, TCP, IP, and Ethernet, as shown in Figure 5-6.

Figure 5-6

Application layer data encapsulation

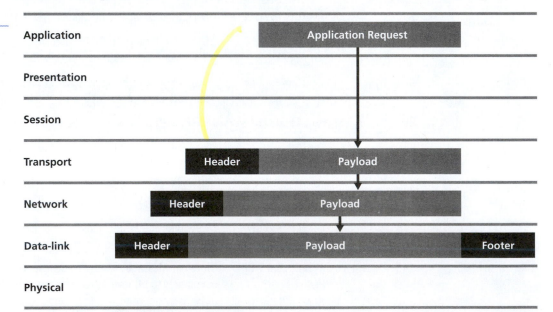

When the packet arrives at its final destination, the networking stack on the receiving computer performs the same steps in reverse. The system passes the incoming packets up through the layers, with each one removing its header and using the header information to pass the contents to the correct protocol at the next higher layer. Finally, the packet arrives at its final terminus, which is an application running on the destination computer, in this case, an e-mail server.

Connecting to a Network

THE BOTTOM LINE

The networking capabilities in Windows 7 have been designed to minimize the threat of intrusion from outside intruders, while providing users with a simple and reliable networking experience. The following sections examine some of the networking tools and concepts in Windows 7.

Networking provides Windows 7 with an open door to a virtually unlimited array of resources, but an open door can let things in as easily as it lets things out. This makes security a primary concern for Windows 7 technical specialists. Windows 7 includes a variety of tools and features that enable users and administrators to manage the operating system's networking capabilities and help protect it against unauthorized access. Many of these features lie "under the hood," and operate invisibly to both users and administrators.

Some of the tools that desktop technicians must use regularly, and the concepts they support, are discussed in the following sections.

Installing Network Support

Windows 7 is usually able to detect a network interface adapter in a computer and automatically install and configure the networking client.

The installation of Windows 7's networking support is usually automatic. When Windows 7 detects a network interface adapter in the computer, either during the operating system installation or afterward, it installs a device driver for the adapter, as well as the components of the default networking stack listed here:

- **Client for Microsoft Networks:** Provides application layer services that enable programs to access shared files and printers on the network.
- **QoS Packet Scheduler:** Enables the network client to prioritize network traffic based on bandwidth availability and changing network conditions.
- **File and Printer Sharing for Microsoft Networks:** Enables the computer to share its files and printers with other users on the network.
- **Internet Protocol Version 6 (TCP/IPv6):** Provides support for the IPv6 network layer protocol, including 128-bit IP addresses.
- **Internet Protocol Version 4 (TCP/IPv4):** Provides support for the IPv4 network layer protocol, including 32-bit IP addresses.
- **Link Layer Topology Discovery Mapper I/O Driver and Link Layer Topology Discovery Responder:** Implement the protocol that enables Windows 7 to compile a map of the computers on the network.

The first time that the computer connects to a network, Windows 7 presents the user with a selection of three network locations. These selections are actually combinations of network discovery and file sharing settings, which determine how much access the workstation user will have to the network and how much access network users will have to the workstation.

These three network location options are as follows:

- **Home:** Indicates that the computer is connected to a private workgroup or HomeGroup network and not directly connected to the Internet. This means that it is safe for the computer to share its files and discover other computers.

TAKE NOTE*

When a Windows 7 computer is set to use the Home, Work, or Public network location, the user can modify the settings manually from the Network and Sharing Center. When the network location is set to Domain, the setting is controlled by domain policy and is not manually configurable. See "Changing the Network Location," later in this lesson for more information.

- **Work:** Indicates that the computer is connected to a small office workgroup network. This means that it is safe for the computer to share its files and discover other computers, but the system cannot create or join a HomeGroup.
- **Public:** Indicates that the computer is connected to a network in a public place, such as an airport or coffee shop "hot spot" for wireless computers, or is connected directly to the Internet without an intervening router. This means that the computer and its shares cannot be seen or accessed from the network, nor can the system create or join a HomeGroup network. In addition, some applications might not be able to access the network.

There is also a fourth option, Domain, which indicates that the computer is connected to an Active Directory Domain Services (AD DS) domain. This option is set automatically when you join the computer to the domain.

Using the Network and Sharing Center

The Network and Sharing Center is a centralized console that provides technical specialists and system administrators with access to most of the major networking tools included with Windows 7.

The Windows 7 Network and Sharing Center provides a central access point for all of the network connections on the computer. Many of the common network configuration and administration tasks that technicians perform on Windows 7 computers start by opening the Network and Sharing Center. As with many Windows tools, there are several ways to open the Network and Sharing Center, two of which are as follows:

- Click Start > Control Panel > Network and Internet > Network and Sharing Center
- Click Start > Search for "Network" > Network and Sharing Center

When the Network and Sharing Center appears, you see a window like the one shown in Figure 5-7.

Figure 5-7

The Network and Sharing Center

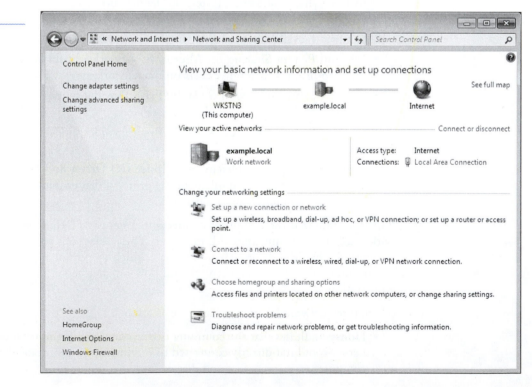

The Network and Sharing Center main window consists of the following elements:

- **Task list (left pane):** Contains links that enable you to manage network adapter settings and configure sharing parameters.
- **Summary network map (top right):** Provides a graphical representation of the computers and networks (represented by icons) in the immediate vicinity of the workstation and their connections (represented by lines). A link also provides access to a complete map of the entire network.
- **View your active networks (middle right):** Displays the name of the network and other information, such as the network location (private, domain, or public), whether the workstation is connected to a local network, the Internet, or both, and the name of the local area connection the system is using to access the network. There are also links that enable you to connect to or disconnect from the network and view the current status of the local area connection.
- **Change your networking settings (bottom right):** Contains switches that enable you to control the sharing and discovery behavior of the network.

UNDERSTANDING NETWORK DISCOVERY

Network Discovery is an important security concept first introduced in Windows Vista. It enables users to control critical network firewall controls with a single switch. Windows Firewall is a feature that was first introduced in the Windows XP Service Pack 2 release, which is now included in Windows 7 as well.

A *firewall* is a software routine that acts as a virtual barrier between a computer and the network to which it is attached. A firewall is essentially a filter that enables certain types of incoming and outgoing traffic to pass through the barrier, while blocking other types.

Firewalls typically base their filtering on the TCP/IP characteristics at the network, transport, and application layers, as follows:

- **IP addresses:** Represent specific computers on the network.
- **Protocol numbers:** Identify the transport layer protocol being used by the packets.
- **Port numbers:** Identify specific applications running on the computer.

If, for example, you want to prevent all computers on the network from accessing your system using the Telnet protocol, you would configure the firewall to block the traffic from all IP addresses using TCP port number 23, the well-known port number associated with Telnet.

Configuring a firewall manually can be an extremely complex task, however. You must be conscious of all the protocols and port numbers used by specific operating system functions and applications. Network Discovery is a Windows 7 feature that simplifies the task of firewall configuration by enabling you to block or allow the protocols and ports needed for the computer to browse and access the network.

Modifying the Network Discovery setting in the Network and Sharing Center controls two functions:

- Whether the computer can see and be seen by the other systems on the network.
- Whether the computer can share its resources and access shared resources on the network.

It is critical to understand that this setting works in both directions. When a Windows 7 computer has Network Discovery turned off, it cannot browse the other computers on the network or access their shares. At the same time, the other computers on the network cannot browse to the Windows 7 computer or access its shares.

The default state of the Network Discovery setting is dependent on the network location, as set manually by the user or automatically by the computer. Computers configured with the Home and Work locations have Network Discovery turned on, and Public computers have it turned off.

TAKE NOTE*

Public is also the default location Windows 7 uses when it cannot detect the network type, because the operating system would prefer to err on the side of caution.

CHANGING THE NETWORK LOCATION

After you select the initial network location during the network interface adapter installation, Windows 7 attempts to detect the type of location whenever you connect to a different network. If, for example, you selected Home when you installed Windows 7 on your laptop computer, and you later take the computer to a coffee shop with a wireless network, Windows 7 will most likely detect the change and alter the network location to Public. This turns the Network Discovery and file sharing options off for greater security.

If, for any reason, the computer fails to detect a network change and you want to manually alter the location setting, you can do so by performing the following procedure.

⊙ CHANGE THE NETWORK LOCATION

GET READY. Log on to Windows 7 using an account with administrative capabilities.

1. Open the Network and Sharing Center. The Network and Sharing Center window appears.
2. In the View your active networks section, click the current network location. The *Set Network Location* page appears, as shown in Figure 5-8.

Figure 5-8

The Set Network Location page

Set Network Location

Select a location for the 'example.local' network

This computer is connected to a network. Windows will automatically apply the correct network settings based on the network's location.

Home network
If all the computers on this network are at your home, and you recognize them, this is a trusted home network. Don't choose this for public places such as coffee shops or airports.

Work network
If all the computers on this network are at your workplace, and you recognize them, this is a trusted work network. Don't choose this for public places such as coffee shops or airports.

Public network
If you don't recognize all the computers on the network (for example, you're in a coffee shop or airport, or you have mobile broadband), this is a public network and is not trusted.

☐ Treat all future networks that I connect to as public, and don't ask me again.
Help me choose

Cancel

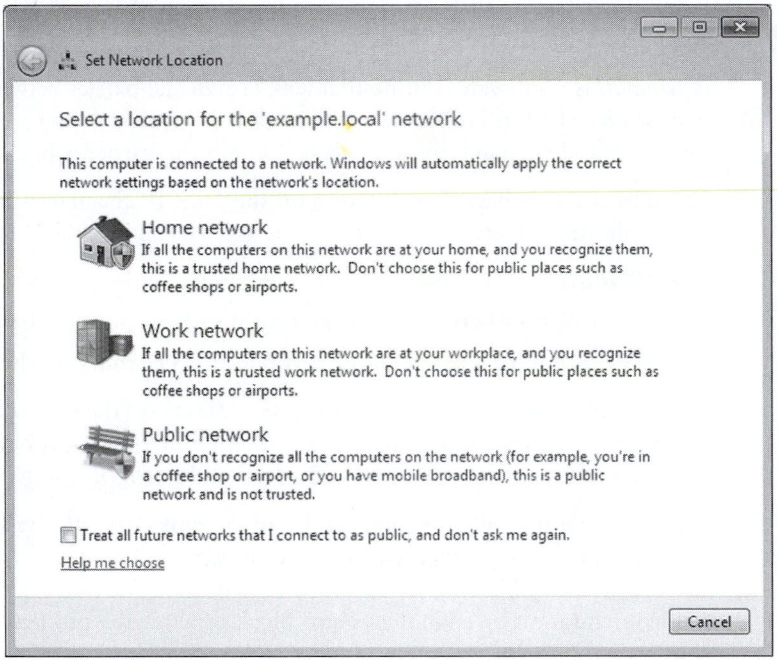

3. Select one of the following network locations. The system connects to the network, reconfigures the Network Discovery settings, and a screen appears, specifying the new network location:
   • Home network
   • Work network
   • Public network
4. Click Close.
5. Close the Network and Sharing Center window.

X REF

For more information on HomeGroup networking, see Lesson 9, "Working with Domains, Workgroups, and HomeGroups."

When you select the Home network location for the first time, the system creates a new HomeGroup network and supplies you with a password for it.

CONFIGURING ADVANCED SHARING SETTINGS

When you are using the Home, Work, or Public network location setting, you can manually change the Network Discovery and other sharing settings by using the following procedure.

→ CONFIGURE ADVANCED SHARING

GET READY. Log on to Windows 7 using an account with administrative capabilities.

1. Open the Network and Sharing Center. The Network and Sharing Center window appears.

2. In the left pane, click Change advanced sharing settings. The Change sharing options for different network profiles dialog box appears.

3. Click the down arrow for the location whose settings you want to modify, to produce the display shown in Figure 5-9.

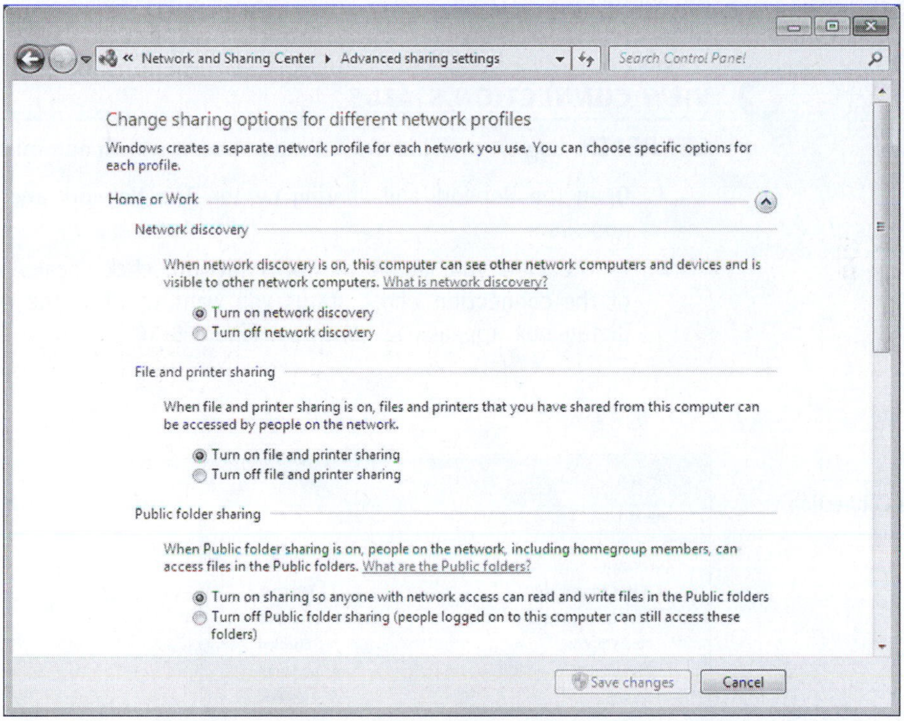

Figure 5-9

The Change sharing options for different network profiles dialog box

4. Configure the following settings by selecting one of the options provided:

   - **Network Discovery:** Enables the computer to see other devices on the network and renders it visible from the network.

   - **File and printer sharing:** Enables network users to access the files and printers shared on the computer.

   - **Public folder sharing:** Enables network users to access the Public folders on the computer.

   - **Media streaming:** Enables network users to access media files on the computer and enables the computer to locate media files on the network.

   - **File sharing connections:** Specifies whether clients accessing the computer's shares must use 128-bit encryption.

   - **Password-protected sharing:** Specifies whether network users accessing the computer's shares must have local user accounts with passwords.

   - **HomeGroup connections:** Specifies whether Windows 7 should manage HomeGroup connections automatically.

5. Click Save Changes. The Network and Sharing Center window reappears.

Managing Network Connections

Windows 7 creates and configures local area connections automatically, but you can also manage and modify the properties of the connections manually.

CERTIFICATION READY?
Configure Networking Settings.
4.3

When Windows 7 detects a network interface adapter, it creates a network connection automatically, installs the TCP/IP networking components, and configures it to use DHCP to obtain IP addresses and other network configuration settings. To view and modify the local area connection properties, use the procedures in the following sections.

VIEWING A CONNECTION'S STATUS

Each local area connection on a Windows 7 system has a status dialog box that displays real-time information about the connection. To view the status of a connection, use the following procedure.

VIEW CONNECTION STATUS

GET READY. Log on to Windows 7 using an account with administrative capabilities.

1. Open the Network and Sharing Center. The Network and Sharing Center window appears.
2. In the View your active networks section, click Local Area Connection or the name of the connection whose status you want to view. The Local Area Connection Status dialog box appears, as shown in Figure 5-10.

Figure 5-10
The Local Area Connection Status dialog box

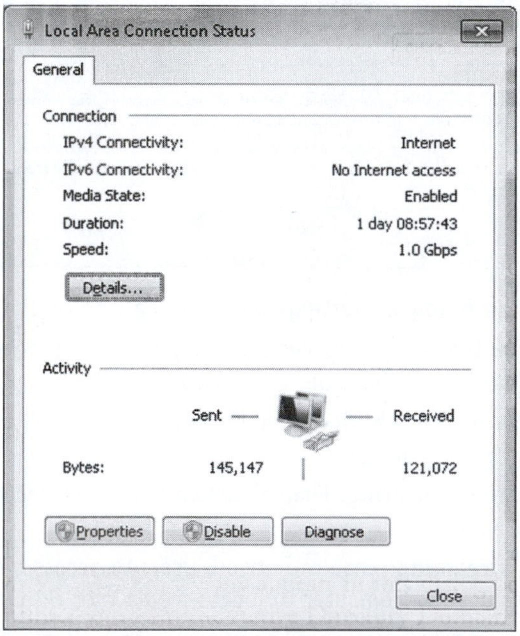

3. Click Details. The Network Connection Details dialog box appears, as shown in Figure 5-11.
4. Click Close to close the Network Connection Details dialog box.
5. Click Close to close the Local Area Connection Status dialog box.

Figure 5-11

The Network Connection
Details dialog box

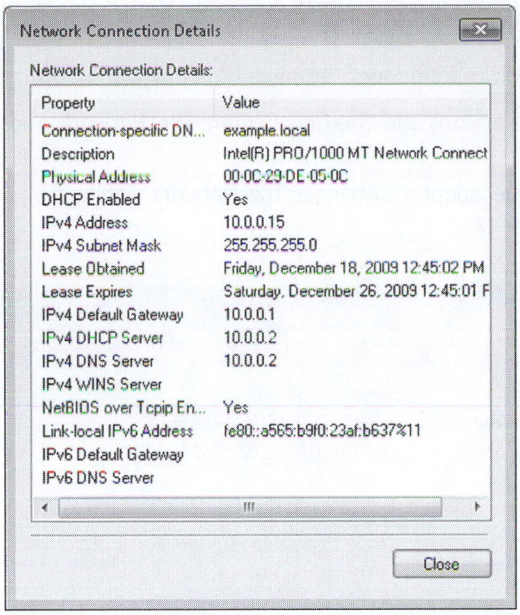

The Local Area Connection Status dialog box displays basic information about the connection, such as its speed, which version(s) of IP it is using, and how long the computer has been connected. In the Activity area, you can see the number of bytes that the computer has sent and received in a real-time display, so you can tell if the network connection is currently functional.

At the bottom of the dialog box are buttons that enable you to perform the following tasks:

- **Properties:** Open the Properties sheet for the network connection.
- **Disable/Enable:** Toggle the operational status of the network connection.
- **Diagnose:** Start Windows Network Diagnostics and attempt to detect any problems affecting the network connection.

TAKE NOTE Disabling a network connection does not affect its configuration settings in any way. The networking hardware is still installed and configured and the TCP/IP settings remain intact. The connection is simply turned off until you turn it back on again, which renders it immediately operational.

The Network Connection Details page displays the configuration settings for the network connection, including the TCP/IP settings obtained using DHCP.

CONFIGURING IPv4 SETTINGS

Most networks today use DHCP to configure the TCP/IP configuration settings of their workstations. DHCP automates the configuration process and prevents the duplication of IP addresses. However, there are still some situations in which it is desirable or necessary to configure the Windows 7 TCP/IP client manually. To do this, use the following procedure.

CERTIFICATION READY?
Configure IPv4 network settings.
4.1

CONFIGURE IPv4 SETTINGS

GET READY. Log on to Windows 7 using an account with administrative capabilities.

1. Open the Network and Sharing Center. The Network and Sharing Center window appears.
2. Click Change adapter settings. The Network Connections window appears, as shown in Figure 5-12.

Figure 5-12

The Network Connections window

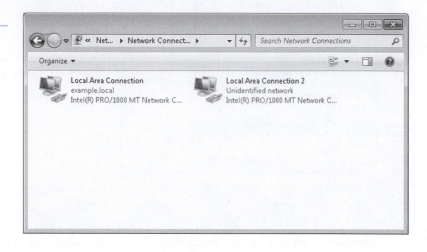

3. Right click the connection you want to manage and, from the context menu, select Properties. The connection's Properties sheet appears.

TAKE NOTE*

You can click the Configure button on the connection's Properties sheet to open the Properties sheet for the network interface adapter hardware. From this sheet, you can configure advanced networking settings, as well as the adapter's hardware resource settings.

4. Select Internet Protocol Version 4 (TCP/IPv4) and click Properties. The Internet Protocol Version 4 (TCP/IPv4) Properties sheet appears, as shown in Figure 5-13.

Figure 5-13

The Internet Protocol Version 4 (TCP/IPv4) Properties sheet

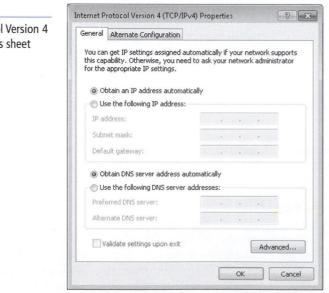

5. Select the Use The Following IP Address option and enter appropriate values for the following parameters:

- **IP address:** A 32-bit IPv4 address, in dotted decimal notation.
- **Subnet Mask:** An appropriate mask indicating which part of the IP address is the network identifier and which part the host identifier.
- **Default Gateway:** The IP address of the router on the local network that the computer should use to access other networks and/or the Internet.

6. Select the Use The Following DNS Server Addresses option and enter appropriate values for the following parameters:

- **Preferred DNS Server:** The IP address of the DNS server the computer should use to resolve host and domain names into IP addresses.
- **Alternate DNS Server:** The IP address of a DNS server that the computer should use if the preferred DNS server is unavailable.

> ➕ **MORE INFORMATION**
>
> Clicking the Advanced button opens the Advanced TCP/IP Settings dialog box, in which you can configure multiple IP addresses, subnet masks, default gateways, DNS servers, and WINS servers for client computers with special requirements.

7. Click OK to close the Internet Protocol Version 4 (TCP/IPv4) Properties sheet.
8. Click OK to close the connection's Properties sheet.

The command-line alternative to this graphical interface is a program called Netsh.exe. Netsh.exe is a powerful tool that you can use interactively or with command-line parameters to configure virtually any Windows 7 networking setting. To configure the basic IPv4 parameters for a network connection, you use the following syntax:

```
netsh interface ipv4 set address connection_name static ip_address
subnet_mask default_gateway
```

An example of an actual command would be as follows:

```
netsh interface ipv4 set address "Local Area Connection" static
192.168.1.23 255.255.255.0 192.168.1.1
```

Then, to configure the DNS server address, you would use the following command syntax:

```
netsh interface ipv4 set dnsservers connection_name static ip_address
```

An example of an actual command would be as follows:

```
netsh interface ipv4 set dnsservers "Local Area Connection" static
192.168.1.99
```

To configure a connection to obtain its settings from a DHCP server, use the following commands:

```
netsh interface ipv4 set address name="Local Area Connection"
source=dhcp
```

```
netsh interface ipv4 set dnsservers name="Local Area Connection"
source=dhcp
```

CONFIGURING IPv6 SETTINGS

Because most computers use IPv6 autoconfiguration or DHCP, manual configuration of the Windows 7 IPv6 implementation is rarely necessary, but it is possible.

The procedure for configuring IPv6 using the graphical interface is the same as that for IPv4, except that, in the Local Area Connection Properties sheet, you select Internet Protocol

CERTIFICATION READY?
Configure IPv6 network settings.
4.2

Version 6 (TCP/IPv6) and click Properties. The Internet Protocol Version 6 (TCP/IPv6) Properties sheet appears, as shown in Figure 5-14.

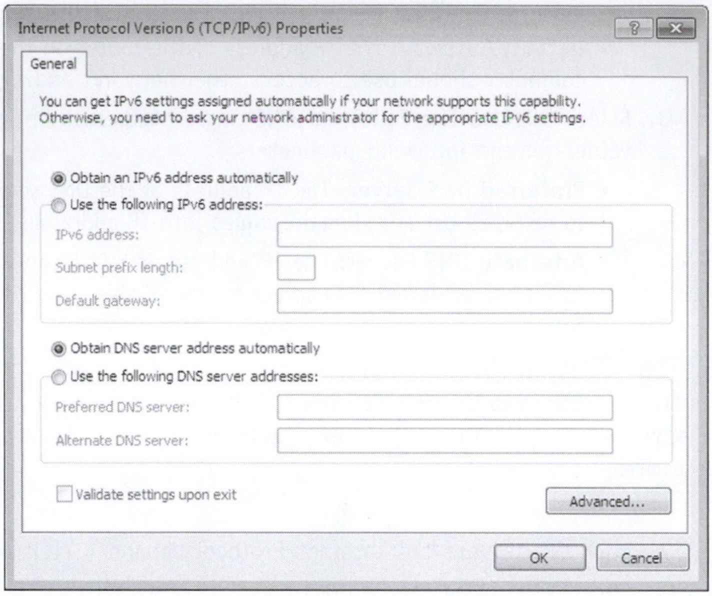

Figure 5-14

The Internet Protocol Version 6 (TCP/IPv6) Properties sheet

To configure IPv6 from the command prompt, you use Netsh.exe in the same way you would for IPv4, substituting the IPv6 parameter for IPv4 and an IPv6 address for the IPv4 address and subnet mask, as in the following example:

```
netsh interface ipv6 set address "Local Area Connection" static
FE80::7166:22E6:1D18:BDAA
```

To configure DNS server addresses, use a command like this:

```
netsh interface ipv6 set dnsservers "Local Area Connection" static
FE80::7166:22E6:1D18:BD01
```

CREATING A NEW NETWORK CONNECTION

Windows 7 creates local area network connections automatically, but desktop technicians frequently have to create other types of connections manually, such as dial-up Internet connections. To do this, use the following procedure.

CREATE A NEW NETWORK CONNECTION

GET READY. Log on to Windows 7 using an account with administrative capabilities. If Windows 7 has not detected and installed your modem, you must install it yourself using the Add New Hardware Wizard, accessible from the Device Manager snap-in.

1. Open the Network and Sharing Center. The Network and Sharing Center window appears.
2. Click Set up a new connection or network. The Setup a Connection or Network Wizard appears, displaying the *Choose a connection option* page, as shown in Figure 5-15.

Figure 5-15

The Choose a connection
option page

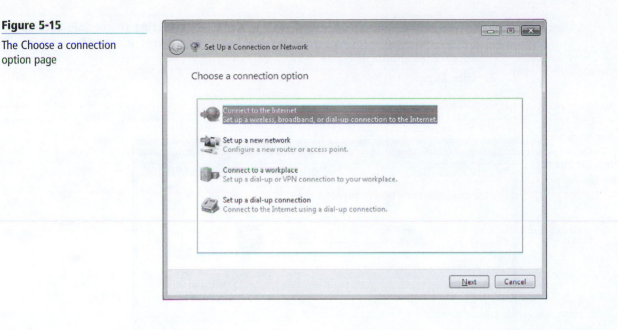

3. Click Set up a dial-up connection and then click Next. The *Type the information from your Internet service provider (ISP)* page appears, as shown in Figure 5-16.

Figure 5-16

The Type the information from
your Internet service provider
(ISP) page appears

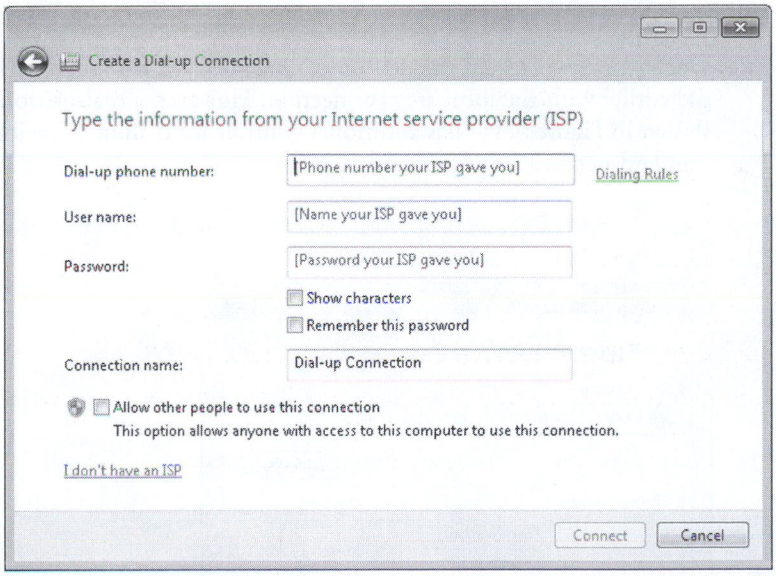

4. Enter the Dial-up phone number, User name, and Password supplied by your ISP. Click the Remember this password check box if you want to avoid typing the password each time you connect to the ISP.

5. Click Connect. The system activates the modem, dials the number you supplied, and attempts to connect to the ISP. If the attempt succeeds, the connection is established and communication with the ISP commences. If the connection attempt does not succeed, a *The Internet Connectivity Test Was Unsuccessful* page appears.

6. To create the dial-up connection without actually connecting to the ISP, click set up the connection anyway. A *The connection to the Internet is ready to use* page appears, as shown in Figure 5-17.

7. Click Close.

Figure 5-17

The Connection to the Internet is ready to use page

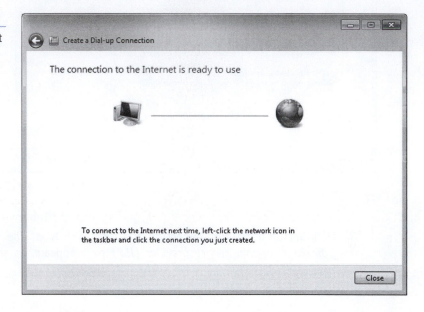

Once you have created the dial-up connection, you can open its Properties sheet, just as you did earlier with the local area connection. However, a dial-up connection's Properties sheet, as shown in Figure 5-18, has additional controls for dialing behavior and sharing, as well as the standard network configuration controls.

Figure 5-18

A dial-up connection's Properties sheet

Using Network Map

Network Map is an administration and diagnostics tool that displays a graphical map of the computers on the network and the connections between them.

Network Map is a tool that first appeared in Windows Vista, and is now included in all of the Windows operating systems. Network Map automatically compiles a graphical representation of the network, including icons representing the computers, printers, and other devices attached to it, and lines representing the connections between these elements.

Network Map uses a protocol called Link-Layer Topology Discovery (LLTD) to discover information about the network and the devices attached to it. LLTD devices called *enumerators* transmit requests for information over the network; and other computers, called *responders*, reply with the requested information. This protocol not only enables the computer to discover the existence of other systems on the network, it also tests the connections between them.

DISPLAYING A NETWORK MAP

The Network and Sharing Center displays a summary map on its main window, but to display a complete map of the network, you must click the See full map link, to open the window shown in Figure 5-19. For Windows 7 to display a full map of the network, the following conditions must be met:

- Network Discovery must be turned on.
- If the computer is a member of a Windows domain, group policy must be configured to permit network mapping.
- Any Windows XP computers on the network must have the LLTD Responder software installed.

Figure 5-19

The Network Map page

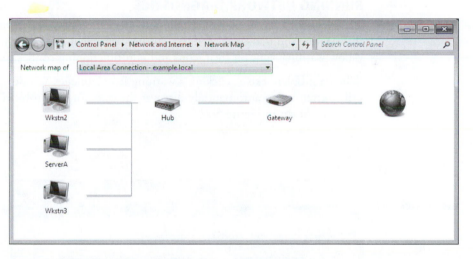

From a security standpoint, it is not a good idea to allow just anyone to access a map of your network. As a result, when a Windows 7 computer is a member of a Windows domain, network mapping is disabled by the default group policy settings. To control network mapping with group policy, you must use the Group Policy Management Console to open an appropriate group policy object (GPO) and navigate to the Computer Configuration > Administrative Templates > Network > Link-Layer Topology Discovery container. There, you will find the following two policies:

- **Turn on Mapper I/O (LLTDIO) driver:** Enables a computer to map other systems on the network.
- **Turn on Responder (RSPNDR) driver:** Enables a computer to be mapped by other systems on the network.

Enabling these policies, as shown in Figure 5-20, allows you to control whether mapping can occur on domain, public, and private networks.

Figure 5-20

Controlling Network Map with Group Policy

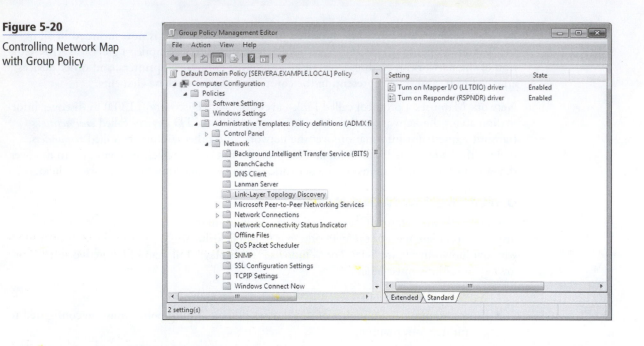

RUNNING NETWORK DIAGNOSTICS

The Network Map display shows not only the existence of the devices on the network, but their status, and that of the connections between them. Improperly configured computers have yellow warning signs on their icons and non-functioning connections have red Xs on them.

When a problem exists, clicking a warning icon launches Windows Network diagnostics. This utility attempts to automatically discover the cause of the problem and displays possible solutions, as shown in Figure 5-21.

Figure 5-21

Running Windows Network Diagnostics

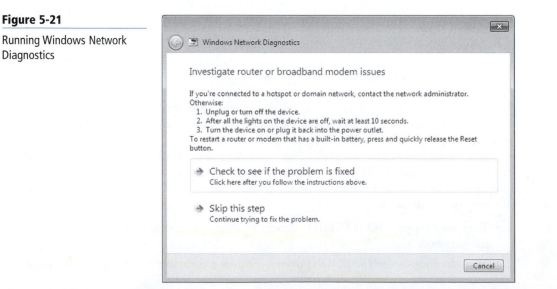

You can also launch Windows Network Diagnostics by opening the Network Connections window, right clicking one of the network connections, and selecting Diagnose from the context menu.

Unlike previous troubleshooting tools, Network Diagnostics does not just display error messages, it tells you in clear language what might be wrong and what you have to do to repair the problem. The Network Diagnostics Framework (NDF) includes troubleshooting routines for wireless as well as wired networks. Problems that the system can diagnose include:

- Broken or detached cable connections
- IP address and subnet mask problems
- Default gateway problems
- DNS and DHCP configuration problems
- Networking hardware configuration problems
- Internet server addresses and service settings

If, after identifying a networking problem, the system can repair it automatically, it provides a link that you can select to have it do so. Otherwise, it displays a list of manual fixes that you can perform to address the problem.

Using TCP/IP Tools

Virtually all network operating systems today include support for TCP/IP protocols, and TCP/IP traditionally includes some basic tools that you can use to troubleshoot network connectivity problems yourself.

The traditional TCP/IP troubleshooting tools originated on UNIX systems, and as a result, they are command-line tools that you run in Windows 7 by opening a Command Prompt window first. The Windows implementations of these utilities generally use the same syntax that they did on UNIX.

This section examines some of the most common TCP/IP utilities and their purposes.

USING IPCONFIG.EXE

UNIX and Linux systems have a program called ifconfig (the name is derived from the words *interface configuration*) that you use to manually configure the properties of network interface adapters, including TCP/IP configuration parameters such as IP addresses. Running ifconfig on a UNIX system with just the name of an interface displays the current configuration information for that interface.

All Windows operating systems, including Windows 7, have a graphical interface for configuring network connections, but the configuration display capabilities of ifconfig have been retained in a command-line tool called Ipconfig.exe.

When you run Ipconfig.exe with the /all parameter at the Windows 7 command prompt, you see a display like the one shown in Figure 5-22.

Figure 5-22

The Ipconfig.exe display

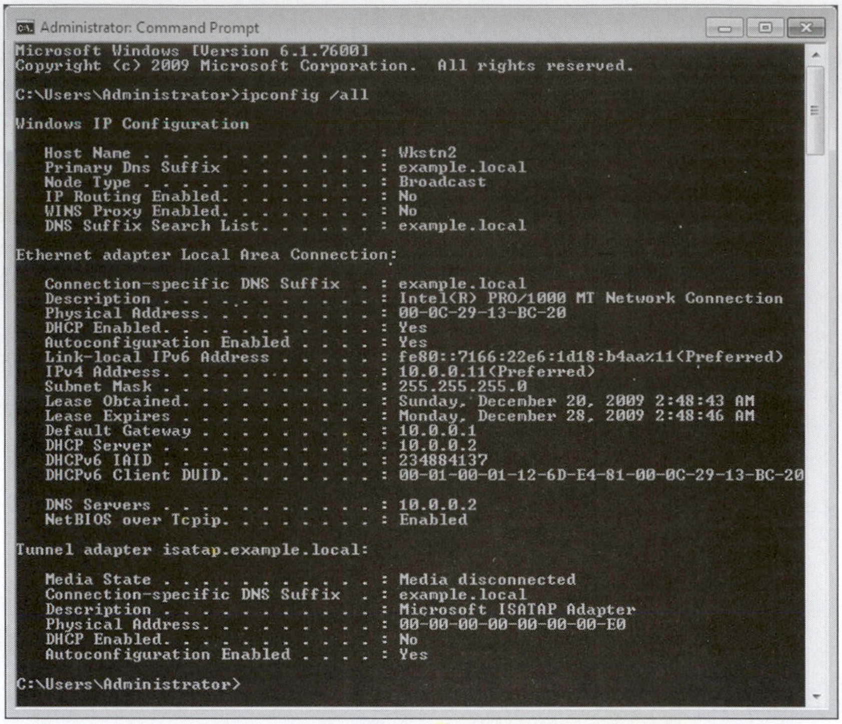

The value of Ipconfig.exe is particularly apparent when a Windows 7 computer autoconfigures its TCP/IP client or uses DHCP to obtain its IP address and other TCP/IP configuration parameters. A DHCP-configured computer does not display any configuration information in the Local Area Connection Properties sheet; it just shows that the DHCP client is activated. One of the few ways to see what settings the DHCP server has assigned to the computer (without examining the DHCP server itself) is to use Ipconfig.exe.

In addition to displaying the DHCP-obtained configuration settings, Ipconfig.exe also enables you to manually release the IP address the system obtained from the DHCP server and renew existing address leases. By running Ipconfig.exe with the `/release` and `/renew` command-line parameters, you can release or renew the IP address assignment of one of the network interfaces in the computer or for all of the interfaces at once.

USING PING.EXE

Ping (Ping.exe) is the most basic of TCP/IP utilities, and it is included in some form with every TCP/IP implementation. On Windows 7 systems, the program is called Ping.exe.

Ping.exe can tell you if the TCP/IP stack of another system on the network is functioning normally. The Ping.exe program generates a series of Echo Request messages using the Internet Control Message Protocol (ICMP) and transmits them to the computer whose name or IP address you specify on the command line. The basic syntax of the Ping program is as follows:

`ping target`

The *target* variable contains the IPv4 or IPv6 address or name of any computer on the network. Because Ping.exe is a TCP/IP utility, the target computer can be running any operating system, not just Windows. You can use DNS host and domain names or Windows NetBIOS names in Ping commands. Ping resolves the name into an IP address before sending the Echo Request messages, and it then displays the address in its output.

TCP/IP computers respond to any Echo Request messages they receive that are addressed to them by generating Echo Reply messages and transmitting them back to the sender. When the pinging computer receives the Echo Reply messages, it produces a display like the one shown in Figure 5-23.

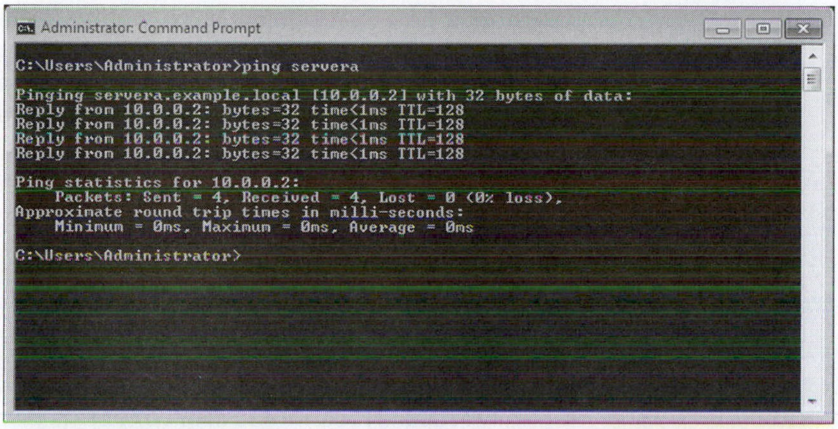

Figure 5-23

The Ping.exe display

In Windows 7's Ping.exe implementation, the display shows the IP address of the computer receiving the Echo Requests, the number of bytes of data included with each request, the elapsed time between the transmission of each request and the receipt of each reply, and the value of the Time To Live (TTL) field in the IP header.

In this example, the target computer was on the same local area network (LAN), so the time measurement is very short—less than 1 millisecond. When pinging a computer on the Internet, the interval is likely to be longer. A successful Ping result like this one indicates that the target computer's networking hardware is functioning properly, as are its TCP/IP protocols, at least as high as the network layer of the OSI model. If a Ping test fails, there might be a firewall blocking the ICMP traffic between the two systems. If there is no firewall, then the Ping test failure indicates that there is a problem in one or both of the computers or in the network medium connecting them.

Ping.exe also has a series of command-line switches that you can use to modify the operational parameters of the program, such as the number of Echo Request messages it generates and the amount of data in each message. To display the syntax of the program, type *ping /?* At the command prompt.

USING TRACERT.EXE

Traceroute is another UNIX program that was designed to display the path that TCP/IP packets take to their final destination. Called traceroute in UNIX, in Windows 7 it is implemented as Tracert.exe. Because of the nature of IP routing, the path from a packet's source to its destination on another network can change from minute to minute, especially on the Internet. Tracert.exe displays a list of the routers that are currently forwarding packets to a particular destination.

Tracert.exe is a variation on Ping.exe. The program uses ICMP Echo Request and Echo Reply messages just like Ping, but it modifies the messages by changing the value of the TTL field in the IP header. The values in the TTL field prevent packets from getting caught in router loops that keep them circulating endlessly around the network. On a Windows 7 computer, the default value for the TTL field is relatively high, 128. Each time a packet passes from one network to another, the router connecting the networks reduces the TTL value by one. If the TTL value ever reaches zero, the router processing the packet discards it and transmits an ICMP error message back to the original sender.

Tracert.exe works by modifying the TTL values in the successive Ping.exe packets that it transmits to a target computer. When you run Tracert.exe from the command prompt with a *target* parameter, the program generates its first set of Echo Request messages with TTL values of 1. When the messages arrive at the first router on their path to the destination, the router decrements the TTL values to 0, discards the packets, and reports the errors to the sender. The error messages contain the router's address, which Tracert.exe displays as the first hop in the path to the destination.

Tracert.exe's second set of Echo Request messages use a TTL value of 2, causing the second router on the path to discard the packets and generate error messages. The Echo Request messages in the third set have a TTL value of 3, and so on. Each set of packets travels one hop farther than the previous set before causing a router to return error messages to the source. The list of routers displayed by the program as the path to the destination is the result of these error messages.

The following is an example of a Tracert.exe display:

```
Tracing route to www.fineartschool.co.uk [173.146.1.1] over a maximum of 30 hops:
1    <10  ms  1    ms  <10  ms   192.168.2.99
2    105  ms  92   ms  98   ms   qrvl-67terminal01.cpandl.com [131.107.24.67.3]
3    101  ms  110  ms  98   ms   qrvl.cpandl.com [131.107.67.1]
4    123  ms  109  ms  118  ms   svcr03-7b.cpandl.com [131.107.103.125]
5    123  ms  112  ms  114  ms   clsm02-2.cpandl.com [131.107.88.26]
6    136  ms  130  ms  133  ms   sl-gw19-pen-6-1-0-T3.fabrikam.com [157.54.116.5]
7    143  ms  126  ms  138  ms   sl-bb10-pen-4-3.fabrikam.com [157.54.5.117]
8    146  ms  129  ms  133  ms   sl-bb20-pen-12-0.fabrikam.com [157.54.5.1]
9    131  ms  128  ms  139  ms   sl-bb20-nyc-13-0.fabrikam.com [157.54.18.38]
10   130  ms  134  ms  134  ms   sl-gw9-nyc-8-0.fabrikam.com [157.54.7.94]
11   147  ms  149  ms  152  ms   sl-demon-1-0.fabrikam.com [157.54.173.10]
12   154  ms  146  ms  145  ms   ny2-backbone-1-ge021.router.fabrikam.com [157.54.173.121]
13   230  ms  225  ms  226  ms   tele-backbone-1-ge023.router.adatum.co.uk [157.60.173.12]
14   233  ms  220  ms  226  ms   tele-core-3-fxp1.router.adatum.co.uk [157.60.252.56]
15   223  ms  224  ms  224  ms   tele-access-1-14.router.adatum.co.uk [157.60.254.245]
16   236  ms  221  ms  226  ms   tele-service-2-165.router.adatum.co.uk [157.60.36.149]
17   220  ms  224  ms  210  ms   www.fineartschool.co.uk [206.73.118.65]

Trace complete.
```

In this example, Tracert.exe displays the path between a computer in Pennsylvania and one in the United Kingdom. Each of the hops contains the elapsed times between the transmission and reception of three sets of Echo Request and Echo Reply packets. In this trace, you can clearly see the point at which the packets begin traveling across the Atlantic Ocean. At hop 13, the elapsed times increase from approximately 150 to 230 milliseconds (ms) and stay in that range for the subsequent hops. This additional delay of only 80 ms is the time it takes the packets to travel the thousands of miles across the Atlantic Ocean.

Ping.exe simply tells you whether two TCP/IP systems are having trouble communicating. It can't pinpoint the location of the problem. A failure to contact a remote computer could be due to a problem in your workstation, in the remote computer, or in any of the routers in between. Tracert.exe can tell you how far your packets are going before they run into the problem.

TAKE NOTE*

Because the configuration of the Internet is constantly changing, there is no guarantee that the route displayed by Tracert.exe is completely accurate. The ICMP messages that execute each step of the Tracert.exe process could conceivably be taking different routes to the same destination, resulting in the display of a composite route between two points that does not actually exist. There is also no way of knowing what path the packets are taking as they return to the source. In addition, routers typically deprioritize ICMP processing in favor of packet forwarding and other more critical router tasks. When a router is busy, it might delay the processing of an Echo Request or Echo Reply packet. The resulting latency numbers will be higher than the delay experienced by actual data packets crossing the network.

USING NSLOOKUP.EXE

The Nslookup.exe command-line utility enables you to generate DNS request messages and transmit them to specific DNS servers on the network. The advantage of Nslookup.exe is that you can test the functionality and the quality of the information on a specific DNS server by specifying it on the command line.

The basic command-line syntax of Nslookup.exe is as follows:

nslookup *DNSname DNSserver*

- *DNSname:* Specifies the DNS name that you want to resolve.
- *DNSserver:* Specifies the DNS name or IP address of the DNS server that you want to query for the name specified in the *DNSname* variable.

There are also many additional parameters that you can include on the command line to control the server query process. The output generated by Nslookup.exe in Windows 7 resembles that shown in Figure 5-24.

Figure 5-24

The Nslookup.exe display

The Nslookup.exe utility has two operational modes: command line and interactive. When you run Nslookup.exe with no command-line parameters, the program displays its own prompt from which you can issue commands to specify the default DNS server to query, resolve multiple names, and configure many other aspects of the program's functionality.

USING NETSTAT.EXE

Netstat.exe is a command-line program that displays status information about the current network connections on a computer running Windows 7 and about the traffic generated by the various TCP/IP protocols. In UNIX, the program is called netstat, and in Windows 7, it is called Netstat.exe.

The syntax for the Windows 7 version of Netstat.exe is as follows:

NETSTAT [*interval*][-a][-b][-e][-f][-n][-o][-p *protocol*][-r][-s][-t]

- *interval:* Specifies the time interval (in seconds) between display refreshes.
- -a: Displays the current network connections and the ports that are currently listening for incoming network connections.
- -b: Displays the executable associated with each active connection and listening port.

- **-e**: Displays Ethernet traffic statistics for the network interface, broken down into bytes, unicast packets, nonunicast packets, discards, errors, and unknown protocols.
- **–f**: When combined with other parameters, causes the program to display foreign addresses as fully qualified domain names.
- **–n**: When combined with other parameters, causes the program to display addresses and port numbers in numerical, rather than alphabetical, form.
- **–o**: Displays the process ID associated with each active connection and listening port.
- **–p** *protocol*: Displays the current active connections for the protocol specified by the *protocol* variable.
- **–r**: Displays the computer's IPv4 and IPv6 routing tables.
- **–s**: Displays detailed network traffic statistics for the IP, ICMP, TCP, and UDP protocols, in both v4 and v6 versions.
- **–t**: Displays the offload state of the current connection.

Part of the default network connection listing displayed by Netstat.exe on a computer running Windows 7 appears in Figure 5-25.

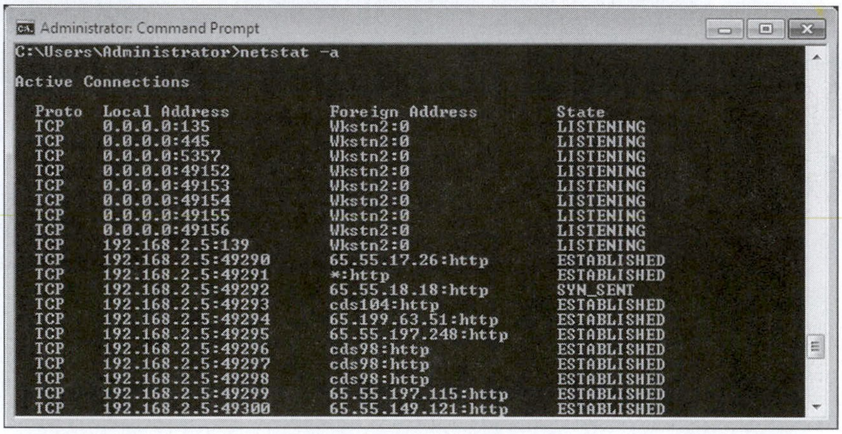

Figure 5-25

The network connection listing in Netstat.exe

The Ethernet interface statistics, as displayed by netstat.exe, are shown in Figure 5-26.

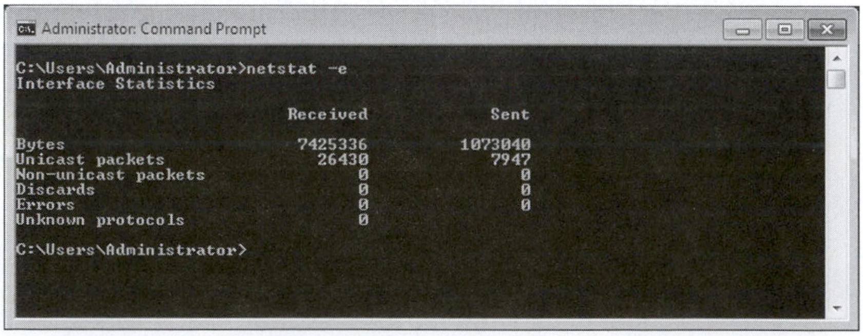

Figure 5-26

The Ethernet interface statistics in Netstat.exe

The routing tables for a computer running Windows 7 appear as shown in Figure 5-27.

Figure 5-27

The IPv4 and IPv6 routing
tables in Netstat.exe

SKILL SUMMARY

IN THIS LESSON YOU LEARNED:

• The networking stack used on Windows 7 computers corresponds roughly to the seven-layer OSI reference model.

• The OSI (Open Systems Interconnection) reference model consists of seven layers: physical, data-link, network, transport, session, presentation, and application.

• Ethernet, the data-link layer protocol used on most LANs, consists of physical layer specifications, a frame format, and a MAC mechanism.

• The network and transport layer protocols work together to provide an end-to-end communication service that achieves the quality of service required by the application requesting network services.

• The functions of the session, presentation, and application layers are often combined into a single application layer protocol.

• Windows 7 includes support for both the IPv4 and IPv6 protocols. IPv6 increases the IP address space from 32 to 128 bits, simplifies the routing process, and improves address autoconfiguration.

• Network Discovery is a Windows 7 feature that simplifies the task of firewall configuration by enabling you to block or allow the protocols and ports needed for the computer to browse and access the network.

• The Network Map utility uses the Link Layer Discovery Protocol (LLTD) to detect network devices and connections.

• Most networks use DHCP to configure their TCP/IP clients, but it is still possible to configure them manually, using a graphical interface or the Netsh.exe command-line utility.

• Windows 7 includes a variety of command-line TCP/IP tools, including Ipconfig.exe, Ping.exe, Tracert.exe, Nslookup.exe, and Netstat.exe.

Knowledge Assessment

Fill in the Blank

Complete the following sentences by writing the correct word or words in the blanks provided.

1. A software routine, which also acts as a filter that blocks certain type of incoming and outgoing traffic, while enabling other types is called a _____.

2. The _____ tool provides a central access point for all of the network controls and connections on a computer running Windows 7.

3. A device that connects one network to another is called a _____.

4. The most common method for illustrating the operations of a networking stack is the _____, which consists of _____ layers.

5. Protocols that do not guarantee delivery of their data, but do operate with a very low overhead that conserve network bandwidth are called _____.

6. The Windows 7 command-line utility that can tell you if the TCP/IP stack of another system on the network is functioning normally is called _____.

7. The Windows 7 command-line utility that enables you to generate DNS request messages and then transmit them to specific DNS servers on the network is called _____.

8. Most networks use _____ to dynamically assign addresses and configure computers to use them.

9. The Windows 7 utility that displays a list of the routers currently forwarding packets to a particular destination is called _____.

10. The top and bottom layers of the OSI model are called the _____ and _____ layers.

True / False

Circle T if the statement is true or F if the statement is false.

T | F 1. The purpose of Network Diagnostics is to display error messages only.

T | F 2. Transport layer protocols are not concerned with addressing packets to the correct system.

T | F 3. The Network Map utility uses a new protocol called Link Layer Topology Discovery (LLTD) to discover information about the network and the devices attached to it.

T | F 4. The protocols that Windows uses by default at the network and transport layers are collectively called TCP/IP.

T | F 5. Home and work computers have Network Discovery turned on, and public computers have it turned off.

T | F 6. There are two basic types of port numbers: ephemeral port numbers and well-known port numbers.

T | F 7. A Windows 7 computer that is connected to a LAN has a hardware address and a computer that is connected to the Internet has an IP address.

T | F 8. The only two layers of the OSI reference model that do not have individual protocols associated with them are the transport layer and the session layer.

T | F 9. Because the configuration of the Internet is constantly changing, the only way you can know for certain what route packets are taking to a specific destination is to use Tracert.exe.

T | F 10. The IPv6 addresses Windows 7 computers use at the network layer are six-byte hexadecimal sequences, hard coded into each network interface adapter by the manufacturer.

Review Questions

1. What is the difference between a hardware address and an IPv4 address?
2. Explain how the process of data encapsulation works on a TCP/IP network when an application sends a message to another computer on the Internet.

Case Scenarios

Scenario 5-1: Using Port Numbers

While you are installing an Internet web server on your company network, the owner of the company tells you that he also wants to build a web server for internal use by the company's employees. This intranet web server will not contain confidential information, but it should not be accessible from the company's Internet Web site. To do this, you create a second site on the web server. The Internet site uses the well-known port number for web servers, which is 80. For the intranet site, you select the port number 283. Assuming that the web server's IP address on the internal network is 10.54.3.145, what should the users on the company network do to access the intranet Web site with Microsoft Internet Explorer?

Scenario 5-2: Configuring TCP/IP Clients

Mark is setting up a small Ethernet network in his home by installing network adapters in three computers running Windows 7 and connecting them to a switch. Mark only uses one of the computers to access the Internet with a dial-up modem, but he wants to be able to access files and his printer from any one of the three systems. After he installs the network interface adapters, he notes that the default networking components have been installed on all three systems, and he sets about configuring their TCP/IP configuration parameters manually. Of the settings on the Internet Protocol Version 4 (TCP/IPv4) Properties sheet, which must Mark configure to provide the network connectivity he desires, and which can he leave blank?

Sharing Resources

OBJECTIVE DOMAIN MATRIX

TECHNOLOGY SKILL	OBJECTIVE DOMAIN	OBJECTIVE NUMBER
Understanding Folder Sharing in Windows 7	Configure shared resources.	5.1
Managing NTFS Permissions	Configure file and folder access.	5.2

KEY TERMS

access control entries (ACEs)

access control list (ACL)

effective permissions

NTFS permissions

print device

printer

printer control language (PCL)

printer driver

print server

security principal

■ Managing Permissions

THE BOTTOM LINE

In Lesson 4, "Working with Devices," you learned how to prepare hard disk drives so that users store files on them. To control access to the disks and other resources, Windows 7 uses *permissions*.

Permissions are privileges granted to specific system entities, such as users, groups, or computers, enabling them to perform a task or access a resource. For example, you can grant a specific user permission to read a file, while denying that same user the permissions needed to modify or delete the file.

Windows 7 has several sets of permissions, which operate independently of each other. As a technical specialist, you should be familiar with the operation of the following four permission systems:

- *NTFS permissions:* Control access to the files and folders stored on disk volumes formatted with the NTFS file system. To access a file, whether on the local system or over a network, a user must have the appropriate NTFS permissions.
- **Share permissions:** Control access to files and folders shared over a network. To access a file over a network, a user must have appropriate share permissions and appropriate NTFS permissions.

TAKE NOTE *

While all of these permissions systems are operating all the time, technicians do not necessarily have to work with them all on a regular basis. In fact, you might not ever have to manually alter a Registry or Active Directory permission. However, many technicians have to work with NTFS and share permissions on a daily basis.

- **Registry permissions:** Control access to specific parts of the Windows registry. An application that modifies registry settings or a user attempting to manually modify the registry must have the appropriate registry permissions.
- **Active Directory permissions:** Control access to specific parts of an Active Directory hierarchy. Although Windows 7 cannot host an Active Directory domain, desktop technicians might require these permissions when servicing computers that are members of a domain.

All of these permission systems operate independently of each other and can conceivably combine to provide increased protection to a specific resource. For example, Alice might grant Ralph the NTFS permissions needed to access the budget spreadsheet stored on her computer. If Ralph sits down at Alice's computer and logs on as himself, he will be able to access that spreadsheet. However, if Ralph is working at his own computer, he will not be able to access the spreadsheet until Alice creates a share containing the file and grants Ralph the proper share permissions.

Understanding the Windows Permission Architecture

Permissions protect files, folders, shares, registry keys, and Active Directory objects.

To store permissions, each of these elements has an ***access control list (ACL)***. An ACL is a collection of individual permissions, in the form of ***access control entries (ACEs)***. Each ACE consists of a ***security principal*** (that is, the name of the user, group, or computer being granted the permissions) and the specific permissions assigned to that security principal. When you manage permissions in any of the Windows 7 permission systems, you are actually creating and modifying the ACEs in an ACL.

It is crucial to understand that, in all of the Windows operating systems, permissions are stored as part of the element being protected, not the security principal being granted access. For example, when you grant a user the NTFS permissions needed to access a file, the ACE you create is stored in the file's ACL; it is not part of the user account. You can move the file to a different location, and its permissions go with it.

To manage permissions in Windows 7, you use the controls in the Security tab of the element's Properties dialog box, like the one shown in Figure 6-1, with the security principals

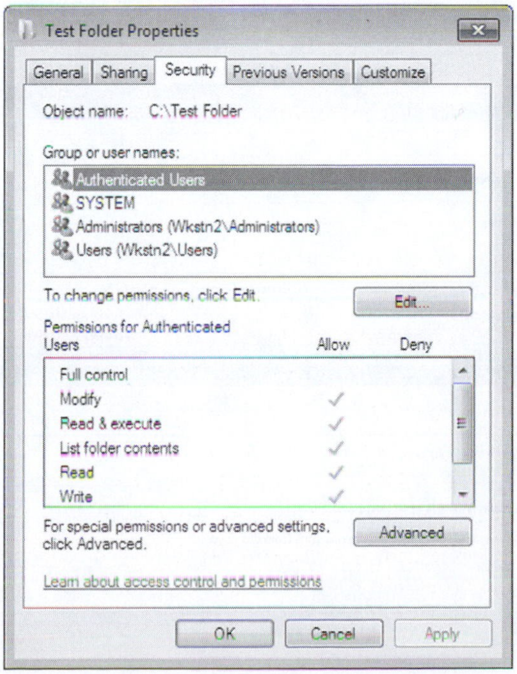

Figure 6-1

The Security tab of a Properties dialog box

listed at the top and the permissions associated with them at the bottom. All of the Windows permission systems use the same interface, although the permissions themselves differ.

UNDERSTANDING STANDARD AND SPECIAL PERMISSIONS

The permissions protecting a particular system element are not like the keys to a lock, which provide either full access or no access at all. Permissions are designed to be granular, enabling you to grant specific degrees of access to security principals.

You can use NTFS permissions to control not only who has access to Alice's spreadsheet, but also the degree to which each user has access. You might grant Ralph permission to read the spreadsheet and also modify it, while Ed can only read it, and Trixie cannot see it at all.

To provide this granularity, each of the Windows permission systems has an assortment of permissions that you can assign to a security principal in any combination. Depending on the permission system you are using, you might have dozens of different permissions available for a single system element.

If this is all starting to sound extremely complex, don't worry. Windows provides precon-figured permission combinations that are suitable for most common access control chores. When you open the Properties dialog box for a system element and look at its Security tab, the permissions you are seeing are called *standard permissions*. Standard permissions are actually combinations of *special permissions*, which provide the most granular control over the element.

For example, the NTFS permission system has 14 special permissions that you can assign to a folder or file. However, there are also 6 standard permissions, which are various com-binations of the 14 special permissions. In most cases, you will only have to work with the standard permissions. Many technicians rarely, if ever, work directly with the special permissions.

If you do find it necessary to work with special permissions directly, Windows makes it pos-sible. When you click the Advanced button on the Security tab of any Properties dialog box, an Advanced Security Settings dialog box appears, as shown in Figure 6-2, which enables you to access the ACEs for the selected system element directly.

Figure 6-2

The Advanced Security Settings dialog box

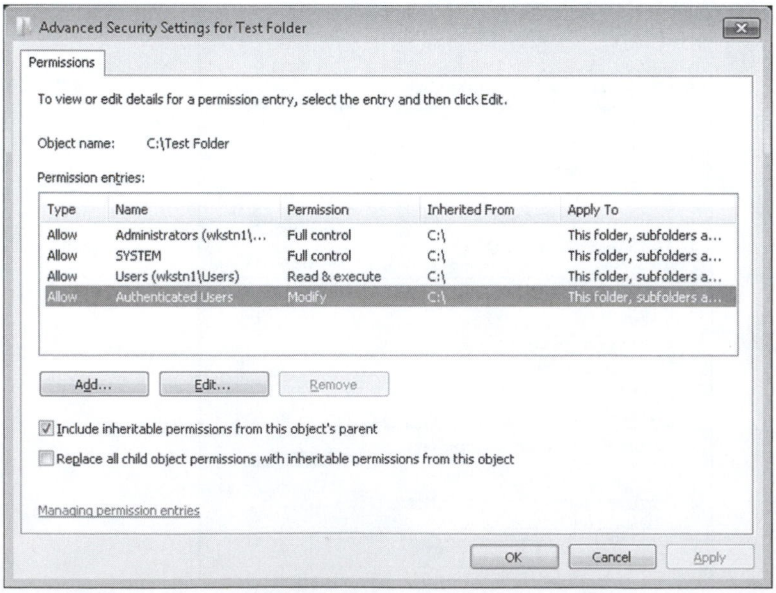

ALLOWING AND DENYING PERMISSIONS

When you assign permissions to a system element, you are, in effect, creating a new ACE in the element's ACL There are two basic types of ACEs: *Allow* and *Deny*. This makes it possible to approach permission management tasks from two directions:

- **Additive:** Start with no permissions and then grant Allow permissions to individual security principals to provide them with the access they need.
- **Subtractive:** Start by granting all possible Allow permissions to individual security principals, providing them with full control over the system element, and then grant them Deny permissions for the access you don't want them to have.

Most administrators prefer the additive approach, because Windows, by default, attempts to limit access to important system elements. In a properly designed permission hierarchy, the use of Deny permissions is often not needed at all. Many administrators frown on their use, because combining Allow and Deny permissions in the same hierarchy can make it difficult to determine the effective permissions for a specific system element.

INHERITING PERMISSIONS

The most important principle in permission management is that permissions tend to run downward through a hierarchy. The tendency of permissions to flow downward through a file system or other hierarchy is called *permission inheritance*. Permission inheritance means that parent elements pass their permissions down to their subordinate elements.

For example, when you grant Alice Allow permissions to the root of the D: drive, all of the files and subfolders on the D: drive inherit those permissions, and Alice can access them. The principle of inheritance simplifies the permission assignment process enormously. Without it, you would have to grant security principals individual Allow permissions for every file, folder, share, object, and key they need to access. With inheritance, you can grant access to an entire file system by creating one set of Allow permissions.

In most cases, whether they do it consciously or not, system administrators take inheritance into account when they design their file systems and Active Directory trees. The location of a system element in a hierarchy is often based on how the administrators plan to assign permissions. For example, the section of a directory tree shown in Figure 6-3 is intended to be a place where network users can temporarily store files that they want other users to access.

Figure 6-3

A sample xfer directory structure

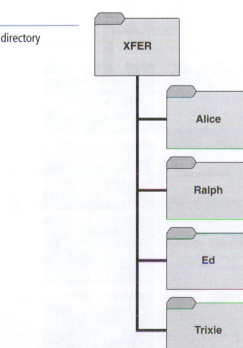

Because the administrator has assigned all users the Allow Read and Allow List Folder Contents standard permissions to the xfer folder, as shown in Figure 6-4, everyone is able to read the files in the xfer directory. Because the assigned permissions run downward, all of the subfolders beneath xfer inherit those permissions, so all of the users can read the files in all of the subfolders as well.

Figure 6-4

Granting Allow permissions to the xfer folder

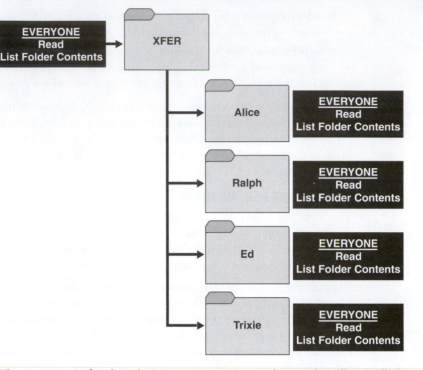

The next step is for the administrator to assign each user the Allow Full Control permission to his or her own subfolder, as shown in Figure 6-5. This enables each user to create, modify, and delete files in his or her own folder, without compromising the security of the other users' folders. Because the user folders are at the bottom of the hierarchy, there are no subfolders to inherit the Full Control permissions.

Figure 6-5

Granting Full Control to individual user folders

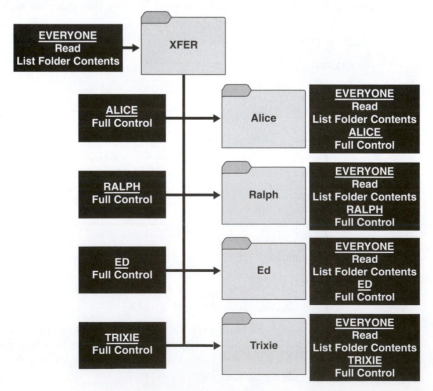

There are some situations in which an administrator might want to prevent subordinate elements from inheriting permissions from their parents. There are two ways to do this:

- **Turn off inheritance:** When you assign special permissions, you can configure an ACE not to pass its permissions down to its subordinate elements. This effectively blocks the inheritance process.
- **Deny permissions:** When you assign a Deny permission to a system element, it overrides any Allow permissions that the element might have inherited from its parent objects.

COPYING AND MOVING NTFS FILES

TAKE NOTE *

It is possible to move NTFS files or folders to a different volume while retaining their existing permissions by using the Robocopy.exe command-line utility included with Windows 7.

NTFS permission inheritance behaves in various ways when you copy and move files and folders to different locations. When you copy NTFS files or folders from one location to another, whether the destination is on the same or a different NTFS volume, the new copy does not take the permissions from its original location with it. Instead, the new copy inherits permissions from its parent folder at the new location.

When moving files or folders, the behavior is different. If you move files or folders to a new location on the same NTFS volume, their existing permissions move with them. If you move files or folders to a different volume, they leave their existing permissions behind and inherit permissions from the parent folder at the new location.

UNDERSTANDING EFFECTIVE PERMISSIONS

A security principal can receive permissions in many different ways, and it is important for an administrator to understand how these permissions interact. *Effective permissions* are the combination of Allow permissions and Deny permissions that a security principal receives for a given system element, whether explicitly assigned, inherited, or received through a group membership. Because a security principal can receive permissions from so many sources, it is not unusual for those permissions to conflict, so there are rules defining how the permissions combine to form the effective permissions. These rules are as follows:

- **Allow permissions are cumulative:** When a security principal receives Allow permissions from more than one source, the permissions are combined to form effective permissions. For example, if Alice receives the Allow Read and Allow List Folder Contents permissions for a particular folder by inheriting them from its parent folder, and receives the Allow Write and Allow Modify permissions to the same folder from a group membership, Alice's effective permissions for the folder are the combination of all four permissions. If you then explicitly grant Alice's user account the Allow Full Control permission, this fifth permission is combined with the other four.
- **Deny permissions override Allow permissions:** When a security principal receives Allow permissions, whether explicitly, by inheritance, or from a group, you can override those permissions by granting the principal Deny permissions of the same type. For example, if Alice receives the Allow Read and Allow List Folder Contents permissions for a particular folder by inheritance, and receives the Allow Write and Allow Modify permissions to the same folder from a group membership, explicitly granting her the Deny permissions to that folder prevents her from accessing it in any way.
- **Explicit permissions take precedence over inherited permissions:** When a security principal receives permissions by inheriting them from a parent or from group memberships, you can override those permissions by explicitly assigning contradicting permissions to the security principal itself. For example, if Alice inherits the Deny Full Access permission for a folder, explicitly assigning her user account the Allow Full Access permission to that folder overrides the denial.

Of course, instead of examining and evaluating all of the possible permission sources, you can just open the Advanced Security Settings dialog box, click the Effective Permissions tab, as shown in Figure 6-6, and select a security principal to display its current effective permissions for the selected file or folder.

Figure 6-6

The Effective Permissions tab of
the Advanced Security Settings
dialog box

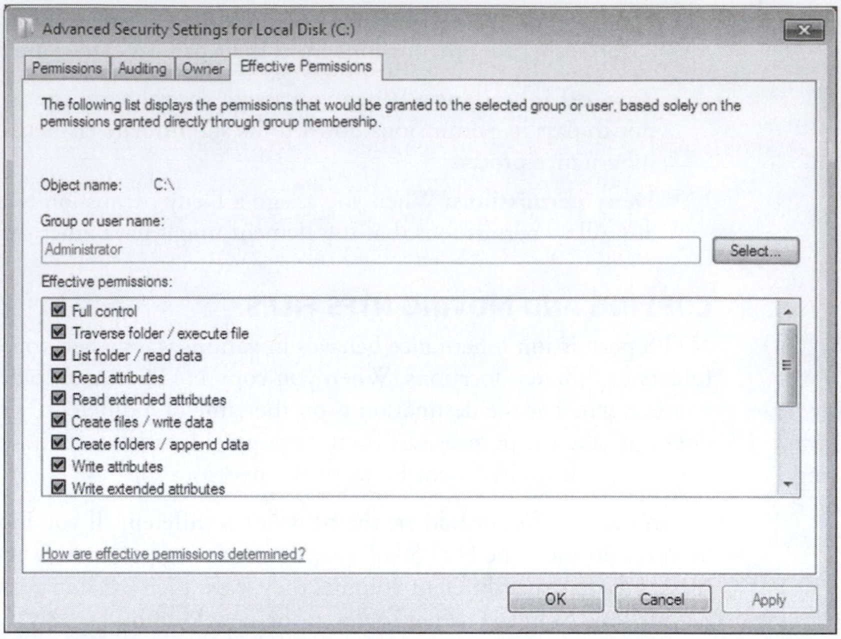

Managing NTFS Permissions

> Windows 7 supports two file systems, NTFS and FAT, but the majority of Windows
> installations today use NTFS.

One of the main advantages of NTFS is that it supports permissions, which FAT does not.
As described earlier in this lesson, every file and folder on an NTFS drive has an ACL that
consists of ACEs, each of which contains a security principal and the permissions assigned to
that principal.

> **+ MORE INFORMATION**
>
> The original 12-bit *file allocation table* file system (now referred to as FAT12) was severely limited in several ways.
> The FAT12 file system was the source of the 8.3 DOS filename limitation, and it originally imposed a volume size
> limitation of 32 megabytes. Subsequent enhancements to the file system increased its address space to 16
> and eventually 32 bits. The resulting FAT32 file system now supports filenames up to 255 characters long and
> volumes up to 8 terabytes in size, but it still has no built-in permissions system. However, the versions of Windows
> supporting FAT32, including Windows 7, impose a FAT32 volume size limit of 32 gigabytes, which is the
> primary reason why most Windows computers today use NTFS. For more information about the FAT file system,
> see Lesson 4, "Working with Disks and Devices."

In the NTFS permission system, the security principals involved are users and groups, which
Windows refers to as *security identifiers (SIDs)*. When a user attempts to access an NTFS file
or folder, the system reads the user's *security access token*, which contains the SIDs for the
user's account and all of the groups to which the user belongs. The system then compares
these SIDs to those stored in the file or folder's ACEs to determine what access the user
should have. This process is called *authorization*.

CERTIFICATION READY?
Configure file and folder
access.
5.2

ASSIGNING STANDARD NTFS PERMISSIONS

Most technical specialists and Windows system administrators work with standard NTFS
permissions almost exclusively. This is because there is no need to work directly with special
permissions for most common access control tasks. To assign standard NTFS permissions, use
the following procedure:

ASSIGN STANDARD NTFS PERMISSIONS

GET READY. Log on to Windows 7 using an account with administrator privileges.

1. Click the Windows Explorer icon on the taskbar. A Windows Explorer window appears.
2. In the Computer container, right click the Local Disk (C:) drive and then, on the context menu, point to New and select Folder. Give the folder the name Test Folder.
3. Right click the Test Folder folder you created and then, from the context menu, select Properties. The Test Folder Properties sheet appears.
4. Click the Security tab. The top half of the resulting display lists all of the security principals currently possessing permissions to the Test Folder folder. The bottom half lists the permissions held by the selected security principal.
5. Click Edit. The Permissions for Test Folder dialog box appears, as shown in Figure 6-7. The interface is the same as that of the Security tab on the Properties sheet, except that the permissions are now represented by check boxes, indicating that you can modify their states.

TAKE NOTE*

The Security tab only appears in Properties dialog boxes if you are running the Professional, Enterprise, or Ultimate edition of Windows 7. The Home Premium, Home Basic, and Starter editions do not support NTFS permissions.

Figure 6-7

The Permissions for Test Folder dialog box

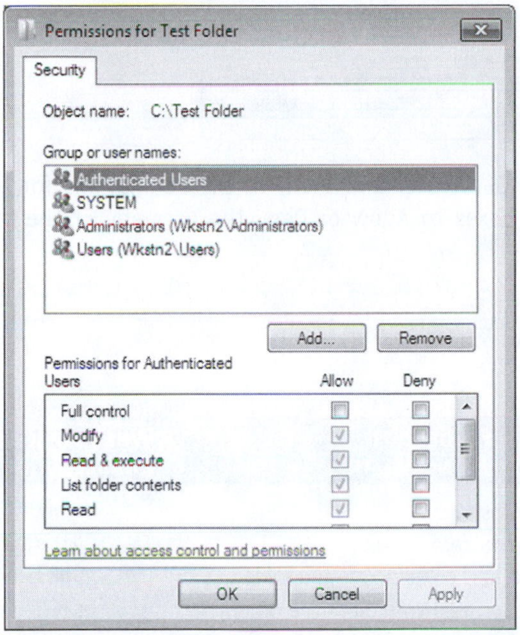

6. Click Add. The Select Users or Groups dialog box appears, as shown in Figure 6-8.

Figure 6-8

The Select Users or Groups dialog box

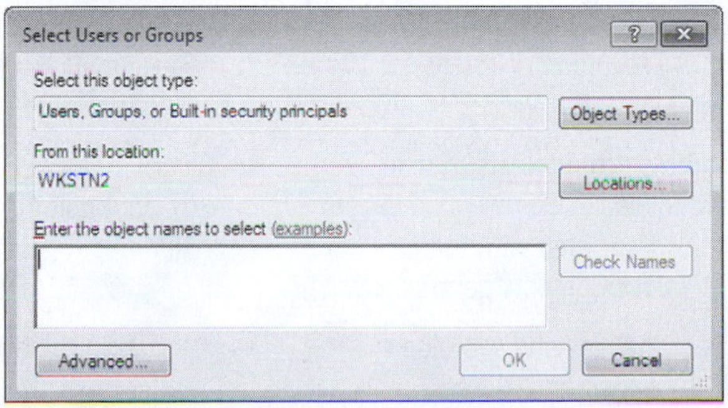

TAKE NOTE*

When you assign permissions on a computer using the Home, Work, or Public network location, you select local user and group accounts to be the security principals that receive the permissions. However, if the computer is a member of an Active Directory Domain Services domain, the default is to assign permissions to domain users, groups, and other objects.

7. In the *Enter the object names to select* text box, type Guest and then click OK. The Guest user account appears on the Permissions for Test Folder dialog box in the *Group or user names* list, as shown in Figure 6-9.

Figure 6-9

The Permissions for Test Folder dialog box, with the Guest user added

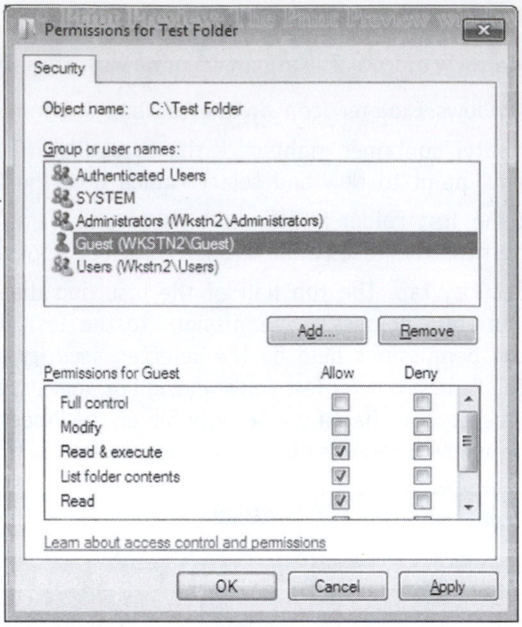

TAKE NOTE *

Assigning permissions to the single folder you created takes only a moment, but for a folder with a large number of subordinate files and subfolders the process can take a long time because the system must modify the ACL of each folder and file.

8. Select the Guest user and then, in the Permissions for Guest box, select or clear the check boxes to Allow or Deny the user any of the standard permissions shown in Table 6-1.

Table 6-1

NTFS Standard Permissions

STANDARD PERMISSION	WHEN APPLIED TO A FOLDER, ENABLES A SECURITY PRINCIPAL TO:	WHEN APPLIED TO A FILE, ENABLES A SECURITY PRINCIPAL TO:
Full Control	Modify the folder permissions. Take ownership of the folder. Delete subfolders and files contained in the folder. Perform all actions associated with all of the other NTFS folder permissions.	Modify the file permissions. Take ownership of the file. Perform all actions associated with all of the other NTFS file permissions.
Modify	Delete the folder. Perform all actions associated with the Write and the Read & Execute permissions.	Modify the file. Delete the file. Perform all actions associated with the Write and the Read & Execute permissions.
Read & Execute	Navigate through restricted folders to reach other files and folders. Perform all actions associated with the Read and List Folder Contents permissions.	Perform all actions associated with the Read permission. Run applications.
List Folder Contents	View the names of the files and subfolders contained in the folder.	Not applicable
Read	See the files and subfolders contained in the folder. View the ownership, permissions, and attributes of the folder.	Read the contents of the file. View the ownership, permissions, and attributes of the file.
Write	Create new files and subfolders inside the folder. Modify the folder attributes. View the ownership and permissions of the folder.	Overwrite the file. Modify the file attributes. View the ownership and permissions of the file.

9. Click OK to close the Permissions for Test Folder dialog box.

10. Click OK to close the Test folder Properties sheet.

Assigning Special NTFS Permissions

If you ever have the need to work with special NTFS permissions directly, Windows 7 provides the tools to do so.

To view and manage the special NTFS permissions for a file or folder, use the following procedure.

ASSIGN SPECIAL NTFS PERMISSIONS

GET READY. Log on to Windows 7 using an account with administrator privileges.

1. Open Windows Explorer and expand the Local Disk (C:) drive.

2. Right click the Test Folder folder you created earlier and then, from the context menu, select Properties. The Test Folder Properties sheet appears.

3. Click the Security tab, and then click Advanced. The Advanced Security Settings for Test Folder dialog box appears. This dialog box is as close as the Windows graphical interface can come to displaying the contents of an ACL. Each of the lines in the *Permission entries* list is essentially an ACE and includes the following information:

   • **Type:** Specifies whether the entry allows or denies the permission.

   • **Name:** Specifies the name of the security principal receiving the permission.

   • **Permission:** Specifies the name of the standard permission being assigned to the security principal. If the entry is used to assign special permissions, the word *Special* appears in this field.

   • **Inherited From:** Specifies whether the permission is inherited, and if so, from where.

   • **Apply To:** Specifies whether the permission is inherited by subordinate objects and if so, by which ones.

4. Click Change Permissions. Another Advanced Security Settings for Test Folder dialog box appears, this one editable, as shown in Figure 6-10. This dialog box also contains the following two check boxes:

   • **Include inheritable permissions from this object's parent:** Specifies whether the file or folder should inherit permissions from parent objects. This check box is

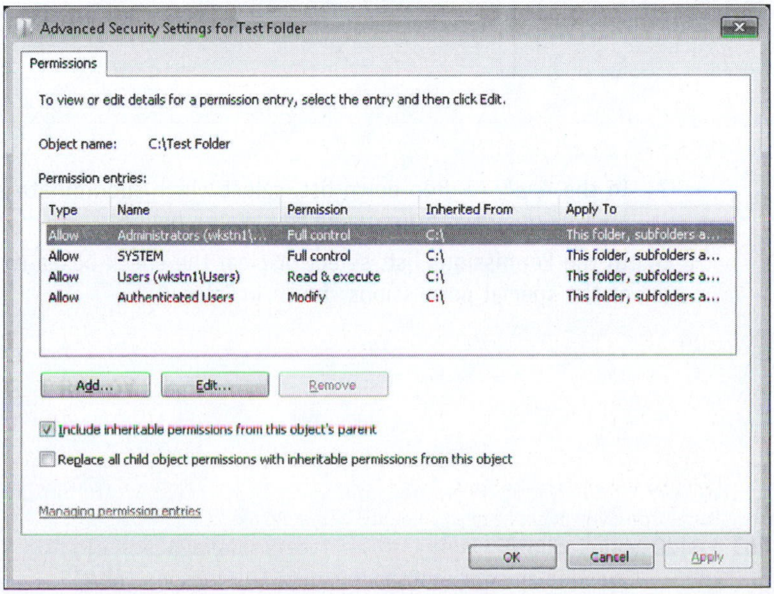

Figure 6-10

The editable Advanced Security Settings for Test Folder page selected by default. Clearing it causes a Windows Security message box to appear, enabling you to choose whether to remove all of the inherited ACEs from the list or copy the inherited permissions from the parent to the file or folder. If you choose the latter, the effective permissions stay the same, but the file or folder is no longer dependent on the parent for permission inheritance. If you change the permissions on the parent objects, the file or folder remains unaffected.

- **Replace all child object permissions with inheritable permissions from this object:** Causes subordinate objects to inherit permissions from this file or folder, to the exclusion of all permissions explicitly assigned to the subordinate objects.

5. Click Add. The Select Users or Groups dialog box appears.

6. In the *Enter the object names to select* text box, type Guest, and then click OK. The Permission Entry for Test Folder dialog box appears, as shown in Figure 6-11.

Figure 6-11

The Permission Entry for Test Folder dialog box

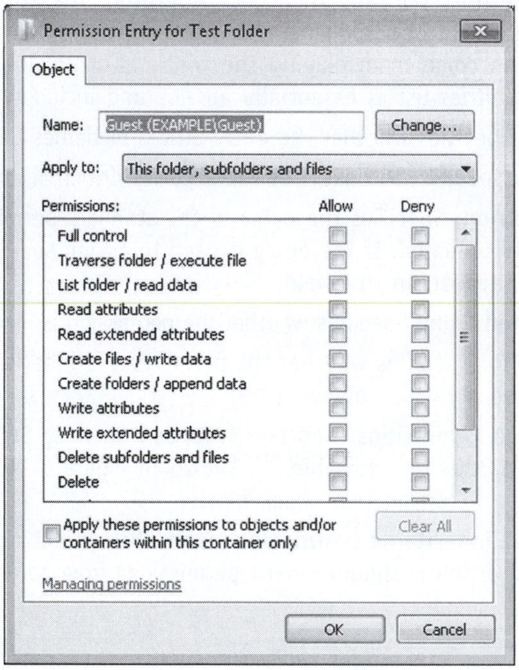

7. In the *Apply to* drop-down list, select which subordinate elements should receive the permissions you assign using this dialog box.

8. In the Permissions list, select or clear the check boxes to Allow or Deny the user any of the special permissions shown in Table 6-2.

Table 6-2

NTFS Special Permissions

SPECIAL PERMISSION	FUNCTIONS
Traverse Folder/Execute File	The Traverse Folder permission allows or denies security principals the ability to move through folders that they do not have permission to access, so as to reach files or folders that they do have permission to access. This permission applies to folders only.
	The Execute File permission allows or denies security principals the ability to run program files. This permission applies to files only.
List Folder/Read Data	The List Folder permission allows or denies security principals the ability to view the file and subfolder names within a folder. This permission applies to folders only.
	The Read Data permission allows or denies security principals the ability to view the contents of a file. This permission applies to files only.
Read Attributes	Allows or denies security principals the ability to view the NTFS attributes of a file or folder.
Read Extended Attributes	Allows or denies security principals the ability to view the extended attributes of a file or folder.
Create Files/Write Data	The Create Files permission allows or denies security principals the ability to create files within the folder. This permission applies to folders only.
	The Write Data permission allows or denies security principals the ability to modify the file and overwrite existing content. This permission applies to files only.
Create Folders/Append Data	The Create Folders permission allows or denies security principals to create subfolders within a folder. This permission applies to folders only.
	The Append Data permission allows or denies security principals the ability to add data to the end of the file but not to modify, delete, or overwrite existing data in the file. This permission applies to files only.
Write Attributes	Allows or denies security principals the ability to modify the NTFS attributes of a file or folder.
Write Extended Attributes	Allows or denies security principals the ability to modify the extended attributes of a file or folder.
Delete Subfolders and Files	Allows or denies security principals the ability to delete subfolders and files, even if the Delete permission has not been granted on the subfolder or file.
Delete	Allows or denies security principals the ability to delete the file or folder.
Read Permissions	Allows or denies security principals the ability to read the permissions for the file or folder.
Change Permissions	Allows or denies security principals the ability to modify the permissions for the file or folder.
Take Ownership	Allows or denies security principals the ability to take ownership of the file or folder.
Synchronize	Allows or denies different threads of multithreaded, multiprocessor programs to wait on the handle for the file or folder and synchronize with another thread that might signal it.

9. Click OK to close the Permission Entry for Test Folder dialog box.
10. Click OK to close the second Advanced Security Settings for Test Folder dialog box.
11. Click OK to close the first Advanced Security Settings for Test Folder dialog box.
12. Click OK to close the Test Folder Properties sheet.

As mentioned earlier in this lesson, standard permissions are combinations of special permissions designed to provide frequently needed access controls. Table 6-3 lists all of the standard permissions and the special permissions that compose them.

Table 6-3

NTFS Standard Permissions and Their Special Permission Equivalents

STANDARD PERMISSION	SPECIAL PERMISSIONS
Read	List Folder/Read Data Read Attributes Read Extended Attributes Read Permissions Synchronize
Read & Execute	List Folder/Read Data Read Attributes Read Extended Attributes Read Permissions Synchronize Traverse Folder/Execute File
Modify	Create Files/Write Data Create Folders/Append Data Delete List Folder/Read Data Read Attributes Read Extended Attributes Read Permissions Synchronize Write Attributes Write Extended Attributes
Write	Create Files/Write Data Create Folders/Append Data Read Permissions Synchronize Write Attributes Write Extended Attributes
List Folder Contents	List Folder/Read Data Read Attributes Read Extended Attributes Read Permissions Synchronize Traverse Folder/Execute File
Full Control	Change Permissions Create Files/Write Data Create Folders/Append Data Delete Delete Subfolders and Files List Folder/Read Data Read Attributes Read Extended Attributes Read Permissions Synchronize Take Ownership Write Attributes Write Extended Attributes

USING ICACLS.EXE

In addition to configuring NTFS permissions graphically, you can also use the Icacls.exe command-line utility. Using Icacls.exe, you can grant or revoke standard or special permissions by allowing or denying them to specific security principals. The syntax for granting permissions is as follows:

```
icacls.exe filespec /grant[:r] security_id:(permissions) [/T][/C][/L][/Q]
```

- *filespec:* Specifies the file or folder whose ACL you want to modify.
- *:r:* Causes the assigned permissions to replace any previously assigned ones. Without the :r switch, the program adds the permissions to the existing ones.
- *security_id:* Specifies the name or security ID of the user or group to whom you want to assign permissions.
- *permissions:* Specifies the permissions you want to assign to the security principal, using the following abbreviations:
  - F (Full Control)
  - M (Modify)
  - RX (Read and Execute)
  - R (Read)
  - W (Write)
- /T: Executes the command on all of the files and subfolders contained in the filespec.
- /C: Proceeds with the operation despite the occurrence of errors.
- /L: Performs the operation on a symbolic link rather than the actual destination.
- /Q: Prevents the program from displaying success messages.

+ MORE INFORMATION

You can also use Icacls.exe to manage special permissions. For more information on using Icacls.exe, see http://technet.microsoft.com/en-us/library/cc753525(WS.10).aspx.

In addition to granting permissions, you can also use the */deny* parameter to assign Deny permissions and the */remove* parameter to erase permissions from an ACL.

Understanding Resource Ownership

As you study the NTFS permission system, it might occur to you that it seems possible to lock out a file or folder—that is, assign a combination of permissions that permits access to no one at all, leaving the file or folder inaccessible. In fact, this is true.

A user with administrative privileges can revoke his or her own permissions, as well as everyone else's, preventing them from accessing a resource. However, the NTFS permissions system includes a "back door" that prevents these orphaned files and folders from remaining permanently inaccessible.

Every file and folder on an NTFS drive has an owner, and the owner always has the ability to modify the permissions for the file or folder, even if the owner has no permissions him- or herself. By default, the owner of a file or folder is the user account that created it. However, any account possessing the Take Ownership special permission (or the Full Control standard permission) can take ownership of the file or folder.

The other purpose for file and folder ownership is to calculate disk quotas. When you set quotas specifying the maximum amount of disk space particular users can consume, Windows calculates a user's current disk consumption by adding up the sizes of all the files and folders that the user owns.

■ Sharing Files and Folders

THE BOTTOM LINE

On a stand-alone Windows 7 computer, the partitions and volumes you create on the hard disks provide a place to store applications and files. However, when you connect the computer to a network, they become a means to share files with other users.

Windows 7 is capable of functioning as both a client and a server on a network, meaning that users can access files on other computers, as well as share files and folders on their own computers with other network users. For network users to be able to access your files, you must first create a network share out of a specific drive or folder. Once you have created a share, users on the network can browse to it in Windows Explorer and access the files there, just as if they were on a local drive.

Understanding Folder Sharing in Windows 7

When compared to pre-Windows Vista versions, Windows 7 provides additional methods for sharing files and folders, as well as additional security mechanisms to protect the computer from intrusion.

CERTIFICATION READY?
Configure shared resources.
5.1

Windows 7 provides three basic methods for sharing the files and folders on the computer: any folder sharing, public folder sharing, and homegroup sharing. Table 6-4 lists the capabilities of each sharing method.

Table 6-4

Windows 7 sharing features

ANY FOLDER SHARING	PUBLIC FOLDER SHARING	HOMEGROUP SHARING
Shares files from any location	Places all shared files in a single location	Shares files from their default library locations
Enables you to set different sharing permissions for individual network users	Uses the same sharing permissions for all network users	Enables you to set the same sharing permissions for all network users or set different sharing permissions for individual users
Access can be limited to network users with a user account and password on your computer	Access can be limited to network users with a user account and password on your computer	Access can be limited to network users with a user account and password on your computer
Individual users can be granted read-only or read-write access to the share	Can be configured as a read-only share or a read-write share	Individual users can be granted read-only or read-write access to the share
Shares files from their original locations	Requires you to copy or move files to be shared to the public folder	Shares files from their original locations

The type of sharing method you elect to use depends on the size and formality of the network to which the computer is connected. For home users, homegroup networking is simple to set up and use. For small business networkers, public folder sharing is often the easiest method, one that users can easily maintain for themselves on a day-to-day basis. For larger networks, Windows domain networks, or any network with more elaborate security requirements, any folder sharing is preferable.

Sharing with Homegroups

> Homegroup networking is a new Windows 7 feature that enables computers configured to use the Home network location to share the contents of their respective libraries among themselves.

Using homegroups, Windows 7 users can share their documents, printers, pictures, music, and videos with other Windows 7 users connected to the same home network. A home network has a single read-only homegroup by default, with the individual users selecting what they want to share.

Homegroups are relatively limited, when compared to any folder sharing, because you can only share the contents of the libraries in the user's profile. However, compared to public folder sharing, homegroups don't require users to copy or move files to a public folder.

In the default homegroup networking configuration, all of the users that join the homegroup have read-only access to all the libraries the other users have elected to share. However, it is possible for each user to configure the system to provide read-write access, and to share libraries only with specific users.

TAKE NOTE *

> Homegroups are designed to share only libraries, but you can extend their capabilities by adding to Windows 7's default libraries. As mentioned in Chapter 1, "Introducing Windows 7," libraries are virtualized folders that enable users to access files from different locations as if they were all in the same place. The Windows 7 libraries point to the standard user profile folders by default, but you can add additional locations to a library as well, and any files at those locations appear in Windows Explorer as part of the library, even though they remain in their original places.

CREATING A HOMEGROUP

When you configure a Windows 7 computer to use the Home network location for the first time, either during the operating system installation or afterward, the computer attempts to detect an existing homegroup on the network. If the system does not detect a homegroup, the Create a Homegroup Wizard appears, displaying the *Share with other home computers running Windows 7* page, as shown in Figure 6-12.

Figure 6-12

The *Share with other home computers running Windows 7* page in the Create a Homegroup Wizard

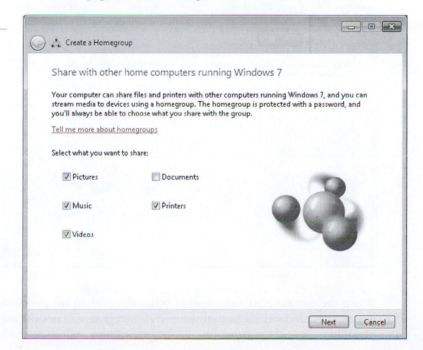

This wizard enables you to select the libraries you want to share, and then displays the *Use this password to add other computers to your homegroup* page, as shown in Figure 6-13. For other computers to join the homegroup, they must supply this same password.

JOINING A HOMEGROUP

When a user selects the Home network location on a Windows 7 computer and the system does detect a homegroup on the network, the Join a Homegroup Wizard appears. This wizard also enables the user to select the libraries to share, and then displays the *Type the homegroup password* page, as shown in Figure 6-14.

When the user supplies the password originally given to the person who created the homegroup, the computer successfully joins the homegroup, shares the selected libraries, and provides access to the shared libraries of the other computers in the homegroup.

WORKING WITH HOMEGROUPS

Once a computer is joined to a homegroup, the shared libraries of the other computers on the network appear in Windows Explorer in the Homegroup container, as shown in Figure 6-15.

Figure 6-15

Homegroup shares in Windows Explorer

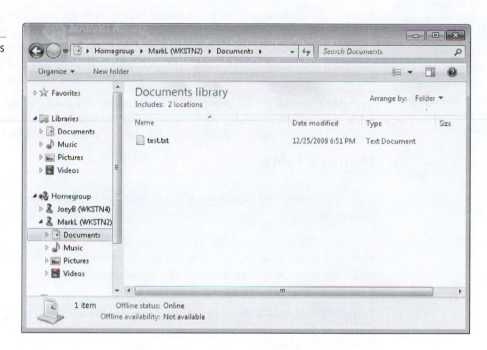

To modify the default homegroup sharing configuration, you select one of your shared libraries in Windows Explorer and click Share in the toolbar, as shown in Figure 6-16. From the menu that appears, you can change other homegroup users' access to the library from Read to Read-Write. You can also limit access to specific homegroup users, or prevent anyone on the network from accessing that library.

Figure 6-16

Modifying homegroup sharing

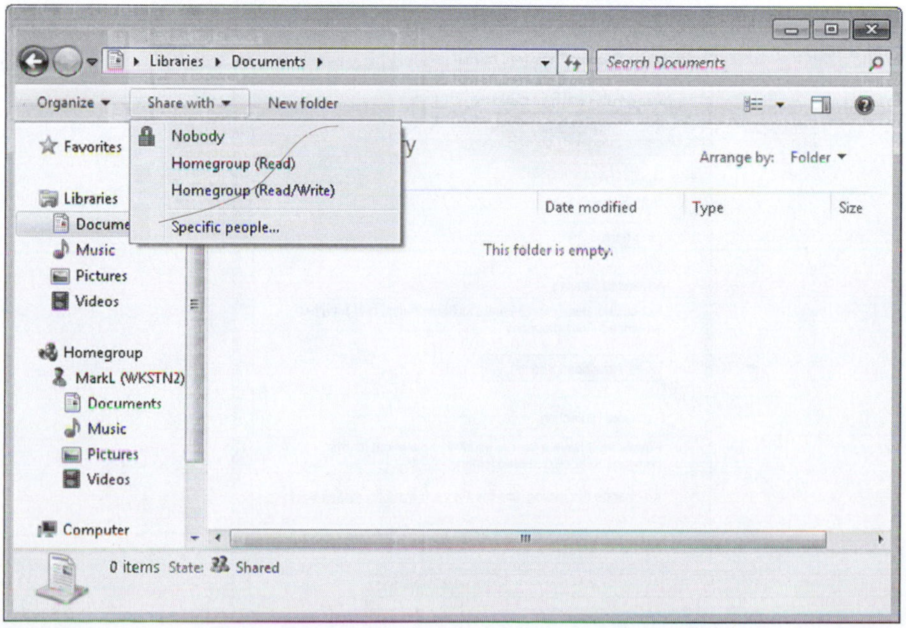

X REF

Windows 7 automatically enables or disables certain network settings, depending on the network location specified during the operating system installation. Before you can share files or folders with network users, you must be sure that Network Discovery and either File Sharing or Public Folder Sharing are enabled. For more information on configuring these options, see Lesson 5, "Connecting to a Network."

Sharing the Public Folder

Sharing files and folders using the public folder is the simplest way to give your clients file-sharing capability.

All you have to do to activate public folder sharing is enable Network Discovery and Public Folder Sharing in the Change sharing options for different network profiles dialog box, accessible from the Network and Sharing Center. Once you have done that, any files and folders that the user copies to the public folder are automatically shared. Users on other network computers can browse to the public share on the client's computer and access any of the files placed there.

Depending on the setting you chose when you enabled public folder sharing, either all network users are granted full read-write access to the folder, or only network users with local user accounts and passwords on the computer can access the public folder.

Sharing a Folder

The real power and flexibility of Windows 7 file sharing is found in the any folder sharing capability.

With any folder sharing, you have full control over what material on the computer is shared, which users are permitted to access the shared material, and what degree of access each user is granted.

To share a folder on a Windows 7 computer, use the following procedure.

⊙ SHARE A FOLDER

GET READY. Log on to Windows 7 using an account with administrator privileges. Make sure that Network Discovery, File and Printer Sharing, and Password Protected Sharing are all turned on.

1. Open Windows Explorer and expand the Local Disk (C:) drive.
2. Right click the Test Folder folder you created earlier and then, from the context menu, select Properties. The Test Folder Properties sheet appears.
3. Click the Sharing tab to display the interface shown in Figure 6-17.

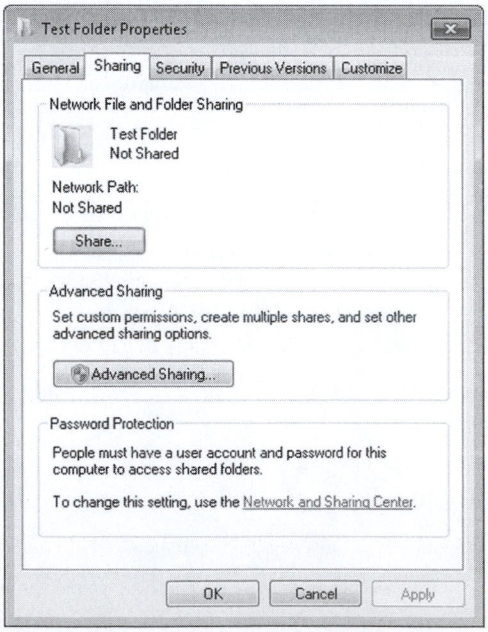

Figure 6-17

The Sharing tab of a folder's Properties sheet

4. Click Advanced Sharing. The Advanced Sharing dialog box appears, as shown in Figure 6-18.

Figure 6-18

The Advanced Sharing dialog box

Advanced Sharing

☐ Share this folder

Settings

Share name:

Add   Remove

Limit the number of simultaneous users to:

Comments:

Permissions   Caching

OK   Cancel   Apply

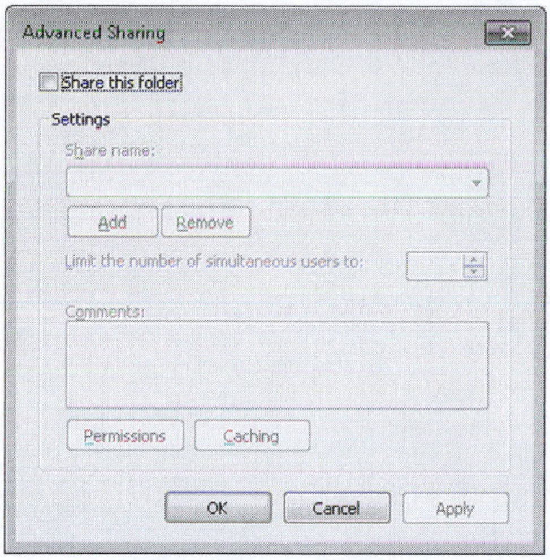

ANOTHER WAY

If you click Share on the Sharing tab, or if you right click a folder and select Share from the context menu, Windows 7 takes you to the File Sharing Wizard, which is a simplified method for creating a share. The wizard is designed for end users and provides a limited set of features, as well as a means for informing network users that a new share is available. Technical specialists will usually want to use the Advanced Sharing interface. It is possible to disable the wizard entirely by clearing the Use Sharing Wizard check box on the View tab of the Folder Options control panel.

5. Select the *Share this folder* check box. By default, the name of the folder you are sharing appears as the name of the share, but you can change the name, if desired, without affecting the original folder.

6. The number of users permitted to access the share simultaneously is 20 by default. To conserve system resources and network bandwidth, you can reduce this number by adjusting the value in the *Limit the number of simultaneous users to* spin box.

➕ MORE INFORMATION

It is possible to create a share that is invisible to users browsing the network simply by appending a dollar symbol ($) to the share name. For example, each drive in the computer has an administrative share that the setup program creates during the operating system installation, called C$, D$, and so on. These shares do not appear in Windows Explorer, but you can still access them by specifying the share name in a command line. Any additional hidden shares that you create are also accessible, though invisible.

7. Click OK to create the share and close the Advanced Sharing dialog box.

8. Click Close to close the Test folder Properties sheet.

If you return to Windows Explorer and browse to the computer in the Network container, you can now see the shared folder there, as shown in Figure 6-19.

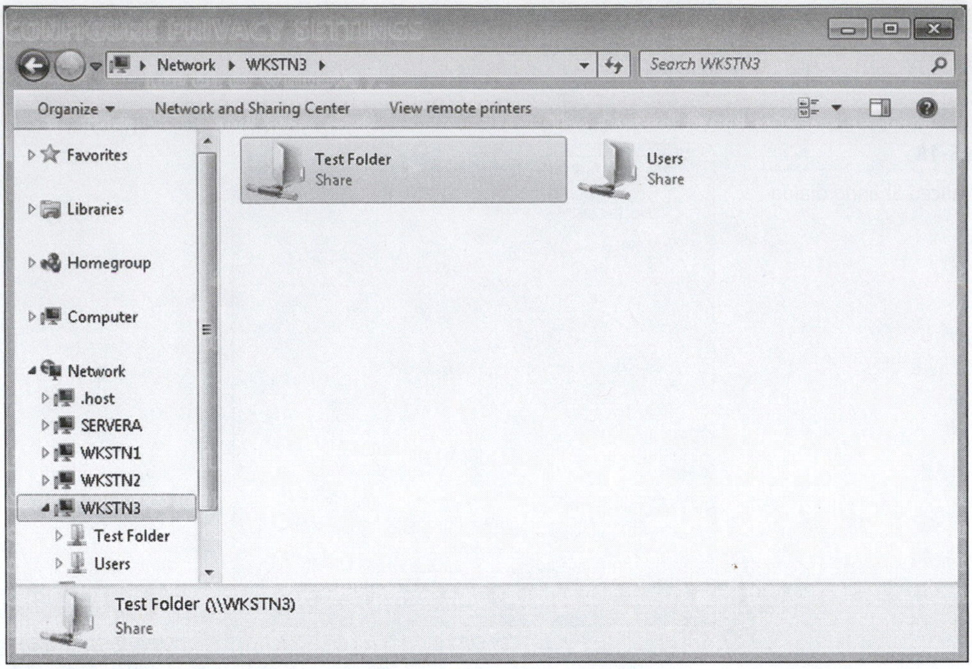

Figure 6-19

A Windows Explorer window displaying a new share

Managing Share Permissions

> Windows 7 shares have their own permission system, which is completely independent from the other Windows permission systems.

For network users to access shares on a Windows 7 computer with Password protected sharing enabled, they must have user accounts on the sharing computer (or in a domain to which both computers are joined) and you must grant them the appropriate permissions.

To set share permissions, use the following procedure.

SET SHARE PERMISSIONS

GET READY. Log on to Windows 7 using an account with administrator privileges. Make sure that Network Discovery, File Sharing, and Password Protected Sharing are all turned on.

1. Open Windows Explorer and expand the Local Disk (C:) drive.

2. Right click the Test Folder folder you created earlier and then, from the context menu, select Properties. The Test Folder Properties sheet appears.

3. Click the Sharing tab and click Advanced Sharing. The Advanced Sharing dialog box appears.

4. Click Permissions. The Permissions for Test Folder dialog box appears, as shown in Figure 6-20. As with all of the Windows permission systems, the top half of the dialog box lists the security principals that have been granted permissions, and the bottom half displays the permissions granted to the selected principal.

Figure 6-20

The Permissions for Test Folder dialog box

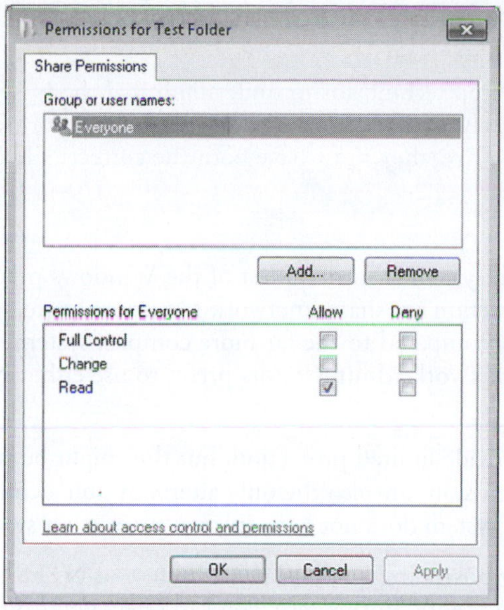

5. Click Add. The Select Users or Groups dialog box appears.

6. In the *Enter the object names to select* text box, type Guest and click OK. The Guest user account is added to the *Group or user names* list.

7. In the Permissions for Guest list, select or clear the check boxes to Allow or Deny the user any of the permissions shown in Table 6-5.

Table 6-5

Share Permissions and Their Functions

SHARE PERMISSION	ALLOWS OR DENIES SECURITY PRINCIPALS THE ABILITY TO:
Read	Display folder names, filenames, file data, and attributes Execute program files Access other folders within the shared folder
Change	Create folders Add files to folders Change data in files Append data to files Change file attributes Delete folders and files Perform all actions permitted by the Read permission
Full Control	Change file permissions Take ownership of files Perform all tasks allowed by the Change permission

8. Click OK to close the Permissions for Test Folder dialog box.

9. Click OK to close the Advanced Sharing dialog box.

10. Click Close to close the Test Folder Properties sheet.

When assigning share permissions, be aware that they do not combine in the same way that NTFS permissions do. If you grant Alice the Allow Read and Allow Change permissions to the C:\Test Folder share, and at a later time deny her all three permissions to the C:\ share, the Deny permissions prevent her from accessing any files on the C:\ share, but she can still access the C:\Test Folder share because of the Allow permissions. In other words, the C:\Test Folder share does not inherit the Deny permissions from the C:\ share.

Combining Share and NTFS Permissions

> It is crucial for desktop technicians to understand that the NTFS and share permission systems are completely separate from each other, and that for network users to access files on a shared NTFS drive, they must have both the correct NTFS and the correct share permissions.

TAKE NOTE*

The Effective Permissions display in the Advanced Security Settings dialog box shows only the effective NTFS permissions, not the share permissions that might also constrain the user's access.

The share permission system is the simplest of the Windows permission systems, and provides only basic protection for shared network resources. Share permissions provide only three levels of access, compared to the far more complex system of NTFS permissions. Generally speaking, network administrators prefer to use either NTFS or share permissions, but not both.

Share permissions provide limited protection, but this might be sufficient on some small networks. Share permissions are also the only alternative on a computer with FAT32 drives, because the FAT file system does not have its own permission system as NTFS does.

On networks already possessing a well-planned system of NTFS permissions, share permissions are not really necessary. In this case, you can safely grant the Full Control share permission to Everyone, and allow the NTFS permissions to provide security. Adding share permissions to the mix only complicates the administration process, without providing any additional security.

■ Working with Printers

> **THE BOTTOM LINE**
>
> The printer is one of the most common external devices you find connected to a PC, but unlike most devices, you do not manage printers using the Device Manager application. Instead, you work with printers using the Printers control panel or the Print Management snap-in for Microsoft Management Console (MMC).

Windows 7, like the other Windows versions, provides a great deal of flexibility in its handling and management of printers. As a client, a Windows 7 computer can have a printer directly attached to one of its ports, or it can access a printer located elsewhere on the network. Windows 7 can also function as a print server, enabling other users on the network to send print jobs to the computer, which feeds them to a printer. The following sections examine the various printer functions possible with Windows 7.

Understanding the Windows Print Architecture

> Printing in the Windows environment involves a number of different roles and components, and the names used to refer to these roles and components can sometimes be confusing. You can avoid confusion by making sure that you understand the terms used for the print components and how they work together.

Printing in Microsoft Windows typically involves the following four components:

- **Print device:** A *print device* is the actual hardware that produces hard copy documents on paper or other print media. Windows 7 supports both *local print devices*, which are directly attached to the computer's parallel, serial, Universal Serial Bus (USB), or IEEE 1394 (FireWire) ports, or *network interface print devices*, which are connected to the network, either directly or through another computer.

- **Printer:** In Windows parlance, a *printer* is the software interface through which a computer communicates with a print device. Windows 7 supports numerous interfaces, including parallel (LPT), serial (COM), USB, IEEE 1394, Infrared Data Access (IrDA), and Bluetooth ports, and network printing services such as lpr, Internet Printing Protocol (IPP), and standard TCP/IP ports.

TAKE NOTE*

The most common misuse of the Windows printing vocabulary is the confusion of the terms printer and print device. Many sources use the term printer to refer to the printing hardware, but in Windows, the two are not equivalent. For example, you can add a printer to a Windows 7 computer without a physical print device being present. The computer can then host the printer, print server, and printer driver. These three components enable the computer to process the print jobs and store them in a print queue until the print device is actually available.

- **Print server:** A *print server* is a computer (or stand-alone device) that receives print jobs from clients and sends them to print devices that are either locally attached or connected to the network.
- **Printer driver:** A *printer driver* is a device driver that converts the print jobs generated by applications into an appropriate string of commands for a specific print device. Printer drivers are designed for a specific print device and provide applications with access to all of the print device's features.

UNDERSTANDING WINDOWS PRINTING

The four printing components work together to process the print jobs produced by Windows applications and turn them into hard copy documents, as shown in Figure 6-21.

Figure 6-21

The Windows print architecture

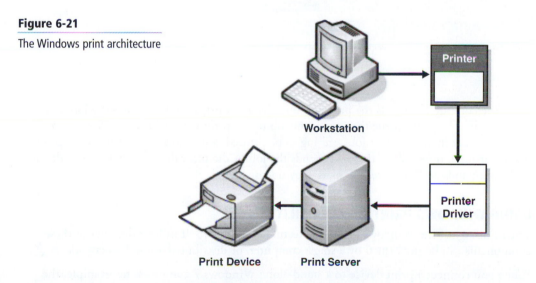

Before you can print documents in Windows, you must install at least one printer. To install a printer in Windows, you must do the following:

- Select a specific manufacturer and model of print device.
- Specify the port (or other interface) the computer will use to access the print device.
- Supply a printer driver specifically created for that print device.

When you print a document in an application, you select the printer that will be the destination for the print job.

The printer is associated with a printer driver that takes the commands generated by the application and converts them into a language understood by the printer, which is called a ***printer control language (PCL)***. PCLs can be standardized, as in the case of the PostScript language, or they can be proprietary languages developed by the print device manager.

The printer driver enables you to configure the print job to use the various capabilities of the print device. These capabilities are typically incorporated into the printer's Properties dialog box, like the one shown in Figure 6-22.

Figure 6-22

A Windows printer's Properties dialog box

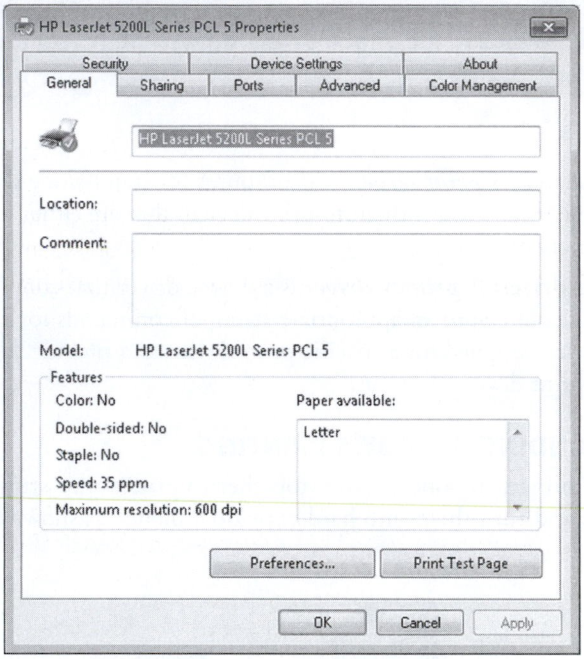

Once the computer converts the print job into the appropriate PCL, it stores the job in a print queue. The print queue then sends the job to the print device when the device is ready to receive it. If there are other jobs waiting to be printed, a new job might wait in the print queue for some time. When the server sends the job to the print device, the device reads the PCL commands and produces the hard copy document.

USING WINDOWS PRINTING FLEXIBILITY

The flexibility of the Windows print architecture manifests itself in how the roles of these components can be performed by a single computer, or distributed around a network.

When you connect a print device to a stand-alone Windows 7 computer, for example, the computer supplies the printer, printer driver, and print server functions. However, you can also connect the computer to a local area network (LAN) and share the printer with other users. In this arrangement, the computer with the print device attached to it functions as a print server. The other computers on the network are the print clients.

In this network printing arrangement, each client supplies its own printer and printer driver. As before, the application sends the print jobs to the printer and the printer driver converts the application commands to PCL commands. The client computer then sends the PCL print jobs over the network to the print server on the computer with the attached print device. Finally, the print server sends the jobs to the print device.

This is only the most basic of network printing arrangements. A multitude of possible variations exist to enable you to create a network printing architecture that supports your organization's printing needs. Some of the more advanced possibilities are as follows:

- **Print devices do not necessarily have to be connected to computers:** Many print devices have integrated network interfaces that enable them to connect directly to the LAN and function as their own print servers. You can also purchase stand-alone print server devices that connect a print device to a network. In these cases, print devices have their own IP addresses, which clients use to communicate with the devices.

- **You can connect a single print server to multiple print devices:** This is called a printer pool. On a busy network with many print clients, the print server can distribute large numbers of incoming jobs among several identical print devices to provide timely service. Alternatively, you can connect print devices that support different forms and paper sizes to a single print server, which will distribute jobs with different requirements to the appropriate print devices.

- **You can connect multiple print servers to a single print device:** By creating multiple print servers, you can configure different priorities, security settings, auditing, and monitoring parameters for different users. For example, you can create a high-priority print server for company executives, while junior users send their jobs to a lower-priority server. This ensures that the executives' jobs get printed first, even if the servers are both connected to the same print device.

Adding a Local Printer

The most common configuration for home, small business, or workgroup users is to connect a print device directly to a computer running Windows 7 or another version of Windows, and then add a printer and printer driver. This enables local users to print their own jobs, and it also makes it possible to share the printer with other network users.

To add a local printer to a Windows 7 computer, use the following procedure.

TAKE NOTE*

This procedure is necessary only if the print device is connected (or will be connected) to the computer by a parallel (LPT) port or serial (COM) port interface. This is because these interfaces are not capable of automatically detecting connected devices. If your print device connects to the computer using USB, IEEE 1394, IrDA, Bluetooth, or any other auto-detecting technology, simply connecting the print device will cause the computer to detect it and install it automatically.

➔ ADD A LOCAL PRINTER

GET READY. Log on to Windows 7 using an account with administrator privileges.

1. Click Start, and then click Control Panel. The Control Panel window appears.
2. Under Hardware and Sound, click View Devices and Printers. The Devices and Printers window appears, as shown in Figure 6-23.

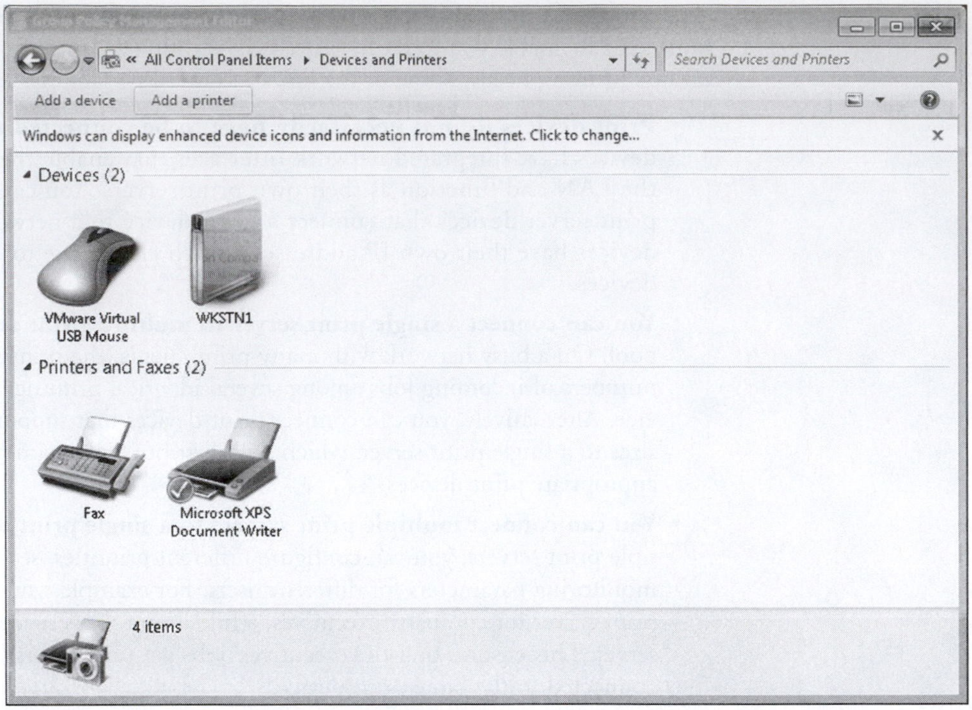

Figure 6-23

The Devices and Printers
control panel

3. Click Add a printer. The Add Printer Wizard appears, displaying the *What type of printer do you want to install?* page appears, as shown in Figure 6-24.

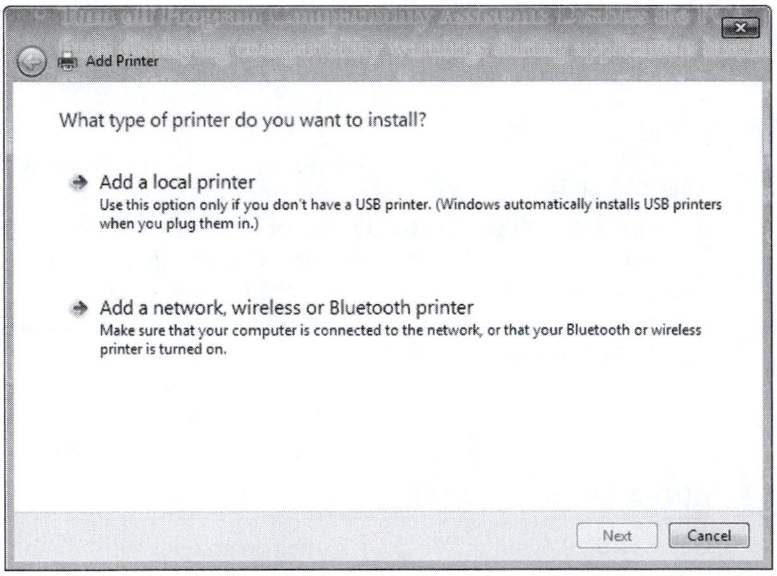

Figure 6-24

The What type of printer do
you want to install? page

4. Click Add a local printer. The *Choose a printer port* page appears, as shown in Figure 6-25.

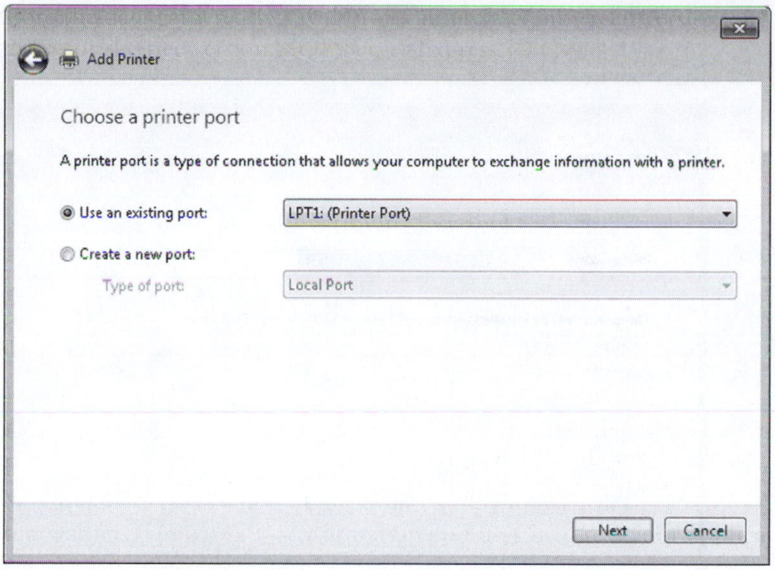

Figure 6-25

The Choose a printer port page

┌───┐
│ 🖶 Add Printer   ⟵ 🗙 │
│   │
│   Choose a printer port   │
│   │
│   A printer port is a type of connection that allows your computer to exchange information with a printer. │
│   │
│   ⦿ Use an existing port: LPT1: (Printer Port)   ▼ │
│   │
│   ○ Create a new port: │
│   Type of port: Local Port   ▼   │
│   │
│   │
│   [Next] [Cancel]   │
└───┘

5. Select the Use an existing port option, and then select the LPT or COM port to which the print device is connected.

6. Click Next to continue. The *Install the printer driver* page appears, as shown in Figure 6-26.

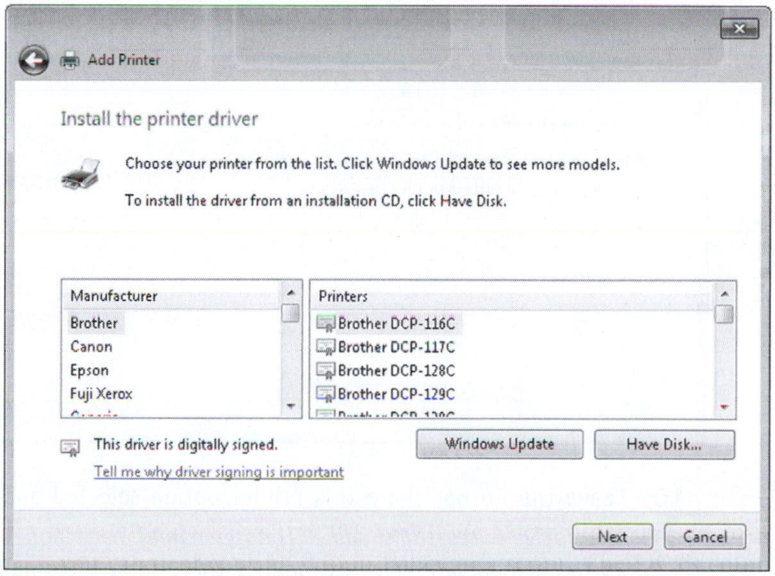

Figure 6-26

The Install the printer driver page

┌───┐
│ 🖶 Add Printer   ⟵ 🗙 │
│   │
│   Install the printer driver   │
│   │
│   🖶   Choose your printer from the list. Click Windows Update to see more models. │
│   │
│   To install the driver from an installation CD, click Have Disk. │
│   │
│   ┌──────────────────┐   ┌─────────────────────────────────┐ │
│   │ Manufacturer   │   │ Printers   │ │
│   │ Brother   │   │ 🖶 Brother DCP-116C   │ │
│   │ Canon   │   │ 🖶 Brother DCP-117C   │ │
│   │ Epson   │   │ 🖶 Brother DCP-128C   │ │
│   │ Fuji Xerox   │   │ 🖶 Brother DCP-129C   │ │
│   └──────────────────┘   └─────────────────────────────────┘ │
│   🖶 This driver is digitally signed.   [Windows Update] [Have Disk...] │
│   Tell me why driver signing is important   │
│   │
│   [Next] [Cancel]   │
└───┘

7. In the Manufacturer column, scroll down and select the manufacturer of your print device. Then, in the Printers column, select the specific model of print device you want to install. If your print device does not appear in the list, you must either click Have Disk, to supply a driver you downloaded or that came with the print device; or Windows Update, to display a selection of drivers available from the Windows Update Web site.

8. Click Next to continue. The *Type a printer name* page appears, as shown in Figure 6-27.

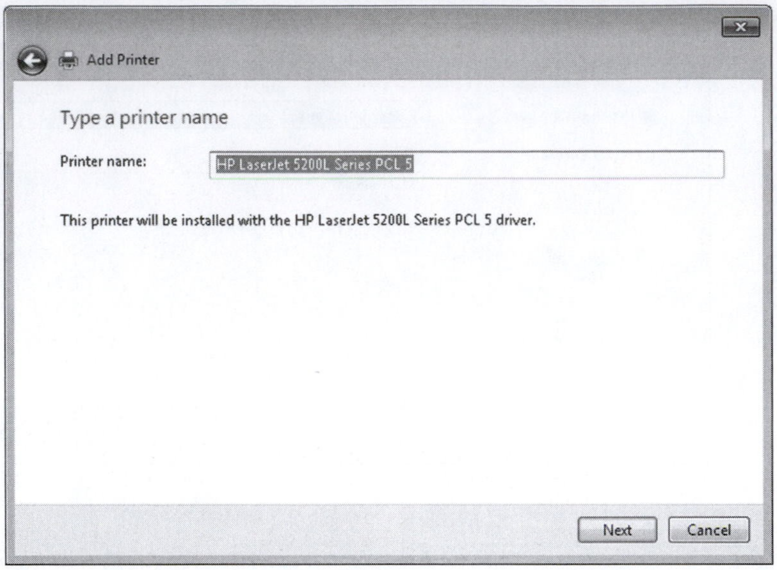

Figure 6-27

The Type a printer name page

9. Type a name for the printer in the Printer name text box and click Next. After a few moments, the *Printer sharing* page appears, as shown in Figure 6-28.

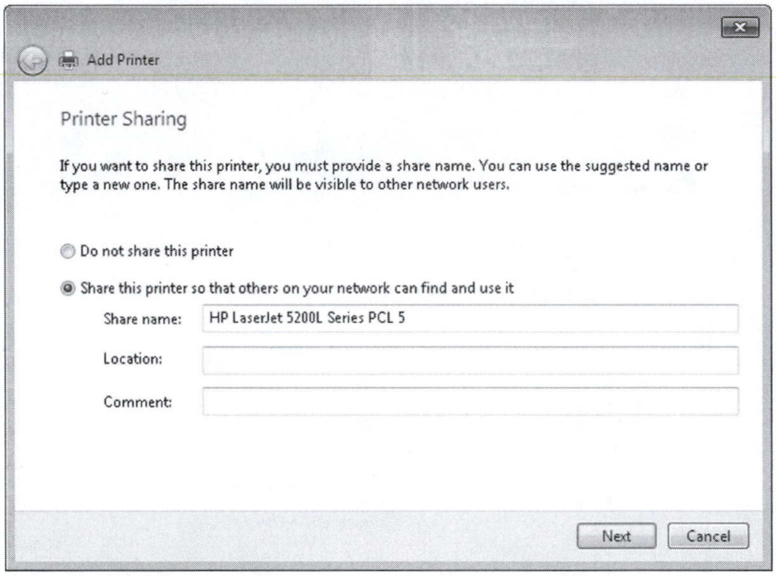

Figure 6-28

The Printer sharing page

10. Leave the Do not share this printer option selected and click Next.

11. The *You've successfully added [printer name]* page appears. If desired, select the *Set as the default printer* check box. If the printer is connected and ready to use, you can also click the Print a test page button.

12. Click Finish. The printer appears in the Devices and Printers control panel.

13. Close the Control Panel window.

At this point, the printer is ready to receive jobs from applications, but this does not necessarily mean that the print device is ready. As stated earlier, you can complete this entire procedure without the print device being attached to the computer, or turned on, or loaded with paper. Jobs that users send to the printer are processed and remain in the print queue until the print device is available for use.

Sharing a Printer

A local printer is, of course, available for use by anyone working at the computer to which it is attached. However, you can also share the printer with other users in a homegroup, workgroup, or domain. When you share a printer connected to a Windows 7 computer, you are essentially using Windows 7 as a print server.

Using Windows 7 as a print server can be a simple or a complex matter, depending on how many clients the server has to support and how much printing they do. For a home, small business, or workgroup, in which a handful of users need occasional access to the printer, no special preparation is necessary. However, if the computer must support heavy printer use, any or all of the following hardware upgrades might be needed:

- **Additional system memory:** Processing print jobs requires system memory, just like any other application. If you plan to run heavy print traffic on a Windows 7 computer, in addition to regular applications, you might want to install extra system memory.
- **Additional disk space:** When a print device is busy, any additional print jobs that arrive at the print server must be stored temporarily on a hard drive until the print device is free to receive them. Depending on the amount of print traffic involved, the print server might require a substantial amount of temporary storage for this purpose.

When in PCL format, print jobs can often be much larger than the document files from which they were generated, especially if they contain graphics. When estimating the amount of disk space required for a print server, be sure that you consider the size of the PCL files, not the application files.

- **Make the computer a dedicated print server:** In addition to memory and disk space, using Windows 7 as a print server requires processor clock cycles, just like any other application. On a computer handling heavy print traffic, standard user applications are likely to experience substantial performance degradation. If you need a print server to handle heavy traffic, you might want to consider using the computer for print server tasks exclusively and move the user(s) elsewhere.

TAKE NOTE *

If you plan to use a Windows computer as a dedicated print server, Windows 7 might not be your best choice as an operating system. As with all of the workstation versions of Windows, Windows 7 is limited to ten simultaneous network connections, so no more than ten clients can print at any one time. If you need a print server that can handle more than ten connections, you must use a server operating system, such as Windows Server 2008 R2.

To share a printer on a Windows 7 computer, you must enable the appropriate settings in the Network and Sharing Center, just as you have to do to share files and folders. To share printers, the following Sharing and Discovery settings must be turned on:

- Network Discovery
- File and Printer Sharing

In addition, if the Password Protected Sharing setting is turned on, users must be logged on and have appropriate permissions to use the printer.

To share a printer that is already installed on a Windows 7 computer, use the following procedure.

SHARE A PRINTER

GET READY. Log on to Windows 7 using an account with administrator privileges.

1. Click Start, and then click Control Panel. The Control Panel window appears.

2. Under Hardware and Sound, click View Devices and Printers. The Devices and Printers window appears.

3. Right click one of the printer icons in the window and then, from the context menu, select Printer Properties. The printer's Properties sheet appears

4. Click the Sharing tab, as shown in Figure 6-29.

Figure 6-29

The Sharing tab of a printer's Properties sheet

> **EPSON LASER LP-6100 Properties**
>
> General | Sharing | Ports | Advanced | Color Management | Security | Optional Settings
>
> You can share this printer with other users on your network. The printer will not be available when the computer is sleeping or turned off.
>
> ☐ Share this printer
>
> Share name: [   ]
>
> ☑ Render print jobs on client computers
>
> ☐ List in the directory
>
> **Drivers**
> If this printer is shared with users running different versions of Windows, you may want to install additional drivers, so that the users do not have to find the print driver when they connect to the shared printer.
>
> [Additional Drivers...]
>
> [OK] [Cancel] [Apply]

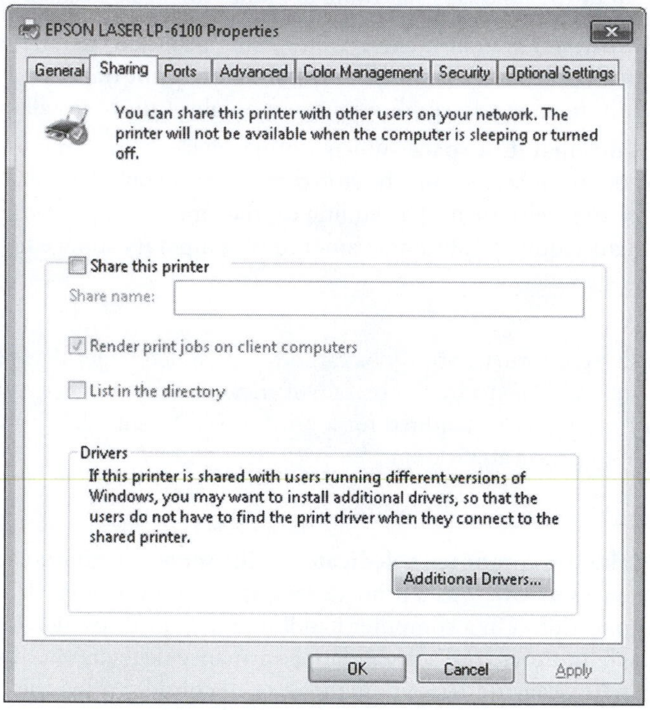

5. Select the Share this printer check box. The printer name appears in the Share name text box. You can accept the default name or supply one of your own. Select the *Render print jobs on client computers* check box if you want to use the printer drivers on the individual client computers. Leaving this box unchecked will force the print server on the computer hosting the printer to process all of the jobs.

TAKE NOTE*

If the computer is a member of an Active Directory domain, an additional *List printer in the directory* check box appears in this dialog box. Selecting this check box creates a new printer object in the Active Directory Domain Services database, which enables domain users to locate the printer by searching the directory.

6. Click Additional Drivers. The Additional Drivers dialog box appears, as shown in Figure 6-30. This dialog box enables you to load printer drivers for other operating system versions, so that clients installing the printer do not have to locate the drivers themselves.

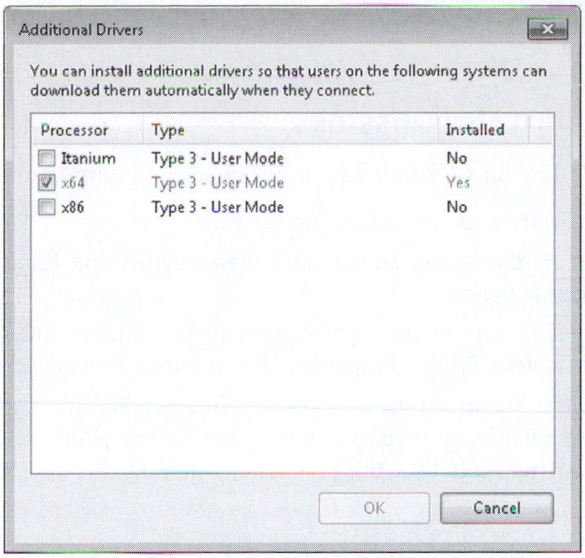

Figure 6-30

The Additional Drivers dialog box

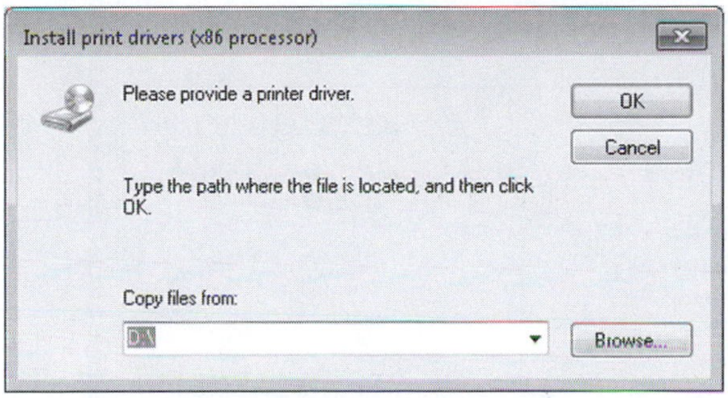

Figure 6-31

An Install Print Drivers dialog box

7. Select any combination of the available check boxes and click OK. For each check box you selected, Windows 7 displays an Install Print Drivers dialog box, as shown in Figure 6-31.

8. In each Install Print Drivers dialog box, type or browse to the location of the printer drivers for the selected operating system, and then click OK.

9. Click OK to close the Additional Drivers dialog box.

10. Click OK to close the Properties sheet for the printer.

11. The printer icon in the Printers control panel now includes a symbol indicating that it has been shared.

Configuring Printer Security

Just like NTFS files and folders, Windows printers have their own permissions, which enable you to control who has access to the printer and to what degree.

When Password Protected Sharing is turned on in the Windows 7 Network and Sharing Center, users must log on to the computer with a user account that requires a password before they can access a shared printer. In addition, the user account must have the appropriate permissions to use the printer.

Printer permissions are much simpler than NTFS permissions; they basically dictate whether users are allowed to merely use the printer, manage documents submitted to the printer, or manage the properties of the printer itself. To assign permissions for a printer, use the following procedure.

 ASSIGN PRINTER PERMISSIONS

GET READY. Log on to Windows 7 using an account with administrator privileges.

1. Click Start, and then click Control Panel. The Control Panel window appears.
2. Under Hardware and Sound, click View Devices and Printers. The Devices and Printers window appears.
3. Right click one of the printer icons in the window and then, from the context menu, select Printer Properties. The printer's Properties sheet appears
4. Click the Security tab, as shown in Figure 6-32. The top half of the display lists all of the security principals currently possessing permissions to the selected printer. The bottom half lists the permissions held by the selected security principal.

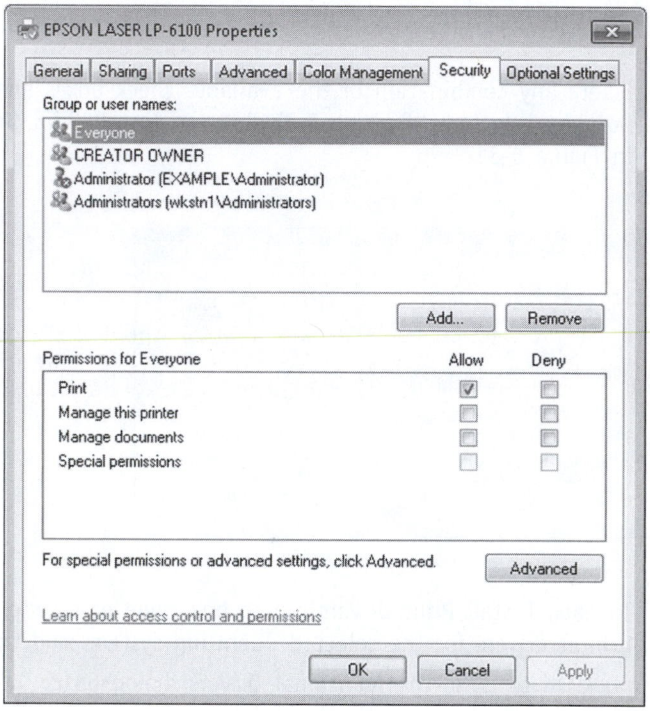

Figure 6-32

The Security tab of a printer's Properties sheet

EPSON LASER LP-6100 Properties

General | Sharing | Ports | Advanced | Color Management | Security | Optional Settings

Group or user names:

- Everyone
- CREATOR OWNER
- Administrator (EXAMPLE\Administrator)
- Administrators (wkstn1\Administrators)

Add...   Remove

Permissions for Everyone   Allow   Deny

Print   ☑   ☐
Manage this printer   ☐   ☐
Manage documents   ☐   ☐
Special permissions   ☐   ☐

For special permissions or advanced settings, click Advanced.   Advanced

Learn about access control and permissions

OK   Cancel   Apply

5. Click Add. The Select Users or Groups dialog box appears.

TAKE NOTE When you assign permissions on a stand-alone computer, you select local user and group accounts to be the security principals that receive the permissions. However, if the computer is a member of an Active Directory Domain Services domain, you assign permissions to domain users, groups, and other objects by default.

6. In the *Enter the object names to select* text box, type a user or group name, and then click OK. The user or group appears in the *Group or user names* list.
7. Select the user or group you added, and select or clear the check boxes in the bottom half of the display to Allow or Deny the user any of the standard permissions shown in Table 6-6.
8. Click OK to close the Properties sheet.

Table 6-6

Standard Printer Permissions

PERMISSION	CAPABILITIES	SPECIAL PERMISSIONS	DEFAULT ASSIGNMENTS
Print	Connect to a printer Print documents Pause, resume, restart, and cancel the user's own documents	Print Read Permissions	Assigned to the Everyone special identity
Manage Printers	Cancel all documents Share a printer Change printer properties Delete a printer Change printer permissions	Print Manage Printers Read Permissions Change Permissions Take Ownership	Assigned to the Administrators group
Manage Documents	Pause, resume, restart, and cancel all users' documents Control job settings for all documents	Manage Documents Read Permissions Change Permissions Take Ownership	Assigned to the Creator Owner special identity

TAKE NOTE*

As with NTFS permissions, there are two types of printer permissions: standard permissions and special permissions. Each of the three standard permissions consists of a combination of special permissions. As with NTFS, you can work directly with the special permissions by clicking Advanced on the Security tab, to display the Advanced Security Settings dialog box.

Accessing a Shared Printer

Once you have shared a printer, it is available to all network users with the appropriate permissions, just as a shared folder is available to the network.

To access a shared printer from Windows 7, use the following procedure.

➜ ADD A NETWORK PRINTER

GET READY. Log on to Windows 7 using any user account.

1. Click Start, and then click Control Panel. The Control Panel window appears.
2. Under Hardware and Sound, click View Devices and Printers. The Devices and Printers window appears.
3. Click Add a printer. The *Choose a local or network printer* page appears.
4. Click Add a network, wireless, or Bluetooth printer. The *Searching for available printers* page appears, as shown in Figure 6-33.

Figure 6-33

The Searching for available printers page

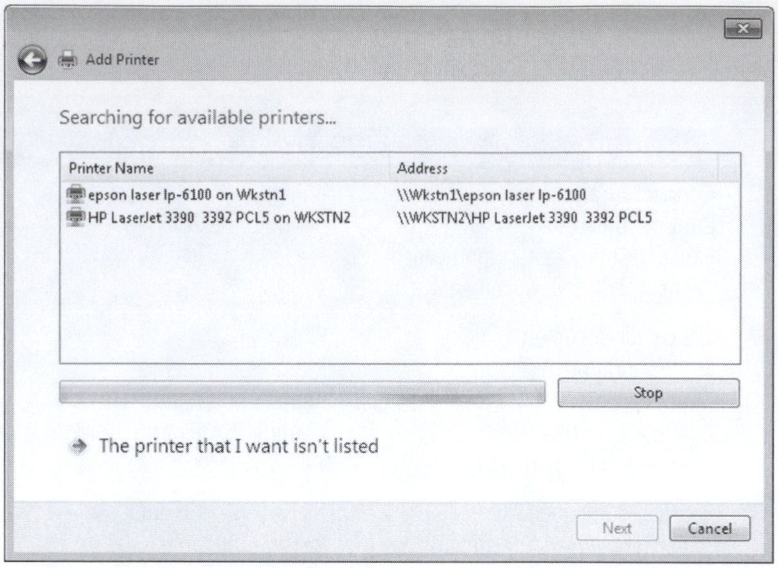

5. Select one of the listed printers and click Next. If the printer you want does not appear, click The printer that I want isn't listed, and the *Find a printer by name or TCP/IP address* page appears, as shown in Figure 6-34. Select the proper radio button to browse for a network printer, type a UNC name or URL for a printer, or enter a printer's IP address or hostname. Then click Next. When you have selected a printer, the *You've successfully added [printer name]* page appears.

Figure 6-34

The Find a printer by name or TCP/IP address page

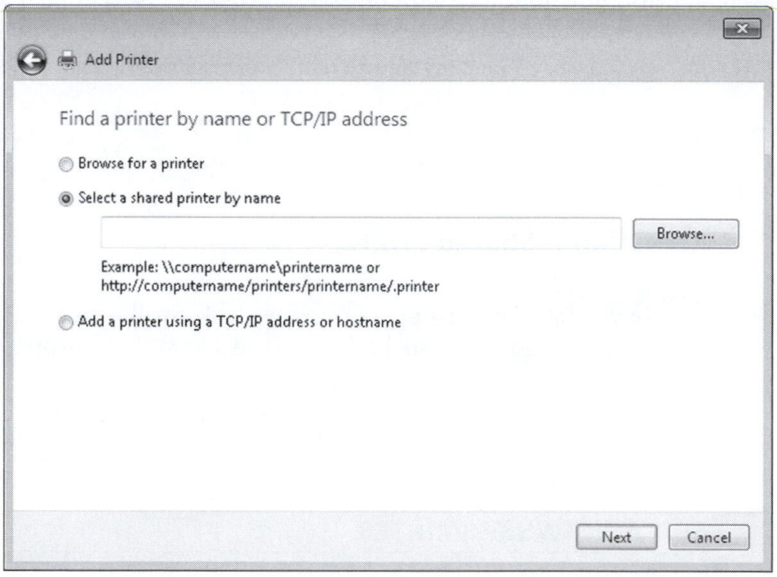

6. Click Next to continue. The final *You've successfully added [printer name]* page appears.

7. If desired, select the *Set as the default printer* check box and click Finish. The printer appears in the Devices and Printers control panel.

8. Close the Control Panel window.

In addition to using the Add Printer wizard, there are several other ways to access shared network printers. When browsing the network in Windows Explorer, you can see the shared printers for each computer on the network, as shown in Figure 6-35. By right clicking a printer in any Windows Explorer window and selecting Connect from the context menu, you can access any printer for which you have the appropriate permissions. Any other Windows 7 mechanism that can display the shared printers on the network provides access to them in the same way.

Figure 6-35

Viewing printers in Windows Explorer

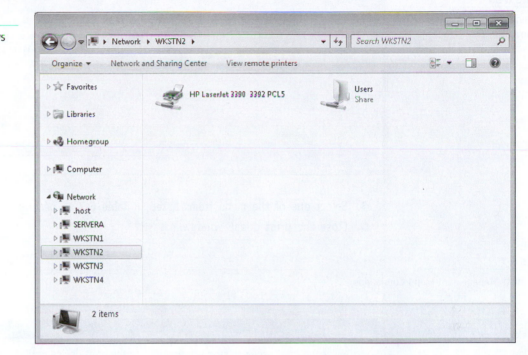

When the computer hosting the printer is a member of an Active Directory Domain Services domain, the ability to locate shared printers is enhanced even further. Opting to list the printer in the Active Directory database creates an object for the printer, and in this object you can specify a lot of information about the print device, including its location and its capabilities.

Recording this information in the printer object makes it possible for users to locate printers by searching the directory for specific characteristics. For example, if a user on a large corporate network needs to find a color duplex printer on the third floor, running a directory search with the appropriate keywords will enable the user to locate the required printer.

Managing Documents

> By default, all printers assign the Allow Print permission to the Everyone special identity, which enables all users to access the printer and manage their own documents. Users that possess the Allow Manage Documents permission can manage any users' documents. To manage documents, you open the print queue window for the printer.

Managing documents refers to pausing, resuming, restarting, and canceling documents that are currently waiting in a print queue. Windows 7 provides a print queue window for every printer, which enables you to view the jobs that are currently waiting to be printed.

To manage documents, use the following procedure.

MANAGE DOCUMENTS

GET READY. Log on to Windows 7 using any user account.

1. Click Start, and then click Control Panel. The Control Panel window appears.
2. Under Hardware and Sound, click View Devices and Printers. The Devices and Printers window appears.

3. Right click one of the printer icons and, from the context menu, select See what's printing. A print queue window named for the printer appears, as shown in Figure 6-36.

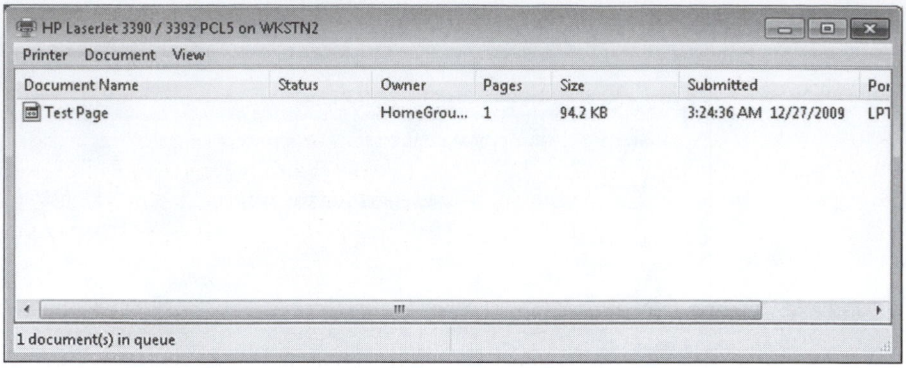

Figure 6-36

A Windows 7 print queue window

4. Select one of the menu items listed in Table 6-7 to perform the associated function.
5. Close the print queue window.

Table 6-7

Document Management Menu Commands

MENU ITEM	FUNCTION
Printer > Pause Printing	Causes the print server to stop sending jobs to the print device until you resume it by selecting the same menu item again. All pending jobs remain in the queue.
Printer > Cancel All Documents	Removes all pending jobs from the queue. Jobs that are in progress complete normally.
Printer > Properties	Opens the Properties sheet for the printer.
Document > Pause	Pauses the selected document, preventing the print server from sending the job to the print device.
Document > Resume	Causes the print server to resume processing a selected document that has previously been paused.
Document > Restart	Causes the print server to discard the current job and restart printing the selected document from the beginning.
Document > Cancel	Causes the print server to remove the selected document from the queue.
Document > Properties	Opens the Properties sheet for the selected job.

TAKE NOTE*

When managing documents, keep in mind that the commands accessible from the print queue window affect only the jobs waiting in the queue, not those currently being processed. For example, a job that is partially transmitted to the print device cannot be completely canceled. The data already in the print device's memory will be printed, even though the remainder of the job was removed from the queue. To stop a job that is currently printing, you must clear the print device's memory (by power cycling or resetting the unit), as well as clear the job from the queue.

Managing Printers

Users with the Allow Manage Printers permission can go beyond just manipulating queued documents and reconfigure the printer itself. Managing a printer refers to altering the operational parameters that affect all users and controlling access to the printer.

Generally speaking, most of the software-based tasks that fall under the category of managing a printer are those you perform once, while setting up the printer for the first time. Day-to-day printer management is more likely to involve clearing print jams, reloading paper, and changing toner or ribbon cartridges. However, the following sections examine some of the printer configuration tasks that typically are the responsibility of a printer manager.

SETTING PRINTER PRIORITIES

In some cases, you might want to give certain users in your organization priority access to a print device so that when a print device is busy, their jobs are processed before those of other users. To do this, you must create multiple printers, associate them with the same print device, and then modify their priorities, as described in the following procedure.

SETTING A PRINTER'S PRIORITY

GET READY. Log on to Windows 7 using an account with the Manage Printer permission.

1. Click Start, and then click Control Panel. The Control Panel window appears.
2. Under Hardware and Sound, click View Devices and Printers. The Devices and Printers window appears.
3. Right click one of the printer icons in the window and then, from the context menu, select Printer Properties. The printer's Properties sheet appears.
4. Click the Advanced tab, as shown in Figure 6-37.

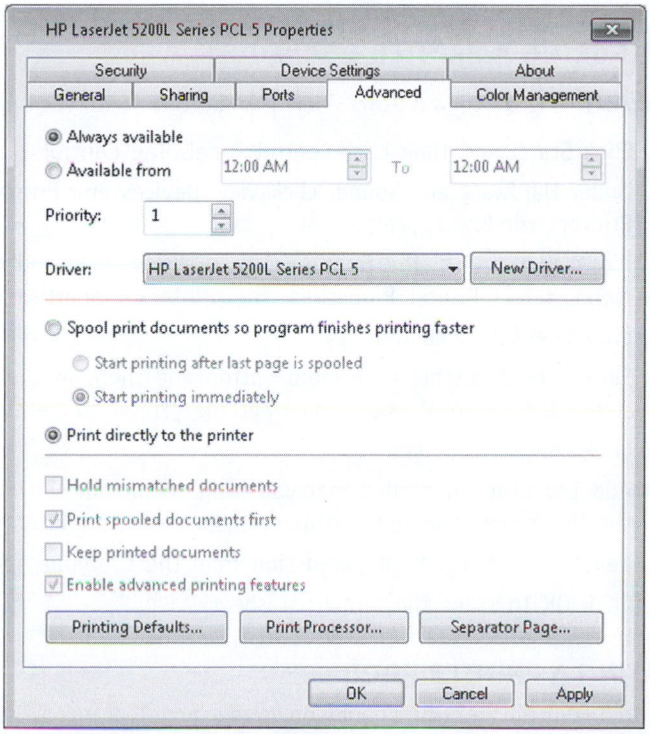

Figure 6-37

The Advanced tab of a printer's Properties sheet

5. Set the Priority spin box to a number representing the highest priority you want to set for the printer. Higher numbers represent higher priorities. The highest possible priority is 99.

TAKE NOTE*

The values of the Priority spin box do not have any absolute significance; they are pertinent only in relation to each other. As long as one printer has a higher priority value than another, its print jobs will be processed first. In other words, it doesn't matter if the high-priority value is 9 or 99, as long as the low-priority value is less than 9.

6. Click the Security tab.

7. Add the users or groups that you want to provide with high-priority access to the printer and assign them the Allow Print permission.

8. Revoke the Allow Print permission from the Everyone special identity.

9. Click OK to close the Properties sheet.

10. Create an identical printer using the same printer driver and pointing to the same print device. Leave the Priority setting to its default value of 1 and leave the default permissions in place.

11. Rename the printers, specifying the priority assigned to each one.

12. Inform the privileged users that they should send their jobs to the high-priority printer. All jobs sent to that printer will be processed before those sent to the other, low-priority printer.

SCHEDULING PRINTER ACCESS

Sometimes, you might want to limit certain users' access to a printer to specific times of the day or night. For example, your organization might have a color laser printer that the company's graphic designers use during business hours, but which you permit other employees to use after 5:00 p.m. To do this, you associate multiple printers with a single print device, much as you did to set different printer priorities.

After creating two printers, both pointing to the same print device, you configure their scheduling using the following procedure.

CONFIGURING A PRINTER'S SCHEDULE

GET READY. Log on to Windows 7 using an account with the Manage Printer permission.

1. Click Start, and then click Control Panel. The Control Panel window appears.

2. Under Hardware and Sound, click View Devices and Printers. The Devices and Printers window appears.

3. Right click one of the printer icons in the window and then, from the context menu, select Printer Properties. The printer's Properties sheet appears.

4. Click the Advanced tab.

5. Select the Available from radio button and then, in the two spin boxes provided, select the range of hours you want the printer to be available.

6. Click the Security tab.

7. Add the users or groups that you want to provide with access to the printer during the hours you selected and grant them the Allow Print permission.

8. Revoke the Allow Print permission from the Everyone special identity.

9. Click OK to close the Properties sheet.

CREATING A PRINTER POOL

As mentioned earlier, a printer pool is an arrangement that increases the production capability of a single printer by connecting it to multiple print devices. When you create a printer pool, the print server sends each incoming job to the first print device it finds that is not busy. This effectively distributes the jobs among the available print devices, providing users with more rapid service.

To create a printer pool, you must have at least two identical print devices, or at least print devices that use the same printer driver. The print devices must be in the same location, because there is no way to tell which print device will process a given document. You must also connect all of the print devices in the pool to the same print server. If the print server is a Windows 7 computer, you can connect the print devices to any viable ports.

To configure a printer pool, use the following procedure.

CREATE A PRINTER POOL

GET READY. Log on to Windows 7 using an account with the Manage Printer permission.

1. Click **Start,** and then click **Control Panel.** The Control Panel window appears.
2. Under **Hardware and Sound,** click **View Devices and Printers.** The Devices and Printers window appears.
3. Right click one of the printer icons in the window and then, from the context menu, select **Printer Properties.** The printer's Properties sheet appears.
4. Click the **Ports** tab, and then select all of the ports to which the print devices are connected.
5. Select the **Enable printer pooling** check box, and then click **OK.**

SKILL SUMMARY

IN THIS LESSON YOU LEARNED:

- Windows 7 has several sets of permissions, which operate independently of each other, including NTFS permissions, share permissions, registry permissions, and Active Directory permissions.

- NTFS permissions enable you to control access to files and folders by specifying just what tasks individual users can perform on them.

- Share permissions provide rudimentary access control for all of the files on a network share.

- The printing architecture in Windows is modular, consisting of the print device, a printer, a print server, and a printer driver.

- A local printer is one that supports a print device directly attached to the computer or attached to the network. A network printer connects to a shared printer hosted by another computer.

- To install a printer, you run the Add Printer wizard and specify the printer driver and port to use.

- A single printer can direct jobs to more than one port, creating a printer pool.

- A single print device can be served by multiple printers, each of which can have unique properties, drivers, settings, permissions, or monitoring characteristics.

- The print queue window enables you to monitor printers for potential signs of trouble.

■ Knowledge Assessment

Fill in the Blank

Complete the following sentences by writing the correct word or words in the blanks provided.

1. If a user has the Deny Full Control permission for the root of the D: drive and the Allow Full Control permission for D:\Documents, then the user's effective permissions for D:\Documents will be _____ Full Control.

2. A user calls the help desk and asks you why she cannot send print jobs to a shared printer that is using Windows 7 as a print server. You determine that the problem is related to the printer permissions. The user cannot send jobs to the printer because she only has the _____ permission for the printer.

3. To share a printer with network users, you must first open the Network and Sharing Center and turn on _____ and _____.

4. In the Windows printing architecture, the two hardware components are called the _____ and the _____.

5. Jack has the Allow Print, Allow Manage Documents, and Allow Manage Printers permissions to a printer with a priority of 1. Jill has the Allow Print permission to a printer with a priority of 10, connected to the same print device. If Jack and Jill both submit a print job at exactly the same time, _____'s print job will be processed first.

6. The primary function of a printer driver is to take printer commands generated by applications and convert them into _____ commands.

7. In the NTFS permission system, _____ permissions are actually combinations of _____ permission.

8. When no users have NTFS permissions to access a particular file, the only person who can regain access to it is the _____.

9. To share a printer, you must be a member of the _____ group.

10. To create a share called DOCS and hide it from network users, you must assign it the name _____.

True / False

Circle T if the statement is true or F if the statement is false.

T | F **1.** Granting users the Manage Printers permissions enables them to submit jobs to the printer.

T | F **2.** All permissions are stored in the access control list of the element being protected.

T | F **3.** A security principal is the person granting permissions to network users.

T | F **4.** NTFS permissions always take precedence over share permissions.

T | F **5.** To create a printer pool, you must create a separate printer for each print device.

T | F **6.** Granting someone the Allow Manage Printers permission enables them to submit jobs to the printer.

T | F **7.** To assign different printer priorities to two different groups, you must create two printers.

T | F **8.** When you move an NTFS file to a location on the same volume, the file's existing permissions move with it.

T | F **9.** When you install a printer for a print device connected to a Windows 7 computer's USB port, you must specify the print device's manufacturer and model.

T | F**10.** When you open a print queue window and cancel the document that is currently printing, the print device stops immediately.

Review Questions

1. You are the administrator of a network with several print devices, all of which are hosted by Windows 7 computers and shared with all of the users on the network. One of the print devices is malfunctioning and must be sent out for repair. What is the most practical way to prevent network users from sending jobs to that printer while the print device is unavailable?

2. A standard user wants to install a USB printer connected to her computer. The drivers for the printer are included with Windows 7. Can the user install the printer without help from an administrator? Why or why not?

■ Case Scenarios

Scenario 6-1: Rescuing Orphaned Files

Heidi, a junior desktop technician, approaches you, her supervisor, ashen-faced. A few minutes earlier, the president of the company called the help desk and asked Heidi to give his new assistant the permissions needed to access his personal budget spreadsheet. As she was attempting to assign the permissions, she accidentally deleted the BUDGET_USERS group from the spreadsheet's access control list. Heidi is now terrified because that group was the only entry in the file's ACL. Now no one can access the spreadsheet file, not even the president or the Administrator account. Is there any way to gain access to the file, and if so, how?

Scenario 6-2: Enhancing Print Performance

You are a desktop support technician for a law firm with a group of ten legal secretaries who provide administrative support to the attorneys. All of the secretaries use a single, shared, high-speed laser printer that is connected to a dedicated Windows 7 print server. The secretaries print multiple copies of large documents on a regular basis, and although the laser printer is fast, it is kept running almost constantly. Sometimes the secretaries have to wait 20 minutes or more after submitting a print job for their documents to reach the top of the queue. The office manager has offered to purchase additional printers for the department. However, the secretaries are accustomed to simply clicking the Print button, and don't like the idea of having to examine multiple print queues to determine which one has the fewest jobs before submitting a document. What can you do to provide the department with a printing solution that will enable the secretaries to utilize additional printers most efficiently?

Scenario 6-3: Assigning Permissions

You are working the help desk for a corporate network and you receive a call from a user named Leo, who is requesting access to the files for a new classified project called Trinity. The Trinity files are stored in a shared folder on a file server, which is locked in a secured underground data storage facility in New Mexico. After verifying that the user has the appropriate security clearance for the project, you create a new group on the file server called TRINITY_USERS and add Leo's user account to that group. Then, you add the TRINITY_USER group to the access control list for the Trinity folder on the file server, and assign the group the following NTFS permissions:

- Allow Modify
- Allow Read & Execute
- Allow List Folder Contents
- Allow Read
- Allow Write

Some time later, Leo calls you back to tell you that while he is able to access the Trinity folder and read the files stored there, he has been unable to save changes back to the server. What is the most likely cause of the problem?

Working with Applications

OBJECTIVE DOMAIN MATRIX

TECHNOLOGY SKILL	OBJECTIVE DOMAIN	OBJECTIVE NUMBER
Configuring Application Compatibility	Configure application compatibility.	3.2
Configuring Application restrictions	Configure application restrictions.	3.3
Configuring Internet Explorer	Configure Internet Explorer.	3.4

KEY TERMS

Application Compatibility Toolkit (ACT)

application control policies (AppLocker)

certification authority (CA)

compatibility fix

compatibility mode

Compatibility View

InPrivate Mode

phishing

Program Compatibility Troubleshooter

protected mode

public key infrastructure (PKI)

RSS feeds

Secure Sockets Layer (SSL)

security zones

shim

SmartScreen Filter

social engineering

software restriction policies

Windows XP Mode

■ Administering Internet Explorer

↓ THE BOTTOM LINE Technical specialists must be familiar with the administrative controls in Internet Explorer to protect users from Internet predators.

Windows 7 includes the latest version of the Internet Explorer web browser, Version 8, which enhances the features introduced in Version 7 and includes some important upgrades of its own. For technical specialists, these changes are likely to result in an increasing number of "user error" calls as users become accustomed to the new tools and the changes to the interface. Internet Explorer 8 also includes security tools that you must know how to configure for maximum effectiveness.

Configuring Internet Explorer

Internet Explorer includes a variety of new features that technical specialists must be able to use and configure.

CERTIFICATION READY?
Configure Internet Explorer.
3.4

As with earlier versions of Internet Explorer, IE satisfies most users' needs with no adjustment. However, some of the new features in IE require configuration. The following sections examine the configuration procedures that desktop technicians might have to perform for their clients.

CONFIGURING COMPATIBILITY VIEW

The standards that developers use when creating Web sites, like most standards, are in a continual state of development. Browsers like IE, therefore, must be designed to properly display pages that conform to the latest version standards. IE 8 operates in a default standards mode that enables it to display pages created using Cascading Style Sheets 2.1 and other standards.

The problem with this regular development is that many of the pages on the Internet still conform to older versions of the standards, and IE 8 might not display them properly. To accommodate these older pages, IE 8 includes a feature called *Compatibility View*, which enables the browser to display older pages properly.

From the user's perspective, the most easily visible indication of Compatibility View is the broken window icon that appears at the right end of the IE address box, as shown in Figure 7-1. When a Web site designed to earlier standards does not display properly, clicking this icon switches IE into Compatibility View mode, which can sometimes improve the appearance of the site. You can also enable Compatibility View by selecting Tools/Compatibility View from the Tools menu or the Tools toolbar button.

Figure 7-1

The IE Compatibility View icon

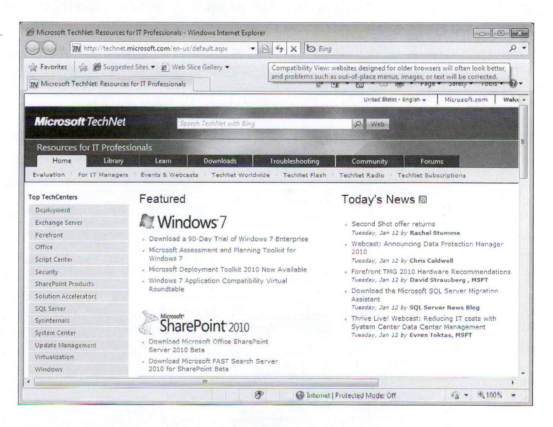

When you select Tools/Compatibility View Settings from the Tools menu or the Tools toolbar button, the Compatibility View Settings dialog box appears, as shown in Figure 7-2. In this dialog box, you can maintain a list of Web sites for which you want to use Compatibility View all of the time.

Figure 7-2

The IE Compatibility View Settings dialog box

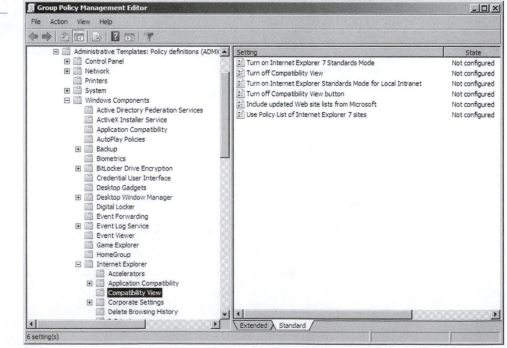

In addition to maintaining individual lists on each computer, Microsoft also maintains its own list of sites that can benefit from Compatibility View. When you select the *Include updated Web site lists from Microsoft* check box on the Compatibility View Settings dialog box, IE includes the Microsoft-supplied sites in the computer's list.

For Web site developers, it is possible to include tags in HTML files that cause IE to view the page in Compatibility View mode. For example, to render a page using the IE Version 7 standards, you can include the following code in the page's HEAD section:

```
<meta http-equiv="X-UA-Compatible" content="IE=7" />
```

For workstations on an Active Directory Domain Services (AD DS) network, administrators can configure Compatibility View settings using Group Policy, as shown in Figure 7-3. The settings are located in the Computer Configuration\Policies\Administrative Templates\Windows Components\Internet Explorer\Compatibility View container.

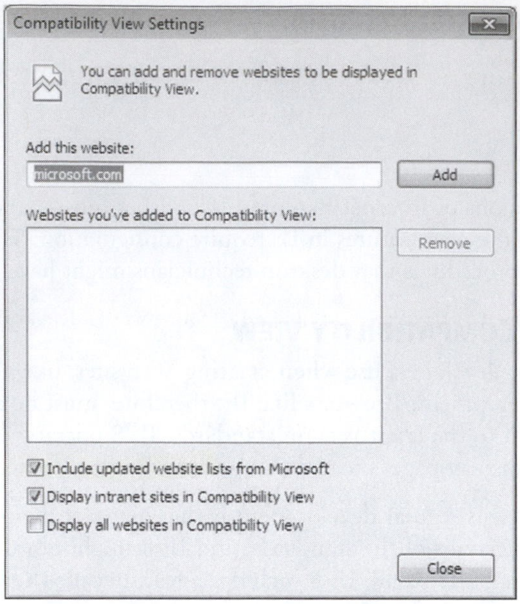

TAKE NOTE*

Any META tags in a web page's code specifying a rendering standard override the presence of the site in the computer's Compatibility View list.

Figure 7-3

Compatibility View Settings in a Group Policy object

The policy settings for Compatibility View are as follows:

- **Turn on Internet Explorer 7 Standards Mode:** Causes IE to render all web pages in the Standards Mode from the previous version of the browser. This improves compatibility with older Web sites, but can negatively affect the appearance of sites designed to the current standard.

- **Turn off Compatibility View:** Disables the Compatibility View feature in IE. The broken view icon does not appear, and users cannot configure the Compatibility View settings.

- **Turn on Internet Explorer Standards Mode for Local Intranet:** Causes IE to display all intranet content using the current Standards Mode, and prevents users from modifying this behavior.

- **Turn off Compatibility View button:** Prevents the broken page icon from appearing on the IE address box.

- **Include updated Web site lists from Microsoft:** Forces IE to use the Microsoft site compatibility lists when displaying web pages.

- **Use Policy List of Internet Explorer 7 sites:** Enables administrators to create a common list of sites that IE should display using Compatibility View mode.

MANAGING ADD-ONS

Internet Explorer is designed to be a versatile platform that can interact with a variety of other resources on the computer, on the network, and on the Internet. One of the ways that IE does this is through the use of add-ons. Add-ons are separate software components, created by Microsoft or third parties, that interact with the basic functions of the web browser. Add-ons can provide an interface between the browser and another software product or between the browser and a specific site on the Internet.

The four basic types of add-ons supported by IE are as follows:

- **Toolbars and Extensions:** Enable the browser to open and manipulate Web sites or file types that IE does not support natively. Some applications add their own toolbars to IE, enabling you to work with their documents within an IE session.

- **Search Providers:** Enable the user to perform searches directly from the IE interface using search engines on the Internet or the local network.

- **Accelerators:** Enable users to send text or other media they select in an IE browser window to another application, such as an email client, or an Internet resource, such as a blog.

- **InPrivate Filtering:** Enables you to import and export XML files containing InPrivate filters.

Microsoft provides a few add-ons with IE in Windows 7, and also maintains gallery sites, from which you can download add-ons created by third parties. Some applications come with their own add-ons, which they install along with the application itself. Some Web sites also make add-ons available directly from their own pages.

To work with the IE add-ons on a particular Windows 7 computer, you open the Manage Add-ons dialog box, as shown in Figure 7-4, by clicking Tools\Manage Add-ons from either the menu bar or the Tools toolbar button.

WARNING As with any Internet download, be sure that you only install add-ons provided by sources that you trust. Add-ons can easily contain various types of malware that can damage your system.

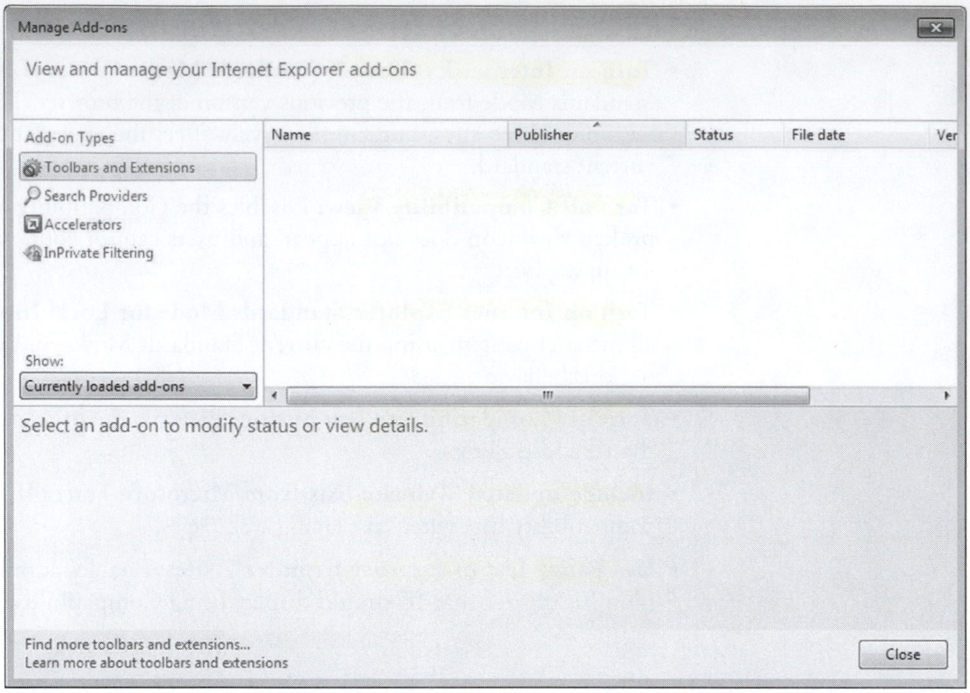

Figure 7-4

The Manage Add-ons dialog box

When you select one of the categories in the Add-on Types list, you see a list of the computer's currently installed add-ons. With the controls that appear on the bottom pane of the dialog box, you can temporarily disable an add-on, remove it permanently, or select it as the default add-on of that type.

CONFIGURING SEARCH OPTIONS

Search providers are one of the most useful types of IE add-on. By default, the Instant Search box found in Internet Explorer enables users to perform searches using Microsoft's Bing engine. To use other search engines, you must first install them to the list of search providers. Search providers are add-ons specifically designed to conform to the syntax required by other search engines.

IE supports virtually any type of search provider, not just the well-known web search engines such as Google. You can also add search providers for specific topics or sites, such as Wikipedia and the *New York Times*. Finally, you can add internal search engines of your own design, so that users can search your corporate intranet.

Adding Search Providers

To add search providers to the Instant Search list, use the following procedure.

➔ **ADD A SEARCH PROVIDER**

GET READY. Log on to Windows 7.

1. Click Start, and then click Internet Explorer. The Internet Explorer window appears.

2. Click the down arrow on the right side of the Instant Search box and then, from the context menu, select Find More Providers. The *Add-ons Gallery: Search Providers* page appears, as shown in Figure 7-5.

Figure 7-5

The Add-ons Gallery: Search Providers page

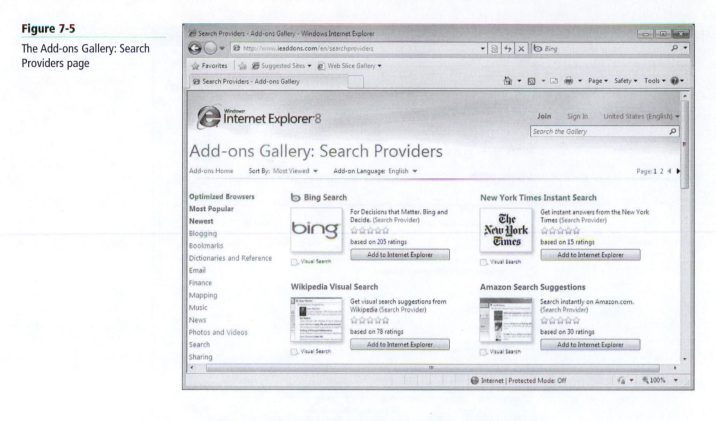

3. Click the Add to Internet Explorer button for one of the Web Search or Topic Search providers. An Add Search Provider dialog box appears, as shown in Figure 7-6.

+ MORE INFORMATION

To add international search providers in other languages, click the See Global Search Guides link, select a country, and then select one of the search providers for that country.

Figure 7-6

The Add Search Provider dialog box

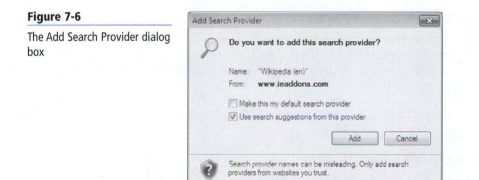

4. If you want the selected provider to replace Bing as the IE default, select the Make this my default search provider check box. If you want the provider to provide suggestions as you type searches, select the Use search suggestions from this provider check box. Then, click Add to add the selected provider to the Instant Search list.

5. To add a search provider that does not appear on the page, click the Create your own search provider link at the bottom of the page. *The Create your own search provider* page appears, as shown in Figure 7-7.

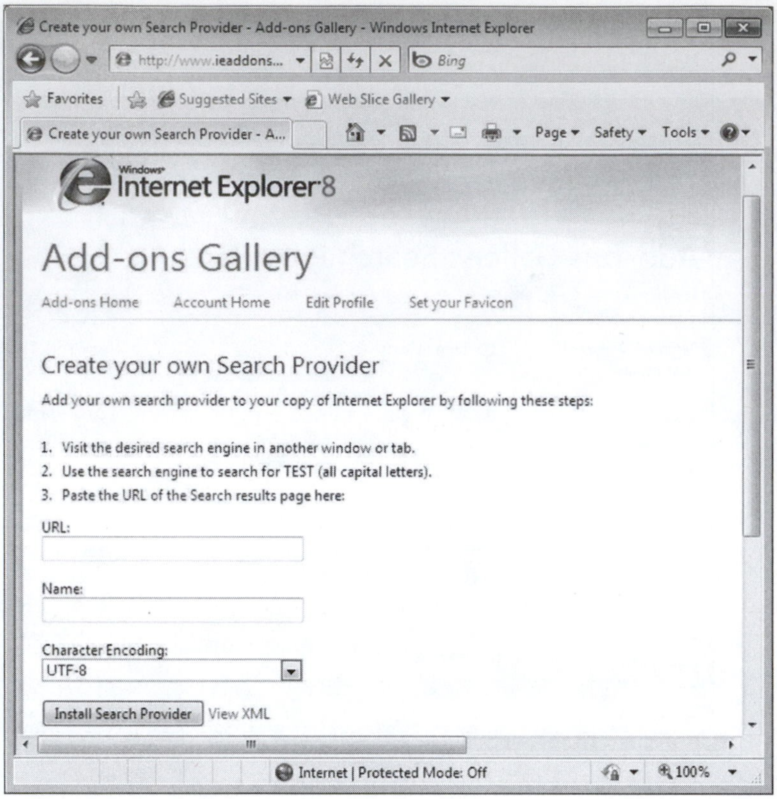

Figure 7-7

The Create your own search provider page

6. Follow the instructions to supply the URL for the search provider you want to add and type a name for the search provider in the Name text box.

7. Click Install Search Provider. IE adds the new search provider to the list.

Once you configure IE with multiple search providers, you can click the down arrow on the right side of the Instant Search box to select the provider you want to use for a particular search.

Specifying a Default Search Provider

When you first open an Internet Explorer window, the Instant Search box displays the name of the default search provider, which initially is *Bing*. Once you have added search providers to the Instant Search list, you can specify a different default provider, using the following procedure.

SPECIFY A DEFAULT SEARCH PROVIDER

GET READY. Log on to Windows 7.

1. Click Start, and then click Internet Explorer. The Internet Explorer window appears.

2. Click the down arrow on the right side of the Instant Search box and then, from the context menu, select Manage Search Providers. The Manage Add-ons dialog box appears, with the Search Providers add-on type selected, as shown in Figure 7-8.

3. In the list of search providers, select the entry you want to set as the default and click the Set as default button. The Instant Search box changes to reflect the new default search provider.

4. Click OK.

Figure 7-8

The Search Providers list in the Manage Add-ons dialog box

Manage Add-ons			
View and manage your Internet Explorer add-ons			

Add-on Types	Name	Status	Listing order	Search suggestions
Toolbars and Extensions	Bing	Default	1	Enabled
Search Providers	Wikipedia (en)		2	Disabled
Accelerators				
InPrivate Filtering				

Select the search provider you want to view or change.

☐ Prevent programs from suggesting changes to my default search provider

Find more search providers...
Learn more about search provider preferences

[Close]

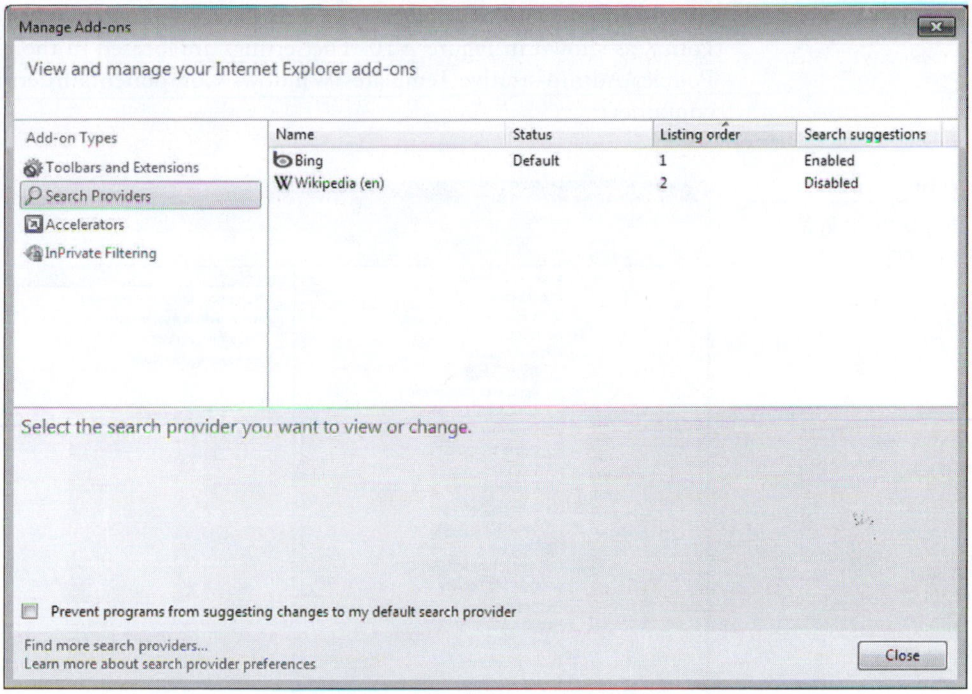

CONFIGURING ACCELERATORS

Like search providers, accelerators enable users to send content to other resources, in the form of applications running on the computer or other sites on the Internet. However, instead of the user typing content into a search box, accelerators enable you to highlight content in a browser window and select the accelerator for the resource you want to receive that content.

By default, IE includes accelerators that enable users to email content, post it to a blog, find it on a map, or translate it to another language. By clicking the *Find more accelerators* link on the Manage Add-ons dialog box, you can install new accelerators from the Microsoft Add-ons Gallery, as shown in Figure 7-9, using them to replace or augment the default ones.

Figure 7-9

Accelerators in the Microsoft Add-ons Gallery

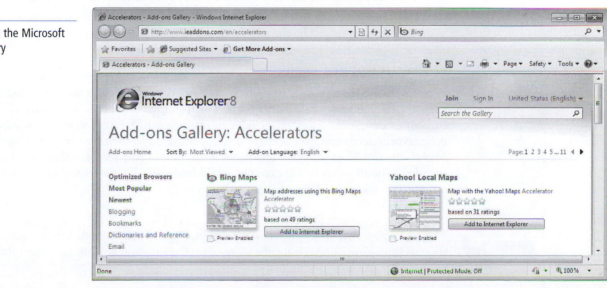

Administrators can control the use of accelerators on Windows 7 computers using Group Policy, as shown in Figure 7-10. The settings are located in the Computer Configuration\ Policies\Administrative Templates\Windows Components\Internet Explorer\Accelerators container.

Figure 7-10

Accelerators Settings in a Group Policy object

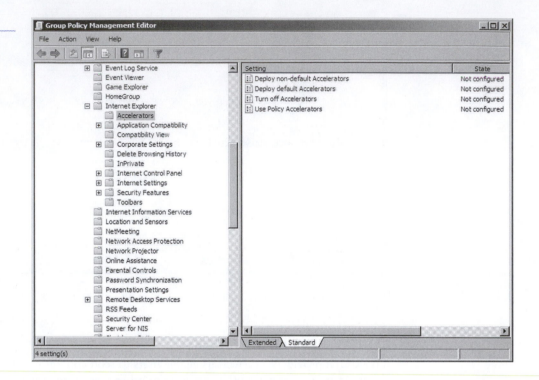

The Accelerators Group Policy settings are as follows:

- **Deploy non-default Accelerators:** Enables administrators to specify additional accelerators to be installed on Windows 7 computers. Users can also add their own non-default accelerators at will, but they cannot modify or remove the accelerators specified by the administrator.

- **Deploy default Accelerators:** Causes Windows 7 computers to deploy the accelerators included with IE by default. Users can also add their own accelerators at will, but they cannot modify or remove the default accelerators.

- **Turn off Accelerators:** Prevents Windows 7 computers from running any IE accelerators.

- **Use Policy Accelerators:** Prevents Windows 7 users from adding any accelerators other than those specified by the administrator in other Group Policy settings.

CONFIGURING RSS FEEDS

Many Web sites that provide frequently changing content, such as news sites and blogs, support a push technology called **RSS feeds**, which simplifies the process of delivering updated content to designated users. IE includes an integrated RSS reader so users can subscribe to their favorite feeds and have updated content delivered to their browsers on a regular basis. Many sites and blogs maintain text-based feeds, but an RSS feed can also push images, audio, or video content to users. For example, audio feeds, also known as *podcasts*, have become an increasingly dominant form of content delivery.

> **TAKE NOTE** *
>
> The initials RSS are most commonly said to stand for Really Simple Syndication, but several competing standards for the technology use the same initials, including Rich Site Summary and RDF Site Summary.

The whole point of an RSS feed is to eliminate the need for users to open multiple Web sites and browse for new content. With an RSS feed, the RSS client automatically retrieves new content from the content provider, enabling users to browse only the new information from their favorite sites.

Before you can receive RSS feeds with IE, however, you must subscribe to them. Subscription is the term used to refer to the process of configuring the RSS client to receive transmissions from a particular site. At the present time, most RSS feeds are available for subscription free of charge, but it is possible that future incarnations of the technology will take the form of services for which you must pay a fee to the content provider.

Subscribing to RSS Feeds

When you access a web page, IE automatically searches for RSS feeds. If IE locates feeds as part of the page, the RSS button on the toolbar changes its color to red. To subscribe to a feed, use the following procedure.

➔ SUBSCRIBE TO AN RSS FEED

GET READY. Log on to Windows 7.

1. Click Start, and then click Internet Explorer. The Internet Explorer window appears.

2. Browse to the Web site providing the feed to which you want to subscribe. When IE detects a feed, the Feeds button in the toolbar turns red.

3. Click the Feeds button. If there is more than one feed associated with the page, select one from the Feeds submenu. The RSS feed page appears, as shown in Figure 7-11. You can always read the current contents of the feed on this page, whether you are subscribed or not.

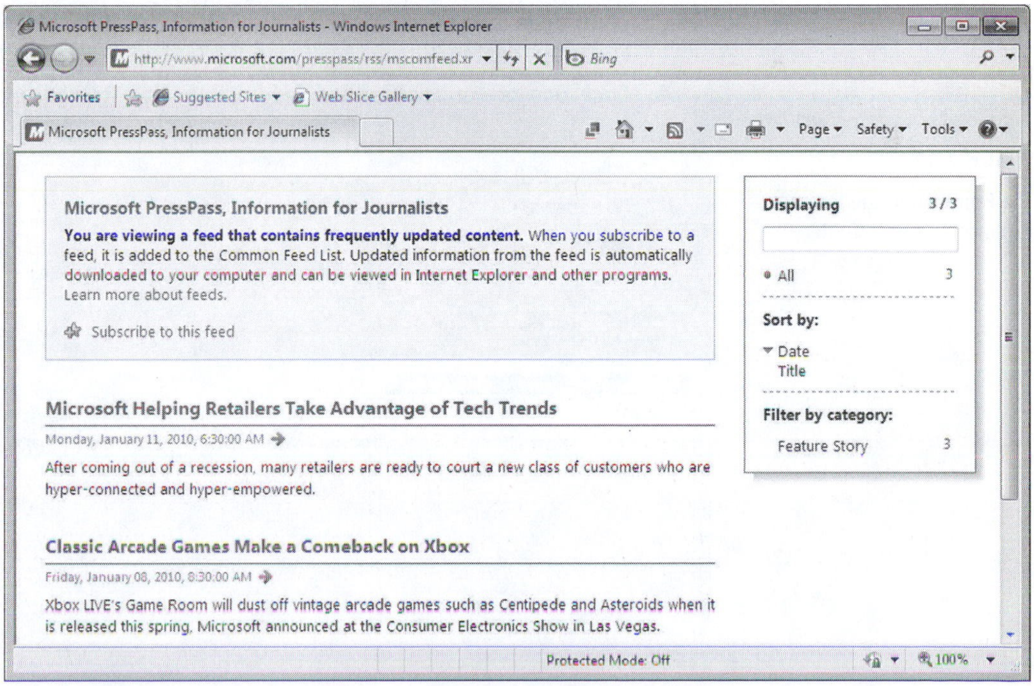

Figure 7-11

An RSS feed page in Internet Explorer

Microsoft PressPass, Information for Journalists - Windows Internet Explorer

http://www.microsoft.com/presspass/rss/mscomfeed.xr   Bing

Favorites   Suggested Sites ▾   Web Slice Gallery ▾

Microsoft PressPass, Information for Journalists   Page ▾ Safety ▾ Tools ▾

Microsoft PressPass, Information for Journalists

You are viewing a feed that contains frequently updated content. When you subscribe to a feed, it is added to the Common Feed List. Updated information from the feed is automatically downloaded to your computer and can be viewed in Internet Explorer and other programs. Learn more about feeds.

⭐ Subscribe to this feed

Microsoft Helping Retailers Take Advantage of Tech Trends

Monday, January 11, 2010, 6:30:00 AM

After coming out of a recession, many retailers are ready to court a new class of customers who are hyper-connected and hyper-empowered.

Classic Arcade Games Make a Comeback on Xbox

Friday, January 08, 2010, 8:30:00 AM

Xbox LIVE's Game Room will dust off vintage arcade games such as Centipede and Asteroids when it is released this spring, Microsoft announced at the Consumer Electronics Show in Las Vegas.

Displaying   3 / 3

• All   3

Sort by:
▾ Date
  Title

Filter by category:

Feature Story   3

Protected Mode: Off   100%

4. Click the Subscribe to this feed link. A Subscribe to this Feed dialog box appears, as shown in Figure 7-12.

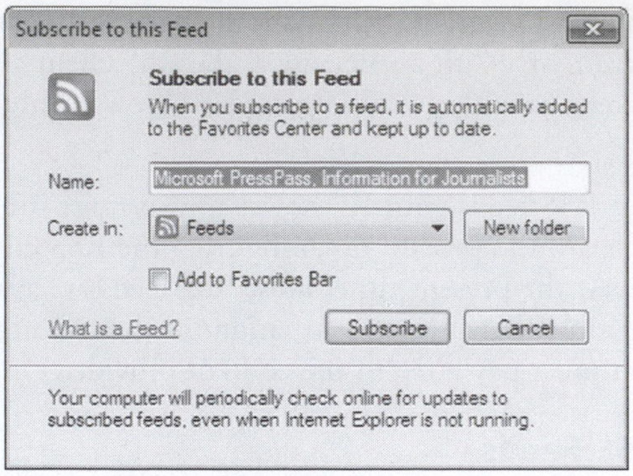

Figure 7-12

An Internet Explorer Subscribe to this Feed dialog box

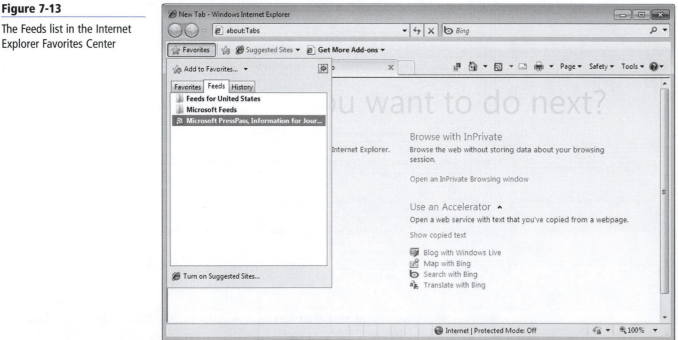

5. In the Name text box, type a name you want to assign to the feed (if it differs from the default).

6. Select the folder to which you want to add the feed, or click New folder to create one. Then click Subscribe. The feed page changes to indicate that you have successfully subscribed to the feed.

Viewing RSS Feeds

Once you have subscribed to RSS feeds, you can view their contents at any time by using the following procedure.

VIEW RSS FEEDS

GET READY. Log on to Windows 7.

1. Click Start, and then click Internet Explorer. The Internet Explorer window appears.

2. Click the Favorites button. The Favorites Center pane appears.

3. In the Favorites Center pane, click the Feeds tab. The pane displays a list of your currently subscribed feeds, as shown in Figure 7-13. To leave the Favorites Center pane open so you can browse through a list of subscriptions, click the Pin the Favorites Center button, on the right side of the menu bar.

4. Click one of your subscribed feeds to display its contents in the main IE window.

Figure 7-13

The Feeds list in the Internet Explorer Favorites Center

Configuring Feed Settings

When you subscribe to an RSS feed using Internet Explorer, the content is updated once every day, by default. You can modify the default update setting for all feeds or for individual feeds. To update the default setting for all feeds, use the following procedure.

CONFIGURE DEFAULT FEED SETTINGS

GET READY. Log on to Windows 7.

1. Click Start, and then click Internet Explorer. The Internet Explorer window appears.
2. Click the Tools button, and then select Internet Options. The Internet Options dialog box appears, as shown in Figure 7-14.

Figure 7-14

The Internet Options dialog box

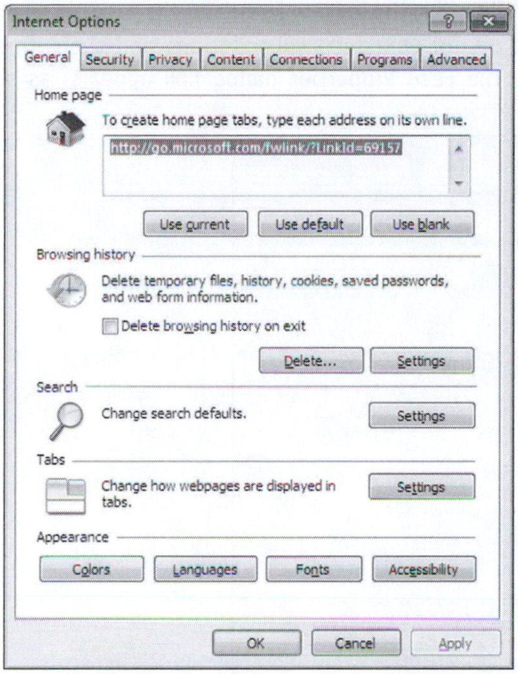

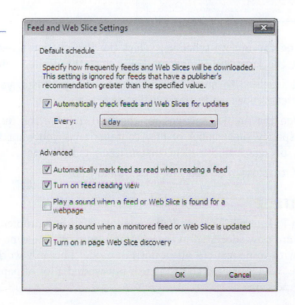

3. Click the Content tab and then, in the Feeds section, click Settings. The Feed and Web Slice Settings dialog box appears, as shown in Figure 7-15.

Figure 7-15

The Feed and Web Slice Settings dialog box

4. In the Every dropdown list, specify the interval at which IE should check the sub-scribed RSS feeds for updates. Then click OK to close the Feed Settings dialog box.

5. Click OK to close the Internet Options dialog box.

To configure the settings for an individual feed, use the following procedure.

CONFIGURE INDIVIDUAL FEED SETTINGS

GET READY. Log on to Windows 7.

1. Click Start, and then click Internet Explorer. The Internet Explorer window appears.

2. Click the Favorites button. The Favorites Center pane appears.

3. In the Favorites Center pane, click the Feeds button. The pane displays a list of your currently subscribed feeds.

4. Right click one of your feed subscriptions and then, from the context menu, select Properties. The Feed Properties dialog box appears, as shown in Figure 7-16.

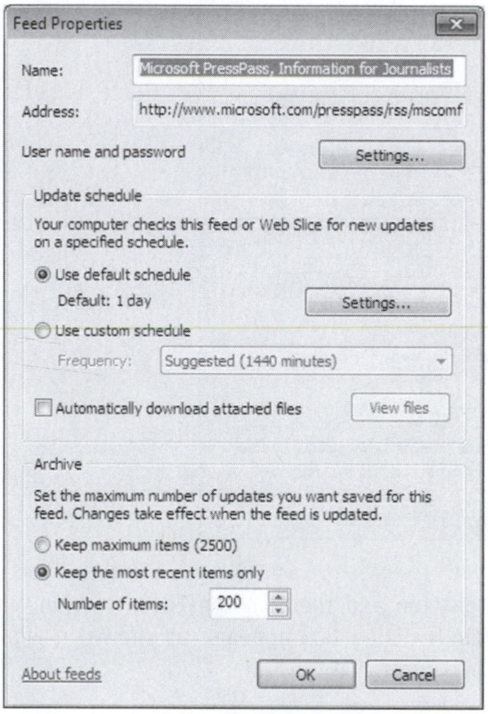

Figure 7-16

The Feed Properties dialog box

5. To change the update schedule, select the Use custom schedule radio button and then, in the Frequency dropdown list, select the desired interval.

6. When subscribing to an RSS feed that includes podcasts, you must also select the Automatically download attached files check box.

7. To change the Archive settings for the feed, change the Number of items spin box to specify the number of new content items you want to retain in the feed window, or select the Keep maximum items radio button.

8. Click OK to close the Feed Properties dialog box.

PRINTING WITH IE

Prior to version 7, Internet Explorer had some long-standing problems with the printing of web pages that are now addressed in the current release. At one time, it was common for web pages to print with some text cut off in portrait mode. The only workaround was to switch to landscape mode, which printed all of the text but wasted a lot of paper and provided an awk-ward reading experience.

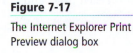

IE now has a Print Preview dialog box, as shown in Figure 7-17, that provides users with greater flexibility, both in viewing and formatting the pages to be printed. For example, the default Shrink To Fit setting reduces each web page to the point that it will fit on a single sheet of paper. No longer is text cut off on the right, and there are no more orphaned lines that print on a second page.

Figure 7-17

The Internet Explorer Print Preview dialog box

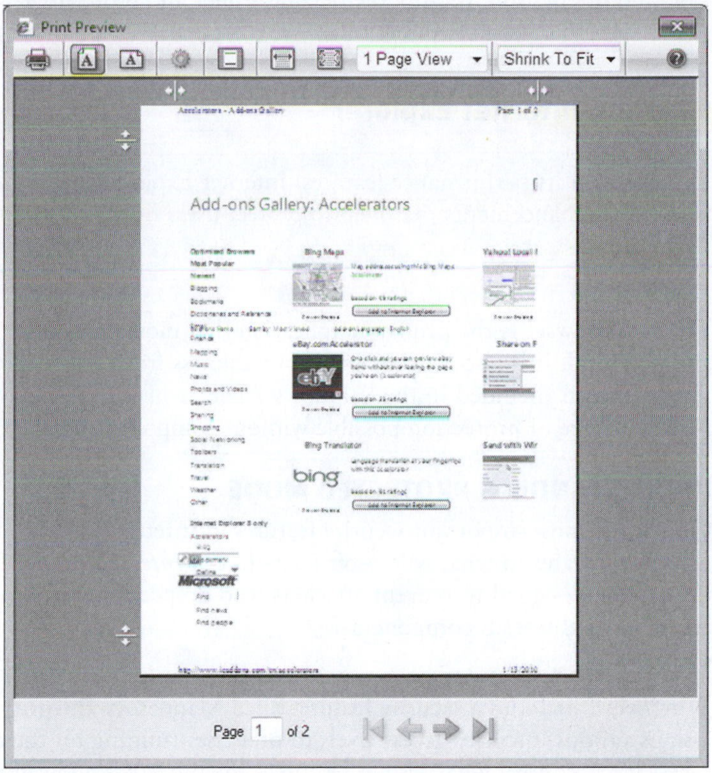

In addition to shrinking web pages to fit the printed page size, you can also make pages larger or smaller by adjusting the sizes using percentages. This enables you to print enlarged pages for easier reading or reduce the size to print multiple web pages on a single sheet of paper.

When you click the down arrow next to the Print button on the toolbar, you can choose from the following options:

- **Print:** The Print dialog box, shown in Figure 7-18, enables you to select a printer, choose the pages you want to print, print multiple copies, and, on the Options tab, print specific frames from a web page.

Figure 7-18

The Internet Explorer Print dialog box

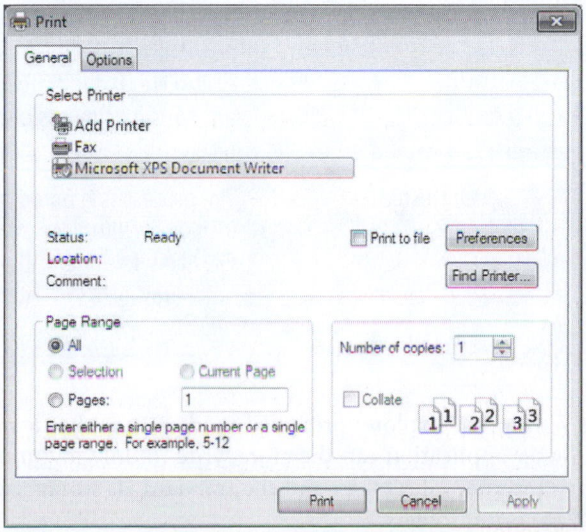

- **Print Preview:** The Print Preview window enables you to view the current web page at various sizes, select the page orientation (portrait or landscape), specify the size at which the web page should print, and dynamically adjust the margins.
- **Page Setup:** The Page Setup dialog box enables you to select a paper size, source tray, and orientation; modify the default header and footer that will print on each page; and adjust the margins numerically.

Securing Internet Explorer

Apart from its performance features, Internet Explorer includes a number of important security enhancements that help to protect users from malware incursions and other Internet dangers.

The web browser is the primary application that most people use to access the Internet, and as a result it is also a major point of weakness from a security perspective. The security improvements included in the Windows 7 release of Internet Explorer provide users with the highest degree of protection possible without compromising their Internet experiences.

UNDERSTANDING PROTECTED MODE

One of the most important security features in Internet Explorer is that, by default, the browser operates in what Microsoft refers to as *protected mode*. Protected mode is an operational state designed to prevent attackers who do penetrate the computer's defenses from accessing vital system components.

Protected mode is essentially a way to run Internet Explorer with highly reduced privileges. Windows 7 includes a security feature called Mandatory Integrity Control (MIC), which assigns various integrity access levels to processes running on the computer. These integrity access levels control what system resources the process is allowed to access. Table 7-1 shows the integrity levels assigned by MIC.

Table 7-1

Mandatory Integrity Control

INTEGRITY ACCESS LEVEL	PRIVILEGE LEVEL	PRIVILEGES
High	Administrator	The process is granted full access to the system, including write access to the Program Files folder and the HKEY_LOCAL_MACHINE registry key.
Medium	User	The process is granted limited access to the system, including write access to user-specific areas, such as the user's Documents folder and the HKEY_CURRENT_USER registry key. All processes that are not explicitly assigned an integrity access level receive this level of access.
Low	Untrusted	The process is granted minimal access to the system, including write access only to the Temporary Internet Files\Low folder and the HKEY_CURRENT_USER\ Software\Microsoft\Internet Explorer/LowRegistry registry key.

TAKE NOTE*

Mandatory Integrity Control is a Windows 7 and Windows Vista feature that is not present in Windows XP. As a result, when you install Internet Explorer 8 on a Windows XP system, it does not run in protected mode.

In Windows 7, Internet Explorer protected mode means that it runs as a low-integrity procedure. The browser application can therefore write to only low-integrity disk locations, such as the Temporary Internet Files folder and the standard IE storage areas, including the History, Cookies, and Favorites folders.

What this means is that even if attackers manage to gain access to the computer through a web browser connection, there is little they can do to damage the system because they do not have access to vital system areas. For example, even if an attacker manages to upload a destructive application to the system, he or she cannot force it to load each time the system starts by adding it to the Startup group.

Protected mode is not a complete defense against malware in itself. IE and Windows 7 have many other security mechanisms that work in combination. Protected mode is designed to limit the damage that attackers can do if they manage to penetrate the other security measures.

Detecting Protected Mode Incompatibilities

Because IE on Windows 7 runs in protected mode by default, it is possible that web-based applications designed to run on IE 6 or earlier versions might not run properly. These applications might be designed to write to a disk area that is inaccessible while in protected mode, or they might not know how to handle the new prompts in IE.

However, you might find that applications that did not run under IE version 7 now do run in IE 8, using the default settings. This is because in IE 7, Web sites in the local intranet zone ran in protected mode by default. In IE 8, Microsoft changed the defaults and disabled protected mode for local intranet sites, as shown in Figure 7-19.

Figure 7-19

Protected mode disabled

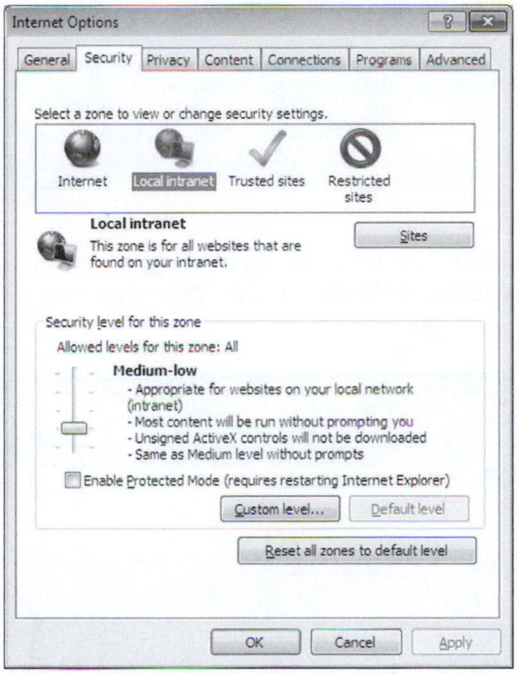

Comprehensive testing of all web-based applications should be an essential part of every Windows 7 or IE deployment. To gather information about application incompatibilities, enable Compatibility Logging using the following procedure.

ENABLE COMPATIBILITY LOGGING USING GROUP POLICY

GET READY. Log on to Windows 7 using an account with administrative capabilities.

1. Click Start, type mmc in the Start Search box, and then press **Enter**. After confirming that you are performing the action, a blank MMC console appears.

2. Click File > Add/Remove Snap-In. The Add or Remove Snap-Ins dialog box appears.

3. In the Available Snap-Ins list, select Group Policy Object Editor, and then click Add. The *Select Group Policy Object* page appears.

4. Click Finish to select the default Local Computer object.

5. Click OK to close the Add or Remove Snap-Ins dialog box.

6. Open the Computer Configuration\Administrative Templates\Windows Components\ Internet Explorer folder or the User Configuration\Administrative Templates\Windows Components\Internet Explorer folder, as shown in Figure 7-20.

Figure 7-20

The Internet Explorer folder

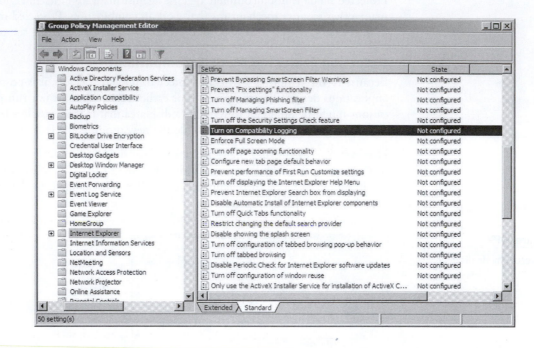

7. Double click the Turn on Compatibility Logging policy. The Turn on Compatibility Logging Properties sheet appears, as shown in Figure 7-21.

Figure 7-21

The Turn on Compatibility Logging Properties sheet

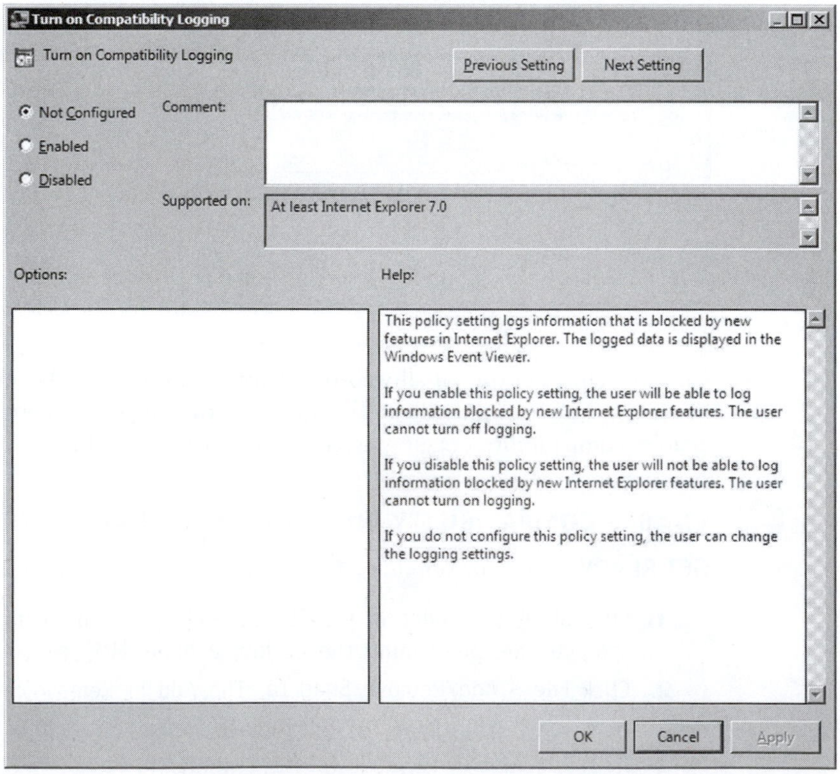

8. Select the Enabled radio button, and then click OK.

9. Close the Group Policy Object Editor console.

Once you enable the Turn on Compatibility Logging policy, Windows 7 begins logging all information blocked by the Internet Explorer security settings. The logged data appears in the Windows Event Viewer console in the Internet Explorer application log.

Resolving Protected Mode Incompatibilities

Once you have determined the exact source of your application's incompatibility, you can use the following techniques to try to resolve the problem:

- **Move the site to the Trusted Sites zone:** IE maintains different security zones that provide applications with different levels of privileges. Sites in the Internet zone run in protected mode with minimal privileges, but if you move them to the Trusted Sites zone, they receive elevated privileges and do not run in protected mode.

- **Disable protected mode in IE:** Although Microsoft does not recommend this practice, you can disable protected mode by selecting a zone and clearing the Enable Protected Mode check box. Disabling protected mode causes IE to apply the medium integrity access level to the zone.

- **Modify the application:** Probably the most difficult and time-consuming option, you can also modify the application itself so that it can run properly using the minimal privileges provided by protected mode.

CONFIGURING SECURITY ZONES

With the appropriate development tools and programming expertise, web-based applications can do virtually anything that traditional software applications do, which can be either a good or a bad thing. For companies developing their own in-house software, web browsers provide a stable, proven technological base. However, a web-based intranet application is likely to require extensive access to system resources. An intranet application might have to install software on the computer, for example, or change system configuration settings.

Granting this type of access is acceptable for an internal application, but you could not grant the same privileges to an Internet Web site. Imagine what it would be like to surf the Internet if every site you accessed had the ability to install any software it wanted on your computer, or modify any of your system configuration settings. Your computer would likely be rendered inoperative within a matter of hours.

To provide different levels of access to specific applications, Internet Explorer divides the addresses accessible with the web browser into several different *security zones*, each of which has a different set of privileges. The four zones are as follows:

- **Internet:** All Web sites that are not listed in the other three zones fall into this zone. Sites in the Internet zone run in protected mode and have minimal access to the computer's drives and configuration settings.

- **Local Intranet:** IE automatically detects sites that originate from the local intranet and places them in this zone. Sites in this zone do not run in protected mode and have significant access to the system, including the ability to run certain scripts, ActiveX controls, and plug-ins.

- **Trusted Sites:** This zone provides the most elevated set of privileges and is intended for sites that you can trust not to damage the computer. By default, there are no sites in this zone; you must add them manually.

- **Restricted Sites:** This zone has the most reduced set of privileges and runs in protected mode. It is intended for Web sites that are known to be malicious, but which users still must access for some reason. As with the Trusted Sites zone, this zone is empty by default.

There are two ways to modify the default zone settings in IE. You can assign Web sites to specific zones, or you can modify the security settings of the zones themselves. These two procedures are described in the following sections.

Adding Sites to a Security Zone

The easiest way to modify the security settings that Internet Explorer imposes on a specific Web site is to manually add the site to a different security zone. The typical procedure is to add a site to the Trusted Sites zone, to increase its privileges, or add it to the Restricted Sites zone, to reduce its privileges. To do this, use the following procedure:

 ADD A SITE TO A SECURITY ZONE

GET READY. Log on to Windows 7.

1. Click Start, and then click Control Panel. The Control Panel window appears.
2. Select Network and Internet > Internet Options. The Internet Properties sheet appears.
3. Click the Security tab, as shown in Figure 7-22.

Figure 7-22

The Security tab of the Internet Properties sheet

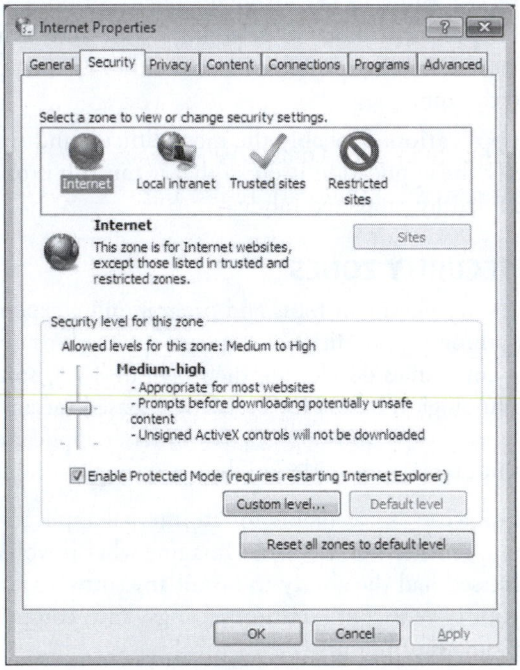

4. Select the zone, either Trusted sites or Restricted sites, to which you want to add a site.
5. Click Sites. The Trusted sites or Restricted sites dialog box appears, as shown in Figure 7-23.

Figure 7-23

The Trusted sites dialog box

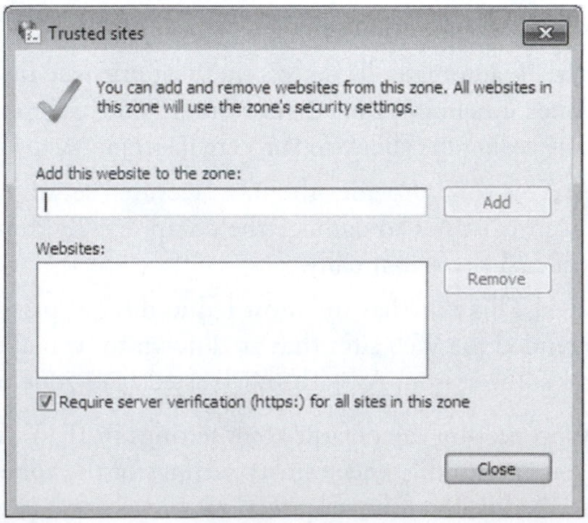

6. Type the URL of the Web site that you want to add to the zone into the *Add this website to the zone* text box, and then click Add. The URL appears in the Web sites list.

7. Click Close to close the *Trusted sites* or *Restricted sites* dialog box.

8. Click OK to close the Internet Properties sheet.

Configuring Zone Security

In addition to placing sites into zones, it is also possible to modify the properties of the zones themselves. Before you do this, however, you should consider that changing a zone's security properties will affect all of the sites in that zone. Decreasing the privileges allocated to a zone could prevent some sites in that zone from functioning properly. Increasing the privileges of a zone could open up security holes that attackers might be able to exploit.

To modify the security properties of a zone, use the following procedure.

⊙ MODIFY SECURITY ZONE SETTINGS

GET READY. Log on to Windows 7.

1. Click Start, and then click Control Panel. The Control Panel window appears.

2. Select Network and Internet > Internet Options. The Internet Properties sheet appears.

3. Click the Security tab.

4. Select the zone for which you want to modify the security settings.

5. In the Security level for this zone box, adjust the slider to increase or decrease the security level for the zone. Moving the slider up increases the protection for the zone and moving the slider down decreases it.

6. Select or clear the Enable protected mode check box, if desired.

7. To exercise more precise control over the zone's security settings, click Custom level. The Security Settings dialog box for the zone appears, as shown in Figure 7-24.

Figure 7-24

The Security Settings dialog box for the Internet zone

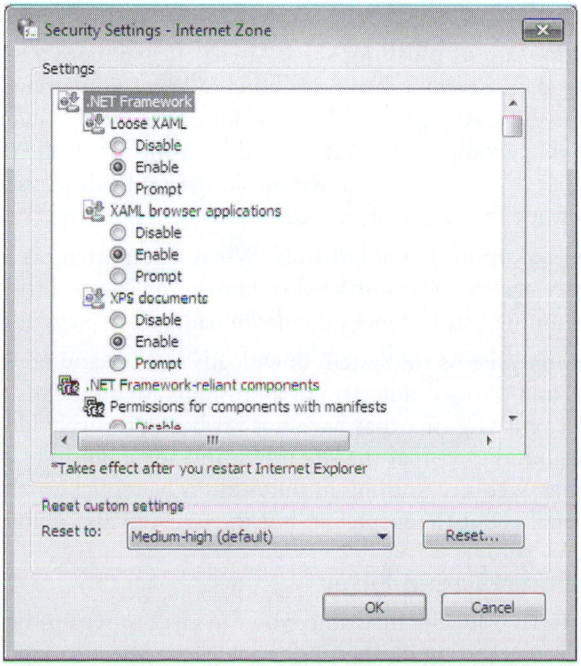

8. Select radio buttons for the individual settings in each of the security categories. The radio buttons typically make it possible to enable a setting, disable it, or prompt the user before enabling it.

9. Click OK to close the Security Settings dialog box.

10. Click OK to close the Internet Properties sheet.

CONFIGURING THE SMARTSCREEN FILTER

Social engineering is a term that describes any attempt to penetrate the security of a system by convincing people to disclose secret information. Many would-be attackers have realized that discovering a user's password with an elaborate software procedure is a lot more difficult than simply calling the user up and asking for it. When asked for information by an authoritative-sounding person saying that they work for the IT department, most people are eager to help and are all too willing to give out information that should be kept confidential.

Phishing is a technique that takes social engineering to a mass scale. Instead of convincing-sounding telephone callers, phishing uses convincing-looking Web sites that urge users to supply personal information, such as passwords and account numbers.

For example, an attacker might send out thousands of email messages directed at customers of a particular bank, urging them to update their account information or risk having their accounts closed. Unsuspecting users click the hyperlink in the email and are taken to a web page that looks very much like that of the actual bank site, but it isn't. The page is part of a bogus site set up by the attacker and probably copied from the bank site. This false site proceeds to ask the user for information such as bank account numbers, PINs, and passwords, which the attacker can then use to access the account.

Defending against phishing is more a matter of educating users than competing in a technological arms race, as is the case with viruses and other types of malware. Internet Explorer 8 includes a component called the *SmartScreen Filter* that examines traffic for evidence of phishing activity and displays a warning to the user if it finds any. It is up to the user to recognize the warning signs and to refrain from supplying confidential information to unknown parties.

Filtering for Phishing Attacks

The IE SmartScreen Filter uses three techniques to identify potential phishing Web sites. These techniques are as follows:

- **Online lookup of phishing sites:** Microsoft maintains a list of known phishing sites that it updates several times every hour. When a user attempts to access a Web site, IE transmits the URL, along with other nonconfidential system information to a Microsoft server, which compares it with the phishing site list. If the online lookup process determines that a Web site is a known phishing site, IE displays a warning. However, the user can continue to the site, if desired.

- **Online lookup of download sites:** When a user attempts to download a file, IE checks the source against Microsoft's list of known malicious software sites. If the source site appears on the list, IE blocks the download and displays a warning.

- **Onsite analysis:** As the system downloads it, IE examines the code of each web page for patterns and phrases indicative of a phishing attempt. This technique provides a means to detect phishing sites that have not yet been positively identified and reported as such. If the scan indicates that the site might include a phishing attempt, IE displays a yellow Suspicious Web site warning in the Address bar. Clicking the warning button displays more detail about the suspicion, but the user can also ignore the warning and proceed.

Disabling SmartScreen Filter

When you run IE 8 for the first time, you can elect to set up the browser by using express settings, or by configuring settings individually, as shown in Figure 7-25.

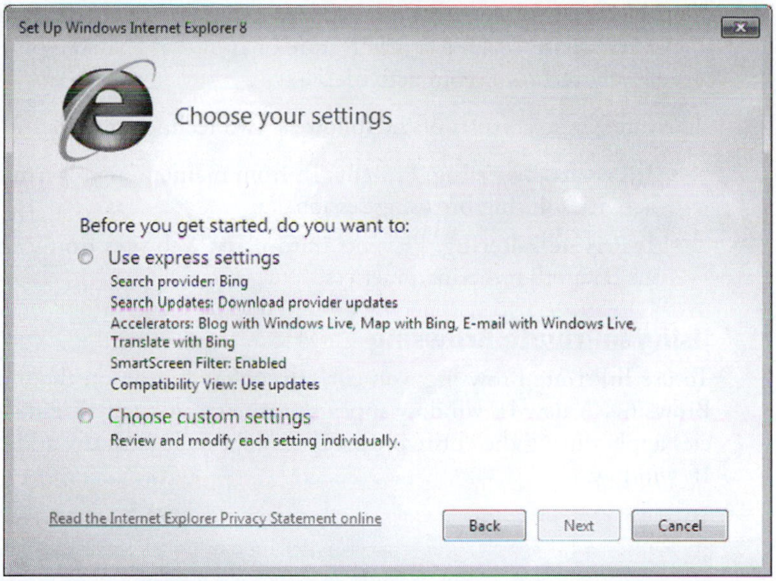

Figure 7-25

Configuring Internet Explorer

> **Set Up Windows Internet Explorer 8**
>
> **Choose your settings**
>
> Before you get started, do you want to:
>
> ○ Use express settings
> Search provider: Bing
> Search Updates: Download provider updates
> Accelerators: Blog with Windows Live, Map with Bing, E-mail with Windows Live, Translate with Bing
> SmartScreen Filter: Enabled
> Compatibility View: Use updates
>
> ○ Choose custom settings
> Review and modify each setting individually.
>
> Read the Internet Explorer Privacy Statement online   [Back] [Next] [Cancel]

The express settings option enables the SmartScreen Filter, but you can disable it at any time by clicking the Safety button on the toolbar and selecting SmartScreen Filter > Turn off SmartScreen Filter, to display the Microsoft SmartScreen Filter dialog box, as shown in Figure 7-26.

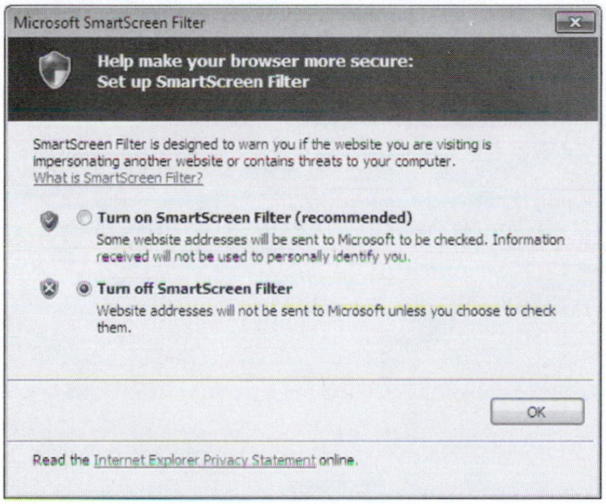

Figure 7-26

The Microsoft SmartScreen Filter dialog box

> **Microsoft SmartScreen Filter**
>
> **Help make your browser more secure: Set up SmartScreen Filter**
>
> SmartScreen Filter is designed to warn you if the website you are visiting is impersonating another website or contains threats to your computer.
> What is SmartScreen Filter?
>
> ○ **Turn on SmartScreen Filter (recommended)**
> Some website addresses will be sent to Microsoft to be checked. Information received will not be used to personally identify you.
>
> ● **Turn off SmartScreen Filter**
> Website addresses will not be sent to Microsoft unless you choose to check them.
>
> [OK]
>
> Read the Internet Explorer Privacy Statement online.

Phishing sites present no danger other than the temptation to reply to requests for confidential information. It is possible to turn the SmartScreen Filter off and remain safe from phishing attempts, as long as you follow one simple rule: Don't trust hyperlinks. Never supply a password or any other confidential information to a Web site unless you type the URL yourself and you are sure that it is correct.

Most successful phishing attempts occur when a user clicks a hyperlink in an email or another Web site. It is a simple matter to create a hyperlink that looks like http://www.woodgrovebank.com, but which actually points to a server run by an evil attacker in another domain. However, as long as you yourself type www.woodgrovebank.com in the browser's Address bar, you are assured of accessing the true Web site of Woodgrove Bank.

USING INPRIVATE MODE

Internet Explorer has always maintained a record of each user's activities, in the form of temporary files, cookies, and a browsing history. The user could delete these elements individually after the fact, but there was no easy way to prevent IE from gathering them all in the first place. *InPrivate Mode* is a new feature of IE 8 that enables you to surf the Internet without leaving any record of your activities.

InPrivate Mode consists of the following two technologies:

- **InPrivate Browsing:** Prevents IE from maintaining a permanent record of the user's activities during browsing session.
- **InPrivate Filtering:** Prevents third-party Web sites from compiling information about an IE user's browsing practices.

Using InPrivate Browsing

To use InPrivate Browsing, you click the Safety button on the toolbar and select InPrivate Browsing. A new IE window appears, as shown in Figure 7-27. The InPrivate Browsing policies apply during the entire browsing session, including any additional tabs you create in that IE window.

Figure 7-27

InPrivate Browsing in Internet Explorer

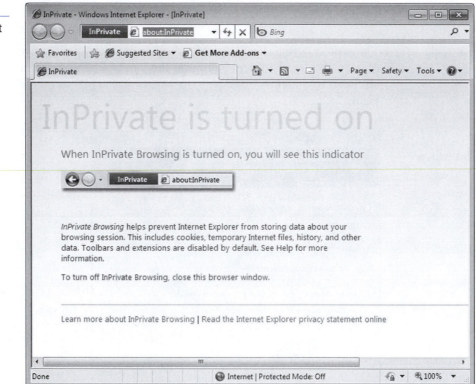

During the browsing session, IE stores some information temporarily, such as that found in cookies and temporary files, and IE deletes it when you terminate the session by closing the browser window. However, there is some information that IE does not store at all, including the browsing history, any data you supply in forms, and address bar and AutoComplete data.

Using InPrivate Filtering

Many Internet Web sites incorporate content from third-party providers, such as advertisements, maps, and videos. As a user browses to various sites that use these same providers, they can build up a profile of the user's browsing habits, and use that information to target them for specific types of ads. InPrivate Filtering enables you to block specific providers—or all providers—from gathering that information.

You can turn InPrivate Filtering on or off by clicking the Safety button in the toolbar and selecting InPrivate Filtering. You can also choose the sites you want to block by selecting

Safety > InPrivate Filtering Settings, to display the InPrivate Filtering Settings dialog box shown in Figure 7-28. In this dialog box, you can select a Web site from the list and choose whether to allow or block it.

Figure 7-28

The InPrivate Filtering Settings dialog box

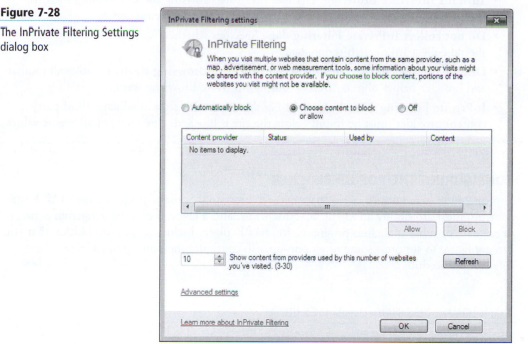

Configuring InPrivate Mode Using Group Policy

AD DS administrators can configure InPrivate Mode settings for Windows 7 users all over the network using Group Policy. The policy settings are located in the Computer Configuration\ Policies\Administrative Templates\Windows Components\Internet Explorer\InPrivate container, as shown in Figure 7-29.

Figure 7-29

InPrivate Settings in a Group Policy object

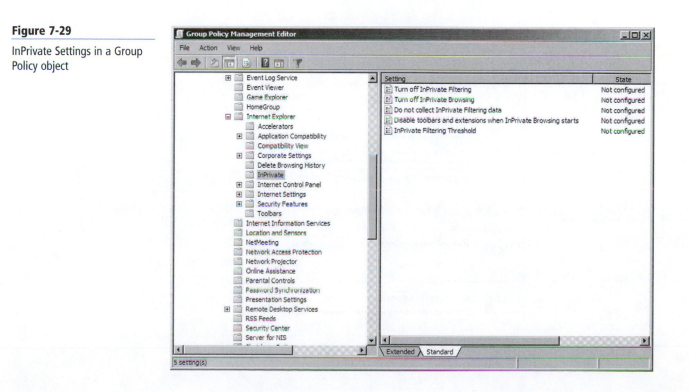

The policy settings for InPrivate Mode are as follows:

- **Turn off InPrivate Filtering:** Disables InPrivate Filtering for all browsing sessions. When you disable the setting, InPrivate Filtering is available for use.
- **Turn off InPrivate Browsing:** Disables InPrivate Browsing for all browsing sessions. When you disable the setting, InPrivate Browsing is available for use.
- **Do not collect InPrivate Filtering data:** Specifies whether Windows 7 computers should collect InPrivate filtering data.
- **Disable toolbars and extensions when InPrivate Browsing starts:** Disables all toolbars and browser helper objects (BHOs) during InPrivate Browsing sessions.
- **InPrivate Filtering Threshold:** Specifies the number of sites in which a third-party content provider must be found before the site is blocked. The range of allowable values is 3 to 30.

CONFIGURING THE POP-UP BLOCKER

Pop-up windows are now a fact of Internet web browsing. Some pop-ups are useful Web site controls, most are simply annoying advertisements, and a few can even be dangerous sources of spyware or other malicious programs. Internet Explorer includes a pop-up blocker that you can configure to suppress some or all pop-ups. To configure the pop-up blocker, use the following procedure.

CONFIGURE THE POP-UP BLOCKER

GET READY. Log on to Windows 7.

1. Click Start, and then click Control Panel. The Control Panel window appears.
2. Select Network and Internet > Internet Options. The Internet Properties sheet appears.
3. Click the Privacy tab, as shown in Figure 7-30.

Figure 7-30

The Privacy tab of the Internet Properties sheet

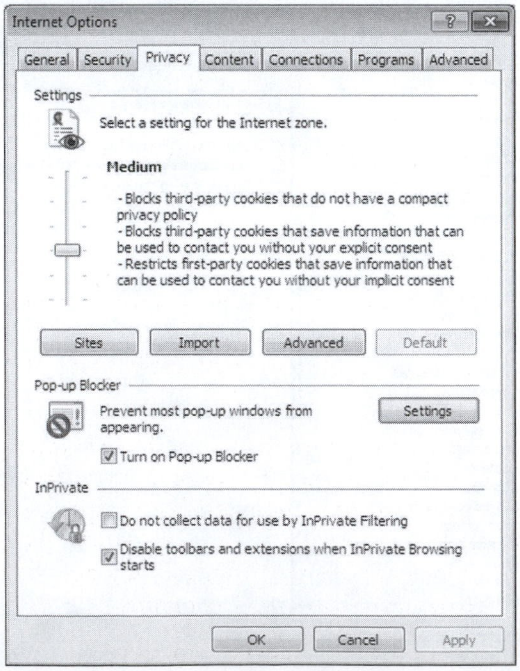

4. Click Settings. The Pop-Up Blocker Settings dialog box appears, as shown in Figure 7-31.

Figure 7-31

The Pop-Up Blocker Settings dialog box

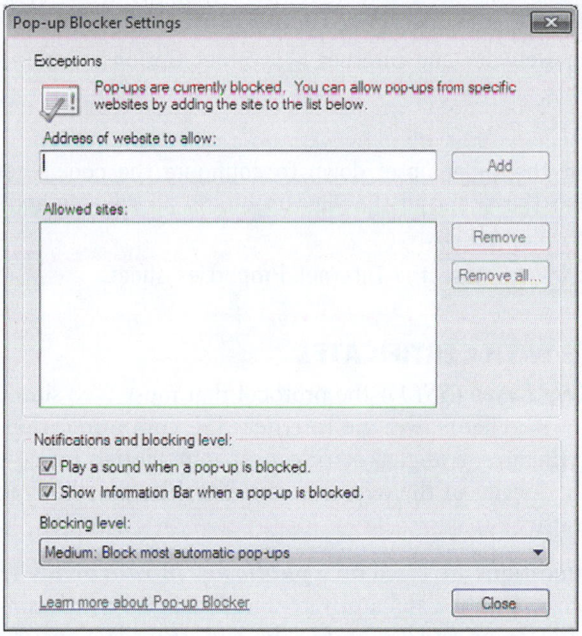

TAKE NOTE*

You can also open the Pop-Up Blocker Settings dialog box by clicking Tools on the toolbar and selecting Pop-Up Blocker > Pop-Up Blocker Settings.

5. To allow pop-ups from a specific Web site, type the URL of the site in the Address of website to allow text box, and then click Add. Repeat the process to add additional sites to the Allowed sites list.

+ MORE INFORMATION

Some Web sites use pop-ups for legitimate reasons. If you are aware of any that your users visit frequently, it is a good idea to add them to the Allowed sites list. This is particularly true if your organization runs intranet sites that use pop-ups.

6. Adjust the Blocking level drop-down list to one of the following settings:
   - **High:** Block all pop-ups.
   - **Medium:** Block most automatic pop-ups.
   - **Low:** Allow pop-ups from secure sites.
7. Click Close to close the Pop-Up Blocker Settings dialog box.
8. Click OK to close the Internet Properties sheet.

CONFIGURING PRIVACY SETTINGS

Another big privacy issue in Internet Explorer is *cookies*. Although the term has other applications in computer networking, in the context of Internet Explorer, a cookie is a file containing information about you or your web-surfing habits that a Web site maintains on your computer.

In some cases, cookies are extremely useful. They can save you keystrokes and remember who you are from one Web site visit to the next. In other cases, however, Web sites use cookies to track your web surfing habits for the purpose of targeting you with specific ad campaigns. Many users resent the idea of outside parties saving data on their local drives and using it for their own purposes. IE includes a variety of privacy settings you can use to limit the ability of Web sites to create cookies on a Windows 7 computer.

To configure these settings, use the following procedure.

CONFIGURE PRIVACY SETTINGS

GET READY. Log on to Windows 7.

1. Click Start, and then click Control Panel. The Control Panel window appears.
2. Select Network and Internet > Internet Options. The Internet Properties sheet appears.
3. Click the Privacy tab.
4. Adjust the slider up or down to configure the cookie settings for the Internet zone. Moving the slider all the way up blocks all cookies and moving it all the way down allows all cookies.
5. Click OK to close the Internet Properties sheet.

BROWSING WITH CERTIFICATES

Secure Sockets Layer (SSL) is the protocol that most Web sites use when establishing secure connections with clients over the Internet. SSL communication is based on the exchange of digital certificates. A digital certificate is a credential, issued by a trusted party, that confirms the identity of the web server and enables the client and the server to exchange encrypted traffic.

SSL communications are based on a *public key infrastructure (PKI)*, which requires two encryption keys: a public and a private one. Data encrypted using the public key can only be decrypted with the private key, and in the same way, data encrypted with the private key can only be encrypted using the public key. A web server participating in a PKI receives a digital certificate from a *certification authority (CA)*, which contains its public key. The server also generates a private key, which it stores locally.

When a web server on the Internet establishes an SSL connection with a client, it transmits its certificate. Then, when the server sends data encrypted with its private key to a client, the fact that the client can successfully decrypt the data using the public key from the certificate confirms the identity of the server. When the client transmits data encrypted using the public key, only the possessor of the private key—the server—can decrypt it.

When a Windows 7 IE user connects to a site that is secured using SSL, a gold lock appears in the address bar, along with the name of the organization to which the CA issued the certificate, as shown in Figure 7-32.

Figure 7-32

A secure connection in IE 8

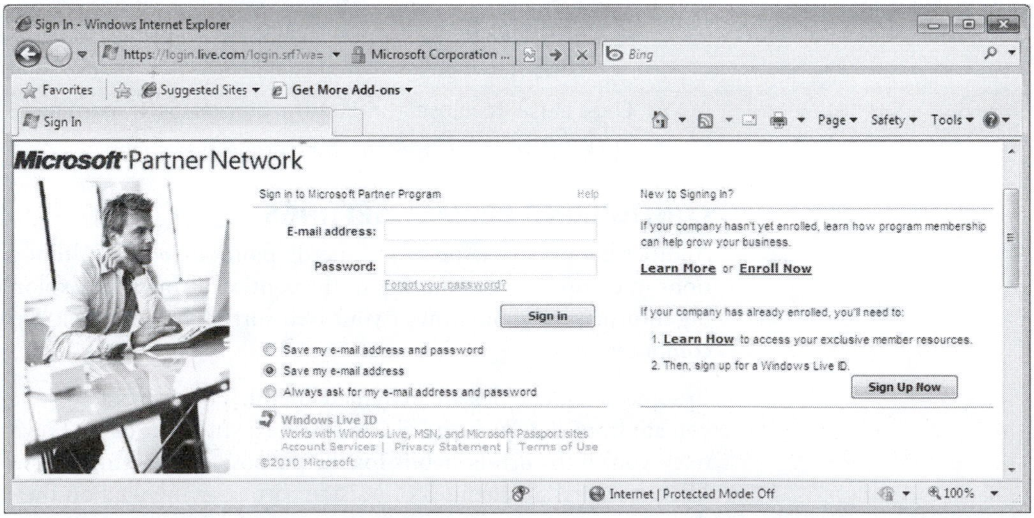

Clicking the lock icon displays more information about the site, including the identity of the CA that issued the certificate, as shown in Figure 7-33.

Figure 7-33

Displaying certificate information in IE 8

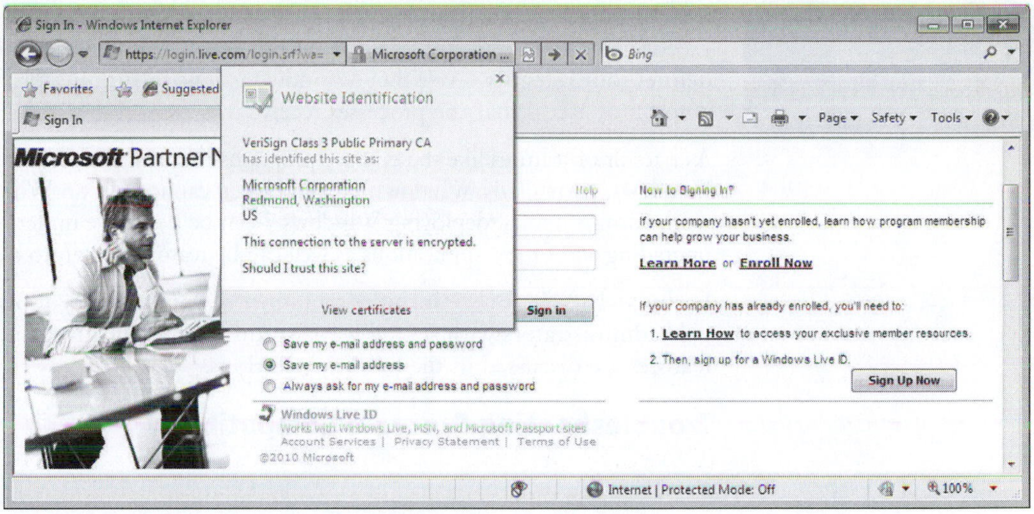

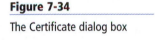

For even more information, you can click the View Certificate link to open the Certificate dialog box, as shown in Figure 7-34. In most cases, the CA is a commercial entity, such as VeriSign or Thawte, which is in the business of issuing certificates to clients. If you trust the CA that issued the certificate, then you should trust the Web site that possesses it.

Figure 7-34

The Certificate dialog box

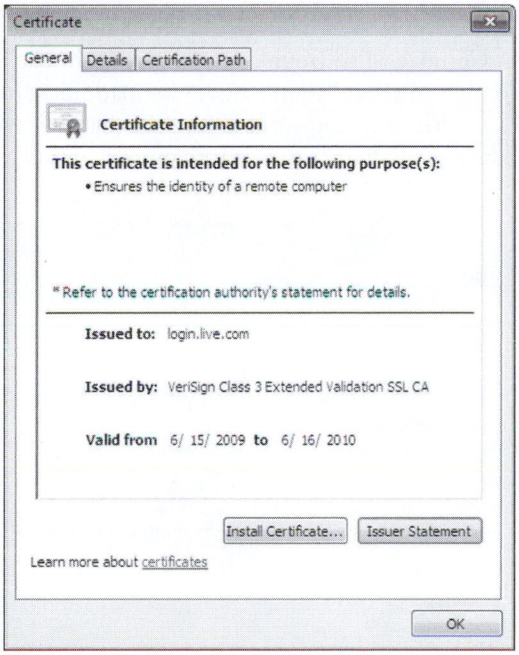

At times, an IE user might connect to a site that has a certificate that is improper in some way. The certificate might have expired, it might be corrupted, it might have been revoked, or it might have a name that is different from that of the site itself. When this occurs, IE blocks access to the site and displays a warning screen stating that there is a problem with the certificate. The user can then opt to close the browser window or ignore the warning and continue on to the site.

Configuring Application Compatibility

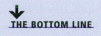

THE BOTTOM LINE

Windows 7 includes a number of new security features that can alter the ability of certain applications to run. Administrators must therefore take measures to ensure the compatibility of their legacy applications.

CERTIFICATION READY?
Configure application
compatibility.
3.2

One example of these features, data execution prevention (DEP), prevents applications from executing code in certain areas of memory. Another, mandatory integrity control (MIC), defines four integrity levels that Windows assigns to running processes, which specify the amount of access that the processes receive to system resources.

As a result of features like these, some programs that run perfectly well in older versions of Windows, particularly Windows XP and earlier, cannot run on Windows 7. For enterprise network administrators, deploying Windows 7 can be a massive undertaking in itself. The prospect of upgrading all of their applications as well can be reason enough to delay or even cancel the project.

Fortunately, Windows 7 includes a number of compatibility tools and features that can provide administrators with several ways to run their applications successfully. These tools and features are discussed in the following sections.

Troubleshooting Program Compatibility

The simplest method of coping with an application compatibility issue in Windows 7 is to run the Program Compatibility Troubleshooter.

The *Program Compatibility Troubleshooter* is a wizard-based solution that users or administrators can use to automatically configure an executable file to use an appropriate Windows 7 compatibility mechanism. Thus, the troubleshooter is not a compatibility mechanism in itself; it is just a method for applying other mechanisms.

To run the Program Compatibility Troubleshooter, you right click an executable file or a shortcut to an executable file and select Troubleshoot Compatibility from the context menu. When the troubleshooter launches, it attempts to determine what is preventing the program from running properly. The troubleshooter then gives you two options, as shown in Figure 7-35.

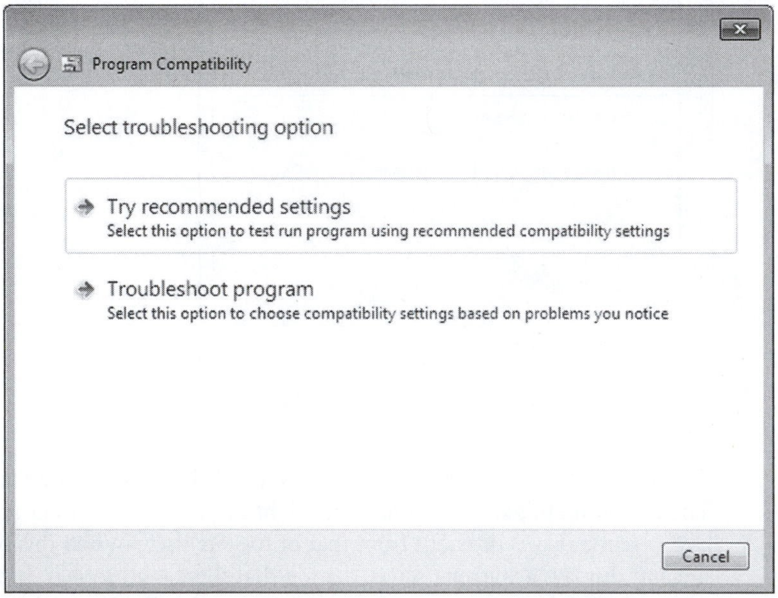

Figure 7-35

The *Select troubleshooting option* page in the Program Compatibility Troubleshooter

Try recommended settings: Implements the compatibility settings that the troubleshooter has determined will resolve the problem and configures the executable to use those settings whenever you run it.

Troubleshoot program: Displays a *What problems do you notice?* page, shown in Figure 7-36, on which you can select the problems you have experienced. The troubleshooter then leads you through a series of pages that further identify the problem and configure the executable with specific compatibility settings.

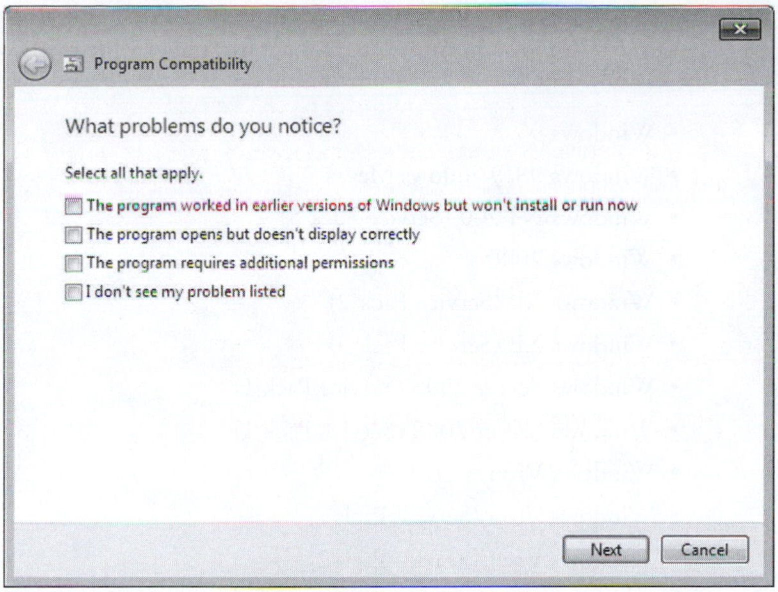

Figure 7-36

The *What problems do you notice?* page in the Program Compatibility Troubleshooter

Setting Compatibility Modes

The Program Compatibility Troubleshooter is essentially a wizard that simplifies the process of selecting compatibility mode settings for an executable. However, you can also configure those same compatibility mode settings manually.

To configure the compatibility mode settings for an application, you must open the Properties sheet for the application's executable file (or a shortcut pointing to that executable file) and select the Compatibility tab, as shown in Figure 7-37.

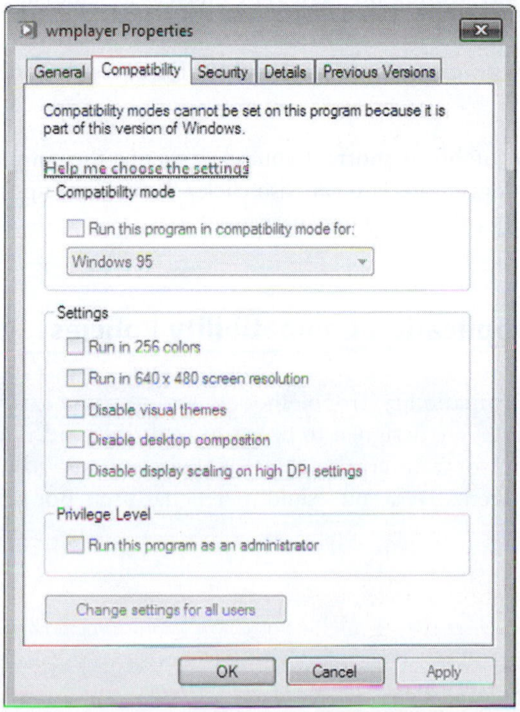

Figure 7-37

The Compatibility tab of an executable's Properties sheet

Selecting the *Run this program in compatibility mode for* check box, you can select a previous version of Windows from the drop-down list, under which you were able to run the program successfully. The Windows emulation modes are as follows:

- Windows 95
- Windows 98/Windows Me
- Windows NT 4.0 (Service Pack 5)
- Windows 2000
- Windows XP (Service Pack 2)
- Windows XP (Service Pack 3)
- Windows Server 2003 (Service Pack 1)
- Windows Server 2008 (Service Pack 1)
- Windows Vista
- Windows Vista (Service Pack 1)
- Windows Vista (Service Pack 2)

This setting does not emulate the earlier operating system version in every way, so the successful execution of the program is not guaranteed, but in many cases, applications that do not run properly in Windows 7 can run with this setting enabled.

In addition to the version emulations, you can also select any or all of the following compatibility mode settings:

- **Run in 256 colors:** Causes the program to run with a limited color depth.
- **Run in 640 × 480 screen resolution:** Causes the program to run at a limited screen resolution.
- **Disable visual themes:** Disables display themes that can interfere with the program's buttons and menus.
- **Disable desktop composition:** Disables transparency and other Aero user interface elements while the program is running.
- **Disable display scaling on high DPI images:** Disables application resizing due to large font sizes.
- **Run this program as an administrator:** Executes the program with elevated privileges.

By default, the executable or shortcut you select retains the compatibility mode settings for the user currently logged on. You can also click Change Settings For All Users to apply the same settings to all of the computers users.

Configuring Application Compatibility Policies

The Program Compatibility Troubleshooter, and to some extent the compatibility mode settings themselves, are designed to be easily accessible and understandable to the end user. However, in some enterprise network environments, administrators manage compatibility issues themselves, and would prefer that users not see Windows 7 compatibility warnings.

To suppress application compatibility warnings, administrators can use the Group Policy settings located in a GPO at Computer Configuration\Administrative Templates\System\Troubleshooting and Diagnostics\Application Compatibility Diagnostics, as shown in Figure 7-38.

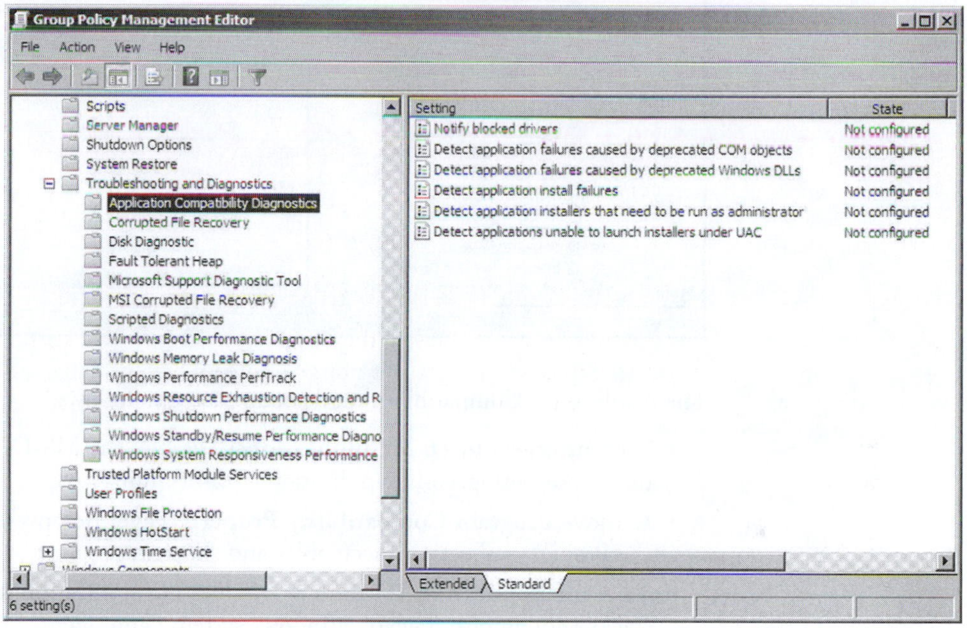

Figure 7-38

The Application Compatibility Diagnostics Group Policy settings

The Application Compatibility Diagnostics settings are as follows:

- **Notify blocked drivers:** Specifies whether the Program Compatibility Assistant (PCA) should notify users when drivers are blocked for compatibility reasons.

- **Detect application failures caused by deprecated com objects:** Specifies whether the PCA should attempt to detect the creation of COM objects that no longer exist in Windows 7.

- **Detect application failures caused by deprecated windows DLLs:** Specifies whether the PCA should detect attempts to load DLLs that no longer exist in Windows 7.

- **Detect application install failures:** Specifies whether the PCA should attempt to detect application installation failures and prompt to restart the installation in compatibility mode.

- **Detect application installers that need to be run as administrator:** Specifies whether the PCA should detect application installations that fail due to a lack of administrative privileges and prompt to restart the installation as an administrator.

- **Detect applications unable to launch installers under UAC:** Specifies whether the PCA should detect the failure of child installer processes to launch due to the lack of elevated privileges.

Administrators can also limit users' access to compatibility mode controls using Group Policy. These settings are located in Computer Configuration\Administrative Templates\Windows Components\Application Compatibility, as shown in Figure 7-39.

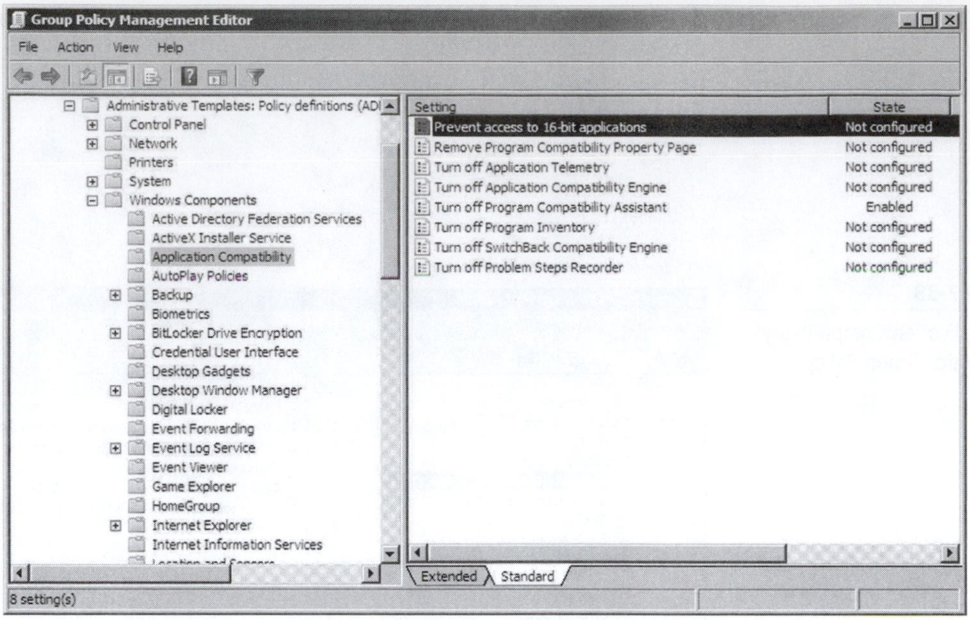

Figure 7-39

The Application Compatibility
Group Policy settings

The Application Compatibility mode controls are as follows:

- **Prevent access to 16-bit applications:** Disables the MS-DOS subsystem on the computer, preventing 16-bit applications from running.
- **Remove Program Compatibility Property Page:** Removes the Compatibility tab from the Properties sheets of executables and shortcuts.
- **Turn off Application Telemetry:** Disables the application telemetry engine, which tracks anonymous usage of Windows system components by applications.
- **Turn off Application Compatibility Engine:** Prevents the computer from looking up applications in the compatibility database, boosting system performance but possibly affecting the execution of legacy applications.
- **Turn off Program Compatibility Assistant:** Disables the PCA, preventing the system from displaying compatibility warnings during application installations and start-ups.
- **Turn off Program Inventory:** Prevents the system from inventorying programs and files and sending the resulting information to Microsoft.
- **Turn off Switchback Compatibility Engine:** Prevents the computer from providing generic compatibility mitigations to older applications, thus boosting performance.
- **Turn off Problem Steps Recorder:** Prevents the computer from capturing the steps taken by the user before experiencing a problem.

Using the Application Compatibility Toolkit

For application incompatibilities that are not readily solvable with the Windows 7 compatibility mode settings, Microsoft has released the Application Compatibility Toolkit, a collection of programs that allow administrators to gather information about incompatibilities between specific applications and Windows 7 and create customized solutions that enable those applications to run.

The *Application Compatibility Toolkit (ACT)* 5.5 is available as a free download from the Microsoft Download Center at http://www.microsoft.com/downloads/details.aspx? FamilyID=24DA89E9-B581-47B0-B45E-492DD6DA2971&displaylang=en. In addition to the toolkit itself, you will also need a computer running SQL Server on your network to store the data gathered by ACT. You can use a commercial version of SQL Server 2005 or 2008, or the free version: SQL Server Express.

The tools included in the kit are as follows:

- Application Compatibility Manager
- Compatibility Administrator
- Internet Explorer Compatibility Test Tool
- Setup Analysis Tool
- Standard User Analyzer

The individual tools are discussed in the following sections.

APPLICATION COMPATIBILITY MANAGER

Designed primarily to help administrators ensure application compatibility for large-scale Windows 7 deployments, Application Compatibility Manager is a tool, shown in Figure 7-40, that gathers compatibility information and uses it to test your applications for compatibility issues.

Figure 7-40

Application Compatibility Manager

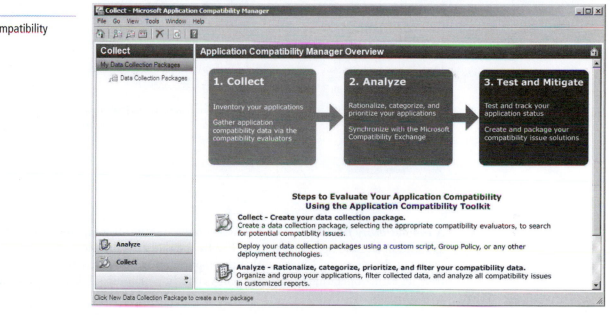

These are the three basic steps of the process:

- **Collect:** To collect information from other computers on the network, you create data collection packages (DCPs), which are Microsoft Windows Installer (.msi) files that you can deploy using Group Policy or a script. The DCPs compile information in log files, which they upload to the ACT computer, which in turn adds them to a SQL database.

- **Analyze:** The analysis of the collected data begins with organization, which can include categorization, prioritization, application assessment, and assignment of deployment status. Once you have organized your data, you can add compatibility issues, derived from the Microsoft Compatibility Exchange, compatibility evaluators, the ACT community, and your own research. You can then add compatibility solutions from the same sources and resolve your compatibility issues. Finally, you can generate detailed reports using the information in your ACT database.

- **Test and Mitigate:** In the final phase of the process, you test your applications in a lab environment to see if the issues you have gathered in your analysis are actual problems on your network. If they are, you can create fixes called mitigation strategies, using the Compatibility Administrator application.

COMPATIBILITY ADMINISTRATOR

Compatibility Administrator, as shown in Figure 7-41, is a central clearinghouse for solutions to known compatibility problems for hundreds of commercial Windows 7 applications. When you select an application in the left pane, the right pane lists existing compatibility fixes.

Figure 7-41

Compatibility Administrator

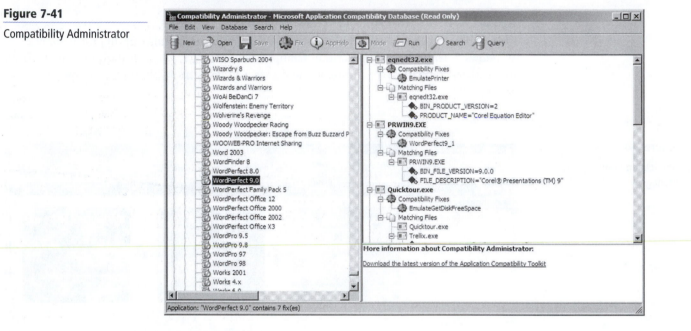

A *compatibility fix*, formerly known as a *shim*, is a software component that sits between an application and the operating system. The fix translates the function calls that the application makes to the operating system so that the application receives the same responses it would get from an earlier operating system version. A collection of compatibility fixes is called a *compatibility mode*.

You can use the Compatibility Administrator to locate fixes for the compatibility issues you discover during your network analysis. The program also includes extensive query capabilities that enable you to search your computers for installed fixes, based on specific applications or fix properties.

If the administrator does not have a fix listed for any of your issues, you can create your own compatibility fixes or compatibility modes.

INTERNET EXPLORER COMPATIBILITY TEST TOOL

The Internet Explorer Compatibility Test Tool is a specialized program that collects compatibility information for web pages and web-based applications. Unlike the Application Compatibility Manager, this is a real-time tool that examines the compatibility of the Web sites you access with Internet Explorer 8.

To use the Internet Explorer Compatibility Test Tool, you simply run the program, click enable, and use Internet Explorer to access the sites you want to test. An icon appears in the IE status bar, indicating that Internet Explorer compatibility evaluation logging is turned on, and log entries begin to appear in the tool's Live Data window, as shown in Figure 7-42.

Figure 7-42

Internet Explorer Compatibility Test Tool

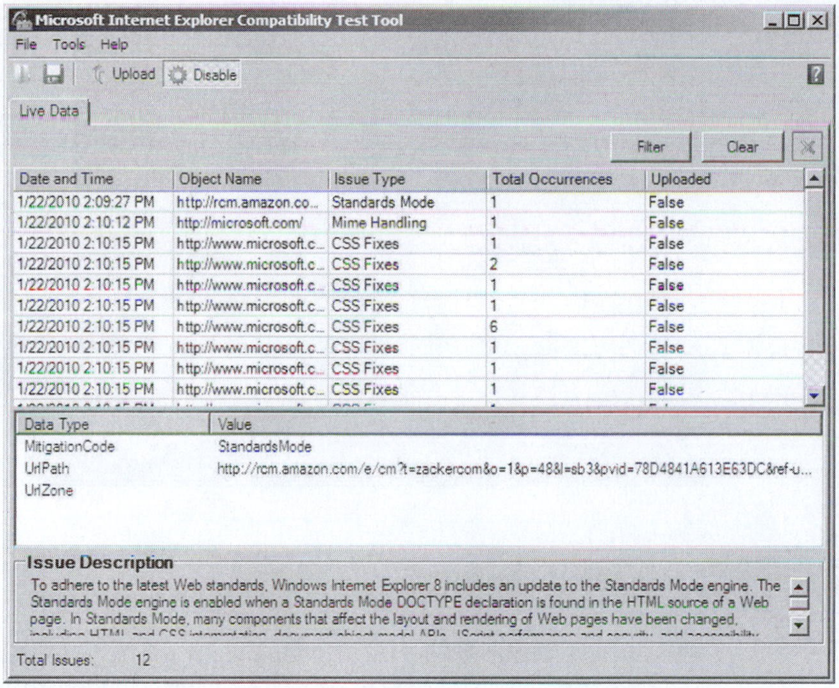

The tool sends the log data it gathers to the ACT Log Processing Service, which adds it to the same ACT database as the information about stand-alone applications that DCPs gather from your workstations.

SETUP ANALYSIS TOOL

The Setup Analysis Tool is a logging tool that is designed to analyze application setup programs for compatibility issues. The tool can detect potential issues such as:

- Installation of kernel mode drivers
- Installation of 16-bit components
- Installation of Graphical Identification and Authentication (GINA) DLLs
- Changes to files or registry keys that exist under Windows Resource Protection (WRP)

STANDARD USER ANALYZER

The Standard User Analyzer is a tool that examines applications for compatibility issues caused by the User Account Control (UAC) feature of Windows 7. UAC can prevent applications from accessing resources that were available to them in previous Windows versions. The Standard User Analyzer identifies these resources, using either a manual or wizard-based format.

To use the Standard User Analyzer, you run the program and use the analyzer's interface to launch your applications, as shown in Figure 7-43.

Figure 7-43

Standard User Analyzer

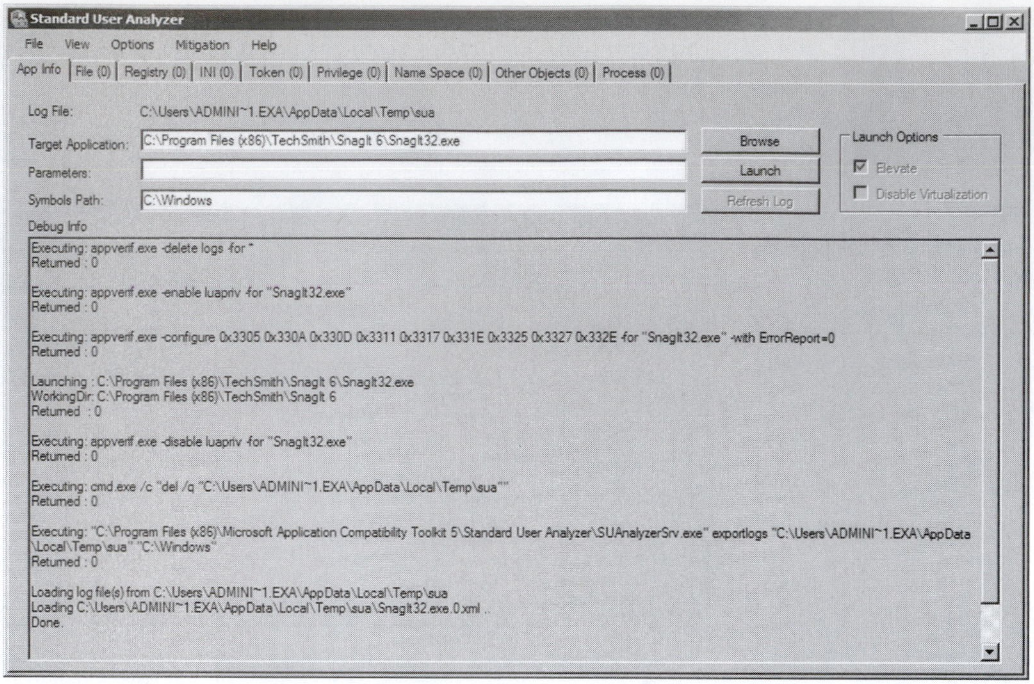

Using Windows XP Mode

> If you have an application that you cannot get to run on Windows 7 any other way, you can use Windows XP Mode to create a virtual machine that runs Windows XP on your Windows 7 system.

Windows XP Mode is a free download that enables a computer running Windows 7 Professional, Enterprise, or Ultimate edition to create a virtual Windows XP machine on which you can run any native Windows XP application.

Windows XP Mode is essentially a Microsoft Virtual PC installation with Windows XP running on a virtual machine. Unlike the other compatibility options discussed in this lesson, Windows XP Mode has some rather extensive hardware requirements, including the following:

- **Processor:** The computer's processor must support hardware virtualization, using either Intel Virtualization Technology (Intel VT-x) or AMD virtualization (AMD-V).
- **BIOS:** The computer's BIOS must support the virtualization capabilities of the processor. In most cases, virtualization is turned off by default, and you must enable it in the BIOS before you install Windows XP Mode.
- **Memory:** The virtual machine created by Windows XP mode requires 256 megabytes (MB) of memory of its own. Thus, the total memory requirement for the computer is 2 gigabytes (GB).

Microsoft's Download Windows XP Mode page, at http://www.microsoft.com/windows/virtual-pc/download.aspx, provides access to the Microsoft Hardware-Assisted Virtualization Detection Tool, which checks your computer for the necessary hardware and the Windows XP Mode downloads.

Once you install both the Windows XP Mode and the Windows Virtual PC files on your Windows 7 computer, you can start the Windows XP Mode client and install your application. Once you have done this, a shortcut for the application then appears in a Virtual Windows XP Applications folder. With the application installed, you can launch it from the Start menu just as you would any other program.

TAKE NOTE*

No matter what processor platform Windows 7 is using, the virtual Windows XP machine is the x86 version of Windows XP Professional SP3. You can therefore only use Windows XP Mode to run x86 applications.

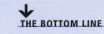

■ Configuring Application Restrictions

↓
THE BOTTOM LINE

In a business environment, administrators often prefer to limit the applications that their users are permitted to run. In Windows 7, there are two ways to do this.

CERTIFICATION READY?
Configure application restrictions.
3.3

Restricting the applications that users can run on their computers is one step toward creating a consistent workstation environment. Workstations that are identically configured are easier to support and limit the possibility of malware infiltration.

Windows 7 supports two mechanisms for restricting applications, both of which you can deploy using Group Policy settings: software restriction policies and AppLocker. These mechanisms are discussed in the following sections.

Using Software Restriction Policies

Software restriction policies are rules that specify which applications users can run.

Software restriction policies are Group Policy settings that enable administrators to specify the programs that are allowed to run on workstations by creating rules of various types. Software restriction policies have been around for years, and their main advantage is that you can create one set of policies that apply to Windows XP and Windows Vista workstations, as well as Windows 7. The disadvantage of software restriction policies is that, unlike the new AppLocker feature, you can only create rules manually and individually.

CREATING RULES

The software restriction policy rules that you can create include:

- **Certificate rules:** Identify applications based on the inclusion of a certificate signed by the software publisher. An application can continue to match this type of rule, even if the executable file is updated, as long as the certificate remains valid.

- **Hash rules:** Identify applications based on a digital fingerprint that remains valid even when the name or location of the executable file changes.

- **Network zone rules:** Identify Windows Installer (.msi) packages downloaded with Internet Explorer based on the security zone of the site from which they are downloaded.

- **Path rules:** Identify applications by specifying a file or folder name or a registry key. The potential vulnerability of this type of rule is that any file can match the rule, as long as it is the correct name or location.

To create rules, you must open a Group Policy object (GPO) and browse to Computer Configuration\Windows Settings\Security Settings\Software Restriction Policies, right click the Software Restriction Polices object and, from the context menu, select Create Software Restriction Policies. The policies appear, as shown in Figure 7-44.

Figure 7-44

Software Restriction Policies

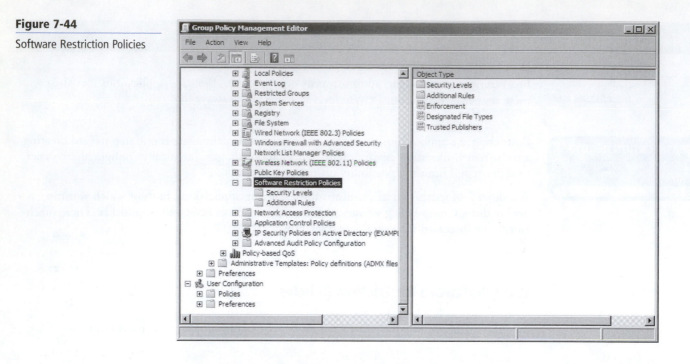

You create new rules of your own in the Additional Rules folder, using a dialog box like the one shown in Figure 7-45.

Figure 7-45

The New Path Rule dialog box

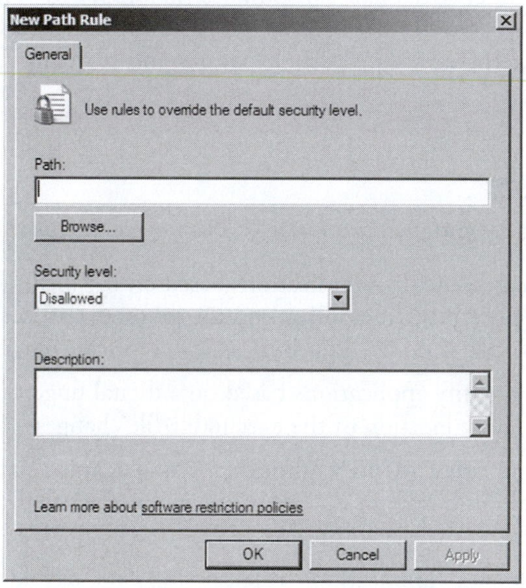

There is also a fifth type of rule—the default rule—which applies when an application does not match any of the other rules you have created. To configure the default rule, you select one of the policies in the Security Levels folder and click Set As Default on its Properties sheet.

TAKE NOTE * The most common way to implement software restriction policies is through Group Policy objects linked to Active Directory Domain Services containers, so that administrators can apply their policy settings to large numbers of computers simultaneously. However, it is also possible to configure software restriction policies on individual computers using Local Security Policy.

CONFIGURING RULE SETTINGS

Software restriction policies can work in three ways, based on the settings you choose for each of the rules. The three possible settings are as follows:

- **Disallowed:** Prevents an application that matches a rule from running.
- **Basic user:** Allows all applications not requiring administrative privileges to run. Allows applications that do require administrative privileges to run only if they match a rule.
- **Unrestricted:** Allows an application that matches a rule to run.

The most restrictive—and the most secure—way to use the settings is to set the default rule to Disallowed and then create additional Unrestricted rules for the applications you want your users to be able to run. This prevents them from launching any applications other than the ones you specify. The reverse of this method is to set the default rule to Unrestricted and use additional Disallowed rules to specify applications that you want to prevent users from running.

Although the most obvious way of using these settings is to create rules for individual applications, there are other alternatives also. You can, for example, create rules that prevent users from running applications from anywhere other than the Program Files folder, and then use NTFS permissions to prevent them from installing new applications to Program Files.

RESOLVING CONFLICTS

It is possible to create rules in such a way that conflicts occur because more than one rule applies to a single application. When this is the case, the more specific rule takes precedence over the less specific. Thus, the order of precedence is as follows:

1. Hash rules
2. Certificate rules
3. Path rules
4. Zone rules
5. Default rule

Using AppLocker

> AppLocker is a new feature in the Windows 7 Enterprise and Ultimate editions that enables administrators to create application restriction rules much more easily.

Software restriction policies can be a powerful tool, but they can also require a great deal of administrative overhead. If you elect to disallow all applications except those matching the rules you create, there are a great many programs in Windows 7 itself that need rules, in addition to the applications you want to install. Administrators must also create the rules manually, which can be an onerous chore.

AppLocker, also known as ***application control policies***, is a new Windows 7 (and Windows Server 2008 R2) feature that is essentially an updated version of the concept implemented in software restriction policies. AppLocker also uses rules, which administrators must manage, but the process of creating the rules is much easier, thanks to a wizard-based interface.

AppLocker is also more flexible than software restriction policies. You can apply AppLocker rules to specific users and groups and also create rules that support all future versions of an application. The primary disadvantage of AppLocker is that you can only apply the policies to computers running Windows 7 and Windows Server 2008 R2.

UNDERSTANDING RULE TYPES

The AppLocker settings are located in Group Policy objects in the Computer Configuration\Windows Settings\Security Settings\Application Control Policies\AppLocker container.

In the AppLocker container, there are three nodes that contain the basic rule types:

- **Executable rules:** Contains rules that apply to files with .exe and .com extensions.
- **Windows Installer rules:** Contains rules that apply to Windows Installer packages with .msi and .msp extensions.
- **Script rules:** Contains rules that apply to script files with .ps1, .bat, .cmd, .vbs, and .js extensions.

TAKE NOTE *

You can also configure AppLocker to use DLL rules, which require administrators to create rules that provide users with access to all of the dynamic link libraries (DLLs) in an application, as well as the executables. This option, while more secure, can incur a significant performance penalty, because AppLocker must confirm access to each of an application's DLLs before it can load. To configure this option, open the Properties sheet for the AppLocker container, click the Advanced tab, and select the *Enable the DLL rule collection* check box.

Each of the rules you create in each of these containers can allow or block access to specific resources, based on one of the following criteria:

- **Publisher:** Identifies code-signed applications by means of a digital signature extracted from an application file. You can also create publisher rules that apply to all future versions of an application.
- **Path:** Identifies applications by specifying a file or folder name. The potential vulnerability of this type of rule is that any file can match the rule, as long as it is the correct name or location.
- **File Hash:** Identifies applications based on a digital fingerprint that remains valid even when the name or location of the executable file changes. This type of rule functions much like its equivalent in software restriction policies; in AppLocker however, the process of creating the rules and generating file hashes is much easier.

CREATING DEFAULT RULES

By default, AppLocker blocks all executables, installer packages, and scripts, except for those specified in Allow rules. Therefore, to use AppLocker, you must create rules that enable users to access the files needed for Windows and the system's installed applications to run. The simplest way to do this is to right click each of the three rules containers and select Create Default Rules from the context menu.

The default rules for each container, as shown in Figure 7-46, are standard rules that you can replicate, modify, or delete as necessary. You can also create your own rules instead, as long as you are careful to provide access to all the resources the computer needs to run Windows.

TAKE NOTE *

To use AppLocker, Windows 7 requires the Application Identity service to be running. By default, this service uses the manual startup type, so you must start it yourself in the Services console before Windows 7 can apply the AppLocker policies. This behavior is deliberate. With AppLocker, it is relatively easy to inadvertently create a set of rules that omits access to executables or other files that Windows needs to run, thus disabling the operating system. If this should occur, simply restarting the computer will cause the operating system to load without the Application Identity service, preventing AppLocker from loading. Only when you are certain that you have configured your rules properly should you change the startup type for the Application Identity service to automatic.

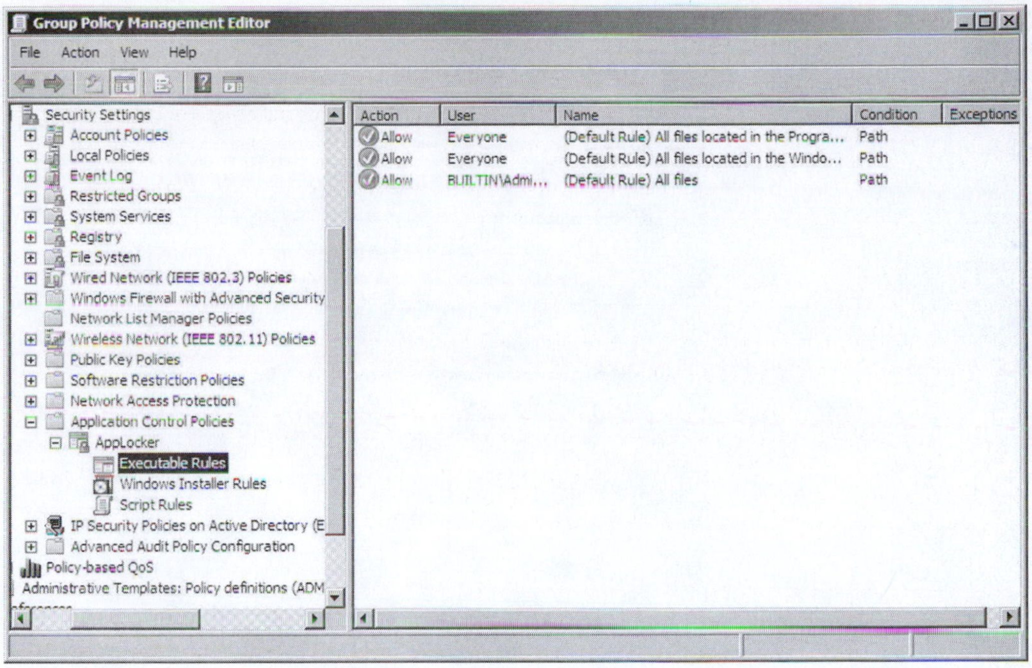

Figure 7-46

The default AppLocker executable rules

CREATING RULES AUTOMATICALLY

The greatest advantage of AppLocker over software restriction policies is the ability to create rules automatically. When you right click one of the three rules containers and select Create Rules Automatically from the context menu, an Automatically Generate Rules Wizard appears, as shown in Figure 7-47.

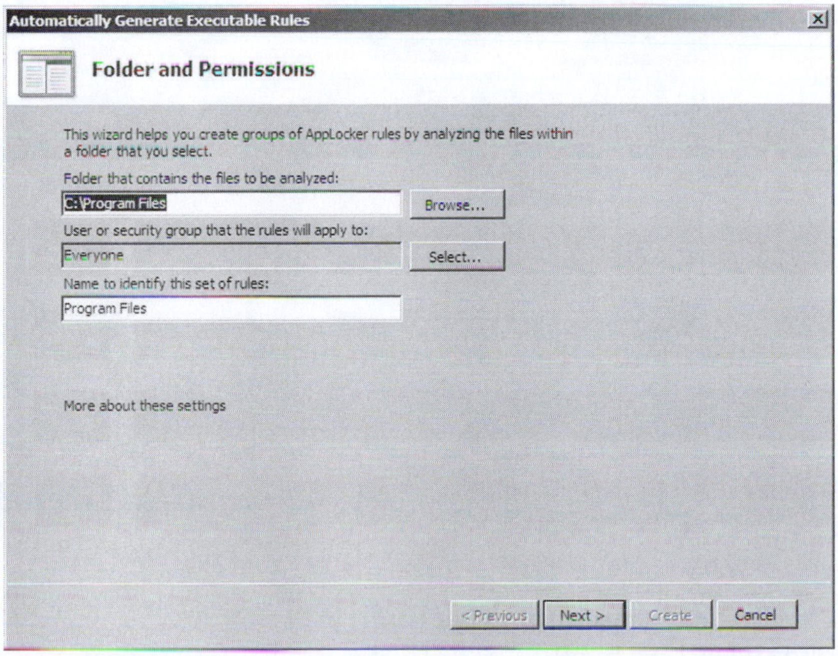

Figure 7-47

The Automatically Generate Executable Rules Wizard

After specifying the folder to be analyzed and the users or groups to which the rules should apply, a *Rule Preferences* page appears, as shown in Figure 7-48, which allows you to select the types of rules you want to create.

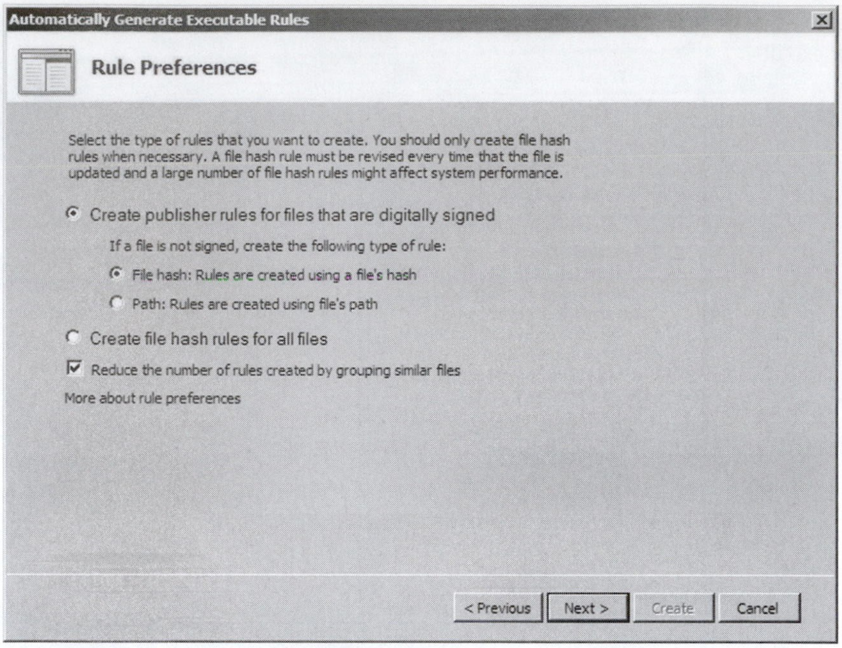

Figure 7-48

The Rule Preferences page of the Automatically Generate Executable Rules Wizard

The wizard then displays a summary of its results in the *Review Rules* page, as shown in Figure 7-49, and adds the rules to the container.

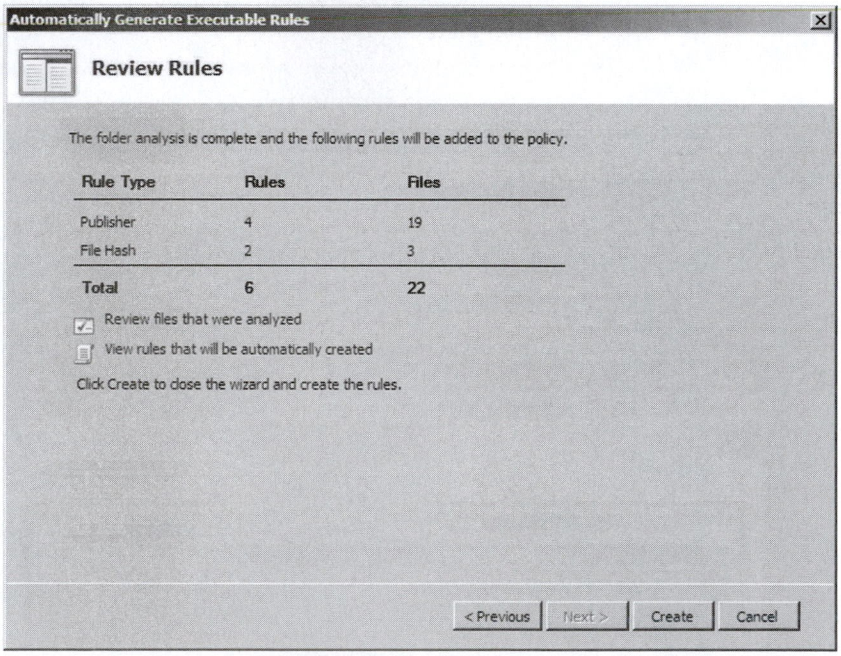

Figure 7-49

The Review Rules page of the Automatically Generate Executable Rules Wizard

CREATING RULES MANUALLY

In addition to creating rules automatically, you can also do it manually using a wizard-based interface that you activate by selecting Create New Rule from the context menu for one of the three rule containers. The wizard prompts you for the following information:

- **Action:** Specifies whether you want to allow or deny the user or group access to the resource. In AppLocker, explicit deny rules always override allow rules.

- **User or group:** Specifies the name of the user or group to which the policy should apply.
- **Conditions:** Specifies whether you want to create a publisher, path, or file hash rule. The wizard generates an additional page for whichever option you select, enabling you to configure its parameters.
- **Exceptions:** Enables you to specify exceptions to the rule you are creating, using any of the three conditions: publisher, path, or file hash.

SKILL SUMMARY

IN THIS LESSON YOU LEARNED:

- Many of the pages on the Internet still conform to old standards, and IE 8 might not display them properly. To accommodate these pages, IE 8 includes a feature called Compatibility View, which enables the browser to display older pages properly.

- One of the ways that IE interacts with other resources is through the use of add-ons. Add-ons are separate software components, created by Microsoft or third parties, that interact with the basic functions of the web browser.

- Accelerators enable users to send content to other resources in the form of applications running on the computer or other sites on the Internet. Accelerators enable you to highlight content in a browser window and select the accelerator for the resource you want to receive that content.

- Many Web sites that provide frequently changing content, such as news sites and blogs, support a push technology called RSS, which simplifies the process of delivering updated content to designated users.

- Protected mode is a way to run Internet Explorer 8 with highly reduced privileges.

- Phishing is a technique that uses convincing-looking Web sites that urge users to supply personal information, such as passwords and account numbers. Internet Explorer 8 includes a SmartScreen Filter that examines traffic for evidence of phishing activity and displays a warning to the user if it finds any.

- To provide different levels of access to specific applications, Internet Explorer divides the addresses accessible with the web browser into several different security zones, each of which has a different set of privileges.

- When a Windows 7 IE user connects to a site that is secured using SSL, a gold lock appears in the address bar, along with the name of the organization to which the CA issued the certificate.

- Windows 7 includes a number of new security features that can alter the ability of certain applications to run. Administrators must therefore take measures to ensure the compatibility of their legacy applications.

- For application incompatibilities that are not readily solvable with the Windows 7 compatibility mode settings, Microsoft has released the Application Compatibility Toolkit.

- Software restriction policies are Group Policy settings that enable administrators to specify the programs that are allowed to run on workstations by creating rules of various types.

- AppLocker is a new feature in the Windows 7 Enterprise and Ultimate editions that enables administrators to create application restriction rules much more easily.

■ Knowledge Assessment

Matching

Complete the following exercise by matching the terms with their corresponding definitions.

- **a.** a collection of compatibility fixes
- **b.** the application compatibility mechanism of last resort in Windows 7
- **c.** prevents Internet Explorer from logging a browser history
- **d.** minimizes access to protected operating system resources
- **e.** a protocol that Internet Explorer uses to establish encrypted connections to servers
- **f.** a rules-based access control mechanism for applications
- **g.** a compatibility fix
- **h.** the process of discovering passwords and other confidential information through trickery
- **i.** a method for classifying Web sites, based on their potential dangers
- **j.** provides protection again phishing Web sites

_____ **1.** InPrivate Mode

_____ **2.** shim

_____ **3.** SmartScreen Filter

_____ **4.** Windows XP Mode

_____ **5.** AppLocker

_____ **6.** security zones

_____ **7.** social engineering

_____ **8.** compatibility mode

_____ **9.** protected mode

_____ **10.** Secure Sockets Layer

Multiple Choice

Select one or more correct answers for each of the following questions.

1. What are the names of the two security zones in Internet Explorer that have no sites in them by default? (Choose all that apply.)
   - **a.** Internet
   - **b.** Local intranet
   - **c.** Trusted sites
   - **d.** Restricted sites

2. Which of the following is NOT one of the add-on types supported by Internet Explorer 8?
   - **a.** Toolbars and Extensions
   - **b.** Search Providers
   - **c.** Accelerators
   - **d.** SmartScreen Filtering

3. Which of the following software restriction policy rule types takes the highest precedence?
   - **a.** Certificate rules
   - **b.** Hash rules
   - **c.** Default rules
   - **d.** Zone rules

4. Which of the following tools are included in the Application Compatibility toolkit 5.5? (Choose all that apply.)
   a. Setup Analysis Tool
   b. Compatibility Administrator
   c. Application Compatibility Manager
   d. Standard User Analyzer

5. The primary function of the SmartScreen Filter in Internet Explorer 8 is to protect users from which of the following forms of malware?
   a. phishing
   b. cookies
   c. viruses
   d. social engineering

6. Which of the following is NOT a requirement that a Windows 7 computer must have to install Windows XP Mode.
   a. A minimum of 2 GB of memory
   b. A processor that supports hardware virtualization
   c. A copy of Windows 7 Professional, Enterprise, or Ultimate
   d. A Windows XP Professional installation disk

7. Which of the following are types of rules you can manually create in AppLocker.
   a. Publisher rules
   b. Certificate rules
   c. Path rules
   d. File hash rules

8. What does a broken window icon in the Internet Explorer 8 address bar indicate?
   a. A failure to successfully download a certificate from the Web site
   b. A web page that is incompatible with Internet Explorer 8
   c. A failure to update a subscribed RSS feed
   d. A failure to print a document from Internet Explorer

9. Which of the following is the tool in Application Compatibility Manager 5.5 that contains a catalog of compatibility fixes for hundreds of applications?
   a. Application Compatibility Manager
   b. Standard User Analyzer
   c. Compatibility Administrator
   d. Setup Analysis Tool

10. Which of the following Windows versions support AppLocker policies? (Choose all that apply.)
    a. Windows 7
    b. Windows Vista
    c. Windows Server 2003
    d. Windows Server 2008 SP2

Review Questions

1. List the three main steps involved in a compatibility study using Application Compatibility Toolkit 5.5 and briefly describe each step.

2. List three ways that you can resolve a web-based application's incompatibility with Internet Explorer 7's protected mode.

■ Case Scenarios

Scenario 7-1: Using the SmartScreen Filter

Several employees at the company you work for have recently been victims of identity theft. These incidents were the result of emails received by the victims requesting that they supply personal bank account information to a Web site or risk having their accounts closed. The Web site was, of course, not legitimate, and attackers used the information collected there to transfer funds from the victims' accounts. The company has recently upgraded all of the company workstations to Windows 7, and you are examining the capabilities of the SmartScreen Filter in the Internet Explorer 8. Your superiors have told you that you can use any of the new IE 8 security features for the company workstations, as long as they do not consume any additional Internet bandwidth.

Explain to your supervisor the various methods IE 8 uses to protect against phishing attacks, and specify which ones you intend to use for the company workstations.

Scenario 7-2: Using AppLocker

Sophie is planning on using AppLocker to control access to applications on a new network she has constructed for the Research and Development department at a major aerospace firm. The software developers in the department have recently deployed a new application called Virtual Wind Tunnel, which is based on government project research and is therefore classified. All of the full-time personnel have sufficient clearance to use the application, but the interns in the department do not. Sophie has placed the user accounts for everyone in the department into a security group called ResDev. The interns are also members of a group called RDint.

How can Sophie use AppLocker to provide everyone in the department with access to the Virtual Wind Tunnel application without changing the group memberships and without having to apply policies to individual users?

Managing and Monitoring Windows 7 Performance

OBJECTIVE DOMAIN MATRIX

Technology Skill	Objective Domain	Objective Number
Updating Windows 7	Configure updates to Windows 7.	7.1
Monitoring Performance	Monitor systems.	7.3
Managing Performance	Configure performance settings.	7.4

KEY TERMS

Background Intelligent Transfer Service (BITS)

baseline

channel

collector

data collector set

events

hotfix

instance

performance counter

performance object

ReadyBoost

SuperFetch

Windows Experience Index

Windows Server Update Services (WSUS)

■ Updating Windows 7

↓ THE BOTTOM LINE

Keeping Windows 7 systems updated with the latest software is one of the primary tasks of the technical specialist, who should be familiar with the types of update releases and the methods for deploying updates.

The process by which software is designed and developed has evolved over the years, not only in the tools and languages used to do the job, but also in the release strategies. At one time, software products were small enough and simple enough to be distributed on a few floppy disks. Today, a Windows operating system release consists of gigabytes of data; this increase in size is a reflection of the software's increased complexity.

273

One of the results of this complexity is that it is no longer practical to issue occasional updates for applications and operating systems. An operating system such as Windows consists of so many elements that, from a developmental standpoint, it is always a work in progress, constantly being updated to correct errors, enhance performance, and add features. Keeping the operating system updated is no longer an optional element of Windows 7 maintenance, justified by the belief that "if it ain't broke, don't fix it." The regular application of operating system updates is imperative, for reasons of compatibility, performance, and most important, security. There is no better way to protect a Windows 7 computer than to make sure to apply all of the latest security updates.

Understanding Update Types

Microsoft updates its operating systems frequently by issuing software updates in several forms.

Microsoft releases operating system updates on the 12th of each month, with occasional, additional releases when an issue (typically involving security) requires an immediate response. The updates that Microsoft releases typically take one of the following forms:

- **Hotfixes:** A *hotfix* is an update consisting of one or more files designed to address a specific problem or issue with the operating system. Some hotfixes are intended for all Windows users, and are released using the Microsoft Update web site, while others are intended for special circumstances and are released only to users experiencing a particular problem.

- **Security Updates:** A security update is a hotfix designed to address a particular vulnerability in Windows 7 security. In addition to the software itself, security updates include a security bulletin and a Knowledge Base article that discuss the nature and severity of the problem.

- **Cumulative Updates (or Rollups):** Over time, Microsoft releases a large number of updates, and a cumulative update is a distribution method that consolidates all of the updates for a particular operating system element or application, such as Internet Explorer or Internet Information Services. Downloading and installing a single rollup is far easier than applying many different updates. Rollups typically undergo more testing than individual hotfixes, and because they are always installed together they provide a more stable platform than individually installed hotfixes.

- **Service Packs:** A service pack is a cumulative set of all updates for a particular operating system version, usually going back to its original release. Unlike updates, service packs can contain new or enhanced features. More than any other type of update, service packs are extensively tested until Microsoft is confident that all users can safely apply them. To a certain degree, service packs are an extension of the operating system release itself. Once a service pack is released, Microsoft and original equipment manufacturer (OEM) providers typically distribute Windows with the service pack integrated into the installation.

In addition to these release types, Microsoft classifies updates using the following categories:

- **Important Updates:** Updates that address important issues that require immediate attention and which all users should install. The Windows Update client always downloads all available important updates by default.

- **Recommended Updates:** Updates that address less-important issues or that apply only to certain users. You can configure Windows Update to download recommended updates along with critical updates, or ignore them.

- **Optional Updates:** Updates that contain enhancements or new features that are not essential for the proper functioning of the operating system.

- **Device Drivers:** Microsoft uses Windows Update to distribute fully tested and digitally signed device drivers for some hardware products.

Evaluating Updates

Despite all of the update testing that Microsoft performs, incompatibilities can occur, and individual testing is strongly recommended.

As mentioned earlier, Microsoft tests its update releases with varying degrees of thoroughness, depending on the complexity of the update and the time factor involved. Service packs can go through months of testing, including an extensive beta testing program, while some security updates are rushed to release because they address a time-critical vulnerability. No matter how much testing Microsoft does, however, it cannot possibly test every combination of hardware and software installed on millions of Windows computers, and incompatibilities do occur.

For this reason, network administrators should perform their own testing before deploying any updates to production computers. The testing methodology is usually dependent on the size of the network and the resources available to its administrators. For a large organization, it is a good idea to perform test deployments on an isolated lab network. This is not practical for most small businesses, though, so they might have to install the update on a single production computer and let it run for a while before performing a deployment to the rest of the network.

TAKE NOTE*

Home users often have no choice but to install updates on their computers, and then see if any problems occur. Fortunately, virtually all Windows updates have uninstall capabilities that enable you to roll a system back to its previous state.

If you are a technical specialist for a large organization, you are more likely to be involved in the actual update testing process than in the creation of the company or departmental policy defining the testing methodology. However, if you service individual customers, you might be forced to decide whether to recommend specific updates for your clients. In this case, it is up to you to remain informed about issues involving the latest update releases. For example, some technicians deliberately avoid installing new service pack releases for several weeks or months, to make sure that major compatibility issues do not appear.

Applying Updates

The Windows Update client enables computers running Windows 7 to automatically download and install operating system updates.

Although it is possible to manually update Windows 7 computers by connecting to the Microsoft Update Web site, the Windows Update client included with Windows 7 makes it possible to configure computers to automatically download and install Windows updates as needed. Because Microsoft digitally signs all of its operating system update releases, any user can install them without the need for administrative privileges. This means that the entire process of downloading and installing updates can occur during nonproduction hours without user intervention.

TAKE NOTE*

Windows XP, Windows Server 2003, and Windows 2000 all include a client called Automatic Updates. For Windows Vista and Windows 7, Microsoft redesigned the client and called it Windows Update.

Unlike the Automatic Updates client in Windows XP, the Windows Update client in Windows 7 is an independent application that can download updates from any of the following three locations:

- **Windows Update:** For individual computers and small networks, it is practical to use the default setting, which causes Windows Update to download its updates directly from the Microsoft Update servers on the Internet.

- **Windows Server Update Services (WSUS):** For medium to large networks, WSUS is a free product that conserves bandwidth by downloading updates from the Internet once and then providing them to Windows Update clients on the local network. WSUS also enables administrators to select the updates they want to release to the clients, thus giving them the opportunity to evaluate and test the updates first, and then schedule the deployment. (See "Understanding WSUS Architectures" later in this lesson.)

- **System Center Configuration Manager (SCCM):** For large enterprise networks, SCCM, formerly known as Systems Management Server (SMS), is a comprehensive network management tool that administrators can use to deploy all types of software products, including operating system updates. SCCM is by far the most advanced and customizable method of deploying updates, but it is a highly complex and expensive product that must be licensed for the appropriate number of clients on the network.

TAKE NOTE* The Windows Update client connects to the Microsoft Update servers on the Internet by default. To use an alternative WSUS or SCCM server on your local network as the source for updates, you must configure the client using local or domain Group Policy settings, as discussed later in this lesson.

Using the Windows Update Client

The Windows Update client included in Windows 7 is a service that launches shortly after the computer starts. Windows Update is a pull client that periodically checks a designated server for the availability of updates.

The Windows Update process consists of three basic stages:

- **Detection:** At scheduled times, the Windows Update client connects to a designated server, either on the Internet or the company network, downloads the server's list of available updates, and compares the list with the computer's current configuration. The client then flags all of the updates that have not yet been installed on the system for download.

TAKE NOTE* The Windows Update client can activate a computer that is on standby when it is time to check for updates. If the computer is turned off at the time of a scheduled update, the detection process will begin the next time the computer starts.

- **Download:** After determining which updates it needs, the client initiates a download using the *Background Intelligent Transfer Service (BITS)*. BITS is an HTTP-based file transfer service that downloads files using only the network's idle bandwidth. This enables Windows Update to perform downloads without affecting other applications that are using the network. BITS downloads are also resumable in the event they are interrupted.

TAKE NOTE* BITS uses whatever idle network bandwidth is available when performing downloads, but it will not initiate a connection on a computer that uses dial-up access to the Internet. In this case, the download process will not start until the user initiates a network connection.

- **Installation:** By default, the Windows Update client installs updates immediately after downloading them. However, you can also configure the client to hold the updates until the user manually triggers the installation.

When you install Windows 7, the Setup program displays the screen shown in Figure 8-1, which prompts you to specify whether you want the client to install all updates automatically, install only important updates, or do nothing and prompt you again later.

Figure 8-1

The Help protect Windows automatically window

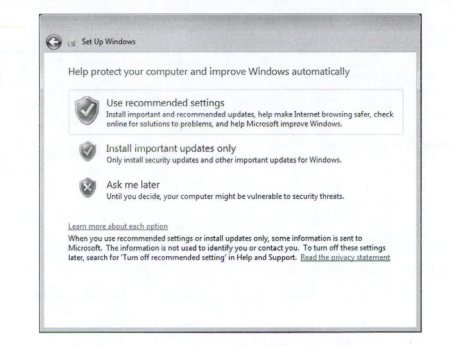

This screen provides only limited access to the Windows Update client. For example, you cannot choose to download updates and select the ones you want to install. Even if you are planning to reconfigure the client later, you might want to select the *Use recommended settings* option.

When you activate the client during the Windows installation, the computer performs an update as soon as it detects a connection to the Internet. This minimizes the system's potential vulnerability by applying the latest security updates as soon as possible after the installation. In addition, Windows Update downloads and installs drivers for hardware devices that have no drivers installed or that are using generic drivers.

Once the operating system is fully installed, you can reconfigure the Windows Update client to make full use of its capabilities. The procedures for using and configuring the Windows Update client are discussed in the following sections.

CONFIGURING THE WINDOWS UPDATE CLIENT

Although it is possible to use the Windows Update client interactivity, its real usefulness is evident when you configure it to take the update process out of the user's hands by automatically downloading and installing operating system updates. There are two methods for configuring the client. You can use the Windows Update control panel or you can use Group Policy settings. Group Policy provides a great deal more flexibility, but for home and small business users, the options found in the Control Panel are usually sufficient.

To configure the Windows Update client with the Control Panel, use the following procedure.

⊙ CONFIGURE WINDOWS UPDATE

GET READY. Log on to Windows 7 using an account with administrative privileges.

1. Click Start, and then click Control Panel. The Control Panel window appears.
2. Click System and Security > Windows Update. The Windows Update window appears, as shown in Figure 8-2.

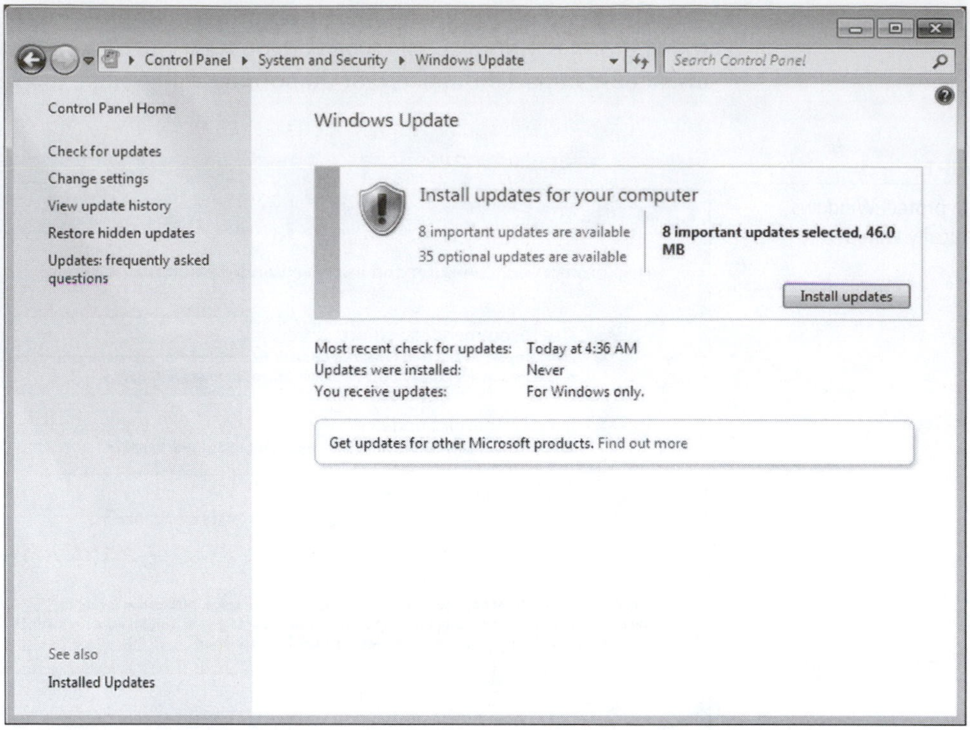

Figure 8-2

The Windows Update window

3. Click Change settings. The *Choose how Windows can install updates* page appears, as shown in Figure 8-3.

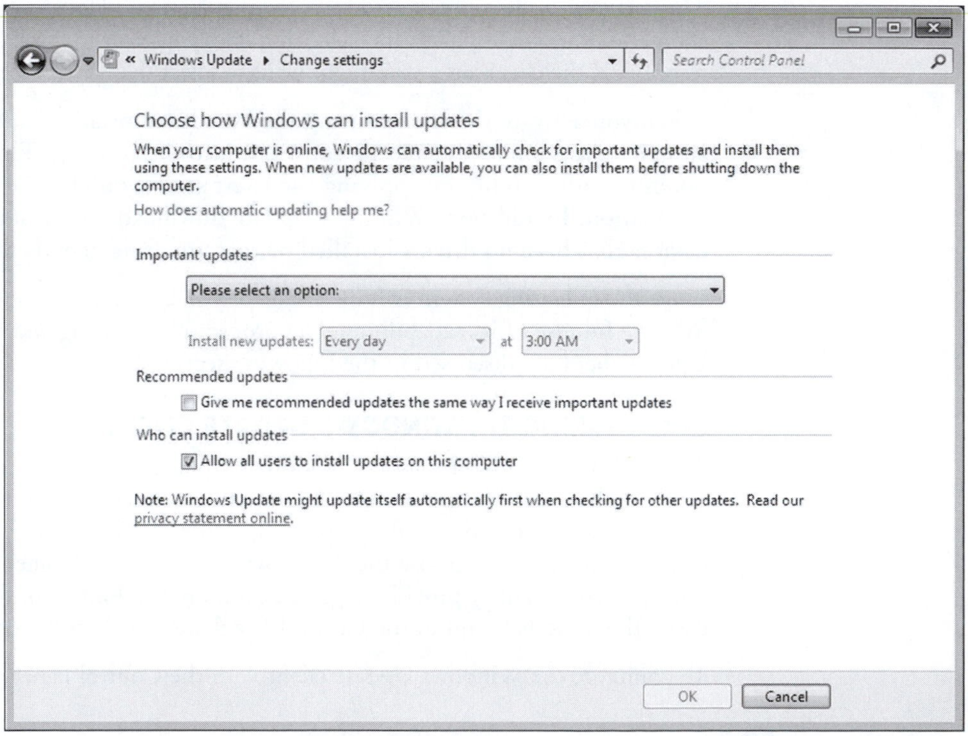

Figure 8-3

The *Choose how Windows can install updates* page

4. Under Important Updates, select one of the following options from the drop-down list:

- Install updates automatically (recommended). If you select this option, use the *Install new updates* drop-down lists to specify the day and time the installations should occur.

- Download updates but let me choose whether to install them.

- Check for updates but let me choose whether to download and install them.
- Never check for updates (not recommended).

5. Select the following additional check boxes as needed:

- Include recommended updates when downloading, installing, or notifying me about updates.
- Allow all users to install updates on this computer.

6. Click **OK**. The system configures the Windows Updates client and performs an immediate update check.

When you select the *Install updates automatically* option, Windows 7 downloads any available updates at the specified time and installs them immediately, even restarting the computer if the updates call for it. To prevent the computer from restarting automatically, you can select the *Download updates but let me choose whether to install them* option. Select *Check for updates but let me choose whether to download and install them* if you want to prevent the computer from accessing the Internet until a user initiates the download.

CONFIGURING WINDOWS UPDATE USING GROUP POLICY

In addition to the Control Panel interface, it is possible to configure the Windows Update client using Group Policy settings. You can use local Group Policy settings to configure the client, but system administrators more commonly distribute the settings using Active Directory Domain Services (AD DS).

Group Policy is the only way to configure the client to check for updates on a local server rather than the Microsoft Update servers on the Internet. There are also other client options that are not accessible through the standard interface.

To configure the Windows Update client using Group Policy, you must open a Group Policy object (GPO) using the Group Policy Management Editor snap-in for Microsoft Management Console, as shown in Figure 8-4. On a stand-alone Windows 7 computer, you can use Local Computer Policy to apply the appropriate settings to the local system.

Figure 8-4

Windows Update policies in the Group Policy Management Editor

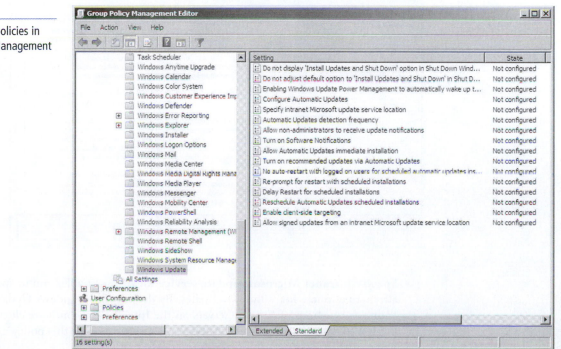

To configure Windows Update using Group Policy, the recommended practice is to create a new Group Policy object (GPO), configure the required settings, and link the GPO to an appropriate AD DS domain, site, or organizational unit object. If you are using multiple WSUS servers, you can distribute the client load among them by creating a separate GPO for each server and linking them to different objects.

The policies that configure the Windows Update client are found in the Computer Configuration > Administrative Templates > Windows Components > Windows Update container of the GPO. The Windows Update policies and their functions are as follows:

- **Do not display 'Install Updates and Shut Down' option in Shut Down Windows dialog box:** Suppresses the stated option when the user shuts down Windows, even when updates are available for installation.

- **Do not adjust default option to 'Install Updates and Shut Down' in Shut Down Windows dialog box:** Specifies whether the stated option should appear as the default choice when shutting down Windows.

- **Enabling Windows Update Power Management to automatically wake up the system to install scheduled updates:** Specifies whether Windows Update will wake up the system from hibernation when there are updates available at the time indicated for installation.

- **Configure Automatic Updates:** Activates the Windows Update client and specifies when and how the client should apply updates, as shown in Figure 8-5. This policy performs the same basic functions as the *Choose how windows can install updates* page in the Windows Update control panel.

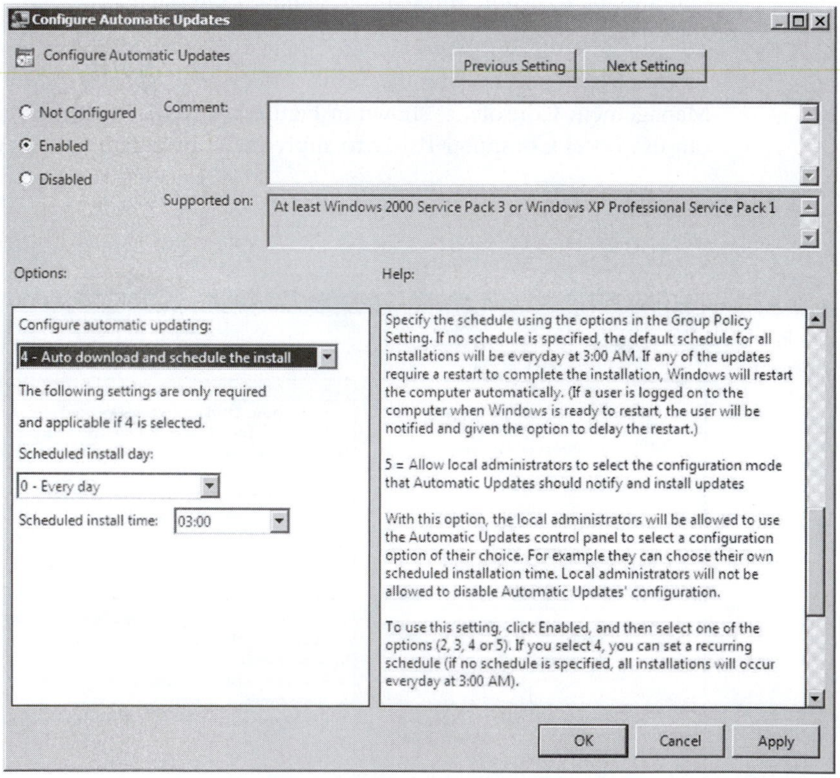

Figure 8-5

The Configure Automatic Updates dialog box

- **Specify intranet Microsoft update service location:** Enables you to specify an alternative source for Windows updates. By default, the Windows Update client connects to Microsoft Update servers on the Internet. To configure clients to check a local WSUS or SCCM server for updates, you must enable this policy and specify the name of the server.

- **Automatic Updates detection frequency:** When the *Specify intranet Microsoft update service location* setting is enabled, specifies the interval (in hours) that Windows Update clients will wait before checking for updates. Clients receiving this setting stagger their frequencies using values zero to twenty percent of the specified interval.

- **Allow non-administrators to receive update notifications:** Specifies whether the notifications that the Windows Update client is configured to generate should be displayed to users without administrative privileges.

- **Turn on Software Notifications:** Specifies whether users should receive enhanced notification messages from the Microsoft Update service.

- **Allow Automatic Updates immediate installation:** Specifies whether the Windows Update client should install updates that do not require a system restart immediately after downloading them.

- **Turn on recommended updates via Automatic Updates:** Specifies whether the Windows Update client should download recommended, as well as important, updates. This policy performs the same function as the *Include recommended updates when downloading, installing, or notifying me about updates* check box on the *Choose how Windows can install updates* page in the Windows Update control panel.

- **No auto-restart with logged on users for scheduled Automatic Updates installations:** Specifies whether the Windows update client should automatically restart the computer after installing an update that requires it. When disabled, a logged-on user must manually restart the computer for the installation of the update to be completed.

- **Re-prompt for restarts with scheduled installations:** Specifies the interval (in minutes) that the Windows Update client will wait after a system restart is postponed before prompting again for a restart.

- **Delay Restart for scheduled installations:** Specifies the interval (in minutes) that the Windows Update client will wait before restarting, after it completes an update installation that requires a restart.

- **Reschedule Automatic Updates scheduled installations:** Specifies the interval (in minutes) that the Windows Update client should wait after starting to install an update whose scheduled installation was missed.

- **Enable client-side targeting:** Specifies the name of the intranet Windows Update service target group to which the computer belongs. This setting is only active when the *Specify intranet Microsoft update service location* setting is enabled.

- **Allow signed updates from an intranet Microsoft update service location:** Enables the Windows Update client to install updates signed by entities other than Microsoft. This setting is only active when the *Specify intranet Microsoft update service location* setting is enabled.

TRIGGERING AN UPDATE

Although the real benefit of the Windows Update client is the ability to automate the update process, it is also possible to manually trigger an update. To trigger an update, use the following procedure.

➔ TRIGGER AN UPDATE

GET READY. Log on to Windows 7 using an account with administrative privileges.

1. Click Start, and then click Control Panel. The Control Panel window appears.

2. Click System and Security > Windows Update. The Windows Update window appears.

3. Click Check for updates. The client connects to the source server and determines whether there are any updates that need to be installed. If the client finds and downloads any updates, a *Download and Install updates for your computer* page appears, as shown in Figure 8-6.

Figure 8-6

The *Download and Install updates for your computer* page

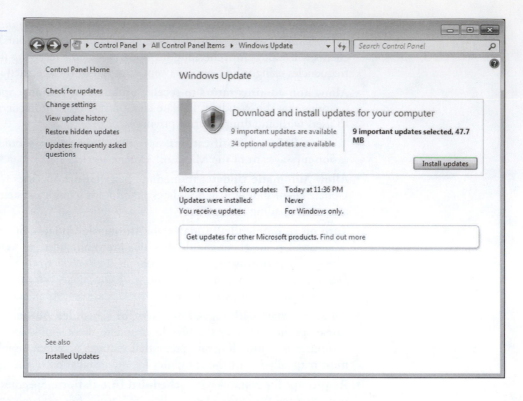

4. Click one of the links specifying how many updates are available. The *Select the updates you want to install* page appears, as shown in Figure 8-7.

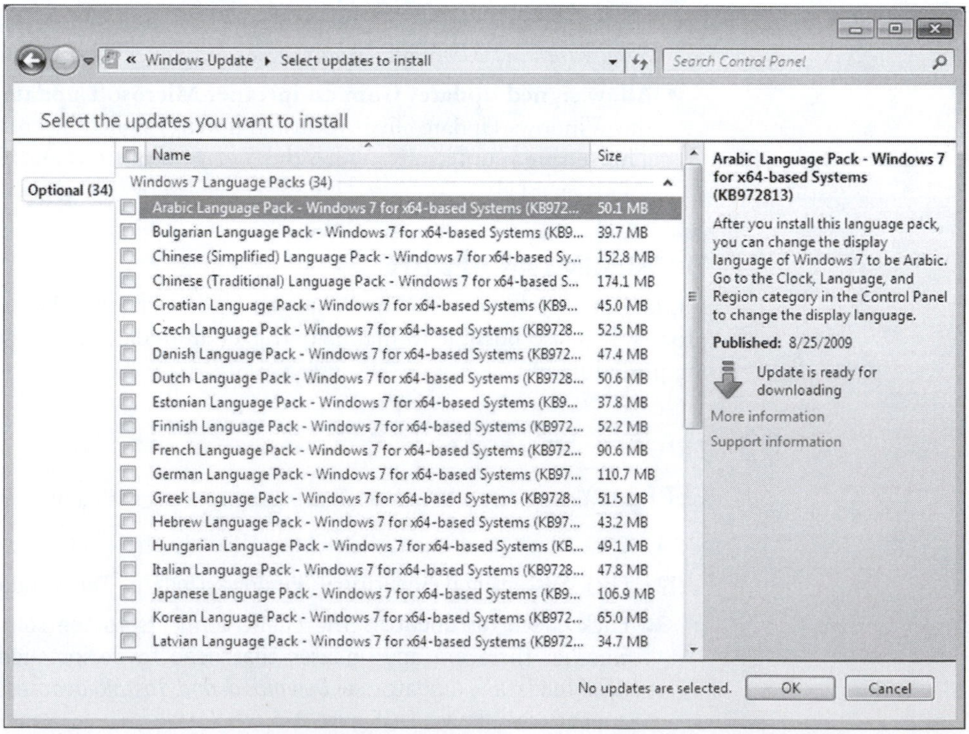

Figure 8-7

The *Select the updates you want to install* page

5. Select each update to display information about its function and links to associated articles on the Internet.

6. Select the check boxes on the Important and Optional tabs for the updates you want to install and click OK. The client installs the selected updates.

HIDING UPDATES

In some cases, there might be updates that you do not want to install on a particular computer. You might have discovered an incompatibility or other problem, or the update might simply not apply to the computer's role or configuration. In this event, you can prevent the unwanted updates from appearing each time you generate an available updates list.

To hide an update, right click its entry on the *Select the updates you want to install* page and, from the context menu, select *Hide update*. That update will no longer appear in the list.

To restore hidden updates to view, open the Windows Update window and click *Restore hidden updates*. The *Restore hidden updates* page appears, as shown in Figure 8-8, in which you can select the individual updates you want to restore. Click Restore, and the selected items will appear in the list of updates available for installation.

Figure 8-8

The *Restore hidden updates* page

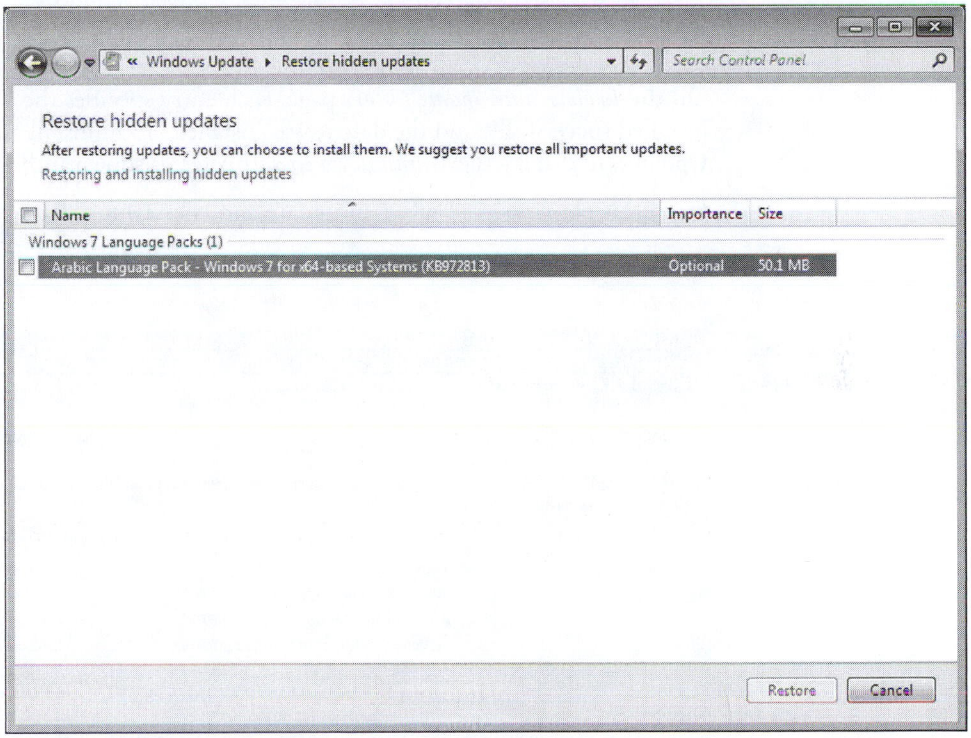

VIEWING THE UPDATE HISTORY

The Windows Update client keeps track of all the updates that have been installed on the computer. This is how the client determines whether it needs to download a particular update. To view the list of installed updates, open the Windows Update window and click *View update history*. The *Review your update history* page appears, as shown in Figure 8-9.

Figure 8-9

The *Review your update history* page

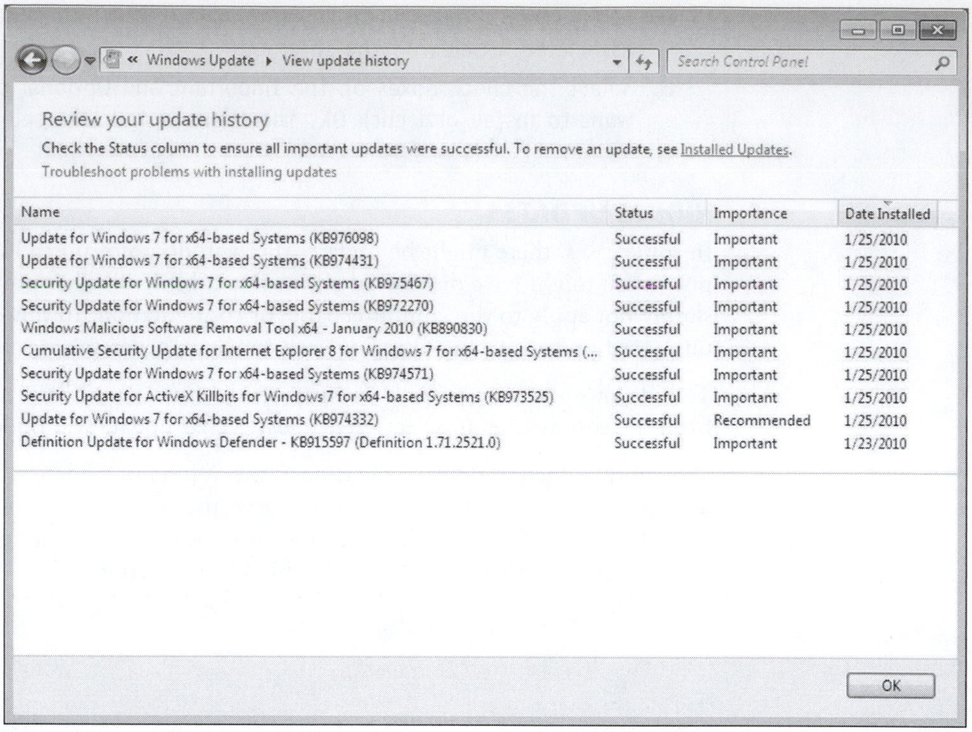

On the *Review your update history* page, each entry specifies the update type, whether it was installed successfully, and the date it was installed. To uninstall an update, click Installed Updates, to display the *Uninstall an update* page, as shown in Figure 8-10.

From this page, you can select an update and click Uninstall on the toolbar to remove it.

Figure 8-10

The *Uninstall an update* page

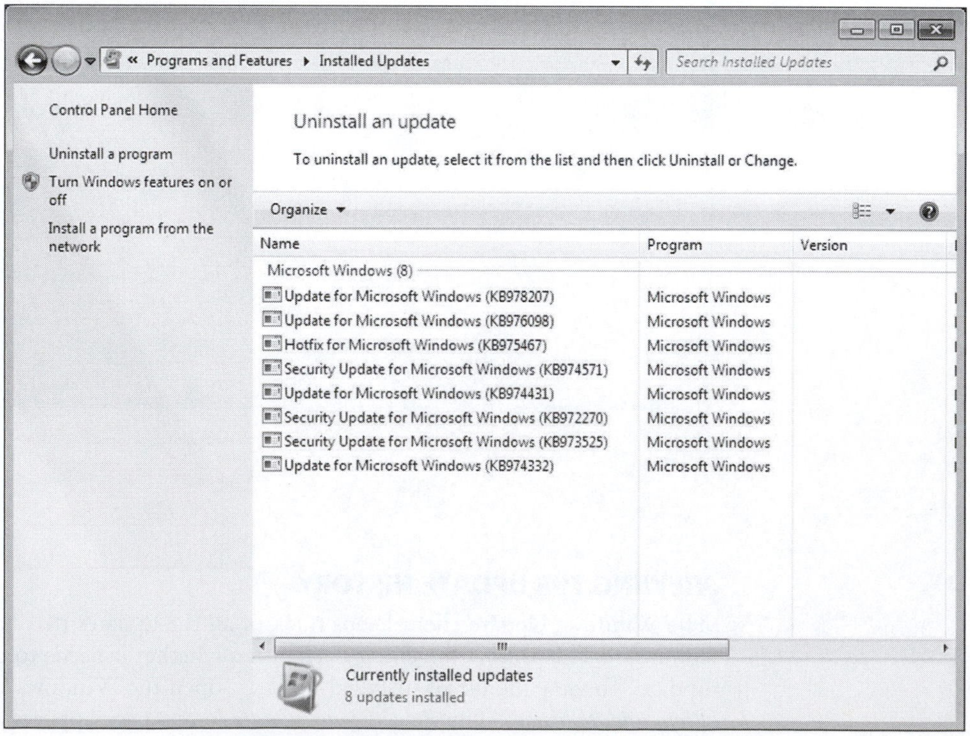

Using Windows Server Update Services

WSUS enables enterprise network administrators to centralize the workstation update process, conserving network bandwidth and exercising greater control over the upgrades distributed to the network.

In an enterprise network environment, where there are hundreds or thousands of computers, Windows Update, in its default configuration, is certainly vastly superior to downloading and installing individual updates on each computer. However, there are still some major drawbacks to this arrangement.

First, having each computer download the same updates independently compounds the amount of Internet bandwidth the systems utilize. In the case of Service Packs, which can run to hundreds of megabytes, the bandwidth needed to update hundreds of computers can be enormous.

Second, Windows Update does not give administrators an opportunity to evaluate the updates before deploying them on production computers. Many administrators prefer to wait some time before installing new updates, to see if any problems arise, while others test the updates themselves on laboratory computers.

Windows Server Update Services (WSUS) is a solution to both these problems. WSUS is a program that downloads updates from the Microsoft Update Web site and stores them for administrative evaluation. An administrator can then select the updates to deploy, and computers on the network download them using a reconfigured Windows Update client. The result is that the WSUS server downloads each update from the Internet only once and then distributes it to the other computers using internal local area network (LAN) bandwidth.

UNDERSTANDING WSUS ARCHITECTURES

WSUS is a highly scalable product that can provide updates to networks of almost any size, using a number of different architectures. In its simplest configuration, a single WSUS server downloads updates from the Microsoft Update Web site, and all of the other computers on the network download the updates from that WSUS server, as shown in Figure 8-11 on the next page. A single WSUS server can support as many as 25,000 clients, so this configuration is suitable for most enterprise networks.

Figure 8-11

The WSUS single server
architecture

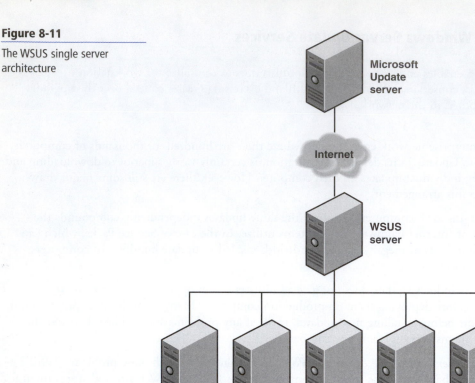

For enterprise networks with remote locations, it might be preferable to run a separate WSUS server at each site. In the multiple independent architecture, each of the WSUS servers has its own connection to the Microsoft Update site, as shown in Figure 8-12, and each maintains its own updates. Administrators at each site manage their own WSUS server configuration and designate the updates they want to release to the production network.

Figure 8-12

The WSUS multiple independent server architecture

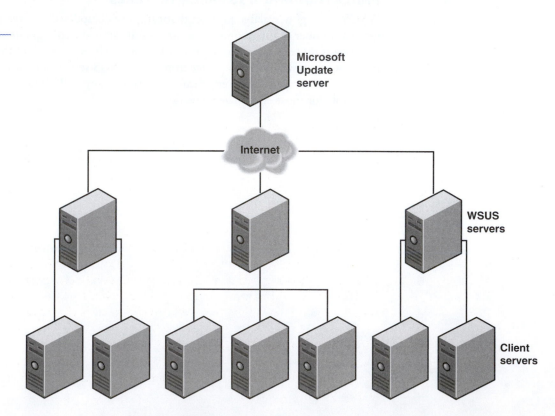

It is also possible to use multiple WSUS servers in a synchronized manner. In this configuration, one central WSUS server downloads updates from the Microsoft Update site, and the other WSUS servers obtain their updates from that first server, as shown in Figure 8-13. This minimizes the amount of Internet bandwidth expended and enables the administrators of the central server to manage the updates for the entire enterprise.

Figure 8-13

The WSUS multiple synchronized server architecture

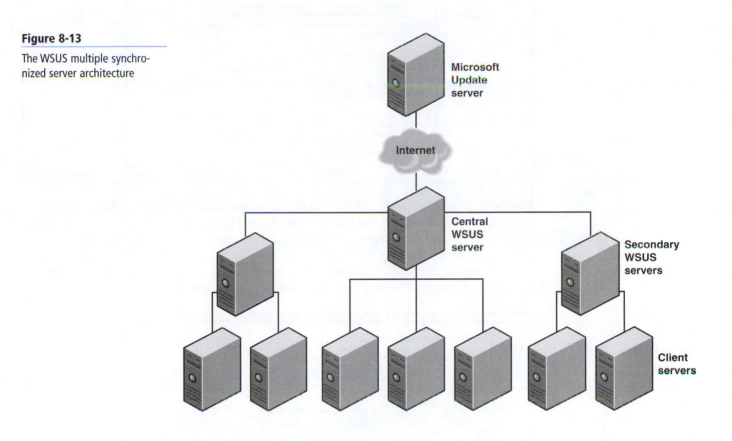

DEPLOYING WSUS

WSUS 3.0 SP2, the latest version of Windows Server Update Services, must be installed on a computer running Windows Server 2008 R2, Windows Server 2008 SP1, or Windows Server 2003 SP1. WSUS is not supplied with any version of the Windows Server operating system, but it is a free download from the Microsoft Web site at http://technet.microsoft.com/en-us/wsus/default.aspx.

Windows Update clients connect to a WSUS server by accessing a Web site, just as they do when connecting to the Microsoft Update site directly. Therefore, before you install WSUS, you must add the Web Server (IIS) role to the computer. WSUS also requires a database, in which it maintains information about its updates and operations. The program can use the Windows Internal Database, which is included with Windows Server, but for larger installations, you might want to use a separate SQL Server database instead.

MANAGING WSUS

Once you have installed WSUS on your server, you use the Update Services console, shown in Figure 8-14, to manage it. WSUS management consists of two main tasks: synchronization and approval of updates.

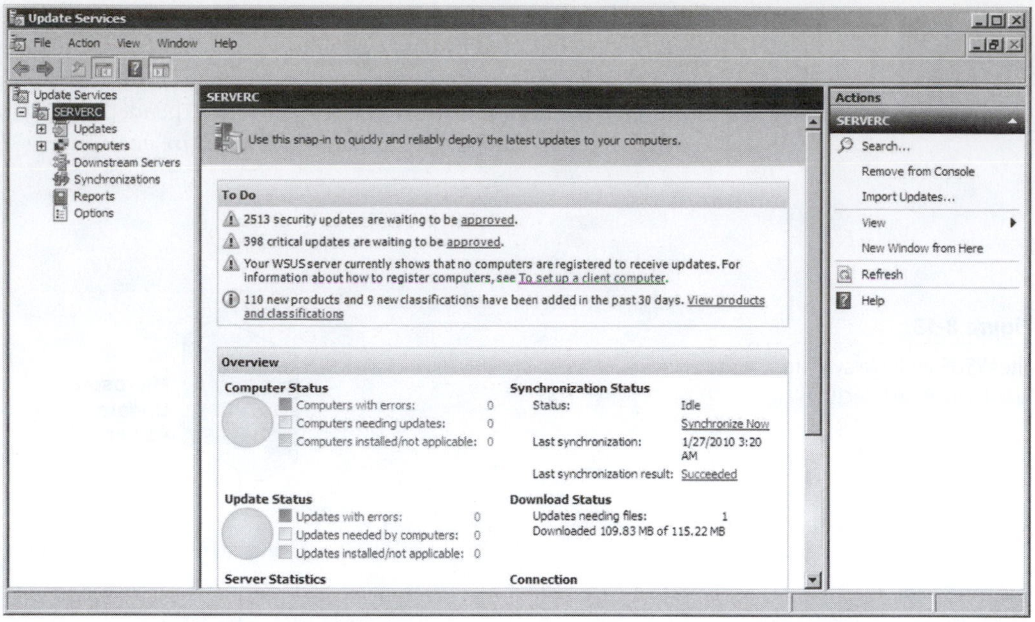

Figure 8-14

The Update Services console

Synchronization is the process by which a WSUS server obtains the updates that it will distribute to clients. When you run the Windows Server Update Services Configuration Wizard, you specify whether you want the server to synchronize with the Microsoft Update servers on the Internet, or with another WSUS server, as shown in Figure 8-15. This is how you implement the various architectural configurations described earlier in this lesson. You can then configure synchronizations to occur automatically, at scheduled intervals.

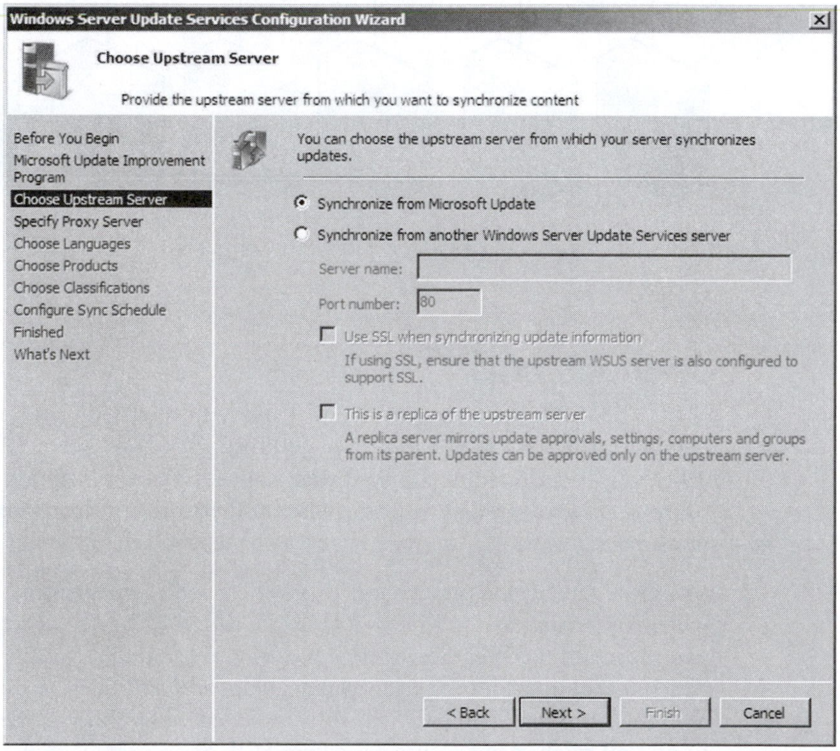

Figure 8-15

The Windows Server Update Services Configuration Wizard

Once the server is synchronized and you have downloaded all of the available updates, you can use the console to read about them and approve specific updates for deployment to Windows Update clients on the network, as shown in Figure 8-16. Depending on your company polices, the approval process might involve researching and testing each update before you deploy it, or you can configure WSUS to automatically approve some or all of the updates.

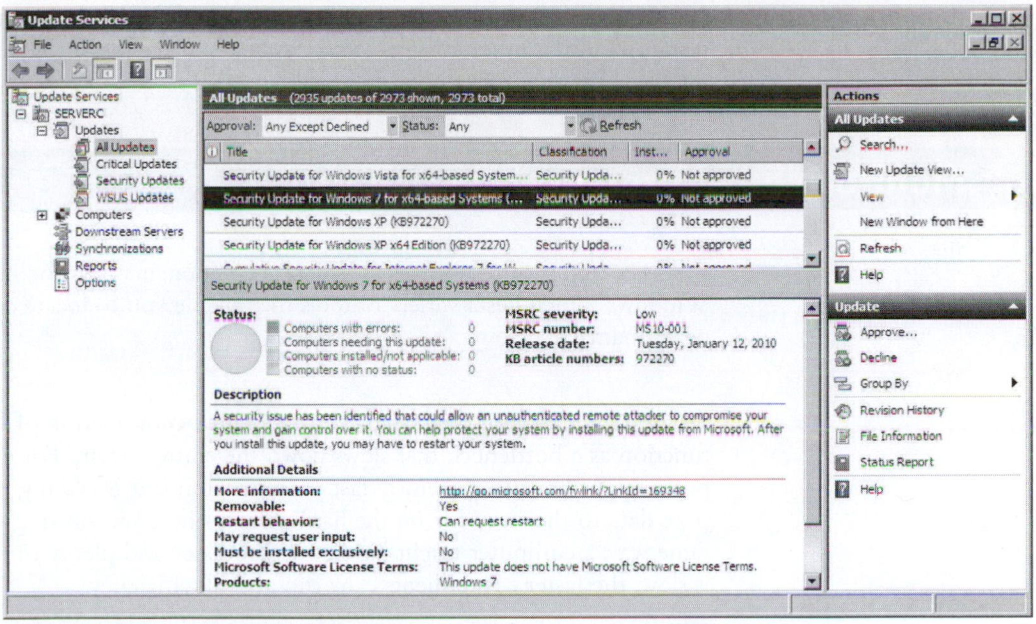

Figure 8-16

Evaluating updates in WSUS

CONFIGURING WSUS CLIENTS

Before the client computers on the network can download updates from the WSUS server, you must configure their Windows Update clients. The Windows Update control panel in Windows 7 does not provide any means of configuring the client to use an internal WSUS server instead of the Microsoft Update Web site, and even if it did, individual client configuration would not be a practical solution for a large enterprise network. To configure the Windows Update clients on your network you must use Group Policy.

The key policy setting for this purpose, as mentioned earlier, is *Specify intranet Microsoft update service location*, as shown in Figure 8-17. This is where you specify the name of the

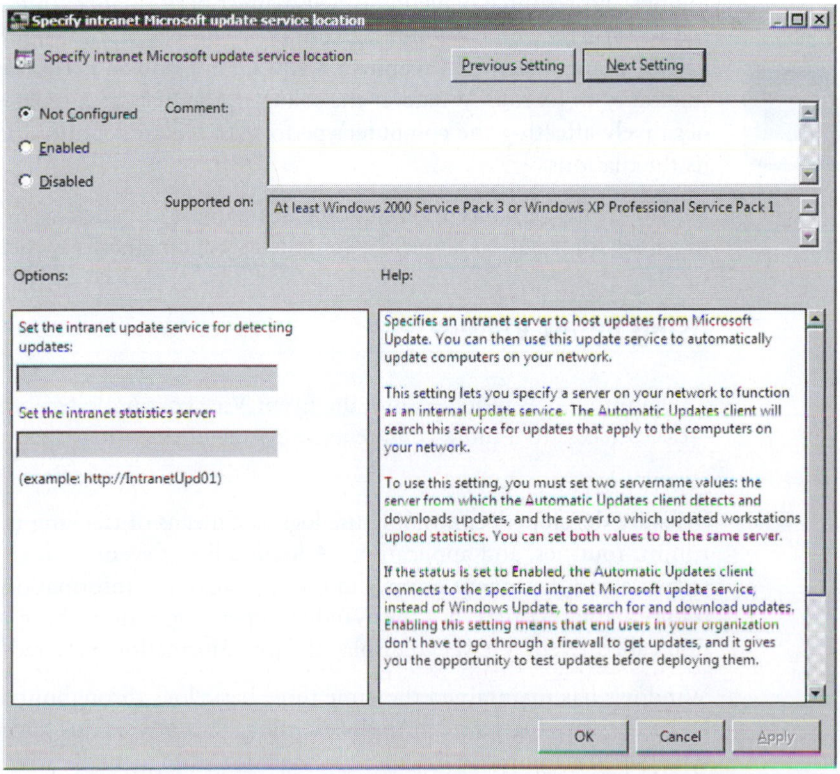

Figure 8-17

The Specify intranet Microsoft update service location dialog box

WSUS server that you want your clients to access. You can then use *Configure Automatic Updates* and the other settings to configure the behavior of the Windows Update clients in the usual manner.

Monitoring Performance

THE BOTTOM LINE

For a computer to perform well, all of its components must be individually efficient. Windows 7 includes a variety of tools that enable you to locate components whose performance is below par.

A computer's level of performance is based on a combination of factors, any of which can function as a bottleneck that slows down the entire system. For example, a Windows 7 computer might have an extremely fast processor, but if it is lacking in memory, it will have to page data to the swap file on the hard drive more often, slowing down the system. In the same way, a computer might have a fast processor and plenty of memory, but if its hard drive is slow, the faster components can't run at peak efficiency.

TAKE NOTE*

Windows 7 includes a wide array of tools for monitoring and managing system performance, but administrators who are not satisfied with the tools provided are free to create their own. Windows Management Instrumentation (WMI) is an interface to managed resources in Windows 7 that administrators can use to create scripts to configure performance parameters, among many other things. WMI classes describe the properties of managed resources in Windows 7 and the actions that WMI can use to manage those resources. Administrators can create WMI scripts using Microsoft Visual Basic, Jscript, or any language supported by the Windows Scripting Host (WSH) engine.

Hardware problems are not the only cause of performance degradations. Software incompatibilities and resource depletion can also affect performance. In essence, the task of optimizing the performance of a Windows 7 computer consists of locating the bottlenecks and eliminating them. This might require a hardware upgrade or a reexamination of the computer's suitability to its role. Whatever the solution, the first step in determining what factors are negatively affecting the computer's performance is to quantify that performance and monitor its fluctuations.

CERTIFICATION READY?
Monitor systems.
7.3

The following sections examine some of the tools provided by Windows 7, which enable you to gather information about the computer's ongoing performance levels.

Using Event Viewer

Beginning in Windows Vista, the Event Viewer console has been enhanced to provide easier access to a more comprehensive array of event logs.

Software developers commonly use logs as a means of tracking the activities of particular algorithms, routines, and applications. A log is a list of events, which can track the activity of the software and document errors and provide analytical information to administrators. Logs are traditionally text files, but the Windows operating systems have long used a graphical application called Event Viewer to display the log information gathered by the operating system.

Windows has maintained the same three basic logs throughout several versions: a System log, a Security log, and an Application log. Recent versions have added a Setup log, and servers performing certain roles have additional logs, such as those tracking DNS and File

Replication activities. The format of these logs has remained consistent, although the Event Viewer has undergone some changes. In Windows Server 2003 and Windows XP, Event Viewer first took the form of an MMC snap-in, rather than an independent application.

In Windows Vista and Windows Server 2008, Microsoft gave the Windows eventing engine its most comprehensive overhaul in many years. Windows Eventing 6.0 includes the following enhancements:

- A new, XML-based log format.
- The addition of a Setup log documenting the operating system's installation and configuration history.
- New logs for key applications and services, including DFS Replication and the Key Management Service.
- Individual logs for Windows components.
- Enhanced querying capabilities that simplify the process of locating specific events.
- The ability to create subscriptions that enable administrators to collect and store specific types of events from other computers on the network.

LAUNCHING THE EVENT VIEWER CONSOLE

The primary function of the Windows Eventing engine is to record information about system activities as they occur and package that information in individual units called *events*. The application you use to view the events is an MMC snap-in called Event Viewer. As with all MMC snap-ins, you can launch the Event Viewer console in a variety of ways, including the following:

- Click Start, then click Control Panel > System and Security > Administrative Tools > Event Viewer.
- Open a blank MMC console and add the Event Viewer snap-in.
- Click Start and type Event Viewer or Eventvwr.msc in the search box.
- Open the Computer Management console and expand the Event Viewer node.

USING THE OVERVIEW AND SUMMARY DISPLAY

When the Event Viewer console appears, you see the Overview and Summary screen shown in Figure 8-18.

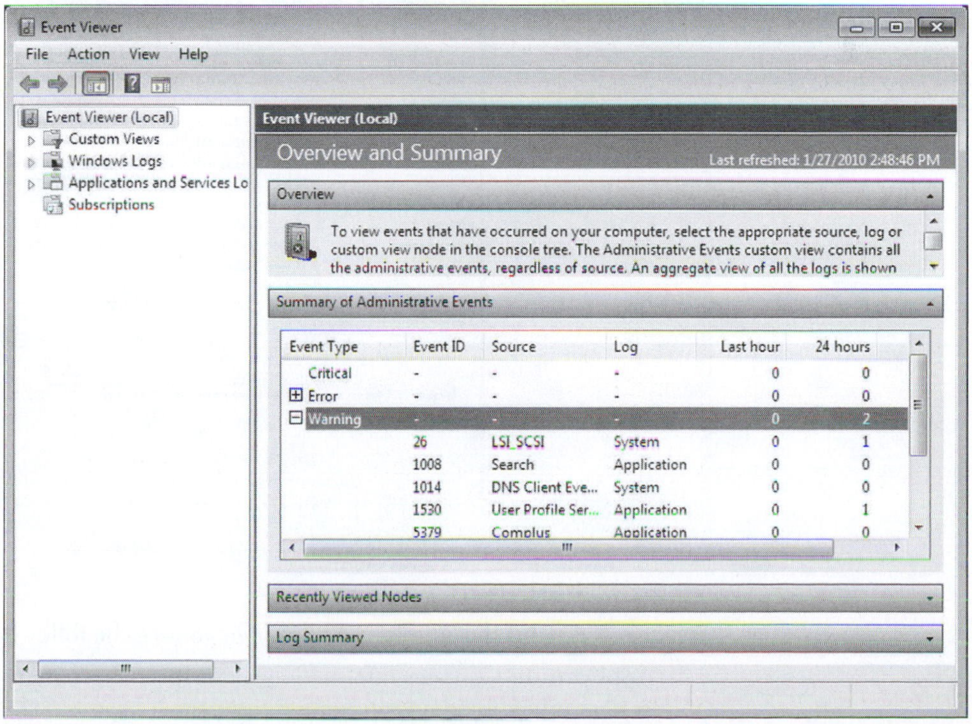

Figure 8-18

The Overview and Summary screen in the Event Viewer console

The Summary of Administrative Events displays the total number of events recorded in the last hour, day, and week, sorted by event type. When you expand an event type, the list is broken down by event ID, as shown in Figure 8-19.

Figure 8-19

The Event ID breakdown in the Event Viewer console

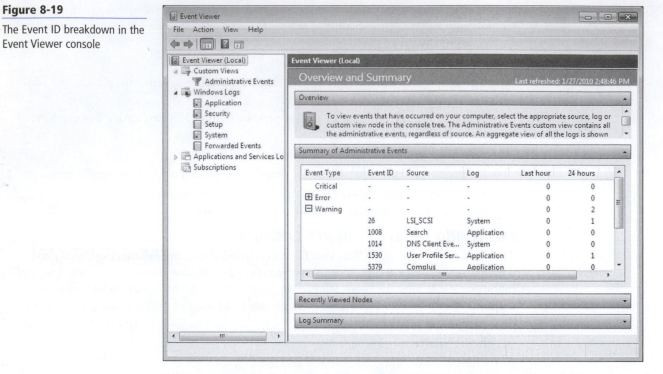

When you double click one of the event IDs, the console creates a filtered custom view that displays only the events having that ID, as shown in Figure 8-20.

Figure 8-20

A custom view in the Event Viewer console

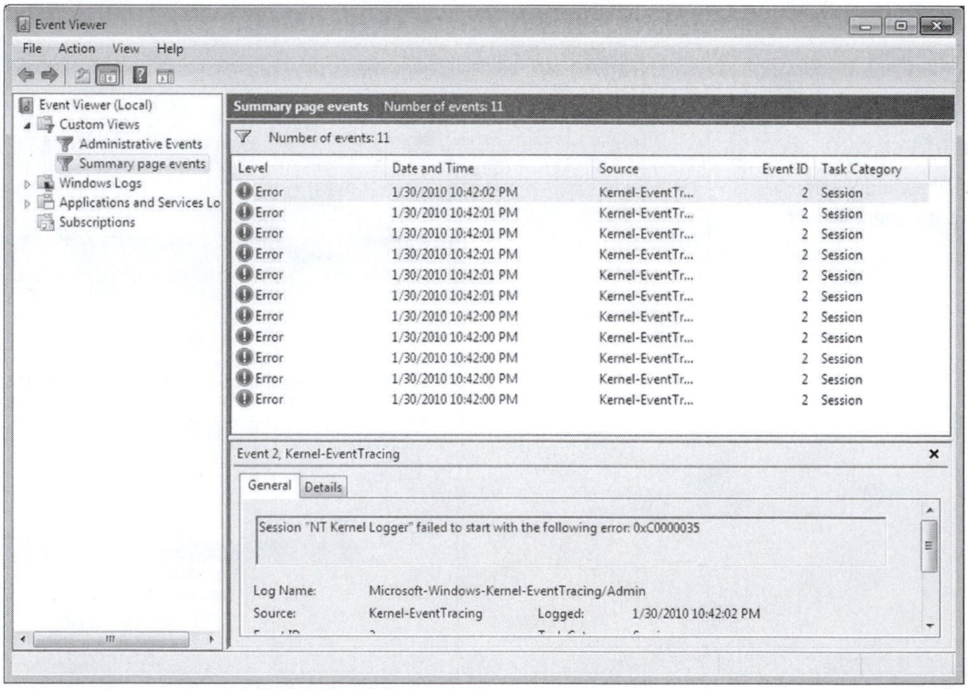

VIEWING WINDOWS LOGS

When you expand the Windows Logs folder, you see the following logs:

- **Application:** Contains information about specific programs running on the computer, as determined by the application developer.

> **TAKE NOTE***
>
> The System log is the primary Windows 7 operational log. You should always view this log first when looking for general information about system problems.

- **Security:** Contains information about security-related events, such as failed logons, attempts to access protected resources, and success or failure of audited events. The events recorded in this log are determined by audit policies, which you can enable using either local computer policies or Group Policy.
- **Setup:** Contains information about the operating system installation and setup history.
- **System:** Contains information about events generated by the operating system, such as services and device drivers. For example, a failure of a service to start or a driver to load during system startup is recorded in the System log.
- **Forwarded Events:** Contains events received from other computers on the network via subscriptions.

Selecting one of the logs causes a list of the events it contains to appear in the details pane, in reverse chronological order, as shown in Figure 8-21.

Figure 8-21

Contents of a log in the Event Viewer console

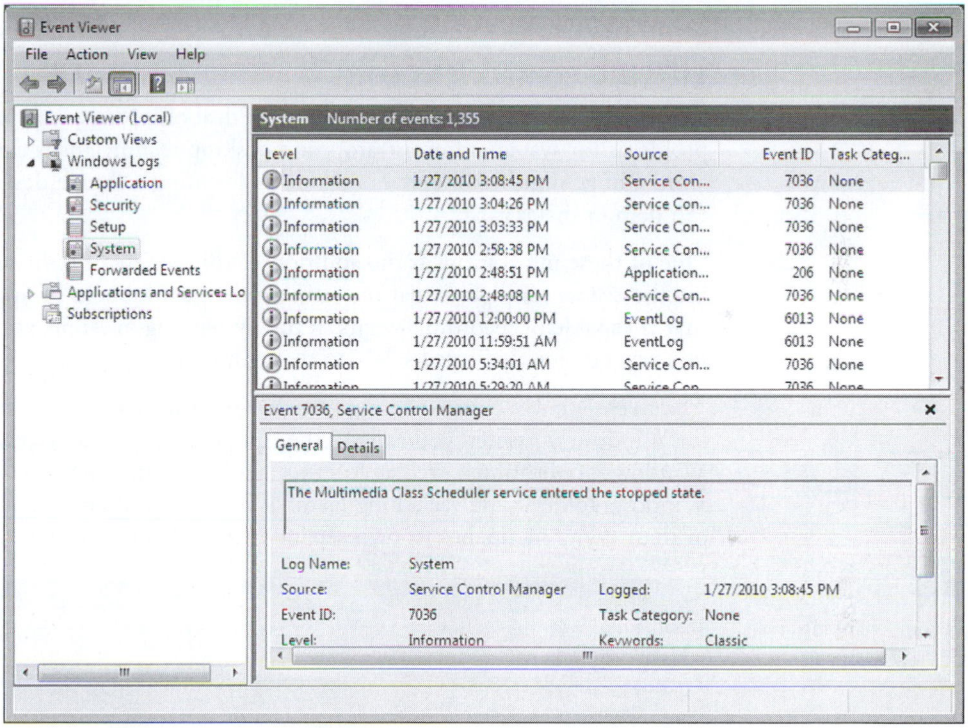

The Windows event logs contain different types of events, which are identified by icons. The four event types are as follows:

- **Information:** An event that describes a change in the state of a component or process as part of a normal operation.
- **Error:** An event that warns of a problem that is not likely to affect the performance of the component or process where the problem occurred, but that could affect the performance of other components or processes on the system.
- **Warning:** An event that warns of a service degradation or an occurrence that can potentially cause a service degradation in the near future, unless you take steps to prevent it.
- **Critical:** An event that warns that an incident resulting in a catastrophic loss of functionality or data in a component or process has occurred.

When you select one of the events in the list of events, its properties appear in the preview pane at the bottom of the list. You can also double click an event to display a separate Event Properties dialog box, as shown in Figure 8-22.

Figure 8-22

An Event Properties dialog box

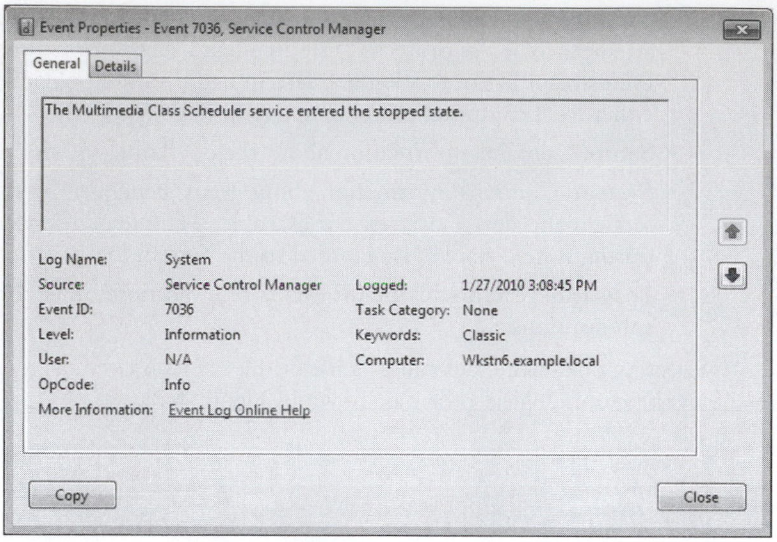

VIEWING COMPONENT LOGS

The Event Viewer console contains a great deal of information, and one of the traditional problems for system administrators and desktop technicians is finding the events they need amid a huge number of entries. Windows Eventing 6.0 includes a number of innovations that can help in this regard.

One of these innovations is the addition of component-specific logs that enable you to examine the events for a particular operating system component or application. Any component that is capable of recording events in the System log or Application log can also record events in a separate log dedicated solely to that component.

The Event Viewer console comes preconfigured with a large collection of component logs for Windows 7. When you expand the Applications and Services Logs folder, you see logs for Windows applications, such as Internet Explorer. Then, when you expand the Microsoft and Windows folders, you see a long list of Windows components, as shown in Figure 8-23. Each of these components has its own separate log, called a *channel*.

Figure 8-23

Windows component logs in the Event Viewer console

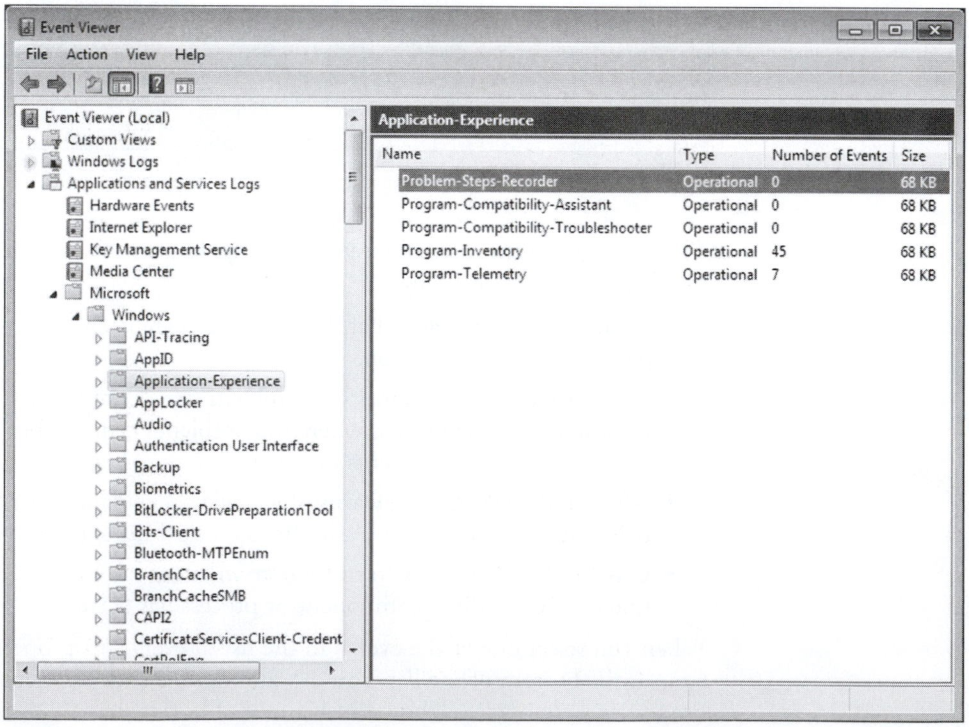

In most cases, the events in the component logs are non-administrative, meaning that they are not indicative of problems or errors. The components continue to save the administrative events to the System log or Application log. The events in the component logs are operational, analytic, or debug events, which means that they are more descriptive entries that document the ongoing activities of the component. The component logs are intended more for use in troubleshooting long-term problems and for software developers seeking debugging information.

CREATING CUSTOM VIEWS

Another means of locating and isolating information about specific events is to use custom views. A custom view is essentially a filtered version of a particular log, configured to display only certain events. The Event Viewer console now has a Custom Views folder in which you can create filtered views and save them for later use.

To create a custom view, use the following procedure.

➔ CREATE A CUSTOM VIEW

GET READY. Log on to Windows 7.

1. Click Start, and then click Control Panel > System and Security > Administrative Tools > Event Viewer. The Event Viewer console appears.
2. Right click the Custom Views folder and then, from the context menu, select Create Custom View. The Create Custom View dialog box appears, as shown in Figure 8-24.

Figure 8-24

The Create Custom View dialog box

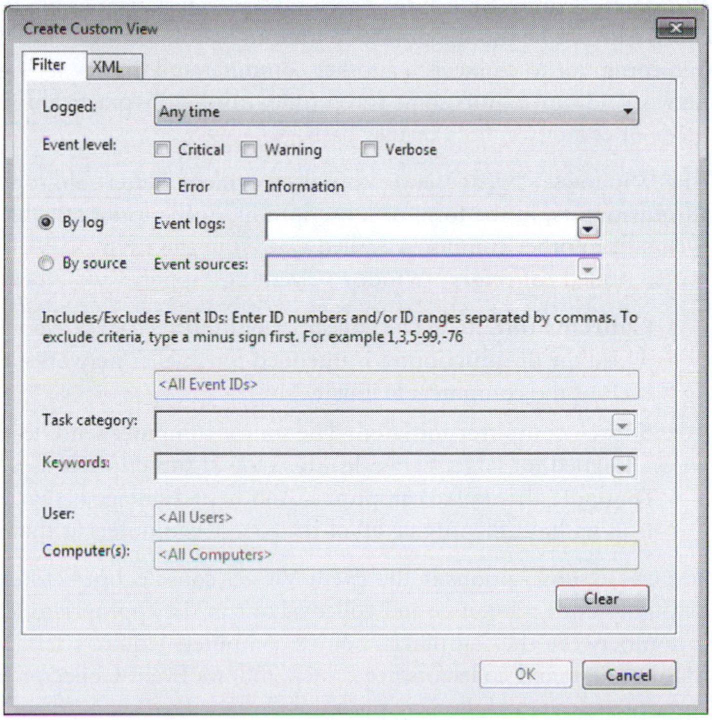

3. From the Logged: drop-down list, select the time interval from which you want to display events.
4. In the Event level: area, select the check boxes for the types of events you want to display.
5. From the By log: drop-down list, select the log(s) from which you want to display events. Alternatively, from the By source: list select the source(s) from which you want to display events.

6. Optionally, you can specify event ID numbers, task categories, keywords, and user credentials to narrow your search.

7. Click OK. The Save Filter to Custom View dialog box appears, as shown in Figure 8-25.

Figure 8-25

The Save Filter to Custom View dialog box

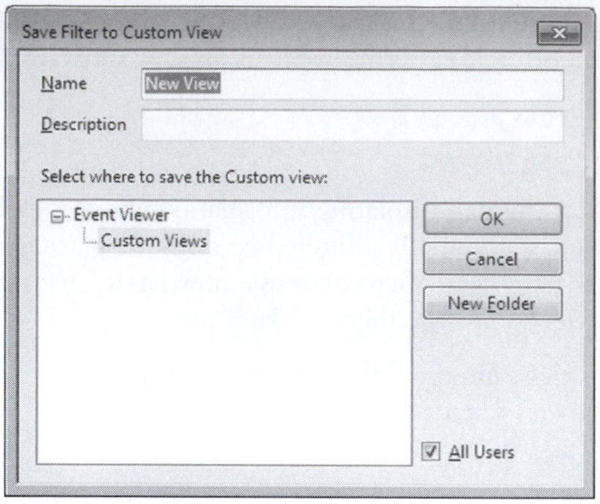

8. Type a name for the view in the Name text box, a description if desired, and select the folder in which you want to create your custom view. Then click OK. The console adds your view to the folder you selected and displays the view in the detail pane.

SUBSCRIBING TO EVENTS

The Event Viewer console can provide an enormous amount of information about a Windows 7 computer, but for a technical specialist responsible for hundreds of workstations, this can be too much information to handle. You can use the Event Viewer console on one computer to connect to another computer and display its logs, but while this saves the network administrators some travel time, it is hardly practical for them to check logs on hundreds of computers on a regular basis.

The Windows 7 Event Viewer console provides a better solution for enterprise network administrators, in the form of subscriptions. Subscriptions enable administrators to receive events from other computers (called *sources*) in the Event Viewer console on their own computers (called ***collectors***). Windows Eventing supports two types of subscriptions:

- **Collector initiated:** The collector computer retrieves events from the source computer. This type of subscription is intended for smaller networks, because you must configure each of the computers manually.

- **Source computer initiated:** The source computer sends events to the collector computer. Designed for larger networks, this type of subscription uses Group Policy settings to configure the source computers. Another advantage is that you can create the subscription without identifying all of the source computers at that time.

You create subscriptions in the Event Viewer console, but before you can do so, you must configure both the source and collector to run the appropriate services needed for communication between the computers. Source computers require a service called Windows Remote Management and collectors need the Windows Event Collector service. To configure the computers, use the following procedures.

On the collector computer:

- Open an elevated command prompt, type the following command, and press Enter:
  ```
  wecutil qc
  ```

On each source computer:

- Open an elevated command prompt, type the following command, and press Enter:
  ```
  winrm quickconfig
  ```

- Open the Computer Management console and, in the Local Users and Groups snap-in, add the computer account for the collector to the local Administrators group.

Event log subscriptions use the Hypertext Transfer Protocol (HTTP), or optionally, the Secure Hypertext Transfer Protocol (HTTPS), for communications. These are the same protocols used by Internet web servers and browsers, so most computers are configured to allow them through their firewalls. However, if you experience communication problems, make sure that the firewalls on the collector and all source computers are configured to allow traffic on TCP port 80 for HTTP or TCP port 443 for HTTPS.

Once you have completed these tasks, you can proceed to create a subscription in the Event Viewer console on the collector computer, using the following procedure.

CREATE AN EVENT SUBSCRIPTION

GET READY. Log on to the Windows 7 computer you have configured as the collector.

1. Click Start, and then click Control Panel > System and Security > Administrative Tools > Event Viewer. The Event Viewer console appears.
2. Right click the Subscriptions node and, from the context menu, select Create Subscription. The Subscription Properties dialog box appears, as shown in Figure 8-26.

Figure 8-26

The Subscription Properties dialog box

Subscription Properties	☒
Subscription name:	
Description:	
Destination log:	Forwarded Events ▼
Subscription type and source computers	
⊙ Collector initiated	Select Computers...
This computer contacts the selected source computers and provides the subscription.	
○ Source computer initiated	Select Computer Groups...
Source computers in the selected groups must be configured through policy or local configuration to contact this computer and receive the subscription.	
Events to collect: <filter not configured>	Select Events... ▼
User account (the selected account must have read access to the source logs):	
Machine Account	
Change user account or configure advanced settings:	Advanced...
	OK Cancel

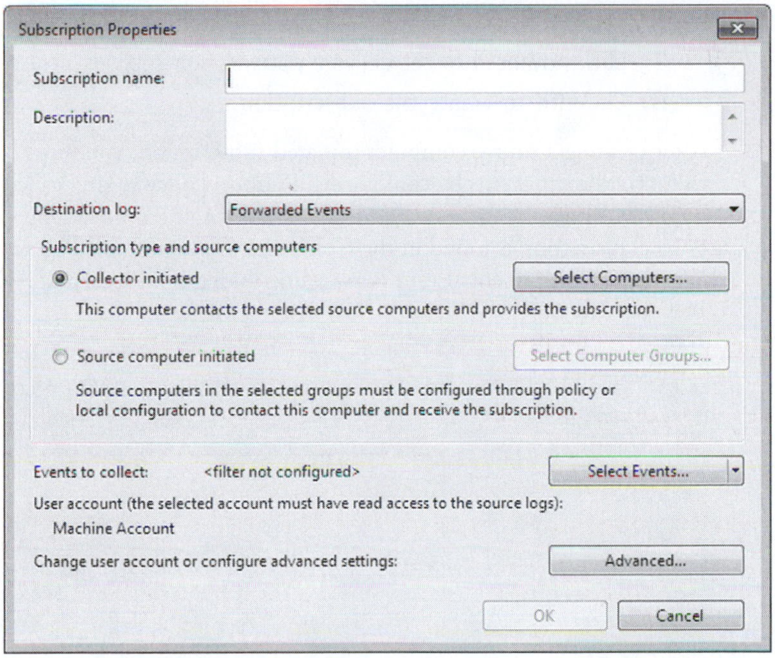

3. In the Subscription Name text box, type a name for the subscription.
4. Select one of the following subscription type options:
   - **Collector initiated:** If you choose this option, you must click Select Computers to display the Computers dialog box, in which you must specify the name of all the source computers from which you want to receive events.
   - **Source computer initiated:** If you choose this option, you must click Select Computer groups to display the Computer Groups dialog box, in which you can specify the names of source computers or the names of security groups into which you will add the computers from which you want to receive events.
5. Click Select Events. The Query Filter dialog box appears, as shown in Figure 8-27.
6. Use the controls to select the events you want the source computers to forward and click OK.

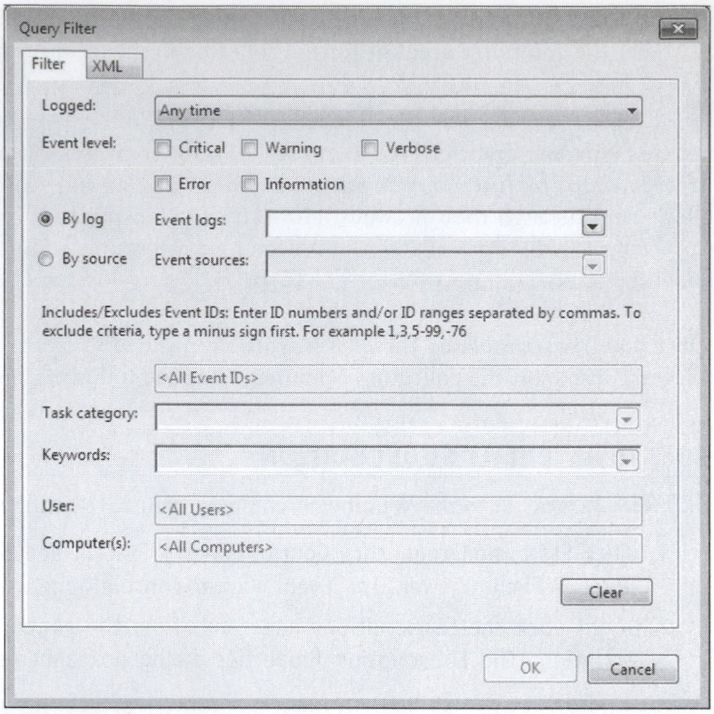

Figure 8-27

The Query Filter dialog box

7. Click **Advanced** to set delivery optimization settings or use HTTPS for additional security.

8. Click **OK** to create the subscription.

After creating a source computer initiated subscription, you must configure the source computers to forward their events by configuring a Group Policy setting called *Configure the server address, refresh interval, and issuer certificate authority of a target Subscription Manager*, as shown in Figure 8-28. This setting is found in the Computer Configuration\Policies\Administrative Templates\Windows Components\Event Forwarding folder of all local and AD DS GPOs.

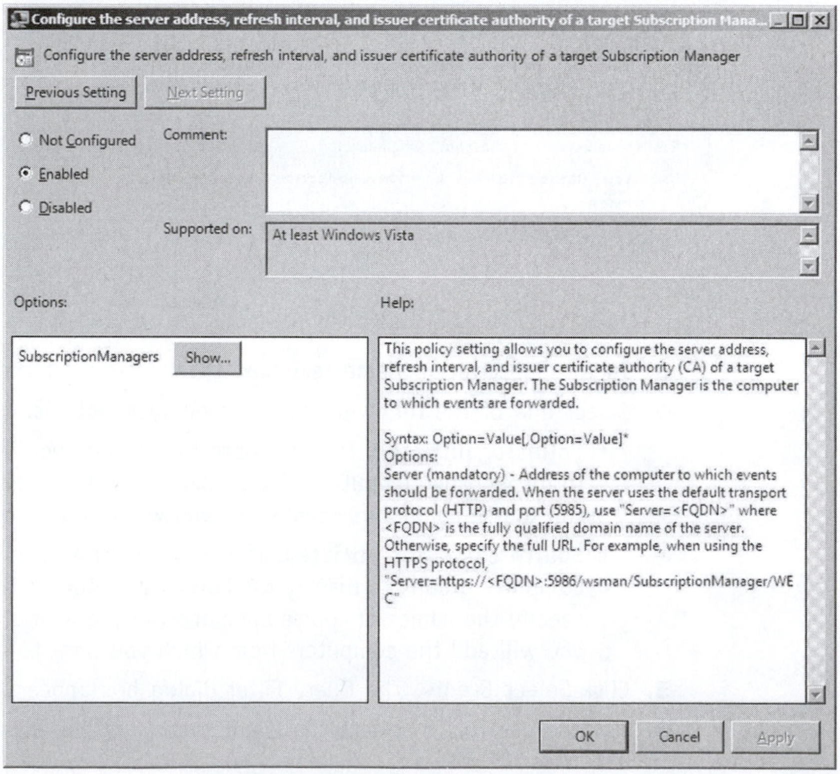

Figure 8-28

The Configure the server address, refresh interval, and issuer certificate authority of a target Subscription Manager dialog box

Using Performance Information and Tools

The System control panel contains a system rating called the ***Windows Experience Index***, which quantifies the capabilities of a Windows 7 computer by breaking it down into categories and assigning each one a rating. One key function of this rating is to help users determine why a particular computer is unable to run the Windows Aero user experience. However, the underlying technology of this tool has other uses as well.

To view the detailed information that Windows 7 uses to determine the system's overall rating, use the following procedure.

⊕ DISPLAY WINDOWS EXPERIENCE INDEX DATA

GET READY. Log on to Windows 7.

1. Click Start, and then click Control Panel > System and Security > System. The *View basic information about your computer* page appears, as shown in Figure 8-29.

Figure 8-29

The View basic information about your computer page

Control Panel ▸ All Control Panel Items ▸ System	Search Control Panel

Control Panel Home

- Device Manager
- Remote settings
- System protection
- Advanced system settings

View basic information about your computer

Windows edition

Windows 7 Enterprise

Copyright © 2009 Microsoft Corporation. All rights reserved.

System

Rating:	**1.0** Windows Experience Index
Processor:	Intel(R) Xeon(R) CPU 3075 @ 2.66GHz 2.66 GHz
Installed memory (RAM):	1.00 GB
System type:	64-bit Operating System
Pen and Touch:	No Pen or Touch Input is available for this Display

Computer name, domain, and workgroup settings

Computer name:	Wkstn6
Full computer name:	Wkstn6.example.local
Computer description:	
Domain:	example.local

See also

Action Center

Windows Update

Performance Information and Tools

Change settings

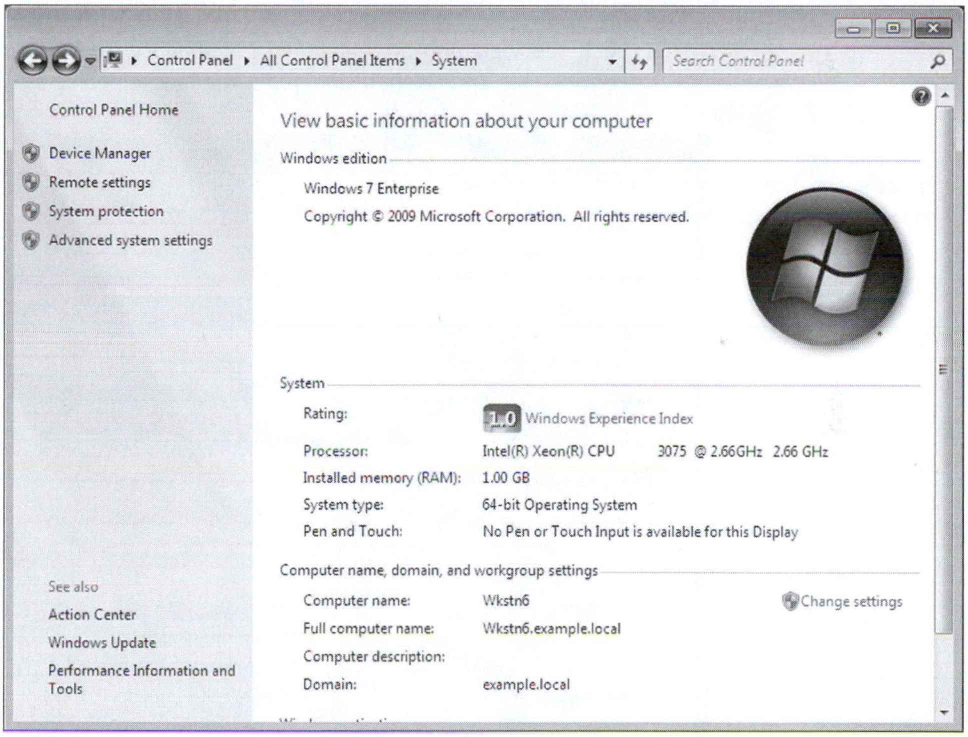

2. In the System section, click the Windows Experience Index link. The *Rate and improve your computer's performance* page appears, as shown in Figure 8-30.

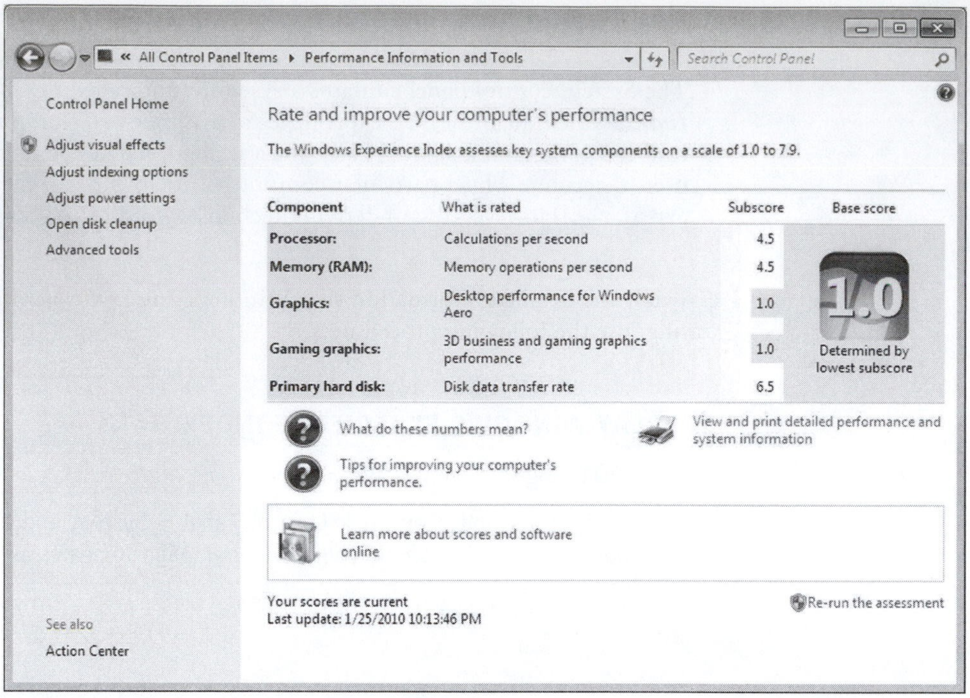

Figure 8-30

The Rate and improve your computer's performance page

3. Click the *View and print detailed performance and system information* link. The *Performance Information and Tools* window appears, as shown in Figure 8-31.

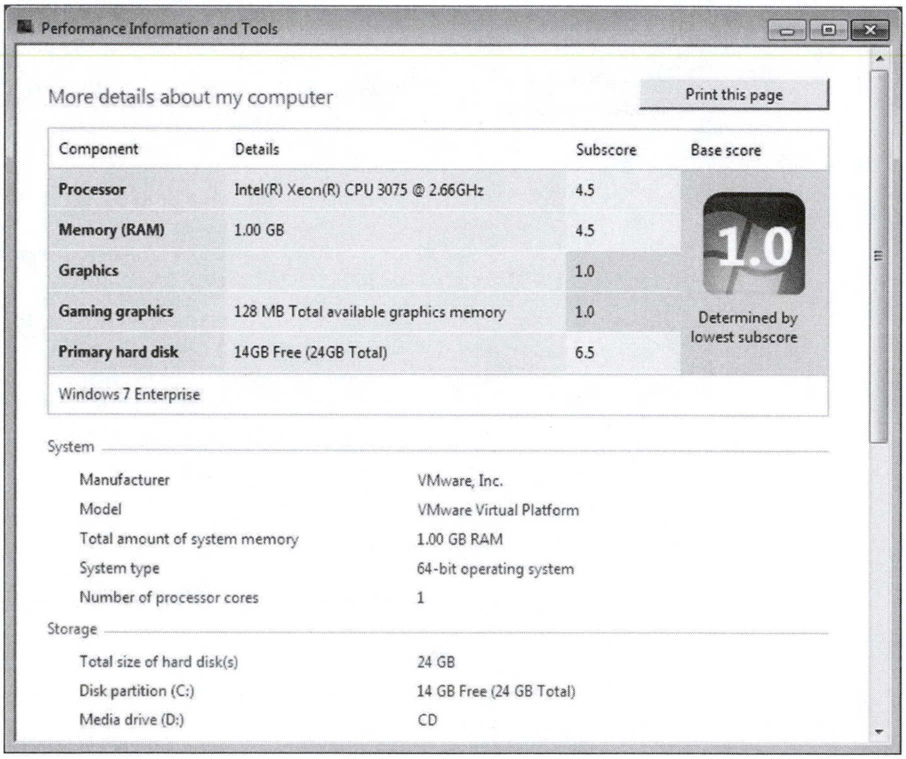

Figure 8-31

The Performance Information and Tools page

The *Performance Information and Tools* page breaks down the computer into the following five components:

- Processor
- Memory (RAM)
- Graphics

- Gaming graphics
- Primary hard disk

The tool assigns each of these areas a numerical score that gauges its performance. The overall system performance rating for the computer, known as the *base score*, is the lowest of the component scores. This is a perfect illustration of the bottleneck concept mentioned earlier. It is the slowest component on the computer that dictates its overall performance level. In the same way that one component can prevent the computer from running Windows Aero, it can also cause a general degradation of performance.

> **TAKE NOTE** *
>
> As a general rule, computers with a base score under 3.0 are unable to run Windows Aero. A computer with a base score of 3.0 or more should be able to run Aero.

One of the best ways to improve the performance of your computer is to try to raise the system's base score. This usually means a hardware upgrade, such as installing additional memory, replacing a graphics adapter, or installing a faster hard drive. However, there are often less invasive (and less expensive) ways to improve performance. Back on the *Rate and improve your computer's performance* page, clicking the *Tips for improving your computer's performance* link opens a help page that contains a number of tips that can help you conserve system resources, thereby enhancing performance.

In addition to the base score and subscores, this window displays a variety of information about the hardware in the computer and the software running on it. For example, the Graphics section of the Performance Information and Tools page provides the following information:

- **Total available graphics memory:** Specifies how much memory is installed on the video adapter and how much system memory is devoted to graphics tasks.
- **Display adapter driver version:** Specifies the version number of the display driver currently installed on the system.
- **Primary monitor resolution:** Specifies the primary resolution at which the computer's monitor is designed to run.
- **DirectX version:** Specifies the version of the DirectX APIs supported by the graphics hardware.

Using the Performance Monitor Console

> A computer's performance level is constantly changing as it performs different combinations of tasks. Monitoring the performance of the various components over a period of time is the only way to get a true picture of the system's capabilities.

While the Performance Information and Tools page provides a snapshot of your computer's performance at a single moment in time, the Performance Monitor console enables you to view much of the same information, but on a continuous, real-time basis. Like Event Viewer, the Performance Monitor console is an MMC snap-in that you can launch in a variety of ways, including the following:

- Click Start, then click Control Panel > System and Security > Administrative Tools > Performance Monitor.
- Open a blank MMC console and add the Performance Monitor snap-in.
- Click Start and type Perfmon.msc in the search box.
- Open the Computer Management console and expand the Performance Monitor node.

Performance Monitor is a tool that can display information for hundreds of different statistics (called **performance counters**) in a variety of ways. You can use Performance Monitor to create a customized graph or report containing any statistics you choose.

When you open the Performance Monitor snap-in, expand the Monitoring Tools node, and select Performance Monitor, the detail pane of the snap-in contains a line graph, updated in real time, showing the current level for the % Processor Time performance counter, as shown in Figure 8-32.

Figure 8-32

The default Performance Monitor display

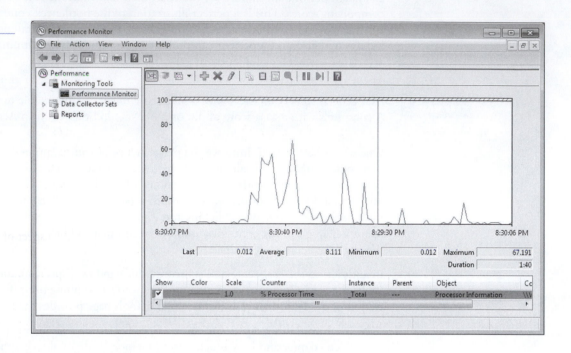

ADDING COUNTERS

The performance counter that appears in Performance Monitor by default is a useful gauge of the computer's performance, but the snap-in includes hundreds of other counters that you can add to the display. To add counters to the Performance Monitor display, click the Add button in the toolbar, or press Ctrl+I to display the Add Counters dialog box, as shown in Figure 8-33.

Figure 8-33

The Add Counters dialog box

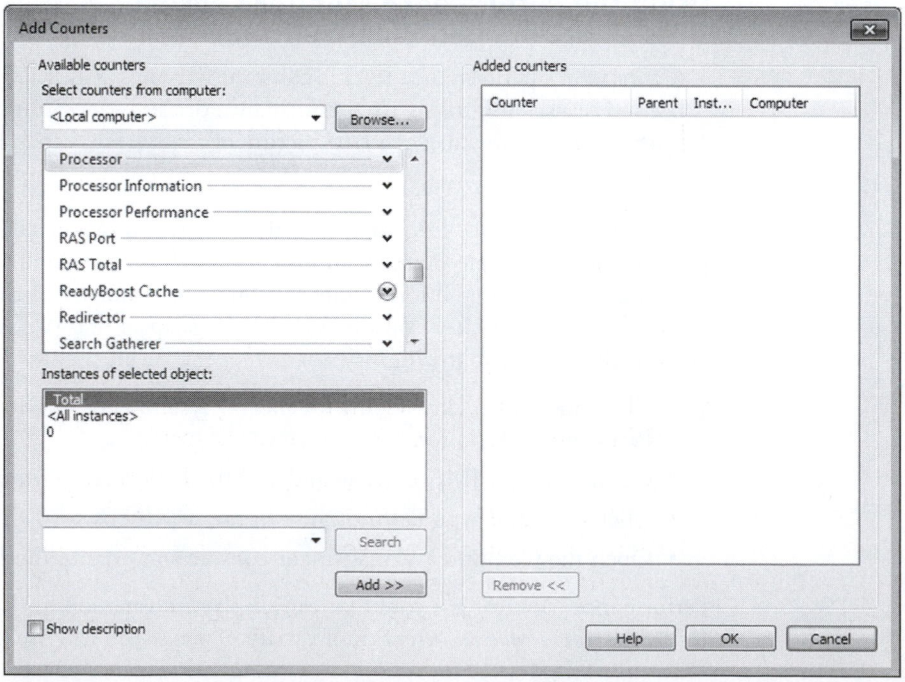

Unlike most MMC snap-ins, Performance Monitor does not insert its most commonly used functions into the MMC console's Action menu. The only methods for accessing Performance Monitor functions are the toolbar buttons, hotkey combinations, and the context menu that appears when you right click the display.

In this dialog box, you have to specify the following four pieces of information to add a counter to the display:

- *Computer:* The name of the computer you want to monitor with the selected counter. Unlike most MMC snap-ins, you cannot redirect the entire focus of Performance Monitor to another computer on the network. Instead, you specify a computer name for each counter you add to the display. This enables you to create a display showing counters for various computers on the network, such as a single graph of processor activity for all of your workstations.
- *Performance object:* A category representing a specific hardware or software component in the computer. Click the down arrow on a performance object to display a selection of performance counters related to that component.
- *Performance counter:* A statistic representing a specific aspect of the selected performance object's activities.
- *Instance:* An element representing a specific occurrence of the selected performance counter. For example, on a computer with two network interface adapters, each counter in the Network Interface performance object would have two instances, one for each adapter, enabling you to track the performance of the two adapters individually. Some counters also have instances such as Total or Average, enabling you to track the performance of all instances combined or the median value of all instances.

Once you have selected a computer name, a performance object, a performance counter in that object, and an instance of that counter, click Add to add the counter to the Added Counters list. The dialog box remains open so that you can add more counters. Click OK when you are finished to update the graph with your selected counters.

Select the *Show description* check box to display a detailed explanation of the selected performance counter.

The performance objects, performance counters, and instances that appear in the Add Counters dialog box depend on the computer's hardware configuration, the software installed on the computer, and the computer's role on the network.

MODIFYING THE GRAPH VIEW

The legend beneath the Performance Monitor graph specifies the line color for the counter, the scale of values for the counter, and other identifying information. When you select a counter in the legend, its current values appear in numerical form at the bottom of the graph. Click the Highlight button in the toolbar (or press Ctrl+H) to change the selected counter to a broad line that is easier to distinguish in the graph.

If your computer is otherwise idle, you will probably notice that the line in the default graph is hovering near the bottom of the scale, which makes it difficult to see its value. You can address this problem by modifying the scale of the graph's Y (i.e., vertical) axis. Click the Properties button in the toolbar (or press Ctrl+Q) to display the Performance Monitor Properties sheet and click the Graph tab, as shown in Figure 8-34. In the *Vertical scale* box, you can reduce the maximum value for the Y axis, thereby using more of the graph to display the counter data.

Figure 8-34

The Graph tab in the Performance Monitor Properties sheet

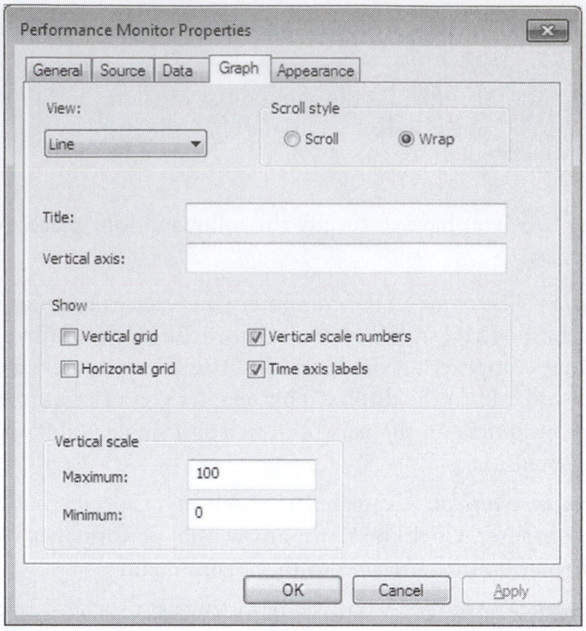

The Performance Monitor Properties sheet contains a number of other controls that you can use to modify the appearance of the graph. For example, on the Graph tab, you can add axis titles and gridlines, and in the Appearance tab, you can control the graph's background and select a different text font.

In the General tab of the Performance Monitor Properties sheet, you can also modify the sample rate of the graph. By default, the graph updates the counter values once every second, but you can increase this value to display data for a longer period of time on a single page of the graph. This can make it easier to detect long-term trends in counter values.

USING OTHER VIEWS

In addition to the line graph, Performance Monitor has two other views of the same data: a histogram view and a report view. You can change the display to one of these views by clicking the Change Graph Type toolbar button. The histogram view is a bar graph with a separate vertical bar for each counter, as shown in Figure 8-35. In this view, it is easier to monitor large numbers of counters because the lines do not overlap.

Figure 8-35

The Performance Monitor histogram view

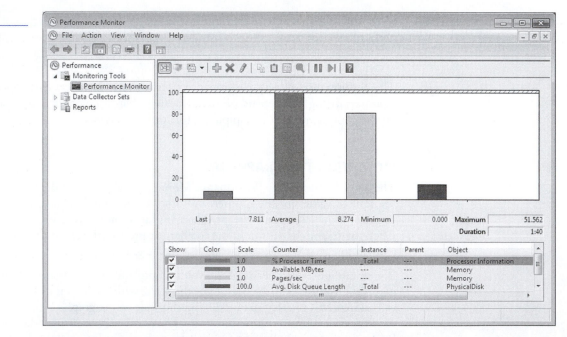

The report view (see Figure 8-36) displays the numerical value for each of the performance counters.

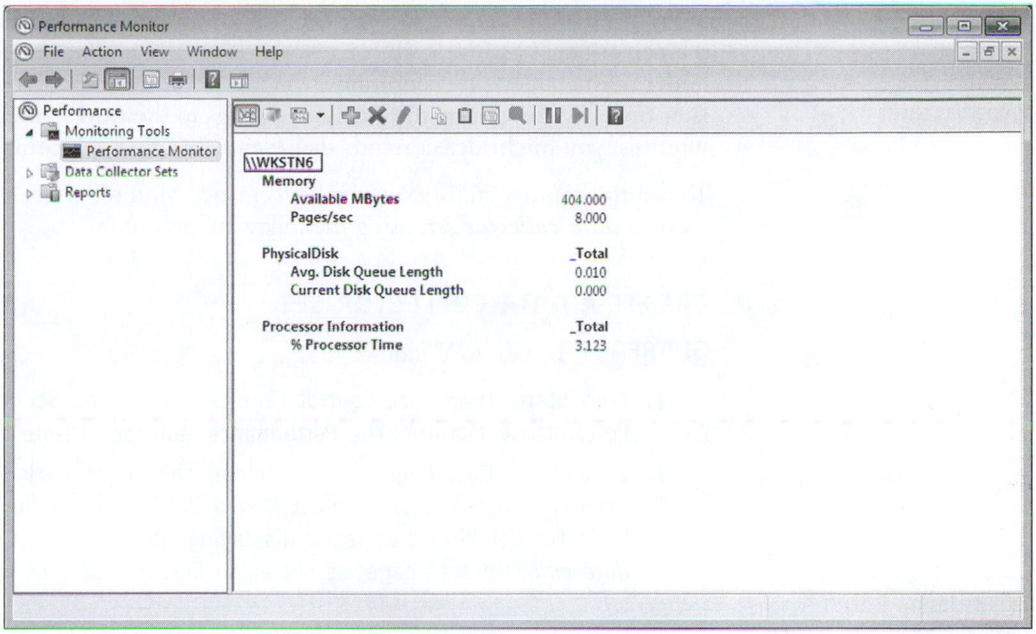

Figure 8-36

The Performance Monitor report view

As with the line graph, the histogram and report views both update their counter values at the interval specified in the General tab of the Performance Monitor Properties sheet. The main drawback of these two views, however, is that they do not display a history of the counter values, only the current value. Each new sampling overwrites the previous one in the display, unlike the line graph, which displays the previous values as well.

CREATING AN EFFECTIVE DISPLAY

In most cases, when users first discover Performance Monitor, they see the dozens of available performance objects and proceed to create a line graph containing dozens of different counters. In most cases, the result is a graph that is hopelessly crowded and incoherent. The number of counters that you can display effectively depends on the size of your monitor and the resolution of your video display.

Consider the following tips when selecting counters:

- **Limit the number of counters:** Too many counters make the graph difficult to understand. To display a large number of statistics, you can display multiple windows in the console and select different counters in each window, or use the histogram or report view to display a large number of counters in a more compact form.

- **Modify the counter display properties:** Depending on the size and capabilities of your monitor, the default colors and line widths that System Monitor uses in its graph might make it difficult to distinguish counters from each other. In the Data tab in the Performance Monitor Properties sheet, you can modify the color, style, and width of each counter's line in the graph to make it easier to distinguish.

- **Choose counters with comparable values:** Performance Monitor imposes no limitations on the combinations of counters you can select for a single graph, but some statistics are not practical to display together because of their disparate values. When a graph contains a counter with a typical value that is under twenty and another counter with a value in the hundreds, it is difficult to arrange the display so that both counters are readable. Choose counters with values that are reasonably comparable so that you can display them legibly. If you must display counters with different value ranges, you may prefer to use the report view over the graph view.

CREATING DATA COLLECTOR SETS

As mentioned earlier, performance bottlenecks can develop over a long period of time, and it can often be difficult to detect them by observing a server's performance levels at one particular point in time. This is why it is a good idea to use tools like Performance Monitor to establish the operational baseline levels for a workstation. A **baseline** is a set of readings, captured under normal operating conditions, which you can save and compare to readings taken at a later time. By comparing the baseline readings to the workstation's current readings at regular intervals, you might detect trends that eventually affect the computer's performance.

To capture counter statistics in the Performance Monitor console for later review, you must create a **data collector set**, using the following procedure.

CREATE A DATA COLLECTOR SET

GET READY. Log on to Windows 7.

1. Click Start. Then click Control Panel > System and Security > Administrative Tools > Performance Monitor. The Performance Monitor console appears.

2. Expand the Data Collector Sets folder. Then right click the User Defined folder and, from the context menu, select New > Data Collector Set. The Create New Data Collector Set Wizard appears, displaying the *How would you like to create this new data collector set?* page, as shown in Figure 8-37.

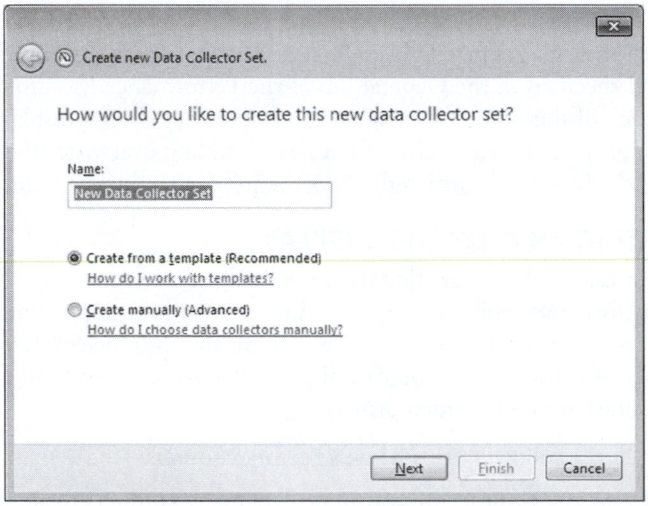

Figure 8-37

The How would you like to create this new data collector set? page in the Create New Data Collector Set wizard

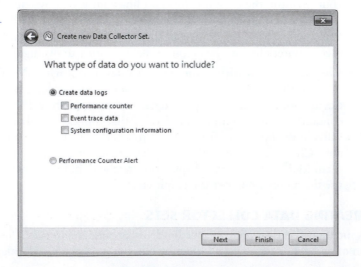

3. In the Name text box, type a name for the data collector set. Then, select the *Create manually (Advanced)* option and click Next. The *What type of data do you want to include?* page appears, as shown in Figure 8-38.

Figure 8-38

The What type of data do you want to include? page in the Create New Data Collector Set wizard

4. Select the *Performance counter* check box and click Next. The *Which performance counters would you like to log?* page appears, as shown in Figure 8-39.

Figure 8-39

The Which performance counters would you like to log? page in the Create New Data Collector Set wizard

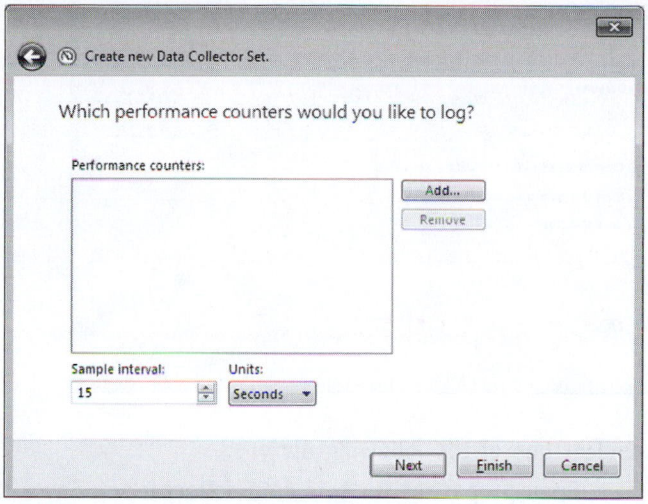

5. Click Add. The standard Add Counters dialog box appears. Select the counters you want to log in the usual manner and click OK. The counters appear in the *Performance counters* box.

> **TAKE NOTE*** You can also use the Create New Data Collector Set wizard to create performance counter alerts, which monitor the values of specific counters and perform a task, such as sending an email to an administrator when the counters reach a specific value.

6. Select the interval at which you want the system to collect samples and click Next. The *Where would you like the data to be saved?* page appears, as shown in Figure 8-40.

Figure 8-40

The Where would you like the data to be saved? page in the Create New Data Collector Set wizard

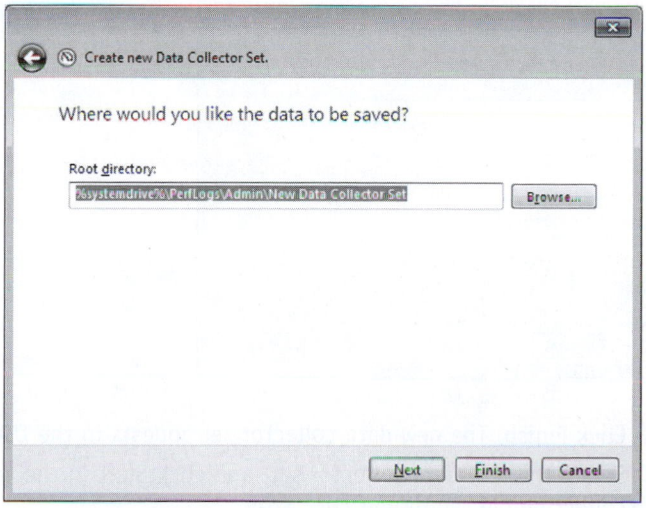

7. Type the name of the data collector set or browse to the folder where you want to store the data collector set and click Next. The *Create the data collector set?* page appears, as shown in Figure 8-41.

8. If the account you are currently using does not have the privileges needed to gather the log information, click Change to display a Performance Monitor dialog box in which you can supply alternative credentials.

Figure 8-41

The Create the data collector set? page in the Create New Data Collector Set wizard

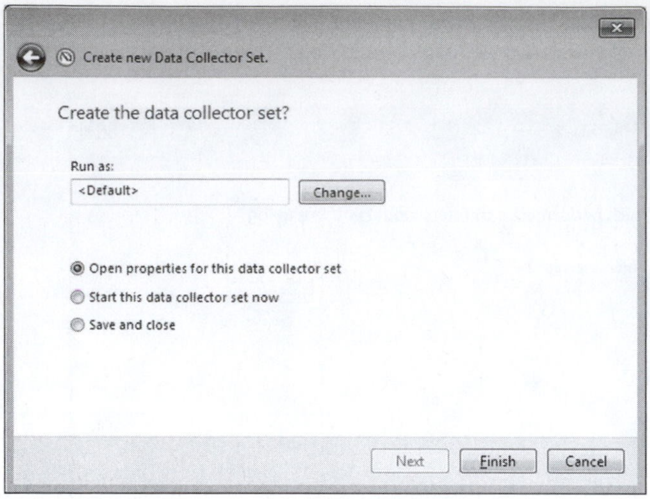

9. Select one of the following options:
   - **Open properties for this data collector set:** Saves the data collector set to the specified location and opens its Properties sheet, as shown in Figure 8-42, for further modifications.
   - **Start this data collector set now:** Saves the data collector set to the specified location and starts collecting data immediately.
   - **Save and close:** Saves the data collector set to the specified location and closes the wizard.

Figure 8-42

The Properties sheet for a data collector set

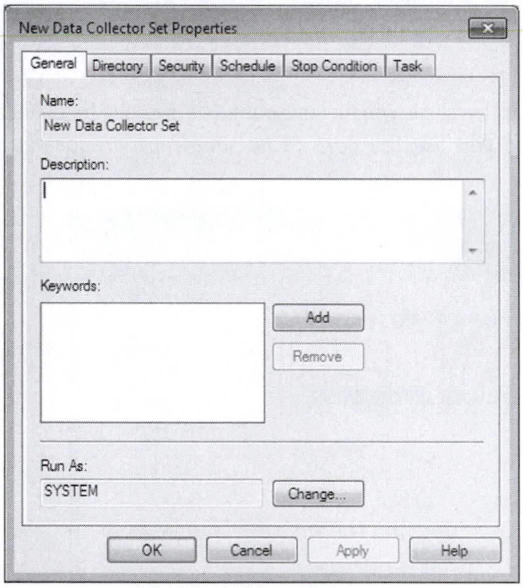

10. Click Finish, The new data collector set appears in the User Defined folder.
11. Select the new data collector set, and click Start in the toolbar. The console begins collecting data until you click Stop.

Once you have captured data using the collector set, you can display the data by double clicking the Performance Monitor file in the folder you specified during its creation. This opens a Performance Monitor window containing a graph of the collected data, as shown in Figure 8-43, instead of real-time activity.

By repeating this process at a later time and comparing the information in the two data collector sets, you can detect performance trends that indicate the presence of bottlenecks.

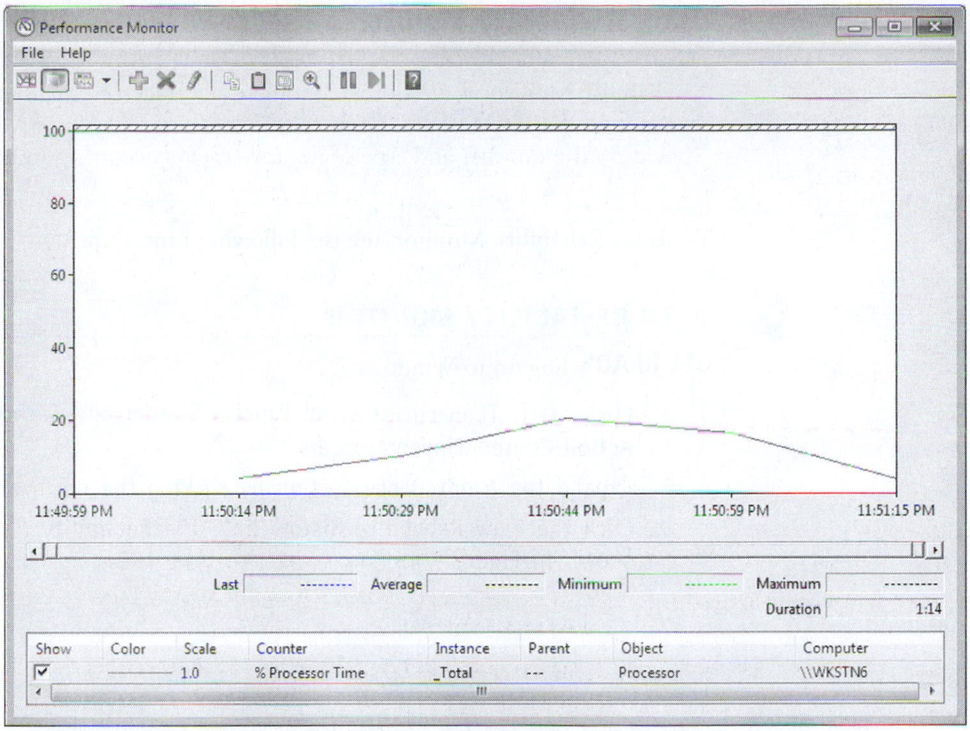

Figure 8-43

Performance Monitor information collected using a data collector set

Figure 8-43

Performance Monitor information collected using a data collector set

CREATING A SYSTEM DIAGNOSTICS REPORT

In addition to its user-configurable capabilities, Performance Monitor also includes preset system diagnostics and system performance reports, which you can generate by expanding the Data Collector Sets\System node, selecting a report, and clicking the Start button in the toolbar.

After allowing the program about 60 seconds to gather data, browse to the Reports\System\ System Diagnostics node to view the report, as shown in Figure 8-44, and examine any failures for system problems.

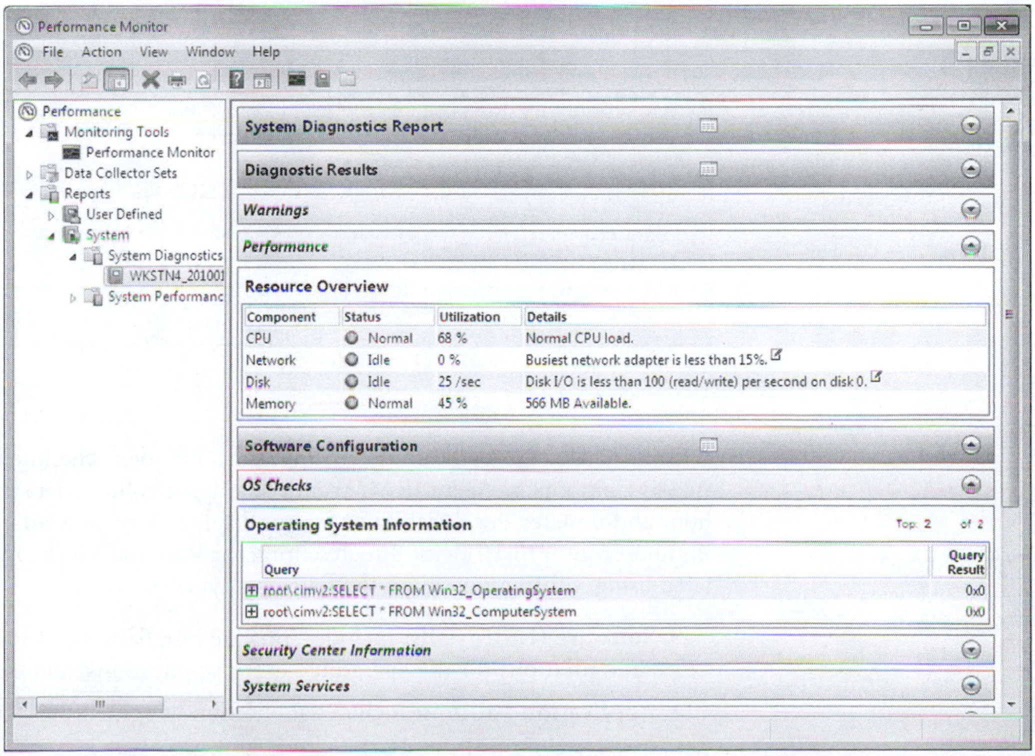

Figure 8-44

A system diagnostics report in Performance Monitor

Using Reliability Monitor

> Reliability Monitor is a tool that automatically tracks events that can have a negative effect on system stability and uses them to calculate a stability index, which is a measurement based on the number and type of negative events occurring in the preceding 28 days.

To access Reliability Monitor, use the following procedure.

⊕ OPEN RELIABILITY MONITOR

GET READY. Log on to Windows 7.

1. Click Start. Then click Control Panel > System and Security > Action Center. The Action Center window appears.
2. Expand the Maintenance section by clicking the down arrow button.
3. Click the View Reliability History link. The Reliability Monitor window appears, as shown in Figure 8-45.

Figure 8-45

The Reliability Monitor window

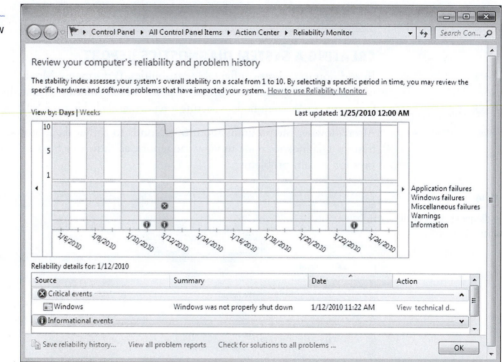

Reliability Monitor gathers information using a hidden scheduled task called Reliability Access Component Agent (RACAgent). The agent collects data from the event logs every hour and updates the Reliability Monitor display every 24 hours. The stability index is a number from 0 to 10 (with 0 representing the least and 10 the most stability) that is calculated using information about the following types of events:

- **Software (Un)Installs:** Includes software installations, uninstallations, updates, and configurations for the operating system, applications, and device drivers.
- **Application Failures:** Includes application hangs, crashes, and terminations of nonresponding applications.

- **Hardware Failures:** Includes disk and memory failures.
- **Windows Failures:** Includes boot failures, operating system crashes, and sleep failures.
- **Miscellaneous Failures:** Includes unrequested system shutdowns.
- **System Clock Changes:** Includes all significant clock time changes. This entry appears only when a significant clock time change has occurred recently.

Pertinent events appear in the System Stability Chart as data points. Clicking one of the points displays information about it in the System Stability Report.

The Reliability Monitor snap-in doesn't actually do anything except present event log information in a different way. It is not possible to configure the snap-in or alter the criteria it uses to evaluate a computer's reliability. If you ever notice that the stability index has decreased, you should check the events that caused the reduction and evaluate for yourself how serious the situation is and what actions you should take, if any.

■ Managing Performance

↓ THE BOTTOM LINE   Windows 7 includes a variety of controls and technologies that enable technical specialists to enhance and fine-tune the performance of their workstations.

CERTIFICATION READY?
Configure performance settings.
7.4

Monitoring performance is of little use unless there is something you can do about it. In Windows 7, there are a variety of tools that you can use to configure the operating system so that it performs better, or to troubleshoot transient lapses in performance. Some of these tools are discussed in the following sections.

Working with Processes

The ability to monitor and manage processes is an important part of Windows 7 troubleshooting, and Microsoft provides a variety of tools that enable you to do these things.

Every application and service running on a Windows 7 computer, including those that are part of the operating system, generates processes or individual tasks that contribute to the overall performance of the system. When performance degrades, the most common method of troubleshooting is to examine the processes running on the computer and the system resources they are consuming.

USING WINDOWS TASK MANAGER

Windows Task Manager is often one of the first tools that many administrators and users turn to when they experience performance problems on a Windows computer. The default Windows Task Manager screen lists the applications currently running on the computer, and lets you switch to them or end them, but Task Manager's true power lies on its other tabs.

The Performance tab, as shown in Figure 8-46, contains graphs that display the computer's processor and memory utilization in real time. The left two graphs display the current readings, and the right displays their recent history. Below the graphs are more detailed real-time statistics in numerical form.

Figure 8-46

The Performance tab in Task Manager

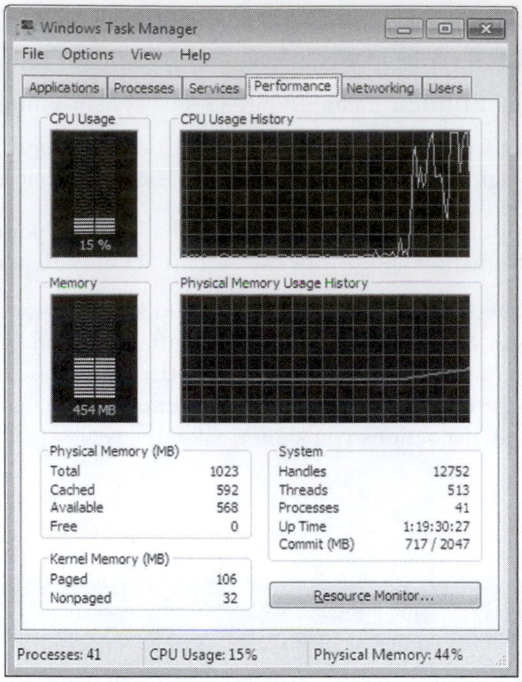

The information on this tab provides an overview of the computer's current performance, which can help administrators locate potential bottlenecks. For example, if, under the computer's normal load, the CPU utilization is consistently approaching 100%, performance can suffer. In such a situation, possible solutions include a faster processor, a second processor, or a reduced application load.

The Processes tab also shows resource utilization, but this tab breaks it down by individual executables, displaying the CPU and memory used by each one, as shown in Figure 8-47. This enables you to determine which processes are responsible for monopolizing the system's resources.

Figure 8-47

The Processes tab in Task Manager

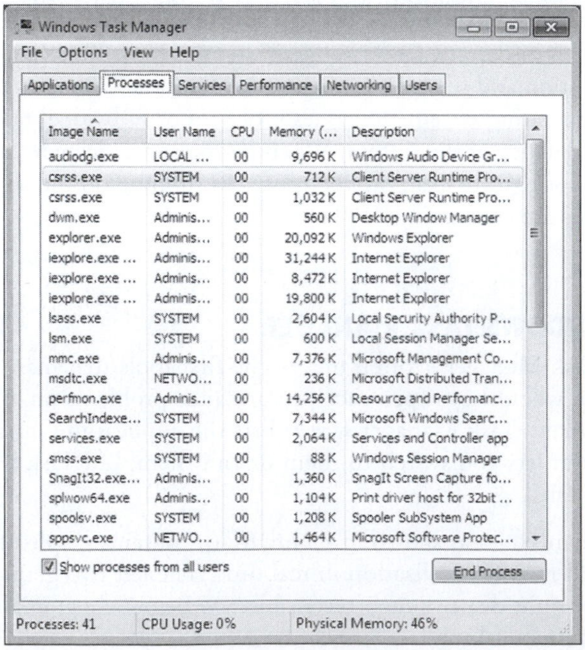

USING RESOURCE MONITOR

When you click the Resource Monitor button on the Task Manager's Performance tab, the Resource Monitor window shown in Figure 8-48 appears, displaying a more comprehensive breakdown of process and performance statistics.

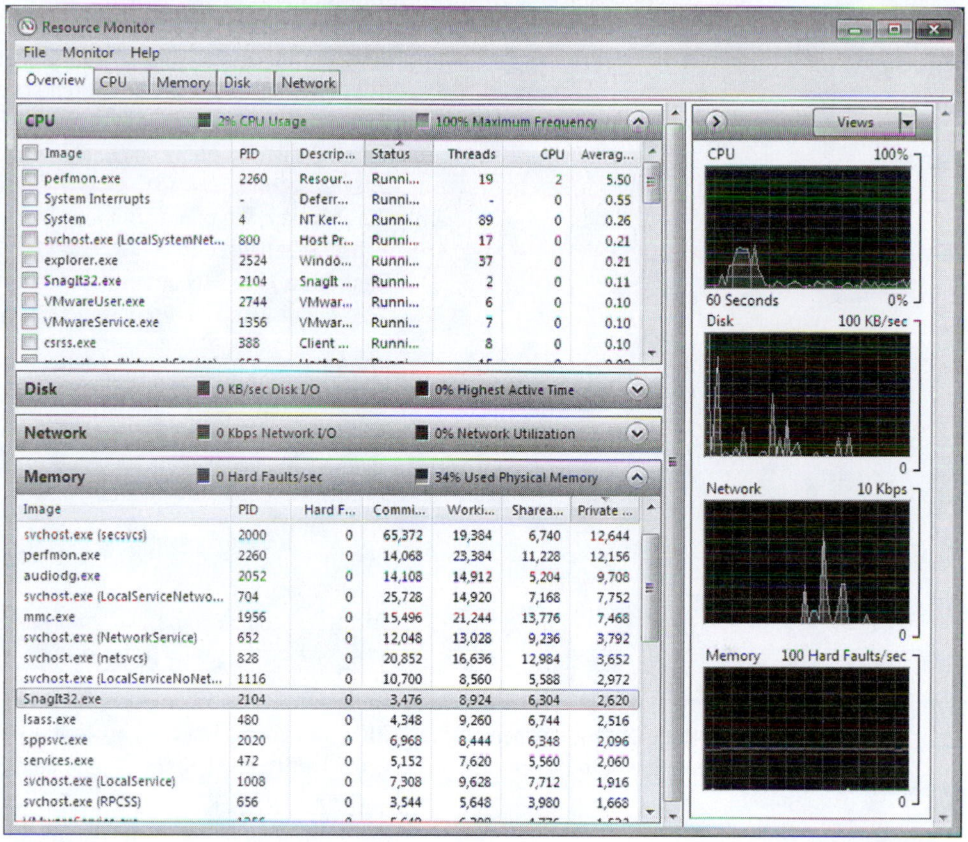

Figure 8-48

The Resource Monitor window

On the Overview tab, there are four real-time line graphs that display information about the main system hardware components. Each of the four components also has a separate, expandable section beside the graphs, displaying more detailed information in text form, such as the resources being utilized by individual applications and processes. Table 8-1 lists the statistics displayed by the graphs and the text sections for each component. Clicking the other tabs displays more extensive information about each one.

Table 8-1

Resource Monitor Overview Statistics

COMPONENT	LINE GRAPH STATISTICS	TEXT STATISTICS
CPU	CPU Usage (%) Maximum Frequency (%)	**Image:** The executable using CPU resources **PID:** The Process ID of the application **Description:** The application using CPU resources **Status:** The current operational status of the application **Threads:** The number of active threads generated by the application **CPU:** The number of CPU cycles currently being used by the application **Average CPU:** The percentage of the total CPU capacity being used by the application

(*continued*)

Table 8-1 *(continued)*

COMPONENT	LINE GRAPH STATISTICS	TEXT STATISTICS
Disk	Total current disk I/O rate (in KB/sec) Highest Active Time (%)	**Image:** The application using disk resources **PID:** The Process ID of the application **File:** The file currently being read or written by the application **Read:** The speed of the current read operation (in bytes/second) **Write:** The speed of the current write operation (in bytes/second) **Total:** The speed of the combined read and write operations (in bytes/second) **I/O Priority:** The priority of the I/O task currently being performed by the application **Response Time:** The interval between the issuance of a command to the disk and its response (in milliseconds)
Network	Current total network I/O (in Kb/sec) Network Utilization (%)	**Image:** The application using network resources **PID:** The Process ID of the application **Address:** The network address or computer name of the system with which the computer is communicating **Send:** The speed of the current network send operation (in bytes/second) **Receive:** The speed of the current network receive operation (in bytes/second) **Total:** The combined bandwidth of the current network send and receive processes (in bytes/second)
Memory	Current hard faults per second Percentage of physical memory currently in use (%)	**Image:** The application using memory resources **PID:** The Process ID of the application **Hard Faults Per Second:** The number of hard faults currently being generated by the application **Commit:** The amount of memory (in KB) committed by the application **Working Set:** The amount of physical memory (in KB) currently being used by the application **Shareable:** The amount of memory (in KB) being used by the application that it can share with other applications **Private:** The amount of memory (in KB) being used by the application that it cannot share with other applications

Examining the resources utilized by specific applications and processes over time can help you determine ways to improve the performance of a computer. For example, if all of the system's physical memory is frequently being utilized, then the system is probably being slowed by a large amount of paging to disk. Increasing the amount of physical memory or reducing the application load will probably improve the overall performance level of the computer.

USING PROCESS EXPLORER

For even greater statistical detail, you can download the Process Explorer application from Microsoft's Web site at http://technet.microsoft.com/en-us/sysinternals/bb896653.aspx. In addition to listing the running programs, Process Explorer can list the files and directories each process has open, as shown in Figure 8-49, as well as open handles and loaded DLLs.

Figure 8-49

Process Explorer

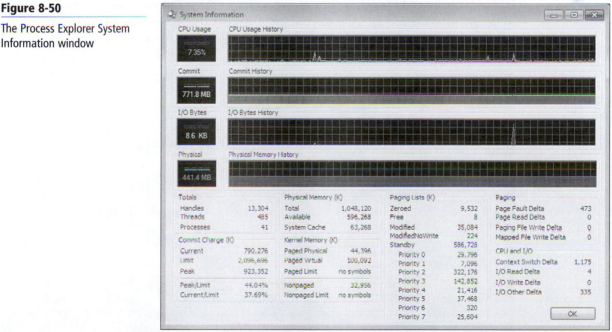

At the top of the display are four mini-graphs displaying the following information:

- CPU Usage History
- Commit History
- I/O Bytes History
- Physical Memory History

Clicking any one of the mini-graphs opens the System Information window shown in Figure 8-50.

Figure 8-50

The Process Explorer System Information window

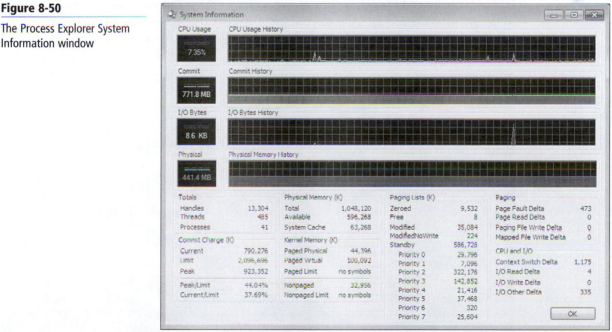

Using the System Configuration Tool

> The System Configuration tool (Msconfig.exe) is designed primarily to configure and troubleshoot the Windows 7 startup process.

The System Configuration tool does not appear in the Start menu; you can only run it by executing the Msconfig.exe program or typing *msconfig* in the Start menu's search box. While the program is not directly involved with performance tuning, you can use it to identify programs and configuration settings that might be having a negative effect on system performance.

When you start the System Configuration tool, you see the General tab, as shown in Figure 8-51, in which you can temporarily set the system's default startup sequence to a diagnostic or selective mode. These modes can help you identify programs loading at startup that are slowing the system down.

Figure 8-51

The General tab in the System Configuration tool

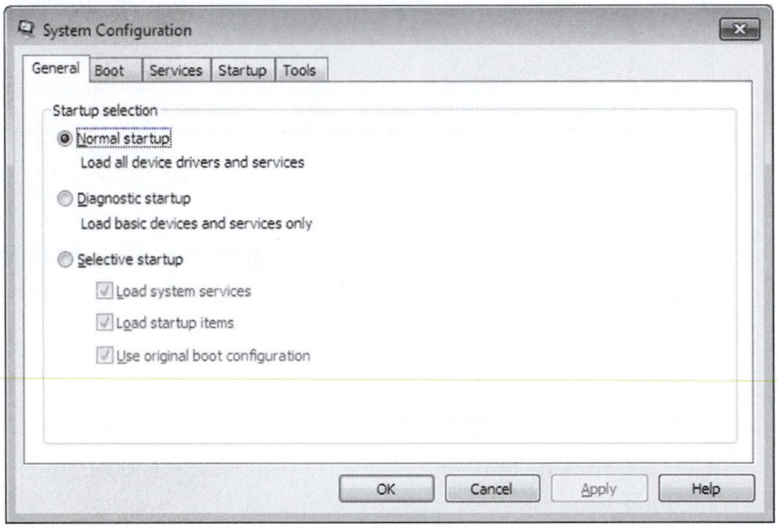

The Boot tab enables you to manage and select the files the computer uses to boot, if there is more than one operating system available. The Startup tab, shown in Figure 8-52, lists the programs configured to execute when the system starts. Many applications add their own utility programs to the startup sequence, programs that the system often does not need to run all the time. With this interface, you can prevent individual programs from launching for testing purposes.

Figure 8-52

The Startup tab in the System Configuration tool

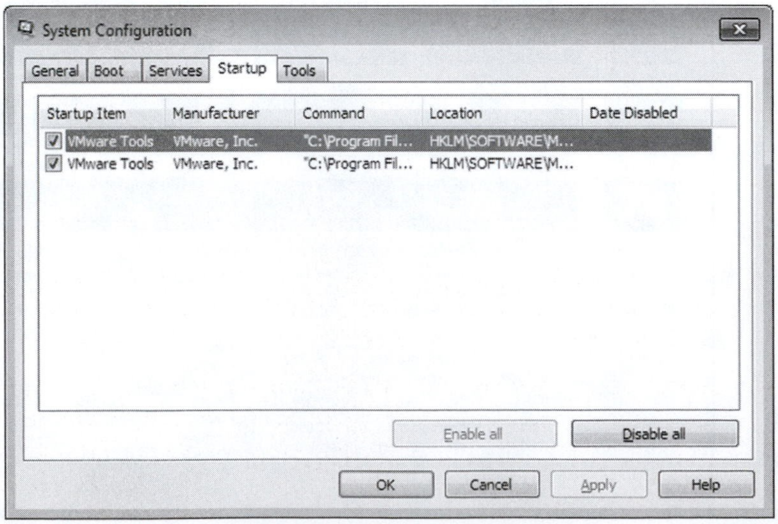

The Services tab provides access to the services running on the computer, just like the Services console discussed in the next section. The Tools tab provides links to many of the configuration and troubleshooting tools in Windows 7.

Managing Services

Windows 7 loads a large number of services automatically when the computer starts. Disabling the services the workstation does not need can free up resources and improve the computer's performance.

In Windows, a service is a program that the computer launches and leaves running continuously in the background. When Windows starts a service automatically, it loads when the system boots, before a user even logs on, so its services are always available.

When you open the Services console in one of the following ways, you can see that Windows 7 installs a lot of services and activates many of them:

- Open the Control Panel and click System and Security > Administrative Tools > Services.
- Open the Start menu and type services in the Search box.
- Open the Computer Management console and click Services and Applications > Services.
- Open the System Configuration tool and click the Services tab.

The Services console, as shown in Figure 8-53, displays each of the services installed on the computer, its current status, its startup type, and the account with which the service accesses the operating system.

Figure 8-53

The Services console

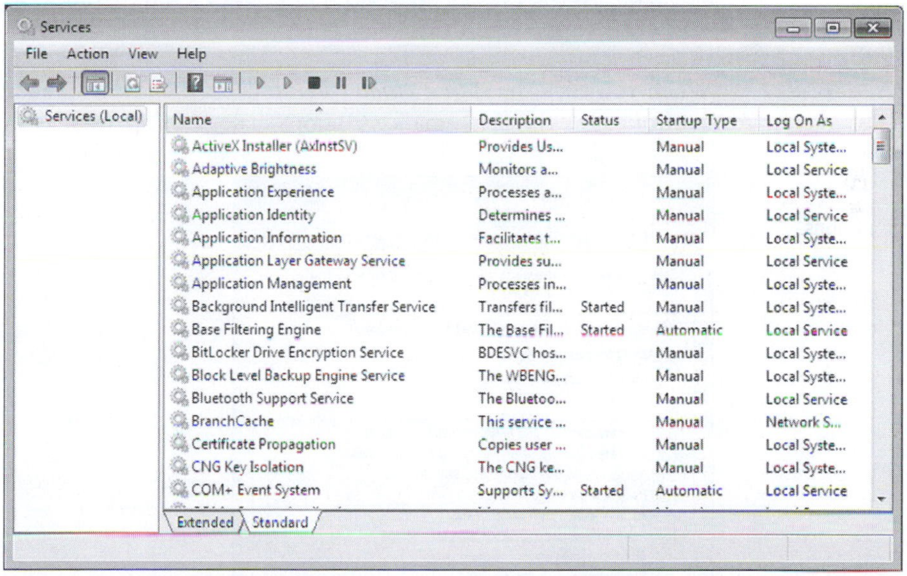

The Status column indicates whether a service is running or not. A service can be installed, but it doesn't have to be running all the time. Only the services with a Started status are consuming memory and processor cycles.

To enhance the performance of the computer, you can stop a currently running service that the computer does not need by right clicking the service and, from the context menu, selecting stop. To prevent the system from automatically starting a service when the system boots, open the service's Properties sheet, as shown in Figure 8-54, and set the Startup Type value to Manual or Disabled.

Figure 8-54

A service's Properties sheet

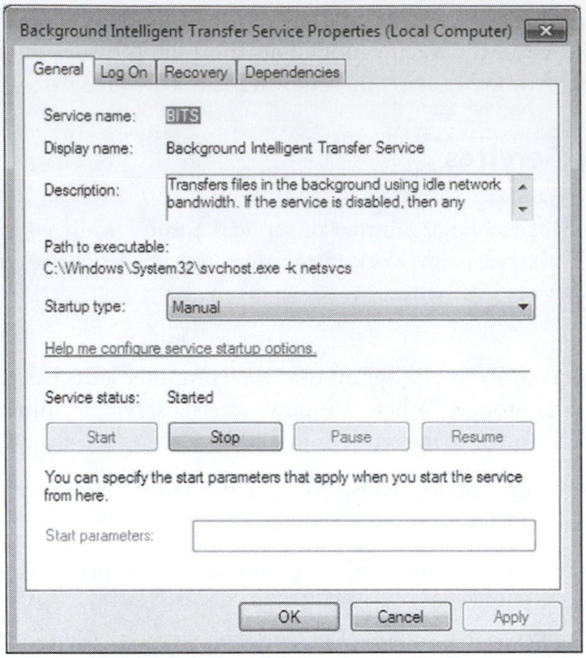

WARNING It might not be immediately clear what services are required to run Windows 7. Services are often dependent on each other, and disabling them can have harmful effects. Be sure to stop services you suspect might not be needed on a nonproduction computer first and test them carefully before stopping them on your production workstations.

To manage services on all of your workstations, you can use the Group Policy settings found in the Computer Configuration\Preferences\Windows Settings\Control Panel Settings\ Services container.

Configuring Performance Option Settings

The Performance Information and Tools control panel, in addition to the monitoring capabilities discussed earlier, also has links to a number of performance tuning tools.

When you click the *Adjust visual effects* link on the Performance Information and Tools control panel, the Performance Options dialog box appears, as shown in Figure 8-55.

Figure 8-55

The Performance Options dialog box

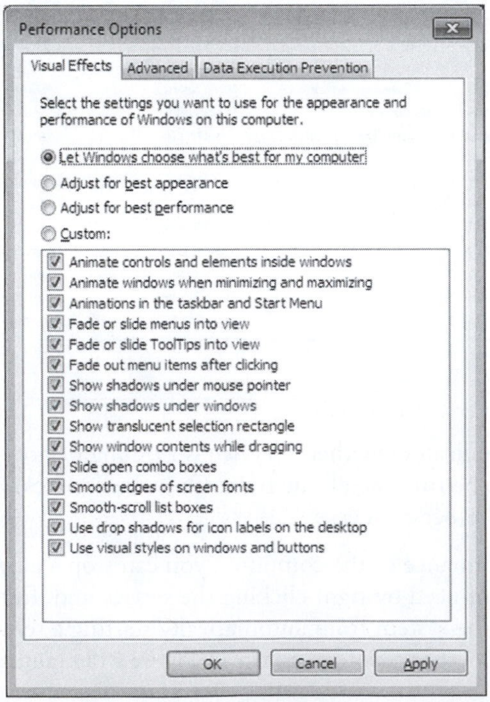

On the Visual Effects tab, you can selectively choose the cosmetic visual elements you want the computer to use. Depending on the computer's graphics hardware, disabling some or all of the visual effects can significantly enhance the system's overall performance.

On the Advanced tab, you can configure the system processor to allocate more resources to running programs or background activities. Clicking the change button opens the Virtual Memory dialog box, as shown in Figure 8-56, on which you can control the size of the paging file for each of the computer's drives.

Figure 8-56

The Virtual Memory dialog box

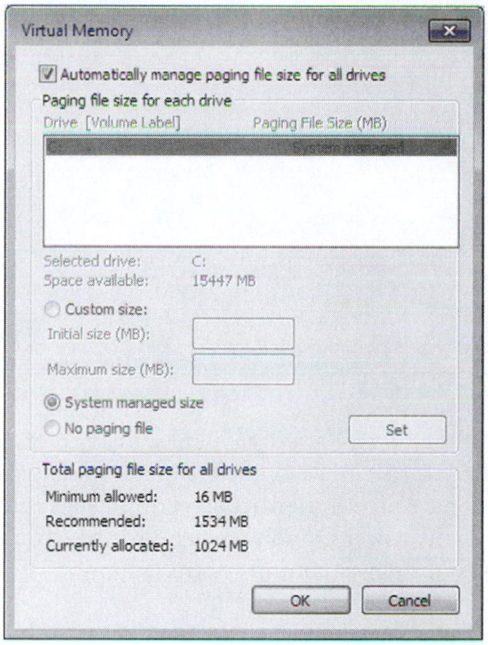

A paging file is an area of disk space that Windows uses to store data that overflows from system memory. This virtual memory enables Windows to run programs that utilize more memory than is available in the system, but at the cost of reduced performance. This is because memory I/O is inherently faster than disk I/O.

In most cases, the default setting, in which Windows automatically manages the paging file sizes, is suitable. However, on a workstation in which memory is the performance bottleneck, you might be able to tweak performance by increasing the size of the paging file.

Configuring Power Settings

The power configuration settings in Windows 7 enable you to throttle various system components to optimize their power utilization, which can also have an effect on system performance.

The Power Options control panel, shown in Figure 8-57, enables you to select a power plan for a Windows 7 computer, and also provides controls that you can use to configure the power plans themselves.

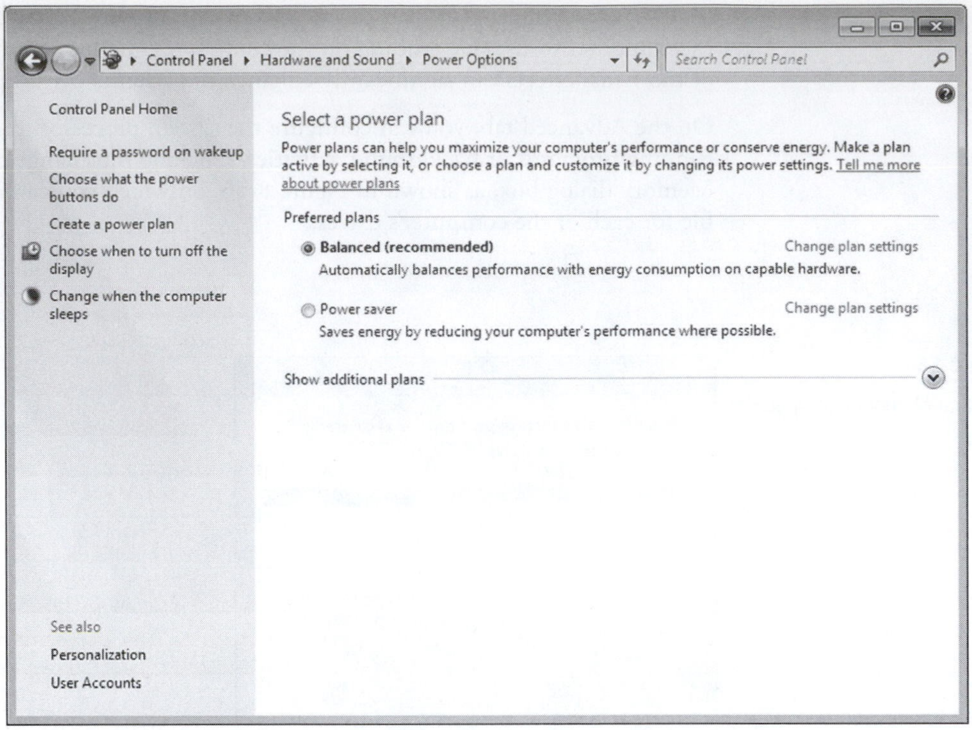

Figure 8-57

The Power Options control panel

When you click one of the *Change power plan* links, the Edit Plan Settings window provides simple controls that let you specify when the computer should turn off the display and go to sleep. These settings have no effect on actual performance, but when you click *Change advanced power settings*, the Power Options dialog box, shown in Figure 8-58, provides more comprehensive access to the power control system.

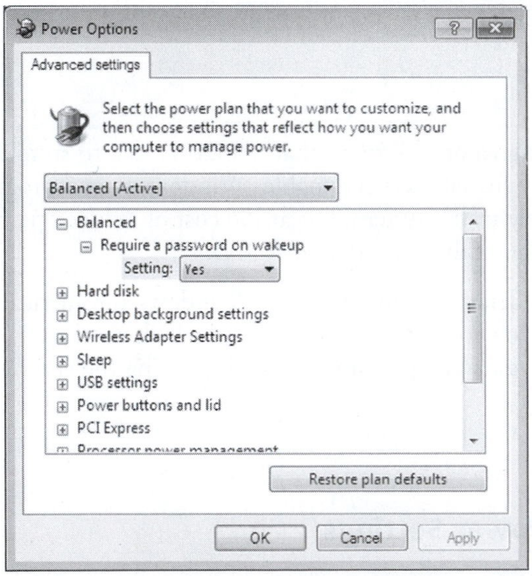

Figure 8-58

The Advanced Settings tab in the Power Options dialog box

Some of the power settings provided in this dialog box have no effect on performance, or at best a temporary effect. For example, hard disks that are turned off require a brief spin-up period before they are operational again, and a computer that is sleeping or hibernating takes some time to wake up.

However, you can also configure elements such as the processor state, which can have a profound effect on the computer's performance. Reducing the Maximum Processor State

percentage conserves power, which is particularly useful for a mobile computer running on batteries, but it can also slow down the entire system, particularly if the processor is the computer's primary performance bottleneck.

Configuring Hard Disk Caching

> Configuring hard disk caching is a trade-off between safety and performance.

In Windows 7, hard disks and other storage devices can cache write data to improve performance. Write caching is when the device stores data sent to the disk in temporary memory until the slower device can catch up.

For example, if you copy a large file to a hard disk, caching the write will return control to the user faster, leaving the write operation to complete in the background. The potential drawback of write caching is that if the device is interrupted—by a power failure, for example—data still cached in memory could be lost before it is written to the disk.

You can configure the write caching behavior for a hard disk by opening its Properties sheet in Device Manager and clicking the Policies tab. Clearing the Enable write caching on the device check box increases data safety, but reduces disk performance; while selecting Turn off Windows write-cache buffer flushing on the device leaves data in the cache for longer periods, improving performance but also increasing the risk of data loss. This latter setting is recommended only for computers that have uninterrupted power supplies.

Using ReadyBoost

> ReadyBoost is a Windows 7 feature that enables you to use the storage space on a USB flash drive to free up system memory for other uses.

Every desktop technician should know that one of the easiest ways to improve the performance of a Windows computer is to install more system memory. However, in many cases this is not possible. A computer might already have the maximum amount of RAM the motherboard can support, or it might not be economically feasible to purchase more memory. In cases like these, Windows 7 includes a feature called ***ReadyBoost***, which you can use to increase a computer's memory capacity using non-volatile memory in the form of a USB flash drive or a flash memory card. While Windows Vista was limited to Secure Digital (SD) cards, Windows 7 enables you to use Compact Flash (CF) and most other memory cards as well.

Non-volatile memory is a storage device with no moving parts that retains its data, even when unpowered. USB drives and SD or CF cards can contain large amounts of non-volatile memory; and the USB interface, while not as fast as the computer's internal memory bus, is fast enough to allow serviceable data transfer speeds.

ReadyBoost does not only add the storage space on the flash drive to the system memory pool, however. If this were the case, removing the drive at the wrong time could cause a catastrophic system failure. Instead, ReadyBoost uses the non-volatile memory for a memory cache, in coordination with the system's SuperFetch mechanism.

SuperFetch is a caching routine that enables Windows 7 to restore user access to applications much faster than Windows XP. All of the Windows operating systems use a virtual memory management technique called paging. When nearly all of the physical memory in a Windows computer is in use, the operating system begins swapping some of the data currently in memory to a paging file on the hard disk. This increases the memory capacity of the computer, but it also slows down some processes because hard disks transfer data much slower than memory chips.

> **+ MORE INFORMATION**
>
> You can easily compare the difference in speed between memory chips and hard disk drives simply by examining their access rates. Hard disk drive access rates are measured in milliseconds, that is, thousandths of a second. By comparison, the access rates of DRAM memory chips are measured in nanoseconds, that is, billionths of a second.

When your computer is, to all appearances, idle, there are usually a variety of tasks occurring in the background. Backups, updates, and virus scans are just a few of the various types of tasks that wait until the system is idle before they run. These background tasks require system memory also, and while they are running, the idle applications that you have open are swapped to the paging file on your hard drive. The result is that when you attempt to use your computer again, there is a delay as the applications are swapped from the paging file back into system memory.

SuperFetch addresses this problem by storing copies of your most frequently used applications in a cache in system memory. With this information in cache memory, the system can recall it almost instantaneously when you try to start working at your idle computer again. The paging delay is eliminated.

USB storage devices are not as fast as system memory, but their seek times are faster than those of hard drives. Therefore, when you use a USB flash drive, ReadyBoost stores the SuperFetch cache on the flash drive, rather than in system memory. This frees up the area of system memory that was formerly used for the cache, and still provides quick access to the cached applications. ReadyBoost is also completely safe, because even if you yank the flash drive out of the system with no warning, you are removing only a copy of the cached information. The same data is also available from the paging file on the hard drive.

ReadyBoost requires a computer with a USB 2.0 interface and a 256 MB or larger flash drive or other storage device that is fast enough to be useful. When you insert the drive into a USB slot, Windows 7 tests the speed of the device and, if it's fast enough, gives you the option of using it for ReadyBoost. In Windows 7, the 4 GB limit for a ReadyBoost drive from Windows Vista has been removed. You can now use as many as eight devices for ReadyBoost, totaling up to 256 GB.

You can also manually configure a flash drive to use ReadyBoost by opening its Properties sheet and clicking the ReadyBoost tab. Using this interface, you can specify how much of the storage space on the device you want to devote to memory caching.

Another way to take advantage of non-volatile memory with Windows 7 is to use hard drives that have flash memory integrated into them. Some hard drives have a traditional disk mechanism plus a small amount of flash memory for use as a cache. Others are completely solid state, with no moving parts at all. ReadyDrive is a variation of ReadyBoost that can use these drives to store data from the paging file, providing an even greater increase in performance.

SKILL SUMMARY

IN THIS LESSON YOU LEARNED:

- Microsoft releases operating system updates on the 12th of each month, with occasional, additional releases when an issue requires an immediate response.
- Microsoft classifies updates using the following categories: Important Updates, Recommended Updates, Optional Updates, and Device Drivers.
- The Windows Update client included with Windows 7 makes it possible to configure computers to automatically download and install Windows updates as needed.
- In addition to the Control Panel interface, it is possible to configure the Windows Update client using Group Policy settings.
- Windows uses a graphical application called Event Viewer to display the log information gathered by the operating system.

- While the Performance Information and Tools page provides a snapshot of your computer's performance at a single moment in time, the Performance Monitor console enables you to view much of the same information, but on a continuous, real-time basis.

- The Resource Monitor program contains four real-time line graphs that display information about four of the main system hardware components. Each component also has a separate, expandable section, displaying more detailed information in text form, such as the resources being utilized by individual applications and processes.

- Performance Monitor can display hundreds of different statistics (called performance counters). You can create a customized graph containing any statistics you choose.

- Reliability Monitor automatically tracks events that can have a negative effect on system stability and uses them to calculate a stability index.

- Windows 7 provides a variety of tools for monitoring and managing processes, including Task Manager, Resource Monitor, and Process Explorer.

- ReadyBoost enables Windows 7 to use the storage space on USB devices to free up system memory for other uses.

■ Knowledge Assessment

Matching

Complete the following exercise by matching the terms with their corresponding definitions.

   a. requires Internet Information Services (IIS)
   b. an update designed to address a specific Windows issue
   c. stores copies of frequently used applications in cache memory
   d. conserves bandwidth during update downloads
   e. captures performance counter data
   f. Performance Monitor statistic
   g. recipient of forwarded events
   h. additional system memory cache
   i. Windows performance rating
   j. Performance Monitor category

_____ **1.** Background Intelligent Transfer Service (BITS).

_____ **2.** performance counter

_____ **3.** ReadyBoost

_____ **4.** Windows Experience Index

_____ **5.** data collector set

_____ **6.** SuperFetch

_____ **7.** Windows Server Update Services (WSUS)

_____ **8.** collector

_____ **9.** performance object

_____ **10.** hotfix

Multiple Choice

Select one or more correct answers for each of the following questions.

1. Performance Monitor can display hundreds of different statistics called _____.
   a. Performance objects
   b. Performance counters
   c. Instances
   d. Histograms

2. Which of the following Group Policy settings must you configure for Windows 7 computers to obtain updates from a WSUS server?
   a. Configure Automatic Updates
   b. Allow signed updates from an intranet Microsoft update service location
   c. Allow Automatic Updates immediate installation
   d. Specify intranet Microsoft update service location

3. Which of the following is not one of the improvements to the ReadyBoost feature that was introduced in Windows 7?
   a. The ability to use flash devices larger than 4 GB
   b. The ability to use multiple USB devices for ReadyBoost
   c. Support for a total of 256 GB of ReadyBoost storage
   d. Support for Secure Digital (SD) memory cards

4. Which of the following is not one of the categories Microsoft uses to classify its update releases?
   a. Optional updates
   b. Security updates
   c. Important updates
   d. Recommended updates

5. Which of the following is required to install Windows Server Update Services on a server?
   a. SQL Server 2005
   b. Internet Information Services (IIS)
   c. Windows Server 2008 R2 Enterprise
   d. Active Directory Domain Services

6. Which of the following is not one of the graphs found in Resource Monitor?
   a. CPU
   b. Disk
   c. Display
   d. Memory

7. Which of the following Event Viewer logs contains no events until you configure auditing policies?
   a. Application
   b. Security
   c. Setup
   d. System

8. In Event Viewer, what is the term used for the Windows component logs in the Applications and Services Logs folder?
   a. instances
   b. events
   c. subscriptions
   d. channels

9. In an event forwarding situation, the source computers must have which of the following services running?
   a. Windows Event Collector
   b. Secure Hypertext Transfer Protocol
   c. Background Intelligent Transfer Service
   d. Windows Remote Management

10. Which of the following is the primary function of the System Configuration tool?
    a. To configure and troubleshoot the Windows 7 startup process
    b. To configure display and virtual memory settings
    c. To configure services
    d. To monitor CPU, Disk, Network, and Memory activity in real time

Review Questions

1. Explain why Performance Monitor counters sometime have multiple instances?

2. The Windows 7 computers on a company network are configured to download and install updates every day at 3:00 a.m. However, the company is currently running three shifts, and there are workers using the computers 24 hours a day. Explain why the update downloads will not interfere with the user's activities.

■ Case Scenario

Scenario 8-1: Using WSUS

You are a newly hired desktop technician at a company with a network of Windows 7 computers. You have been given the task of configuring several new computers to automatically download and install updates on a nightly basis. The company has recently installed a server running Windows Server Update Services (WSUS), which the IT director wants all of the workstations to use to retrieve their updates. The director plans to install Active Directory servers on the network in the near future, but they are not available yet. Describe the procedure you must perform to configure the Windows update client on the computers.

9 LESSON

Working with Workgroups and Domains

OBJECTIVE DOMAIN MATRIX

TECHNOLOGY SKILL	OBJECTIVE DOMAIN	OBJECTIVE NUMBER
Introducing User Account Control	Configure user account control (UAC).	5.3

KEY TERMS

Active Directory	domain	secure desktop
Admin Approval Mode	domain controller	special identity
authentication	elevation prompt	User Account Control (UAC)
authorization	group	user profile
credential prompt	mandatory user profile	user rights
directory service	roaming user profile	workgroup

■ Working with Users and Groups

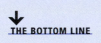

THE BOTTOM LINE

The user account is the fundamental unit of identity in Windows operating systems. In computer terminology, the term *user* has two meanings; it can refer to the human being operating the computer, or it can be an operating system element that represents a single human user.

From a programming perspective, a user account is a relatively simple construct, no more than a collection of properties that apply to the human being or other entity that the user account represents. These properties can include information about the user, such as names and contact information, and identifying characteristics, such as passwords.

+ MORE INFORMATION

Most user accounts represent humans, but Windows also employs user accounts to provide system processes and applications with access to secured resources. These accounts are no different from standard user accounts structurally; the only difference is that they are created and managed automatically by the operating system or an application.

As an operating system element, the user account and its properties are vital components in two of the most important Windows functions:

- *Authentication:* The process of verifying that the identity of the person operating the computer matches that of the user account the person is using to gain access. Typically, to be authenticated, the human user must supply some piece of information associated with the user account, such as a password; demonstrate some personal characteristic, such as a fingerprint; or prove access to an identifying possession, such as a smart card.

- *Authorization:* The process of granting an authenticated user a specific degree of access to a specific computer or data resources. In Windows, a user account provides access to permissions that grant the human user access to files and folders, printers, and other resources.

The first thing a human user does with a Windows system is authenticate him- or herself—a process typically referred to as logging on. The human user specifies the name of a user account and supplies a password or other identifying token. Once the authentication is successful, the person is known by that username throughout the Windows session, and the operating system grants access to specific resources using that name.

As the authenticated user begins working with the operating system, the authorization process occurs whenever the user attempts to access certain resources or perform specific tasks. All of the Windows permission systems, including NTFS, share, registry, and **Active Directory** permissions, are user based. The access control list (ACL) for each permission-protected resource contains a list of users and the degree of access each user is granted to that resource.

Another user-based Windows element, completely separate from the permission systems, is called *user rights*. User rights are specific operating system tasks, such as Shut Down the System or Allow Log On Through Terminal Services, which can only be performed by certain users designated by a system administrator.

A *group* is another type of entity that Windows uses to represent a collection of users. System administrators can create groups for any reason and with any name, and then use them just as they would a user account. Any permissions or user rights that an administrator assigns to a group are automatically inherited by all of the members of the group.

➕ MORE INFORMATION

The concept of group inheritance is one of the fundamental principles of network administration. On all but the smallest networks, administrators typically assign permissions to groups, rather than individual users, and then control access by adjusting group memberships. For example, if a person performing a particular job needs access to a variety of different network resources, it might take an administrator some time to assign all of the rights and permissions that person needs to an individual user account. Later, if that job should be taken over by another person, the administrator has to go through the entire process again twice, once to remove the rights and permissions from the old user's account and once to grant the same rights and permissions to the new user. By creating a group to represent the job, the administrator only has to grant the rights and permissions to the group once. When someone new takes over the job, the administrator only has to remove the departed user from the group and add the new user.

Understanding Local and Domain Users

The concept of users and groups is complicated in Windows because there are two completely separate user account systems: local users and domain users. Which user account system a Windows computer uses depends on whether it is a member of a workgroup or an Active Directory domain.

Windows 7 supports three types of networks: homegroups, workgroups, and domains, as described in the following sections.

INTRODUCING THE HOMEGROUP

New in Windows 7, a homegroup is a simplified networking paradigm that enables users connected to a home network to share the contents of their libraries without the need for creating user accounts and permissions. For more information on creating and using homegroups, see "Sharing with Homegroups" in Chapter 6, "Sharing Resources."

INTRODUCING THE WORKGROUP

A *workgroup* is a collection of computers that are all peers. A peer network is one in which every computer can function as both a server by sharing its resources with other computers, and a client by accessing the shared resources on other computers.

On a workgroup network, each computer has its own set of users and groups that it uses to control access to its own resources. For example, if you want to use one computer to access resources on all four of the other computers on a five-node workgroup network, you must have a user account on each of those four computers. As you connect to each computer, you are authenticated and authorized by each one. If effect, you are logging on to each computer individually.

> **TAKE NOTE***
>
> Although it is technically a separate authentication process every time a workgroup computer accesses another computer, this does not necessarily mean that users have to supply account names and passwords each time they connect to another computer. If a user has accounts with the same name and password on multiple workgroup computers, then the authentications occur automatically, with no user intervention. This is called *passthrough authentication*. If the passwords for the accounts are different, however, a manual authentication is necessary for each one.

INTRODUCING THE DOMAIN

A *domain* is a collection of computers that all utilize a central directory service for authentication and authorization. A *directory service* is a collection of logical objects that represent various types of network resources, such as computers, applications, users, and groups. Each object consists of attributes that contain information about the object.

> **TAKE NOTE***
>
> Do not confuse an Active Directory Domain Services (AD DS) domain with a Domain Name System (DNS) domain. An AD DS domain is a collection of Windows computers that are all joined to the Windows directory service. A DNS domain is a collection of Internet host names used by computers that can be running any operating system.

To create a domain, you must have at least one Windows server with the Active Directory Domain Services (AD DS) directory service installed. This server is called a *domain controller*. Each of the computers then joins the domain and is represented by a computer object. In the same way, administrators create user objects that represent human users. In Windows networking, the main difference between a domain and a workgroup is that users log on to the domain once, rather than each computer individually. When users attempt to access network resources, the individual computers hosting the resources send authorization requests to the domain controller, rather than handling the authorizations themselves.

DIFFERENTIATING LOCAL AND DOMAIN USERS

The primary advantage of a domain over a workgroup is that administrators only have to create one user account for each person, while workgroups can require many different user accounts for one person. If, on a workgroup network, a user's password is lost or compromised, someone must change that password on every computer where that user has an account. On a domain, there is only one user account for each person, so only one password change is needed.

Windows 7 computers always have a need for local user accounts, for administrative access to the system, if for no other reason. For networking purposes, though, it is typical to use local user accounts or domain user accounts, but not both. Workgroup networks are typically small and informal, with users administering their own computers. Domain networks are usually larger and have dedicated network administrators responsible for managing user accounts and controlling access to network resources.

Local and domain users are different in several important ways. You use different tools to create and manage the two types of users, and the user accounts themselves are different in composition. As mentioned earlier, a user account consists of attributes, which contain information about the user. Domain users have many more attributes than local users.

As a demonstration of this, Figures 9-1 and 9-2 contain the Properties sheets of a local user account and a domain user account. Notice that the Properties sheet for the local user has

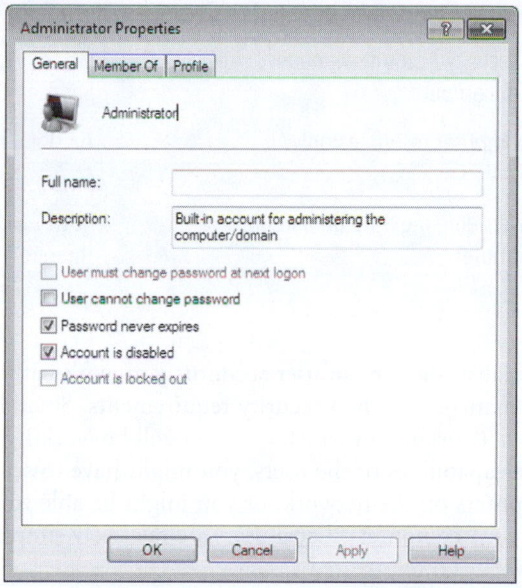

Figure 9-1

The Properties sheet for a local user

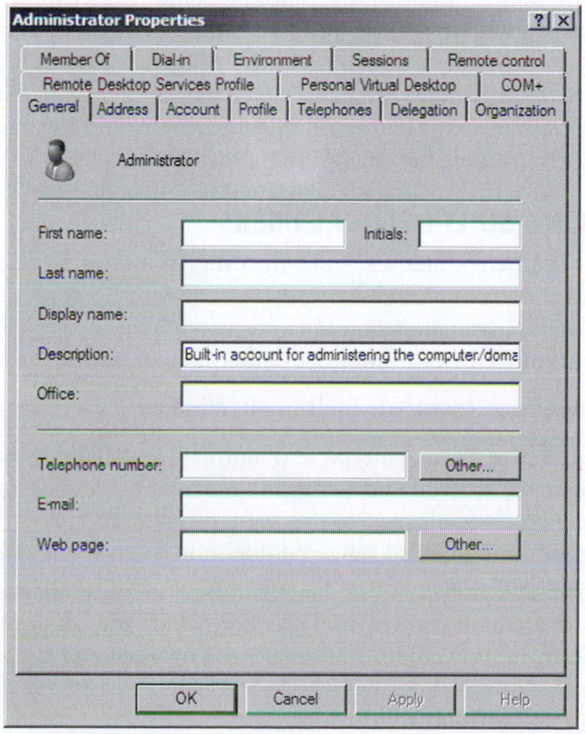

Figure 9-2

The Properties sheet for a domain user

only 3 tabs, while the domain user's sheet has 15. This means that the domain user account can store a great deal more information about the user and can access many more different kinds of network resources.

Table 9-1 lists some of the other differences between local and domain users.

Table 9-1

Frequently Asked Questions About Local and Domain Users

QUESTION	LOCAL USERS	DOMAIN USERS
What tools do you use to manage the user accounts?	The User Accounts control panel or the Local Users and Groups snap-in for Microsoft Management Console (MMC)	The Active Directory Users and Computers MMC snap-in
Where are the user accounts stored?	In the Security Account Manager (SAM) on the local computer	On the Active Directory Domain Services domain controllers
What can you access with the user account?	Local computer resources only	All domain and network resources
What restrictions are there on the user name?	Each username must be unique on the computer	Each username must be unique in the directory

As a technical specialist, the type of user accounts you work with depends on the nature of the networks you manage and their security requirements. Small businesses are more likely to use workgroup networking, in which case you will be working with local user accounts. Depending on the capabilities of the users, you might have to set up all of the user accounts for all of the computers on the network, or you might be able to show the users how to create accounts on their own computers. Local users are relatively simple to create and manage, and a workgroup network is often treated casually.

If your client is a medium or large business, it is more likely to be running an AD DS domain, in which case you will be working primarily with domain user accounts. The question of whether to host a Windows domain is a major decision that an organization usually makes when they are designing and installing the network. Hosting a Windows domain is a costly undertaking, both in terms of the additional hardware and software required and in terms of the time and effort needed for planning and deployment.

INTRODUCING BUILT-IN LOCAL USERS

As mentioned earlier, Windows 7 (like the other Windows workstation operating systems) always has a need for local user accounts. When you perform a standard interactive installation of Windows 7, you are required to create one user account. In addition, the Setup program automatically creates a number of other user accounts.

The following user accounts are built-in on Windows 7:

- **Administrator:** During a typical Windows 7 installation, the Setup program creates an Administrator account and makes it a member of the Administrators group, giving it complete access to all areas of the operating system. However, the Setup program leaves the account in a disabled state and does not assign it a password.
- **New User Account:** During the operating system installation process, the installer must specify the name for a new user account, which the Setup program creates and adds to the Administrators group. This grants the new account full access to the operating system. The installer decides whether to assign a password to this account. Windows 7 uses this account for its initial logons.

- **Guest:** This account is designed for users who require only temporary access to the computer and who do not need high levels of access. The Guest account is disabled, by default, and is a member only of the Guests group, which provides it with only the most rudimentary access to the system.

In addition to these accounts, Windows 7 also creates a number of system and service accounts, none of which you have to manipulate directly.

After the Windows 7 installation is completed, you might want to consider enabling the Administrator account and assigning it a strong password. This will provide you with administrative access to the system, even if your main user account becomes compromised.

Understanding Local and Domain Groups

Just as there are local and domain users, there are local and domain groups as well. Whether local or domain, a group is essentially just a collection of users and, in some cases, other groups. As mentioned earlier, by assigning rights and permissions to a group, you assign those rights and permissions to all of its members.

USING LOCAL GROUPS

When compared to domain groups, local groups are quite simple and are defined more by what they cannot do than what they can do. Local groups are subject to the following restrictions:

- You can only use local groups on the computer where you create them.
- Only local users from the same computer can be members of local groups.
- When the computer is a member of an AD DS domain, local groups can have domain users and domain global groups as members.
- Local groups cannot have other local groups as members. However, they can have domain groups as members.
- You can only assign permissions to local groups when you are controlling access to resources on the local computer.
- You cannot create local groups on a Windows server computer that is functioning as a domain controller.

INTRODUCING BUILT-IN LOCAL GROUPS

Windows 7 includes a number of built-in local groups that are already equipped with the permissions and rights needed to perform certain tasks. You can enable users to perform these tasks simply by adding them to the appropriate group. Table 9-2 lists the Windows 7 built-in local groups and the capabilities they provide to their members.

Some of the built-in local groups in Windows 7, such as Administrators, Backup Operators, and Remote Desktop Users, are created for the convenience of system administrators so that they can easily grant certain privileges to users. Other groups, such as IIS_USRS and Replicator, are designed to support automated functions that create their own system user accounts. There is no need to manually add users to these groups.

Table 9-2

Windows 7 Built-in Local Groups and Their Capabilities

BUILT-IN LOCAL GROUP	FUNCTION
Administrators	Members have full administrative access to the entire operating system. By default, the Administrator user and the user account created during the operating system installation are both members of this group.
Backup Operators	Members have user rights enabling them to override permissions for the sole purpose of backing up and restoring files, folders, and other operating system elements.
Cryptographic Operators	Members are capable of performing cryptographic operations.
Distributed COM Users	Members are capable of launching, activating, and using distributed COM objects.
Event Log Readers	Members can read the computer's event logs.
Guests	Members have no default user rights. By default, the Guest user account is a member of this group.
IIS_IUSRS	Group used to provide privileges to dedicated Internet Information Services users.
Network Configuration Operators	Members have privileges that enable them to modify the computer's network configuration settings.
Performance Log Users	Members have privileges that enable them to schedule the logging of performance counters, enable trace providers, and collect event traces on this computer, both locally and from remote locations.
Performance Monitor Users	Members have privileges that enable them to monitor performance counter data on the computer, both locally and from remote locations.
Power Users	Members possess no additional capabilities in Windows 7. In previous Windows versions, the Power Users group provided privileges for a limited number of administrative functions, but in Windows 7, the group is included solely for reasons of backwards compatibility.
Remote Desktop Users	Members can log on to the computer from remote locations using Terminal Services or Remote Desktop.
Replicator	When the computer is joined to a domain, this group provides the access needed for file replication functions. The only member should be a user account dedicated solely to the replication process.
Users	Members can perform most common tasks, such as running applications, using local and network printers, and locking the server. However, members are prevented from making many system-wide configuration changes, whether they do so accidentally or deliberately.
Offer Remote Assistance Helpers	Members can offer remote assistance to other users of the computer.

The built-in local groups in Windows 7, although created by the operating system, are groups like any other. You can modify their properties, change their names, and assign new rights and permissions to them. However, it's a better idea to create your own groups and assign whatever additional rights and permissions you need to them. You can make a single user a member of multiple groups, and the permissions from all of the groups will be combined according to the rules specified in Lesson 6.

INTRODUCING SPECIAL IDENTITIES

Another type of element in Windows 7 (and all other Windows operating systems) is a special identity, which functions like a group. A *special identity* is essentially a placeholder for a collection of users with similar characteristics. For example, the Authenticated Users special identity represents all of the users that are logged on to the computer at a given instant. You can assign rights and permissions to a special identity just as you would to a group.

When the access control list (ACL) for a system resource contains a special identity in one of its access control entries (ACEs), the system substitutes the users that conform to the special identity at the moment the ACL is processed.

TAKE NOTE*

It's important to understand that the set of computers represented by a special identity can change from minute to minute. The Authenticated Users special identity changes every time a user logs on or off, for example. When you assign rights and permissions to a special identity, the users who receive those rights and permissions are not those who conform to the special identity at the time you make the assignment, but rather those who conform to the special identity at the time the special identity is read from the ACL.

Table 9-3 lists the special identities included in Windows 7.

Table 9-3

Windows 7 Special Identities and Their Constituents

SPECIAL IDENTITY	FUNCTION
Anonymous Logon	Includes all users who have connected to the computer without authenticating.
Authenticated Users	Includes all users with a valid local user account whose identities have been authenticated. The Guest user is not included in the Authenticated Users special identity, even if it has a password.
Batch	Includes all users who are currently logged on through a batch facility such as a task scheduler job.
Console Logon	Includes all users that are logged on to the computer's physical console.
Creator Group	Includes the primary group of the user who created or most recently took ownership of the resource.
Creator Owner	Includes only the user who created or most recently took ownership of a resource.
Dialup	Includes all users who are currently logged on through a dial-up connection.
Everyone	Includes all members of the Authenticated Users special identity plus the Guest user account.
Interactive	Includes all users who are currently logged on locally or through a Remote Desktop connection.
IUSR	Account used to provide anonymous access to web pages through Internet Information Services (IIS).
Local Service	Provides all services configured to run as a local service with the same privileges as the Users group.
Network	Includes all users who are currently logged on through a network connection.
Network Service	Provides all services configured to run as a network service with the same privileges as the Users group.
Owner Rights	Represents the current owner of an object.
Remote Interactive Logon	Includes all users who are currently logged on through a Remote Desktop connection.
Service	Includes all security principals who have logged on as a service.
System	Provides the operating system with all of the privileges it needs to function.
Terminal Server User	Includes all users who are currently logged on to a Terminal Services server that is in Terminal Services version 4.0 application compatibility mode.
The Organization Certificate	Account used by the default IIS user.

Creating and Managing Local Users and Groups

↓ THE BOTTOM LINE

Windows 7 provides two separate interfaces for creating and managing local user accounts: the User Accounts control panel and the Local Users and Groups snap-in for the Microsoft Management Console (MMC). Both of these interfaces provide access to the same Security Account Manager (SAM) where the user and group information is stored, so any changes you make using one interface will appear in the other.

Microsoft designed the User Accounts control panel and the Local Users and Groups snap-in for computer users with different levels of expertise, and they provide different degrees of access to the Security Account Manager, as follows:

- **User Accounts:** Microsoft designed the User Accounts control panel for relatively inexperienced end users; it provides a simplified interface with extremely limited access to user accounts. With this interface, it is possible to create local user accounts and modify their basic attributes, but you cannot create groups or manage group memberships (except for the Administrators group).
- **Local Users and Groups:** Microsoft includes this MMC snap-in as part of the Computer Management console; it provides full access to local users and groups, as well as all of their attributes. Designed more for the technical specialist or system administrator, this interface is not difficult to use, but it does provide access to controls that beginning users generally do not need.

TAKE NOTE *

Both the User Accounts control panel and the Local Users and Groups snap-in are capable of working with local users and local groups only. You cannot create and manage domain users and groups using these tools. To work with domain users and groups, you must use a domain tool, such as Active Directory Users and Groups, which is supplied with the server operating system that is hosting the Active Directory domain.

Using the User Accounts Control Panel

As described earlier, the first local user account on a Windows 7 computer is the one created during the operating system installation process. The Setup program prompts the installer for an account name, and creates a new user account with administrative privileges. The program also creates the Administrator and Guest accounts, both of which are disabled by default.

When the Windows 7 installation process is completed, the system restarts. Because only one user account is available, the computer automatically logs on using that account. This account has administrative privileges, so at this point you can create additional user accounts or modify the existing ones.

CREATING A NEW USER ACCOUNT

To create a new user account with the User Accounts control panel, use the following procedure.

 CREATE A NEW USER ACCOUNT

GET READY. Log on to Windows 7 using an account with administrator privileges.

TAKE NOTE *

This procedure is valid only on Windows 7 computers that are part of a workgroup. When you join a computer to an AD DS domain, you can only create new local user accounts with the Local Users and Groups snap-in.

1. Click Start, and then click Control Panel. The Control Panel window appears.

2. Click User Accounts and Family Safety. The User Accounts and Family Safety window appears, as shown in Figure 9-3.

Figure 9-3

The User Accounts and Family Safety window

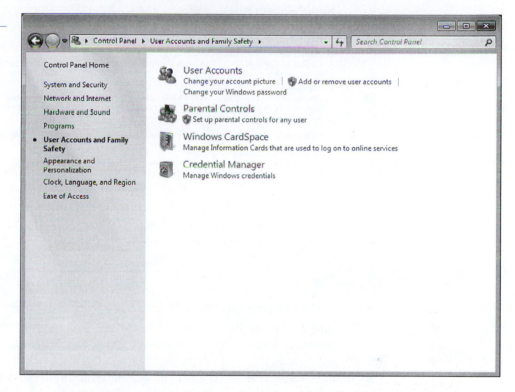

3. Click Add or remove user accounts. The *Choose the account you would like to change* page appears, as shown in Figure 9-4.

Figure 9-4

The Choose the account you would like to change page

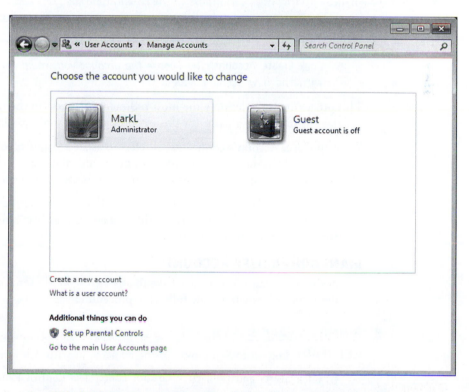

4. Click Create a new account. The *Name the account and choose the account type* page appears, as shown in Figure 9-5.

Figure 9-5

The Name the account and choose the account type page

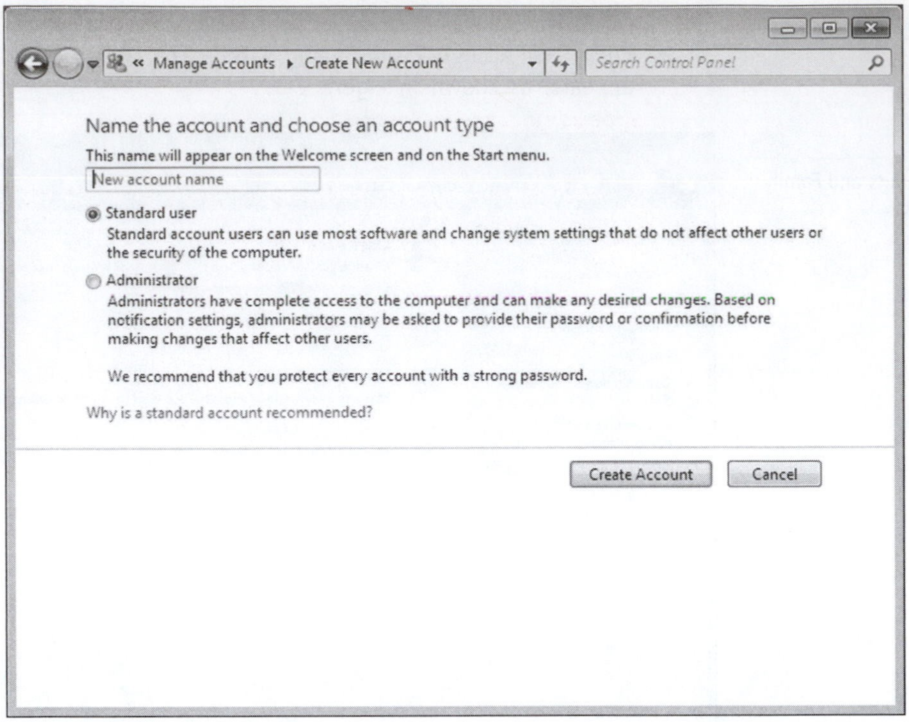

5. Type a name for the new account in the text box, and then choose the appropriate radio button to specify whether the account should be a Standard user or an Administrator.

TAKE NOTE* Recommended network practices call for administrators to use a standardized system for creating user account names. For example, smaller networks often use the first name followed by the first letter of the surname, such as JohnD. For larger networks with a greater chance of name duplication, use of the first initial plus the surname is common, such as JDoe. The purpose of standardizing usernames in this way is to enable any administrator to determine the account name for any user.

WARNING Following this procedure creates an account that is capable of logging on to the system without supplying a password. For security purposes, in all but the most informal circumstances, you should assign a password to all user accounts immediately after creating them.

6. Click Create Account. The *Choose the account you would like to change* page reappears, with the new account added.

This procedure provides only the most rudimentary access to the user account attributes. Apart from supplying a name for the account, all you can do is specify the account type.

What the User Accounts control panel refers to as an account type is actually a group membership. Selecting the Standard user option adds the user account to the local Users group, while selecting the Administrator option adds the account to the Administrators group.

Most critically, when you create a new user account with this procedure, the account is not protected by a password. You must modify the account after creating it to specify a password or change any of its other attributes.

MANAGING A USER ACCOUNT

To see the modifications you can make to an existing local user account with the User Accounts control panel, use the following procedure:

MANAGE USER ACCOUNTS

GET READY. Log on to Windows 7 using an account with Administrator privileges.

1. Click Start, and then click Control Panel. The Control Panel window appears.
2. Click User Accounts and Family Safety. The User Accounts and Family Safety window appears.

3. Click Add or remove user accounts. The *Choose the account you would like to change* page appears.

4. Click one of the existing accounts. The *Make changes to [user's] account* page appears, as shown in Figure 9-6.

Figure 9-6

The Make changes to [user's] account page

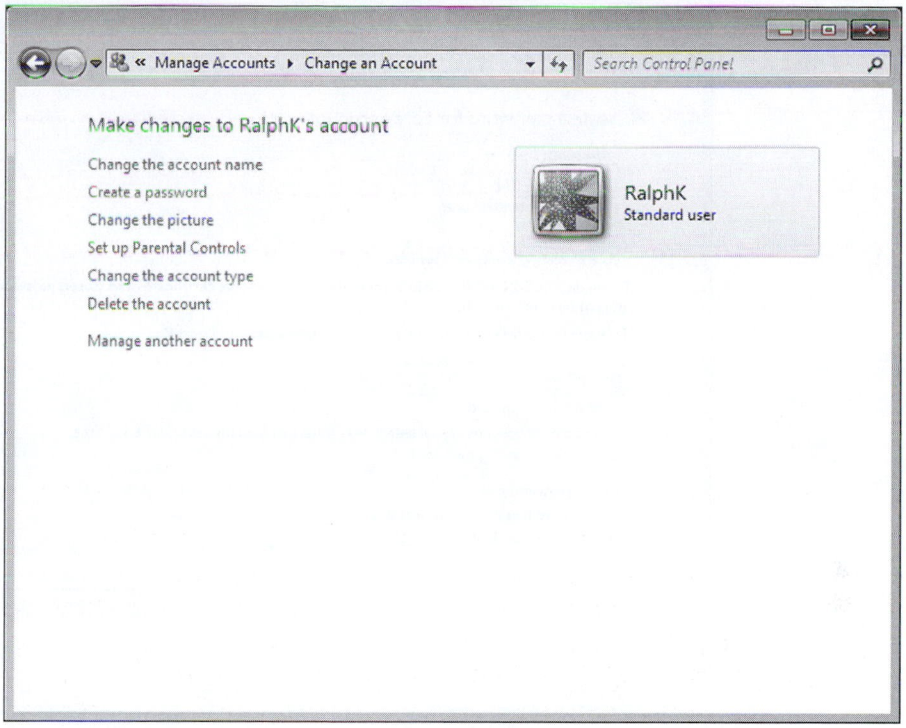

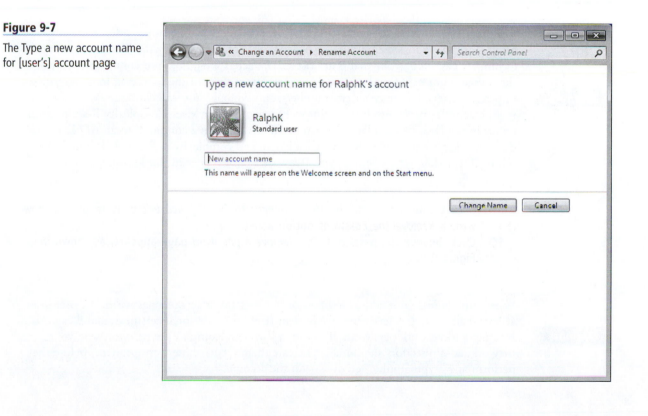

5. Click Change the account name. The *Type a new account name for [user] account* page appears, as shown in Figure 9-7.

Figure 9-7

The Type a new account name for [user's] account page

6. Type a new name for the account in the text box, and then click Change Name. The *Make changes to [user's] account* page reappears.

7. Click Create a password. The *Create a password for [user's] account* page appears, as shown in Figure 9-8.

Figure 9-8

The Create a password for [user's] account page

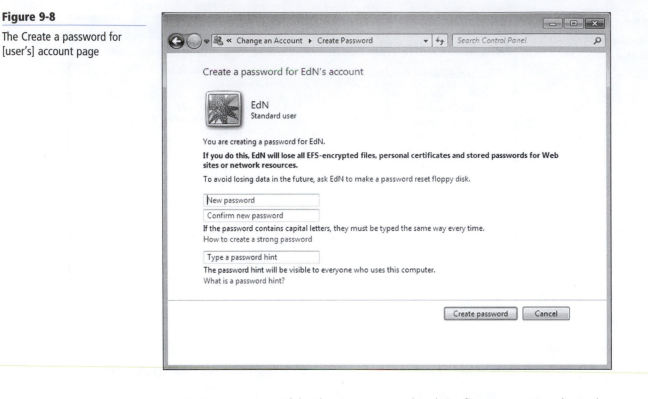

8. Type a password in the *New password* and *Confirm new password* text boxes and, if desired, supply a password hint.

TAKE NOTE *

Although Windows 7 does not require them by default in workgroup mode, Microsoft recommends that you use complex passwords for all user accounts. By the Windows definition, a complex password is one that is at least six characters long, does not contain any part of the user account name, and contains characters from three of the following four categories: uppercase letters, lowercase letters, numbers, and symbols. You can configure Windows 7 to require complex passwords by enabling the Password Must Meet Complexity Requirements policy in the Local System Policies snap-in. When you join a computer to an AD DS domain, the system enables the password length and complexity policies by default. For more information, see "Working with Password Policies" later in this lesson.

9. Click Create password. The *Make changes to [user's] account* page reappears, now with a *Remove the password* option added.

10. Click Remove the password. The *Remove a password* page appears, as shown in Figure 9-9.

TAKE NOTE *

When an administrator adds, modifies, or removes a user account password, the user loses access to all existing Encrypting File System (EFS) files, personal certificates, and cached Internet and network passwords. Therefore, if you are going to use passwords on your network, administrators should always create them (or have users create them) before they perform any cryptographic activities with the account.

Figure 9-9

The Remove a password page

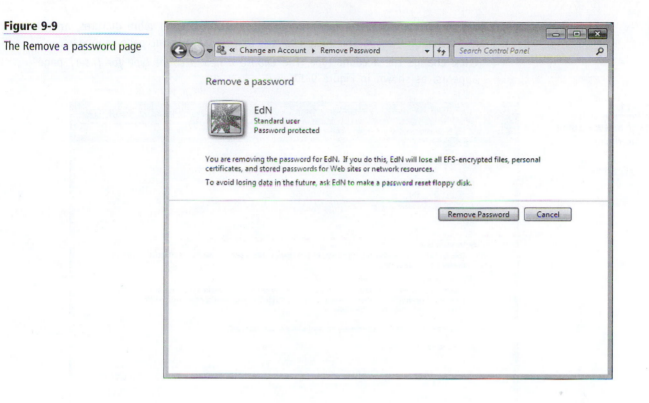

11. Click Remove Password. The *Make changes to [user's] account* page reappears.

12. Click Change the picture. The *Choose a new picture for [user's] account* page appears, as shown in Figure 9-10.

Figure 9-10

The Choose a new picture for [user's] account page

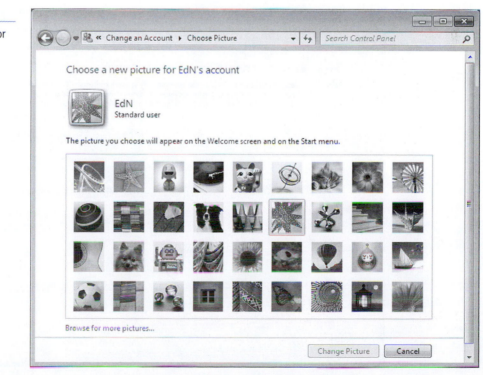

13. Select a new picture for the account, or click Browse for more pictures, and then click Change Picture. The *Make changes to [user's] account* page reappears.

14. Click Change the account type. The *Choose a new account type for [user]* page appears, as shown in Figure 9-11.

Figure 9-11

The Choose a new account type for [user] page

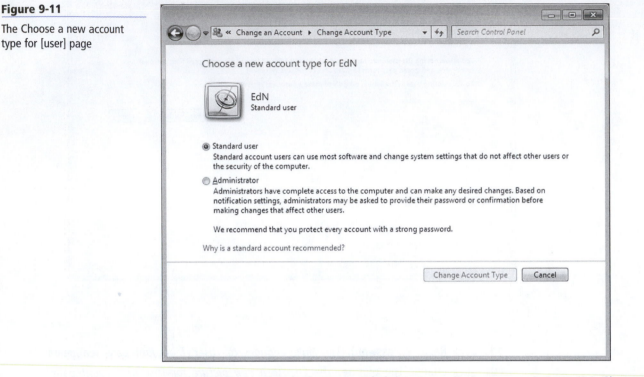

15. Select the Standard user or Administrator radio button, and then click Change Account Type. The *Make changes to [user's] account* page reappears.

16. Click Delete the account. The *Do you want to keep [user's] files?* page appears, as shown in Figure 9-12.

Figure 9-12

The Do you want to keep [user's] files? page

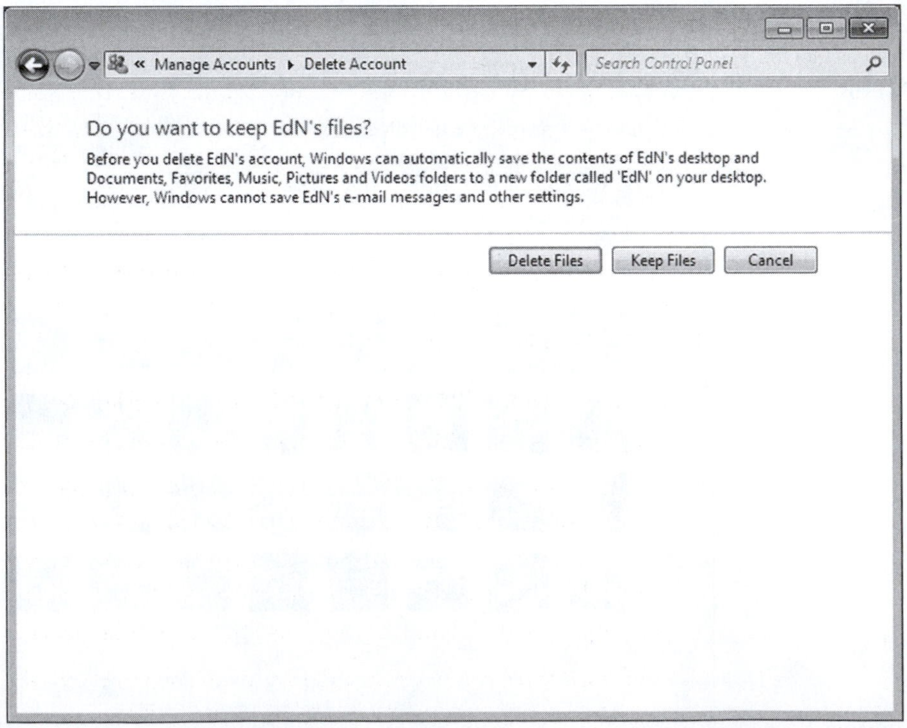

17. Click Delete Files to delete the user profile, or click Keep Files to save it to the desktop. The *Are you sure you want to delete [user's] account?* page appears, as shown in Figure 9-13.

Figure 9-13

The Are you sure you want to delete [user's] account? page

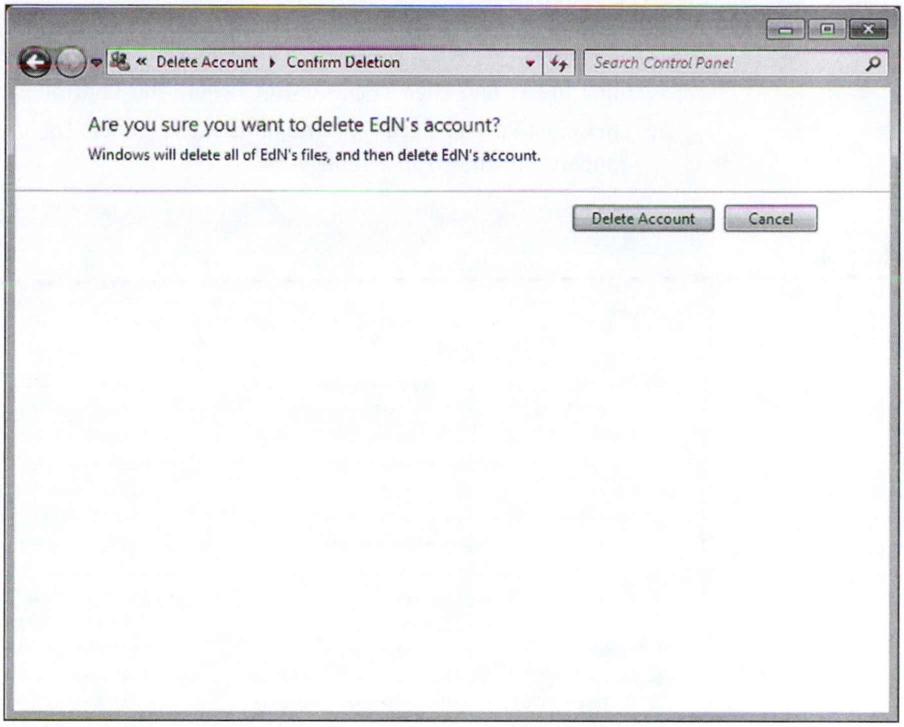

18. Click Delete Account. The *Choose the account you would like to change* page reappears.

19. Close the User Accounts control panel window.

Using the Local Users and Groups Snap-In

As you might have noticed in the previous sections, the User Accounts control panel provides only partial access to local user accounts, and no access to groups other than the Users and Administrators groups. The Local Users and Groups snap-in, on the other hand, provides full access to all of the local user and group accounts on the computer.

By default, the Local Users and Groups snap-in is part of the Computer Management console. However, you can also load the snap-in by itself, or create your own MMC console with any combination of snap-ins you wish.

OPENING THE LOCAL USERS AND GROUPS SNAP-IN

You can open the Local Users and Groups snap-in in one of three basic ways:

- Open the Control Panel from the Start menu and select System and Security > Administrative Tools > Computer Management
- Launch Microsoft Management Console (Mmc.exe), choose File > Add/Remove Snap-In, and then select the Local Users and Groups snap-in.
- Open the Start menu and type Lusrmgr.msc in the search box.

Each of these three methods provides access to the same snap-in and the same controls for creating, managing, and deleting local users and groups.

CREATING A LOCAL USER

To create a local user account with the Local Users and Groups snap-in, use the following procedure.

⊕ CREATE A NEW USER

GET READY. Log on to Windows 7 using an account with Administrator privileges.

1. Click Start, and then click Control Panel. The Control Panel window appears.
2. Click System and Security > Administrative Tools. The Administrative Tools window appears, as shown in Figure 9-14.

Figure 9-14

The Administrative Tools window

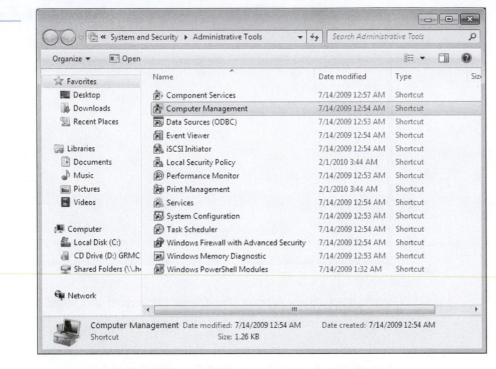

3. Double click Computer Management. The Computer Management window appears, as shown in Figure 9-15.

Figure 9-15

The Computer Management window

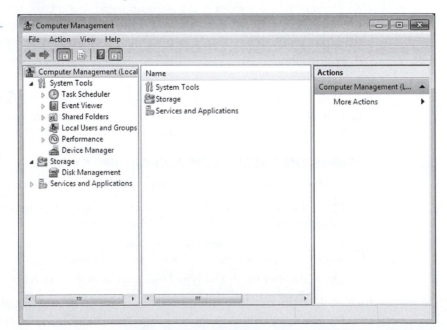

4. In the scope (left) pane of the console, expand the Local Users and Groups node and click Users. A list of the current local users appears in the details (middle) pane, as shown in Figure 9-16.

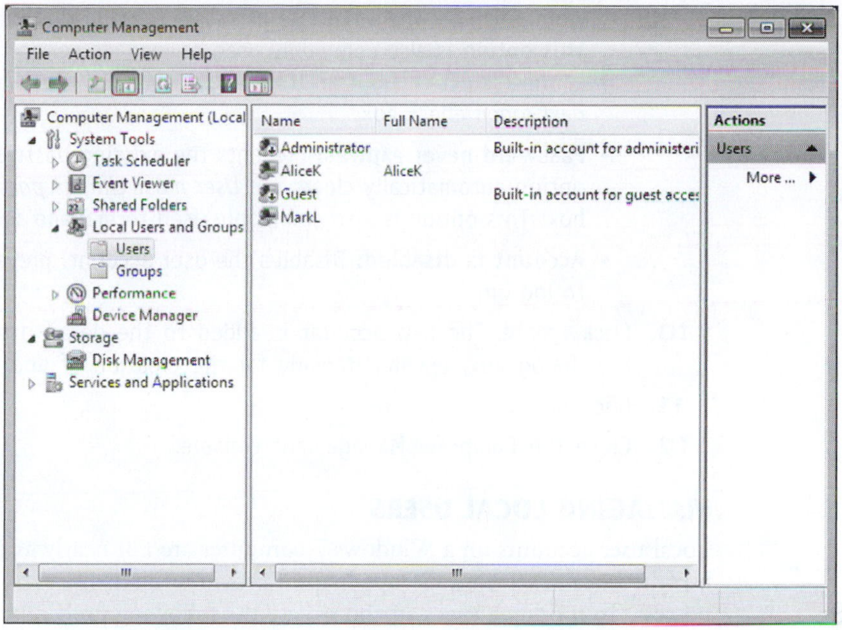

Figure 9-16

The Local Users and Groups snap-in

5. Right click the Users folder and, from the context menu, select New User. The New User dialog box appears, as shown in Figure 9-17.

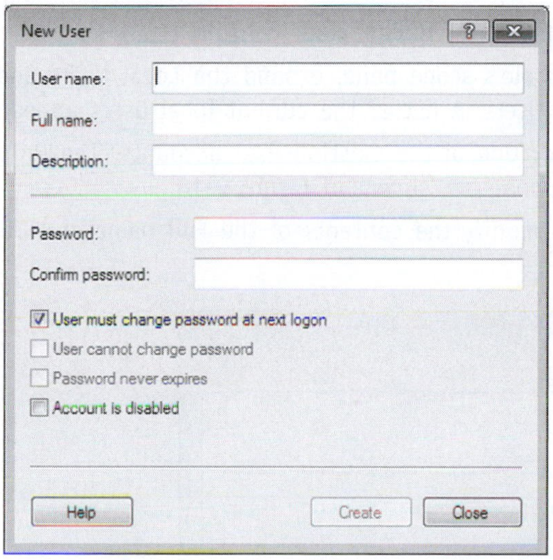

Figure 9-17

The New User dialog box

6. In the User name text box, type the name you want to assign to the user account. This is the only required field in the dialog box.

7. Specify a Full name and a Description for the account, if desired.

8. In the Password and Confirm password text boxes, type a password for the account, if desired.

9. Select or clear the four check boxes to control the following functions:

   • **User must change password at next logon:** Forces the new user to change the password after logging on for the first time. Select this option if you want to assign an initial password and have users control their own passwords after the first logon. You cannot select this option if you have selected the *Password never* *expires* check box. Selecting this option automatically clears the *User cannot change password* check box.

- **User cannot change password:** Prevents the user from changing the account password. Select this option if you want to retain control over the account password, such as when multiple users are logging on with the same user account. This option is also commonly used to manage service account passwords. You cannot select this option if you have selected the *User must change password at next logon* check box.

- **Password never expires:** Prevents the existing password from ever expiring. This option automatically clears the *User must change password at next logon* check box. This option is also commonly used to manage service account passwords.

- **Account is disabled:** Disables the user account, preventing anyone from using it to log on.

10. Click Create. The new account is added to the detail pane and the console clears the dialog box, leaving it ready for the creation of another user account.

11. Click Close.

12. Close the Computer Management console.

MANAGING LOCAL USERS

Local user accounts on a Windows 7 computer are not nearly as complex as domain users, but the Local Users and Groups snap-in provides full access to all of the attributes they do possess. To modify a user's attributes, use the following procedure.

➔ MANAGE A USER

GET READY. Log on to Windows 7 using an account with administrator privileges.

1. Open the Computer Management console.

2. In the console's scope pane, expand the Local Users and Groups subheading, and then click Users. A list of the current local users appears in the details pane.

3. Double click one of the existing user accounts. The Properties sheet for the user account appears, as shown in Figure 9-18.

4. If desired, modify the contents of the Full name and Description text boxes.

Figure 9-18

A user's Properties sheet

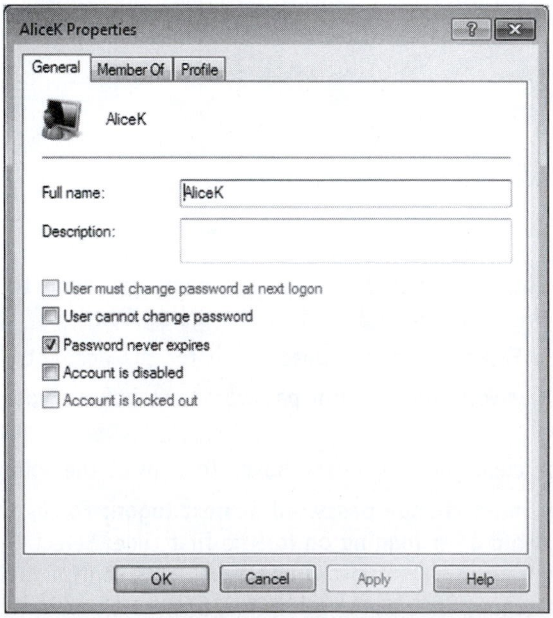

5. Select or clear any of the following check boxes:

- **User must change password at next logon:** Forces the new user to change the password after logging on for the first time. Select this option if you want to assign an initial password and have users control their own passwords after the first logon. You cannot select this option if you have selected the *Password never expires* check box. Selecting this option automatically clears the *User cannot change password* check box.

- **User cannot change password:** Prevents the user from changing the account password. Select this option if you want to retain control over the account password, such as when multiple users are logging on with the same user account. This option is also commonly used to manage service account passwords. You cannot select this option if you have selected the *User must change password at next logon* check box.

- **Password never expires:** Prevents the existing password from ever expiring. This option automatically clears the *User must change password at next logon* check box. This option is also commonly used to manage service account passwords.

- **Account is disabled:** Disables the user account, preventing anyone from using it to log on.

- **Account is locked out:** When selected, indicates that the account has been disabled because the number of unsuccessful logon attempts specified in the local system policies has been exceeded. Clear the check box to unlock the account.

6. Click the Member Of tab. The interface shown in Figure 9-19 appears.

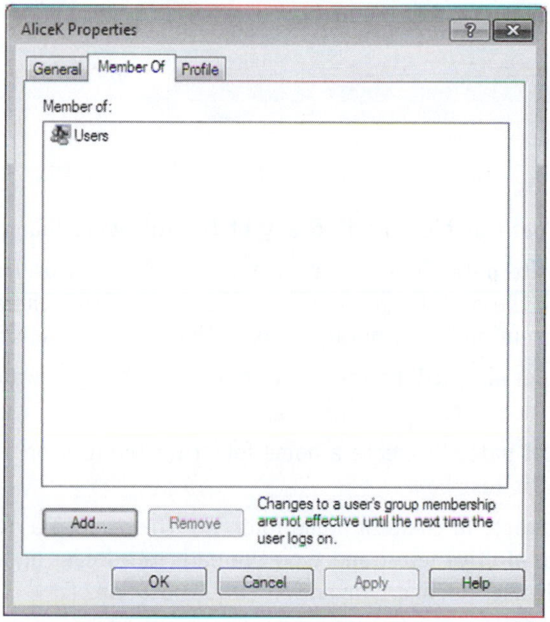

Figure 9-19

The Member Of tab of a user's Properties sheet

7. To add the user to a group, click the Add button. The Select Groups dialog box appears, as shown in Figure 9-20.

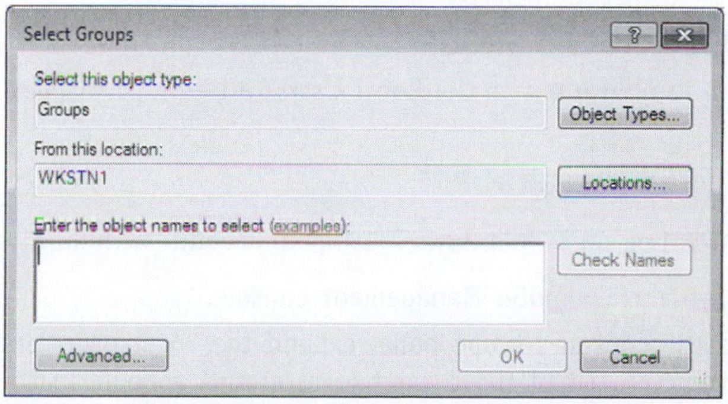

Figure 9-20

The Select Groups dialog box

8. Type the name of the local group to which you want to add the user in the text box, and then click OK. The group is added to the Member Of list. You can also type part of the group name and click Check Names to complete the name or click Advanced to search for groups.

9. Click the Profile tab. The interface shown in Figure 9-21 appears.

Figure 9-21

The Profile tab of a user's Properties sheet

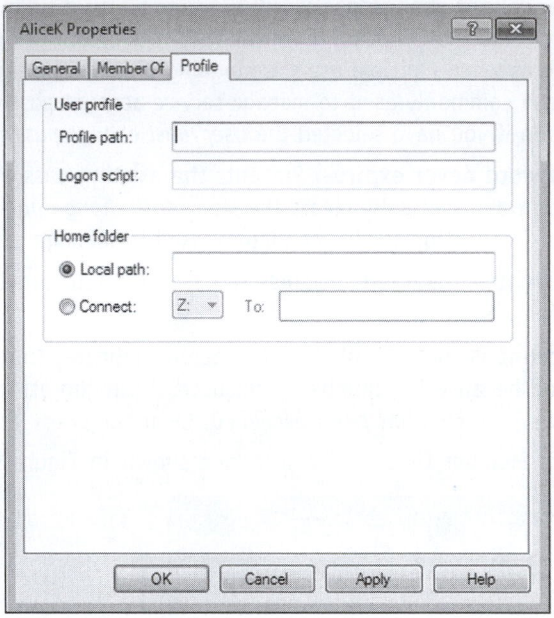

10. Type a path or filename into any of the following four text boxes as needed:
    • **Profile path:** To assign a roaming or mandatory user profile to the account, type the path to the profile stored on a network share using Universal Naming Convention (UNC) notation, as in the example \\server\share\folder.
    • **Logon script:** Type the name of a script that you want to execute whenever the user logs on.
    • **Local path:** To create a home folder for the user on a local drive, specify the path in this text box.
    • **Connect:** To create a home folder for the user on a network drive, select an unused drive letter and type the path to a folder on a network share using Universal Naming Convention (UNC) notation.

11. Click OK to save your changes and close the Properties sheet.

12. Close the Computer Management console.

X REF

For more information on roaming and mandatory user profiles, see "Understanding User Profiles" later in this lesson.

CREATING A LOCAL GROUP

To create a local group with the Local Users and Groups snap-in, use the following procedure.

➔ **CREATE A LOCAL GROUP**

GET READY. Log on to Windows 7 using an account with administrator privileges.

1. Open the Computer Management console.

2. In the console's scope pane, expand the Local Users and Groups node and click Groups. A list of the current local groups appears in the details pane.

3. Right click the Groups folder and then, from the context menu, select New Group. The New Group dialog box appears, as shown in Figure 9-22.

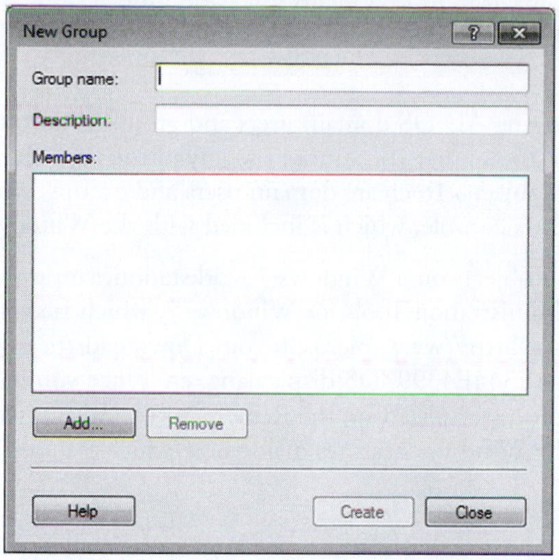

Figure 9-22

The New Group dialog box

4. In the Group name text box, type the name you want to assign to the group. This is the only required field in the dialog box.

5. If desired, specify a Description for the group.

6. Click the Add button. The Select Users dialog box appears, as shown in Figure 9-23.

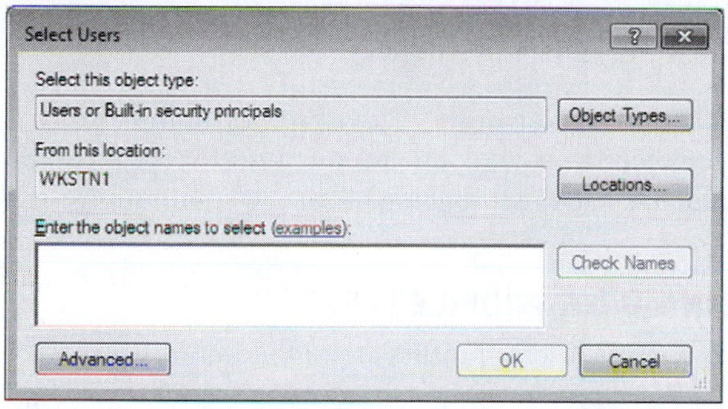

Figure 9-23

The Select Users dialog box

7. Type the names of the users that you want to add to the group, separated by semicolons, in the text box, and then click OK. The users are added to the Members list. You can also type part of a username and click Check Names to complete the name or click Advanced to search for users.

8. Click Create to create the group and populate it with the user(s) you specified. The console then clears the dialog box, leaving it ready for the creation of another group.

9. Click Close.

10. Close the Computer Management console.

Local groups have no attributes other than a member's list, so the only modifications you can make when you open an existing group are to add or remove members. As noted earlier in this lesson, local groups cannot have other local groups as members, but if the computer is a member of a Windows domain, a local group can have domain users and domain groups as members.

> **TAKE NOTE** ★
>
> To add domain objects to a local group, you click the Add button on the group's Properties sheet and, when the Select Users dialog box appears, change the Object Types and Location settings to those of the domain. Then, you can select domain users and groups just as you did local users in the previous procedure.

Working with Domain Users and Groups

> To create and manage AD DS domain users and groups on a Windows 7 workstation, you must install the Remote Server Administration Tools for Windows 7 package.

Creating and managing AD DS domain users and groups is beyond the scope of the 70-680 exam, but suffice it to say that you cannot use any of the tools discussed so far in this lesson to work with domain objects. To create domain users and groups, you use the Active Directory Users and Computers console, which is included with the Windows Server operating systems.

To manage domain objects on a Windows 7 workstation, you must download and install Remote Server Administration Tools for Windows 7, which is available from the Microsoft Download Center at http://www.microsoft.com/Downloads/details.aspx?familyid=7D2F6AD7-656B-4313-A005-4E344E43997D&displaylang=en. Once you have installed the appropriate package for your processor platform, the Remote Server Administration Tools are available for activation in the Windows Features dialog box, which is accessible from the Programs control panel.

Understanding User Profiles

> As discussed in Lesson 2, "Installing Windows 7," a *user profile* is a series of folders, associated with a specific user account, that contain personal documents, user-specific registry settings, Internet favorites, and other personalized information—everything that provides a user's familiar working environment. On a Windows 7 computer, user profiles are stored in the Users folder, in subfolders named for the user accounts.

On computers running Windows 7, user profiles automatically create and maintain the desktop settings for each user's work environment on the local computer. The system creates a new user profile for each user logging on to the computer for the first time.

RECOGNIZING USER PROFILE TYPES

The three main types of user profiles are as follows:

- **Local user profile:** A profile that Windows 7 automatically creates when each user logs on at the computer for the first time. The local user profile is stored on the computer's local hard disk.
- **Roaming user profile:** A copy of a local user profile that is stored on a shared server drive, making it accessible from anywhere on the network.
- **Mandatory user profile:** A roaming profile that users cannot change. Administrators use mandatory user profiles to enforce particular desktop settings for individuals or for a group of users. A fourth variation, called a super-mandatory profile, requires the user to access the server-based profile, or the logon fails.

USING ROAMING PROFILES

To support users who work at multiple computers on the same network, administrators can create roaming user profiles. A *roaming user profile* is simply a copy of a local user profile that is stored on a network share (to which the user has appropriate permissions), so that the user can access it from any computer on the network. No matter which computer a user logs on from, he or she always receives the files and desktop settings from the profile stored on the server.

To enable a user to access a roaming user profile, rather than a local profile, you must open the user's Properties sheet to the Profile tab and specify the location of the roaming profile in the Profile Path field. Then, the next time the user logs on, Windows 7 accesses the roaming user profile in the following manner:

1. During the user's first logon, the computer copies the entire contents of the roaming profile to the appropriate subfolder in the Users folder on the local drive. Having the roaming user profile contents stored on the local drive enables the user access to the profile during later logons, even if the server containing the roaming profile is unavailable.

2. The computer applies the roaming user profile settings to the computer, making it the active profile.

3. As the user works, the system saves any changes he or she makes to the user profile to the copy on the local drive.

4. When the user logs off, the computer replicates any changes made to the local copy of the user profile back to the server where the roaming profile is stored.

5. The next time the user logs on at the same computer, the system compares the contents of the locally stored profile with the roaming profile stored on the server. The computer copies only the roaming profile components that have changed to the copy on the local drive, which makes the logon process shorter and more efficient.

You should create roaming user profiles on a file server that you back up frequently, so that you always have copies of your users' most recent profiles. To improve logon performance for a busy network, place the users' roaming profiles folder on a member server instead of a domain controller.

USING MANDATORY PROFILES

A *mandatory user profile* is simply a read-only roaming user profile. Users receive files and desktop settings from a server-based profile, just as they would with any roaming profile, and they can modify their desktop environments while they are logged on. However, because the profile is read-only, the system cannot save any profile changes back to the server when the users log off. The next time the user logs on, the server-based profile will be the same as during the previous logon.

Windows 7 downloads the mandatory profile settings to the local computer each time the user logs on. You can assign one mandatory profile to multiple users who require the same desktop settings, such as a group of users who all do the same job. Because the profile never changes, you do not have to worry about one user making changes that affect all of the other users. Also, a mandatory profile makes it possible to modify the desktop environment for multiple users by changing only one profile.

To create a mandatory user profile, you rename the Ntuser.dat file in the folder containing the roaming profile to Ntuser.man. The Ntuser.dat file consists of the Windows 7 system registry settings that apply to the individual user account and contains the user environment settings, such as those controlling the appearance of the desktop. Renaming this file with a .man extension makes it read-only, preventing the client computers from saving changes to the profile when a user logs off.

⚠ **WARNING** When you create roaming profiles, you must be conscious of the Windows version running on your various network workstations. Windows 7 user profiles are not compatible with earlier versions of Windows; and in the same way, profiles from DOS-based Windows versions (such as Windows Me) are not compatible with Windows XP and other NT-based Windows versions.

■ Introducing User Account Control

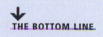
THE BOTTOM LINE

One of the most common Windows security problems arises from the fact that many users perform their everyday computing tasks with more system access than they actually need. Logging on as Administrator or as a user that is a member of the Administrators group grants the user full access to all areas of the operating system. This degree of system access is not necessary to run many of the applications and perform many of the tasks users require every day; it is needed only for certain administrative functions, such as installing system-wide software or configuring system parameters.

CERTIFICATION READY?
Configure user account
control (UAC).
5.3

For most users, logging on with administrative privileges all the time is simply a matter of convenience. Microsoft recommends logging on as a standard user, and using administrative privileges only when you need them. However, many technical specialists who do this frequently find themselves encountering situations in which they need administrative access. There is a surprisingly large number of common, and even mundane, Windows tasks that require administrative access, and the inability to perform those tasks can negatively affect a user's productivity.

In the past, the recommended practices when a user account has insufficient access to perform a task are as follows:

- Ask a user with the required access to perform the task.
- Log off the computer and log on again with an administrative account.
- Use the Run As feature to access a particular system function with administrative privileges.

Many users find these solutions too inconvenient, however, and they find themselves adding their standard user accounts to the Administrators group, just to avoid the repeated interruptions.

The two main problems with this practice are:

1. **It grants users the ability to make system-wide configuration changes, install unauthorized software, and potentially compromise the security of the network.** For a corporate installation, this can be a major problem. Allowing end users to configure their own systems makes it extremely difficult for technical specialists to troubleshoot problems. Many organizations prefer to enforce strict control over desktop computers to maintain a standard system configuration throughout the enterprise.

2. **A computer running with administrative privileges is left wide open to exploits by all kinds of malware.** If, for example, a user unknowingly downloads an infected file, the potential for damage to the system is far greater if the user is logged on as an administrator at the time, rather than if the user is logged on as a standard user. The same would be true if a burglar broke into the basement of a three-story building. The potential for loss is far greater if all of the interior doors are unlocked than if the burglar can't leave the basement.

Understanding User Account Control

Microsoft decided to solve these problems by keeping all Windows 7 users from accessing the system using administrative privileges unless those privileges are required to perform the task at hand. The mechanism that does this is called *User Account Control (UAC)*.

When a user logs on to Windows 7, the system issues a token, which indicates the user's access level. Whenever the system authorizes the user to perform a particular activity, it consults the token to see if the user has the required privileges. In previous versions of Windows, standard users received standard user tokens and members of the Administrators group received administrative tokens. Every activity performed by an administrative user was therefore authorized using the administrative token, resulting in the problems described earlier.

On a Windows 7 computer running User Account Control (UAC), a standard user still receives a standard user token, but an administrative user receives two tokens: one for standard user access and one for administrative user access. By default, the standard and administrative users both run using the standard user token most of the time.

UNDERSTANDING RECOMMENDED UAC PRACTICES

Despite the introduction of UAC, Microsoft still recommends that all Windows users log on with a standard user account, except when they are logging on for administrative purposes only. As compared to earlier Windows versions, Windows 7 and UAC simplify the process by which standard users can gain administrative access, making the use of standard user accounts less frustrating, even for system administrators.

PERFORMING ADMINISTRATIVE TASKS WITH A STANDARD USER ACCOUNT

When a standard user attempts to perform a task that requires administrative privileges, the system displays a ***credential prompt***, as shown in Figure 9-24, requesting that the user supply the name and password for an account with administrative privileges.

Figure 9-24

A UAC credential prompt

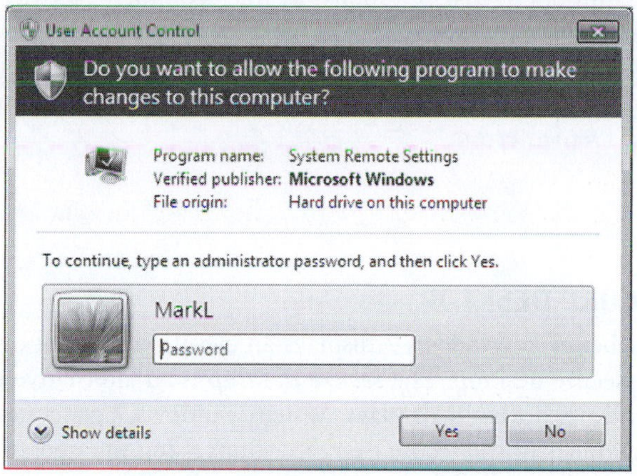
User Account Control
Do you want to allow the following program to make changes to this computer?
Program name: System Remote Settings
Verified publisher: Microsoft Windows
File origin: Hard drive on this computer
To continue, type an administrator password, and then click Yes.
MarkL
Password
Show details
Yes
No

PERFORMING ADMINISTRATIVE TASKS WITH AN ADMINISTRATIVE ACCOUNT

When an administrator attempts to perform a task that requires administrative access, the system switches the account from the standard user token to the administrative token. This is known as ***Admin Approval Mode***.

MORE INFORMATION

The decision to run all users with a standard user token was not one that Microsoft made unilaterally. Part of the process of developing UAC involved working with the software developers both at Microsoft and at third-party companies to minimize the number and type of administrative-level access requests made by applications.

Before the system permits the user to employ the administrative token, it might require the human user to confirm that he or she is actually trying to perform an administrative task. To do this, the system generates an elevation prompt. An ***elevation prompt*** is the message box shown in Figure 9-25. This confirmation prevents unauthorized processes, such as those initiated by malware, from accessing the system using administrative privileges.

Figure 9-25

A UAC elevation prompt

User Account Control
Do you want to allow the following program to make changes to this computer?
Program name: Sysinternals Utilities
Verified publisher: Microsoft Corporation
File origin: Network drive
Show details
Yes
No
Change when these notifications appear

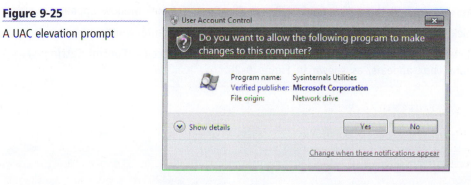

In Windows 7, administrators are faced with elevation prompts far less frequently than they are in Windows Vista. In response to complaints from users, Microsoft has modified the default UAC behavior in Windows 7 so that elevation prompts only appear when an application attempts to perform an administrative task. Operating system administration tasks do not generate elevation prompts.

> **TAKE NOTE** *
>
> The system component that is responsible for recognizing the need for elevated privileges and generating elevation prompts is called the Application Information Service (AIS). AIS is a Windows 7 service that has to be running for UAC to function properly. Disabling this service prevents applications that require administrative access from launching, resulting in Access Denied errors.

WARNING It is still possible for a malware program to imitate the secure desktop and create its own artificial elevation or credential prompt, but an artificial prompt cannot provide the program with genuine access to administrative functions. The only possible danger is that a malware program could use an artificial credential prompt to harvest administrative account names and passwords from unsuspecting users.

USING SECURE DESKTOP

By default, whenever Windows 7 displays an elevation prompt or a credential prompt, it does so using the secure desktop. The *secure desktop* is an alternative to the interactive user desktop that Windows normally displays. When Windows 7 generates an elevation or credential prompt, it switches to the secure desktop, suppressing the operation of all other desktop controls and permitting only Windows processes to interact with the prompt. The object of this is to prevent malware from automating a response to the elevation or credential prompt and bypassing the human reply.

Configuring User Account Control

> All versions of Windows 7 enable User Account Control by default, but it is possible to configure several of its properties, or even disable it completely.

When Windows 7 starts, if the AIS service is not running and UAC is disabled, the Windows Security Center warns you of its absence and gives you the opportunity to turn it on.

In Windows 7, there are now four UAC settings available through the Control Panel, as compared to the simple on/off switch in Windows Vista. To configure UAC through the Control Panel, use the following procedure.

→ CONFIGURE UAC SETTINGS

GET READY. Log on to Windows 7 using an account with administrator privileges.

1. Click Start, and then click Control Panel. The Control Panel window appears.
2. Click System and Security > Action Center. The Action Center window appears.
3. Click Change User Account Control settings. The User Account Control Settings dialog box appears, as shown in Figure 9-26.

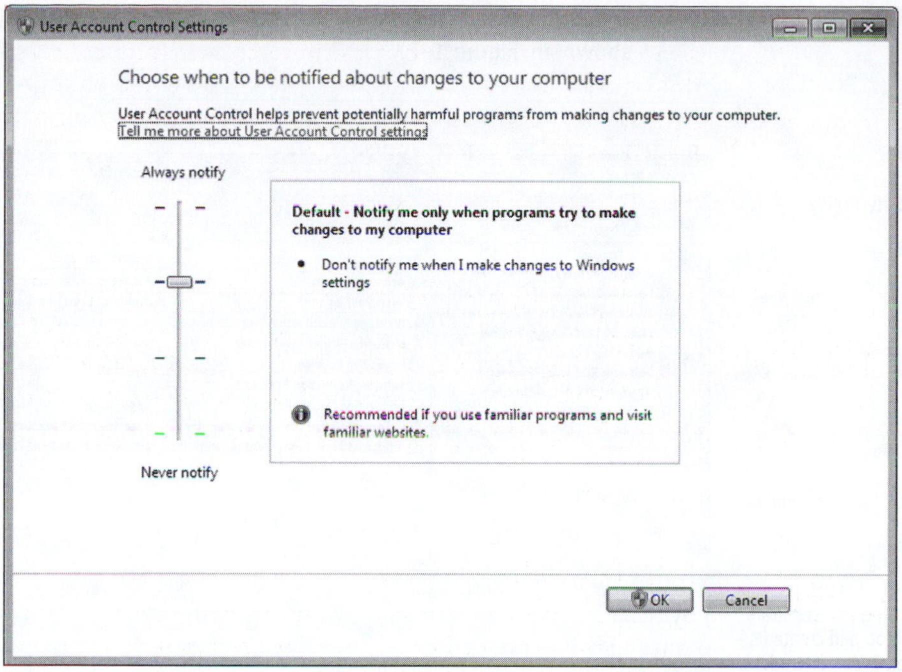

Figure 9-26

The User Account Control
Settings dialog box

4. Adjust the slider to one of the following settings and click OK:

   • Always notify me

   • Notify me only when programs try to make changes to my computer

   • Notify me only when programs try to make changes to my computer (do not dim my desktop)

   • Never notify me

5. Close the Action Center window.

While the UAC controls in Windows 7 are improved, the most granular control over UAC properties is still through Local Security Policy or, on an AD DS network, Group Policy.

To configure UAC properties using Local Security Policy, use the following procedure.

CONFIGURE UAC LOCAL SECURITY POLICIES

GET READY. Log on to Windows 7 using an account with administrator privileges.

1. Click Start, and then click Control Panel. The Control Panel window appears.

2. Click System and Security > Administrative Tools. The Administrative Tools window appears.

3. Double click Local Security Policy. The Local Security Policy console appears, as shown in Figure 9-27.

Figure 9-27

The Local Security Policy console

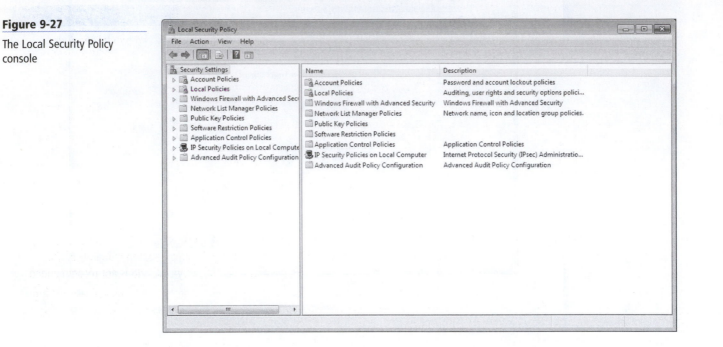

4. Expand the Local Policies header, and then click Security Options. A list of Security Options policies appears in the details pane, as shown in Figure 9-28.

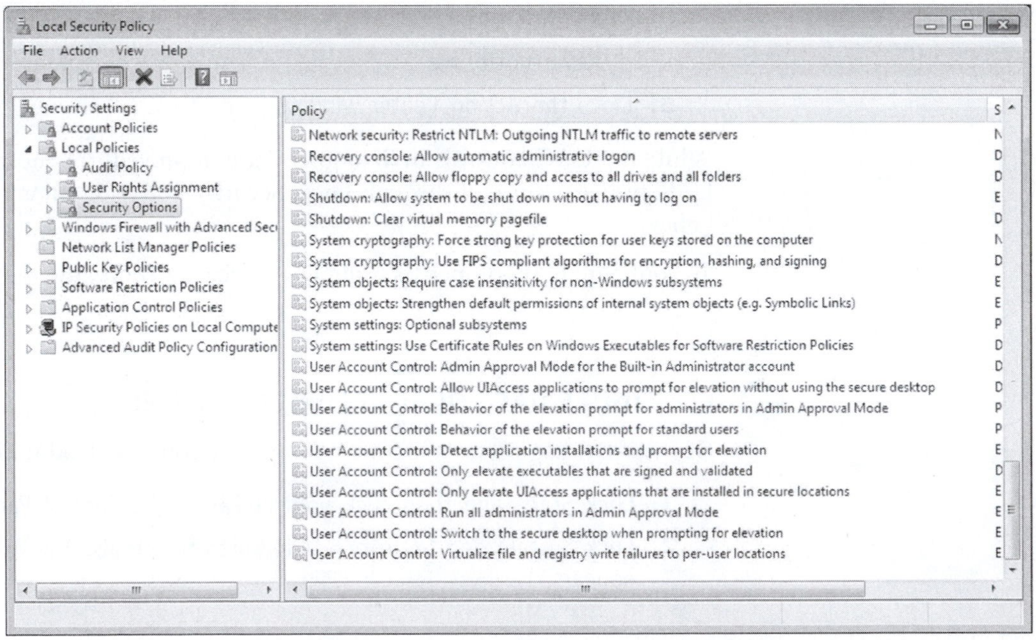

Figure 9-28

The Security Options list

5. Scroll down to the bottom of the policy list until you see the nine policies with the User Account Control prefix, as described in Table 9-4.

Table 9-4

UAC Local Security Policy Settings

POLICY SETTING	VALUES AND FUNCTIONS
User Account Control: Admin Approval Mode for the Built-in Administrator account	When enabled, the built-in Administrator account is issued two tokens during logon and runs in Admin Approval Mode. This is the default setting, except in cases of upgrades from Windows XP systems in which the built-in Administrator account is the only active member of the Administrators group. When disabled, the built-in Administrator account receives only an administrative token and runs with full administrative access at all times.
User Account Control: Allow UIAccess applications to prompt for elevation without using the secure desktop	When enabled, causes User Interface Accessibility programs to disable the secure desktop when displaying elevation prompts. When disabled, elevation prompts use the secure desktop, unless the *User Account Control: Switch to the Secure Desktop when Prompting for Elevation* policy is enabled.
User Account Control: Behavior of the elevation prompt for administrators in Admin Approval Mode	When set to *Elevate without prompting*, administrative users are elevated to the administrative token with no consent or credentials from the human user. This setting, in effect, disables the security provided by UAC and is not recommended. When set to *Prompt for consent on the secure desktop*, administrative users are elevated to the administrative token only after the presentation of an elevation prompt on the secure desktop and the consent of the human user. When set to *Prompt for credentials on the secure desktop*, administrative users are elevated to the administrative token only after the presentation of a credential prompt on the secure desktop, to which the user must supply a valid administrative account name and password, even if he or she is already logged on using such an account. When set to *Prompt for consent*, administrative users are elevated to the administrative token only after the presentation of an elevation prompt and the consent of the human user. This is the default setting. When set to *Prompt for credentials*, administrative users are elevated to the administrative token only after the presentation of a credential prompt, to which the user must supply a valid administrative account name and password, even if he or she is already logged on using such an account.
User Account Control: Behavior of the elevation prompt for standard users	When set to *Automatically deny elevation requests*, suppresses the credential prompt and prevents standard users from being elevated to an administrative token. Standard users can perform administrative tasks only by using the Run As program or by logging on using an administrative account. This is the default setting for the Windows 7 Enterprise edition. When set to *Prompt for credentials on the secure desktop*, standard users attempting to perform an administrative function receive a credential prompt on the secure desktop, to which the user must supply a valid administrative account name and password. When set to *Prompt for credentials*, standard users attempting to perform an administrative function receive a credential prompt, to which the user must supply a valid administrative account name and password. This is the default setting for the Windows 7 Home Basic, Home Premium, Professional, and Ultimate editions.

(*continued*)

Table 9-4 (*continued*)

POLICY SETTING	VALUES AND FUNCTIONS
User Account Control: Detect application installations and prompt for elevation	When enabled, an attempt to install an application causes standard users to receive a credential prompt and administrative users to receive an elevation prompt. The user must supply authentication credentials or consent before the installation can proceed. This is the default setting. When disabled, elevation and credential prompts are suppressed during application installations, and the installations will fail. This setting is for use on enterprise desktops that use an automated installation technology, such as Microsoft System Center Configuration Manager.
User Account Control: Only elevate executables that are signed and validated	When enabled, requires successful public key infrastructure (PKI) signature verifications on all interactive applications that request administrative access. Unsigned applications will not run. When disabled, both signed and unsigned applications will run. This is the default setting.
User Account Control: Only elevate UIAccess applications that are Installed in secure locations	When enabled, Windows 7 will provide access to the protected system user interface only if the executable is located in the Program Files or Windows folder on the system drive. If the executable is not located in one of these folders, access will be denied, despite a positive response to the elevation prompt. This is the default setting. When disabled, the folder location checks are omitted, so any application can be granted access to the protected system user interface upon successful completion of the elevation prompt.
User Account Control: Run all administrators in Admin Approval Mode	When enabled, standard users receive credential prompts and administrative users receive elevation prompts, when either one requests administrative privileges. This policy essentially turns UAC on and off. A change in the value of this policy does not take effect until the system is restarted. This is the default setting. When disabled, the AIS service is disabled and does not automatically start. This turns UAC off and prevents elevation and credential prompts from appearing. When the system starts, the Windows Security Center warns the user that operating system security is reduced and provides the ability to activate UAC.
User Account Control: Switch to the secure desktop when prompting for elevation	When enabled, causes Windows 7 to display all elevation prompts on the secure desktop, which can receive messages only from Windows processes. This is the default setting. When disabled, causes Windows 7 to display all elevation prompts on the interactive user desktop.
User Account Control: Virtualize file and registry write failures to per-user locations	When enabled, allows non-UAC-compliant applications to run by redirecting write requests to protected locations, such as the Program Files and Windows folders or the HKLM\Software registry key, to alternative locations in the registry and file system. This process is called virtualization. This is the default setting. When disabled, virtualization is disabled, and non-UAC-compliant applications attempting to write to protected locations will fail to run. This setting is recommended only when the system is running UAC-compliant applications exclusively.

6. Double click one of the User Account Control policies. The Properties sheet for the policy appears, as shown in Figure 9-29.

Figure 9-29

The Properties sheet of a UAC policy

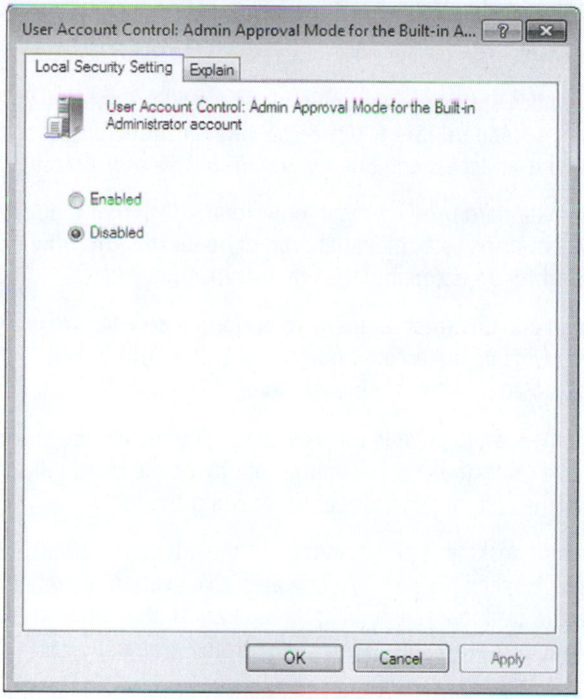

If you are working on an AD DS network, you can configure the same UAC policies for multiple computers simultaneously by creating a Group Policy object, configuring the same policy settings, and applying it to a domain, site, or organizational unit object.

7. Select the radio button (or drop-down list option) for the setting you want the policy to use, and then click OK. The Properties sheet closes.

8. Repeat Steps 6 and 7 to configure other policies, if desired.

9. Close the Local Security Policy console and the Administrative Tools window.

SKILL SUMMARY

IN THIS LESSON YOU LEARNED:

- The user account is the fundamental unit of identity in Windows operating systems.

- A group is an identifying token that Windows uses to represent a collection of users.

- A workgroup is a collection of computers that are all peers. A peer network is one in which every computer can function as both a server by sharing its resources with other computers and as a client by accessing the shared resources on other computers.

- A domain is a collection of computers that all utilize a central directory service for authentication and authorization.

- Windows 7 includes a number of built-in local groups that are already equipped with the permissions and rights needed to perform certain tasks.

- A special identity is essentially a placeholder for a collection of users with a similar characteristic.

- Windows 7 provides two separate interfaces for creating and managing local user accounts: the User Accounts (or user Accounts and Family Safety) control panel and the Local Users and Group snap-in for the Microsoft Management Console (MMC).

(continued)

SKILL SUMMARY (*continued*)

- A roaming user profile is simply a copy of a local user profile that is stored on a network share, so that the user can access it from any computer on the network.

- A mandatory user profile is simply a read-only roaming user profile.

- On a Windows 7 computer running User Account Control (UAC), a standard user still receives a standard user token, but an administrative user receives two tokens: one for standard user access and one for administrative user access.

- When a standard user attempts to perform a task that requires administrative privileges, the system displays a credential prompt, requesting that the user supply the name and password for an account with administrative privileges.

- When an administrator attempts to perform a task that requires administrative access, the system switches the account from the standard user token to the administrative token. This is known as Admin Approval Mode.

- Before the system permits the user to employ the administrative token for an application task, it requires the user to confirm that he or she is actually trying to perform the task. To do this, the system generates an elevation prompt.

- The secure desktop is an alternative to the interactive user desktop that Windows normally displays. When Windows 7 generates an elevation or credential prompt, it switches to the secure desktop, suppressing the operation of all other desktop controls and permitting only Windows processes to interact with the prompt.

- User Account Control is enabled by default in all Windows 7 installations, but it is possible to configure its properties, or even disable it completely, using Local Security Policy.

■ Knowledge Assessment

Matching

Complete the following exercise by matching the terms with their corresponding definitions.

- a. switches an account from the standard user token to the administrative token
- b. displayed when a regular user requires administrative access
- c. confirmation of a user's identity
- d. suppresses the operation of all controls except the UAC prompt
- e. enables users to access their desktops from any workstation
- f. grants a user a specific degree of access to a resource
- g. hosts an AD DS domain
- h. displayed when an administrator requires administrative access
- i. placeholder for a collection of users with a similar characteristic
- j. a profile that multiple users can run simultaneously

_____ 1. credential prompt

_____ 2. roaming user profile

_____ 3. Admin Approval Mode

_____ 4. special identity

_____ 5. authentication

———— **6.** elevation prompt

———— **7.** mandatory user profile

———— **8.** secure desktop

———— **9.** authorization

———— **10.** domain controller

Multiple Choice

Select one or more correct answers for each of the following questions.

1. What is the term used to describe a read-only copy of a user profile stored on a network share?
   a. mandatory profile
   b. super-mandatory profile
   c. roaming profile
   d. search profile

2. When you create a new user account with the User Accounts control panel, you can only add it to which of the following groups? (Choose all that apply.)
   a. Administrators
   b. Users
   c. Power Users
   d. Guests

3. When you log on to a newly installed Windows 7 computer for the first time, why can you not use the Administrator account?
   a. Local Security Policy prevents its use.
   b. The Administrator account has no password.
   c. There is no Administrator account.
   d. The Administrator account is disabled.

4. Which of the following statements is true?
   a. The User Accounts control panel can create local users and local groups only.
   b. The User Accounts control panel can create local and domain users.
   c. The User Accounts control panel can create local users only.
   d. The User Accounts control panel can create local users, local groups, domain users, and domain groups.

5. Which of the following actions can you NOT perform from the Control Panel?
   a. Disable UAC
   b. Disable secure desktop
   c. Disable elevation prompts for operating system tasks only
   d. Disable elevation prompts for application tasks only

6. Which of the following can be members of local groups? (Choose all that apply.)
   a. Local users
   b. Domain users
   c. Other local groups
   d. Domain groups

7. Which of the following built-in Windows 7 accounts are special identities? (Choose all that apply.)
   a. Administrators
   b. Everyone
   c. Authenticated Users
   d. IIS_IUSRS

8. Under which of the following conditions are Windows 7 local user accounts required to use complex passwords?
   a. When the computer is joined to a domain
   b. When one of the Account Lockout Policy settings is enabled in Local Security Policy
   c. When the accounts are members of the Administrators group
   d. When UAC is disabled

9. Which of the following Windows 7 built-in local groups does not provide members with any additional privileges?
   a. Backup Operators
   b. Cryptographic Operators
   c. Power Users
   d. Remote Desktop Users

10. Which of the following is the default UAC setting for a computer that is not joined to an AD DS domain?
    a. Always notify me
    b. Notify me only when programs try to make changes to my computer
    c. Notify me only when programs try to make changes to my computer (do not dim my desktop)
    d. Never notify me

Review Questions

1. Explain why it is recommended that administrators not disable the *User Account Control: Switch to the secure desktop when prompting for elevation* policy.

2. Explain how a special identity differs from a local group.

■ Case Scenario

Scenario 9-1: Configuring UAC

You are a system administrator for a company network running all Windows 7 workstations, and you rely on User Account Control to minimize the possibility of system infiltration by unauthorized software. Many of the department employees spend most of their time performing administrative tasks for the network and therefore require administrative access to their systems. The IS department for the company headquarters also uses an "open office" design, meaning that employees are constantly wandering around to each others' work areas, often leaving their workstations logged on.

You are concerned about the danger of unattended workstations being used to gain administrative access to the systems. What changes can you make to the UAC configuration to minimize this possibility? Explain how these changes would enhance the security of the systems.

Securing Windows 7

OBJECTIVE DOMAIN MATRIX

Technology Skill	Objective Domain	Objective Number
Introducing Windows Firewall	Configure Windows Firewall.	4.4
Using the Encrypting File System	Configure file and folder access.	5.2
Authenticating and Authorizing Users	Configure authentication and authorization.	5.4

KEY TERMS

authenticated exception

brute force

filter

firewall

malware

multifactor authentication

Personal Identity Verification (PIV)

private key

public key

rules

spyware

user rights

Windows Biometric Framework

■ Authenticating and Authorizing Users

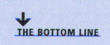

THE BOTTOM LINE

As mentioned in Lesson 9, "Working with Workgroups and Domains," authentication and authorization are two of the most important functions of Windows 7. Authentication confirms the identification of a user accessing computer or network resources, and authorization specifies which resources the user is permitted to access.

Network resources require varying levels of security, and technical specialists are often responsible for seeing to it that users have access only to the information they need to do their jobs, and no more. Authentication is crucial to this process, because before you can provide access to protected resources, you must confirm the identity of those to whom you are providing access.

CERTIFICATION READY?
Configure authentication
and authorization.
5.4

The user authentication process is typically based on one or more of the following:

- **Something the user knows:** A secret shared between the user and management—usually in the form of a password—is the simplest and most common form of authentication. However, users can forget, share, or otherwise compromise passwords, often without knowing it.

- **Something the user has:** A token of some kind, carried by the user, such as a smart card, can serve as proof of identity. While tokens can easily be lost or stolen, users are typically aware of the loss, and the time during which the system is compromised is brief.

- **Something the user is:** Biometric identification is the use of physical characteristics to confirm a user's identity. Fingerprints are the most commonly used biometric identifier, but there are also technologies that are based on ocular scans, facial recognition, and other characteristics.

Because each of these identification methods has inherent weaknesses, networks requiring high security often use more than one. For example, a network that issues smart cards to users nearly always requires some sort of password as well. This technique is known as *multifactor authentication*.

Authentication is nearly always a balance between security and convenience, and nowhere is this truer than in user authentication. As a technical specialist responsible for network security, you could conceivably demand that your users log on each day by typing 72-character passwords, scanning security bracelets permanently fastened to their wrists, and having their identities confirmed with a blood sample. There are, however, likely to be objections to this treatment from users.

Working with Passwords

Passwords are the most common user identifier on Windows networks, primarily because they do not require any additional hardware or software. Passwords can provide excellent security as well, as long as they are used properly.

When left to their own devices, users tend to employ password policies that can compromise their effectiveness as a security mechanism. Potential intruders can obtain passwords in two possible ways: by cracking them or by discovering them.

Cracking is the process of repeatedly guessing passwords until you find the right one. Cracking is a mathematical process in which a software program tries all of the possible passwords until it finds the right one. This is sometimes known as a *brute force* process.

Password discovery is a process in which the intruder tries to guess a password based on the user's personal information, or tries to dupe the user into supplying the password. This is also known as social engineering.

These methods are possible only when users compromise their passwords in some way. Some of the ways in which users can weaken the security of their passwords are as follows:

- **Short passwords:** Shorter passwords are mathematically easier to guess. A three-character alphabetical password has 26^3 or 17,576 possible values. Increasing the password to seven characters increases the number of possible values to 26^7 or over eight billion password combinations.

- **Simple passwords:** Passwords that use only lowercase characters are also mathematically easier to guess than those that use mixed lowercase and uppercase characters. A seven-character password using upper and lowercase characters would have 52^7 or over one trillion possible values. Passwords that use numerical characters and symbols as well increase their strength even further.

- **Unchanging passwords:** A brute force attack takes time to try every possible password combination, so changing passwords forces an attacker to start all over. The fewer the possible password combinations an attacker has to try, the more frequently you should change the password.

- **Predictable passwords:** Users often select passwords based on predicable values, such as birthdays, social security numbers, or names of children and pets. Attackers that have access to this type of information can make more educated password guesses.

Windows 7 includes features that can provide users with a more convenient password experience, and also compel them to obey network password selection and maintenance policies that minimize these potential weaknesses. Some of these features are discussed in the following sections.

CONFIGURING PASSWORD POLICIES

Windows 7 supports a number of Group Policy settings that administrators can use to enforce password security practices on individual computers or on Active Directory Domain Services (AD DS) networks. By enforcing these password practices, you can ensure that your systems remain secure, even though the end users are responsible for their own passwords.

To configure password policies using Local Security Policy, use the following procedure.

⊘ CONFIGURE PASSWORD POLICIES

GET READY. Log on to Windows 7 using an account with administrator privileges.

1. Click Start, and then click Control Panel. The Control Panel window appears.
2. Click System and Security > Administrative Tools. The Administrative Tools window appears.
3. Double click Local Security Policy. The Local Security Policy console appears, as shown in Figure 10-1.

Figure 10-1

The Local Security Policy console

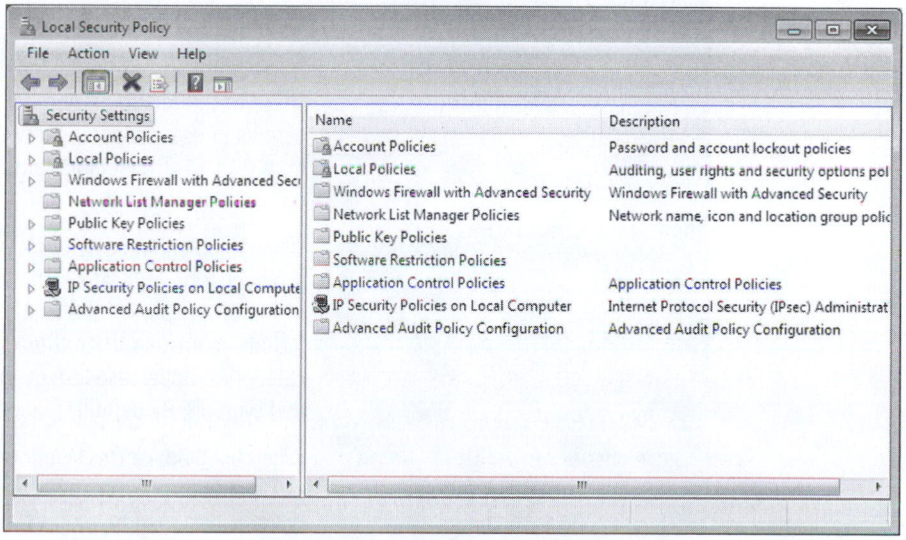

4. Expand the Account Policies header, and then click Password Policy. A list of password policies appears in the details pane, as shown in Figure 10-2.

Figure 10-2

Password Policies in the Local
Security Policy console

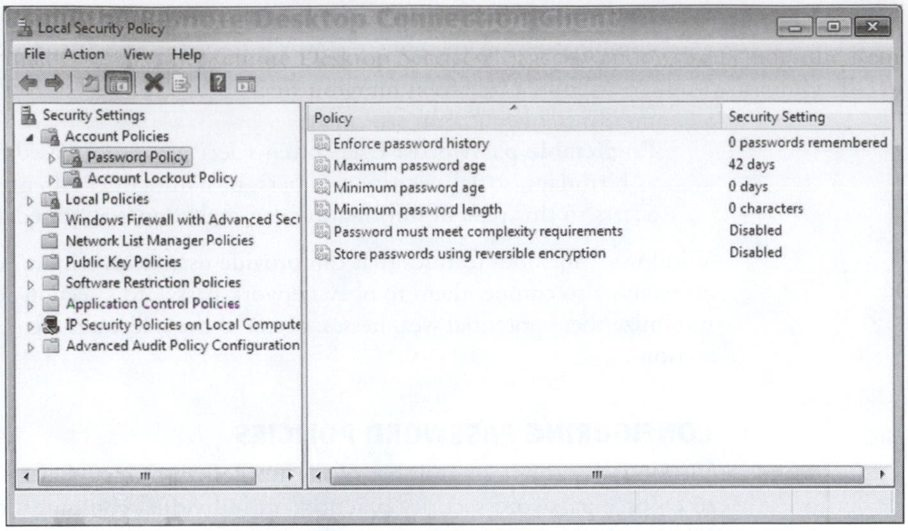

5. Double click one of the password policies described in Table 10-1. The Properties sheet for the policy appears, as shown in Figure 10-3.

Table 10-1

Windows Password Policy
Settings

PASSWORD POLICY SETTINGS	VALUES AND FUNCTION
Enforce password history	Specifies the number of unique passwords that users have to supply before Windows 7 permits them to reuse an old password. Possible values range from 0 to 24. The default value is 0.
Maximum password age	Specifies how long a single password can be used before Windows 7 forces the user to change it. Possible values range from 0 to 999. A value of 0 causes the password never to expire. The default value is 42 days.
Minimum password age	Specifies how long a single password must be used before Windows 7 permits the user to change it. Possible values range from 0 to 998. The default value is 0 days, which enables the user to change the password immediately.
Minimum password length	Specifies the minimum number of characters Windows 7 permits in user-supplied passwords. Possible values range from 0 to 14. The default value is 0, which means that no password is required.
Password must meet complexity requirements	When enabled, indicates that passwords supplied by users must be at least six characters long, with no duplication of any part of the user's account name; and must include characters from at least three of the following four categories: uppercase letters, lowercase letters, numbers, and symbols. By default, this policy is disabled.
Store passwords using reversible encryption	When enabled, causes Windows 7 to store user account passwords using a less effective encryption algorithm. This policy is designed to support authentication protocols that require access to the user's password, such as the Challenge Handshake Authentication Protocol (CHAP). From a security perspective, this policy is functionally equivalent to using plaintext passwords. The default value is disabled.

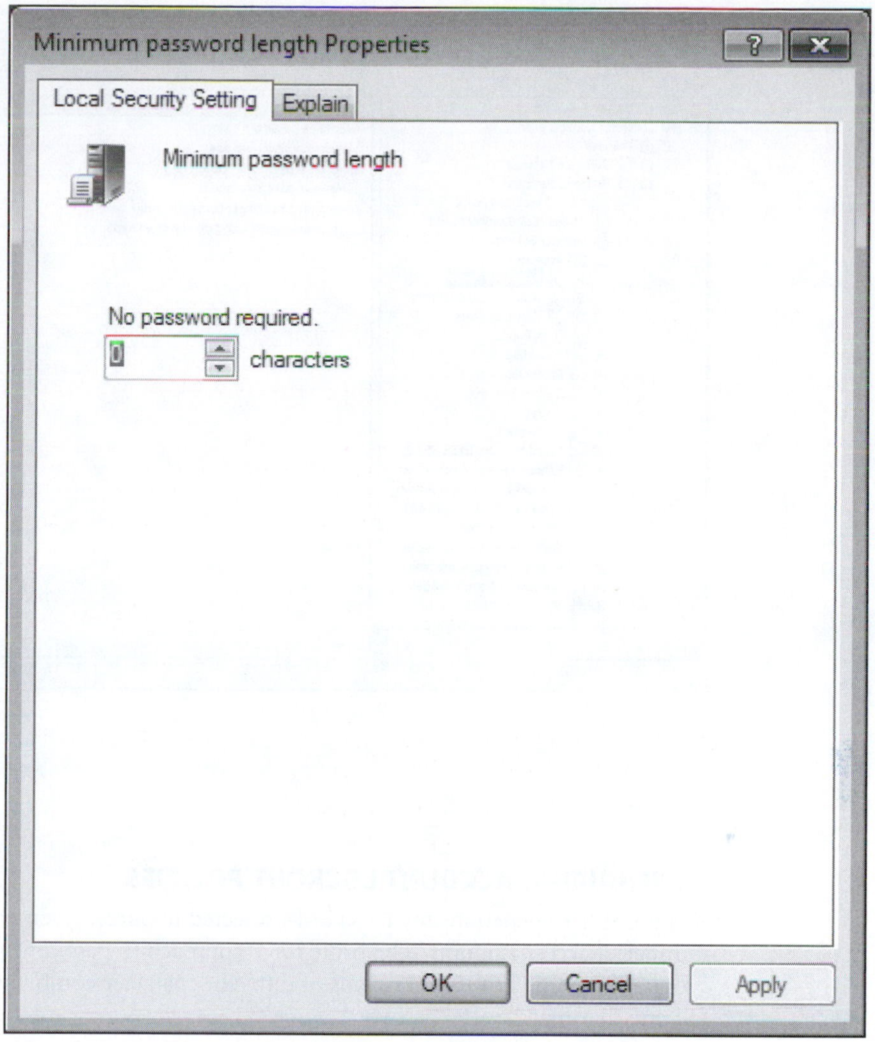

Figure 10-3

The Properties sheet of a password policy

---

6. Configure the policy by setting a value using the spin box, radio button, or other control, and then click OK. The Properties sheet closes.

7. Repeat Steps 5 and 6 to configure other policies, if desired.

8. Close the Local Security Policy console and the Administrative Tools window.

In an enterprise network environment, technical specialists generally prefer to configure these settings using AD DS Group Policy, so they can distribute them to large numbers of workstations simultaneously. To configure password policies on an AD DS network, you must run the Group Policy Management Editor console and create a Group Policy object, which you then link to a domain, site, or organizational unit object in your AD DS tree. The password policies in a GPO are located in the Computer Configuration\Policies\Windows Settings\Security Settings\Account Policies\Password Policies node, as shown in Figure 10-4. The policy settings themselves are exactly the same.

TAKE NOTE*

The Group Policy Management Editor console is supplied with the Windows Server operating systems and installed automatically on AD DS domain controllers. To manage AD DS Group Policy settings on a Windows 7 workstation, you must download and install the Remote Server Administration Tools for Windows 7 package. For more information, see "Working with Domain Users and Groups" in Lesson 9, "Working with Workgroups and Domains."

Figure 10-4

Password Policies in an AD DS
Group Policy object

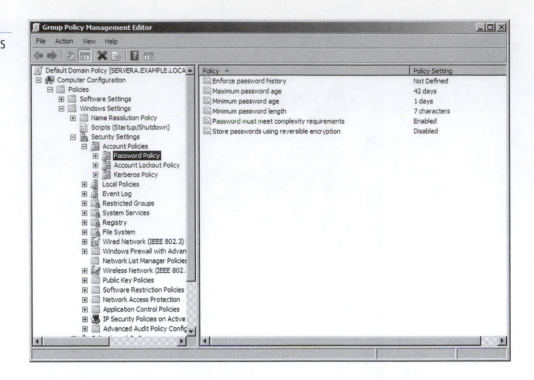

CONFIGURING ACCOUNT LOCKOUT POLICIES

It is possible to penetrate any password-protected resource, given enough time and an unlimited number of access attempts. The brute force approach to password penetration is supported by programs designed to try thousands of different character combinations in an attempt to find the one that matches the password.

Windows 7 can protect against brute force password penetration techniques by limiting the number of unsuccessful logon attempts allowed by each user account. When a potential infiltrator exceeds the number of allowed attempts, the system locks the account for a set period of time. To impose these limits, you can use Local Security Policy for stand-alone computers or Group Policy for AD DS networks.

To set account lockout parameters using Local Security Policy, use the following procedure.

CONFIGURE ACCOUNT LOCKOUT POLICIES

GET READY. Log on to Windows 7 using an account with administrator privileges.

1. Click Start, and then click Control Panel. The Control Panel window appears.
2. Click System and Security > Administrative Tools. The Administrative Tools window appears.
3. Double click Local Security Policy. The Local Security Policy console appears.
4. Expand the Account Policies header, and then click Account Lockout Policy. A list of policies appears in the details pane, as shown in Figure 10-5.

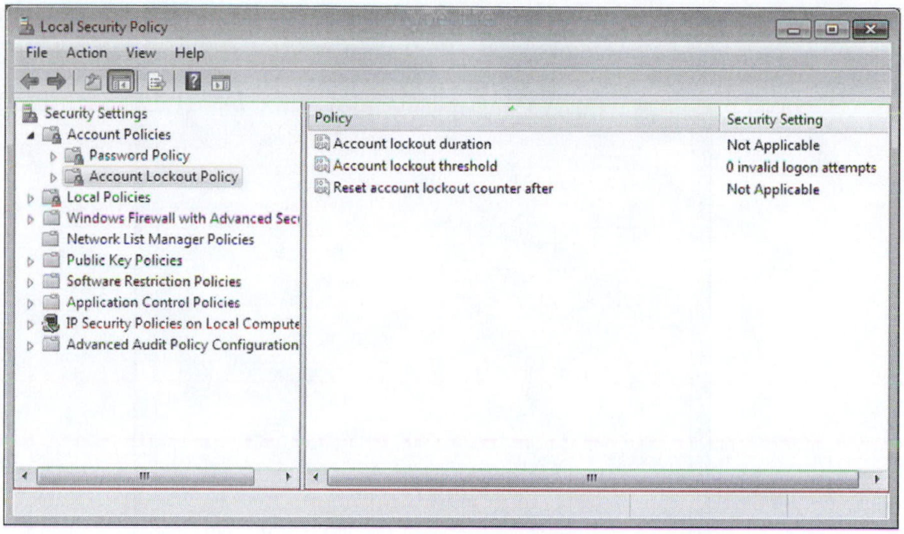

Figure 10-5

Account Lockout Policies in the Local Security Policy console

5. Double click one of the policies described in Table 10-2. The Properties sheet for the policy appears, as shown in Figure 10-6.

6. Configure the policy by setting a value using the spin box, radio button, or other control, and then click OK. The Properties sheet closes.

7. Repeat Steps 5 and 6 to configure other policies, if desired.

8. Close the Local Security Policy console and the Administrative Tools window.

Table 10-2

Windows Account Lockout Policy Settings

ACCOUNT LOCKOUT POLICY SETTING	VALUES AND FUNCTION
Account lockout duration	Determines the period of time that must pass after a lockout before Windows 7 automatically unlocks a user's account. The policy is not set by default, as it is viable only in conjunction with the Account Lockout Threshold policy. Possible values range from 0 to 99999 minutes (about 10 weeks). A low setting (5 to 15 minutes) is usually sufficient to reduce attacks significantly without unreasonably affecting legitimate users who are mistakenly locked out. A value of 0 requires an administrator to unlock the account manually. When the Account Lockout Threshold policy is activated, this policy is activated as well and set to a default value of 30 minutes.
Account lockout threshold	Specifies the number of invalid logon attempts that will trigger an account lockout. Possible values range from 0 to 999. A value that is too low (as few as three, for example) may cause lockouts due to normal user error during logon. A value of 0 prevents accounts from ever being locked out. The default value is 0.
Reset account lockout counter after	Specifies the period of time that must pass after an invalid logon attempt before the lockout counter resets to zero. Possible values range from 1 to 99999 minutes, and must be less than or equal to the account lockout duration. When the Account lockout threshold policy is activated, this policy is activated as well and set to a default value of 30.

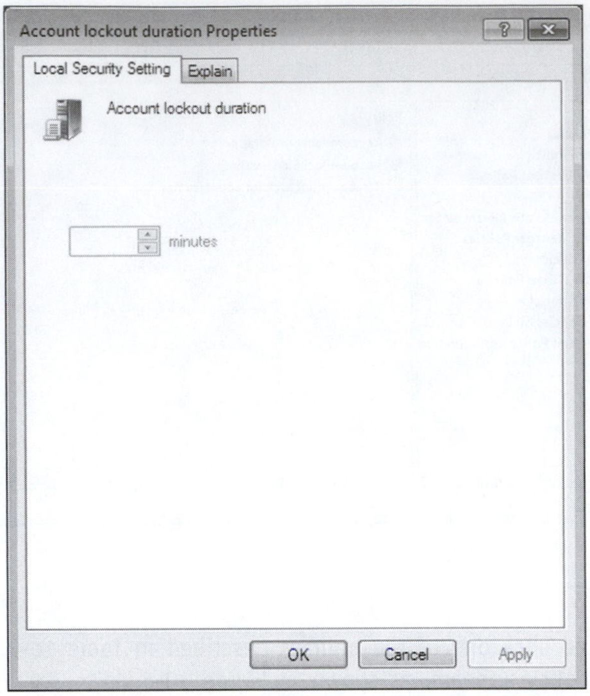

Figure 10-6

The Properties sheet of an
account lockout policy

TAKE NOTE * As with password policies, you can also deploy account lockout policies on an AD DS network using Group Policy.

USING CREDENTIAL MANAGER

Users and administrators alike often become frustrated when forced to re-enter passwords
whenever they have to access a protected resource. This is one reason why Microsoft modified
the default behavior of User Account Control in Windows 7 to eliminate elevation prompts
for administrative operating system tasks.

Credential Manager is a Windows 7 tool that stores the usernames and passwords people supply to servers and Web sites in a protected area called the Windows Vault. When a user selects
the *Remember my credentials* check box while authenticating in Windows Explorer, Internet
Explorer, or Remote Desktop Connection, as shown in Figure 10-7, the system adds the
credentials to the Windows Vault.

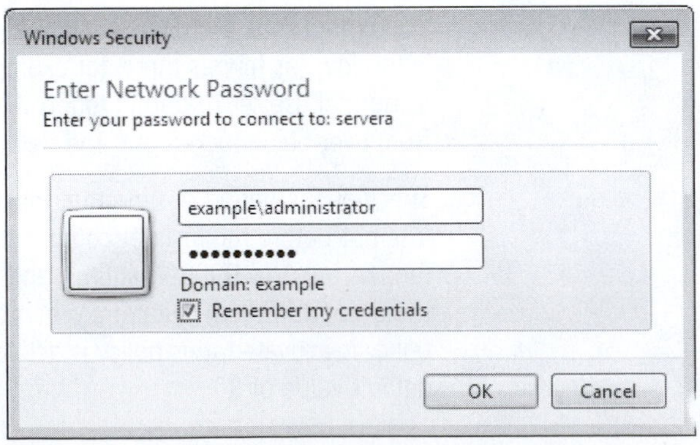

Figure 10-7

Credential Manager

From the Credential Manager window in Control Panel, you can see the resources for which the Windows Vault contains credentials, as shown in Figure 10-8, although you cannot view the passwords themselves.

Figure 10-8

Credential Manager

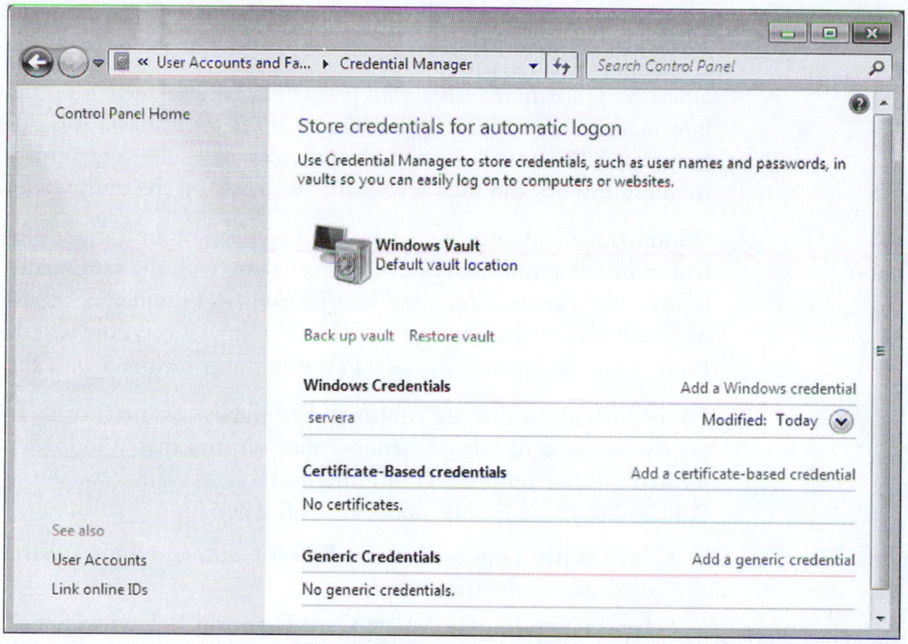

It is also possible to add credentials directly to the vault using Credential Manager, by clicking *Add a Windows credential*, or one of the similar links. The interface shown in Figure 10-9 then appears, in which you can specify the address of a resource and the credentials that go with it. In the same way, you can specify a resource and select a certificate from the computer's store.

Finally, you can back up the contents of the Windows Vault from Credential Manager and restore it to the same or another computer, to protect the credentials or migrate them.

Figure 10-9

The Add a Windows Credential window

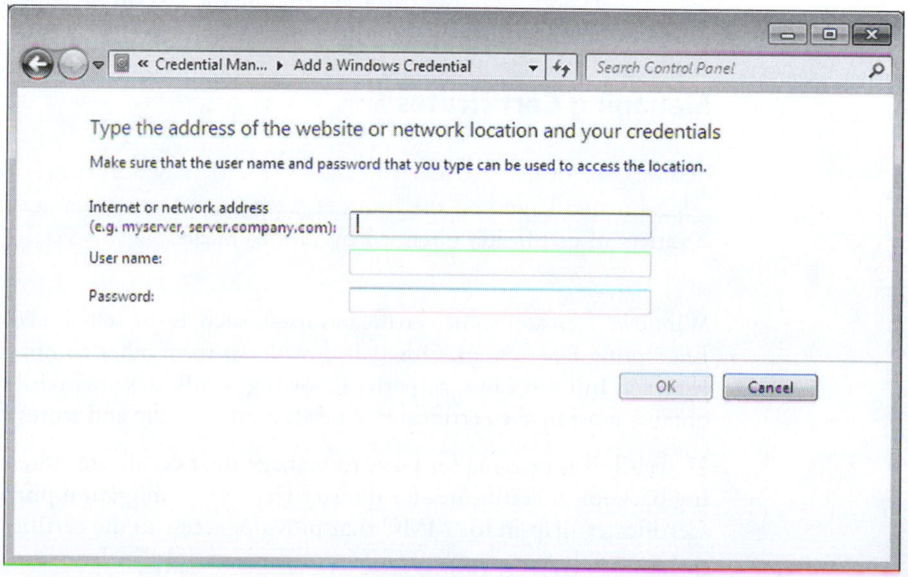

Using Smart Cards

Smart cards provide a high-security alternative to passwords for user authentication.

A smart card is a credit card-like device that contains a chip, on which is stored a digital certificate that serves as an identifier for a particular user. On a computer equipped with a card reader, a user can authenticate him- or herself by specifying a username and inserting the smart card.

Smart cards are more secure than passwords, because there is no practical way to duplicate the information they contain by guessing or brute force attack. It is possible for users to have their smart cards lost or stolen, but in most cases, they know when this occurs and can report the loss. An administrator can then revoke the certificate on the card, rendering it invalid and useless.

Windows has supported smart card authentication for some time, but until Windows 7, you had to install a third-party device driver along with the card reader hardware. By including support for the *Personal Identity Verification (PIV)* standard, published by the National Institute of Standards and Technology (NIST), Windows 7 can now obtain drivers for PIV smart cards from Windows Update, or use a PIV minidriver included with the operating system.

For organizations that are committed to the use of smart cards for authentication, there are two smart card-related Group Policy settings that Windows 7 supports. These settings, located in the Computer Configuration\Policies\Windows Settings\Security Settings\Local Policies\Security Options node, are as follows:

- **Interactive Logon: Require Smart Card:** Configures Windows 7 to allow only smart card user authentications.
- **Interactive Logon: Smart Card Removal Behavior:** Specifies how Windows 7 should behave when a user removes the smart card from the reader while logged on to the computer. The possible values are as follows:
  - **No action:** Enables the user to remove the smart card without affecting the session. This is the default setting.
  - **Lock Workstation:** Disables the workstation while leaving the session open until the user reinserts the smart card. This enables the user to leave the workstation temporarily without leaving the smart card and without having to log off.
  - **Force Logoff:** Causes the workstation to log the user off as soon as the smart card is removed.
  - **Disconnect if a Remote Desktop Services session:** Disconnects the computer from the Remote Desktop Services server without logging the user off from the session. The user can then resume the session by reinserting the smart card at the same or another computer.

Managing Certificates

Windows 7 uses digital certificates for a variety of authentication tasks, internally, on the local network, and on the Internet. Every user account has a certificate store containing a variety of certificates obtained by various means.

Windows 7 creates some certificates itself, such as the self-signed certificate it uses for the Encrypting File System. Others it downloads from other computers, such as servers on the Internet. In most cases, activities involving certificates are invisible to the user. Windows 7 obtains most of the certificates it needs automatically and stores them for future use.

However, it is possible for users to manage their certificate stores directly, including creating backups of certificates for disaster recovery or migration purposes. Windows 7 includes a Certificates snap-in for MMC that provides access to the certificate store, but the snap-in is not accessible from the Start menu or the Control Panel.

To access the Certificates snap-in, type certmgr.msc in the Start menu's search box. This loads the snap-in and points it at the current user account, as shown in Figure 10-10.

Figure 10-10

The Certificates snap-in

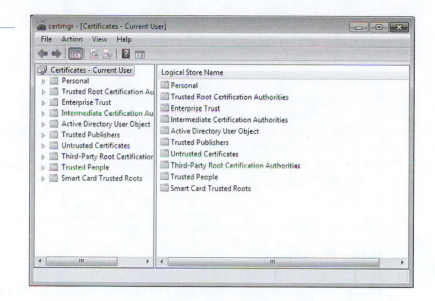

Double clicking one of the certificates in the store displays a Certificate dialog box like the one shown in Figure 10-11. This dialog box contains information about the certificate and the data stored in it.

Figure 10-11

A Certificate dialog box

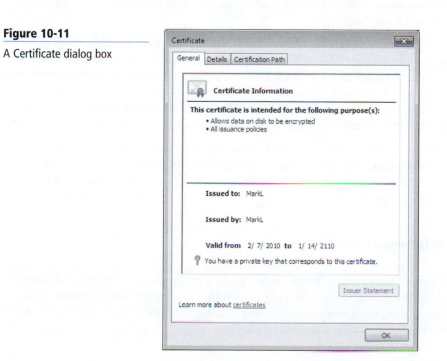

To back up a certificate to a file, right click it in the snap-in and, in the context menu, select All Tasks > Export, to launch the Certificate Export Wizard. This wizard prompts you to select a format for the file, as shown in Figure 10-12, and the location where you want to save it.

Figure 10-12

The Export File Format page in the Certificate Export Wizard

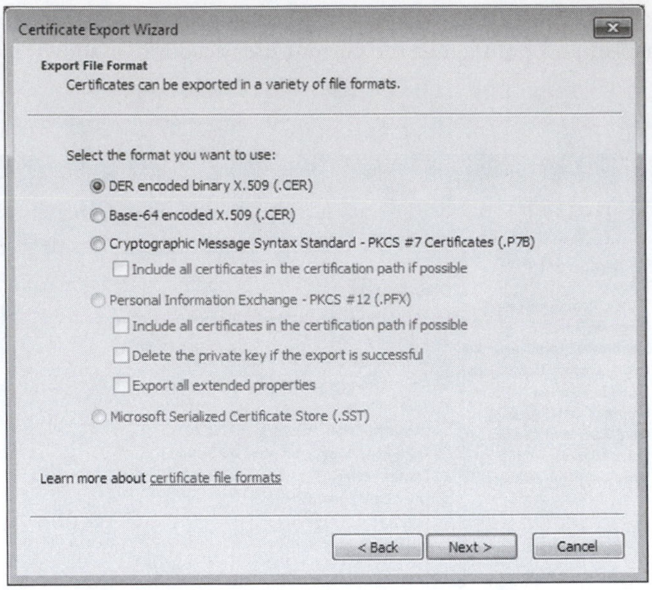

Using Biometrics

> Biometric authentication uses a scan of a physical characteristics to confirm the identity of a user.

Biometric authentication is theoretically more secure than a token-based or secret-based authentication method because the identifying characteristic is difficult or impossible to duplicate. The grisly stories of severed body parts being used to fool biometric scanners are (hopefully) fictitious because the technology exists to confirm that a finger or other appendage is still connected to a living body.

There are a great many third-party biometric authentication solutions available, most of which take the form of fingerprint scanners for laptop computers. Prior to Windows 7, the operating system included no support for biometric devices at all, and required the third-party vendor to supply a complete software solution along with the hardware. However, Windows 7 includes a new component called the ***Windows Biometric Framework***, which provides a core biometric functionality and a Biometric Device control panel.

Even with the Windows Biometric Framework, however, the reliability of these technologies and the security they provide can vary widely. Most biometric solutions include a secondary authentication method, such as a password or a smart card, for when the biometric scan fails. Others are multifactor solutions, requiring both a biometric scan and another form of authentication.

Elevating Privileges

> Since the Windows Vista release, Microsoft has made a concerted effort to persuade users not to log on to Windows for their everyday tasks using an administrative account. This practice not only makes accidental configuration changes more possible, it also increases the likelihood of intrusion by malevolent attackers.

The preferred mechanism for performing tasks that require administrative privileges is to use the Run As feature to execute a program using another account. Shortcuts in the Start menu have a *Run as administrator* option in their context menus, which causes standard users to receive a credential prompt and administrators to receive an elevation prompt, according to the system's normal User Account Control (UAC) practices.

It is also possible to use the Runas.exe command-line program to execute an application using any other account. The syntax for the Runas.exe program is as follows:

```
runas [/user:domain\user] [/profile] [/noprofile] [/savecred]
[/smartcard] [/env] [/netonly] [/trustlevel] [/showtrustlevels]
"program.exe /parameter"
```

- **/user:domain\user:** Specifies the account that Runas.exe should use to execute the program. The account can be specified in the form *domain\user* or *user@domain*. The domain variable can also be the name of a stand-alone workstation and *user* a local user account.
- **/profile:** Causes the Runas.exe program to load the profile of the account specified by the /user parameter. This is the default value.
- **/noprofile:** Prevents the Runas.exe program from loading the profile of the account specified by the /user parameter. Without the profile, the program cannot access the EFS-encrypted files belonging to the account specified by the /user parameter.
- **/savecred:** Causes the Runas.exe program to save the credentials for the account specified by the /user parameter in the Windows Vault or, in the case of a previously saved account, to use the credentials saved in the vault.
- **/smartcard:** Specifies that the credentials for the account specified by the \user parameter will be supplied using a smart card.
- **/env:** Causes the Runas.exe program to use the current environment, rather than the one of the account specified by the /user parameter.
- **/netonly:** Specifies that the credentials of the account specified by the /user variable are for remote access only.
- **"program.exe /parameter":** Specifies the name of the application that Runas. exe should run with elevated privileges, along with any of the application's necessary command-line parameters.

A typical example of a Runas command line would appear as follows:

```
runas /user:example\administrator "notepad.exe \script.vbs"
```

When you run the command, the program prompts for the password to the Administrator account, loads the user profile for the account, executes Notepad.exe, and then loads the Script.vbs file.

Troubleshooting Authentication Issues

The most common problem related to authentication experienced by Windows 7 users is password loss. There is no way for a user or an administrator to read a password from a user account on a Windows system, whether it is stored in the Security Account Manager (SAM), the Windows Vault, or an AD DS domain controller.

When a user loses a Windows 7 account password, there is no way to reclaim it; the only solution is to reset (i.e., change) the password. There are two ways of doing this: either the user resets his or her own password or an administrator resets it.

To reset your own password, you must supply the old one first. If you cannot do this, because you have lost or forgotten the old password, the only solution is to use a password reset disk. The password reset disk supplies the old password for you, enabling you to reset the password to a new value.

The problem with this solution is that you must have created a password-reset disk before losing your password. In the User Accounts control panel, the *Make changes to your user account* page for each user has a link that enables the user to run the Forgotten Password Wizard and create a password reset disk, using a floppy disk or a USB flash drive, as shown in Figure 10-13.

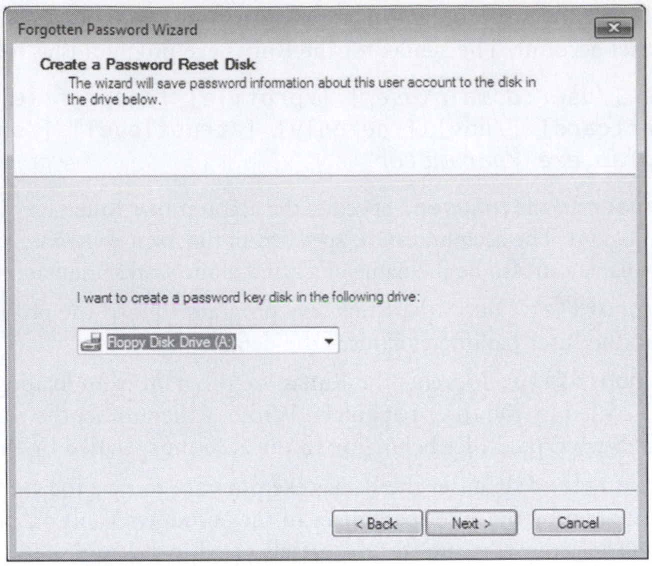

Figure 10-13

The Create a Password Reset Disk page in the Forgotten Password Wizard

When a user loses his or her password, and does not have a password reset disk, the only alternative is for an administrator to reset the password, using either the Local Users and Groups snap-in or the *Manage Accounts* page of the User Accounts control panel. Administrators can reset passwords without having to supply the old password first.

The problem, however, is that an administrative reset causes the user to lose access to all EFS-encrypted files, all certificates in the user's personal certificate store, and all passwords stored in the Windows Vault. These passwords might be recoverable from a backup of the Windows Vault or the EFS key, but it would be a lot easier if the user had created a password-reset disk in the first place.

Authorizing Users

Authentication confirms a user's identity. Authorization grants the user access to certain resources.

A successful authentication confirms that a user is who he or she purports to be, but logging on successfully does not guarantee access to system resources. Some authenticated users have full access to the system, while others might have almost none. The difference between the two is the resources that they are authorized to access.

USING PERMISSIONS

The most commonly used mechanisms for authorizing users in Windows 7 are the NTFS, share, and registry permission systems. By adjusting permissions in the protected resources, administrators can specify who should have access to them and what degree of access users should receive.

For more information on managing permissions, see Lesson 6, "Sharing Resources."

CONFIGURING USER RIGHTS

Some people confuse the concept of user permissions with that of user rights; in Windows 7, these are two different concepts. In Windows 7, *user rights* are policies that define specific operating system functions. For example, in order to sit down at a Windows 7 computer and log on, users must not only have accounts, they also must possess the *Allow log on locally* user right.

Administrators can assign user rights to individual users, but as with permissions, this is rare. The more practical alternative is to assign user rights to groups and then add individual users to the groups as needed.

In fact, Windows 7 does this for you, by default. The built-in local groups on a computer running Windows 7 receive their special capabilities through default user rights assignments. For example, the Remote Desktop Users group has been assigned the *Allow log on through Remote Desktop Services* user right.

To assign user rights to users or groups, you can open the Local Security Policy snap-in on a Windows 7 workstation and browse to Security Settings\Local Policies\User Rights Assignment, as shown in Figure 10-14. In an AD DS environment, you open a GPO and browse to the Computer Configuration\Policies\Windows Settings\Security Settings\Local Policies\User Rights Assignment node. In both interfaces, there are 44 user rights assignments that you can grant to local or domain users and groups.

Figure 10-14

User Rights Assignments

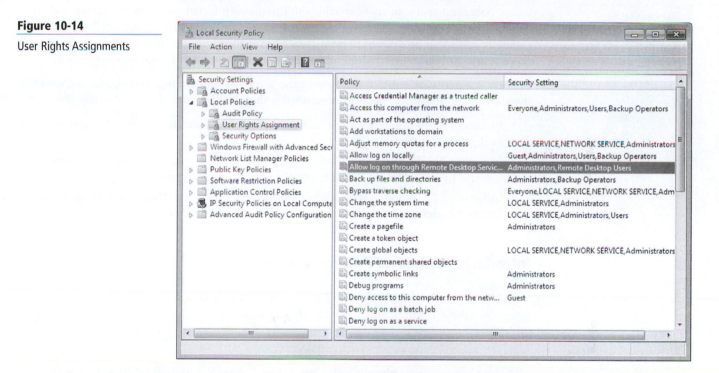

■ Defending Against Malware

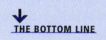

THE BOTTOM LINE

Malware is one of the primary threats to Windows 7 security, and the operating system includes a variety of tools that you can use to combat it. The following sections examine these tools and how to implement and configure them.

Windows 7 holds security as one its primary goals. Beginning with the Windows XP Service Pack 2 release, Windows has monitored the state of the security mechanisms included with the operating system and warns the user if any components are misconfigured, outdated, or not functioning.

Chief among the threats to Windows 7 computers is malicious software created specifically for the purpose of infiltrating or damaging a computer system without the user's knowledge or consent. This type of software includes a variety of technologies, including viruses, Trojan horses, worms, spyware, and adware. The term most commonly used to collectively refer to these malicious software technologies is *malware*.

The types of malware to which Windows 7 is susceptible range from the relatively innocuous to the extremely destructive. The effects it can have on a Windows 7 computer include the following:

- Collect usage information about the computer user and transmit to an Internet server.
- Display advertisements on the user's system.
- Use the system's email address book to send spam.
- Attach code to document files that spreads to other files on any system opening the document.
- Install and run a program that enables a remote user to take control of the system.
- Damage or destroy the files stored on the computer.
- Infiltrate the computer's boot sector and spread to other systems.

Malware is, in most cases, introduced onto a computer by a deliberate action on the part of a user. Someone opens an email attachment, installs an infected program, or accesses a dangerous Web site, and the malicious code is introduced to the system. Windows 7 includes a variety of tools that attempt to prevent users from inadvertently infecting their computers and also attempt to block the activities of malicious software programs once they are present.

Security is a pervasive concern throughout the Windows 7 operating system, and as a result there are some Windows 7 security mechanisms that are discussed elsewhere in this text:

- In Lesson 7, "Working with Applications," you learn about the security features included in Internet Explorer 8.
- In Lesson 9, "Working with Workgroups and Domains," you learn how User Account Control helps to prevent malware from obtaining administrative privileges.
- In Lesson 12, "Working with Mobile Computers," you learn about the security features specifically designed for use on mobile and wireless computers.

Introducing Windows 7 Action Center

> The Windows 7 Action Center ensures that your system is protected from malware intrusion by notifying you if any of the Windows 7 security mechanisms are not running properly.

Like the Network and Sharing Center, the Action Center is a centralized console that enables users and administrators to access, monitor, and configure the various Windows 7 security mechanisms. The primary function of the Action Center is to provide an automatic notification system that alerts users when the system is vulnerable.

Action Center is a service that starts automatically and runs continuously on Windows 7 computers, by default. The service constantly monitors the different security mechanisms running on the computer. If Action Center detects a mechanism that is not functioning properly for any of several reasons, it displays an icon in the notification area (formerly known as the taskbar tray) to inform the user of the condition, as shown in Figure 10-15.

Figure 10-15

The Action Center menu in the notification area

2 important messages

Find an antivirus program online (Important)

Set up Windows Update (Important)

Open Action Center

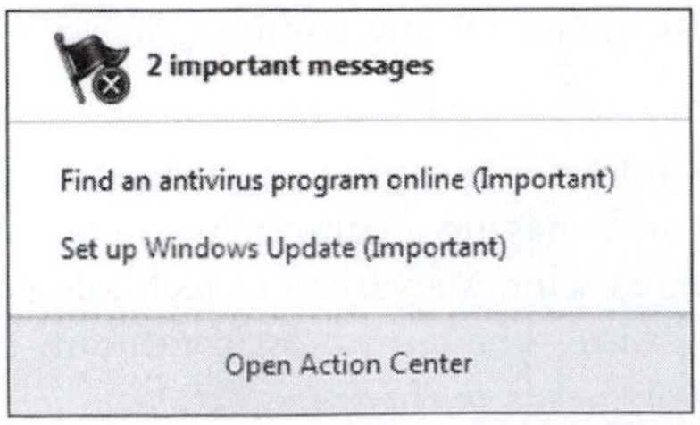

TAKE NOTE*

The Windows 7 Action Center is not limited to monitoring Microsoft security solutions. The service can also monitor third-party programs for their currency and operational status.

ACCESSING ACTION CENTER

When the user clicks the notification area icon to open the Action Center window (or clicks Start > Control Panel > System and Security > Action Center), the system displays information about the problems it has discovered, and links possible solutions.

For example, the Action Center window shown in Figure 10-16 contains a Virus Protection warning. Clicking *Find a program online* opens a web page on Microsoft's site linking to various providers of virus protection software. In the same way, clicking *Change settings* in the Windows Update warning box opens a Choose a Windows Update option dialog box, from which you can activate the Windows Update client.

Figure 10-16

The Action Center window

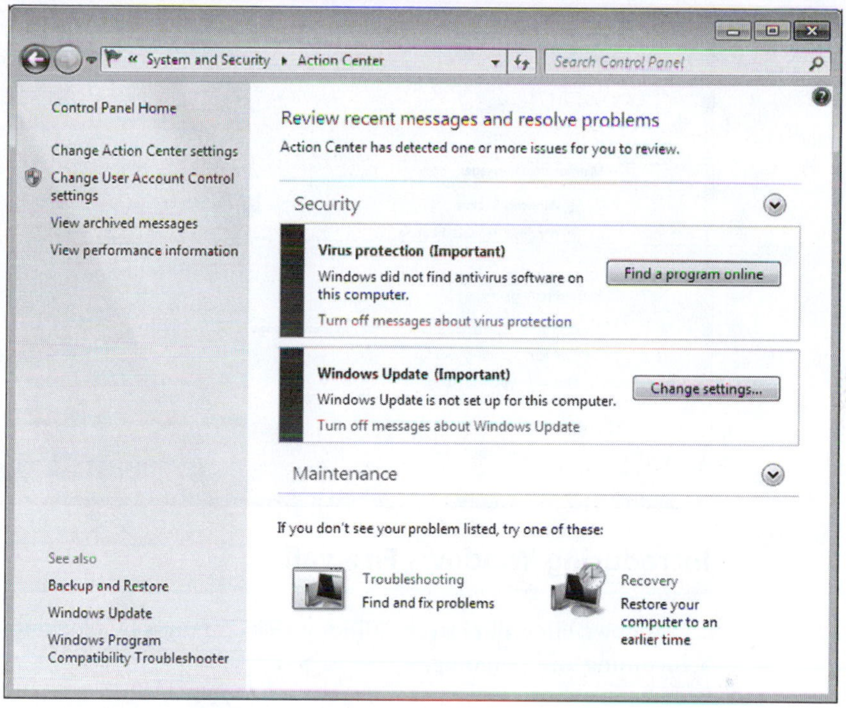

The Action Center window is divided into two main sections: Security and Maintenance. The Security section, in addition to monitoring the computer's security status, provides users with a single point of access to information about Windows 7 security, in the form of the following indicators:

- Network firewall
- Windows Update
- Virus Protection
- Spyware and unwanted software protection
- Internet security settings
- User Account Control
- Network Access Protection

The Maintenance section contains these indicators:

- Check for solutions to problem reports
- Backup
- Check for updates
- Troubleshooting: System Maintenance

Each of these indicators displays the current status of the security or maintenance feature and, if appropriate, supplies a link to the controls for that feature.

Links to other related features appear on the left side of the window, including a link to the Change Action Center Settings window, as shown in Figure 10-17. From this window, you can control which messages appear in the Action Center interface.

Figure 10-17

The Change Action Center Settings window

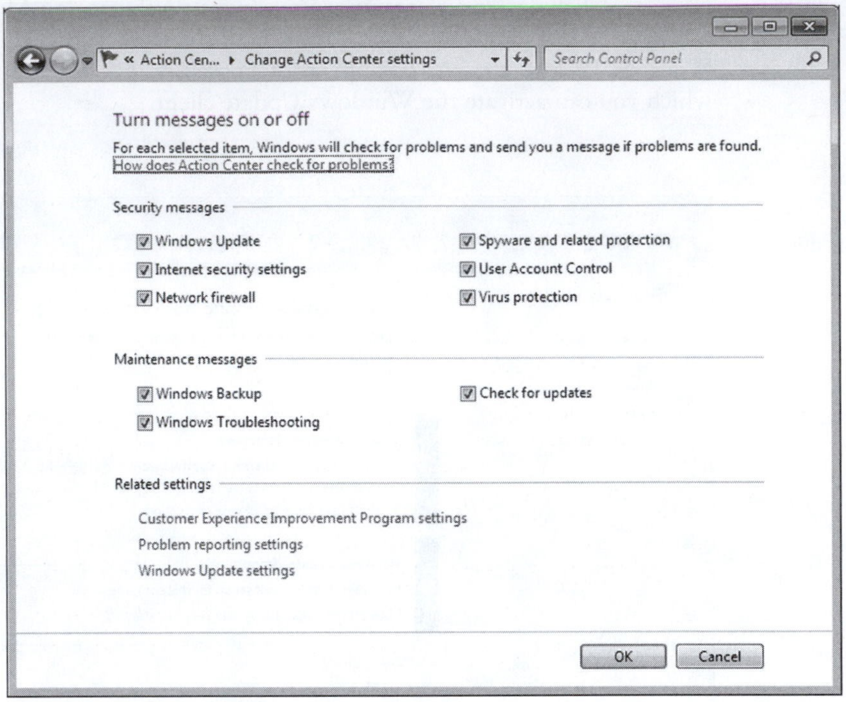

Introducing Windows Firewall

Windows Firewall protects Windows 7 computers by blocking dangerous traffic, both incoming and outgoing.

As discussed in Lesson 5, "Connecting to a Network," a *firewall* is a software program that protects a computer by allowing certain types of network traffic in and out of the system while blocking others. Firewalls are essentially packet filters that examine the contents of packets and the traffic patterns to and from the network to determine which packets should be allowed passage through the filter.

CERTIFICATION READY?
Configure Windows Firewall.
4.4

Network connections are all but ubiquitous in the computing world these days. All business computers are networked, and virtually all home computers have an Internet connection. Many homes have local area networks as well. Network connections provide Windows 7 users with access to virtually unlimited resources, but any door that allows data out can also allow data in. Some of the hazards that firewalls protect against are as follows:

- Trojan horse applications that users inadvertently download and run can open a connection to a computer on the Internet, enabling an attacker on the outside to run programs or store data on the system.
- A mobile computer can be compromised while connected to a public network and then brought onto a private network, compromising the resources there.
- Network scanner applications can probe systems for unguarded ports, which are essentially unlocked doors that attackers can use to gain access to the system.
- Attackers that obtain passwords by illicit means, such as social engineering, can use remote access technologies to log on to a computer from another location and compromise its data and programming.

UNDERSTANDING FIREWALLS

As noted in Lesson 5, firewalls typically base their filtering on the TCP/IP characteristics at the network, transport, and application layers, as follows:

- **IP addresses:** Represent specific computers on the network.
- **Protocol numbers:** Identify the transport layer protocol being used by the packets.
- **Port numbers:** Identify specific applications running on the computer.

To filter traffic, firewalls use *rules* that specify which packets are allowed to pass through the firewall and which are blocked. Firewalls can work in two ways, as follows:

- Admit all traffic, except that which conforms to the applied rules
- Block all traffic, except that which conforms to the applied rules

Generally speaking, blocking all traffic by default is the more secure arrangement. From the firewall administrator's standpoint, you start with a completely blocked system, and then start testing your applications. When an application fails to function properly because network access is blocked, you create a rule that opens up the ports the application needs to communicate.

This is the method that the Windows Firewall service in Windows 7 uses by default for incoming network traffic. The default rules preconfigured into the firewall are designed to admit the traffic used by standard Windows networking functions, such as file and printer sharing. For outgoing network traffic, Windows Firewall uses the other method, allowing all traffic to pass except that which conforms to a rule.

MONITORING WINDOWS FIREWALL

Windows Firewall is one of the programs monitored by the Action Center service. The main Action Center window indicates whether Windows Firewall is running, and also whether any third-party firewall products are running.

When you open the Start menu and click Control Panel > System and Security > Windows Firewall, a Windows Firewall window appears, displaying the firewall's status in greater detail, as shown in Figure 10-18.

Figure 10-18

The Windows Firewall window

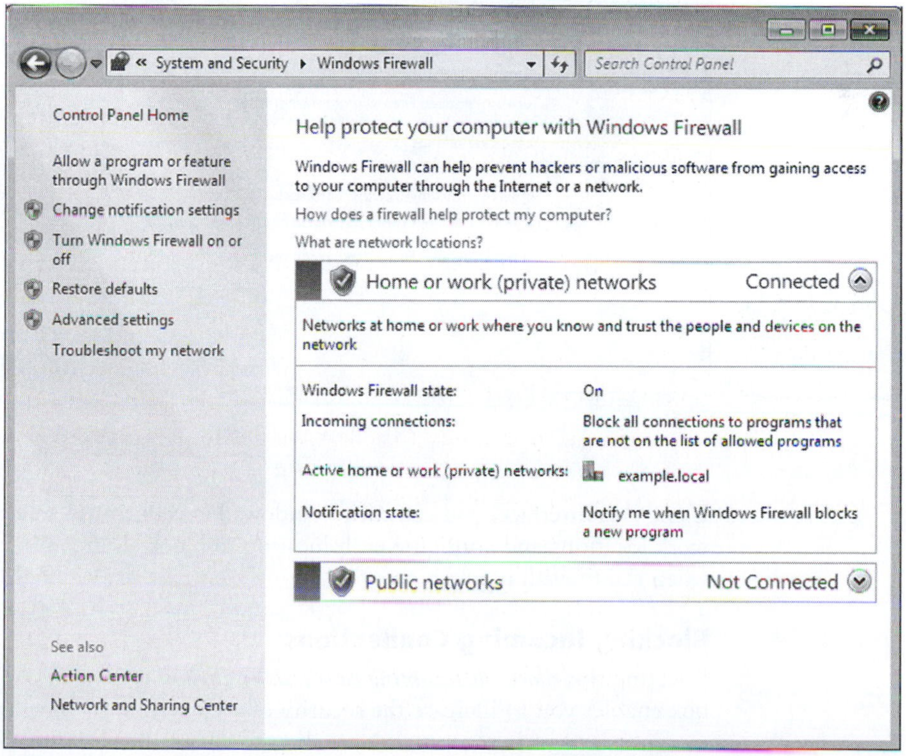

The Windows Firewall window contains expandable headings for the computer's network locations: home or work, public, and domain (if the computer is joined to an AD DS domain). Each of the headings contains the following information:

- Whether the computer is connected to a domain, private, or public network
- Whether the Windows Firewall service is currently turned on or off
- Whether inbound and outbound connections are blocked
- Whether users are notified when a program is blocked

Windows Firewall maintains a separate profile for each of the network locations, so you can have a different firewall configuration for each one. Whenever you are working with Windows Firewall settings, you must be conscious of the profile to which the settings apply.

USING THE WINDOWS FIREWALL CONTROL PANEL

On the left side of the Windows Firewall window is a series of links that enable you to change the firewall notification settings, configure Windows Firewall to allow a specific program through its barrier, turn Windows Firewall on and off, and configure advanced firewall settings.

Clicking *Change notification settings* or *Turn Windows firewall on or off* displays the *Customize settings for each type of network* dialog box, as shown in Figure 10-19. As in the Windows firewall window, controls for the domain profile only appear when the computer is joined to an AD DS domain.

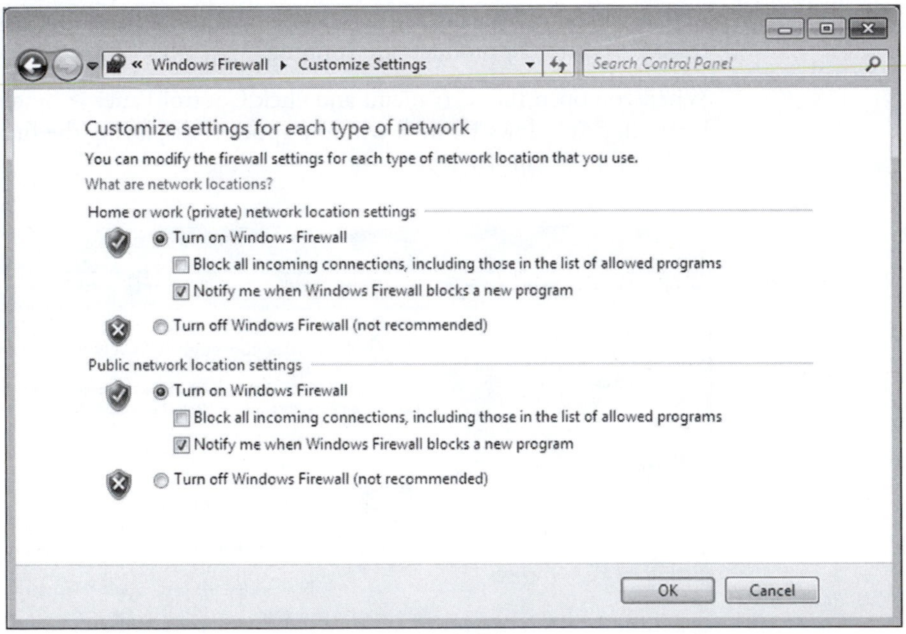

Figure 10-19

The Customize settings for each type of network dialog box

Using this interface, you can turn Windows Firewall completely on or off for each of the network locations and configure each location to block all incoming traffic and notify the user when the firewall blocks a program.

Blocking Incoming Connections

Selecting the *Block all incoming connections, including those in the list of allowed programs* check box enables you to increase the security of your system by blocking all unsolicited attempts to connect to your computer. Note, however, that this does not prevent you from performing common networking tasks, such as accessing Web sites and sending or receiving emails. These activities are not unsolicited connection attempts; they begin with the client contacting the server first. When the firewall detects the outgoing traffic from your web browser to a web server on the Internet, for example, it knows that it should admit the incoming response from the server.

Allowing Programs through the Firewall

Users might want to modify the firewall settings in other ways also, typically because a specific application requires access to a port not anticipated by the firewall's preconfigured rules. Clicking *Allow a program or feature through Windows Firewall* opens the *Allow programs to communicate through Windows Firewall* dialog box, as shown in Figure 10-20. In this dialog box, you can open up a port through the firewall for specific programs and features installed on the computer, simply by selecting the appropriate check boxes.

Figure 10-20

The Allow programs to communicate through Windows Firewall dialog box

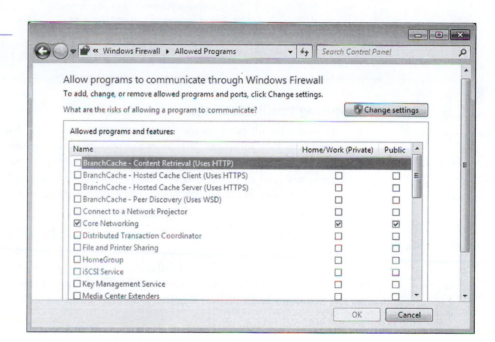

Opening a port in your firewall is an inherently dangerous activity. The more holes you make in a wall, the greater the likelihood that intruders will get in. For this reason, the Windows Firewall controls in the Windows 7 Control Panel are quite limited, more so than in Windows Vista. In Windows 7, you cannot open up specific port numbers using Control Panel; you can only select from a list of installed applications and features. For full access to Windows Firewall, you must use the Windows Firewall with Advanced Security console, as discussed in the next section.

USING THE WINDOWS FIREWALL WITH ADVANCED SECURITY CONSOLE

The Windows Firewall with Advanced Security console provides direct access to the rules that control the behavior of Windows Firewall. To access the console, open Control Panel from the Start menu, and then click *System* and *Security* > *Administrative Tools* > *Windows Firewall with Advanced Security*. The Windows Firewall with Advanced Security console appears, as shown in Figure 10-21.

Figure 10-21

The Windows Firewall with Advanced Security console

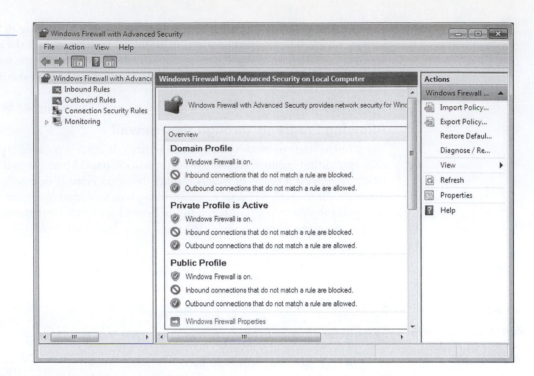

Configuring Profile Settings

At the top of the details pane, in the Overview section, are status displays for the computer's three possible network locations. Windows Firewall maintains separate profiles for each of the three possible network locations: domain, private, and public. If you connect the computer to a different network, as in the case of a laptop computer that you bring to an Internet "hot spot" in a coffee shop, Windows Firewall loads a different configuration for that profile and a different set of rules.

As you can tell from the Overview display, the default Windows Firewall settings call for the same basic configuration for all three profiles: the firewall is turned on, incoming traffic is blocked unless it matches a rule, and outgoing traffic is allowed unless it matches a rule. You can change this default behavior by clicking the Windows Firewall Properties link, which displays the Windows Firewall with Advanced Security on Local Computer Properties sheet, as shown in Figure 10-22.

Figure 10-22

The Windows Firewall with Advanced Security on Local Computer Properties sheet

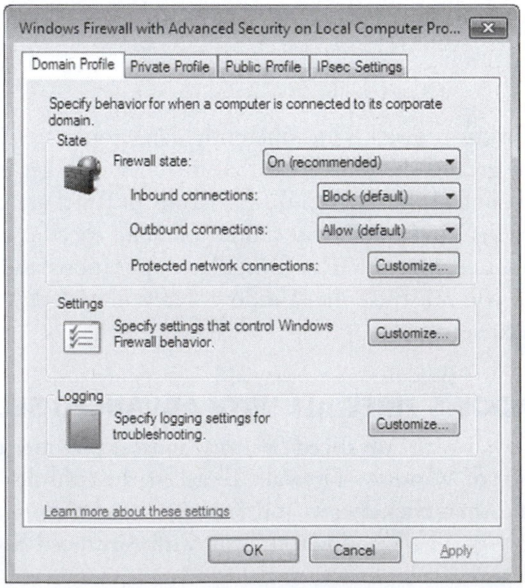

In this Properties sheet, each of the three location profiles has a tab with identical controls that enable you to modify the default profile settings. You can, for example, configure the firewall to shut down completely when it is connected to a domain network, and turn the firewall on with its most protective settings when you connect the computer to a public network. You can also configure the firewall's notification option, which specifies whether the firewall should display a message to the user when it blocks a program, and its logging behavior.

The most important settings in the Properties sheet are those that establish the default behavior for each profile, because these settings determine the nature of the rules that Windows Firewall will use. In the default settings, *Inbound connections* is set to Block, so the rules you create must allow certain types of traffic to pass through the firewall. If you change the default to allow inbound connections, then you must create rules that block certain types of traffic. The setting for *Outbound connections* are the opposite, by default.

Creating Rules

Selecting programs in the Windows Firewall control panel is a relatively friendly method for working with firewall rules. In the Windows Firewall with Advanced Security console, you can work with the rules in their raw form. Selecting either Inbound Rules or Outbound Rules in the scope pane displays a list of all the rules operating in that direction, as shown in Figure 10-23. The rules that are currently operational have a check mark in a green circle, while the rules not in force are grayed out.

TAKE NOTE*

It is important to remember that in the Windows Firewall with Advanced Security console, you are always working with a complete list of rules for all of the profiles, while in the Windows Firewall Settings dialog box, you are working only with the rules that apply to the currently active profile.

Figure 10-23

The Inbound Rules list in the Windows Firewall with Advanced Security console

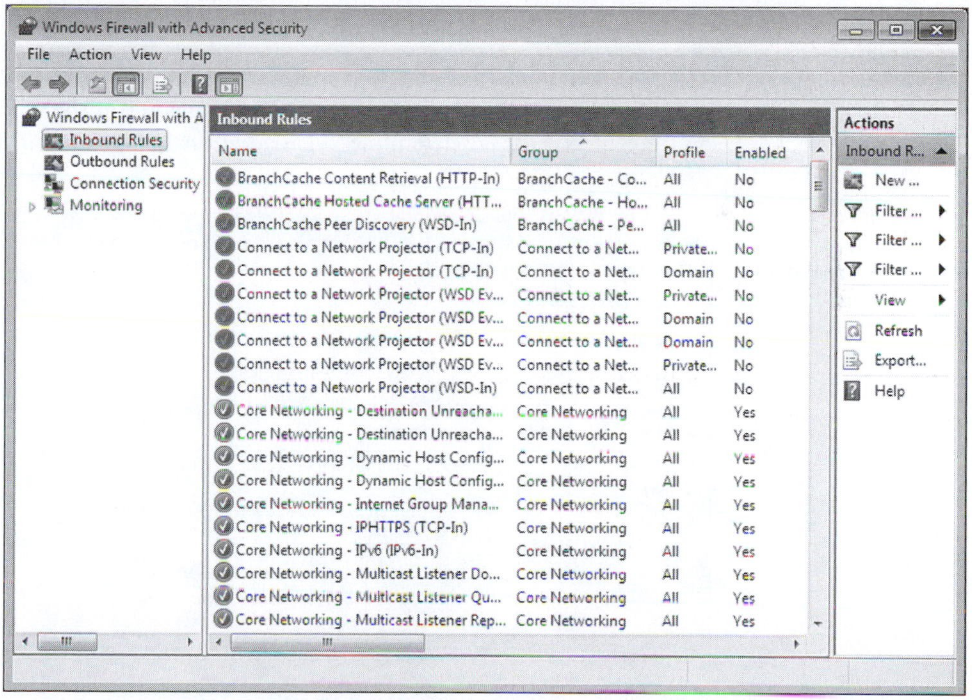

The default rules for three profiles differ, with the public profile providing the most secure environment and the private profile the least. Table 10-3 lists some of the primary networking services in Windows 7 and their default firewall settings for each profile. This is a highly simplified list, as most of these services use a variety of protocols that all require their own rules for incoming and outgoing traffic. When you modify the default networking behavior in Windows 7—such as when you enable Network Discovery in the Advanced Sharing Settings control panel—the controls change the default settings for the Windows Firewall rules.

Table 10-3

Default Windows Firewall Rules Settings

SERVICE	PRIVATE	PUBLIC	DOMAIN
Core Networking	Enabled	Enabled	Enabled
File and Printer Sharing	Enabled	Disabled	Disabled
Homegroup	Disabled	N/A	N/A
Network Discovery	Enabled	Disabled	Disabled
Remote Desktop	Disabled	Disabled	Disabled

TAKE NOTE *

Whenever a network service fails to function as expected, checking the rules for that service in the Windows Firewall with Advanced Security console should be one your first troubleshooting steps.

Creating new rules with this interface provides a great deal more flexibility than the Windows Firewall control panel. When you right click the *Inbound Rules* or *Outbound Rules* node and select *New Rule* from the context menu, the New Rule Wizard, shown in Figure 10-24, takes you through the process of configuring the following sets of parameters:

- **Rule Type:** Specifies whether you want to create a program rule, a port rule, a variant on one of the predefined rules, or a custom rule. This selection determines which of the following pages the wizard displays.
- **Program:** Specifies whether the rule applies to all programs, to one specific program, or to a specific service.

TAKE NOTE *

The New Inbound Rule and New Outbound Rule Wizards are adaptive, meaning that you will not see all of the pages listed here each time you run the wizard. The option you select on the Rule Type page determines what additional pages appear next.

Figure 10-24

The New Inbound Rule Wizard

New Inbound Rule Wizard

Rule Type

Select the type of firewall rule to create.

Steps:
- Rule Type
- Program
- Action
- Profile
- Name

What type of rule would you like to create?

○ **Program**
Rule that controls connections for a program.

○ **Port**
Rule that controls connections for a TCP or UDP port.

○ **Predefined:**

BranchCache - Content Retrieval (Uses HTTP)

Rule that controls connections for a Windows experience.

○ **Custom**
Custom rule.

Learn more about rule types

< Back   Next >   Cancel

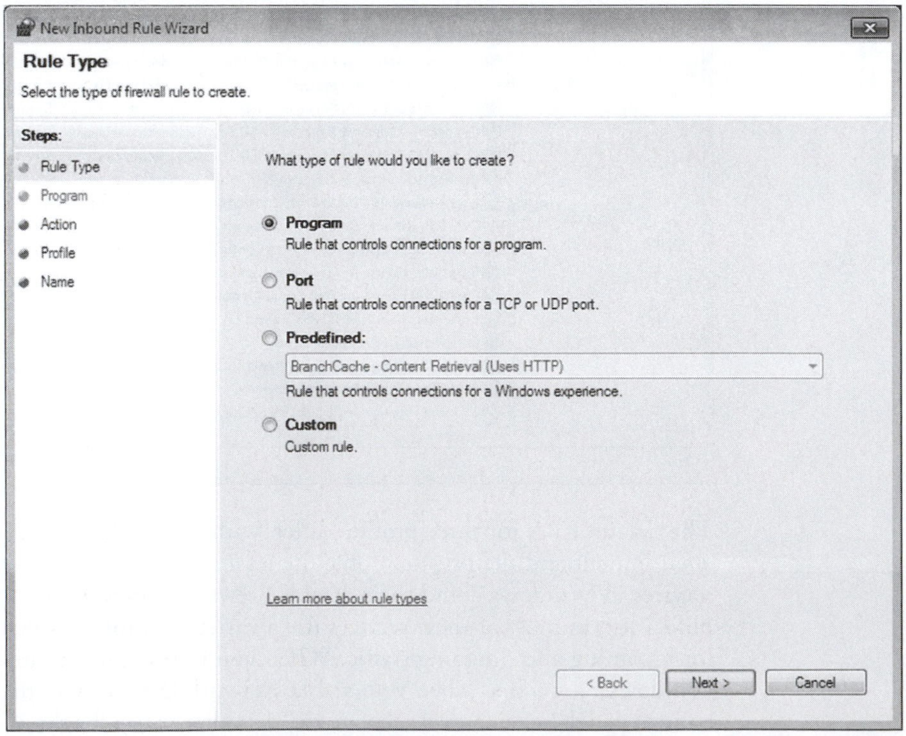

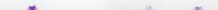

- **Protocol and Ports:** Specifies the protocol and the local and remote ports to which the rule applies. This enables you to specify the exact types of traffic that the rule should block or allow.
- **Scope:** Specifies the IP addresses of the local and remote systems to which the rule applies. This enables you to block or allow traffic between specific computers.
- **Action:** Specifies the action the firewall should take when a packet matches the rule. You configure the rule to allow traffic if it is blocked by default, or block traffic if it is allowed by default. You can also configure the rule to allow traffic only when the connection between the communicating computers is secured using IPsec. This is called an *authenticated exception*.
- **Profile:** Specifies the profile(s) to which the rule should apply: domain, private, and/or public.
- **Name:** Specifies a name and (optionally) a description for the rule.

The rules you can create using the New Rule Wizards range from simple program rules to highly complex and specific rules that block or allow only specific types of traffic between specific computers. The more complicated the rules become, however, the more you have to know about TCP/IP communications in general and the specific behavior of your applications. Modifying the default firewall settings to accommodate some special applications is relatively simple, but creating an entirely new firewall configuration is a formidable task.

Using Filters

Although what a firewall does is sometimes referred to as packet filtering, in the Windows Firewall with Advanced Security console, the term *filter* is used to refer to a feature that enables you to display rules according to the profile they apply to, their current state, or the group to which they belong.

For example, to display only the rules that apply to the public profile, click *Action > Filter By Profile > Filter By Public Profile*. The display changes to show only the rules that apply to the public profile. In the same way, you can apply a filter that causes the console to display only the rules that are currently turned on, or the rules that belong to a particular group. Click *Action > Clear All Filters* to return to the default display showing all of the rules.

Creating Connection Security Rules

Windows 7 includes a feature in Windows Firewall that incorporates IPsec data protection into the Windows Firewall. The IP Security (IPsec) standards are a collection of documents that define a method for securing data while it is in transit over a TCP/IP network. IPsec includes a connection establishment routine, during which computers authenticate each other before transmitting data, and a technique called *tunneling*, in which data packets are encapsulated within other packets for their protection.

> **⊕ MORE INFORMATION**
>
> Data protection technologies such as the Windows 7 Encrypting File System (EFS) and BitLocker protect data while it is stored on a drive. However, they do nothing to protect data while it is being transmitted over the network, because they both decrypt the data before sending it. IPsec, by contrast, protects data while it is in transit.

In addition to inbound and outbound rules, the Windows Firewall with Advanced Security console enables you to create connection security rules, using the New Connection Security Rule Wizard. Connection security rules define the type of protection you want to apply to the communications that conform to Windows Firewall rules.

When you right click the *Connection Security Rules* node and select *New Rule* from the context menu, the New Connection Security Rule Wizard, shown in Figure 10-25, takes you through the process of configuring the following sets of parameters:

- **Rule Type:** Specifies the basic function of the rule, such as to isolate computers based on authentication criteria, to exempt certain computers (such as infrastructure servers) from authentication, to authenticate two specific computers or groups of computers, or to tunnel communications between two computers. You can also create custom rules combining these functions.

- **Endpoints:** Specifies the IP addresses of the computer that will establish a secured connection before transmitting any data.

- **Requirements:** Specifies whether authentication between two computers should be requested or required in each direction.

- **Authentication Method:** Specifies the type of authentication the computers should use when establishing a connection.

- **Profile:** Specifies the profile(s) to which the rule should apply: domain, private, and/or public.

- **Name:** Specifies a name and (optionally) a description for the rule.

Figure 10-25

The New Connection Security Rule Wizard

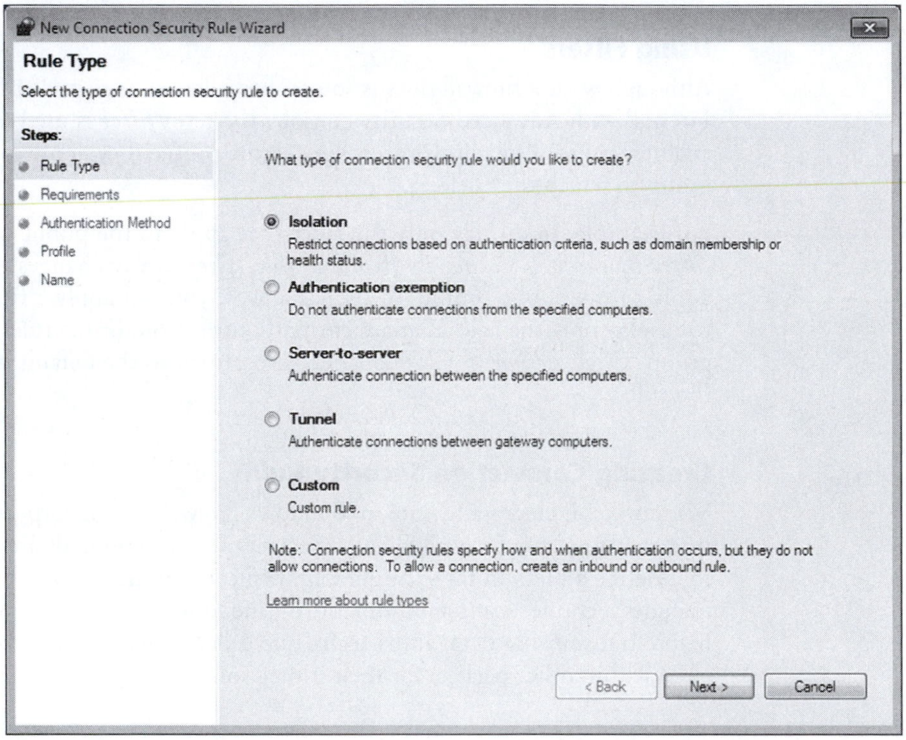

CONFIGURING WINDOWS FIREWALL WITH GROUP POLICY

As with many other Windows 7 features, configuring Windows Firewall on individual computers is not practical in an enterprise network environment. However, it is possible to configure firewall settings on Windows workstations using Group Policy.

When you browse to the Computer Configuration\Policies\Windows Settings\Security Settings\ Windows Firewall with Advanced Security node in a GPO, you see the interface shown in Figure 10-26, which is similar to that of the Windows Firewall with Advanced Security console.

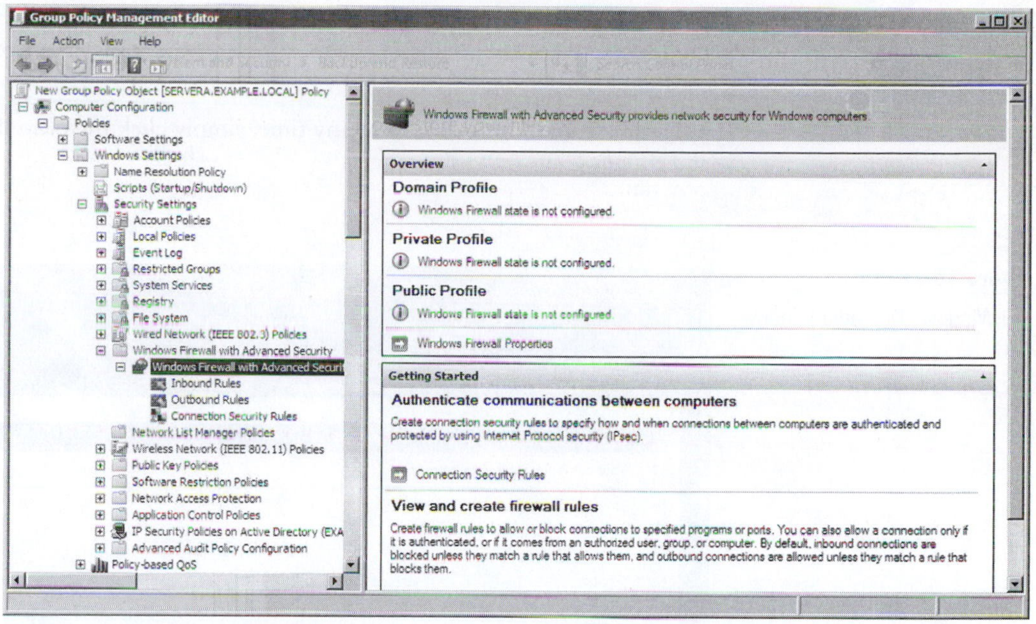

Figure 10-26

The Windows Firewall with Advanced Security node in a GPO

Clicking *Windows Firewall Properties* opens a dialog box with the same controls as the Windows Firewall with Advanced Security on Local Computer Properties sheet and clicking *Inbound Rules and Outbound Rules* launches the same wizards as the console.

Introducing Windows Defender

Windows Defender is a Windows 7 application that prevents the infiltration of spyware into the system.

Originally, the people who created and disseminated viruses and other types of malware did so purely out of gratuitous vandalism. Today, the primary motive is profit, and this has led to the development of new kinds of malware. *Spyware*, for example, is a type of software that gathers information about computer users and transmits it back to the attacker.

The type of information spyware can gather ranges from the trivial to the critical. Some programs simply collect information about users' web surfing habits, the better to target potential customers with their marketing efforts. Others collect personal and confidential information about the computer's users, including passwords and account numbers, which attackers can use for identity theft and other crimes. In addition to compromising the security of a computer, spyware can also affect its performance by consuming system resources.

Windows 7 includes an application called Windows Defender that helps to defend against spyware by scanning the places where it most commonly infiltrates a computer. Spyware is typically a program that is installed along with other software that the user deliberately downloads and installs. To be effective, spyware has to be running all the time, so the installer typically places the program in one of the standard Windows preloading mechanisms, such as the Startup folder and the Run key in the registry. Windows Defender has a set of predefined definitions that it searches for in these places, which help it to identify specific threats.

Windows Defender also includes real-time monitoring, which attempts to prevent spyware from infiltrating the computer as it is installed. When Defender detects a potentially dangerous installation, it alerts and prompts the user to ignore, quarantine, or remove the program, or add it to an Always Allow list that permits it to run on the computer.

Windows Defender runs by default on Windows 7 computers, and performs a scan every day at 2:00 a.m. Windows Update also supplies Defender with signature updates on a regular basis, to keep the program current. When you open the main Windows Defender window,

 **WARNING** Windows Defender is not a full-featured antivirus program, as it cannot detect or remove true viruses, Trojans, and other types of malware. Windows 7 does not include a comprehensive antivirus solution, and Microsoft recommends that you purchase and install a third-party antivirus product. In fact, Windows Action Center monitors the computer for the presence of antivirus software and warns users when it fails to find it, even when Windows Defender is present and running.

as shown in Figure 10-27, by typing *Windows Defender* on the Start menu's search box, the program displays the results of the most recent scan, as well as information about the current configuration settings.

To perform an additional scan at any time, simply click the *Scan* link at the top of the window, and the program starts running.

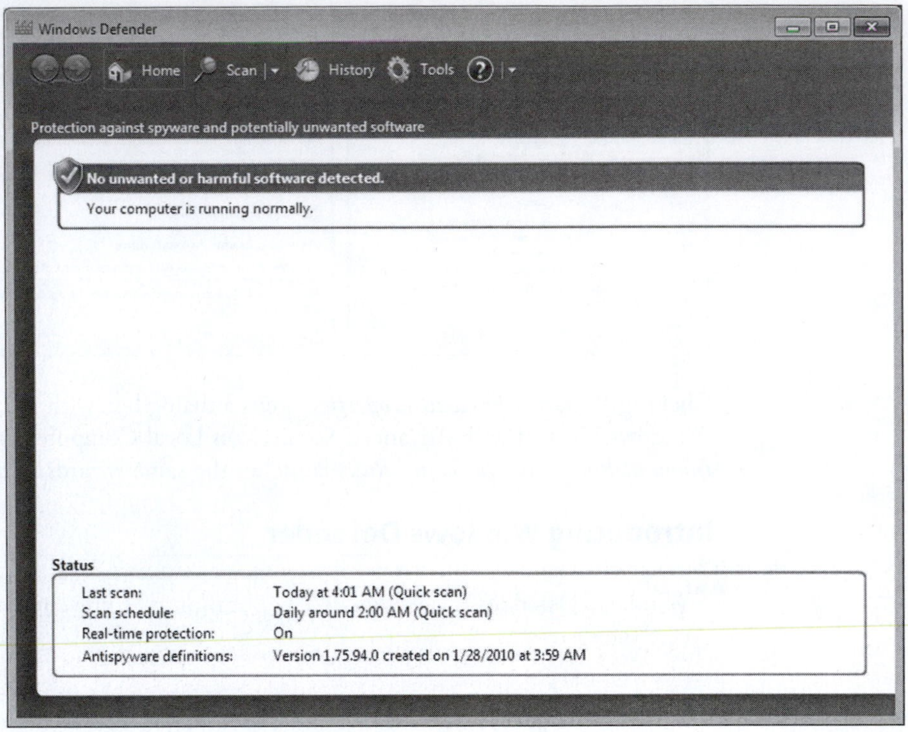

Figure 10-27

The Windows Defender window

CONFIGURING WINDOWS DEFENDER

You can modify the configuration of Windows Defender by using the following procedure.

➔ CONFIGURE WINDOWS DEFENDER

GET READY. Log on to Windows 7 using an account with administrative capabilities.

1. Click Start, and then type Defender in the search box. A Windows Defender link appears in the search results.

TAKE NOTE* Unlike Windows Vista, Windows Defender is difficult to find in Windows 7. There is no shortcut in the Start menu, and it only appears in the Control Panel when you select the *Large icons* or *Small icons* view.

2. Click Windows Defender. The Windows Defender window appears. This window shows the current status of Windows Defender and indicates whether the program has detected any unwanted or harmful software.
3. Click Tools. The *Tools and Settings* page appears, as shown in Figure 10-28.

Figure 10-28

The Windows Defender Tools
and Settings page

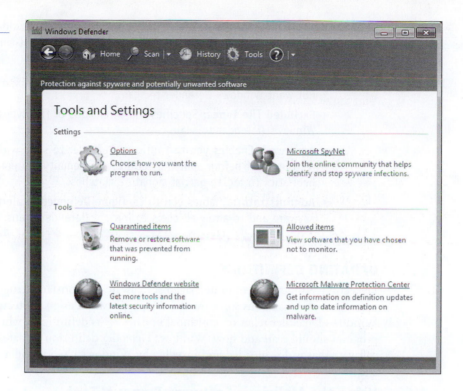

4. Click Options. The *Options* page appears, as shown in Figure 10-29.

Figure 10-29

The Windows Defender Options
page

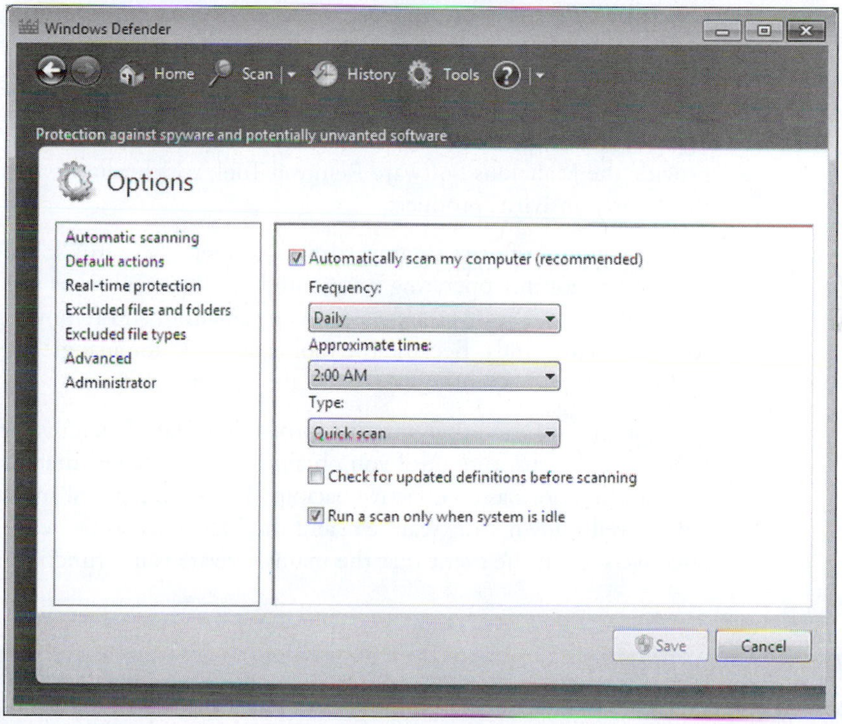

5. Modify the configuration settings for any of the following items and click Save.
   - **Automatic scanning:** Specifies if, when, and how often Defender should scan the system. You can also configure the program to download updated definitions before scanning.
   - **Default actions:** Specifies what action Defender should take when it detects items at each of the alert levels.

- **Real-time protection:** Specifies whether Defender should provide real-time protection and enables you to specify which types of real-time protection Defender should provide.
- **Excluded files and folders:** Specifies the names of files and folders that you do not want Windows Defender to scan.
- **Excluded file types:** Specifies the extensions of file types that you do not want Windows Defender to scan.
- **Advanced:** Enables you to configure Defender to scan within archives, create a restore point before applying actions, scan email and removable drives, and use heuristics to locate partial signature matches.
- **Administrator:** Enables you to configure Defender to alert all users if it detects spyware and to allow all users to initiate Defender scans.

6. Close the Windows Defender window.

UPDATING DEFINITIONS

Protecting Windows 7 computers against malware is a constant struggle between the attackers who create the malicious software and the people who design protective software. As a result, Windows Defender relies on continual updates to its definitions, which determine what the program should scan and how. Windows Defender definition updates are included in the software that is downloaded and installed by Windows Updates on a regular basis.

Using the Malicious Software Removal Tool

The Malicious Software Removal Tool is a one-time virus scanner program that Microsoft distributes with its monthly updates.

As stated earlier, Windows 7 does not include a full-featured antivirus program, and Microsoft strongly recommends that users obtain and install one. However, Microsoft does provide the Malicious Software Removal Tool, which can serve as a substitute or a backup to third-party antivirus products.

The Malicious Software Removal Tool is a single user virus scanner that Microsoft supplies in each of its monthly operating system updates. The tool scans the system for viruses and other forms of malware immediately after its installation, and removes any potentially damaging software that it finds. Because the tool is designed for a single use only, there are no controls, and it is not permanently installed in the operating system.

For systems with no other antivirus protection, the Malicious Software Removal Tool can function as a substitute until you obtain one. For systems that already have antivirus software, the tool functions as an effective backup. There are types of malware that are capable of disabling well-known virus scanners, and the Malicious Software Removal Tool can provide an effective scan in the event that the main software is not functioning.

■ Protecting Sensitive Data

↓
THE BOTTOM LINE Windows 7 includes tools like Encrypting File System (EFS) and BitLocker, which make it possible to prevent data theft using cryptography.

Malware is not the only threat to the security of a Windows 7 computer. The primary reason for having security tools such as Windows Firewall and Windows Defender is to protect the data on a computer. However, tools like these can do nothing to prevent simple, old-fashioned

TAKE NOTE *

BitLocker drive encryption is a particularly useful protection mechanism for portable computers, and is therefore covered in Lesson 12, "Using Mobile Computers."

attacks, such as when someone sits down at a computer while the user is at lunch and copies that person's data, or if someone simply steals the entire computer.

Windows 7 includes other tools that you can use to protect your clients' data from more direct attacks, such as those discussed in the following sections.

Using the Encrypting File System

> The Encrypting File System (EFS) protects users' data by encrypting and decrypting it on the fly as the user works.

CERTIFICATION READY?
Configure file and folder access.
5.2

The Encrypting File System (EFS) is a feature of NTFS that encodes the files on a computer so that even if an intruder can obtain a file, he or she will be unable to read it. The entire system is keyed to a specific user account, using the public and private keys that are the basis of the Windows public key infrastructure (PKI). The user who creates a file is the only person who can read it.

As the user works, EFS encrypts the files he or she creates using a key generated from the user's *public key*. Data encrypted with this key can be decrypted only by the user's personal encryption certificate, which is generated using his or her *private key*.

TAKE NOTE * Only the Professional, Enterprise, and Ultimate editions of Windows 7 support EFS. The Home Basic and Home Premium editions do not support EFS.

When the user logs on to the computer, the system gains access to the keys that are necessary to encrypt and decrypt the EFS-protected data. To the user, the encryption process is completely invisible, and usually does not have a major impact on system performance. The user creates, accesses, and saves files in the normal manner, unaware that the cryptographic processes are taking place.

If another user logs on to the computer, he or she has no access to the other user's private key, and therefore cannot decrypt the encrypted files. An attacker can conceivably sit down at the computer and try to copy the files off to a flash drive, but he or she will receive an "Access Denied" error message, just as if he or she lacked the appropriate NTFS permissions for the files.

There are two main restrictions when implementing EFS:

- EFS is a feature of the NTFS file system, so you cannot use EFS on FAT drives.
- You cannot use EFS to encrypt files that have already been compressed using NTFS compression.

ENCRYPTING A FOLDER WITH EFS

In Windows 7, you can use Windows Explorer to encrypt or disable EFS on any individual files or folders, as long as they are on an NTFS drive. To encrypt a file or folder, use the following procedure.

⊙ ENCRYPT A FOLDER

GET READY. Log on to Windows 7.

1. Click Start, and then click All Programs > Accessories > Windows Explorer. The Windows Explorer window appears.
2. Right click a file or folder and then, from the context menu, select Properties. The Properties sheet for the file or folder appears, as shown in Figure 10-30.

Figure 10-30

A folder's Properties sheet

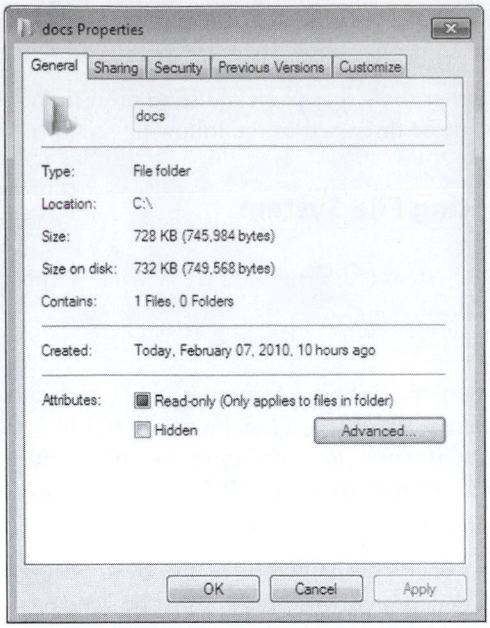

3. On the General tab, click Advanced. The Advanced Attributes dialog box appears, as shown in Figure 10-31.

Figure 10-31

The Advanced Attributes dialog box

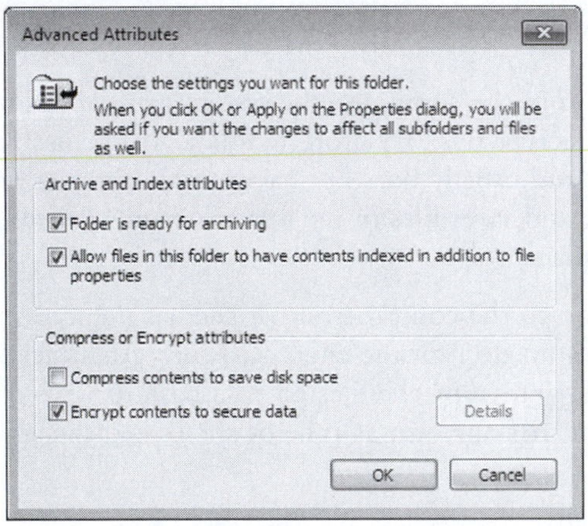

4. Select the Encrypt contents to secure data check box, and then click OK.

5. Click OK to close the Properties sheet. If you selected a folder that contains files or subfolders, a Confirm Attribute Changes dialog box appears, as shown in Figure 10-32, asking you to choose whether to apply changes to the folder only, or to the folder and all of its subfolders and files.

Figure 10-32

A Confirm Attribute Changes dialog box

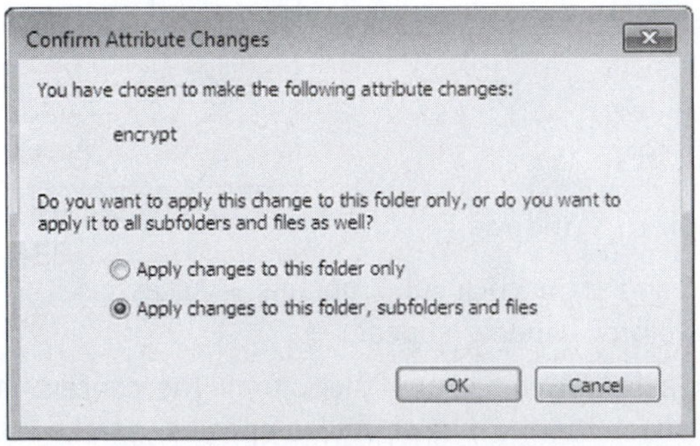

6. Select a confirmation option and click OK. Depending on how many files and folders there are to be encrypted, the process could take several minutes.

DETERMINING WHETHER A FILE OR FOLDER IS ENCRYPTED

Technical specialists commonly receive calls from users who are unable to access their files because they have been encrypted using EFS and the user is unaware of this fact. To resolve the problem, you must first determine whether the files are encrypted or not, and whether the user has the proper NTFS permissions.

Windows Explorer displays the names of encrypted files in green, by default, but this setting is easily changed in the Folder Options dialog box. To verify that a folder or file is encrypted, use the following procedure.

VIEW THE ENCRYPTION ATTRIBUTE

GET READY. Log on to Windows 7.

1. Click Start, and then click All Programs > Accessories > Windows Explorer. The Windows Explorer window appears.
2. Right click a file or folder and then, from the context menu, select Properties. The Properties sheet for the file or folder appears.
3. On the General tab, click Advanced. The Advanced Attributes dialog box appears. If the *Encrypt contents to secure data* check box is selected, the file or folder is encrypted.
4. Click OK to close the Advanced Attributes dialog box.
5. Click OK to close the Properties sheet.

Configuring Parental Controls

> Parental control enables parents to limit their children's access to specific Internet sites, games, and applications.

Just as parents often want to control what their children watch on television, they also may want to control their child's computing habits. Windows 7, in its Home Premium edition and above, includes parental controls that you can use to exercise the following restrictions:

- Enforce time limits for computer use.
- Restrict access to games by rating, content, or title.
- Allow or block specific applications.

SETTING UP USERS

Parental controls are based on user accounts, so parents must create accounts for all family members and enforce their use.

Windows 7 Parental Controls are keyed to user accounts, so the first thing parents have to do is create separate accounts for their children and make sure the family becomes accustomed to logging on and off of their accounts whenever they use the computer. In many cases, this is the most difficult part of the process. Many families are accustomed to using a single account, often one with administrative privileges, and leaving it logged on at all times. This obviously poses dangers both to the operating system and to the parents' ideas of what children should and should not be permitted to see.

For more information on creating user accounts, see Lesson 9, "Working with Workgroups and Domains."

In addition to creating user accounts for everyone in the family, parents must make sure that all of the accounts on the computer have passwords and that the passwords remain secure. If an account with administrative privileges does not have a password, then a child can simply log on using that account and modify or turn off the parental controls.

SETTING UP PARENTAL CONTROLS

After creating user accounts, you can then impose restrictions on those accounts.

Once you have created user accounts for the children whose access you want to restrict, use the following procedure to configure Parental Controls.

SET UP PARENTAL CONTROLS

GET READY. Log on to Windows 7 using an account with administrative capabilities.

1. Click Start, and then click Control Panel. The Control Panel window appears.
2. Click User Accounts and Family Safety > Parental Controls. The *Choose a user and set up Parental Controls* page appears, as shown in Figure 10-33.

Figure 10-33

The Choose a user and set up Parental Controls page

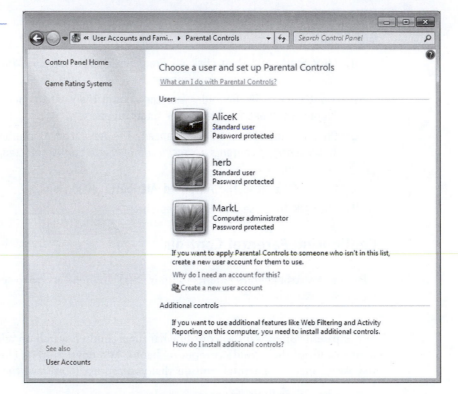

3. Select the account for which you want to configure parental controls. The *User Controls* page appears, as shown in Figure 10-34.

Figure 10-34

The User Controls page

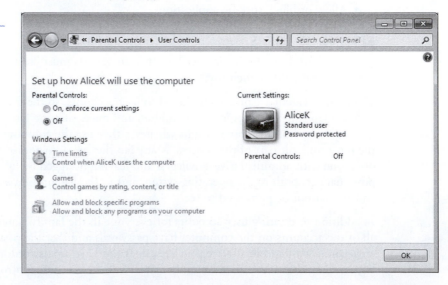

4. Click the On, enforce current settings radio button to enforce the current setting. By default, the Parental Control engine compiles activity reports about the accounts under its protection, but you can turn them off by clicking the Off radio button under Activity Reporting.

5. To impose computer time limits, under Windows Settings, click Time limits. The *Time Restrictions* page appears, as shown in Figure 10-35. Specify in the grid what hours of the day the user is permitted access to the computer.

Figure 10-35

The Time Restrictions page

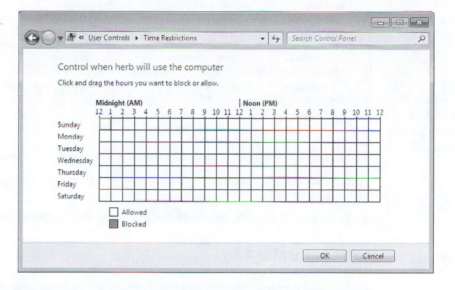

6. To control access to games, under Windows Settings, click Games. The *Game Controls* page appears, as shown in Figure 10-36, where you can do the following:
   - Specify whether the user can play games
   - Allow and block games according to ratings
   - Create a list of games to be allowed or blocked

Figure 10-36

The Game Controls page

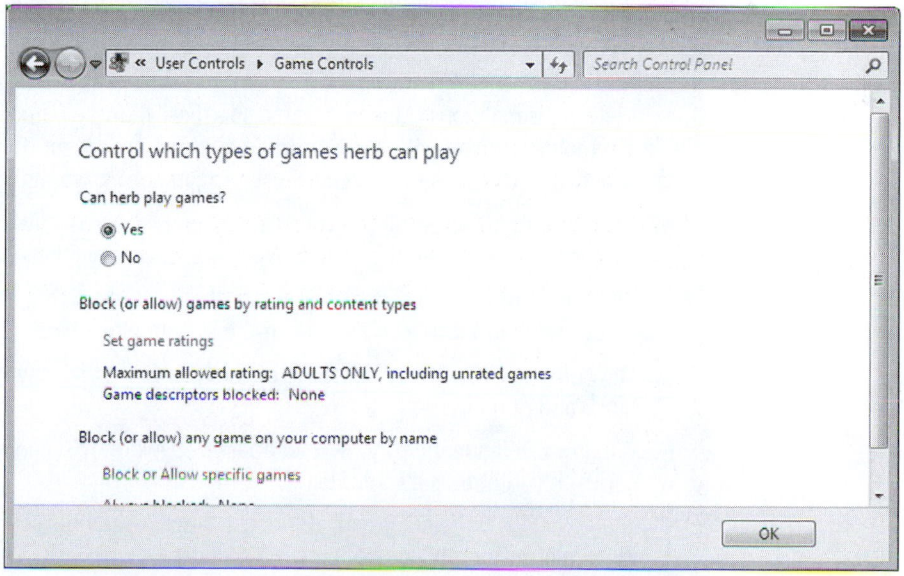

7. To control access to applications, under Windows Settings, click Allow and block specific programs. The *Application Restrictions* page appears, as shown in Figure 10-37, on which you can create a list of the only applications the user is permitted to run.

Figure 10-37

The Application Restrictions page

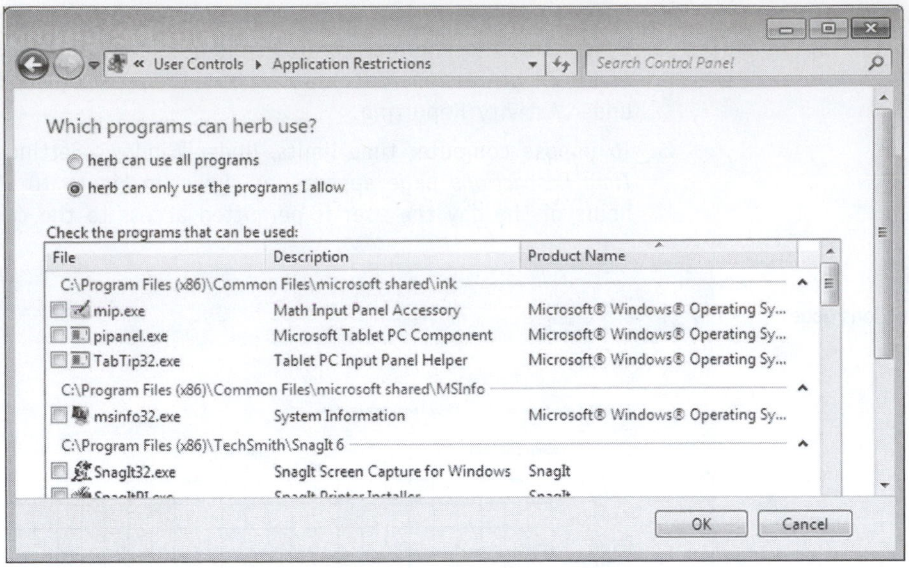

TAKE NOTE*

In Windows Vista, you can use Parental Controls to specify what Internet sites users are permitted to access. This capability has been removed in Windows 7, in which you must use a third-party provider to obtain this functionality.

8. Click OK after configuring each page, and then click OK again to close the User Controls page.
9. Repeat the entire procedure for any other user accounts you want to control.

SKILL SUMMARY

IN THIS LESSON YOU LEARNED:

- Windows 7 supports a number of Group Policy settings that administrators can use to enforce password security practices on individual computers or on Active Directory Domain Services (AD DS) networks.
- Credential Manager is a Windows 7 tool that stores the usernames and passwords people supply to servers and Web sites in a protected area called the Windows Vault.
- The most commonly used mechanisms for authorizing users in Windows 7 are the NTFS, share, and registry permission systems. You can also assign user rights to provide access to operating system activities.
- Malware is malicious software created specifically for the purpose of infiltrating or damaging a computer system without the user's knowledge or consent. This type of software includes a variety of technologies, including viruses, Trojan horses, worms, spyware, and adware.
- Action Center is a centralized console that enables users and administrators to access, monitor, and configure the various Windows 7 security mechanisms.
- Windows Firewall is a software program that protects a computer by allowing certain types of network traffic in and out of the system while blocking others.
- You configure Windows Firewall by creating rules that specify what types of traffic to block and/or allow.
- Windows Defender helps to defend against spyware by scanning the places where it most commonly infiltrates a computer.
- The Malicious Software Removal Tool is a single user virus scanner that Microsoft supplies in each of its monthly operating system updates.
- The Encrypting File System (EFS) is a feature of NTFS that encodes the files on a computer so that even if an intruder can obtain a file, he or she will be unable to read it.
- Windows 7, in its Home Premium and higher editions, includes parental controls that you can use to exercise restrictions over other users' computing habits.

■ Knowledge Assessment

Matching

Complete the following exercise by matching the terms with their corresponding definitions.

    a. automated password guessing
    b. Windows authorization mechanism
    c. passwords plus smartcards
    d. stored in a digital certificate
    e. standard for smart card support
    f. decrypts data encrypted with a certificate
    g. firewall exceptions
    h. standard for fingerprint scanners and other devices
    i. potentially destructive software
    j. firewall rule requiring IPsec

_____ **1.** multifactor authentication

_____ **2.** malware

_____ **3.** brute force

_____ **4.** Personal Identity Verification (PIV)

_____ **5.** private key

_____ **6.** Windows Biometric Framework

_____ **7.** user rights

_____ **8.** authenticated exception

_____ **9.** public key

_____ **10.** rules

Multiple Choice

Select one or more correct answers for each of the following questions.

1. Which of the following account lockout policy modifications could you make to ensure that user passwords cannot be intercepted by analyzing captured packets?
    a. Increase the Enforce Password History value
    b. Enable the Password Must Meet Complexity Requirements setting
    c. Decrease the Account Lockout Threshold value
    d. Disable the Store Passwords Using Reversible Encryption policy

2. Which of the following mechanisms is most often used in firewall rules to allow traffic on to the network?
    a. hardware addresses
    b. IP addresses
    c. protocol numbers
    d. port numbers

3. Which of the following NTFS features is incompatible with EFS encryption?
    a. compression
    b. IPsec
    c. permissions
    d. parental controls

4. Which of the following command-line parameters will prevent a program executed using Runas.exe from accessing the elevated user's encrypted files?
   a. /env
   b. /noprofile
   c. /showcred
   d. /profile

5. Which of the following actions can you NOT perform from the Windows Firewall control panel? (Choose all that apply.)
   a. Allow a program through the firewall in all three profiles
   b. Manage firewall exceptions for the domain profile
   c. Create firewall exceptions based on port numbers
   d. Turn Windows firewall off for all three profiles

6. Which of the following policy modifications would make it harder for intruders to penetrate user passwords by a brute force attack? (Choose all that apply.)
   a. Increase the value of the Reset Account Logon Counter After policy
   b. Enable the Password Must Meet Complexity Requirements policy
   c. Increase the Account Lockout Threshold value
   d. Reduce the value of the Minimum Password Age policy

7. Connection security rules require that network traffic allowed through the firewall use which of the following security mechanisms?
   a. EFS
   b. IPsec
   c. UAC
   d. PIV

8. Which of the following statements about Windows Defender is true?
   a. Windows Defender uses rules that you create to control its scans.
   b. Windows Defender can detect spyware that is already present on the system, but it cannot prevent the infiltration of new spyware.
   c. Windows Defender eliminates the need for third-party anti-virus software.
   d. Windows Defender requires definition updates that are supplied free with the regularly scheduled Windows Update downloads.

9. Which of the parental controls has been removed from Windows 7?
   a. Application restrictions
   b. User time limits
   c. Restricted access to games
   d. Internet filtering

10. The built-in local groups on a Windows 7 workstation receive their special capabilities through which of the following mechanisms?
    a. parental controls
    b. Windows firewall rules
    c. NTFS permissions
    d. user rights

Review Questions

1. List the basic tasks that a parent must perform to successfully implement Parental Controls on a computer running Windows 7, so that the children all have an equal amount of computer time and are prevented from playing inappropriate games.

2. For each of the following Password Policy and Account Lockout Policy settings, specify whether increasing the policy value increases or decreases the security provided by that setting:
   • Account Lockout Threshold
   • Enforce Password History

- Reset Account Lockout Counter After
- Maximum Password Age
- Account Lockout Duration
- Minimum Password Length

Case Scenarios

Scenario 10-1: Using Password and Account Lockout Policies

You are working on a corporate network owned by a company with several government contracts to develop classified technology. You have been assigned the task to create a set of password and account policy settings that meet the following criteria:

- Users must change passwords every four weeks and cannot reuse the same passwords for one year.
- User passwords must be at least 12 characters long, case sensitive, and consist of letters, numbers, and symbols.
- Users are allowed no more than three unsuccessful logon attempts before the account is permanently locked down until released by an administrator.

In the following table, enter the values for the policies that will meet these requirements.

POLICY SETTING	VALUE
Enforce Password History	
Maximum Password Age	
Minimum Password Age	
Minimum Password Length	
Password Must Meet Complexity Requirements	
Store Passwords Using Reversible Encryption	
Account Lockout Threshold	
Account Lockout Duration	
Reset Account Lockout Counter After	

Scenario 10-2: Configuring Windows Firewall

You are a desktop technician in the IT department of a small corporation. Today is the day of the company picnic and, as the junior member of the department, you have been left in charge of the entire corporate network while everyone else is out of the office. Shortly after 2:00 p.m., an email arrives from the company's biggest customer, complaining that they can't access the web server they use to place their orders. After checking the web server logs, it seems clear that the server is undergoing a denial-of-service attack because there are suddenly hundreds of Internet computers repeatedly trying to access it. What temporary modifications could you make to Windows Firewall on the Windows 7 computer that stands between the web server and the Internet that would allow customers to access the web server while blocking the attackers?

Administering Windows 7

Technology Skill	Objective Domain	Objective Number
Using Remote Access Technologies	Configure remote management.	4.5
Using BranchCache	Configure BranchCache.	5.5
Using Backup and Restore	Configure backup.	8.1
Performing a System	Configure system recovery options.	8.2
Restoring Files	Configure file recovery options.	8.3

KEY TERMS

Boot Configuration Data (BCD)	Power-on self-test (POST)	system restore point
BranchCache	Remote Assistance	volume shadow copies
distributed cache mode	Remote Desktop	Windows Recovery Environment (Windows RE)
hosted cache mode	Remote Desktop Protocol (RDP)	
incremental backup	system image backup	Windows Remote Management

■ Understanding Troubleshooting Practices

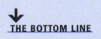
THE BOTTOM LINE

Troubleshooting is a primary function of the Windows 7 technical specialist. Users call for help because something doesn't work or they've done something wrong, and it is up to you to determine what the problem is and how to fix it.

Many technical specialists have troubleshooting skills that are largely intuitive, and this is fine. However, when troubleshooting a problem in a professional environment, whether it's a corporate enterprise network, a help desk in a retail store, or a freelance consultancy, it is important to have a set troubleshooting procedure. This will enable you to explain to the client what you've done, share your findings with your colleagues, and account for your time and effort.

Many troubleshooting calls stem from user error, that is, people who are using the software or hardware improperly. These can often be cleared up immediately with some remedial user training. When you are faced with what appears to be a serious problem, however, you should follow a set troubleshooting procedure that consists of steps similar to the following:

1. Establish the symptoms.

2. Identify the affected area.

3. Establish what has changed.

4. Select the most probable cause.

5. Implement a solution.

6. Test the result.

7. Document the solution.

Various desktop technicians might use slightly different steps or perform them in a slightly different order, but the overall process should be similar. The following sections examine each of these steps.

Establishing the Symptoms

> Have the user explain the problem and assign it a priority.

The first step in troubleshooting any problem is to determine exactly what is going wrong. Depending on the situation, you might also have to note the effects of the problem so that you can assign it a priority. In a business environment, the support staff often receives more calls for help than they can handle at one time. In these cases, it is essential to establish a system of priorities that dictates which calls are addressed first. Just as in the emergency department of a hospital, priorities should not necessarily be based on who is first in line. The severity of the problem and its potential for wide-reaching effects should determine who receives attention first. However, it is also not wise to ignore the political reality that senior management problems are often addressed before those of the rank and file.

Some of the guidelines you might use to establish service priorities are as follows:

- **Shared resources take precedence over individual resources:** A problem with a computer that prevents other users from performing their jobs should take precedence over one that affects only a single user.

- **Network-wide problems take precedence over workgroup or departmental problems:** A problem with a computer that provides services to the entire network, such as a file or print server, should take precedence over a problem with a departmental resource.

- **Departmental issues should be rated according to the function of the department:** A problem with a computer belonging to a department that is critical to the organization, such as order entry or a customer service call center, should take precedence over a problem with a computer belonging to a department that can better tolerate a period of downtime, such as research and development.

- **System-wide problems take precedence over application problems:** A problem that puts an entire computer out of commission and prevents a user from getting any work done should take precedence over a problem a user is experiencing with a single device or application.

It sometimes can be difficult to determine the exact nature of a problem from a description supplied by a relatively inexperienced user. Part of the process of narrowing down the cause of a problem involves obtaining accurate information about what has occurred. Users are often vague about what they were doing when they experienced the problem, or even what the indications of the problem were. For example, in many cases, users call for help because they received an error message, but they neglect to write down the exact wording of the message. Training users in the proper procedures for documenting and reporting problems is often part of the desktop technician's job. It might not be any help now, but it can be beneficial the next time a user receives an error.

Begin by asking the user questions like these:

- What exactly were you doing when the problem occurred?
- What were you doing just before the problem occurred?
- Were you ever able to complete the task you were performing successfully? If so, what has changed?
- Have you had any other problems with your computer lately?
- Was the computer behaving normally just before the problem occurred?
- Has any hardware or software been installed, removed, or reconfigured recently?
- Did you or anyone else do anything to try to resolve the problem?

Identifying the Affected Area

Isolate the hardware or software component that is the source of the problem.

The next step in troubleshooting a network problem is to see whether it can be duplicated. Computer problems that can be reproduced are far easier to fix, primarily because you can easily test to see whether a solution was successful. However, many problems are intermittent or might occur for only a short period of time. In these cases, you might have to leave the incident open until the problem occurs again. In some instances, having the user reproduce the problem can lead to a solution. User error is a common cause of problems that might at first seem to be hardware related.

If you can duplicate a problem, you can set about finding the source of the difficulty. For example, if a user has trouble opening a file in a word processing application, the difficulty might lie in the file itself, in the application, or in the disk drive where the file is stored. The process of isolating the location of the problem consists of logically and methodically eliminating elements that are not the cause.

If you can duplicate the problem, you can begin to isolate the cause by reproducing the conditions under which the problem occurred. To do this, use a procedure like the following:

1. Have the user reproduce the problem on the computer repeatedly, to determine whether the user's actions are causing the error.

2. If possible, sit at the computer yourself and perform the same task. If the problem does not occur, the cause might lie in how the user is performing a particular task. Watch the user carefully to see if he or she is doing something wrong. It is possible that you and the user are performing the same task in different ways and that the user's method is exposing a problem that yours does not.

3. If the problem recurs when you perform the task, log off from the user's account, log on using a different account, and repeat the task. If the problem does not recur, the user is probably lacking the rights or permissions needed to perform the task.

4. If the problem recurs, and the computer is connected to a network, try to perform the same task on a similarly equipped computer connected to the same network. If you cannot reproduce the problem on another computer, you know that the cause lies in the user's computer. If the problem occurs on another computer, then there is likely to be a network problem that is affecting both computers.

Establishing What Has Changed

> Ask the user if the computer has recently been upgraded or reconfigured.

When a computer that used to work properly now does not, it stands to reason that some change has occurred. When a user reports a problem, it is important to determine how the computing environment changed immediately before the malfunction. Unfortunately, getting this information from the user can often be difficult. The response to the question "Has anything changed on the computer recently?" is nearly always "No." Only later will the user remember to mention that a major hardware or software upgrade was performed just before the problem occurred. In an organization with properly established maintenance and documentation procedures, you should be able to determine whether the user's computer has been upgraded or modified recently. IT or departmental records are the first place to look for information like this.

Major changes, such as the installation of new hardware or software, are obvious possible sources of the problem, but you must be aware of causes produced by more subtle changes as well. Tracking down the source of a networking problem can often be a form of detective work, and learning to "interrogate" your "suspects" properly can be an important part of the troubleshooting process.

Selecting the Most Probable Cause

> Look for the simplest possible causes of the problem first.

Once you have narrowed down the possible sources of the problem, you can begin to compile a list of possible causes. Almost any computer problem can have many possible causes, and it is up to you to determine which is the most likely culprit.

There's an old medical school axiom that says when you hear hoofbeats, think horses, not zebras. In the context of computer troubleshooting, this means that when you look for the possible causes of a problem, start with the obvious first. For example, if a computer fails to print a document, do not start by checking the drivers and the printer configuration; check the simple things first, such as whether the printer is plugged in and connected to the computer. You also must work methodically and document everything so that you do not duplicate your efforts.

Implementing a Solution

> Try different solutions until the problem is solved.

After you isolate the problem, try to determine whether hardware or software is the culprit. If it is a hardware problem, you might replace the unit that is at fault or use an alternative that you know is functioning properly. Printing problems, for example, might force you to repair or replace the printer itself. If the problem is inside the computer, you might need to start replacing components, such as hard drives, until the defective component is found. If you determine that the problem is caused by software, try reinstalling the application.

In some cases, the process of isolating the source of a problem includes resolving the problem. For example, if you determine that a printer cable is bad by replacing it with a new one, then the replacement resolves the problem. In other cases, however, the resolution might be more involved, such as one that requires reinstalling an application or even the operating system. Because the user may need to use the computer to complete important tasks, you might have to wait to resolve the problem until a later time, when the computer is not in use and after you have had a chance to back up its data. Sometimes you can use an interim solution, such as a substitute computer, until you can definitively resolve the problem.

Testing the Results

Try to recreate the problem to make sure that the solution is effective.

After implementing a resolution to the problem, you should return to the beginning of the process and repeat the task that originally caused the problem. If the problem no longer occurs, you should test any other functions related to the changes you made to ensure that solving one problem has not created another. At this point, the time you have spent documenting the troubleshooting process becomes worthwhile. Repeat the procedures used to duplicate the problem exactly to ensure that the trouble the user originally experienced has been completely eliminated, and not just temporarily masked. If the problem was intermittent to begin with, it might take some time to ascertain whether the solution has been effective. It might be necessary to check with the user several times to make sure that the problem is not recurring.

Documenting the Solution

Keep a complete record of the entire troubleshooting process.

Although it is presented here as a separate step, the process of documenting all of the actions you perform should begin as soon as the user calls for help. A well-organized technical support organization should have a system in place in which each problem call is registered as a trouble ticket that eventually contains a complete record of the problem and the steps taken to isolate and resolve it. In many cases, a technical support organization operates using tiers, which are groups of technicians with different skill levels. Calls come in to the first tier, and if the problem is sufficiently complex or the first-tier technician cannot resolve it, the call is escalated to the second tier, which is composed of senior technicians. As long as all who are involved in the process document their activities, there should be no problem when one technician hands off the trouble ticket to another. In addition, keeping careful notes prevents people from duplicating one another's efforts.

The final phase of the troubleshooting process is to explain to the user what happened and why. Of course, the average computer user is probably not interested in hearing all the technical details, but it is a good idea to let users know whether their actions caused the problem, exacerbated it, or made it more difficult to resolve. Educating users can lead to a quicker resolution next time or can even prevent a problem from occurring altogether.

■ Using Troubleshooting Tools

↓ THE BOTTOM LINE   Repairing anything requires the right tools and the ability to use them properly.

Windows 7 includes a variety of tools that can aid in the troubleshooting process, some of which were discussed earlier in this book. Table 11-1 lists these tools, along with the lesson that covered the tool.

Table 11-1

Windows 7 Troubleshooting Tools

TOOL	FUNCTION	LOCATION
Upgrade Advisor	Determines whether a computer can run Windows 7 and identifies components that could be upgraded to provide better performance.	Lesson 1
Windows PE	Provides a pre-installation environment from which you can use command-line tools to work with drivers, disks, and network resources.	Lesson 2
Windows Easy Transfer	Enables you to back up and restore user profile information. In the event of a catastrophic malfunction that requires a reinstallation of the operating system, you can use this tool to preserve the user's personalized working environment.	Lesson 2
Performance Information and Tools	Assigns a numerical score to each of the computer's main components, enabling you to identify bottlenecks that affect system performance.	Lesson 8
Disk Management snap-in	Displays information about the storage devices installed in the computer and provides tools for managing partitions and volumes.	Lesson 4
Properties sheets	Shares, disk drives, and most other components in a Windows computer have a Properties sheet that contains a Security tab, which is where you work with the permissions that control access to the component.	Lessons 4, 6
Windows Backup	Performs backups of selected document files. Before performing any major procedure on a client's computer, you should perform a backup of important files.	Lesson 11
User Accounts control panel	Enables you to create and manage local user accounts.	Lesson 9
Local Users and Groups snap-in	Provides comprehensive control over local users and groups.	Lesson 9
Local Security Policies console	Provides access to granular controls that enable you to set system security policies and regulate access to specific system functions.	Lessons 7, 8, 9
Group Policy Object Editor	Provides access to controls that enable you to configure an extensive collection of local and Active Directory Domain Services policies for specific Windows features and components.	Lessons 7, 8, 9
Device Manager	Enables you to view information about and manage the drivers for all of the hardware devices installed in the computer.	Lesson 4
Network and Sharing Center	Provides a central point of access for most Windows 7 networking components and tools.	Lesson 5
Network Map	Provides a graphical depiction of the network topology.	Lesson 5
Network Diagnostics	Displays networking error messages, and specifies in plain language what might be wrong and how to repair the problem.	Lesson 5
Ipconfig.exe	Displays configuration data for all of the network interfaces in the computer.	Lesson 5
Ping.exe	Tests network connections to other TCP/IP systems.	Lesson 5
Tracert.exe	Displays the names of the routers on the path taken by packets to a specific destination.	Lesson 5
Nslookup.exe	Enables you to send customized DNS requests to a specific DNS server.	Lesson 5

(*continued*)

Table 11-1 (*continued*)

TOOL	FUNCTION	LOCATION
Windows Action Center	Provides a central point of access for most Windows 7 security and maintenance components and tools.	Lesson 10
Windows Firewall	Enables you to control what types of network traffic are permitted to enter and leave a computer.	Lesson 10
Windows Update	Enables you to configure a computer to automatically download and install operating system updates.	Lesson 8
Windows Defender	Prevents the infiltration of spyware into a Windows 7 system.	Lesson 10
Malicious Software Removal Tool	A single use virus scanner that Microsoft updates monthly.	Lesson 10
Parental Controls	Enables you to limit the system access granted to specific users.	Lesson 10
Event Viewer	Displays log information about operating system components.	Lesson 8
Performance Monitor	Displays continuous real-time information about the performance of specific system hardware and software components.	Lesson 8

Using Remote Access Technologies

Remote access technologies enable a user on one computer to effectively take control of another computer on the network. For desktop technicians, this capability can save many hours of travel time.

A main objective for desktop technicians working on large corporate networks is to minimize the amount of travel from site to site to work on individual computers. Some of the troubleshooting tools included with Windows 7 are capable of managing services on remote computers as well as on the local system. For example, most MMC snap-ins have this capability, enabling technicians to work on systems throughout the enterprise without traveling. However, most snap-ins are specialized tools used only for certain administration tasks. For comprehensive access to a remote computer, Windows 7 includes two tools that are extremely useful to the desktop technician: Remote Assistance and Remote Desktop.

CERTIFICATION READY?
Configure remote management.
4.5

USING MICROSOFT MANAGEMENT CONSOLE

The shortcuts to various Microsoft Management Console (MMC) tools that appear in the Start menu and the Control Panel of a computer running Windows 7 are all configured to manage resources on the local system. However, many of the snap-ins supplied with Windows 7 enable you to manage other Windows computers on the network as well. There are two ways to access a remote computer using an MMC snap-in, as follows:

- Redirect an existing snap-in to another system.
- Create a custom console with snap-ins directed to other systems.

To connect to and manage another system using an MMC snap-in, you must launch the console with an account that has administrative credentials on the remote computer. The exact permissions required depend on the functions performed by the snap-in. If your credentials do not provide the proper permissions on the target computer, you will be able to load the snap-in, but you will not be able to read information from or modify settings on the target computer.

Redirecting a Snap-in

A snap-in that is directed at a specific system typically has a Connect To Another Computer command in its Action menu. Selecting this command opens a Select Computer dialog box, as shown in Figure 11-1, in which you can specify or browse to another computer on the network. Once you select the name of the computer you want to manage and click OK, the snap-in element in the scope pane changes to reflect the name of the computer you selected.

Select Computer

Select the computer you want to view event logs on.

○ Local computer (the computer this console is running on)

● Another computer: [   ]   Browse...

☐ Connect as another user: <none>   Set User ...

OK   Cancel

Not every snap-in has the ability to connect to a remote computer, because some do not need it. For example, the Active Directory Domain Services consoles automatically locate a domain controller for the current domain and access the directory service from there. There is no need to specify a computer name. However, you will find Change Domain and Change Domain Controller commands in the Action menu in these consoles, which enable you to manage a different domain or select a specific domain controller in the present domain.

Creating a Remote Console

Connecting to a remote computer by redirecting an existing console is convenient for impromptu management tasks, but it is limited by the fact that you can access only one computer at a time. You also have to open the console and redirect it every time you want to access the remote system. A more permanent solution is to create a custom console with snap-ins that are already directed at other computers.

When you add a snap-in to a custom console, you select the computer you want to manage with that snap-in. You can also add multiple copies of the same snap-in to a custom console, with each one pointed at a different computer. This adds a whole new dimension to MMC's functionality. Not only can you create custom consoles containing a variety of tools, you can also create consoles containing tools for a variety of computers. For example, you can create a single console containing multiple instances of the Event Viewer snap-in, with each one pointing to a different computer. This enables you to monitor the event logs for computers all over the network from a single console.

USING REMOTE ASSISTANCE

Remote Assistance is a Windows 7 feature that enables an administrator, trainer, or technical specialist at one location to connect to a distant user's computer, chat with the user, and either view all of the user's activities or take complete control of the system. Remote Assistance eliminates the need for administrative personnel to travel to a user's location for any of the following reasons:

- **Technical support:** A desktop technician can use Remote Assistance to connect to a remote computer to modify configuration parameters, install new software, or troubleshoot user problems.

- **Troubleshooting:** By connecting in read-only mode, an expert can observe a remote user's activities and determine whether improper procedures are the source of problems the user is experiencing. The expert can also connect in interactive mode to try to recreate the problem or to modify system settings to resolve it. This is far more efficient than trying to give instructions to inexperienced users over the telephone.

- **Training:** Trainers and help desk personnel can demonstrate procedures to users right on their systems, without having to travel to their locations.

TAKE NOTE * In Microsoft interfaces and documentation, the person connecting to a client using Remote Assistance is referred to as an expert or a helper.

To receive remote assistance, the computer running Windows 7 must be configured to use the Remote Assistance feature in one of the following ways:

- **Using Control Panel:** Open the System and Security control panel and click *Allow Remote Access*. In the System Properties sheet, select the *Allow Remote Assistance connections to this computer* check box, as shown in Figure 11-2. By clicking the *Advanced* button, the user can specify whether the expert can take control of the computer or simply view activities on the computer. The user can also specify the amount of time that the invitation for remote assistance remains valid.

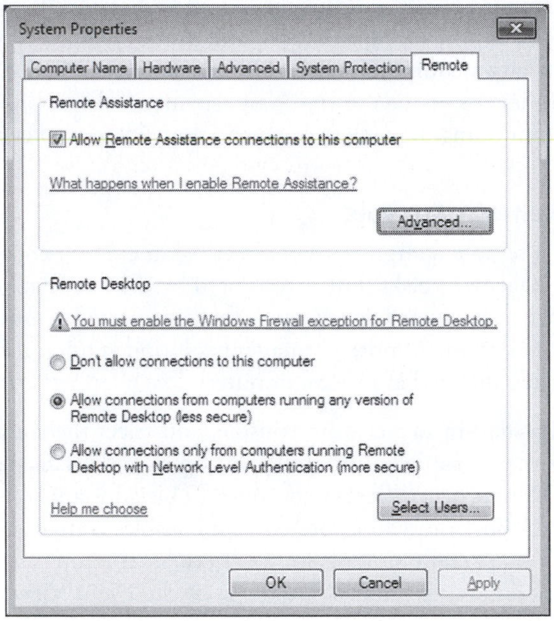

Figure 11-2

The Remote tab of the System Properties sheet

- **Using Group Policy:** Use the Group Policy Object Editor console to access the computer's Local Computer Policy settings. Browse to the Computer Configuration > Administrative Templates > System > Remote Assistance container and enable the Solicited Remote Assistance policy, as shown in Figure 11-3. The Solicited Remote Assistance policy also enables you to specify the degree of control the expert receives over the client computer, the duration of the invitation, and the method for sending email invitations. The Offer Remote Assistance policy enables you to specify the names of users or groups that can function as experts, and whether those experts can perform tasks or just observe. You can also configure these same settings in Group Policy object (GPO) linked to an Active Directory Domain Services (AD DS) domain, site, or organizational unit object.

Figure 11-3

The Solicited Remote Assistance policy in the Group Policy Object Editor console

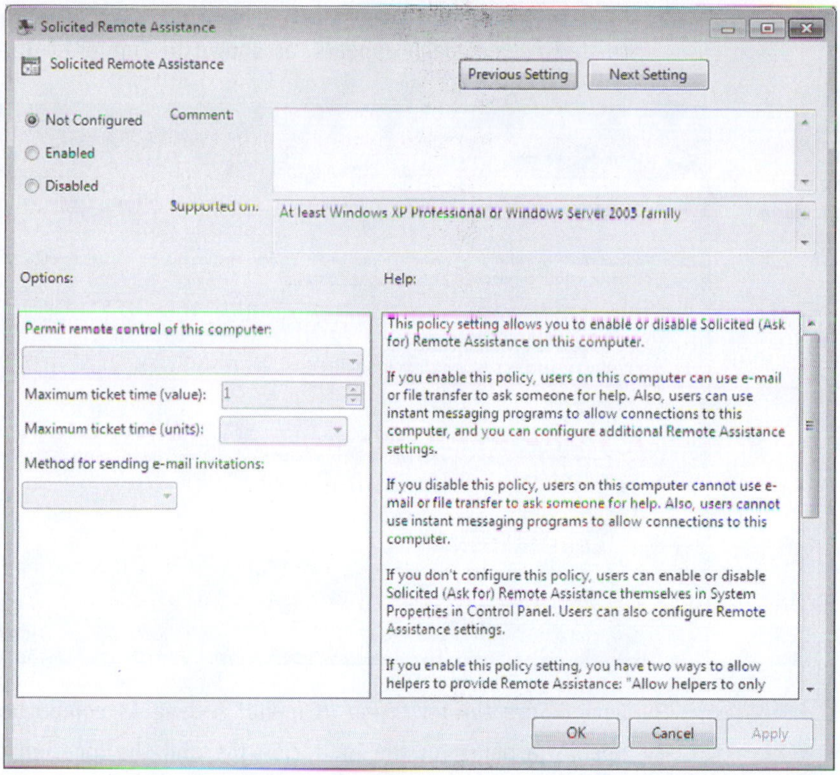

It is also possible for an expert to initiate a Remote Assistance connection to the client by specifying the client's computer name or IP address. However, Windows 7 cannot establish the session unless the client approves the connection.

Creating an Invitation

To request a Remote Assistance session, a client must issue an invitation and send it to a particular expert. The client can send the invitation using email, or save it as a file to be sent to the expert in some other manner. To create an invitation, use the following procedure.

CREATE AN INVITATION

GET READY. Log on to Windows 7.

1. Click Start, and then click All Programs > Maintenance > Windows Remote Assistance. The Windows Remote Assistance Wizard appears, displaying the *Do you want to ask for or offer help?* page, as shown in Figure 11-4.

Figure 11-4

The Do you want to ask for or offer help? page in the Windows Remote Assistance wizard

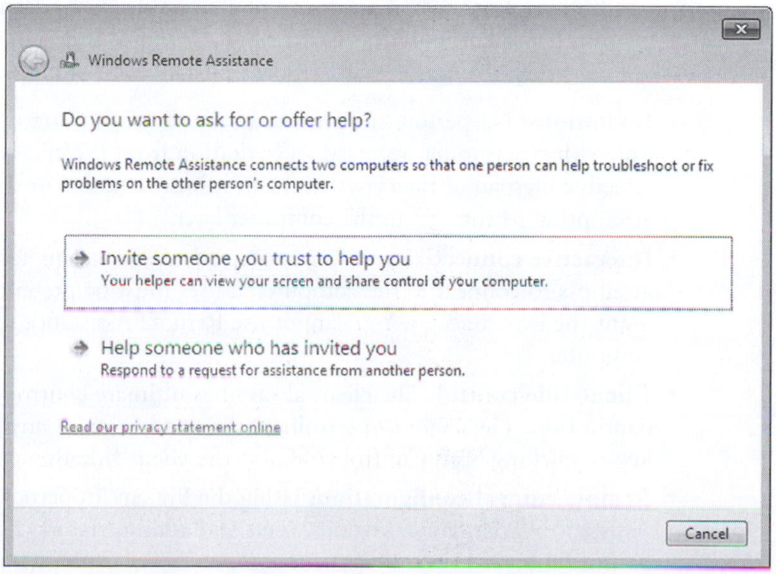

2. Click Invite someone you trust to help you. The *How do you want to invite your trusted helper?* page appears, as shown in Figure 11-5.

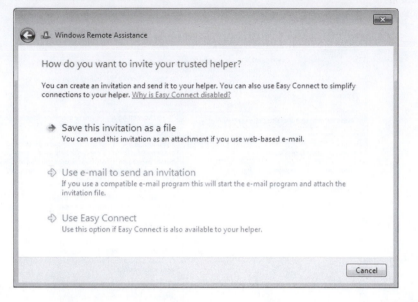

3. Select *Save the invitation as a file*. A Save As combo box appears.
4. Specify a name for the invitation file and the location of the folder in which the wizard should create the invitation and click Save.
5. The Windows Remote Assistance window appears, displaying the password you must supply to the helper or expert.

Once the expert receives the invitation, invoking it launches the Remote Assistance application, which enables the expert to connect to the remote computer. Using this interface, the user and the expert can talk or type messages to each other and, by default, the expert can see everything that the user is doing on the computer. If the client computer is configured to allow remote control, the expert can also click the Take Control button and operate the client computer interactively.

Securing Remote Assistance

Because an expert offering remote assistance to another user can perform virtually any activity on the remote computer that the local user can, this feature can be a significant security hazard. An unauthorized user who takes control of a computer using Remote Assistance can cause almost unlimited damage. However, Remote Assistance is designed to minimize the dangers. Some of the protective features of Remote Assistance are as follows:

- **Invitations:** No person can connect to another computer using Remote Assistance unless that person has received an invitation from the client. Clients can configure the effective lifespan of their invitations in minutes, hours, or days to prevent experts from attempting to connect to the computer later.

- **Interactive connectivity:** When an expert accepts an invitation from a client and attempts to connect to the computer, a user must be present at the client console to grant the expert access. You cannot use Remote Assistance to connect to an unattended computer.

- **Client-side control:** The client always has ultimate control over a Remote Assistance connection. The client can terminate the connection at any time, by pressing the Esc key or clicking Stop Control (ESC) in the client-side Remote Assistance page.

- **Remote control configuration:** Using the System Properties sheet or the Remote Assistance Group Policy settings, users and administrators can specify whether experts are permitted to take control of client computers. An expert who has read-only access cannot modify the computer's configuration in any way using Remote Assistance. The group policies also enable administrators to expert status to grant specific, so that no one else can use Remote Assistance to connect to a client computer, even with the client's permission.

- **Firewalls:** Remote Assistance uses Transmission Control Protocol (TCP) port number 3389 for all its network communications. For networks that use Remote Assistance internally and are also connected to the Internet, it is recommended that network administrators block this port in their firewalls to prevent users outside the network from taking control of computers that request remote assistance. However, it is also possible to provide remote assistance to clients over the Internet, which would require leaving port 3389 open.

USING REMOTE DESKTOP

While Remote Assistance is intended to enable users to obtain interactive help from other users, *Remote Desktop* is an administrative feature that enables users to access computers from remote locations, with no interaction required at the remote site. Remote Desktop is essentially a remote control program for Windows computers; there are no invitations and no read-only capabilities. When you connect to a computer using Remote Desktop, you can operate the remote computer as though you were sitting at the console and perform most configuration and application tasks.

> ➕ **MORE INFORMATION**
>
> One of the most useful applications of Remote Desktop is to connect to servers, such as those in a locked closet or data center, that are not otherwise easily accessible. In fact, some administrators run their servers without monitors or input devices once the initial installation and configuration of the computer is complete, relying solely on Remote Desktop access for everyday monitoring and maintenance.

Remote Desktop is essentially an implementation of the Remote Desktop Services (formerly known as Terminal Services) technology built into the Windows server operating systems. When you use Remote Desktop Services on a server to host a large number of clients, you must purchase licenses for them. However, Windows 7 allows a single Remote Desktop connection for administrative purposes, without the need for a separate license.

The Remote Desktop Connection client communicates with a host computer using the *Remote Desktop Protocol (RDP)*. This protocol essentially transmits screen information, keystrokes, and mouse movements between the two computers. Any applications you launch in the client are still running on the remote computer, using its processor, memory, and storage resources.

When you connect to a computer using Remote Desktop, you must log on, just as you would if you were sitting at the console, meaning that you must have a user account and the appropriate privileges to access the host system. After you log on, the system displays the desktop configuration associated with your user account, and you can then proceed to work as you normally would.

Activating Remote Desktop

By default, the Remote Desktop Services service that powers the server side of Remote Desktop is not started on computers running Windows 7. Before you can connect to a distant computer using Remote Desktop, you must start it using the controls on the Remote tab of the System Properties sheet, which you access from the Control Panel. Select one of the Allow Connections options, depending on your security needs, and click *OK*.

Because Remote Desktop requires the remote user to perform a standard logon, it is inherently more secure than Remote Assistance, and needs no special security measures such as invitations and session passwords. However, you can also click *Select Users* on the Remote tab to display a Remote Desktop Users dialog box, in which you can specify the names of the users or groups that are permitted to access the computer using Remote Desktop. All users with Administrator privileges are granted access by default.

Using the Remote Desktop Connection Client

In addition to the Remote Desktop Services service, Windows 7 includes the Remote Desktop Connection client program needed to connect to a host computer. To connect to a remote computer with the client, use the following procedure.

RUN THE REMOTE DESKTOP CLIENT

GET READY. Log on to Windows 7.

1. Click Start, and then click All Programs > Accessories > Remote Desktop Connection. The Remote Desktop Connection dialog box appears, as shown in Figure 11-6.

Figure 11-6

The Remote Desktop Connection dialog box

2. Click Options. The dialog box expands to show additional controls, as shown in Figure 11-7.

Figure 11-7

The General tab in the expanded Remote Desktop Connection dialog box

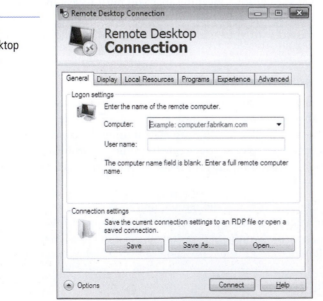

3. On the General tab, type the name of the host computer you want to access in the Computer text box. Then click the Display tab, as shown in Figure 11-8.

Figure 11-8

The Display tab in the Remote Desktop Connection dialog box

Figure 11-8

The Display tab in the Remote Desktop Connection dialog box

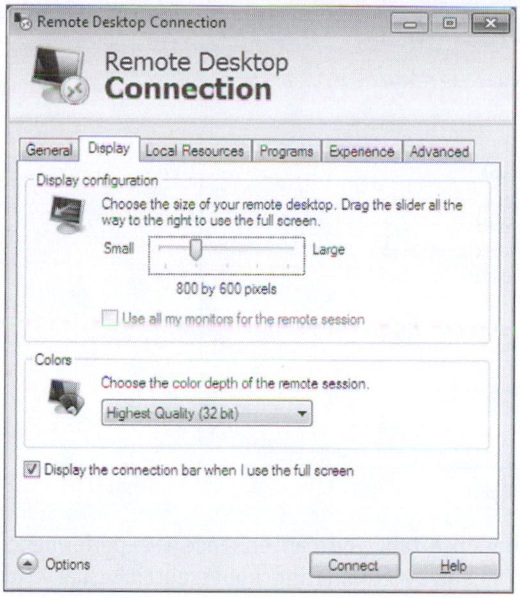

4. In the *Remote desktop size* box, use the slider to select the desired size for the image of the host computer's desktop that will appear on the client system. In the Colors box, select the desired color depth using the drop-down list. Then click the Local Resources tab, as shown in Figure 11-9.

Figure 11-9

The Local Resources tab in the Remote Desktop Connection dialog box

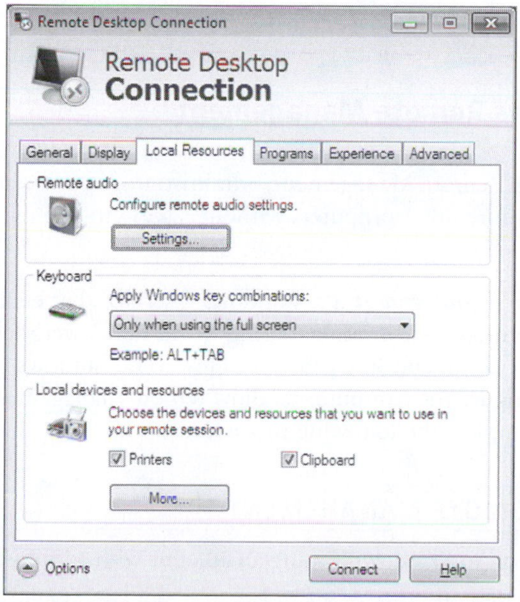

5. Using the controls provided, specify which of the resources on the remote computer you want to bring to your local computer, including sound, printers, clipboard, smart cards, serial ports, drives, and other Plug and Play devices. In the Keyboard box, specify how you want the client to handle the Windows key combinations you press on your local computer. Then click the Experience tab, as shown in Figure 11-10.

Figure 11-10

The Experience tab in the Remote Desktop Connection dialog box

6. On the Experience tab, you can enhance the performance of the Remote Desktop Connection client by eliminating nonessential visual effects from the display information transmitted over the network. Select one of the network connection speeds from the drop-down list or choose the items you want to suppress by clearing their check boxes.

7. Click Connect to initiate the connection process. A Windows Security dialog box appears.

8. Supply User Name and Password values to log on to the remote computer, and then click OK. A Remote Desktop window appears containing an image of the remote computer's desktop.

Using Windows Remote Management

Using Windows Remote Management, administrators can execute programs from the command line on remote computers without having to open a Remote Desktop session.

Windows Remote Management is a Windows 7 service that enables administrators to execute commands on remote computers, using Windows PowerShell or the Windows Remote Shell (WinRS.exe) command-line program. However, Windows 7 does not start the service by default or configure the computer to allow remote management communications. To do this, you must complete the following procedure.

CONFIGURE REMOTE MANAGEMENT

GET READY. Log on to Windows 7 using an account with administrative privileges.

1. Click Start, and then click All Programs > Accessories. Right click Command Prompt and, from the context menu, select *Run as administrator*. An Administrator: Command Prompt window appears.

TAKE NOTE*

If you are working on a computer that is a member of a workgroup, a User Account Control message box appears, in which you must click *Yes* to continue.

2. From the command prompt, type the following command and press Enter:

   winrm quickconfig

3. The command prompts you to start the WinRM service, as shown in Figure 11-11. Type y and press Enter to continue.

Figure 11-11

Starting the WinRM service

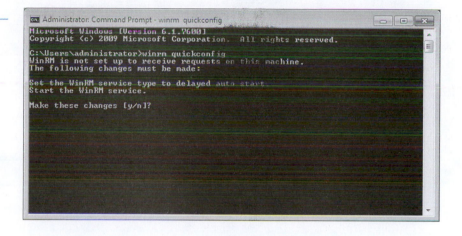

```
Administrator: Command Prompt - winrm  quickconfig

Microsoft Windows [Version 6.1.7600]
Copyright (c) 2009 Microsoft Corporation.  All rights reserved.

C:\Users\administrator>winrm quickconfig
WinRM is not set up to receive requests on this machine.
The following changes must be made:

Set the WinRM service type to delayed auto start.
Start the WinRM service.

Make these changes [y/n]?
```

4. The command prompts you to create a listener for incoming remote management requests and configure the required firewall exception. Type y and press Enter to continue, as shown in Figure 11-12.

5. Close the Administrator: Command Prompt window.

Figure 11-12

Configuring a listener and firewall exception

```
Administrator: Command Prompt

C:\Users\administrator>winrm quickconfig
WinRM is not set up to receive requests on this machine.
The following changes must be made:

Set the WinRM service type to delayed auto start.
Start the WinRM service.

Make these changes [y/n]? y

WinRM has been updated to receive requests.

WinRM service type changed successfully.
WinRM service started.
WinRM is not set up to allow remote access to this machine for management.
The following changes must be made:

Enable the WinRM firewall exception.

Make these changes [y/n]? y

WinRM has been updated for remote management.

WinRM firewall exception enabled.

C:\Users\administrator>
```

In addition to this manual method, you can also configure Windows Remote Management using the Group Policy settings found in the Computer Configuration\Policies\Administrative Templates\Windows Components\Windows Remote Management (WinRM) container of every Group Policy object (GPO), as shown in Figure 11-13.

Figure 11-13

Windows Remote Management
Group Policy settings

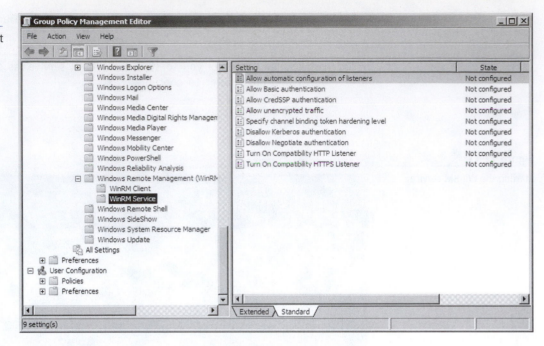

USING WINRS.EXE

Once you have configured the Remote Management service, you can execute commands on other computers that have been similarly configured. To execute a command from the Windows 7 command prompt, you must use the WinRS.exe program.

To use WinRS.exe, you frame the command you want to execute on the remote computer as follows:

`winrs –r:computer [-u:user] [-p:password] command`

- **–r:computer:** Specifies the name of the computer on which you want to execute the command, using a NetBIOS name or a fully qualified domain name (FQDN).
- **–u:user:** Specifies the account on the remote computer that you want to use to execute the command.
- **–p:password:** Specifies the password associated with the account specified in the –u parameter. If you do not specify a password on the command line, WinRS.exe prompts you for one before executing the command.
- **command:** Specifies the command (with arguments) that you want to execute on the remote computer.

You can configure the behavior of WinRS.exe using the Group Policy settings found in the Computer Configuration\Policies\Administrative Templates\Windows Components\ Windows Remote Shell container of every Group Policy object (GPO), as shown in Figure 11-14.

Figure 11-14

Windows Remote Shell Group
Policy settings

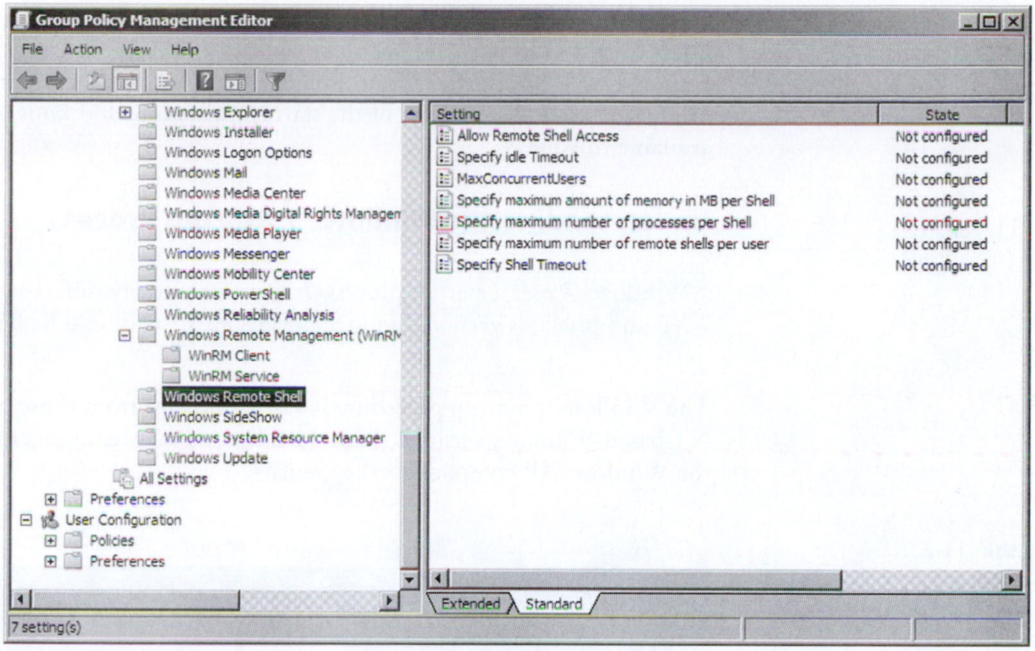

[screenshot: Group Policy Management Editor]

File Action View Help

Setting	State
Allow Remote Shell Access	Not configured
Specify idle Timeout	Not configured
MaxConcurrentUsers	Not configured
Specify maximum amount of memory in MB per Shell	Not configured
Specify maximum number of processes per Shell	Not configured
Specify maximum number of remote shells per user	Not configured
Specify Shell Timeout	Not configured

Windows Explorer
Windows Installer
Windows Logon Options
Windows Mail
Windows Media Center
Windows Media Digital Rights Managem
Windows Media Player
Windows Messenger
Windows Mobility Center
Windows PowerShell
Windows Reliability Analysis
Windows Remote Management (WinRM
    WinRM Client
    WinRM Service
    Windows Remote Shell
Windows SideShow
Windows System Resource Manager
Windows Update
All Settings
Preferences
User Configuration
    Policies
    Preferences

Extended Standard

7 setting(s)

USING POWERSHELL REMOTE COMMANDS

It is also possible to execute commands on remote computers using Windows PowerShell version 2, the version included with Windows 7. Like WinRS.exe, PowerShell requires the Windows Remote Management service to be configured and running on both computers. The configuration parameters are exactly the same.

To execute a PowerShell command on a remote computer, you must open an elevated PowerShell session and use the following syntax:

```
icm computer {command}
```

- ***computer:*** Specifies the name of the computer on which you want to execute the command.
- ***{command}:*** Specifies the PowerShell command you want to execute on the remote computer. The command must be enclosed in curly brackets.

➕ **MORE INFORMATION**

The icm command is an alias for the Invoke-Command cmdlet, which you can use in its place if desired. For information on the other parameters supported by the Invoke-Command cmdlet, see the help screens for the cmdlet.

■ Troubleshooting Installation and Startup Issues

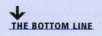
THE BOTTOM LINE

Learning the troubleshooting process is better than learning to fix specific problems. However, troubleshooting startup problems can be difficult because the usual tools are unavailable.

This lesson has so far concentrated on general troubleshooting procedures and the troubleshooting tools that Windows 7 provides. This is in keeping with the belief that, to become an efficient troubleshooter, it is better to concentrate on learning the general process than dealing with specific problems. After all, there are an unlimited number of things that can go wrong on a computer and, as the old saying goes, giving a man a fish feeds him for a day, but teaching him to fish feeds him for life.

One of the more difficult types of problem to troubleshoot is one that prevents the computer from starting properly because you don't have access to all of the troubleshooting tools included with Windows 7. To troubleshoot a Windows 7 computer that fails to start, you must have an understanding of the startup procedure and knowledge of the tools that are available to you.

Understanding the Windows 7 Startup Process

Windows 7 uses a startup process that is substantially different from those of Windows XP and previous versions, and technical specialists should be familiar with the changes.

The Windows 7 startup procedure is vastly different from those of Windows XP and other NT-based Windows versions. Table 11-2 lists the new components found in Windows 7, and the Windows XP components they replace.

Table 11-2

Windows XP and Windows 7 Startup Components

WINDOWS 7 COMPONENT	FUNCTION	WINDOWS XP COMPONENT
Windows Boot Manager Windows Boot Loader	Displays the boot menu and loads the kernel	NTLDR
Boot Configuration Data (BCD) registry file	Contains the boot options displayed on the boot menu	Boot.ini
Merged into the kernel, as hardware profiles are no longer needed	Detects hardware and loads the appropriate hardware profile	Ntdetect.com
Windows Recovery Environment (Windows RE)	Provides limited access to operating system tools	Recovery Console

The Windows 7 startup process consists of the following steps:

1. ***Power-on self-test (POST)* phase:** When you first turn the computer on, it loads the BIOS or Extensible Firmware Interface (EFI) and runs a hardware self-test procedure that detects the devices installed in the system and configures them using settings stored in non-volatile memory. After the main POST, any devices with their own BIOS firmware (such as video display adapters) can run their own self-test procedures.

2. **Initial startup phase:** On BIOS-equipped computers, the system reads the BIOS settings to determine which hardware device it should use to boot the computer. When booting from a hard disk, the system loads the master boot record (MBR) from the disk and locates the active (bootable) partition. The system then loads and runs a stub program called Bootmgr, which switches the processor from real mode to protected mode and loads the Windows Boot Manager application. EFI computers have their own built-in boot manager, which Windows 7 configures to run the same Windows Boot Manager application, eliminating the need for the interim disk location steps.

3. **Windows Boot Manager phase:** The system reads the ***Boot Configuration Data (BCD)*** registry file, which contains the system's boot menu information, and provides the user with access to the boot menu, as shown in Figure 11-15. If there is only one operating system installed on the computer, the boot menu only appears when the user presses the a key just after the POST, or presses the F8 key to display the Advanced Boot Options menu. If there are multiple operating systems installed, the boot menu appears, providing the user with 30 seconds to select one of the operating systems before it loads the default.

Figure 11-15

The Windows 7 boot menu

```
                        Windows Boot Manager

Choose an operating system to start, or press TAB to select a tool:
(Use the arrow keys to highlight your choice, then press ENTER.)


    Windows 7                                                      >
    MyVHD




To specify an advanced option for this choice, press F8.
Seconds until the highlighted choice will be started automatically: 11



Tools:

    Windows Memory Diagnostic




 ENTER=Choose                   TAB=Menu                   ESC=Cancel
```

4. **Windows Boot Loader phase:** The system initiates the memory paging process and loads various operating system elements into memory, such as the Windows kernel, the hardware abstraction layer (HAL), the system registry hive, and boot class device drivers, but it does not actually run them.

5. **Kernel loading phase:** The system runs the Windows Executive (consisting of the Windows kernel and the HAL), which processes the registry hive and initializes the drivers and services specified there. The kernel then starts the Session Manager, which loads the kernel-mode part of the Win32 subsystem, causing the system to switch from text mode to graphics mode. Then the kernel loads the user-mode portion of Win32, which provides applications with indirect, protected access to the system hardware. At this time, the system also performs delayed rename operations resulting from system updates that must replace files that were in use when the update was installed. Finally, the kernel creates additional virtual memory paging files and starts the Logon Manager.

6. **Logon phase:** The system loads the Service Control Manager (SCM) and the Local Security Authority (LSA), and then presents the logon user interface (LogonUI). The interface passes the credentials supplied by the user to the LSA for authentication, and the SCM loads the Plug and Play services and drivers that are configured for autoloading. If the authentication is successful, the Logon Manager launches Userinit.exe, which is responsible for applying group policy settings and running the programs in the Startup group, and then loads the Windows Explorer shell, which provides the Windows desktop.

Troubleshooting Startup Failures

The first step in troubleshooting a startup failure is determining exactly where in the startup process the failure is occurring.

The symptoms of a startup failure differ depending on where in the process the failure occurs. Therefore, the first step to take when a Windows 7 computer fails to start is to determine exactly where in the startup sequence the problem is occurring.

POST FAILURES

One of the most fundamental questions a troubleshooter can ask is whether a problem is being caused by a hardware or a software failure. If a computer fails to make it through the POST successfully, the problem is unquestionably hardware-related. In most cases, the BIOS will display an error message or produce a series of beeps identifying the exact problem that is causing the failure. Consult the BIOS documentation for more information on its error messages and/or beep codes.

> **+ MORE INFORMATION**
>
> Some BIOS programs enable you to select between a "quick" POST and an extended "diagnostic" sequence. At the first sign of a hardware problem, you should switch to the diagnostic mode to gather as much information as possible about the problem.

INITIAL STARTUP FAILURES

A failure during the initial startup phase typically results in a "Non-system disk or disk error," which means that there is an issue with the BIOS configuration, the storage subsystem, or the file system. Startup failures that occur before the progress bar appears are typically caused by one of the following problems:

- **Incorrect BIOS Settings:** If the boot settings in the BIOS are misconfigured, the system might be attempting to boot from the wrong device. For example, if the BIOS is configured to boot from the CD or DVD drive, and there is no bootable disk in the drive, the computer will be unable to start.

- **Hardware faults:** If anyone has recently worked inside the computer's case, you might want to begin by checking the hard drive's power and data connections. Also, if there is an internal problem with the hard disk, such as corruption of the MBR, the system might not be able to locate the active partition.

- **Missing startup files:** If some of the required startup files are missing or damaged, the computer will fail to boot. This could be due to the installation of another operating system over Windows 7, accidental deletion of system files, or data corruption on the hard disk.

- **Data corruption:** Corrupted data on a disk drive can be the result of a hardware fault, environmental factors (such as magnetic fields), or some form of malware.

Resolving these problems can require the replacement of a hardware component, but in many cases you can repair them using the specialized recovery tools provided with Windows 7, as discussed later in this lesson.

DRIVER AND SERVICE FAILURES

The appearance of the progress bar indicates that the kernel has loaded successfully. When a startup failure occurs after the progress bar appears, but before the logon user interface appears, the problem could be hardware-related, but it is most likely due to an issue with one of the drivers or services that the kernel is attempting to load. Resolving the problem is a matter of determining which of the drivers or services is at fault.

To locate the offending driver or service, you must first attempt to get the computer started by using the Last Known Good Configuration option, Safe Mode, or other means. Then you can examine the event logs, enable the boot log, and run the System Information tool to gather information on what is affecting the startup sequence. Finally, use Device Manager or the Services console to disable the offending drivers or services. Once you are able to get the computer started in normal node, you can begin to examine the problematic driver or service, perhaps replacing them with an updated version or rolling back to a previous one.

LOGON FAILURES

When the startup process fails after the user has supplied logon credentials, the problem is most likely due to one of the applications running from the Startup group. The simplest way to prevent the startup applications from running is to hold down the Shift key when logging on, until the icons appear on the desktop. When you do this, the startup applications do not load, but only for that session.

Once the system is started, you can try loading each of the startup applications in turn to see which one is causing the problem. After isolating the offending application, you can see about reconfiguring, upgrading, or uninstalling it, so that the problem is eliminated.

Using Recovery Tools

Windows 7 includes specialized tools for diagnosing and repairing startup problems.

Windows 7 has many tools that you can use for troubleshooting system and network problems, but if the computer fails to start, these tools are not available. Fortunately, Windows 7 includes a special working environment that you can use when the system fails to start, as well as a selection of tools that you can use in that environment.

USING ALTERNATE BOOT OPTIONS

In many cases, just getting the computer to start can be half of the troubleshooting battle. Once the computer is started, you have access to the configuration interface and the Windows 7 troubleshooting tools that can help you solve the problem. If the problem is hardware-related, you are unlikely to get the system started until you repair or replace the malfunctioning component. However, if the startup problem occurs after the progress bar appears, you can probably get the system started in one of the following ways:

- **To suppress drivers and services:** Press F8 repeatedly, immediately after the POST completes and before the progress bar appears. From the Advanced Boot Options menu, shown in Figure 11-16, select Last Known Good Configuration or, if that does not work, one of the Safe Mode options.

Figure 11-16

The Advanced Boot Options menu

```
                        Advanced Boot Options

Choose Advanced Options for: Windows 7
(Use the arrow keys to highlight your choice.)

    Repair Your Computer

    Safe Mode
    Safe Mode with Networking
    Safe Mode with Command Prompt

    Enable Boot Logging
    Enable low-resolution video (640x480)
    Last Known Good Configuration (advanced)
    Directory Services Restore Mode
    Debugging Mode
    Disable automatic restart on system failure
    Disable Driver Signature Enforcement

    Start Windows Normally

Description: View a list of system recovery tools you can use to repair
            startup problems, run diagnostics, or restore your system.

ENTER=Choose                                              ESC=Cancel
```

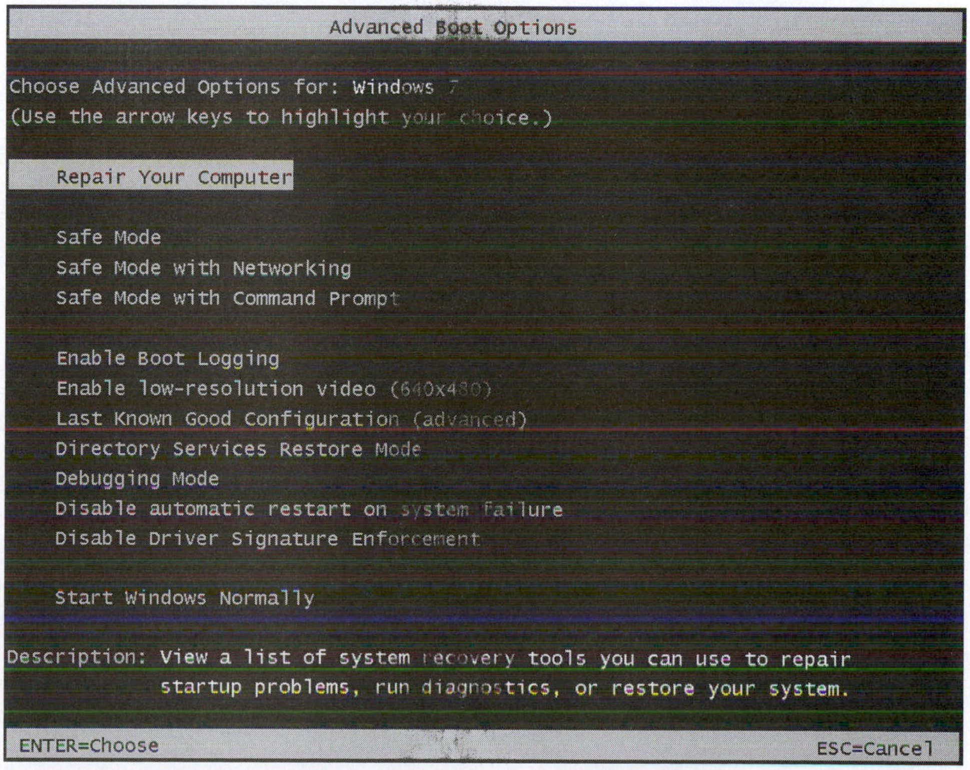

- **To suppress startup applications:** Press the Shift key while logging on and hold it down until the icons appear on the desktop.

The Last Known Good Configuration option reverses all of the system configuration, driver, and registry changes you made since the computer last booted successfully. The Safe Mode options start the computer with a minimal set of generic drivers, just those needed to run the system. Once the system is running, you can exercise control over it and gather information about the startup process using the tools covered in the following sections.

USING THE STARTUP AND RECOVERY DIALOG BOX

The Startup and Recovery dialog box provides basic controls that enable you to configure the Windows 7 startup process by modifying the BCD registry file. To open the Startup and Recovery dialog box, use the following procedure.

OPEN THE STARTUP AND RECOVERY DIALOG BOX

GET READY. Log on to Windows 7.

1. Click Start, and then click Control Panel > System and Security > System. The System control panel appears.
2. Click Advanced System Settings. After confirming your action, the System Properties sheet appears.
3. Click the Advanced tab, as shown in Figure 11-17.

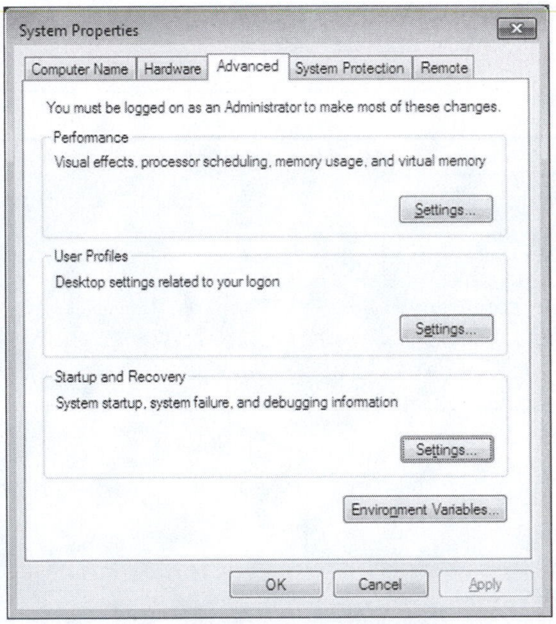

Figure 11-17

The Advanced tab of the System Properties sheet

4. In the Startup and Recovery box, click Settings. The Startup and Recovery dialog box appears, as shown in Figure 11-18.

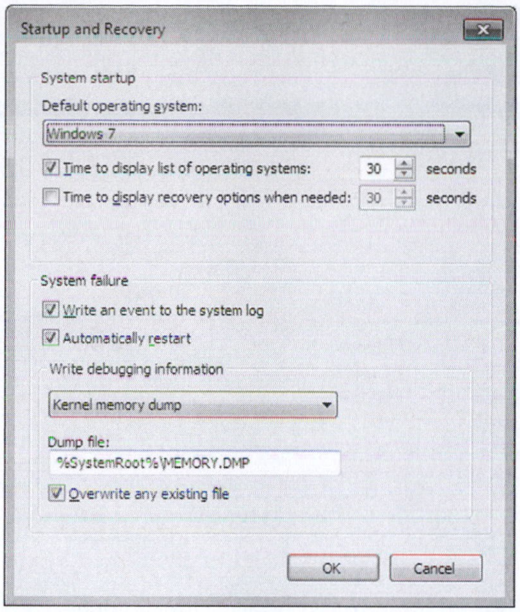

Figure 11-18

The Startup and Recovery dialog box

> **Startup and Recovery**
>
> System startup
>
> Default operating system:
>
> [Windows 7 ▾]
>
> ☑ Time to display list of operating systems: [30 ⬍] seconds
> ☐ Time to display recovery options when needed: [30 ⬍] seconds
>
> System failure
>
> ☑ Write an event to the system log
> ☑ Automatically restart
>
> Write debugging information
>
> [Kernel memory dump ▾]
>
> Dump file:
> [%SystemRoot%\MEMORY.DMP]
> ☑ Overwrite any existing file
>
> [OK] [Cancel]

In this dialog box, you can specify which operating system to load on a dual boot computer, and also specify how long the boot menu and recovery options menu appear by default. You can also exercise control over the computer's logging behavior during system startup.

USING THE SYSTEM CONFIGURATION TOOL

If you can get Windows 7 to start in Safe Mode, the System Configuration tool enables you to exercise a great deal of control over the startup process. You can select the type of startup to perform, configure a variety of BCD registry file settings, and specify individual applications and services to be omitted from the startup sequence.

> **➕ MORE INFORMATION**
>
> While the System Configuration tool provides more access to the BCD registry settings than the Startup and Recovery dialog box, it is not the most comprehensive BCD editing tool available. To exercise complete control over the BCD, you must use the BCDEdit.exe tool from the command line in Windows 7 or Windows RE.

X REF

For more information on using the General and Startup tabs to address system performance issues, see "Using the System Configuration Tool," in Lesson 8, "Managing and Monitoring Windows 7 Performance."

To start the System Configuration tool, click Start, type *msconfig* in the search box, and press Enter. The System Configuration dialog box appears. The dialog box contains the following tabs:

- **General:** Provides controls that enable you to perform a normal, diagnostic, or selective startup sequence. You can use these options to suppress specific parts of the startup process in the hope of bypassing the component causing the problem.
- **Boot:** Controls BCD registry settings that enable you to select the operating system to install and configure a limited boot sequence, as shown in Figure 11-19. Clicking *Advanced options* displays a BOOT Advanced Options dialog box, which you can use to control the system hardware used during the startup sequence.

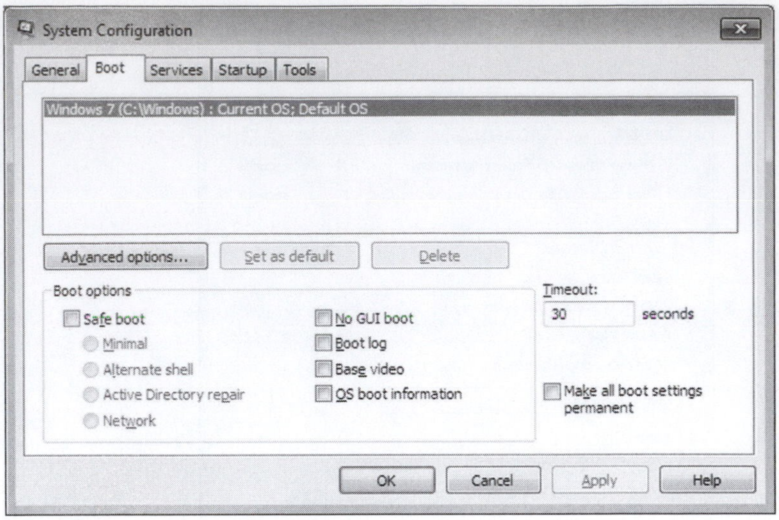

Figure 11-19

The Boot tab in the System Configuration dialog box

- **Services:** Enables you to select the services that will run during the startup sequence, as shown in Figure 11-20. By disabling all of the services and then enabling them one at a time as you repeatedly restart the computer, you can determine which service is causing a startup failure.

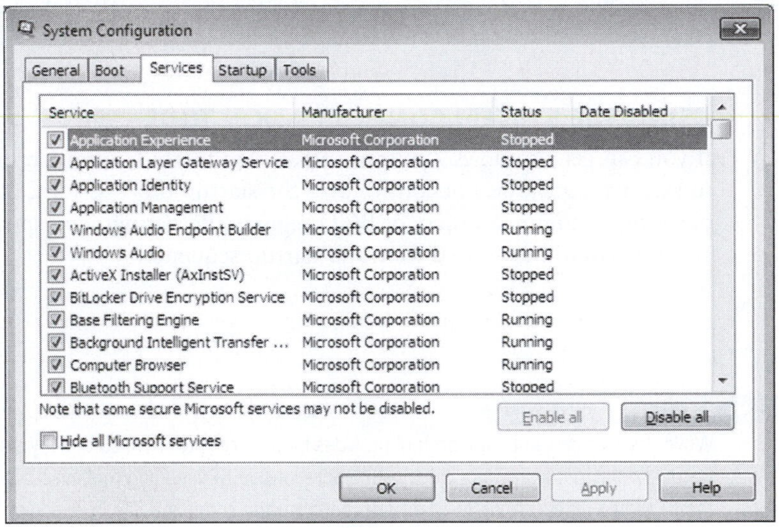

Figure 11-20

The Services tab in the System Configuration dialog box

- **Startup:** Enables you to select the startup applications that will run during the startup sequence. By disabling all of the startup applications and then enabling them one at a time as you repeatedly restart the computer, you can determine which application is causing a startup failure.
- **Tools:** Enables you to launch a variety of Windows 7 configuration and troubleshooting tools, as shown in Figure 11-21.

TAKE NOTE*

When you make changes to the system startup configuration using the System Configuration tool, Windows 7 displays a message when users log on, reminding them of the changes, so they do not forget to restore the original configuration.

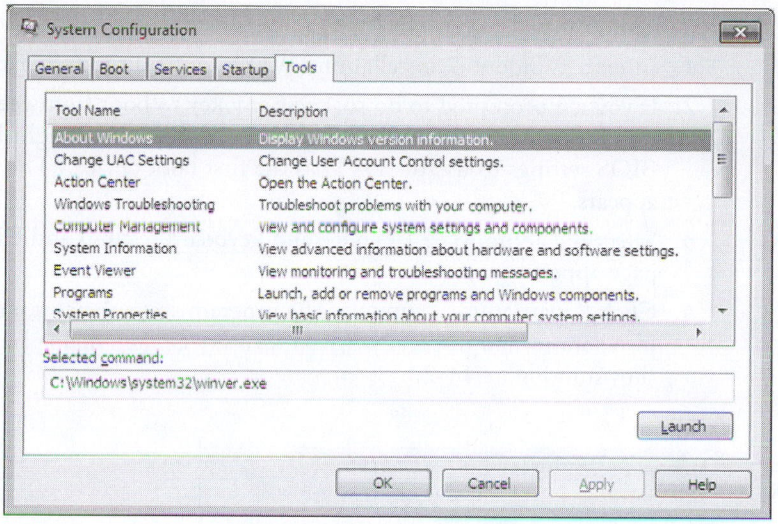

Figure 11-21

The Tools tab in the System Configuration dialog box

ENABLING BOOT LOGGING

Boot logging gathers information about the most recent startup process and saves it to a text file for later examination. However, boot logging is not enabled by default. To enable boot logging, use the following procedure.

ENABLE BOOT LOGGING

1. Turn the computer on.

2. When the POST completes, press the F8 key repeatedly until the Advanced Boot Options menu appears.

3. Select Enable Boot Logging. The system creates a log file in the \Windows folder called Ntblog.txt.

4. The startup procedure continues, adding information to the log file as it proceeds.

The boot log contains a list of all the files that Windows 7 attempts to load during the startup process, along with a status indicator specifying whether each file loaded successfully. If you enable boot logging during a normal startup, and then perform a Safe Mode startup, the system will append the Safe Mode startup information to the existing log. This enables you to compare the two startup sequences and determine which files are required for a successful, normal startup that are not required for a Safe Mode startup. If the Safe Mode startup is successful and a normal one is not, then one of those files must be causing the problem.

USING WINDOWS RE

As you learned in Lesson 2, "Installing Windows 7," the Windows 7 installation process uses the Windows Preinstallation Environment (Windows PE) to boot the system for the first time and initiate the Setup program. Windows PE is a stripped-down operating system that, unlike the DOS environment used in previous Windows versions, supports the same drivers used in a complete Windows 7 installation, as well as a subset of the Win32 application programming interface (API).

For computers that already have the operating system installed, Windows 7 includes the *Windows Recovery Environment (Windows RE)*, which is essentially the same as Windows PE. By booting into Windows RE, you bypass all of the drivers, applications, and services that can be the source of a startup problem. Windows RE also provides access to a collection of recovery tools that can identify and even repair many of the problems that can prevent the system from starting.

To run Windows RE, use the following procedure:

1. Insert a Windows 7 installation DVD into the drive and restart the computer.

2. If you are prompted to do so, press any key to boot from the DVD. (If the system fails to prompt and boots from the hard disk instead, you might have to modify your system BIOS settings to use the DVD as the first boot device.) The Install Windows wizard appears.

3. Select the appropriate language and keyboard settings and click Next. The *Install Now* page appears.

4. Click Repair Your Computer. The program scans the computer's drives for Windows 7 installations and displays a *System Recovery Options* dialog box containing the results, as shown in Figure 11-22.

Figure 11-22

The System Recovery Options dialog box

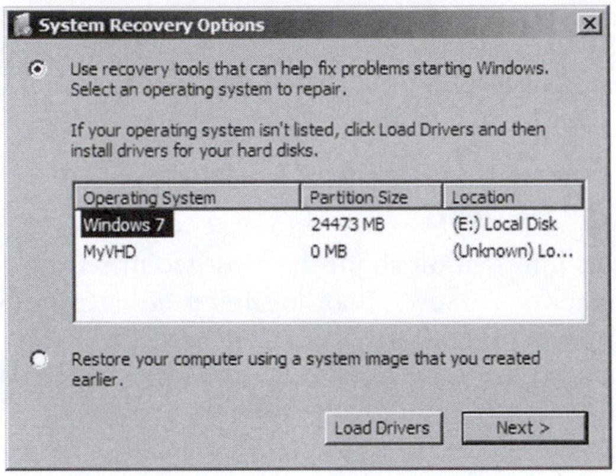

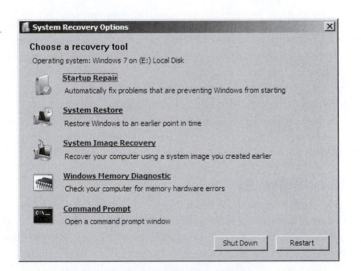

5. Select the instance of the operating system you want to repair, and then click Next. The *Choose a recovery tool* dialog box appears, as shown in Figure 11-23.

6. Click one of the links to launch a recovery tool.

Figure 11-23

The Choose a Recovery Tool dialog box

USING THE SYSTEM RECOVERY TOOLS

When you load Windows RE from the Windows 7 installation DVD, the system provides you with a choice of recovery tools, including the following:

- **Startup Repair:** An automated troubleshooting tool that is capable of diagnosing and repairing a variety of problems that can prevent Windows 7 from starting, including BCD problems and missing startup files. The prompts displayed by the tool vary,

---

TAKE NOTE*

If Windows 7 experienced a startup failure immediately before you booted from the DVD, the Startup Repair tool will load automatically.

depending on the conditions it detects, but all of its activities are logged in a file called SRTTrail.txt, located in the \Windows\System32\LogFiles\SRT folder. When the cause of a startup problem is not immediately apparent, this should be the first tool you use.

- **System Restore:** Enables you to access the restore points on the computer, whether manually or automatically created, and use them to restore the system to an earlier state. This is the same functionality available in the System Restore application, accessible from the System Tools program group in Windows 7 (in normal or safe mode).
- **System Image Recovery:** Enables you to perform a full restoration of your computer, using an image you previously created with the Backup and Restore control panel.
- **Windows Memory Diagnostic:** Tests the computer's memory for hardware errors.
- **Command Prompt:** Displays a command prompt, from which you can run a variety of text-based tools included with Windows RE.

Using BranchCache

THE BOTTOM LINE

BranchCache is a new feature in Windows 7 and Windows Server 2008 R2 that enables networks with computers at remote locations to conserve bandwidth by storing frequently accessed files on local drives.

CERTIFICATION READY?
Configure BranchCache.
5.5

Caching is a process in which computers copy frequently used data to an intermediate storage medium so they can satisfy subsequent requests for the same data more quickly or less expensively. For example, virtually all computers have an area of high-speed memory between the system processor and the main system memory that functions as a cache. Repeated requests for the same data can be satisfied more quickly from the cache memory than the slower main memory. BranchCache works in much the same way, except that it is a disk storage cache that reduces the traffic between branch office computers and a server at another site.

Wide area network (WAN) connections between offices are slower and more expensive than the local area network (LAN) connections within an office. When a computer in a branch office requires a file stored on a server at the main office, the server must transmit the file over a WAN connection. If twenty computers at the branch office require that same file, the server must transmit it twenty times, using twenty times the WAN bandwidth.

BranchCache is a feature that can store a copy of the file on a computer at the branch office site, so that the server only has to transmit the files over the WAN connection once. All of the subsequent requests access the file from the cache on the local network.

Understanding Network Infrastructure Requirements

To use BranchCache, you must have a server running Windows Server 2008 R2 at the home office and computers running Windows Server 2008 R2 or Windows 7 at the branch office.

BranchCache is a new feature introduced in Windows Server 2008 R2 and Windows 7 Enterprise and Ultimate editions; only computers running those operating systems can use it. The content server that stores the data initially must be running Windows Server 2008 R2. The workstations at the branch office that access the data must be running Windows 7.

BranchCache is a client/server application that supports two operational modes, as follows:

- *Distributed cache mode:* Each Windows 7 workstation on the branch office network caches data from the content server on its local drive and shares that cached data with other local workstations.

• *Hosted cache mode:* Windows 7 workstations on the branch office network cache data from the content server on a branch office server, enabling other workstations to access the cached data from there.

Obviously, the major difference between the two modes is the need for a second, branch-office server in hosted cache mode, which makes the caching process more efficient, but which adds to the expense of the implementation. In distributed cache mode, each workstation is responsible for maintaining its own cache and processing cache requests from the other workstations on the local network.

Understanding BranchCache Communications

BranchCache clients and servers exchange relatively small messages among themselves to coordinate their caching activities.

BranchCache supports file requests using Server Message Blocks (SMB), the standard Windows file-sharing protocol; Hypertext Transfer Protocol (HTTP), the standard proto-col for web communications; and the Background Intelligent Transfer Service (BITS). The BranchCache communications process is as follows:

1. **Client request (BranchCache):** A branch office workstation requests a file from the content server, and identifies itself as a BranchCache client.

2. **Server reply (metadata):** The server replies to the client, not with the requested file, but with a message containing metadata that describes the file. The metadata is much smaller than the requested file, reducing the amount of WAN bandwidth consumed.

3. **Client cache check:** Using the metadata supplied by the server, the client sends messages to the local caching computers, asking if the requested file is available locally.

4. **Caching computer reply:** In hosted cache mode, the local caching server replies to the client, indicating whether the requested file is available in its cache. In distributed cache mode, caching workstations only reply in the positive. If the client workstation receives no replies, it assumes that the requested file is not cached locally.

5. **Client request (non-BranchCache):** The client issues another file request, this time without the BranchCache identifier, and sends it either to a local caching computer or the content server.

6. **Server reply (data):** The computer receiving the request replies by sending the requested file to the client.

7. **Client data cache:** On receiving the requested file, the client caches it for use by other branch office workstations. In hosted cache mode, the client caches the file on the branch office server. In distributed cache mode, the client caches the file on its own local disk.

As a result of this process, the traffic transmitted over the WAN consists primarily of small messages containing client requests and metadata replies, as well as one single copy of every requested file.

It is critical to understand that BranchCache is a read-only caching application. The metadata messages described here occur only when branch office clients are requesting files from the content server, not when they are writing modified files back to the server. BranchCache does not support write caching, which is a far more complicated process, because the systems must account for the possibility of conflicts between multiple versions of the same file.

Configuring BranchCache Settings

To implement BranchCache on your network, you must install the appropriate modules on your server(s) and configure Group Policy settings on both servers and clients.

BranchCache requires a minimum of one content server and one or more branch office workstations. You can install additional content servers at any location that serves files to branch offices.

At the branch office, BranchCache in distributed cache mode can typically support up to 50 workstations. To use hosted cache mode, you must have a branch office server at each location where there are branch office workstations.

CONFIGURING A CONTENT SERVER

To use BranchCache on your network, your files must be stored on a content server running Windows Server 2008 R2. To support SMB requests, the server must have the BranchCache for Network Files role service installed in the File Services role. To support HTTP and BITS requests, you must install the BranchCache feature.

Once you have installed the required BranchCache modules, you must configure a Group Policy setting called Hash Publication for BranchCache. This setting is located in the Computer Configuration\Policies\Administrative Templates\Network\Lanman Server node of a Group Policy object (GPO) or in Local Computer Policy.

The Hash Publication for BranchCache setting, shown in Figure 11-24, enables the server to respond to file requests from BranchCache clients with metadata instead of the files themselves. In this setting, you can stipulate that the server publish hash metadata for all of its shared files or for only the shares you select.

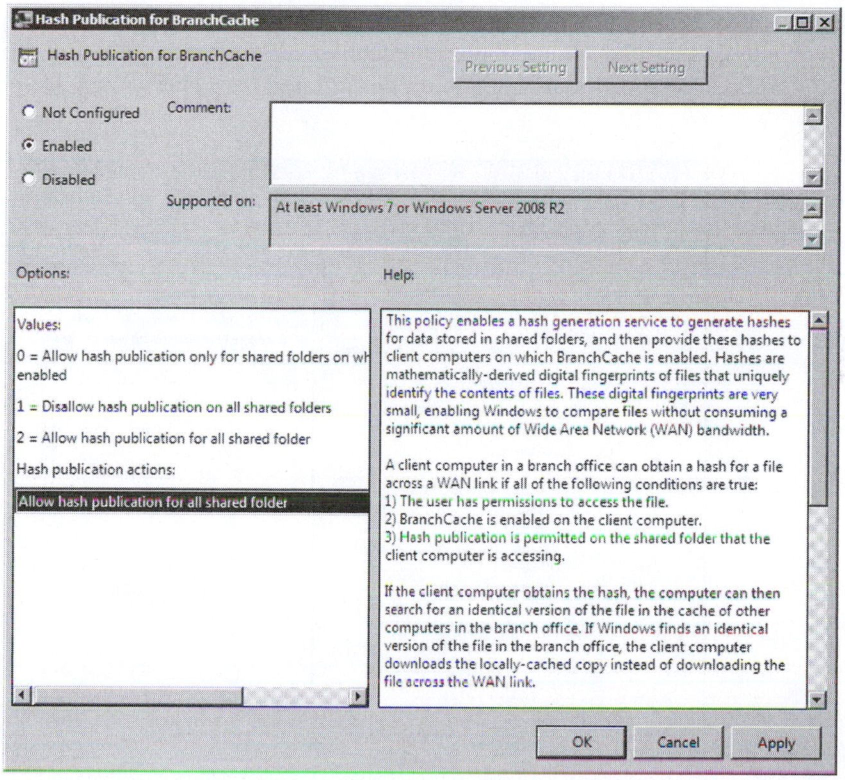

Figure 11-24

The Hash Publication for BranchCache setting in Group Policy

If you select the *Allow hash publication only for shared folders on which BranchCache is enabled* option, you must configure each share for which you want to enable BranchCache by opening the share's Properties sheet in the Share and Storage Management console, clicking Advanced, and selecting an appropriate option on the Caching tab of the Advanced dialog box, as shown in Figure 11-25.

Figure 11-25

The Caching tab of the
Advanced dialog box

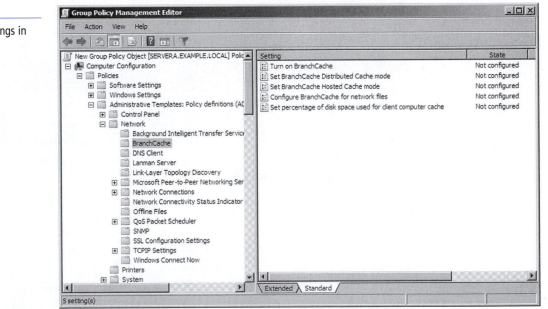

CONFIGURING BRANCHCACHE CLIENTS

BranchCache client computers must be running Windows 7 or Windows Server 2008 R2.
BranchCache is enabled by default in Windows 7. To use a computer running Windows
Server 2008 R2 as a BranchCache client, you must install the BranchCache feature.

To configure BranchCache clients, you must configure the appropriate Group Policy settings found in the Computer Configuration\Policies\Administrative Templates\Network\
BranchCache node of a GPO or in Local Computer Policy, as shown in Figure 11-26.

Figure 11-26

The BranchCache settings in
Group Policy

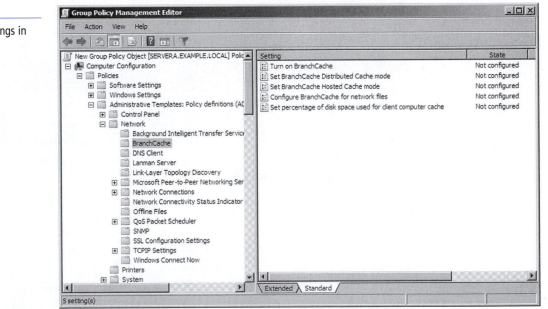

The BranchCache Group Policy settings are as follows:

- **Turn on BranchCache:** Enables BranchCache on the client computer. Enabling this
  setting along with either *Set BranchCache Distributed Cache mode* or *Set BranchCache
  Hosted Cache mode* configures the client to use one of those operational modes. Enabling
  this setting without either one of the mode settings configures the client to cache server
  data on its local drive only, without accessing caches on other computers.

- **Set BranchCache Distributed Cache mode:** When enabled along with the *Turn on BranchCache* setting, configures the client to function in distributed cache mode.

- **Set BranchCache Hosted Cache mode:** When enabled along with the *Turn on BranchCache* setting, configures the client to function in a hosted cache mode. In the *Enter the location of the hosted cache* field, you must specify the address of the computer that will function as the hosted cache server on the branch office network.

- **Configure BranchCache for network files:** When enabled, this setting controls the round trip network latency value that BranchCache uses to differentiate local from remote servers. The default setting is 80 ms. When you decrease the value, the client caches more files; increasing the value causes it to cache fewer files.

- **Set percentage of disk space used for client computer cache:** When enabled, this setting specifies the maximum amount of total disk space that the computer should devote to the BranchCache cache. The default value is 5 percent.

CONFIGURING A HOSTED CACHE MODE SERVER

To use hosted cache mode on your branch office network, you must have a server running Windows Server 2008 R2 with the BranchCache feature installed. You must also configure the *Turn on BranchCache* and *Set BranchCache Hosted Cache mode* Group Policy settings.

The hosted cache mode server must also have a digital certificate issued by a certification authority (CA) that the BranchCache clients trust. You can install an internal CA on the network and use it to issue the certificate, or obtain a certificate from a commercial, third-party CA.

Once you have obtained the certificate, you must use the Certificates snap-in on the hosted cache server to import it. Finally, you must link the certificate to the BranchCache service by opening an elevated command prompt and typing the following command, replacing the thumbprint variable with the thumbprint value from the certificate you imported:

```
netsh http add sslcert ipport=0.0.0.0:443 certhash=thumbprint
appid={d673f5ee-a714-454d-8de2-492e4c1bd8f8}
```

Configuring Data Protection

THE BOTTOM LINE Protecting data from unauthorized access is important, but it is equally critical to protect it from accidental loss or deliberate destruction. To do this, you must create system backups at regular intervals.

Larger, and even some medium-sized, organizations have network-based backup systems that enable multiple workstations to transmit their data to a backup device on the network, such as a magnetic tape drive. Depending on the amount of data involved and the type of storage device, these network backup solutions can easily cost tens of thousands of dollars.

For stand-alone systems or small networks, Windows 7 includes backup tools that you can use to protect your data by copying it to a network drive, another hard disk drive, a USB flash drive, or a series of writable CDs or DVDs. Windows 7 also includes a variety of other tools that you can use to recover from data loss or other system disasters.

Using Backup and Restore

The Windows 7 Backup and Restore control panel enables users to easily set up a repeating regimen of backup jobs using a wizard-based interface.

CERTIFICATION READY?
Configure Backup.
8.1

The backup program included with Windows seems to change significantly with every version of the operating system. The backup program included with Windows XP was capable of getting the job done, but suffered from some serious drawbacks. The software was limited in the types of backup devices it could use, and scheduling repeated backup jobs was difficult.

In Windows Vista, creating a repeating backup job is a simple matter of running the wizard, selecting the files to back up, and selecting the medium you want to use to store the backups. However, the backup program in Vista backs up only document files, not application or operating system files, and there is no way to avoid the wizard and manually create a backup job. To perform a full backup of the entire system, you must use Complete PC, a separate utility.

CREATING A BACKUP JOB

The Windows 7 Backup and Restore control panel integrates the wizard-based file and folder backup and the system image backup capabilities into one program. To create a backup job with the Backup and Restore control panel, use the following procedure.

CREATE A BACKUP JOB

GET READY. Log on to Windows 7 using an account with administrative privileges.

1. Click Start, and then click Control Panel > System and Security > Backup and Restore. The Backup and Restore control panel appears, as shown in Figure 11-27.

Figure 11-27
The Backup and Restore control panel

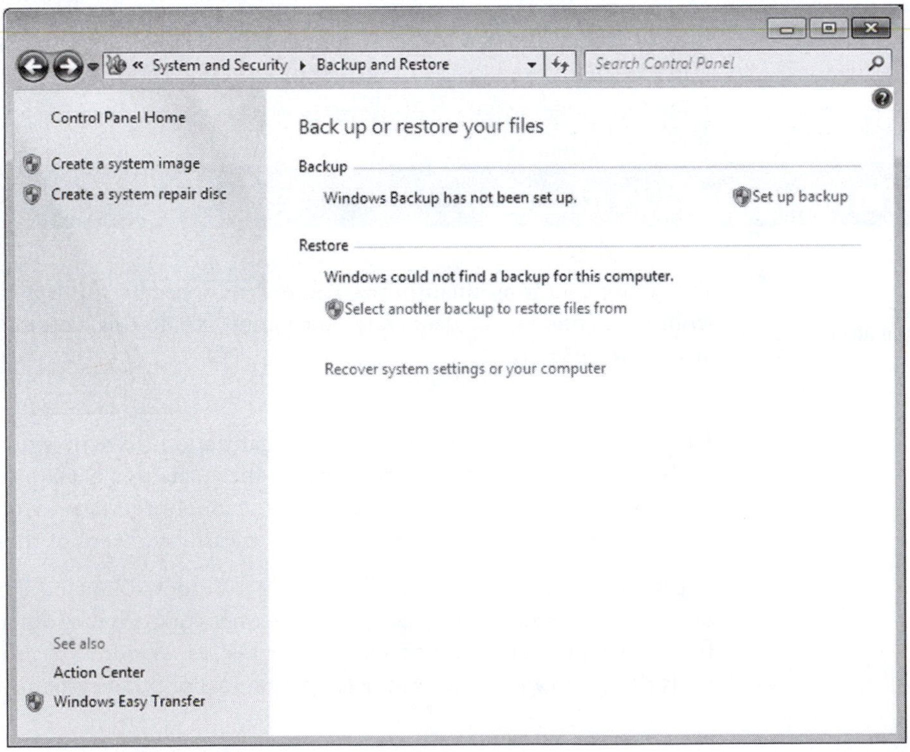

2. Click Set up backup. The *Select where you want to save your backup* page appears, as shown in Figure 11-28.

Figure 11-28

The Select where you want to save your backup page

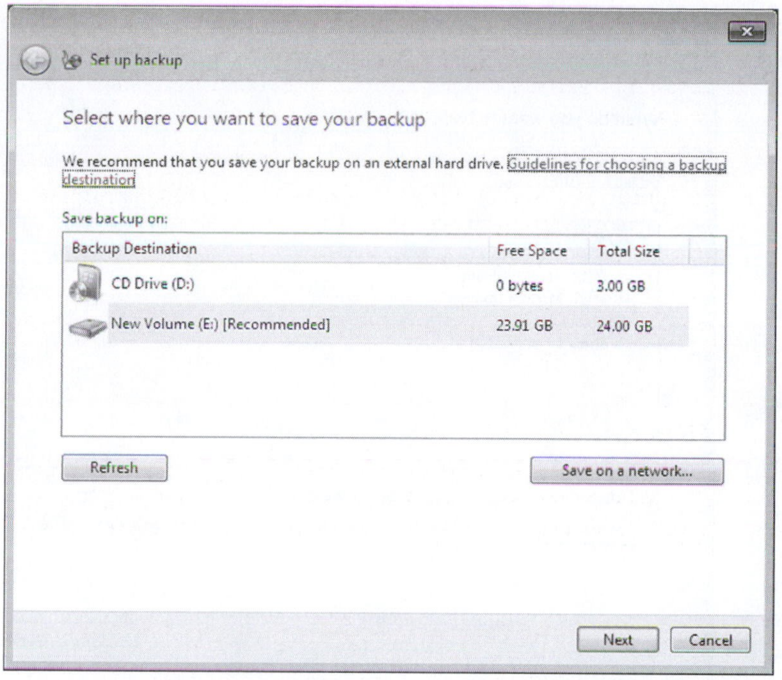

3. Select one of the destinations in the *Save backup on* list and click Next. Windows Backup supports internal and external hard disks, USB flash drives, writable DVD-ROM and CD-ROM drives, and network locations, subject to the limitations shown in Table 11-3. The *What do you want to back up?* page appears.

Table 11-3

Windows 7 Backup Devices

DEVICE	WINDOWS 7 EDITIONS SUPPORTED	BACKUPS SUPPORTED
Internal hard disks	All editions	Files/folders and system images
External hard disks	All editions	Files/folders and system images
DVD-ROMs	All editions	Files/folders and unscheduled system images
CD-ROMs	All editions	Files/folders and unscheduled system images
USB flash drives	All editions	Files/folders only
Network locations	Windows 7 Professional, Enterprise, and Ultimate only	Files/folders and system images

4. Select one of the following options and click Next. The *Review your backup settings* page appears.

   • **Let Windows choose (recommended):** Backs up files in libraries and in the default windows folders. This setting also creates a system image backup.

   • **Let me choose:** Displays a second *What do you want to back up?* page, as shown in Figure 11-29, on which you can select the files and folders you want to back up. You can also opt to perform a system image backup as well.

Figure 11-29

The second What do you want
to back up? page

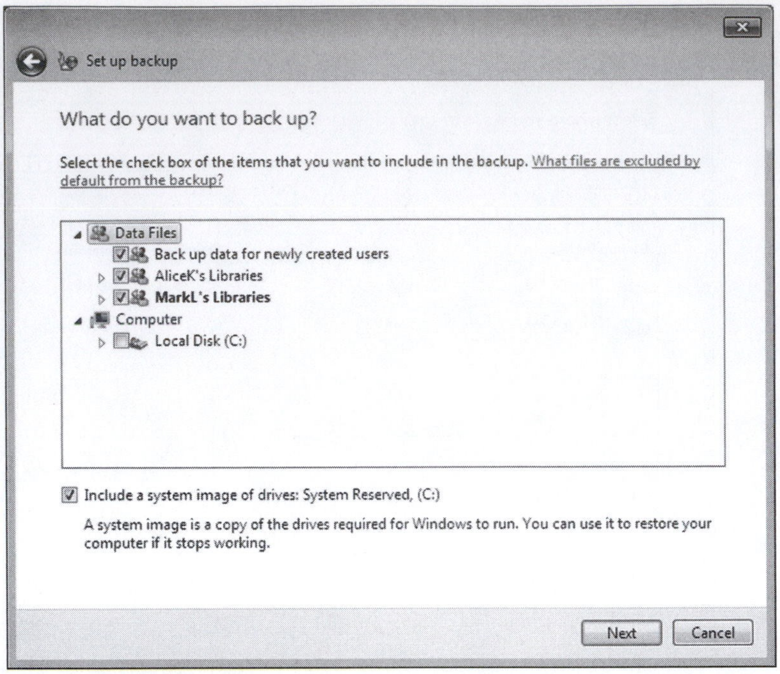

5. To change the default (weekly) job schedule, click Change schedule. The *How often do you want to back up?* page appears, as shown in Figure 11-30.

Figure 11-30

The How often do you want to
back up? page

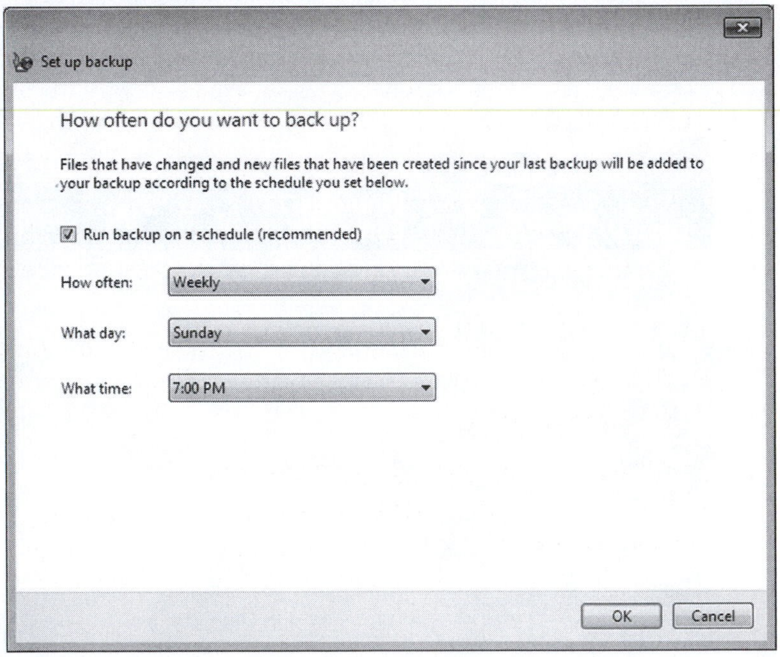

6. In the *How often* drop-down list, specify whether you want the job to run daily, weekly, or monthly. In the *What day* drop-down list, specify the day of the week or the monthly date that you want the job to run. In the *What time* drop-down list, specify the time of day that you want the job to run. To perform a one-time job, clear the Run backup on a schedule (recommended) check box. Then click OK.

7. Click Save settings and run backup. The program creates the backup job, executes it for the first time, and schedules it to repeat at the interval you selected. The Backup and Restore control panel now displays the status of the backup job, as shown in Figure 11-31.

Figure 11-31

The Backup and Restore control panel, displaying the backup job status

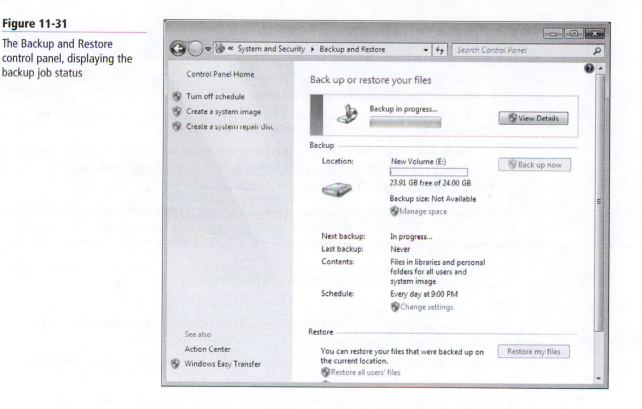

The file and folder backup process stores the selected files in compressed archives with a .zip extension, minimizing the amount of storage space consumed on the backup medium. Windows Backup also conserves space, as well as time, by performing incremental backups automatically.

An **_incremental backup_** is a type of job that backs up only the files that have changed since the last backup was performed. Windows Backup saves multiple versions of each file that changes, but it does not back up multiple copies of unchanged files. It is possible to restore previous versions of modified files; the program only deletes older versions when the backup medium runs out of space.

Because Windows Backup is designed for use with random access storage devices, it always provides the latest version of every file when performing a restore, unless you specifically select an older version.

CREATING A SYSTEM IMAGE BACKUP

As mentioned earlier, you cannot use the file and folder backup capability in the Backup and Restore control panel to protect the entire system. Even when you use the _Let me choose_ option and select the files you want to back up, you cannot select operating system files, such as those in the Windows folder.

To back up the entire system disk, you must perform a **_system image backup_**, which is a separate backup of the computer's system disk and the reserved partition that Windows 7 creates on the disk during installation. Unlike the file and folder backup, which simply copies files to a compressed archive, a system image backup saves each block of the selected targets to a virtual hard disk (VHD) file on the backup device.

You can create a system image backup as part of your regular scheduled backup job, or you can create one separately on demand, but you cannot schedule a system image backup through the Backup and Restore control panel. You can, however, schedule a job from the command prompt, using the Wbadmin.exe utility.

To perform a system image backup, use the following procedure.

➔ CREATE A SYSTEM IMAGE BACKUP

GET READY. Log on to Windows 7 using an account with administrative privileges.

1. Click Start, and then click Control Panel > System and Security > Backup and Restore. The Backup and Restore control panel appears.
2. Click Create a system image. The *Where do you want to save the backup?* page appears.
3. Select one of the destination options and the device where you want to save the backup, and then click Next. The *Confirm your backup settings* page appears.
4. Click Start backup. The backup job starts.

As with file and folder backups, system image backups use incremental jobs by default. However, the incrementals in this type of job simply replace the older versions of files with new ones. The program does not retain copies of older versions.

To restore the computer from a system image backup, you must boot the system into the Windows Recovery Environment (Windows RE). You can do this in either of the following ways:

- Start the computer using a Windows 7 installation disk and, after selecting your language settings, choose *Repair Your Computer*.
- Restart the computer and press F8 as Windows loads. Then, from the Advanced Boot Options menu, select *Repair Your Computer*.

In either case, you will have to specify the location of the backup, and then you will be able to restore the system to the computer.

CREATING A SYSTEM REPAIR DISK

In addition to performing backups and restores, the Backup and Restore control panel can also create a system repair disk, which enables you to access system recovery options if you do not have a Windows 7 installation disk or a recovery partition.

To create a system repair disk, use the following procedure.

➔ CREATE A SYSTEM REPAIR DISK

GET READY. Log on to Windows 7 using an account with administrative privileges.

1. Click Start, and then click Control Panel > System and Security > Backup and Restore. The Backup and Restore control panel appears.
2. Click Create a system repair disc. The *Create a system repair disc* dialog box appears, as shown in Figure 11-32.

Figure 11-32

The Create a system repair disc dialog box

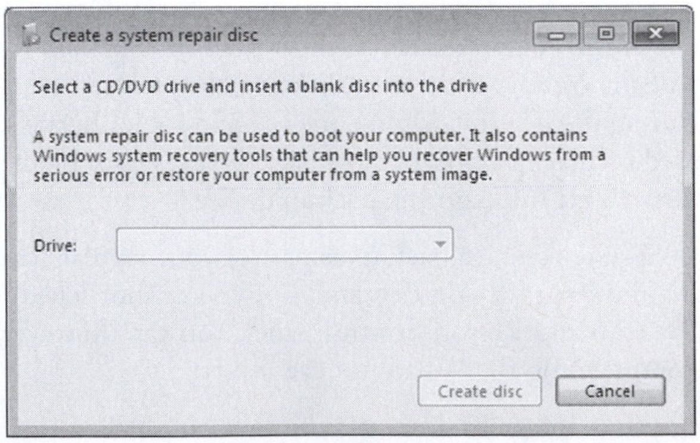

3. Insert a blank DVD-ROM disk into your DVD burner.

4. In the *Drive* drop-down list, select the drive letter corresponding to your DVD burner and click Create disc. The system creates the system repair disk and displays a *Using the system repair disc* page.

5. Click Close.

Store the system repair disk in a safe place, in case you experience a system failure. To use the disk, you simply insert the disk in the drive and boot the system. Windows 7 then displays system recovery options.

CERTIFICATION READY?
Configure file recovery options.
8.3

RESTORING FILES

Once you have completed a file and folder backup job, you can restore specific files from that job at any time. To perform a restore, use the following procedure.

⊕ RESTORE FILES

GET READY. Log on to Windows 7 using an account with administrative privileges.

1. Click Start, and then click Control Panel > System and Security > Backup and Restore. The Backup and Restore control panel appears.

2. Click Restore my files. The *Browse or search your backup for files and folders to restore* page appears, as shown in Figure 11-33.

Figure 11-33

The Browse or search your backup for files and folders to restore page

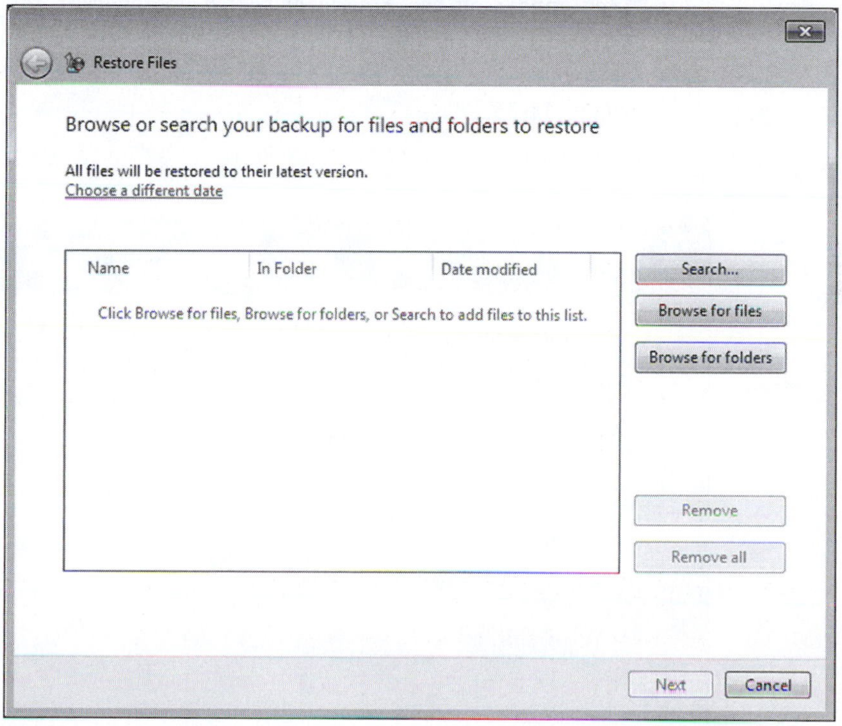

3. Click Browse for files. The *Browse the backup for files* combo box appears, as shown in Figure 11-34.

Figure 11-34

The Browse the backup for files combo box

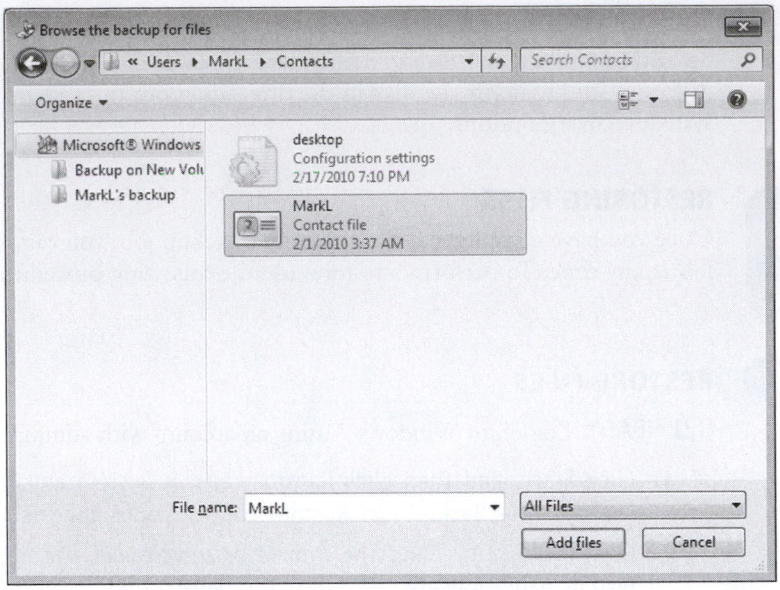

4. Browse to and select the files you want to restore and click Add files. The files appear on the *Browse or search your backup for files and folders to restore* page.

5. Click Next. The *Where do you want to restore your files?* page appears, as shown in Figure 11-35.

Figure 11-35

The Where do you want to restore your files? page

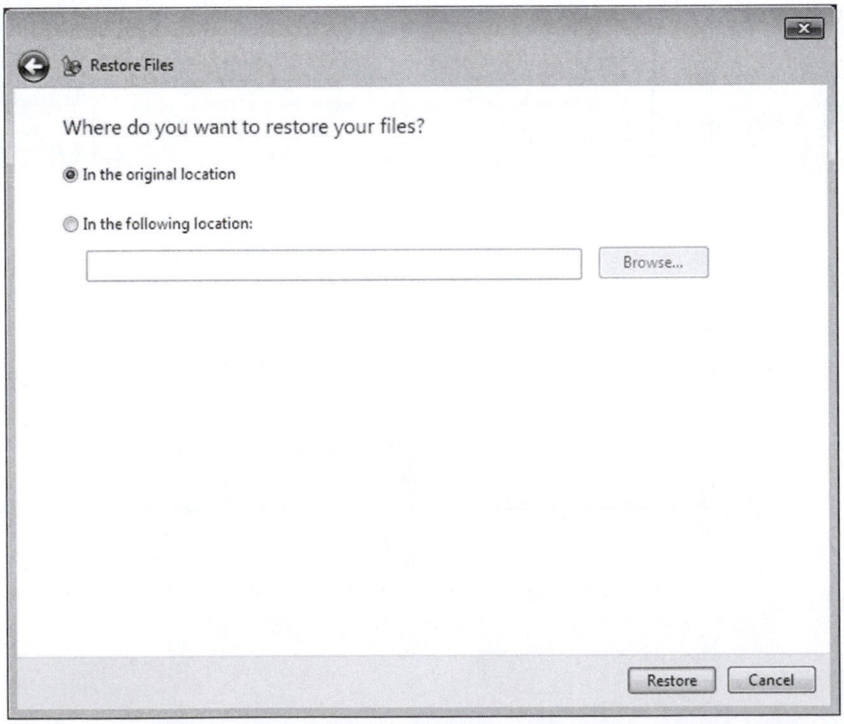

6. Leave the default In the original location option selected or select In the following location and type or browse to the destination for the restore.

7. Click Restore. The program restores the selected files. If files of the same name exist at the destination, the Copy File dialog box appears, as shown in Figure 11-36.

8. Select one of the file copy options to continue. A *Your files have been restored* page appears.

9. Click Finish.

Figure 11-36

The Copy File dialog box

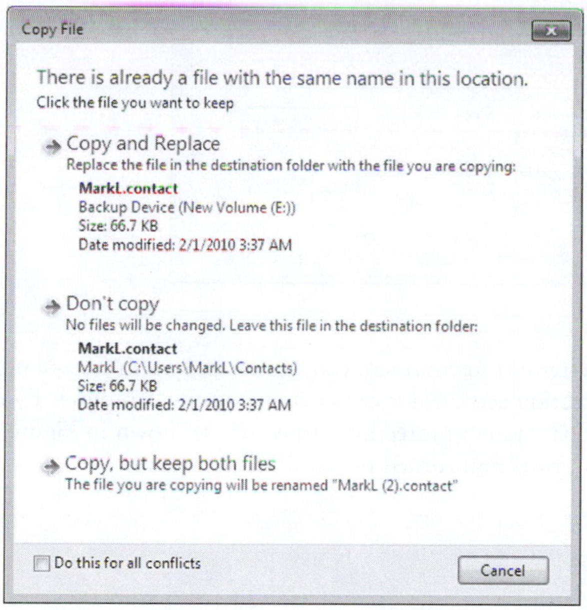

PERFORMING A SYSTEM RESTORE

Windows 7 automatically creates system restore points on a regular basis, including whenever a backup job runs and whenever Windows Update installs operating system updates. A *system restore point* is a copy of various operating system configuration settings and registry information from a specific point in time. If you experience a problem related to a particular change in the system configuration, you can use the Backup and Restore control panel to restore the computer to the system settings of a time of your choosing.

CERTIFICATION READY?
Configure system
recovery options.
8.2

TAKE NOTE*

Performing a system restore is not the same thing as performing a system image restore. A system restore sets the operating system back to a previous state while it's running. A system image restore completely replaces the operating system with an offline copy, and therefore requires that you boot the computer to the Windows RE environment, using a Windows 7 installation disk or its equivalent. For more information, see "Using Recovery Tools," earlier in this lesson.

The primary interface for creating and configuring system protection behavior is the System Protection tab of the System Properties sheet, as shown in Figure 11-37. You can open the System Properties sheet by clicking *Advanced system settings* on the System control panel.

Figure 11-37

The System Protection tab of the System Properties sheet

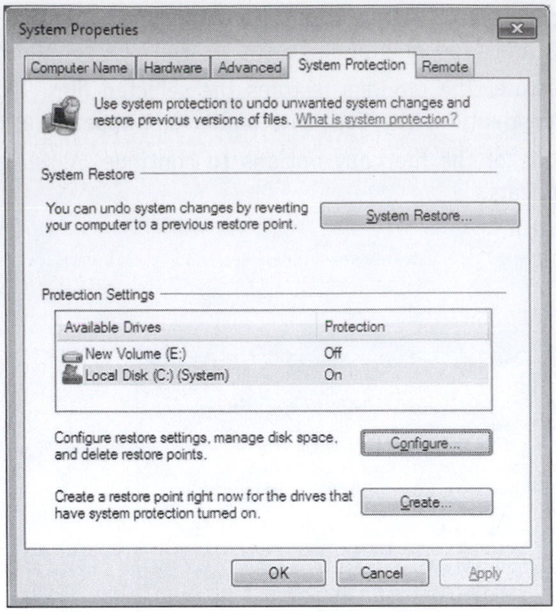

From the System Protection tab, you can create system restore points at will, as well as configure the protection settings for each volume on the computer. By default, the system volume (usually C:) has system protection turned on, as shown in Figure 11-38. All other volumes have system protection turned off until you turn it on.

Figure 11-38

The System Protection for Local Disk (C:) dialog box

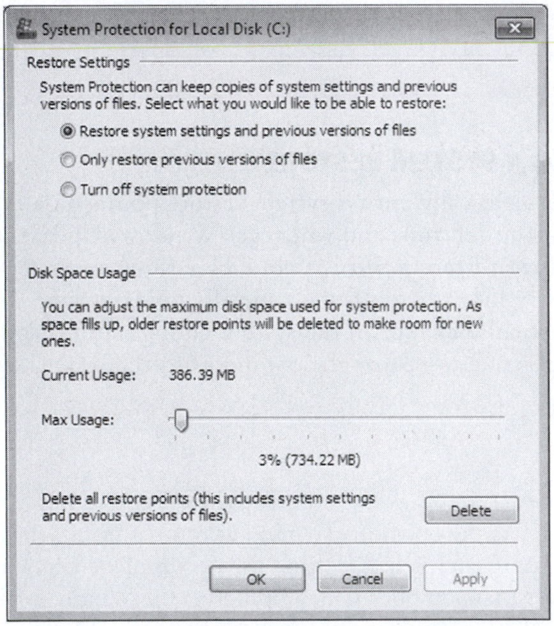

To perform a system restore, use the following procedure.

PERFORM A SYSTEM RESTORE

GET READY. Log on to Windows 7 using an account with administrative privileges.

1. Click Start, and then click Control Panel > System and Security > Backup and Restore. The Backup and Restore control panel appears.

2. Click *Recover system settings or your computer*. The *Restore this computer to an earlier point in time* page appears, as shown in Figure 11-39.

Figure 11-39

The Restore this computer to an earlier point in time page

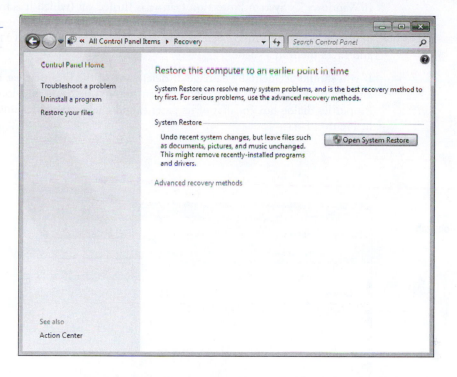

3. Click *Open System Restore*. The System Restore Wizard appears, displaying the *Restore system files and settings* page.

4. Click *Next* to continue. The *Restore your computer to the state it was in before the selected event* page appears, as shown in Figure 11-40.

Figure 11-40

The Restore your computer to the state it was in before the selected event page

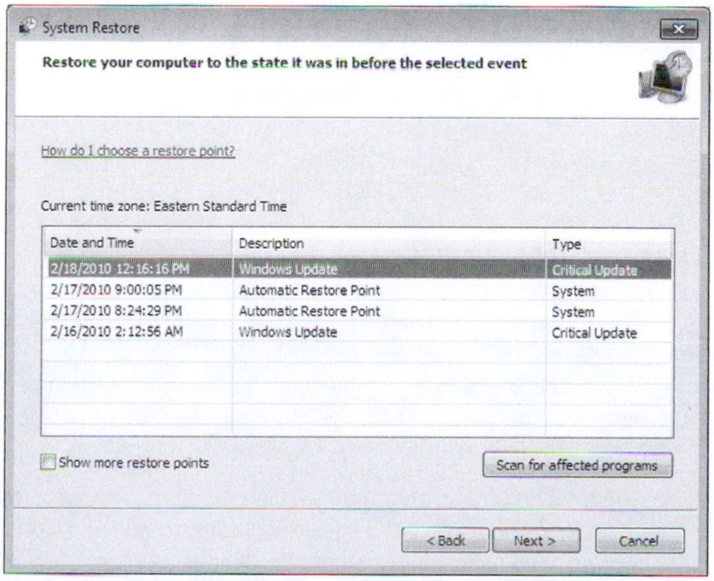

5. Select one of the listed restore points and click *Next*. The *Confirm your restore point* page appears.

6. Click *Finish*. A warning message, indicating that once the system restore process begins, it cannot be interrupted.

7. Click *Yes*. The wizard restores the system to the selected point and restarts.

RESTORING PREVIOUS VERSIONS

Volume shadow copies are duplicates of files that Windows creates as part of a restore point. If Windows 7's System Protection feature is turned on (which it is by default for the system disk), the system automatically creates restore points at periodic intervals. During the creation of a restore point, Windows creates shadow copies of files that have been added or modified and saves them in a cache.

If you should accidentally damage or delete one of the files that has been protected with either a backup or a shadow copy, you can restore one of the previous versions by opening its Properties dialog box (or that of its parent) and clicking the Previous Versions tab, as shown in Figure 11-41.

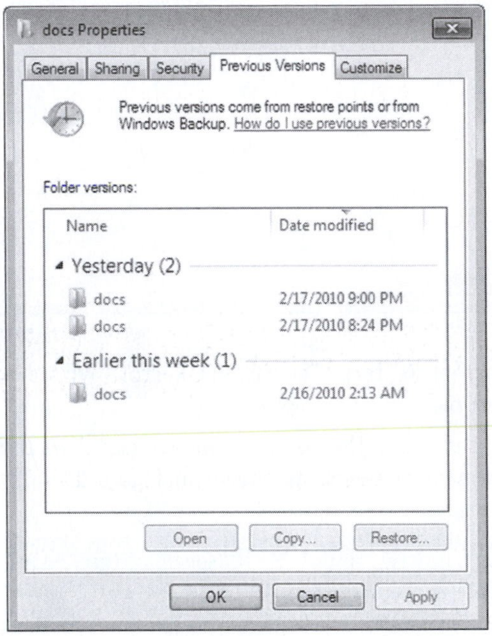

Figure 11-41

The Previous Versions tab of a Properties sheet

SKILL SUMMARY

IN THIS LESSON YOU LEARNED:

- When troubleshooting a problem in a professional environment, whether it's a corporate enterprise network, a help desk in a retail store, or a freelance consultancy, it is important to have a set troubleshooting procedure.

- The troubleshooting procedure should include the following: Establish the symptoms. Identify the affected area. Establish what has changed. Select the most probable cause. Implement a solution. Test the result. Document the solution.

- Remote Assistance is a Windows 7 feature that enables an administrator, trainer, or desktop technician at one location to connect to a distant user's computer, chat with the user, and either view all the user's activities or take complete control of the system.

- Remote Desktop is an administrative feature that enables users to access computers from remote locations, with no interaction required at the remote site.

- To troubleshoot a Windows 7 computer that fails to start, you must have an understanding of the startup procedure, and knowledge of the tools that are available.

- Windows RE is a stripped-down operating system that supports the same drivers used in a complete Windows 7 installation, as well as a subset of the Win32 application programming interface (API).

- BranchCache is a new feature in Windows 7 and Windows Server 2008 R2 that enables networks with computers at remote locations to conserve bandwidth by storing frequently accessed files on local drives.

- The Backup and Restore control panel protects users' document files and enables them to restore single files as needed.

- System image backups protect the entire system, enabling you to restore the computer in the event of a catastrophic failure.

- Volume shadow copies are duplicates of files that Windows creates as part of a restore point. If a user should accidentally damage or delete one of the files, they can restore one of the previous versions.

Knowledge Assessment

Matching

Complete the following exercise by matching the terms with their corresponding definitions.

a. conserves WAN bandwidth
b. files cached on each client
c. files cached on a central server
d. files changed since the last backup job
e. based on the former Terminal Services
f. configuration settings and registry information
g. executes PowerShell commands on remote computers
h. previous versions
i. accessible from a Window 7 installation disk
j. saves data to a VHD file

_____ 1. Remote Desktop

_____ 2. system image backup

_____ 3. BranchCache

_____ 4. distributed cache mode

_____ 5. volume shadow copies

_____ 6. incremental backup

_____ 7. Windows RE

_____ 8. hosted cache mode

_____ 9. Windows Remote Management

_____ 10. system restore point

Multiple Choice

Select one or more correct answers for each of the following questions.

1. Which of the following service priority guidelines are not accurate?
   a. Network-wide problems take precedence over workgroup or departmental problems.
   b. System-wide problems take precedence over application problems.
   c. Shared resources take precedence over individual resources.
   d. You should rate departmental issues according to how the issues affect senior management.

2. Place these troubleshooting steps in the correct order, using the procedure described in this lesson as your guide:
   a. Document the solution
   b. Establish the symptoms
   c. Test the result
   d. Select the most probable cause

3. Which of the following Windows 7 tools does not aid in the network troubleshooting process?
   a. User Accounts control panel
   b. Network Diagnostics
   c. Ipconfig.exe
   d. Tracert.exe

4. Which of the following Windows 7 tools does not aid in the hardware troubleshooting process?
   a. Device Manager
   b. Upgrade Advisor
   c. Nslookup.exe
   d. Performance Monitor

5. Which of the following operating systems cannot use BranchCache? (Choose all that are correct.)
   a. Windows Vista
   b. Windows Server 2008
   c. Windows Server 2008 R2
   d. Windows 7

6. When you load Windows RE from the Windows 7 installation DVD, the system provides you with a choice of recovery tools; which of the following is not included?
   a. System Restore
   b. System Image Recovery
   c. Windows Easy Transfer
   d. Command Prompt

7. Place the following steps of the Windows 7 startup process in their proper order:
   a. Windows Boot Manager phase
   b. Windows Boot Loader phase
   c. Power-on self-test (POST) phase
   d. Initial startup phase

8. Which Windows XP Startup component is no longer needed in Windows 7?
   a. Recovery Console
   b. Ntdetect.com
   c. Boot.ini
   d. NTLDR

9. BranchCache is a client/server application that supports which of the following two operational modes?
   a. Content Server cache mode
   b. Workstation cache mode
   c. Distributed cache mode
   d. Hosted cache mode

10. For stand-alone systems or small networks, Windows 7 includes backup tools that you can use to protect your data. Which of the following devices do the Windows 7 backup tools not permit for backup storage?
    a. An online backup service
    b. Another hard disk drive
    c. A USB flash drive
    d. A series of writable CDs or DVDs

Review Questions

1. Give three reasons why the Remote Assistance tool is safe to use, despite the fact that it can provide a remote user with control over a computer.

2. Place the following phases of the Windows 7 startup sequence in the correct order:

   Logon phase

   Windows Boot Loader phase

   Initial startup phase

   Power-on self-test (POST) phase

   Windows Boot Manager phase

   Kernel loading phase

■ Case Scenarios

Scenario 11-1: Assigning Troubleshooting Priorities

During a busy shift at the help desk at Litware, Inc., a call comes in at 9:05 a.m. from an angry user whose mouse is not working. At 9:07 a.m., the vice president of the Marketing department calls to report that the hard drive in the file server where the company's ad campaigns are stored has failed. At 9:15 a.m., the manager of the Order Entry department calls to report that the email server that delivers the product orders generated through the company's Web site is down. Between 9:25 and 9:45 a.m., four users on the LAN in the Sales department call to report that they cannot access the company intranet server containing the health insurance forms they need. As the help desk manager, which of these four problems should you address first? Explain your answer, and why you did not choose the other three.

Scenario 11-2: Isolating the Problem

You are a freelance computer consultant providing desktop support to a client, Ralph, with a small business network that you designed and installed. The network consists of five Windows 7 computers connected to a single switch, which is in turn connected to a DSL router, providing Internet access to all of the computers. Ralph calls to report that Internet Explorer is unable to connect to any site on the Internet.

Following are three tasks that you will ask Ralph to perform. Explain how each of the tasks can help you to isolate the component that is causing the problem:

1. Ask Ralph to open a Command Prompt window and try to ping a server on the Internet.

2. Ask Ralph to try to connect to a share on another one of the network's computers.

3. Ask Ralph to log on to one of the other computers on the network and try to access the Internet using Internet Explorer.

12 LESSON

Using Mobile Computers

OBJECTIVE DOMAIN MATRIX

TECHNOLOGY SKILL	OBJECTIVE DOMAIN	OBJECTIVE NUMBER
Configuring Windows 7 Wireless Networking	Configure networking settings.	4.3
Using BitLocker	Configure BitLocker and BitLocker To Go.	6.1
Introducing DirectAccess	Configure DirectAccess.	6.2
Opening Windows Mobility Center	Configure mobility options.	6.3
Using Remote Network Connections	Configure remote connections.	6.4

KEY TERMS

Advanced Configuration and Power Interface (ACPI)

Advanced Encryption System (AES)

BitLocker Drive Encryption

data recovery agent (DRA)

DirectAccess

IEEE 802.11

IKEv2 Mobility and Multihoming (MOBIKE)

Institute of Electrical and Electronic Engineers (IEEE)

Internet Key Exchange, Version 2 (IKEv2)

IPsec

Layer 2 Tunneling Protocol (L2TP)

multiple-input multiple-output (MIMO)

Offline Files

Point-to-Point Protocol (PPP)

Point-to-Point Tunneling Protocol (PPTP)

Secure Password (EAP-MSCHAPv2)

Secure Socket Tunneling Protocol (SSTP)

spatial multiplexing

Temporal Key Integrity Protocol (TKIP)

transparent caching

Trusted Platform Module (TPM)

tunneling

virtual private network (VPN)

VPN Reconnect

WiFi Protected Access (WPA and WPA2)

Wired Equivalent Privacy (WEP)

Using Windows 7 on a Mobile Computer

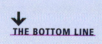

THE BOTTOM LINE | Mobile computing devices present special configuration challenges for technical specialists.

Mobile computing devices are an increasingly popular option for all classes of computer users. Today's laptop computers have performance capabilities comparable to desktops, and many people use them in place of a standard desktop. Although no special procedures or considerations are necessary to install Windows 7 on a laptop computer, technical specialists should be aware of some special configuration settings for laptops, such as power and display options.

In addition to standard laptops, consumers have the option of purchasing tablet PCs from several manufacturers. A tablet PC looks a lot like a standard laptop except that the screen is reversible, so that it faces outward when the user closes the lid. The screen on a tablet PC is also touch sensitive, so that a user can write directly on the LCD panel with a stylus. The standard Windows 7 editions include all of the special software needed for the tablet PC hardware, including a sophisticated handwriting recognition engine that enables the computer to interpret the stylus movements into text and commands. These features also have some specialized configuration settings.

In addition to fully capable computers using the laptop form factor, handheld devices, such as smartphones, are taking the mobile computing world by storm. Too make full use of these devices users must synchronize them with the data on their main computers, and this requires proper configuration.

The following sections examine some the configuration settings that desktop technicians should know how to use when working with mobile devices.

Using Wireless Networking

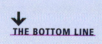

THE BOTTOM LINE | Most mobile computers sold today have wireless networking capabilities. Desktop technicians should be aware of the security issues involved in wireless networking and the configuration tasks required to support them.

Wireless networking technologies have existed for a long time, but only the improvements of the past few years have made wireless networks practical for the average user. In the past, the biggest obstacle to home and small business networking was the expense and inconvenience of installing network cables. Today, many families and organizations with multiple computers use wireless networks to share printers, data, and Internet connections, and in no situation are these wireless technologies more useful than when users are working with mobile computers.

Wireless networks enable laptop users to wander around the home, school, or office, sharing information and collaborating at will. Windows 7 includes full support for wireless networking but, unlike wired network connections that Windows 7 can often install and configure automatically, wireless connections require configuration, which is a job often left to the technical specialist.

Understanding Wireless Security

Wireless networks are subject to many of the same security threats as cabled networks, but the medium they use makes it easier for attackers to penetrate them.

Establishing a wireless connection is not difficult, but establishing a secure one can be. Wired networks typically rely on physical security to protect the privacy of their communications. A potential intruder must have physical access to the network cable to connect to the network. This is not the case with wireless networks. If a wireless network is not properly secured, an intruder in a car parked outside can use a laptop to gain full access to the network's communications.

Connecting to a wireless network can grant an attacker access to resources on an organization's internal network, or it might enable the attacker to access the Internet while hiding his or her identity. Some of the specific types of attacks to which an unsecured wireless network is subject are as follows:

- **Eavesdropping:** Attackers can capture traffic as a wireless computer communicates with a wireless access point (WAP). Depending on the type of antennae the devices use and their transmitting power, an attacker might be able to eavesdrop from hundreds or thousands of feet away.

- **Masquerading:** Attackers might be able to gain access to restricted network resources by impersonating authorized wireless users. This enables the attacker to engage in illegal activities or attack hosts on remote networks while disguised with another identity.

- **Attacks against wireless clients:** Attackers can launch a network-based attack on a wireless computer that is connected to an ad hoc or untrusted wireless network.

- **Denial of service:** Attackers can jam the wireless frequencies by using a transmitter, preventing legitimate users from successfully communicating with a WAP.

- **Data tampering:** Attackers can delete, replay, or modify wireless communications with a man-in-the-middle attack, which is when an intruder intercepts network communications and modifies the contents of the packets before sending them on to their destination.

The concerns over the abuse of wireless networks are far from theoretical. Intruders have a wide variety of tools available for detecting, connecting to, and abusing wireless networks. As with most aspects of security, technologies are available that you can use to limit the vulnerabilities presented by wireless networks. Specifically, you must configure the network computers so that all wireless communications are authenticated and encrypted. This provides protection similar to that offered by the physical security of wired networks.

EVALUATING WIRELESS NETWORKING HARDWARE

The 802.11 standards published by the *Institute of Electrical and Electronic Engineers (IEEE)* dictate the frequencies, transmission speeds, and ranges of wireless networking products. Table 12-1 lists the *IEEE 802.11* standards and their capabilities.

Table 12-1

IEEE Wireless Networking Standards

IEEE STANDARD	RELEASE DATE	STATUS	DATA RATE	INDOOR RANGE	OUTDOOR RANGE
802.11a	1999	Ratified	54 Mb/sec	~30 meters	~100 meters
802.11b	1999	Ratified	11 Mb/sec	~35 meters	~110 meters
802.11g	2003	Ratified	54 Mb/sec	~35 meters	~110 meters
802.11n	2009	Ratified	600 Mb/sec (4×4 MIMO)	~70 meters	~250 meters

Most of the wireless networking hardware now available supports the 802.11b and 802.11g standards. There are also many 802.11n products on the market, some of which are based on the draft standard, while others are certified as conforming to the ratified standard published in late 2009.

+ MORE INFORMATION

IEEE 802.11n equipment increases wireless networking speeds by using multiple transmitter and receiver antennae on each device in a process called *multiple-input multiple-output (MIMO)*. For example, a device using a 2×2 MIMO format has two transmitters and two receivers, operating at different frequencies. The sending system splits its data into two signals for transmission, and the receiving device reassembles the signals into a single data stream. This process is called *spatial multiplexing*. The only potential drawback to this arrangement is the depletion of the available frequency bandwidth by having too many devices in proximity to each other.

As a general rule, devices supporting the newer, faster standards are capable of falling back to slower speeds when necessary. For example, an 802.11g WAP will almost always support computers with 802.11b hardware as well. If you're involved in hardware evaluation or selection, compatibility problems among the basic 802.11 standards are relatively rare. The possibility of purchasing incompatible hardware is likely only if you adopt a proprietary technology.

There is, however, another compatibility factor to consider apart from the IEEE 802.11 standards, and that is the security protocols that the wireless devices support. Two main security protocols are used in the wireless LAN devices on the market today: *Wired Equivalent Privacy (WEP)* and *WiFi Protected Access (WPA* and *WPA2)*. WEP has been around for some time and is supported by virtually all wireless LAN products. WPA and WPA2 are comparatively recent, and some older devices do not support them.

Unfortunately, wireless devices cannot fall back from one security protocol to another. You must decide to use WEP or WPA on your network, and all of your devices must support the one you choose. WPA and WPA2 are inherently more secure than WEP, so they are usually preferable, but if the network has any devices that do not support WPA, you must either replace those devices or settle for WEP.

USING WIRED EQUIVALENT PRIVACY

WEP is a wireless security protocol that helps protect transmitted information by using a security setting, called a shared secret or a shared key, to encrypt network traffic before sending it. To use WEP, administrators must configure all of the devices on the wireless network with the same shared secret key. The devices use that key to encrypt all of their transmissions. Any outside party who gains possession of that key can, at the very least, read the contents of the transmitted packets, and at worst, participate on the network.

Unfortunately, the cryptography used by WEP is relatively weak, and programs that can analyze captured traffic and derive the key from it are readily available. These factors have resulted in WEP becoming one of the most frequently cracked network encryption protocols today.

In addition to its weak cryptography, another factor contributing to WEP's vulnerability is that the protocol standard doesn't provide any mechanism for automatically changing the shared secret. On wireless networks with hundreds of hosts, manually changing the shared secret on a regular basis is a practical impossibility. Therefore, on most WEP networks, the same shared secret tends to stay in place indefinitely. As with any cryptographic function, the longer a system uses the same code, the more time an attacker has to penetrate that code. A static WEP installation that uses the same permanent key gives attackers sufficient opportunity to crack the shared secret and all the time they need to gain access to the network.

If administrators could change the shared secret on a regular basis, however, they would be able to prevent an attacker from gathering enough data to crack the WEP key, and this would significantly improve WEP's privacy. There are techniques for dynamically and automatically changing the shared secret to dramatically reduce WEP's weaknesses, such as the 802.1X authentication protocol.

SELECTING AN AUTHENTICATION METHOD

The initial WEP standards provided for two types of computer authentication:

- **Open system:** Enables any client to connect without providing a password.
- **Shared secret:** Requires wireless clients to authenticate by using a secret key.

Fortunately, choosing between open system and shared secret authentication is easy: always use open system authentication. On the surface this might seem illogical, because open system authentication does not require any proof of identity while shared key authentication requires knowledge of a secret key. However, shared secret authentication actually weakens security because most WEP client implementations use the same secret key for both authentication and WEP encryption. If a malicious user captures the authentication key and manages to penetrate its code, then the WEP encryption key is compromised as well.

Therefore, although shared secret authentication is stronger than open system for authentication, it weakens the WEP encryption. If you use open system authentication, any computer can easily join your network. However, without the WEP encryption key the unauthorized clients cannot send or receive wireless communications, and they will not be able to abuse the wireless network.

USING WIFI PROTECTED ACCESS

To address the weaknesses of WEP, the WiFi Alliance, a consortium of the leading wireless network equipment vendors, developed WiFi Protected Access (WPA). WPA can use the same authentication mechanisms and encryption algorithms as WEP, which enables manufacturers to add support for WPA to existing products with a simple software or firmware upgrade.

There are two encryption options for WPA, as follows:

- *Temporal Key Integrity Protocol (TKIP):* Implemented in the original WPA standard, TKIP encrypts data using the RC4 algorithm with a 128-bit key. This is the same algorithm as WEP, but TKIP virtually eliminates WEP's most exploited vulnerability by using a unique encryption key for each packet.
- *Advanced Encryption System (AES):* Implemented in the WPA2 standard, AES uses a different and more secure encryption algorithm, called CCMP. However, while it is possible to upgrade some legacy WEP equipment to support WPA-TKIP, most equipment cannot be upgraded to support AES. As a result, a wireless network will probably not be able to use AES encryption unless the organization chooses equipment that specifically supports it.

In its current form, WPA has two operational modes, as follows:

- **WPA-Personal:** Also known as WPA-PSK or preshared key mode, an administrator selects a passphrase that is automatically associated with the dynamically generated security settings. This passphrase is stored with the network settings in the WAP and on each of the networked computers. Only wireless devices with the WPA passphrase can join the network and decrypt network transmissions.
- **WPA-Enterprise:** Also known as WPA-802.1X or WPA-RADIUS, requires an authentication server using Remote Authentication Dial-In User Service (RADIUS) and the 802.1X authentication protocol, as implemented in the Network Policy and Access Services role in Windows Server 2008 R2. Although more difficult to implement and configure, the use of RADIUS and 802.1X is more secure. This combination provides centralized administration, auditing, and logging, and eliminates the need for a shared passphrase, which is a potential vulnerability.

Configuring Windows 7 Wireless Networking

Wireless networking equipment must be configured before computers can connect to the network safely and securely.

The process of configuring a wireless network adapter on a Windows 7 computer can vary depending on the hardware involved. Some wireless adapters are supported directly by Windows 7, and the setup process is simply a matter of installing the hardware and letting the operating system detect it and install a device driver. However, some wireless adapters include their own configuration software, which you must install before you can configure the adapter.

To manually configure the adapter settings for a specific network, use the following procedure.

CERTIFICATION READY?
Configure networking settings.
4.3

➡️ **CONFIGURE A WIRELESS ADAPTER**

GET READY. Install the wireless network adapter by inserting it into a PCI or PC Card slot, or connecting it to a USB port. Then start the computer and log on to Windows 7.

1. Click Start, and then click Control Panel > Network and Internet > Network and Sharing Center. The Network and Sharing Center control panel appears, as shown in Figure 12-1.

Figure 12-1

The Network and Sharing Center control panel

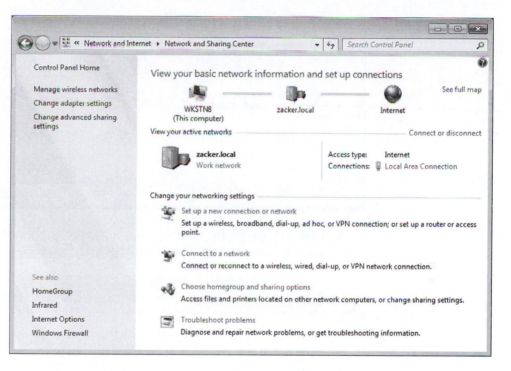

2. Click Manage wireless networks. The Manage Wireless Networks window appears, as shown in Figure 12-2.

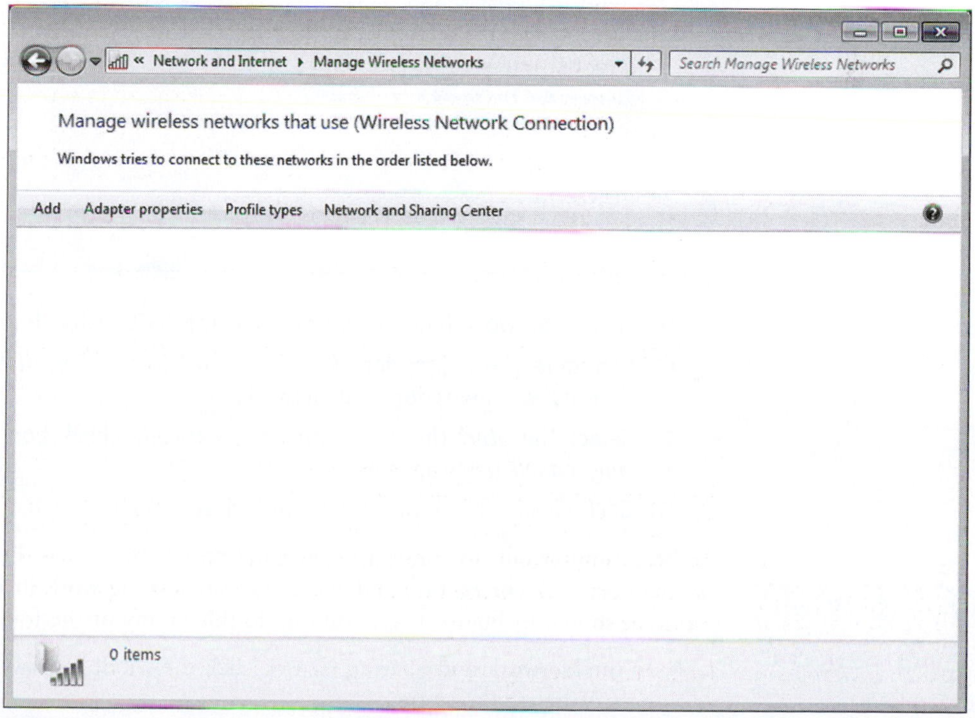

Figure 12-2

The Manage Wireless Networks window

3. Click Add. The *How do you want to add a network?* page appears, as shown in Figure 12-3.

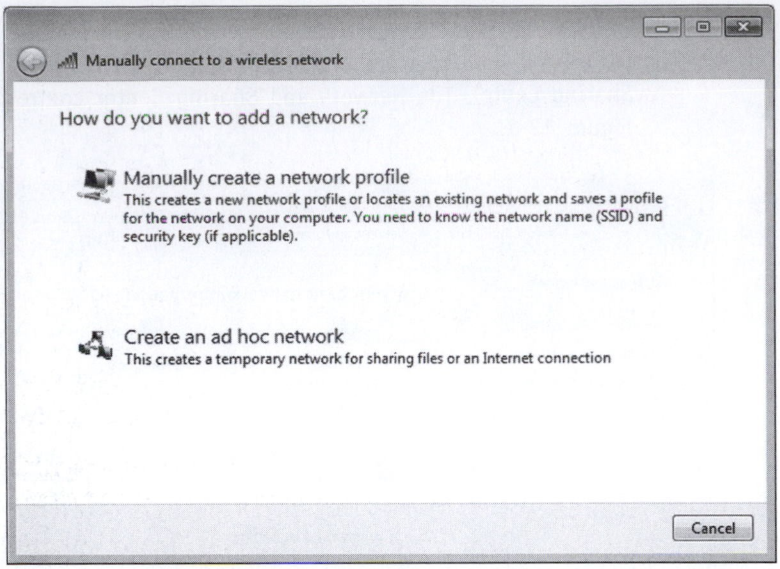

Figure 12-3

The How do you want to add a network? page

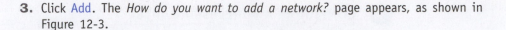

Manually connect to a wireless network

How do you want to add a network?

Manually create a network profile
This creates a new network profile or locates an existing network and saves a profile for the network on your computer. You need to know the network name (SSID) and security key (if applicable).

Create an ad hoc network
This creates a temporary network for sharing files or an Internet connection

Cancel

4. Click Manually create a network profile. The *Enter information for the wireless network you want to add* page appears, as shown in Figure 12-4.

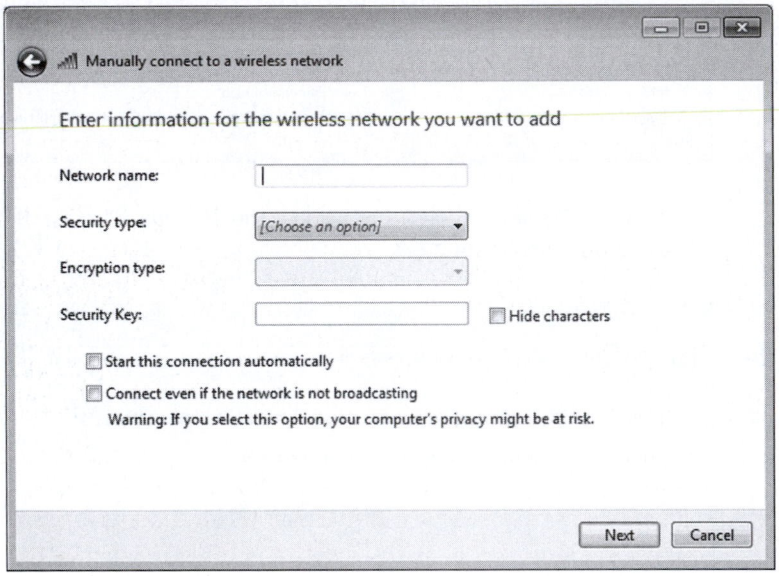

Figure 12-4

The Enter information for the wireless network you want to add page

Manually connect to a wireless network

Enter information for the wireless network you want to add

Network name: |

Security type: [Choose an option]

Encryption type:

Security Key: ☐ Hide characters

☐ Start this connection automatically

☐ Connect even if the network is not broadcasting
   Warning: If you select this option, your computer's privacy might be at risk.

Next   Cancel

5. In the Network Name text box, type the SSID value for the network.

6. Configure the appropriate security values in the *Security type*, *Encryption type*, and *Security key* fields for your network.

7. Select the *Start this connection automatically* check box and click Next. The *Successfully added* page appears.

8. Click Close. The network you created appears in the list of networks.

If the computer fails to connect to the wireless network, open the Status dialog box for the wireless network connection and check the Wireless Network Properties sheet for the network, as shown in Figure 12-5. You can do this in any of the following ways:

• In the Network and Sharing Center, click the wireless network connection, and then click Wireless Properties.

Figure 12-5

The Wireless Network
Properties sheet

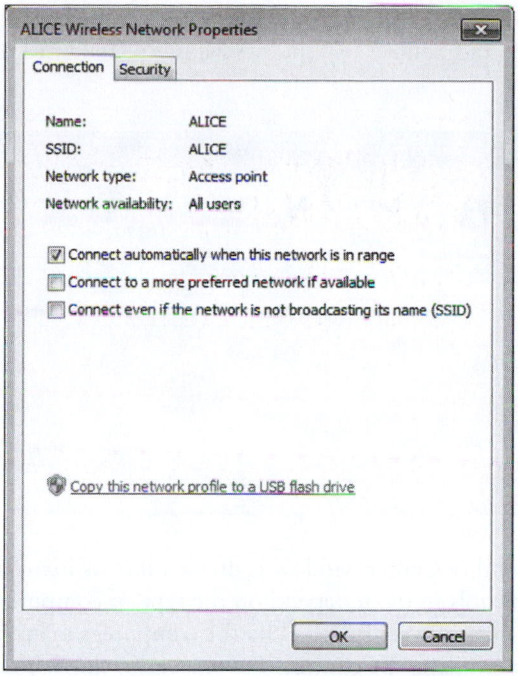

[Figure: ALICE Wireless Network Properties dialog box]

ALICE Wireless Network Properties

Connection | Security

Name: ALICE
SSID: ALICE
Network type: Access point
Network availability: All users

☑ Connect automatically when this network is in range
☐ Connect to a more preferred network if available
☐ Connect even if the network is not broadcasting its name (SSID)

Copy this network profile to a USB flash drive

OK | Cancel

- In the Network Connections window, double click the wireless network connection and then, from the Status dialog box, click Wireless Properties.
- On the Manage Wireless Networks page, double click the network profile you created.

In most cases, wireless connection failures are due to misconfigured security settings. In the Wireless Properties sheet, you can select the security protocol and type of encryption the network uses, and specify the *Security key* value. All of these settings must match the values of the access point to which you are trying to connect, even when its interface may use slightly different terminology for those settings.

Using Windows Mobility Controls

↓
THE BOTTOM LINE

The Windows Mobility Center provides users with convenient access to Windows 7's most frequently used configuration settings.

Windows 7 includes a number of special tools designed specifically for mobile PCs, and particularly laptop computers. Some of these tools take advantage of features that are unique to mobile computers, while others simply consolidate frequently used settings into a single interface.

Opening Windows Mobility Center

Windows Mobility Center provides users with quick access to the configuration settings most commonly adjusted by mobile computer users.

Windows Mobility Center is a shell application. It performs no special functions of its own; it simply provides a central point of access for many of the configuration settings that mobile computer users need frequently. These settings are located in various control panel applets, but placing them in a single window enables users to make adjustments quickly and easily. This is particularly beneficial to business users who give presentations with their laptop computers.

CERTIFICATION READY?
Configure mobility options.
6.3

To open the Windows Mobility Center on a mobile computer, click Start, then click Control Panel > Hardware and Sound > Windows Mobility Center to display the window shown in Figure 12-6.

Figure 12-6

The Windows Mobility Center

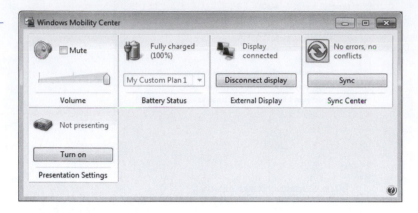

The Windows Mobility Center window is divided into as many as eight tiles. The tiles that appear and the controls in them depend on the type of computer you are using, its hardware components, and the software supplied by the computer's manufacturer. You can modify configuration settings by using the controls that appear in the Windows Mobility Center window or by clicking the icon in one of the tiles to open the corresponding control panel applet.

The eight tiles that can appear in the Windows Mobility Center are as follows:

- **Brightness:** Enables the user to adjust the brightness of the computer's display.
- **Volume:** Enables the user to adjust the volume of the computer's speakers, or mute them completely.
- **Battery Status:** Displays the computer's current power status (AC or battery) and the battery's charge, and allows the user to select one of the computer's power plans.
- **Wireless Network:** Displays the status of the computer's wireless network connection and enables the user to turn the wireless network adapter on or off.
- **Screen Orientation:** On a tablet PC, enables the user to toggle the computer's display orientation between portrait and landscape.
- **External Display:** Enables the user to connect an external display to the computer and modify the display settings.
- **Sync Center:** Enables the user to set up a sync partnership, start a sync event, or monitor the status of a sync event in progress.
- **Presentation Settings:** When turned on, prevents presentations from being interrupted by screen savers and alarms, or attempts to put the computer to sleep. This tile also enables the user to adjust the settings most often used during a presentation, such as the screen saver, speaker volume, and desktop background.

Configuring Mobile Display Options

To accommodate presentation audiences and other situations, mobile users are likely to adjust their display settings more frequently than desktop users.

One of the biggest benefits of mobile computing is the ability to collaborate with other users, bringing your data and your applications with you. Most laptop computers have the capability to connect an external display device, making it possible for a group of users to view the desktop without having to crowd around a single screen. Many people use this external display capability to give lectures, presentations, or demonstrations, using a variety of external display technologies.

Desktop technicians should be familiar with the computer capabilities, configuration settings, and controls used to manage the display options, as discussed in the following settings.

CONNECTING AN EXTERNAL DISPLAY

In most cases, the ability to connect an external display to a laptop computer depends on the system's hardware and software. Many laptops include VGA (Video Graphics Array), DVI (Digital Visual Interface), and/or S-Video connectors that enable you to attach an external display to the computer, and drivers that enable you to configure the properties of each display separately.

At its simplest, an external display can be a standard desktop monitor—analog or digital, LCD or CRT—connected to the laptop and configured to mirror the image on the laptop's own LCD display. If the computer has an S-Video jack, it is also possible to connect a similarly equipped television set. The user can then work with the computer in the normal manner, and a small group of observers can follow the user's action on the external monitor. However, for more elaborate presentations or large audiences, many users employ a display projector, which is a device that uses computer display technology to project an image on a large screen or wall.

Installing the hardware is simply a matter of connecting the external display to the computer using whatever port is provided. VGA and DVI ports are designed for computer monitors. CRTs and lower-end LCD monitors use the standard 15-pin VGA port, while many newer and more advanced LCD monitors use the 29-pin DVI connector. However, some DVI monitors come with an adapter that enables you to plug them into a computer with only a VGA port.

Laptop computers that have a VGA or DVI port for an external monitor typically have a video adapter that is capable of supporting two display configurations. This adapter, plus the device driver that goes with it, enables you to configure the displays using different resolutions, if necessary, and to choose how to use the two displays.

> **+ MORE INFORMATION**
>
> On a desktop computer, you can use either a single video adapter that supports two monitor connections, or two separate video adapters that are designed to work together. On a laptop, however, there is no way to add a second video adapter, so your computer must have an adapter that supports two displays.

CONFIGURING MULTIPLE DISPLAYS

When a Windows 7 computer supports two displays, the standard Display Settings dialog box is modified to contain two icons representing the two displays. By clicking one of the icons, or selecting it from the drop-down list just below the icons, you can configure each display separately.

When you run Windows 7 with two displays, you have two basic configuration choices. You can use the second monitor to display a mirror image of the first, as you would for a presentation, or you can extend the main display to the secondary monitor, creating a single large desktop. This second option enables you to move screen elements, such as icons and windows, from one monitor to the other, creating a huge work environment.

To create a single desktop out of both monitors, use the following procedure.

➡ CONFIGURE AN EXTENDED DESKTOP

GET READY. Using a laptop computer, log on to Windows 7. Connect an external monitor to the computer, using its VGA or DVI port.

1. Click Start, and then click Control Panel > Appearance and Personalization > Display. The Display control panel appears, as shown in Figure 12-7.

Figure 12-7

The Display control panel

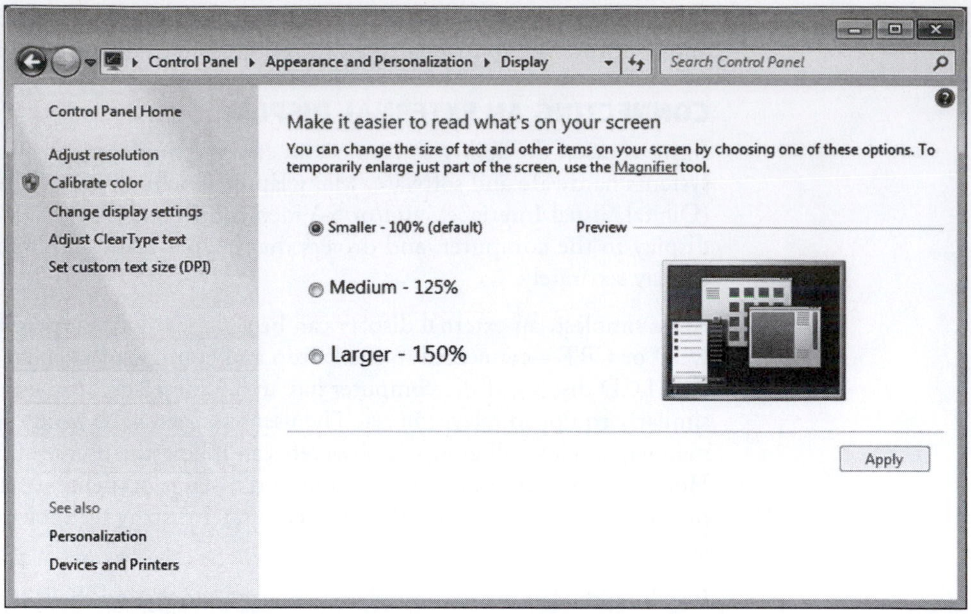

2. Click Change Display Settings. The *Change the appearance of your displays* page appears, as shown in Figure 12-8.

Figure 12-8

The Change the appearance of your displays page

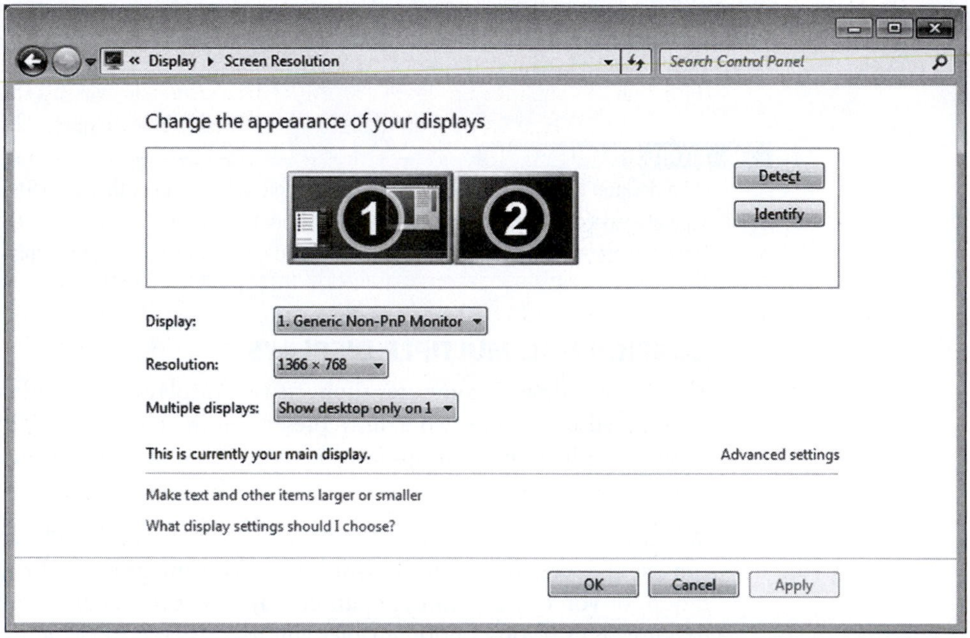

3. Click the display icon for the computer's internal monitor (the one marked with a "1"). Make sure the *This is currently your main display* indicator appears.

4. Click the display icon for the external monitor (the one marked with a "2").

5. In the Multiple Displays drop-down list, select *Extend these displays*, as shown in Figure 12-9.

6. Adjust the resolution setting for the external monitor, if necessary.

7. Click OK to apply the settings.

TAKE NOTE

To mirror the internal display on the external display, select *Duplicate these displays*.

Figure 12-9

Extending the display to a
second monitor

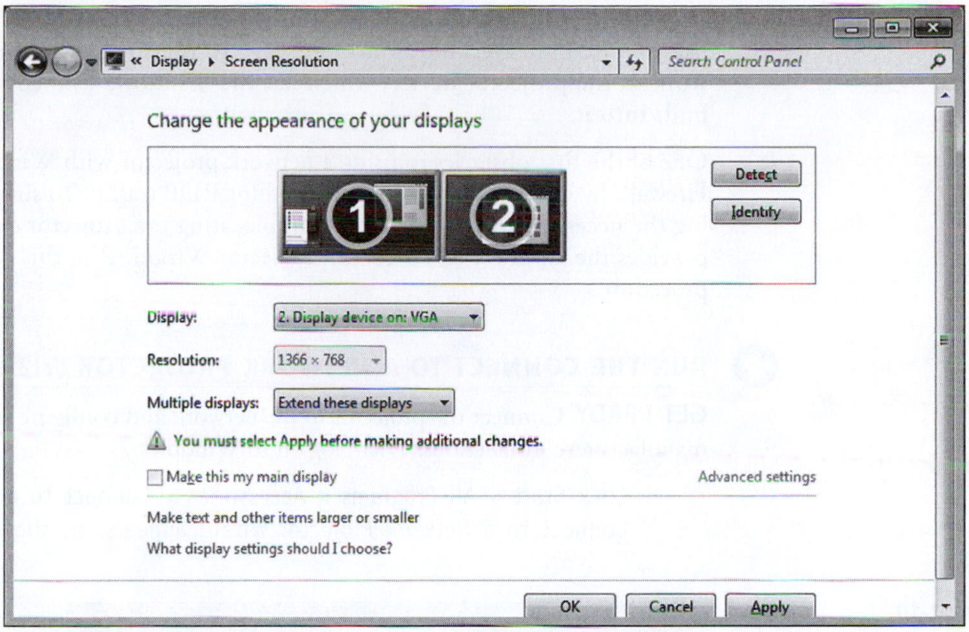

Depending on the size and capabilities of the external monitor, and the size of the audience that will be using it, you might want to use a resolution setting that is different from that of your main monitor. Selecting one of the icons in the Display Settings dialog box enables you to configure the parameters for that display only.

Keep in mind, however, that using different screen resolutions on mirrored displays can have unpredictable results. If the resolution setting for your external display is substantially lower than that for the internal one, you might find yourself moving screen elements on the internal display to locations that are invisible on the external display. Always test your display configuration settings before using them in a presentation or other critical environment.

USING A DISPLAY PROJECTOR

For presentations to larger audiences, many portable computer users prefer to use a display projector as an external display, instead of a standard monitor. A display projector is a device that works like a monitor, except that instead of displaying an image on a screen, it projects a live image of the computer's desktop onto a screen.

Most display projectors can connect to a computer's VGA or DVI port, just like a regular monitor. Others have S-Video and RCA ports for greater flexibility in connecting to variously equipped computers. Some of the more advanced (and expensive) models can even connect directly to a network, either wired or wireless, enabling any computer on the network to send its desktop display to the projector.

Selecting the Display Monitor

Unlike external monitors, projectors are designed to mirror the computer's desktop, not extend it. Laptop computers with external monitor ports typically have some sort of keyboard mechanism that allows you to select whether the computer should send the desktop to the internal LCD panel, the projector, or both. However, Windows 7 simplifies this selection process by displaying a dialog box when you connect a projector, asking you which display(s) you want to use.

Connecting to a Network Projector

Network projectors offer a different situation because they do not connect directly to the video display adapter, and they are not automatically detectible by Windows 7. Instead of simply directing the monitor signal out through a VGA or DVI port, the computer uses the Remote Desktop Protocol (RDP) to transmit the monitor signals over the network to the projector device, which has the Windows Embedded CE operating system built into it.

One of the first obstacles to using a network projector with Windows 7 is that Windows Firewall, by default, blocks the port used for RDP traffic. To simplify the process of configuring the necessary firewall exceptions and locating the projector on the network, Windows 7 provides the Connect to a Network Projector Wizard. Run this wizard using the following procedure.

→ RUN THE CONNECT TO A NETWORK PROJECTOR WIZARD

GET READY. Connect the projector to the network and configure it according to the manufacturer's instructions. Then, log on to Windows 7.

1. Click Start > All Programs > Accessories > Connect to a Network Projector. The Connect to a Network Projector Wizard appears, as shown in Figure 12-10.

Figure 12-10

The Connect to a Network Projector page

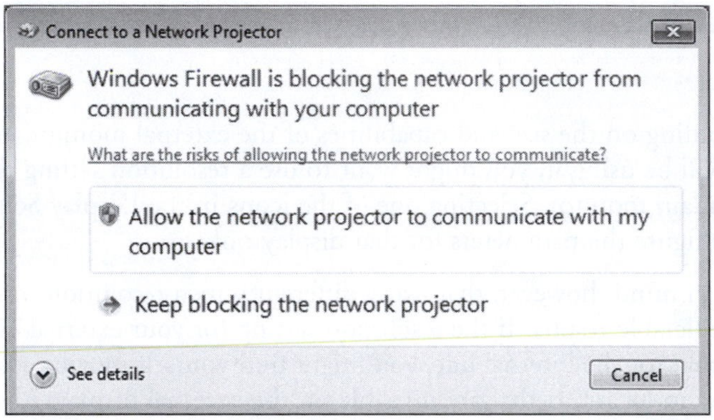

2. Click Allow the network projector to communicate with my computer to create exceptions in the Windows Firewall that will permit communications with the projector. The *How do you want to connect to a network projector?* page appears, as shown in Figure 12-11.

Figure 12-11

The How do you want to connect to a network projector? page

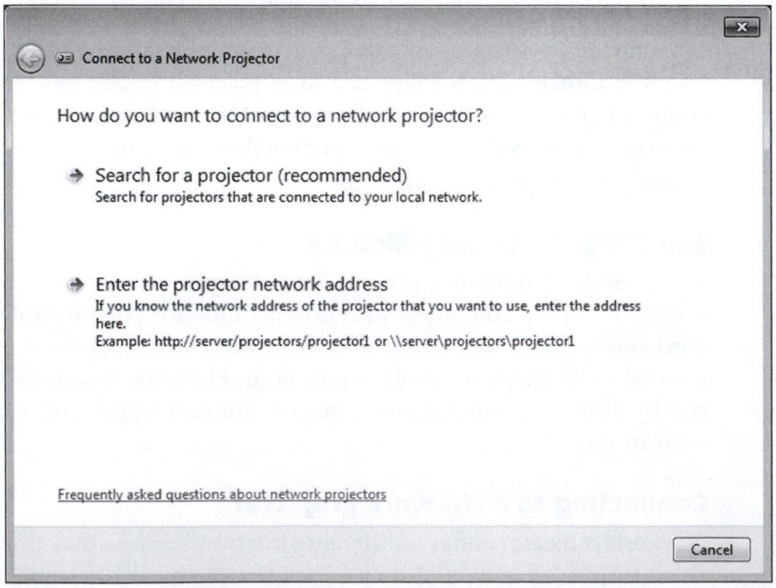

3. Click Search for a projector (recommended). The wizard searches for a projector on the network and prompts you for a password if one is required. You can also click Enter the projector network address to display the *Enter the network address of a network projector* page, as shown in Figure 12-12, in which you can manually supply the projector's network address and password.

4. Click Connect to establish the connection to the projector.

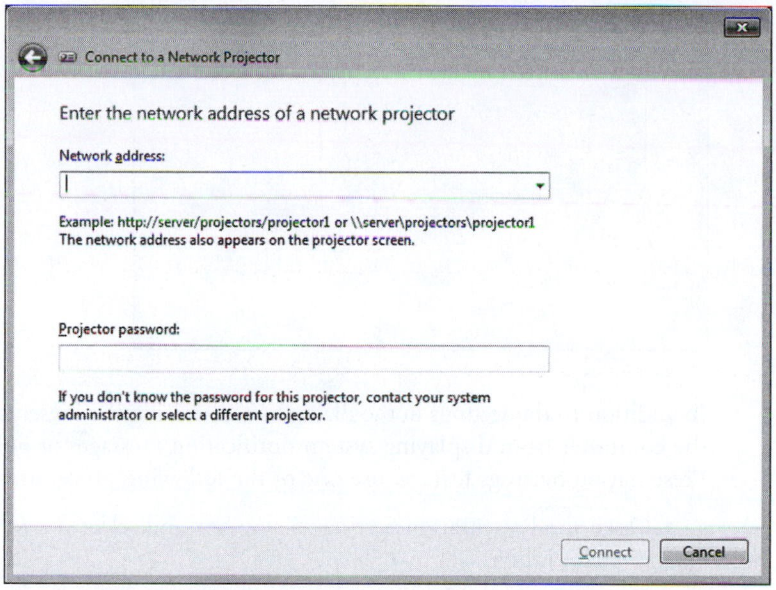

Figure 12-12

The Enter the network address of a network projector page

Configuring Presentation Settings

> The Presentation Settings dialog box provides quick access to the most common adjustments performed by presenters.

Windows 7 designers have attempted to anticipate the needs of many types of computer users. For people who use their mobile computers to give presentations to an audience, few things are more unwelcome than an unexpected system event, such as an error message or a screen saver kicking in. Depending on the audience and the type of presentation, the result of problems like these can range from simple embarrassment to lost sales.

Windows 7 includes a dialog box that bundles together the configuration settings that users most often adjust before giving a presentation, and makes it possible to activate all of the settings with a single switch.

To configure the presentation settings for a computer, use the following procedure.

➔ CONFIGURE PRESENTATION SETTINGS

GET READY. Log on to Windows 7 using an account with administrative privileges.

1. Click Start, and then click Control Panel > Hardware and Sound > Windows Mobility Center > Adjust Settings Before Giving a Presentation. The Presentation Settings dialog box appears, as shown in Figure 12-13.

2. Use the controls to turn off the screen saver, adjust the speaker volume, or display an alternate desktop background when the Presentation Settings feature is activated.

3. Click OK to save your settings.

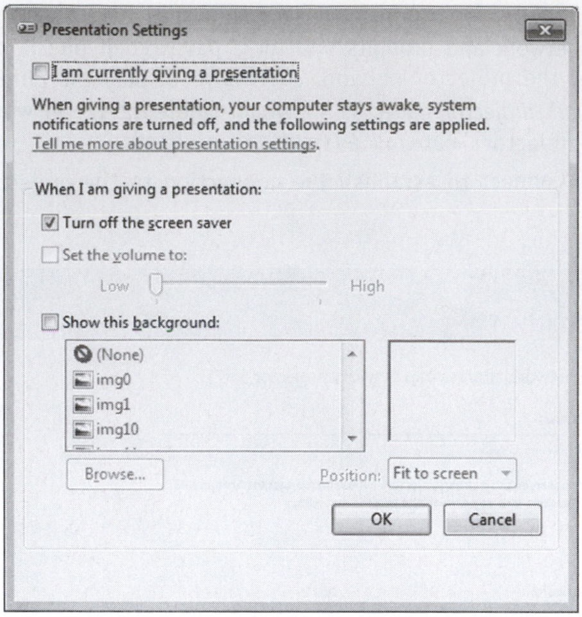

Figure 12-13

The Presentation Settings
dialog box

In addition to the settings in the dialog box, activating the Presentation Settings feature prevents the computer from displaying system notification messages or going to sleep. To activate the Presentation Settings feature, use one of the following procedures:

- Open the Presentation Settings dialog box and select the *I am currently giving a presentation* check box.
- Open Windows Mobility Center and, in the Presentation Settings tile, click *Turn on*.

Configuring Power Options

Windows 7 enables you to fine-tune the power consumption of a mobile computer by configuring individual components to operate at lower power levels.

Power conservation is a critical issue for laptop users who rely on batteries, particularly when using the computer for a presentation. Running out of power in the middle of a demonstration could be disastrous, so it is important for users to be aware of the computer's power level and its power consumption.

To conserve battery power as much as possible, virtually all laptops made today include the hardware and firmware elements needed to dynamically adjust the power consumption of individual components. Some computer components, such as processors and LCD panels, can operate at various power levels, while other devices can be shut down completely when not in use. Windows 7 includes extensive controls called power plans that enable you to create power usage profiles for a laptop computer and assign different profiles depending on whether the computer is plugged in to an AC power source or running on batteries.

MONITORING BATTERY POWER

By default, the Windows 7 desktop contains a power icon in the notification area. When you click that icon, the system displays the following information:

- Whether the computer is currently using AC or battery power
- When running on battery power, the percentage of the battery charge remaining and the amount of time left until the battery is drained
- The power plan currently in use

You can also click *More power options* to open the Power Options control panel, or right click the icon to open the Windows Mobility Center or the Power Options control panel.

WORKING WITH POWER PLANS

Power management is the process of balancing conservation versus performance. Windows 7 includes extensive power management capabilities, including support for the *Advanced Configuration and Power Interface (ACPI)* and the ability to configure all power settings in three ways, using graphical control panel settings, Group Policy, or the command prompt.

The Power Options control panel is the primary interactive power configuration interface. From this control panel you can select the power plan that the computer should use; modify the settings for the default power plans; and create new, custom power plans of your own.

A power plan is a combination of power management settings that provides a balance between power consumption and system performance. Windows 7 includes three default power plans: Balanced (recommended), Power Saver, and High Performance, as shown in Figure 12-14.

Figure 12-14

The Power Options control panel

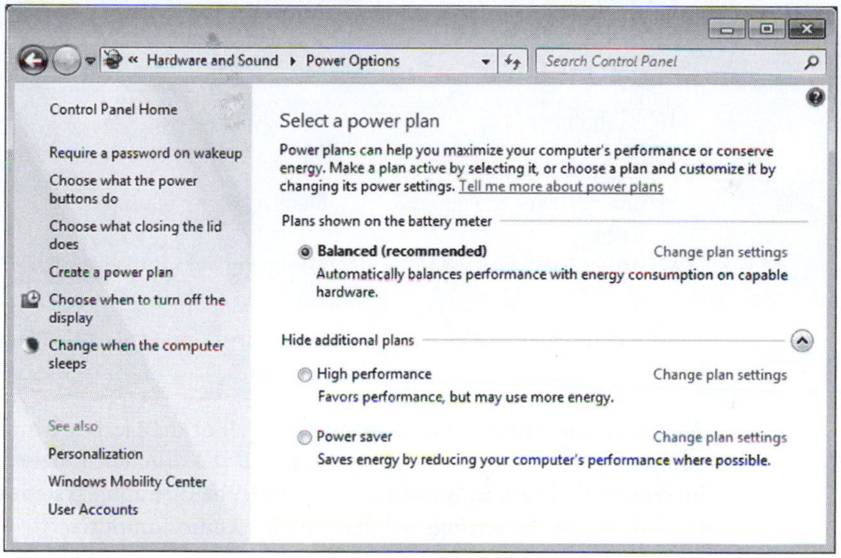

TAKE NOTE The Power Options control panel does not display the High Performance plan by default. You must click the *Show additional plans* down arrow for it to appear.

To select one of the default power plans, you can use any of the following procedures:

- Open the Windows Mobility Center and then, in the Battery Status tile, select one of the plans from the drop-down list.
- Click Start, click Control Panel > Hardware and Sound > Power Options, and then select the radio button for the desired plan.
- Open the Mobile PC control panel, click Power Options, and then select the radio button for the desired plan.
- Click the power icon in the notification area, and then select one of the plans from the menu that appears.

Each power plan consists of two sets of settings, one for when the computer is plugged into an AC power source and one for when the computer is running on battery power. Table 12-2 lists the primary settings for each of the power plans.

Table 12-2

Default Power Plan Settings

POWER SETTING	POWER SAVER	BALANCED	HIGH PERFORMANCE
Turn off the display	2 minutes (battery) 5 minutes (AC)	5 minutes (battery) 10 minutes (AC)	10 minutes (battery) 15 minutes (AC)
Put the computer to sleep	10 minutes (battery) 15 minutes (AC)	15 minutes (battery) 30 minutes (AC)	Never (battery) Never (AC)
Turn off hard disk	5 minutes (battery) 20 minutes (AC)	10 minutes (battery) 20 minutes (AC)	20 minutes (battery) 20 minutes (AC)
Minimum processor state	5% (battery) 5% (AC)	5% (battery) 5% (AC)	5% (battery) 100% (AC)
System cooling policy	Passive (battery) Passive (AC)	Passive (battery) Active (AC)	Active (battery) Active (AC)
Maximum processor state	100% (battery) 100% (AC)	100% (battery) 100% (AC)	100% (battery) 100% (AC)
Wireless adapter power saving mode	Maximum Power Saving (battery) Maximum Performance (AC)	Medium Power Saving (battery) Maximum Performance (AC)	Maximum Performance (battery) Maximum Performance (AC)

As you can see from the data in the table, all of the plans are more conservative when the computer is running on battery power, and the differences between the plan settings are incremental. There is, however, no way for the operating system to know exactly what effect the various power settings will have on a specific computer.

The LCD panel on a laptop with a large, widescreen display will obviously use more power than one with a smaller display, so turning the display off will conserve more battery power. In the same way, hard disk drives, processors, and other components can vary greatly in their power consumption levels. It is up to the user to determine what effect each of the power plans has on a specific computer.

Using the Power Options control panel, you can modify any of the individual settings in a power plan, or you can create a new power plan of your own. To create a custom power plan, use the following procedure.

CREATE A CUSTOM POWER PLAN

GET READY. Log on to Windows 7 using an account with administrative privileges.

1. Click Start, and then click Control Panel > Hardware and Sound > Power Options. The Power Options control panel appears.
2. Click Create a power plan. The Create a power plan wizard appears, as shown in Figure 12-15.

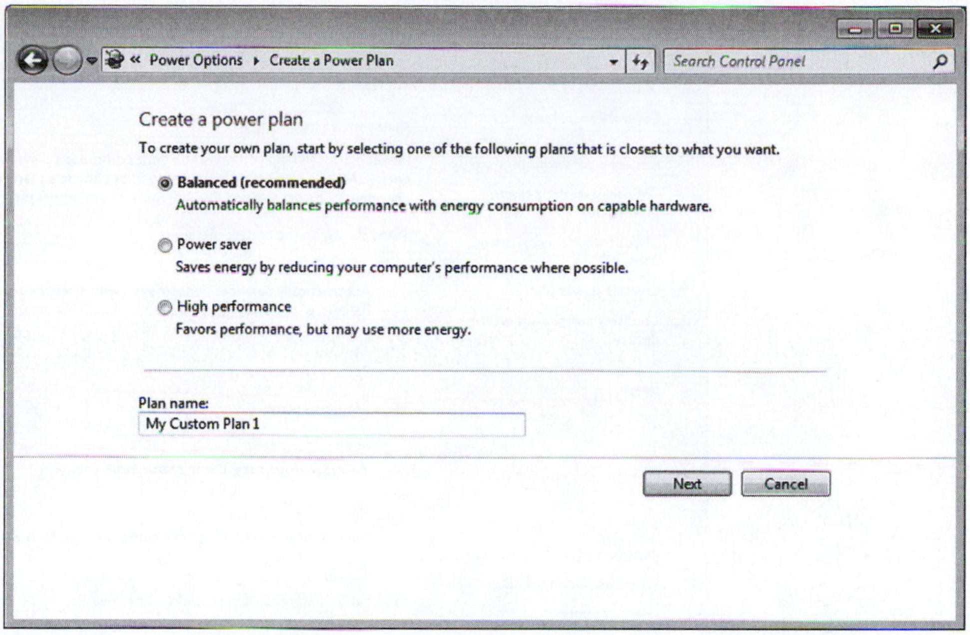

Figure 12-15

The Create a power plan
wizard

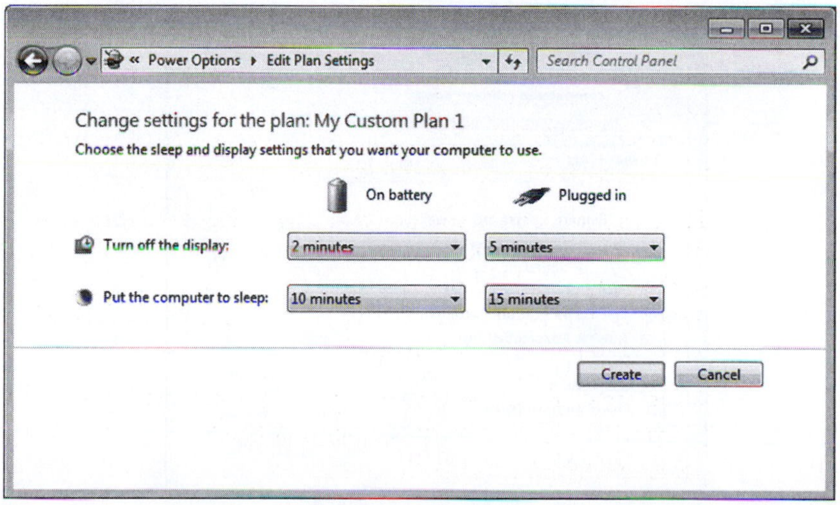

Figure 12-16

The Change settings for the
plan page

3. Select the radio button for the default power plan that will be the basis for your new plan.

4. Type a name for your power plan in the *Plan name* text box. Then click Next. The *Change settings for the plan* page appears, as shown in Figure 12-16.

5. Modify the display and sleep settings as desired for the *On battery* and *Plugged in* power states. Then click Create.

6. The *Select a power plan* page appears, with the new plan you created listed as one of the options, as shown in Figure 12-17.

Figure 12-17

The Select a power plan page

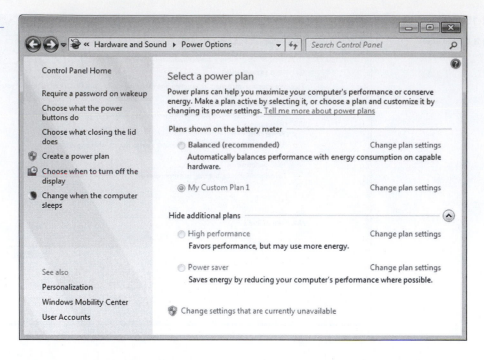

7. Click Change plan settings. The *Change settings for the plan* page appears again.
8. Click Change advanced power settings. The *Advanced settings* dialog box appears, as shown in Figure 12-18.
9. Modify any of the settings as desired and click OK.
10. Click Save Changes to close the *Change settings for the plan* page.

Figure 12-18

The Advanced settings page

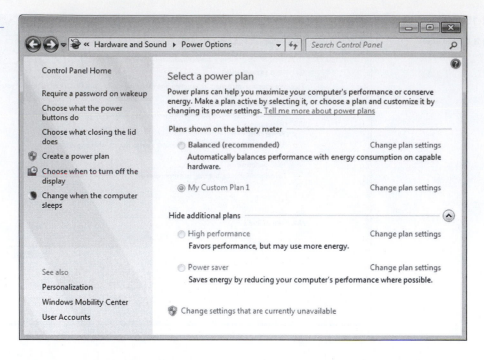

CONFIGURING POWER POLICIES

It is also possible for administrators to configure workstation power options using Group Policy. The Computer Configuration\Policies\Administrative Templates\System\Power Management container in every GPO, as shown in Figure 12-19, contains settings that duplicate all of the controls in the Power Options control panel.

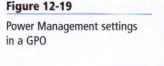

Figure 12-19

Power Management settings
in a GPO

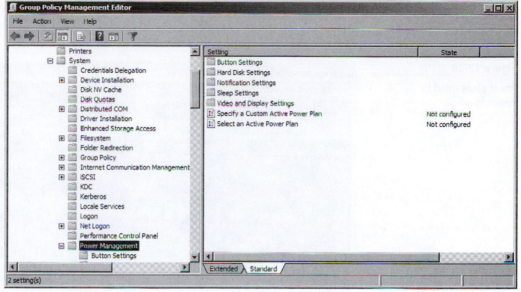

There are a few Power Management settings in Group Policy that you cannot configure
through the Control Panel. In the Sleep Settings container, the following six settings appear:

- Allow Applications To Prevent Automatic Sleep (Plugged In)
- Allow Applications To Prevent Automatic Sleep (On Battery)
- Allow Automatic Sleep With Open Network Files (Plugged In)
- Allow Automatic Sleep With Open Network Files (On Battery)
- Turn On The Ability For Applications To Prevent Sleep Transition (Plugged In)
- Turn On The Ability For Applications To Prevent Sleep Transition (On Battery)

These settings enable you to control whether a workstation can go to sleep when applications
are active or network files are open.

USING POWERCFG.EXE

Powercfg.exe is the command-line program for the Windows 7 power management system.
As the most comprehensive power management interface, Powercfg.exe can configure settings
that are not available from the Control Panel or in Group Policy.

One of the most valuable capabilities of Powercfg.exe is the ability to export entire power
management plans to a file, and then import them on another computer.

To export a power plan, use the following procedure.

⊙ EXPORT A POWER PLAN

GET READY. Log on to Windows 7 using an account with administrative privileges.

1. Click Start, and then click All Programs > Accessories > Command Prompt. The
   Command Prompt window appears.

2. In the Command Prompt window, type powercfg.exe –list and press Enter, as shown in Figure 12-20. The program displays the power plans on the computer.

Figure 12-20

Power plans listed by Powercfg.exe

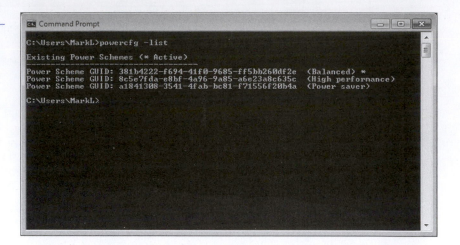

3. Type the following command and press Enter, as shown in Figure 12-21 where *GUID* is the GUID value for the plan you want to export, as displayed in the list:

powercfg.exe -export *power.pow GUID*

4. Close the Command Prompt window.

Figure 12-21

Exporting a power plan with Powercfg.exe

After transferring the file to another computer, you can import it using the following command:

powercfg.exe –import *power.pow*

Synchronizing Data

> Mobile devices enable users to take their data with them wherever they go, but this creates a version control problem.

Mobile computer users often connect to a network when they are in the office, and then take their computers with them when they go home or travel on business. Once the computer disconnects from the network, however, access to the network drives and the files they contain is interrupted. Fortunately, Windows 7 includes the ability to store copies of network files on the local drive for use when the computer is disconnected. This feature is called Offline Files. Windows 7 also makes it possible to maintain copies of files on handheld devices, such as smartphones and PDAs running Windows Phone.

The key to this offline files capability is the synchronization process that occurs when the computer or other device reconnects to the network. Simply copying the files to the mobile device is not enough. Users would have to remember to copy their revised documents back to the network drive after reconnecting. Synchronization is a process in which Windows 7 compares the offline version of a file with the network version, and makes sure that the most recent revisions are present in both places.

Two types of synchronization are supported by Windows 7, as follows:

- **One-way synchronization:** Data moves in one direction only, from the source to the destination. The system replicates any changes users make to the source files to the destination, but changes to the destination files are not replicated to the source. This is recommended for scenarios such as synchronizing music files on a computer with a portable music player.

- **Two-way synchronization:** Data moves in both directions. Changes users make to either copy of the files are replicated to the other system. In the event that both copies have changed, the system prompts the user to resolve the conflict by selecting one of the two versions. This is recommended for scenarios such as copying network-based document files to a mobile system for offline use.

The following sections describe the tools and procedures you can use to ensure that mobile computers synchronize their data reliably.

USING OFFLINE FILES

Offline Files is a form of fault tolerance that individual users can employ to maintain access to their server files, even in the event of a network service failure. Windows 7 workstations copy server-based folders that users designate for offline use to the local drive, and the users work with the copies, which remain accessible whether the computer is connected to the network or not.

If the network connection fails, or the user undocks a portable computer, access to the offline files continues uninterrupted. When the computer reconnects to the network, a synchronization procedure occurs that replicates the files between server and workstation in whichever direction is necessary. If there is a version conflict, such as when users have modified both copies of a file, the system prompts the user to specify which copy to retain.

To synchronize a Windows 7 computer with a network folder you simply browse to the folder using Windows Explorer, right click the folder name, and select Always Available Offline from the context menu. Windows 7 then establishes the partnership and copies the contents of the selected folder to the local hard drive.

Although it is an effective fault tolerance mechanism, primary control of Offline Files rests with the user, which makes it a less suitable solution for an enterprise network than other measures, such as File Redirection.

Configuring Share Caching

Administrators can configure shares to prevent users from saving offline copies. When you create a share using the Advanced Sharing dialog box, clicking Caching opens the Offline Settings dialog box, as shown in Figure 12-22. Here you can specify which files and programs users are permitted to select for storage in the Offline Files cache.

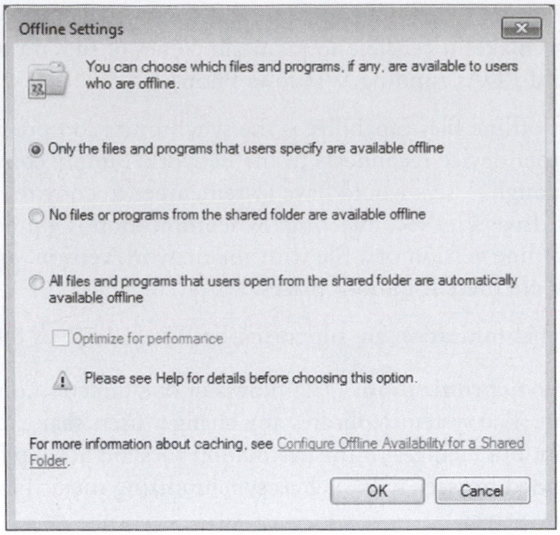

Figure 12-22

The Offline Settings dialog box

Configuring Offline File Policies

Administrators can use Group Policy to configure Offline Files behavior on Windows 7 workstations. The Computer Configuration\Policies\Administrative Templates\Network\Offline Files container in every Group Policy object (GPO) has 28 policy settings, as shown in Figure 12-23.

Using these settings, administrators can control whether workstations are permitted to use Offline Files, how much disk space to allocate to the Offline files cache, whether to encrypt the contents of the cache, and when synchronization events should occur.

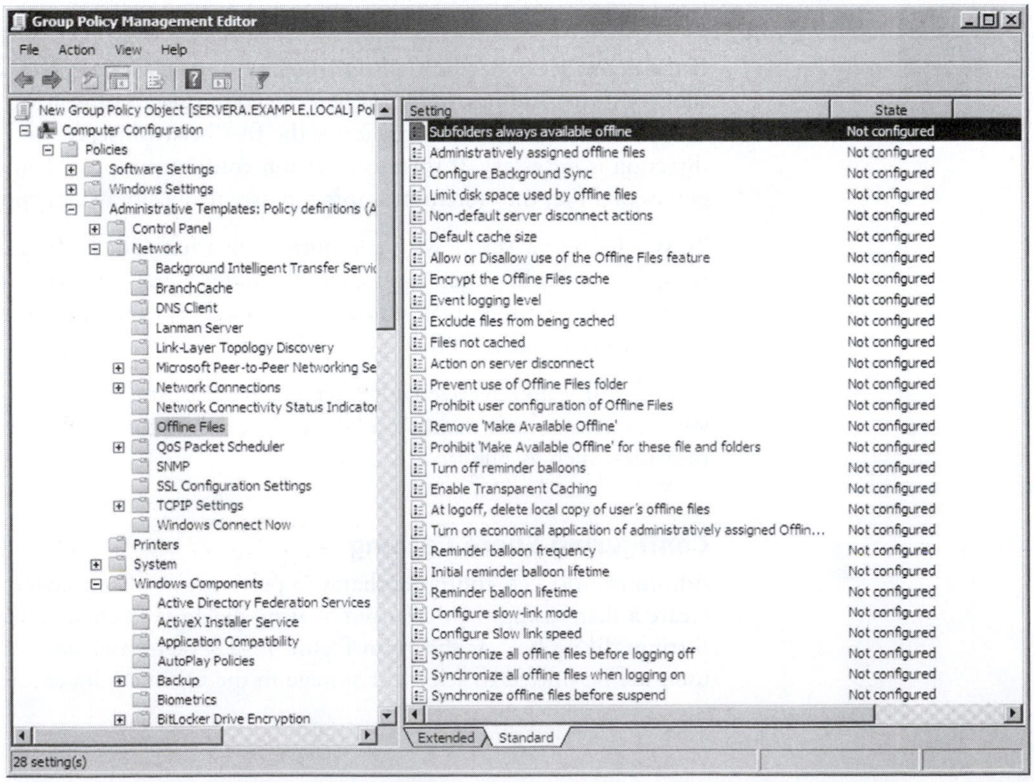

Figure 12-23

The Offline Files Group Policy settings

Using Transparent Caching

The Enable Transparent Caching policy setting, shown in Figure 12-24, causes Windows 7 to save copies of files users access from remote servers on a local drive, whether or not the files are configured as offline files. Unlike Offline Files, the cached files do not remain available when the computer is disconnected from the network, but they do provide the users with faster repeat access, while conserving network bandwidth.

Figure 12-24

The Enable Transparent
Caching policy setting

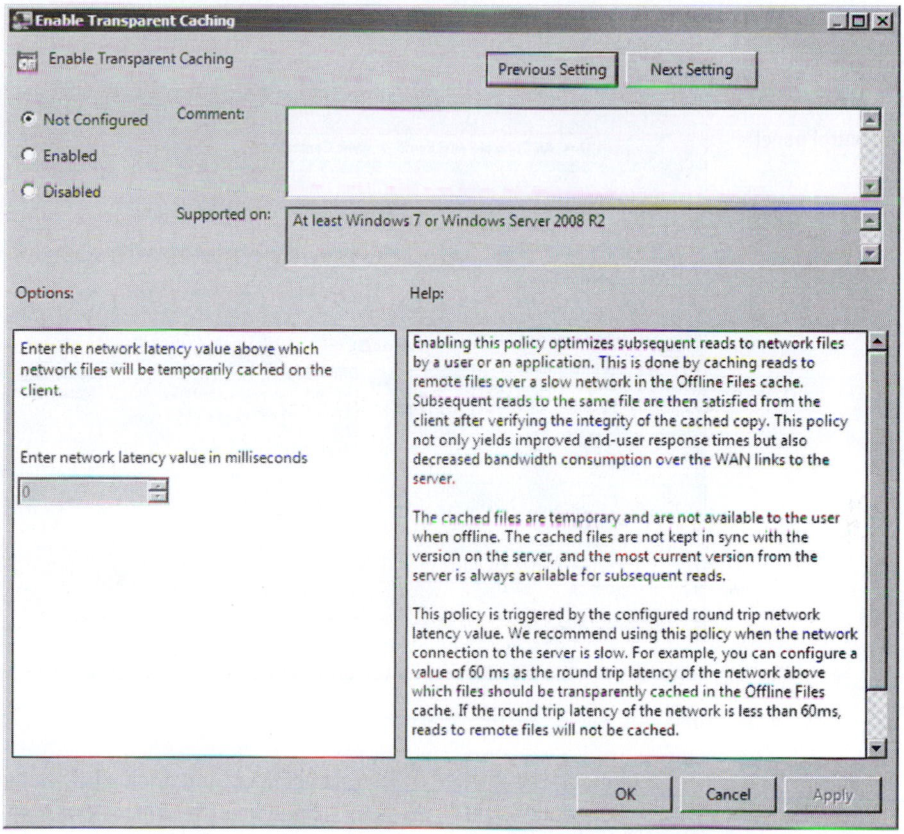

Transparent caching is functionally similar to the BranchCache feature discussed in Lesson 11, "Administering Windows 7," except that each Windows 7 workstation has exclusive use of its own cache; it does not share the cached files with other clients.

Windows 7 decides whether to cache a file based on the network latency value for the connection between the workstation and the server. Transparent caching is designed primarily for clients and servers connected by relatively slow wide area network (WAN) connections. The network latency value is the round time transmission time between the client and the server. The default value for the policy setting is 32,000 milliseconds, or 32 seconds.

USING SYNC CENTER

Sync Center is an application that functions as a central control panel for all of a Windows 7 computer's synchronization partnerships, including those with network drives and mobile devices. Sync partnerships are pairs of folders or devices that are configured to synchronize their data on a regular basis. You can use Sync Center to establish synchronization partnerships, schedule synchronizations, monitor synchronization events, and manage synchronization conflicts.

Once you have established the partnership, you can configure its synchronization schedule. To configure a sync partnership, use the following procedure.

→ **CONFIGURE A SYNC PARTNERSHIP**

GET READY. Log on to Windows 7 using an account with administrative privileges. Then create a sync partnership with a folder on a network drive.

1. Click Start, and then click Control Panel > Hardware and Sound > Windows Mobility Center. The Windows Mobility Center window appears.

2. Click the icon in the Sync Center pane. The Sync Center control panel appears, displaying the *View sync partnerships* page, as shown in Figure 12-25.

Figure 12-25

The Sync Center control panel

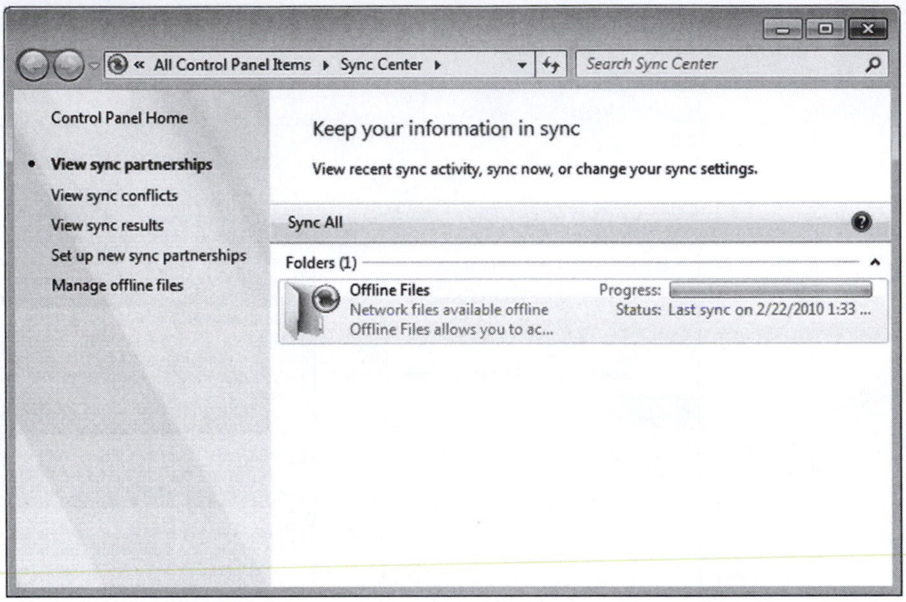

3. Select the Offline Files partnership, and then click Schedule. The Offline Files Sync Schedule wizard appears, displaying the *Which items do you want to sync on this schedule?* page, as shown in Figure 12-26.

Figure 12-26

The Which items do you want to sync on this schedule? page

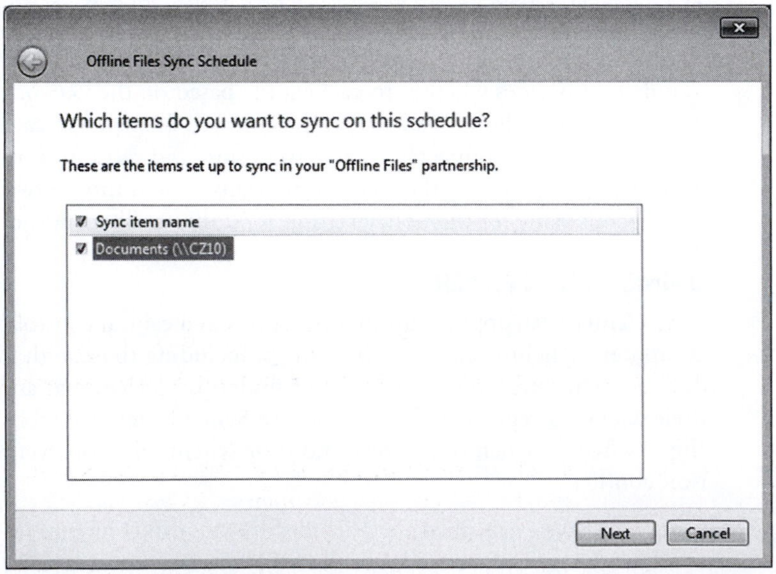

4. Select the network folder whose synchronization you want to schedule, and then click Next. The *When do you want this sync to begin?* page appears, as shown in Figure 12-27.

Figure 12-27

The When do you want this sync to begin? page

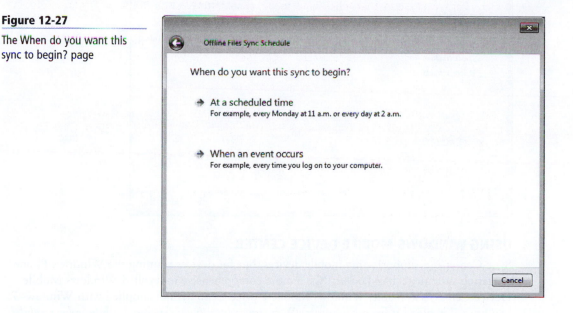

5. Select one of the following options, configure its properties, and then click Next.
   - **At a scheduled time:** Using the interface shown in Figure 12-28, specify a date and time for the synchronization and a repeat interval. You can also click More Options to specify conditions under which the scheduled synchronization should or should not occur.

Figure 12-28

The Sync Center Scheduled time interface

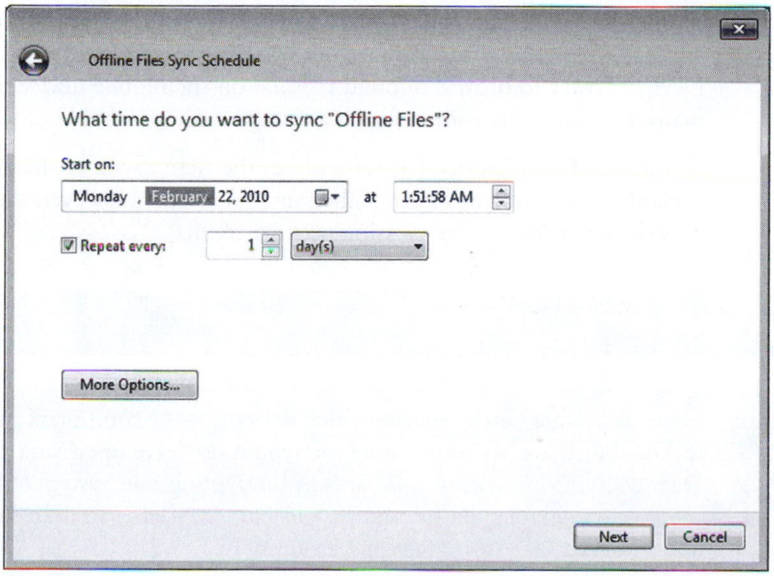

   - **When an event occurs:** Using the interface shown in Figure 12-29, select an event or action that you want to trigger a synchronization, such as logging on to Windows or when the system has been idle for specified amount of time.
6. Specify a name for the schedule, and then click Save Schedule.

Figure 12-29

The Sync Center Event or
Action interface

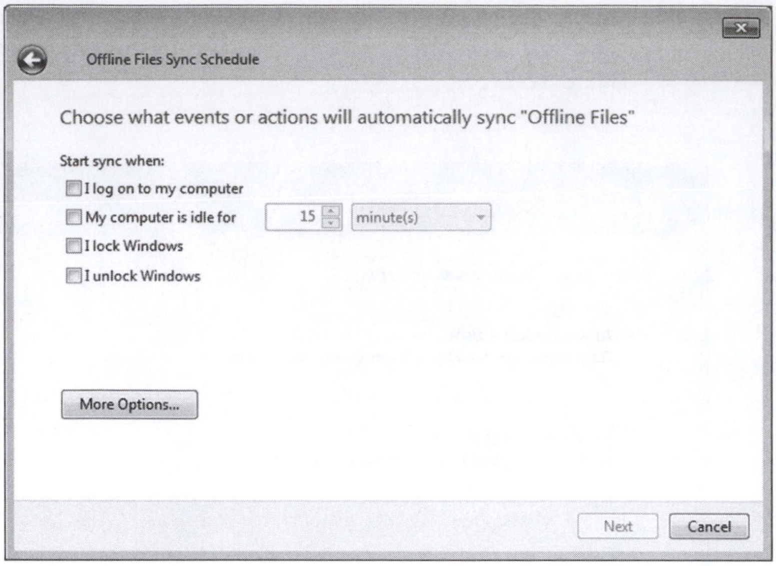

[Offline Files Sync Schedule dialog box]

Choose what events or actions will automatically sync "Offline Files"

Start sync when:

☐ I log on to my computer
☐ My computer is idle for   15 ▴▾   minute(s)   ▾
☐ I lock Windows
☐ I unlock Windows

[More Options...]

[Next] [Cancel]

USING WINDOWS MOBILE DEVICE CENTER

Sync Center can support some mobile devices, but for devices running the Windows Phone operating system, such as Pocket PCs, a more comprehensive tool called Windows Mobile Device Center is available. Windows Mobile Device Center is not supplied with Windows 7; you must download it from Microsoft's Web site at *http://www.microsoft.com/windowsmobile/ en-us/downloads/microsoft/device-center-download.mspx*, or use Windows Update.

TAKE NOTE*

Windows Mobile Device Center appears in Windows Update only if a supported mobile device is connected to your computer (either wirelessly using Bluetooth or by using a USB cable). To be supported, the device must be running Windows Mobile 2003 or later.

Using Windows Mobile Device Center, you cannot only synchronize data files with the mobile device, you can also synchronize certain types of application data, such as email, calendar appointments, and contact information. In addition, you can use Windows Mobile Device Center to browse through the files on the mobile device, access them as needed, and manage multimedia content, such as image, audio, and video files.

Windows Mobile Device Center replaces the ActiveSync application from earlier Windows versions, and performs many of the same functions. However, the interface has been redesigned to provide a more pleasing user experience.

Using BitLocker

THE BOTTOM LINE

Firewalls enable you to specify which doors to your computers are left open and which are locked, but there are some doors that you must leave open, and these require security also. Data encryption mechanisms, such as Encrypting File System (EFS) and BitLocker Drive Encryption, enable you to protect your data, so that even if an intruder gets through the door, they cannot steal the valuables inside.

CERTIFICATION READY?
Configure BitLocker and
BitLocker To Go.

6.1

Encrypting File System, which has been available since Windows 2000, enables users to protect specific files and folders, so that no one else can access them. ***BitLocker Drive Encryption***, on the other hand, is a feature, first released in Windows Vista and now available in the Windows 7 Enterprise and Ultimate editions, that makes it possible to encrypt an entire volume.

The full volume encryption provided by BitLocker has distinct advantages, including the following:

- **Increased data protection:** BitLocker encrypts all of the files on a volume, including operating system and application files, as well as paging files and temporary files, which can also contain sensitive information.
- **Integrity checking:** BitLocker can perform an integrity check before it permits the system to start, ensuring that the system BIOS, master boot record, boot sector, Boot Manager, and Windows Loader have not been compromised. This means that if someone steals a server, or removes its hard drive and tries to install it in another computer, they will be unable to access any of the volume data.

Unlike EFS, BitLocker is not designed to protect files for specific users, so that other users cannot access them. Instead, BitLocker protects entire volumes from being compromised by unauthorized persons. For example, if someone alters the server's boot components, such as by stealing the hard drive and installing it into another computer, BitLocker will lock the protected volumes, preventing all access. However, when the system boots successfully under normal conditions, the BitLocker volumes are accessible to anyone. You must still protect your files and folders using the standard Windows 7 tools, such as NTFS permissions and EFS.

Understanding BitLocker Requirements

To use BitLocker, you must have a computer with the appropriate hardware, and prepare it properly before you install Windows 7.

BitLocker can operate in several modes, depending on the degree of security the computer requires. With one exception, all of the available BitLocker modes require the computer to have a *Trusted Platform Module (TPM)* and a system BIOS that is compatible with its use. The TPM is a dedicated cryptographic processor chip that the system uses to store the BitLocker encryption keys.

BitLocker has five operational modes, which define the steps involved in the system boot process. These modes, in descending order from most to least secure, are as follows:

- **TPM + startup PIN + startup key:** The system stores the BitLocker volume encryption key on the TPM chip, but an administrator must supply a personal identification number (PIN) and insert a USB flash drive containing a startup key before the system can unlock the BitLocker volume and complete the system boot sequence.
- **TPM + startup key:** The system stores the BitLocker volume encryption key on the TPM chip, but an administrator must insert a USB flash drive containing a startup key before the system can unlock the BitLocker volume and complete the system boot sequence.
- **TPM + startup PIN:** The system stores the BitLocker volume encryption key on the TPM chip, but an administrator must supply a PIN before the system can unlock the BitLocker volume and complete the system boot sequence.
- **Startup key only:** The BitLocker configuration process stores a startup key on a USB flash drive, which the administrator must insert each time the system boots. This mode does not require the server to have a TPM chip, but it must have a system BIOS that supports access to the USB flash drive before the operating system loads.
- **TPM only:** The system stores the BitLocker volume encryption key on the TPM chip and accesses it automatically when the chip has determined that the boot environment is unmodified. This unlocks the protected volume and the computer continues to boot. No administrative interaction is required during the system boot sequence.

When you enable BitLocker using the BitLocker Drive Encryption control panel, you can select the TPM + startup key, TPM + startup PIN, or TPM only option. To use the TPM + startup PIN + startup key option, you must first configure the *Require additional authentication at startup* Group Policy setting, found in the Computer Configuration\Policies\ Administrative Templates\Windows Components\BitLocker Drive Encryption\Operating System Drives container, as shown in Figure 12-30.

+ MORE INFORMATION

According to Microsoft, there is no "back door" in the BitLocker encryption mechanism that would allow third parties (including government and law enforcement agencies) to access a protected volume. However, Microsoft has not made the source code available that would enable independent security analysts to confirm or refute this assertion.

Figure 12-30

Configuring BitLocker to require a TPM plus a startup key and a startup PIN

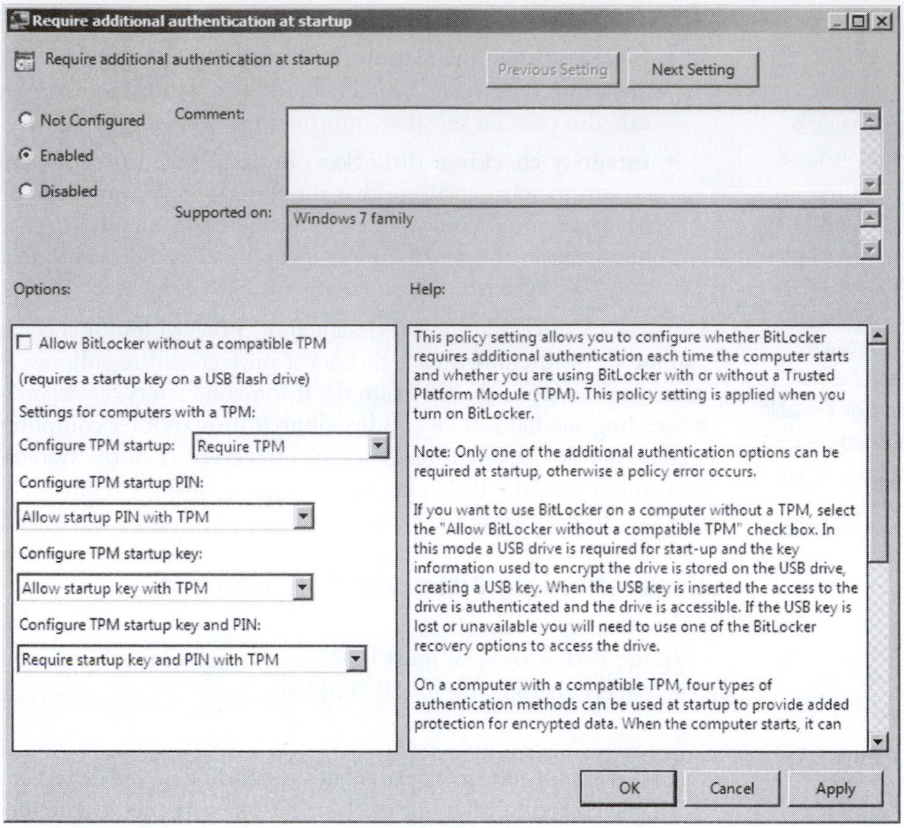

To run BitLocker without a TPM chip, you must configure the same policy, as shown in Figure 12-31.

Figure 12-31

Configuring BitLocker to run a startup key and a startup PIN

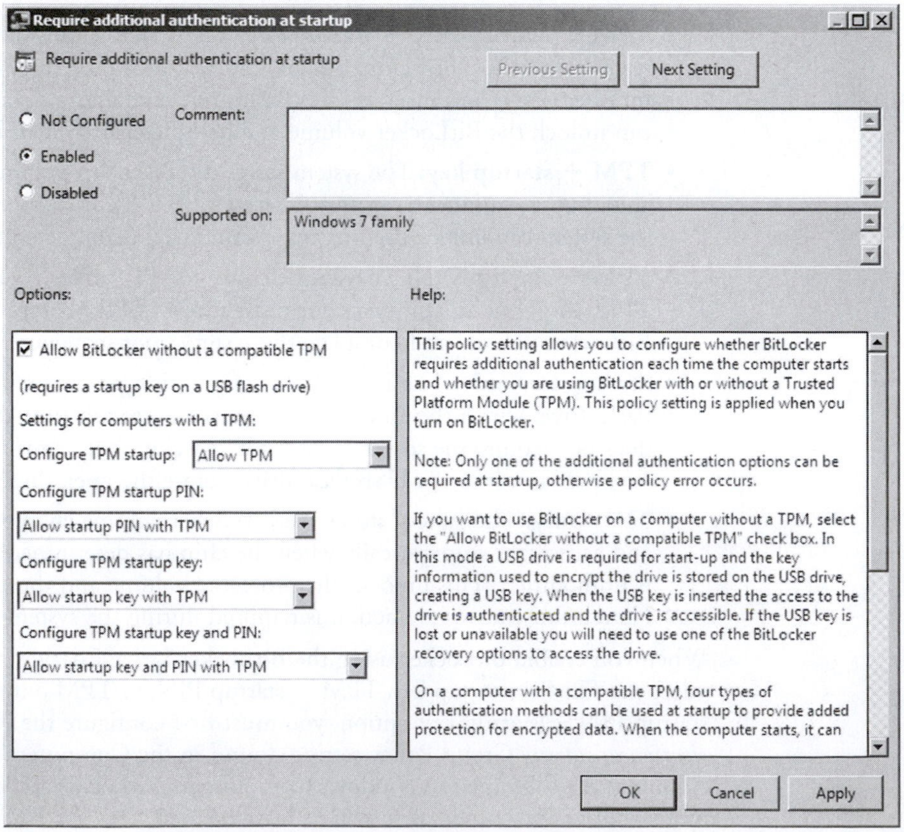

Turning On BitLocker

> Once you have configured the required Group Policy settings, you can turn BitLocker on.

The procedure for enabling BitLocker on a computer without a TPM is as follows.

TURN ON BITLOCKER

GET READY. Log on to Windows 7 using an account with administrative privileges.

1. Click Start, then click Control Panel > System and Security > BitLocker Drive Encryption. The BitLocker Drive Encryption control panel appears, as shown in Figure 12-32.

Figure 12-32

The BitLocker Drive Encryption control panel

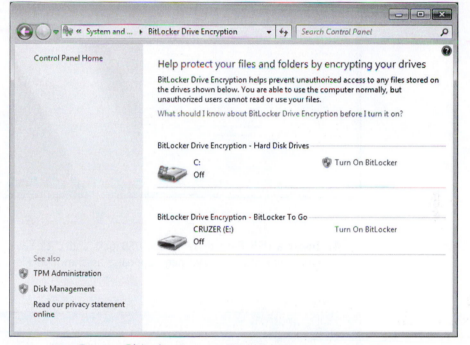

2. Click Turn on BitLocker for your hard disk drives. The *Set BitLocker startup preferences* page appears, as shown in Figure 12-33.

Figure 12-33

The Set BitLocker startup preferences page

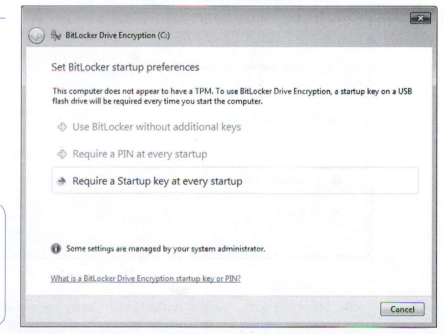

+ MORE INFORMATION

If your computer has a TPM chip, Windows 7 provides a Trusted Platform Module (TPM) Management console that you can use to change the chip's password and modify its properties.

3. Click Require a Startup key at every startup. A *Save your Startup key* page appears, as shown in Figure 12-34.

Figure 12-34

The Save your Startup key page

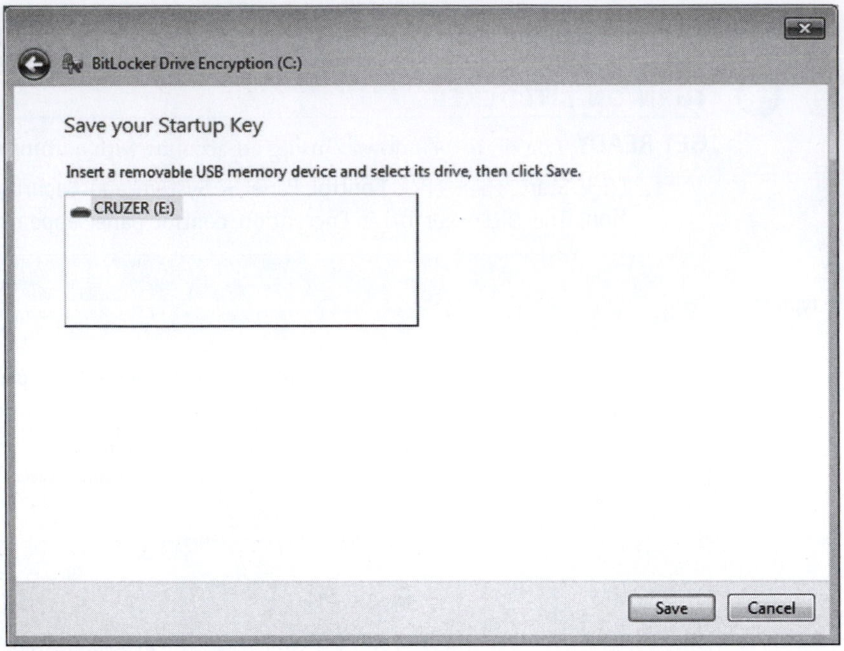

4. Insert a USB flash drive into a USB port and click Save. The *How do you want to store your recovery key?* page appears, as shown in Figure 12-35.

Figure 12-35

The How do you want to store your recovery key? page

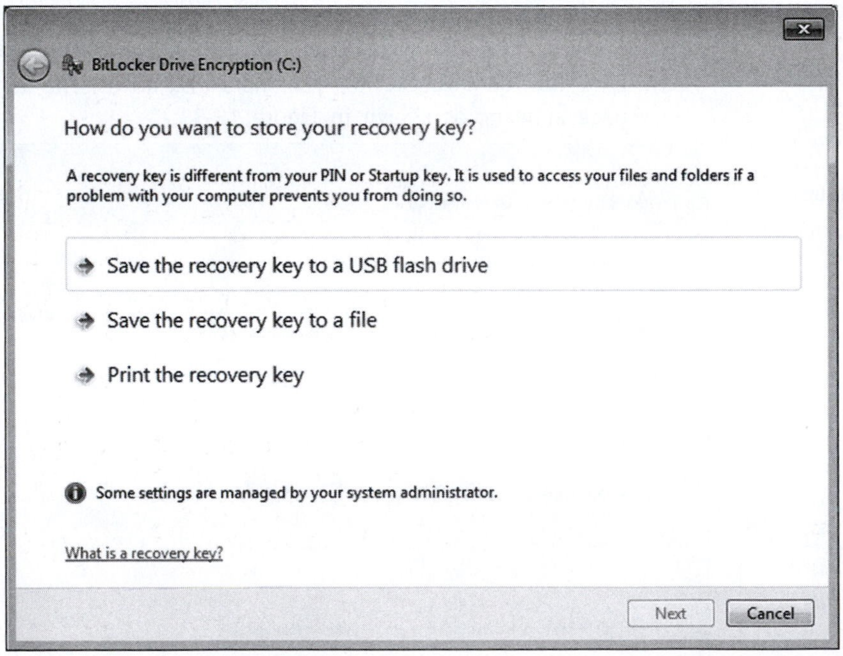

5. Select one of the options to save your recovery key and click Next. The *Are you ready to encrypt this drive?* page appears, as shown in Figure 12-36.

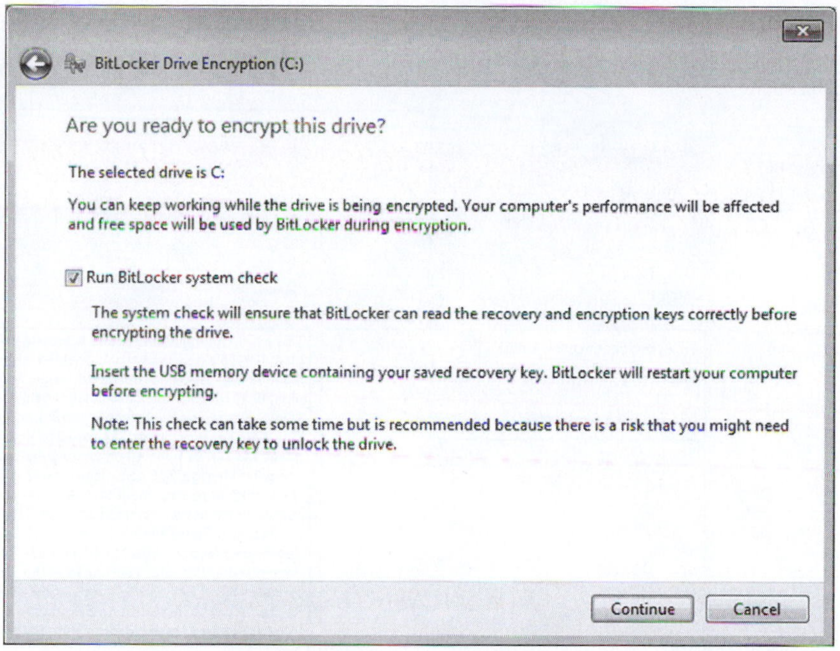

Figure 12-36

The Are you ready to encrypt
this drive? page

6. Click Continue. The wizard performs a system check and then restarts the computer.

7. Log on to the computer. Windows 7 proceeds to encrypt the disk.

Once the encryption process is completed, you can open the BitLocker Drive Encryption control panel to ensure that the volume is encrypted or to turn off BitLocker, such as when performing a BIOS upgrade or other system maintenance.

Using Data Recovery Agents

If a user loses the startup key and/or startup PIN needed to boot a system with BitLocker enabled, the system enters recovery mode. In this mode, the user can supply the recovery key created during the BitLocker configuration process and gain access to the system. If the user loses the recovery key as well, it is still possible for a user who has been designated as a data recovery agent to recover the data on the drive.

A *data recovery agent (DRA)* is a user account that an administrator has authorized to recover BitLocker drives for an entire organization with a digital certificate on a smart card. In most cases, administrators of Active Directory Domain Services (AD DS) networks use DRAs to ensure access to their BitLocker-protected systems, to avoid having to maintain large numbers of individual keys and PINs.

To create a DRA, you must first add the user account you want to designate to the Computer Configuration\Policies\Windows Settings\Security Settings\Public Key Policies\BitLocker Drive Encryption container in a GPO or to the system's Local Security Policy. Then, you must configure the Provide the unique identifiers for your organization policy setting in the Computer Configuration\Policies\Administrative Templates\Windows Components\BitLocker Drive Encryption container with unique identification fields for your BitLocker drives, as shown in Figure 12-37.

Finally, you must enable DRA recovery for each type of BitLocker resource you want to recover, by configuring the following policies:

- Choose how BitLocker-protected operating system drives can be recovered.
- Choose how BitLocker-protected fixed drives can be recovered.
- Choose how BitLocker-protected removable drives can be recovered.

Figure 12-37

The Provide the unique identifiers for your organization Group Policy setting

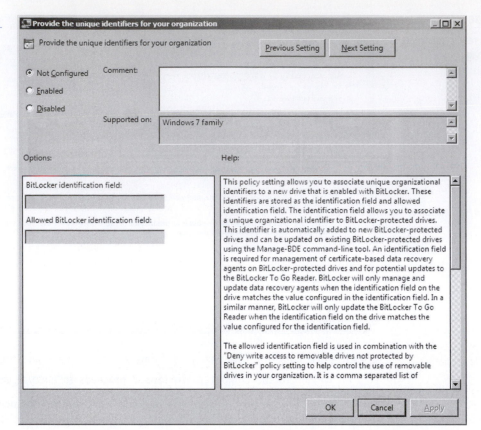

These policies, as shown in Figure 12-38, enable you to specify how BitLocker systems should store their recovery information, and also enable you to store it in the AD DS database.

Figure 12-38

The Choose how BitLocker-protected operating system drives can be recovered Group Policy setting

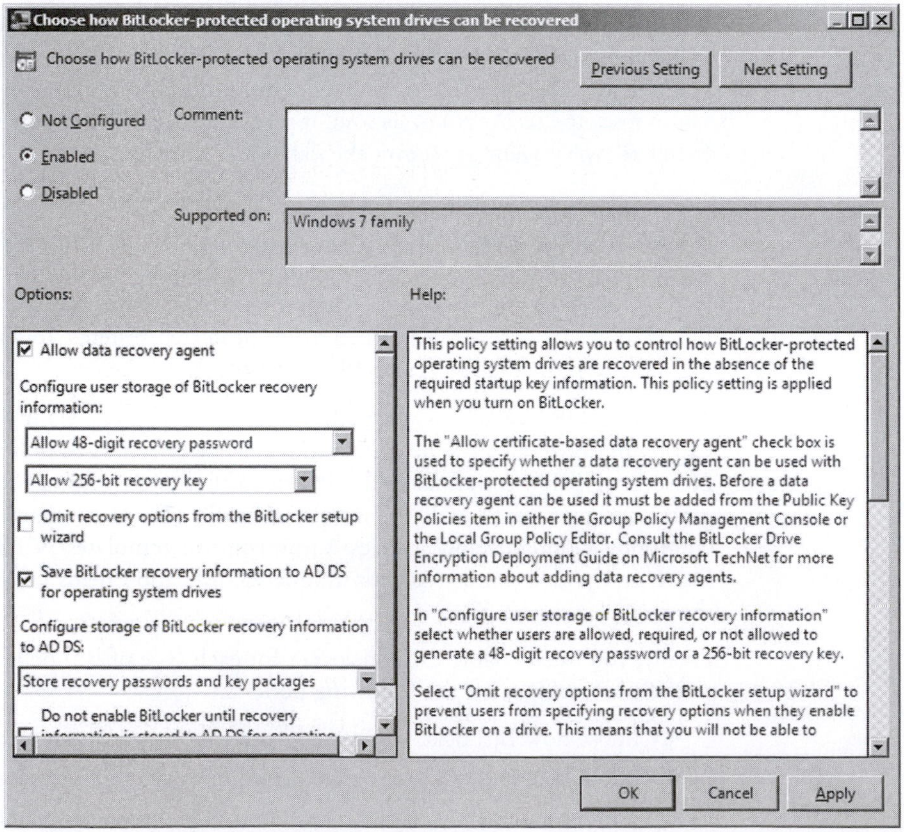

Using BitLocker To Go

> BitLocker To Go is a new feature in Windows 7 that enables users to encrypt removable USB devices, such as flash drives and external hard disks.

While BitLocker has always supported the encryption of removable drives, BitLocker To Go enables you to use the encrypted device on other computers without having to perform an involved recovery process. Because the system is not using the removable drive as a boot device, a TPM chip is not required.

To use BitLocker To Go, you insert the removable drive and open the BitLocker Drive Encryption control panel. The device appears in the interface, with a *Turn on BitLocker* link just like that of the computer's hard disk drive.

To control BitLocker To Go behavior, you use the policy settings in the Computer Configuration\Policies\Administrative Templates\Windows Components\BitLocker Drive Encryption\Removable Data Drives container, as shown in Figure 12-39.

Figure 12-39

The BitLocker Removable Data Drives Group Policy settings

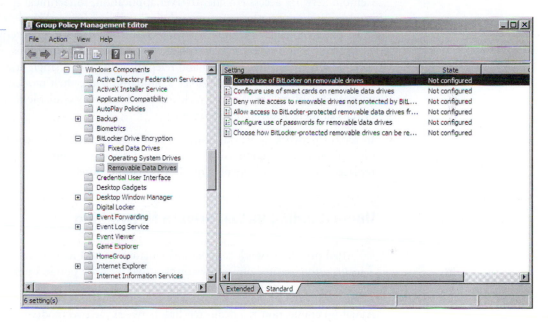

These policy settings are as follows:

- **Control use of BitLocker on removable drives:** Specifies whether users are permitted to add BitLocker encryption to removable drives and whether they can remove BitLocker from drives that are already encrypted.
- **Configure use of smart cards on removable data drives:** Specifies whether users can or must use a smart card to access a removable drive.
- **Deny write access to removable drives not protected by BitLocker:** Prevents users from saving data to removable drives that are not encrypted using BitLocker.
- **Allow access to BitLocker-protected removable data drives from earlier versions of Windows:** Specifies whether FAT-formatted removable BitLocker drives are accessible from previous Windows versions.
- **Configure use of passwords for removable data drives:** Specifies whether removable BitLocker drives must be password-protected.
- **Choose how BitLocker-protected removable drives can be recovered:** Specifies whether DRAs can access the data on removable BitLocker drives.

■ Using Remote Network Connections

THE BOTTOM LINE

Windows supports two types of remote client connections: dial-up, which typically uses standard asynchronous modems and telephone lines, and virtual private networking, which uses the Internet as the medium connecting the client to the remote access server. In addition, Windows 7 adds support for a new type of remote connection called DirectAccess, which eliminates the need to manually establish a connection to a remote server.

CERTIFICATION READY?
Configure remote connections.
6.4

While new technologies such as BranchCache aid technical specialists in maintaining permanent or semi-permanent links between remote sites, they do not address the other type of remote user: the traveling or telecommuting worker who must connect to the company network from a remote site. These workers do not have permanent connections, so they cannot log on to the network in the usual manner. However, Windows provides a number of remote solutions that enable these users to access network resources from any location with a telephone line or an Internet connection.

Remote network access is a client/server application, so technical specialists must plan and implement a server infrastructure at the network site before Windows 7 clients can connect to it. The first step in planning a remote access solution for an enterprise network is to decide which connection type you plan to use. To use dial-up connections, you must equip your servers with at least one modem and telephone line. For a single-user connection, as for an administrator dialing in from home, a standard off-the-shelf modem is suitable. For multiple connections, there are modular rack-mounted modems available that enable you to connect dozens of users at once, if necessary.

In today's networking world, however, hardware and telephone costs and the near-ubiquity of high-speed Internet connections have caused dial-up remote connections to be almost entirely replaced by virtual private network (VPN) connections.

Understanding Virtual Private Networking

Virtual private network connections violate standard networking concepts to provide security for private connections transmitted over the public Internet.

A dial-up connection is a dedicated link between the two modems that remains in place during the entire session, as shown in Figure 12-40. The client and the server establish a *Point-to-Point Protocol (PPP)* connection, during which the server authenticates the client and the computers negotiate a set of communication parameters they have in common. PPP takes the place of the Ethernet protocol at the data-link layer, by encapsulating the datagrams created by the Internet Protocol (IP) at the network layer, to prepare them for their transmission. PPP is much simpler than Ethernet because the two computers are using a dedicated connection, and there is no need to address each packet to a particular destination, as they must do on a local area network (LAN).

Figure 12-40

A dial-up remote access connection

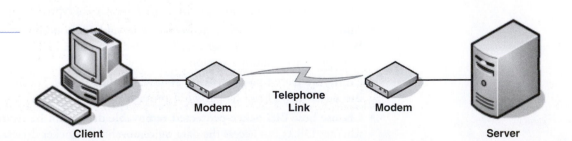

In a *virtual private network (VPN)* connection, the remote client and the remote access server are both connected to the Internet, using local service providers, as shown in Figure 12-41. This eliminates the expense of long distance telephone charges common to dial-up connections, as well as the additional hardware expense, since both computers most likely have Internet connections already. The client establishes a connection to the server using the Internet as a network medium and, after authentication, the server grants the client access to the network.

Figure 12-41

A VPN remote access connection

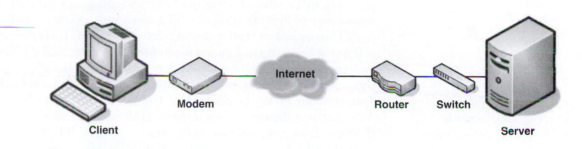

While it is theoretically possible for someone to tap into the telephone line used by a dial-up connection, intercept the analog signals exchanged by the two modems, convert them into digital data packets, and access the data, it is not likely to occur, and remote connections are almost never compromised in this manner. Therefore, the data transmitted during a dial-up connection is considered to be relatively secure.

A VPN is another matter, however, because the client and the server transmit their data over the Internet, which makes the data packets accessible to anyone with the equipment needed to capture them. For this reason, VPN clients and servers use a specialized protocol when establishing a connection, which encapsulates their data packets inside another packet, a process called *tunneling*. The VPN protocol establishes a virtual connection, or tunnel, between the client and the server, which encrypts data encapsulated inside.

In the tunneling process, the two computers establish a PPP connection, just as they would in a dial-up connection, but instead of transmitting the PPP packets over the Internet as they are, they encapsulate the packets again using one of the VPN protocols supported by the Windows operating systems. As shown in Figure 12-42, the original PPP data packet generated by the computer consists of a network layer IP datagram, encapsulated in a data-link layer PPP frame. The system then encapsulates the entire frame in another IP datagram, which the VPN protocol encrypts and encapsulates one more time, for transmission over the network.

Figure 12-42

VPN protocol encapsulation

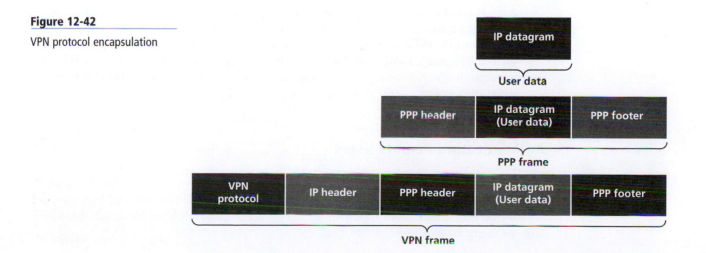

Having a data-link layer frame inside a network layer datagram is a violation of the Open System Interconnection (OSI) reference model's most basic principles, but this is what makes tunneling an effective carrier mechanism for private data transmitted over a public network. Intruders can intercept the transmitted packets, but they cannot decrypt the inner PPP frame, which prevents them from obtaining any of the information inside.

The VPN protocols that Windows Server 2008 supports are as follows:

- *Point-to-Point Tunneling Protocol (PPTP):* The oldest and least secure of the VPN protocols, PPTP takes advantage of the authentication, compression, and encryption mechanisms of PPP, tunneling the PPP frame within a Generic Routing Encapsulation (GRE) header and encrypting it with Microsoft Point-to-Point Encryption (MPPE) using encryption keys generated during the authentication process. PPTP can provide data protection, but not other services, such as packet origin identification or data integrity checking. For authentication, PPTP supports only the Microsoft Challenge Handshake Authentication Protocol version 1 (MS-CHAP v1), Microsoft Challenge Handshake Authentication Protocol version 2 (MS-CHAP v2), Extensible Authentication Protocol (EAP), or Protected Extensible Authentication Protocol (PEAP). Although it can use them (with EAP), one of the advantages of PPTP is that it does not require the use of certificates. In most cases, organizations use PPTP as a fallback protocol for clients running non-Windows operating systems.

- *Layer 2 Tunneling Protocol (L2TP):* L2TP relies on the IP security extensions (IPsec) for encryption, and as a result performs a double encapsulation. The system adds an L2DP header to the PPP frame and packages it with the User Datagram Protocol (UDP). Then it encapsulates the UDP datagram with the IPsec Encapsulating Security Payload (ESP) protocol, encrypting the contents using the Data Encryption Standard (DES) or Triple DES (3DES) algorithm, with encryption keys generated during IPSec's Internet Key Exchange (IKE) negotiation process. L2TP/IPsec can use certificates or preshared keys for authentication, although administrators typically use the latter only for testing. The end result is that the L2TP/IPsec combination provides a more complete set of services than PPTP, including packet origin identification, data integrity checking, and replay protection. For VPN connections involving Windows XP clients, L2TP/IPsec is the preferred protocol.

- *Secure Socket Tunneling Protocol (SSTP):* Introduced in Windows Server 2008 and supported only by clients running Windows Vista SP1 or later, SSTP encapsulates PPP traffic using the Secure Sockets Layer (SSL) protocol supported by virtually all web servers. The advantage of this is that administrators do not have to open an additional external firewall port in the server because SSTP uses the same TCP port 443 as SSL. SSTP uses certificates for authentication, with the EAP-TLS authentication protocol, and in addition to data encryption, provides integrity checking and enhanced key negotiation services.

- *Internet Key Exchange, Version 2 (IKEv2):* New in Windows 7 and Windows Server 2008 R2, IKEv2 uses TCP port 500 and provides support for IPv6 and the new VPN Reconnect feature, as well as authentication by EAP, using PEAP, EAP-MSCHAPv2, or smart cards. IKEv2 does not support the older authentication mechanisms, however, such as PAP and CHAP. By default, Windows 7 computers use IKEv2 when attempting to connect to remote access servers, only falling back to the other protocols when the server does not support it as well.

Authenticating Remote Users

Windows remote access connections use an authentication system that is entirely separate from the Kerberos authentication system that clients on the local network use. However, authentication is even more important for remote access clients than for local ones, because of the increased likelihood of intrusion.

All remote access connections, whether dial-up or VPN, use PPP to package their data, and the PPP connection establishment process includes a sequence in which the client and the server negotiate the use of a specific authentication protocol. In this sequence, each computer sends a list of the authentication protocols it supports to the other, and the two then agree to use the strongest protocol they have in common.

In Windows 7, you configure the authentication method a VPN connection uses on the Security tab of the connection's Properties sheet, as shown in Figure 12-43. The options are as follows:

- **Use Extensible Authentication Protocol (EAP):** EAP is a shell protocol that provides a framework for the use of various types of authentication mechanisms. The primary advantage of EAP is that it enables a computer to use mechanisms other than passwords for authentication, including public key certificates and smart cards, as well as providing an extensible environment for third-party authentication mechanisms. Windows 7 supports three types of EAP-based authentication: Protected EAP (PEAP), *Secure Password (EAP-MSCHAPv2)*, and Smart Card or other certificates. EAP-MSCHAPv2, the default selection for new connections and the strongest password-based mechanism in Windows 7, requires a certificate only at the server. The Smart Card or other certificates option requires the clients, as well as the server, to have a certificate, stored either on a smart card or in the computer's certificate store.

- **Allow these protocols:** Provides support for the Password Authentication Protocol (PAP), Challenge Handshake Authentication Protocol (CHAP), and Microsoft Challenge Handshake Authentication Protocol Version 2 (MSCHAPv2), which are included to provide support for down-level clients. These protocols apply only to PPTP, L2TP, and SSTP connections; IKEv2 connections must use EAP-MSCHAPv2 or a certificate.

Figure 12-43

The Security tab of a connection's Properties sheet

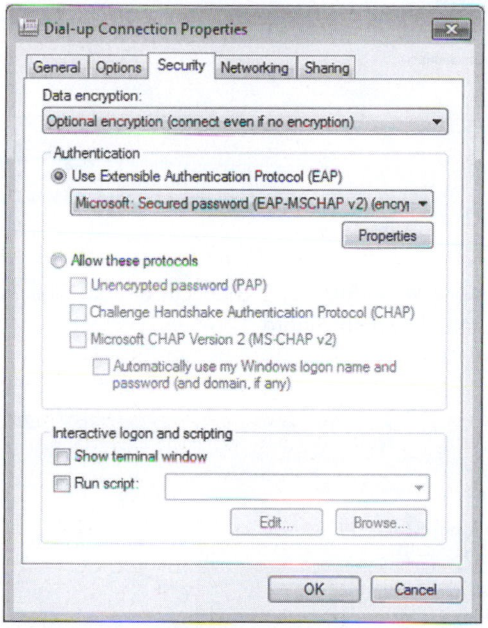

Creating a VPN Connection

> To connect a computer running Windows 7 to a remote access server, you must create a new VPN or dial-up connection.

In Windows 7, the Network Connections window contains a local area connection for every network interface adapter installed in the computer. The Windows installation program creates these connections automatically, but to connect to a dial-up or VPN server, you must create additional connections manually.

To create a VPN connection, use the following procedure.

→ **CREATE A VPN CONNECTION**

GET READY. Log on to Windows 7 using an account with administrative privileges.

1. Click Start, then click Control Panel > Network and Internet > Network and Sharing Center. The Network and Sharing Center control panel appears.

2. Click Set up a new connection or network. The Set Up a Connection or Network Wizard appears, displaying the *Choose a connection option* page, as shown in Figure 12-44.

Figure 12-44

The Choose a connection option page

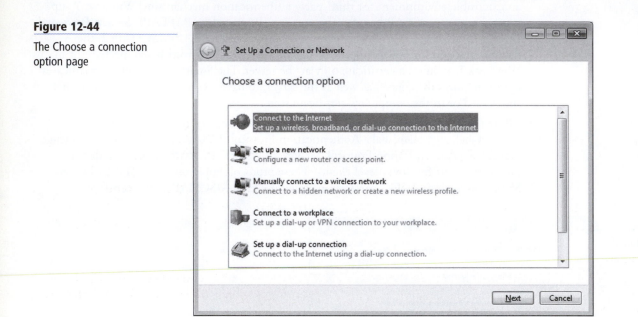

3. Click Connect to a workplace, and then click Next. The *How do you want to connect?* page appears, as shown in Figure 12-45.

Figure 12-45

The How do you want to connect? page

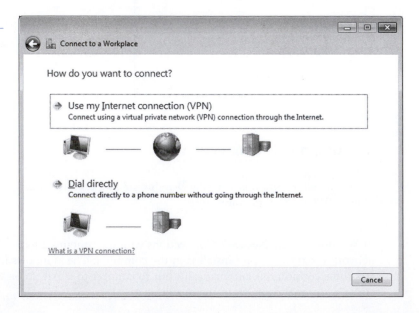

4. Click Use my Internet connection (VPN). The *Type the Internet address to connect to* page appears, as shown in Figure 12-46.

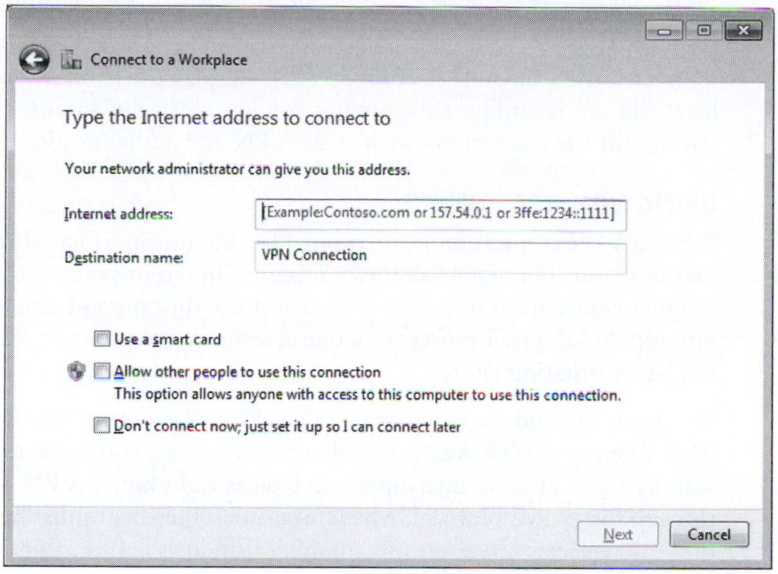

Figure 12-46

The Type the Internet address to connect to page

5. In the *Internet address* text box, type the fully qualified domain name or IP address of the remote server to which you want to connect.

6. In the *Destination name* text box, type a descriptive name for the connection.

TAKE NOTE *

The process of configuring a dial-up connection is essentially like that of creating a VPN connection, except that for a dial-up, you must specify a phone number to call and configure other dialing criteria.

7. Select the Don't connect now; just set it up so I can connect later check box and click Next. The *Type your user name and password* page appears, as shown in Figure 12-47.

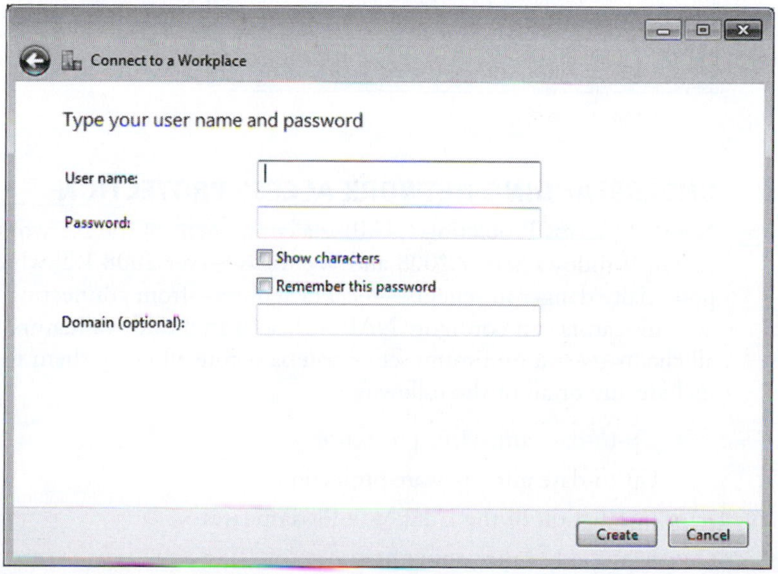

Figure 12-47

The Type your user name and password page

8. In the *User name, Password,* and *Domain* text boxes, type the credentials you will use to connect to the server. Then click Create. A *The connection is ready to use* page appears.

9. Click Close. The new connection is added to the Network Connections window.

Once you have created the connection, you can open the Network Connections window, right click the icon and select Properties to display the connection's Properties sheet. From here, you can reconfigure the options you just set in the wizard, plus configure all of the other settings for the connection, such as the VPN and authentication protocols it should use.

USING VPN RECONNECT

When a VPN connection is interrupted for any reason, it has always been necessary for the user to manually re-establish the connection. In recent years, the growing use of wireless Internet connections in public places has made this more of a problem. When a connection is interrupted, or a user moves from one access point to another, reconnecting to a VPN server can be an irritating chore.

Windows 7 includes a new feature called **VPN Reconnect**, based on the **IKEv2 Mobility and Multihoming (MOBIKE)** protocol, which enables a computer to reconnect to a VPN server automatically, after an interruption as long as eight hours. VPN only works with connections that use the IKEv2 protocol, which means that the client must be running Windows 7 and the remote access server must be running Windows Server 2008 R2.

To configure VPN Reconnect, you open the Properties sheet for a VPN connection, click the Security tab, and click Advanced settings. In the Advanced Properties dialog box that appears, click the IKEv2 tab and select the Mobility check box, as shown in Figure 12-48. The default network outage time is 30 minutes, but you can configure it to be as short as 5 minutes or as long as 8 hours.

Figure 12-48

Enabling VPN Reconnect

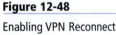

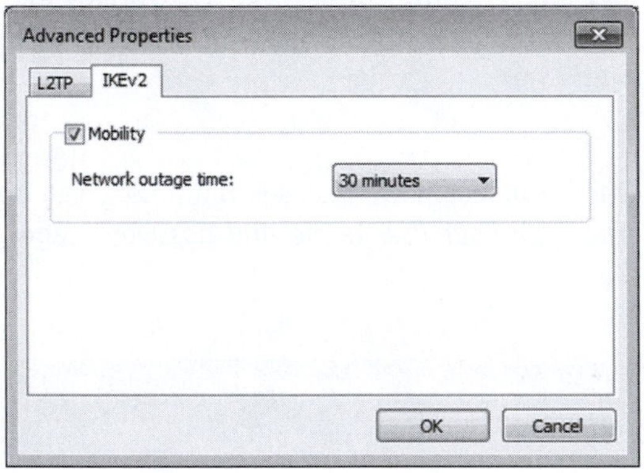

UNDERSTANDING NETWORK ACCESS PROTECTION

Network Access Protection (NAP) is a component of the Network Policy and Access Services role in Windows Server 2008 and Windows Server 2008 R2, which is designed to prevent potentially dangerous clients—local or remote—from connecting to the network. Server administrators can configure NAP with security health validators (SHVs) that ensure that all clients meet a minimum set of criteria before allowing them to connect. The criteria can include any or all of the following:

- Up-to-date anti-virus protection
- Up-to-date anti-spyware protection
- Installation of the latest Windows updates
- A properly functioning firewall

If a client does not meet all of the required criteria in the SHV, the NAP server can simply deny it access, or it can begin a process of remediation, in which the client is essentially quarantined to an isolated network that provides access only to the resources it needs to bring it into compliance.

These resources can include Windows Server Update Services (WSUS) and a server to provide updates for malware protection. It is also possible for administrators to configure Windows 7 clients to perform remediative actions themselves in this situation, such as turning on Windows Firewall or running Windows Update.

Using Remote Desktop

In Lesson 11, "Administering Windows 7," you learned how you can use Remote Desktop to connect to computers on the network and administer them from any location. It is also possible to use this Remote Desktop technology to provide clients with access to network computers and individual applications, even when the clients are at a remote location.

Windows Server 2008 R2 includes a role called Remote Desktop Services, which provides clients with access to server resources in a variety of ways. The Remote Desktop Session Host role service functions much like the Remote Desktop Services service in Windows 7, except that it can provide multiple (licensed) users with access to the server desktop.

To provide remote clients with this type of access, using their standard Internet connections, there is a role service called Remote Desktop Gateway. Users at remote sites can use the standard Remote Desktop Connection client included with Windows 7 to connect to the gateway, and the gateway provides access to the Remote Desktop server.

TAKE NOTE*

Prior to Windows Server 2008 R2, Remote Desktop Services was known as Terminal Services, and the Remote Desktop Gateway as the Terminal Services Gateway. The services are essentially the same; only the names have been changed.

To access Remote Desktop Services using an Internet connection, you must open the Remote Desktop Connection client, click the *Options* arrow, click the *Advanced* tab, and then click *Settings* to display the RD Server Gateway Settings dialog box, as shown in Figure 12-49. Here, you specify the name or address of the Remote Desktop Gateway server and specify how you intend to log on.

Figure 12-49

The RD Server Gateway Settings dialog box

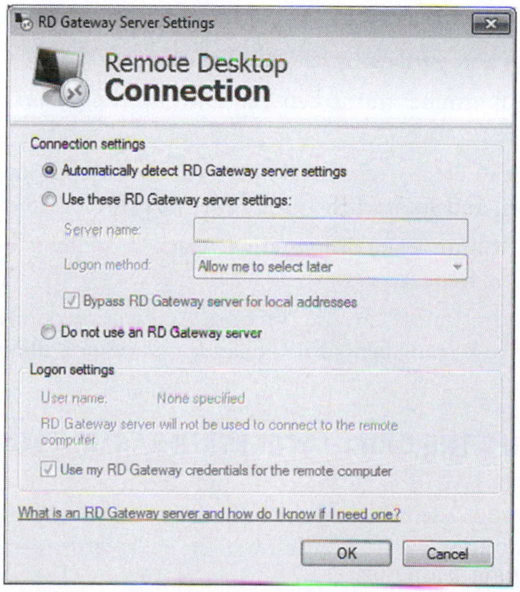

Another new feature introduced in Windows Server 2008 is RemoteApp, which enables clients to access individual applications running on a Remote Desktop server. Unlike the standard Remote Desktop session, which creates a full-featured desktop at the client, RemoteApp enables servers to publish applications that appear on the client in separate windows, no different in appearance from applications running on the local computer.

Introducing DirectAccess

DirectAccess is a new feature in Windows 7 and Windows Server 2008 R2 that enables remote users to automatically connect to the company network whenever they have Internet access.

CERTIFICATION READY?
Configure DirectAccess.
6.2

For many end-users, the entire concept of network computing is difficult to comprehend. There are people who don't know which resources are on their local drives and which are on network servers, and what's more, they don't care. They just want to be able to turn the machine on and know that it will work.

This issue can be particularly vexing for users who are traveling or working from home and don't have immediate access to technical support. A VPN connection can provide them with access to the company network, but they have to remember to initiate the connection first. And if the connection should fail while they are working, they have to re-establish it, a process that can take several minutes each time.

Windows 7 and Windows Server 2008 R2 include a new remote access solution called *DirectAccess*, which addresses these problems by enabling clients to remain connected to their host networks whenever they have access to the Internet, reconnecting automatically whenever it is necessary.

UNDERSTANDING DIRECTACCESS BENEFITS

Designed as a replacement for VPNs, DirectAccess eliminates the need for client users to manually establish wide area connections to their networks. As soon as the client computer accesses the Internet, the system automatically initiates the connection to the network. If the client becomes disconnected from the Internet, such as when the user wanders out of range of a WiFi hot spot, DirectAccess re-establishes the network connection as soon as the client regains access to the Internet.

DirectAccess provides many other benefits to users and administrators, including the following:

- **Bidirectional:** Network administrators can initiate connections to client computers to install updates and perform maintenance tasks.
- **Encrypted:** All intranet traffic between DirectAccess clients and servers is encrypted using the IPsec protocols.
- **Authenticated:** DirectAccess clients perform both a computer authentication and a user authentication, and support the use of smart cards or biometric devices.
- **Authorized:** Administrators can grant DirectAccess clients full intranet access or limit them to specific resources.
- **Verified:** Administrators can use Network Access Protection (NAP) and Network Policy Server (NPS) to screen clients for the latest updates for allowing them access to the network.

UNDERSTANDING THE DIRECTACCESS INFRASTRUCTURE

DirectAccess is all but invisible to the client, but the cost of this invisibility is a complicated communications process with a long list of back end infrastructure requirements. Chiefly that DirectAccess is only supported by Windows 7 in its Enterprise and Ultimate editions and by Windows Server 2008 R2.

For this reason, the adoption of the new technology is likely to be relatively slow. Many organizations are deploying Windows 7 workstations, but upgrading servers is typically a slower and more careful process, and it might be some time before many organizations have all of the necessary components in place.

DirectAccess and IPv6

DirectAccess is also heavily reliant on IPv6, the new version of the Internet Protocol that expands the IP address space from 32 bits to 128 bits. Because IPv6 addresses are globally routable, a DirectAccess client can use the same address wherever it happens to be in the world.

IPv6 is not yet deployed universally, however. Many networks still rely on IPv4, most notably the Internet. Therefore, DirectAccess also relies on a variety of transition technologies that enable IPv4 networks to carry IPv6 traffic. These technologies are as follows:

- **6to4:** Provides IPv6 connectivity over IPv4 networks for hosts with public IP addresses.
- **Teredo:** Provides IPv6 connectivity over IPv4 networks for hosts with private IP addresses behind a Network Address Translation (NAT) router.
- **IP-HTTPS:** Provides Secure Sockets Layer (SSL) tunneling as a backup for systems that cannot use 6to4 or Teredo.
- **Intra-Site Automatic Tunnel Addressing Protocol (ISATAP):** Provides IPv6 connectivity for IPv4 intranets.
- **Network Address Translation–Protocol Translation (NAT-PT):** A hardware device that enables DirectAccess clients to access IPv4 applications.

DirectAccess and IPsec

IPsec is a collection of IP extensions that provide additional security for network communications. DirectAccess relies on IPsec to authenticate users and computers and to encrypt data exchanged by clients and servers.

IPsec uses tunneling to protect communications between computers connecting over a private network. During the DirectAccess connection process, the client uses one IPsec tunnel to access the DNS server and AD DS domain controller on the host network. Then the systems negotiate the creation of a second tunnel that provides the client with access to the other resources on the network.

IPsec consists of two protocols, Authenticated Header (AH) and Encapsulating Security Payload (ESP), and two operational modes: transport mode and tunnel mode. Windows 7 and Windows Server 2008 R2 both include full support for IPsec, but if other servers on your network do not, DirectAccess has ways to work around that limitation.

The way in which the host network uses IPsec is dependent on the access model you elect to use. If all of the servers on your network support IPv6, then DirectAccess clients can establish connections that go through the DirectAccess server and all the way to their application servers, using IPsec in transport mode. This is called the end-to-end access model, as shown in Figure 12-50.

Figure 12-50

The end-to-end access model

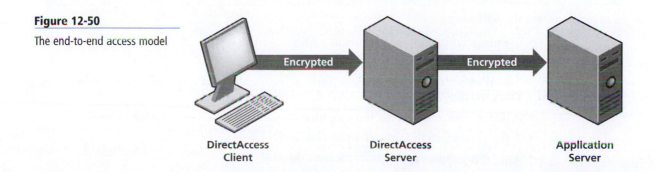

DirectAccess   DirectAccess   Application
Client   Server   Server

To keep IPsec traffic off the company intranet, you can use the end-to-edge access model, as shown in Figure 12-51. In this model, DirectAccess clients establish tunnel mode connections to an IPsec gateway server (which might or might not be the same computer functioning as the DirectAccess server). The gateway server then forwards the traffic to the applications servers in the intranet.

Figure 12-51

The end-to-edge access model

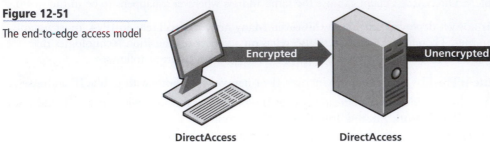

A third model, called modified end-to-edge, adds an additional IPsec tunnel that goes all the way to the application server, as shown in Figure 12-52, enabling clients to perform another authentication directly with the application server.

Figure 12-52

The modified end-to-edge access model

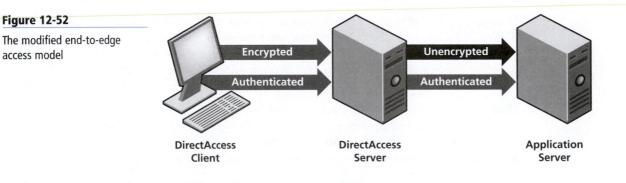

DirectAccess Server Requirements

The primary access point for DirectAccess clients on the host network is a DirectAccess server, which you create by installing the DirectAccess Management Console feature using Server Manager. The DirectAccess server must be running Windows Server 2008 R2, and must also have the following:

- Membership in an AD DS domain
- Two network interface adapters installed
- Two IPv4 addresses that are consecutive, static, public, and resolvable by the Internet DNS, for Toredo support
- A direct connection to the Internet (that does not use NAT or a similar technology)
- A direct connection to the company intranet
- The Group Policy Management feature installed

In addition to the DirectAccess server, the host network must also have the following:

- An AD DS domain with at least one domain controller running Windows Server 2008 R2
- A Windows server functioning as an enterprise root or enterprise subordinate certification authority
- An AD DS security group containing the computer objects for all of the DirectAccess clients as members, so that they can receive Group Policy settings
- A network detection server that hosts a Web site on the company intranet, which clients use to confirm their connections
- Transition technologies that enable clients to use IPv6 to access the DirectAccess server, the AD DS domain controller, and the application servers they need
- Firewall exceptions that enable the clients to access all of the servers they need, using the appropriate protocols

DirectAccess Client Requirements

DirectAccess clients must be running Windows 7 Enterprise, Windows 7 Ultimate, or Windows Server 2008 R2, and they must be joined to the same domain as the DirectAccess server. You must deploy the client computers on the company network first, so they can join the domain and receive certificates and Group Policy settings, before you send them out into the field.

ESTABLISHING A DIRECTACCESS CONNECTION

The DirectAccess connection establishment process is invisible to the user on the client computer, but there is a great deal going on behind the scenes. The individual steps of the connection process are as follows:

1. The client attempts to connect to a designated network detection server on the intranet. A successful connection indicates that the client is connected to the host network locally. If the client fails to connect to the server, then the DirectAccess connection establishment process begins.
2. The client connects to the DirectAccess server on the host network using IPv6. If a connection using IPv6 natively is not possible, the systems fall back to 6to4, Toredo, or, if necessary, IP-HTTPS.
3. The client and the DirectAccess server authenticate each other using their computer certificates. This occurs before the user logon and provides the client with access to the domain controller and the DNS server on the intranet.
4. The client establishes a second connection through the DirectAccess server to the domain controller and performs a standard AD DS user authentication, using NTLMv2 credentials and the Kerberos V5 authentication protocol.
5. The DirectAccess server uses AD DS group memberships to authorize the client computer and user to access the intranet.
6. If required, the client submits a health certificate to a Network Policy Server (NPS) on the host network, to verify its compliance with existing policies.
7. The client begins to access application servers and other resources in the intranet, using the DirectAccess server as a gateway.

CONFIGURING DIRECTACCESS

The process of installing and configuring DirectAccess is relatively simple, and again favors the simplicity of the client side. In Windows Server 2008 R2, you install DirectAccess by adding the DirectAccess Management Console feature and running the setup procedure in that console. This configures the server and also creates the Group Policy settings needed to configure the DirectAccess clients. There is no separate installation procedure for the clients; you simple have to ensure that they receive the Group Policy settings.

When you initiate the DirectAccess Setup process, the console performs a prerequisite check and displays any errors that you must resolve before the procedure can continue, as shown in Figure 12-53.

Figure 12-53

The DirectAccess prerequisite check on Windows Server 2008 R2

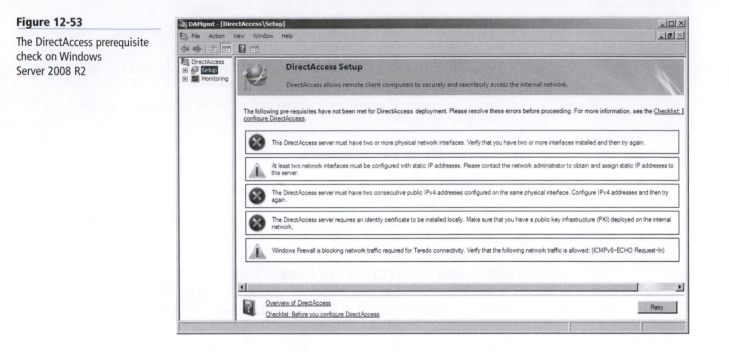

When you have met all the prerequisites, a diagram appears, as shown in Figure 12-54, which takes you through the four steps of the setup.

Figure 12-54

The DirectAccess setup diagram on Windows Server 2008 R2

The four steps are as follows:

1. The *DirectAccess Client Setup* page appears, as shown in Figure 12-55, in which you specify the security group to which you've added the client computers as members.

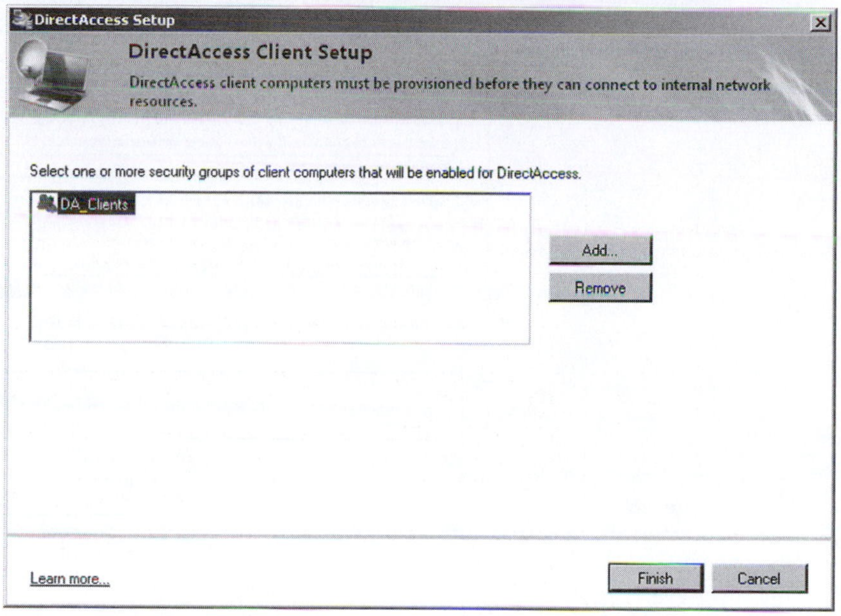

Figure 12-55

The DirectAccess Client Setup page on Windows Server 2008 R2

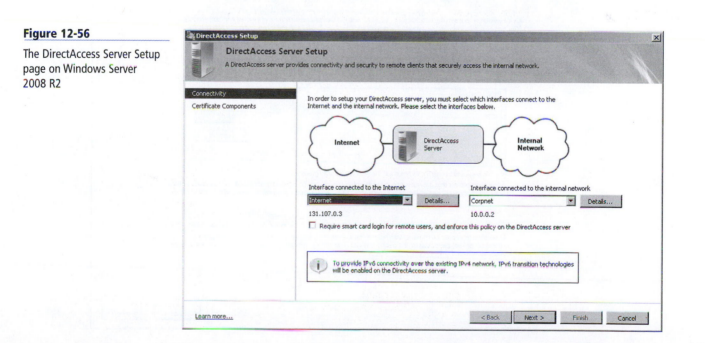

2. The *DirectAccess Server Setup* page appears, as shown in Figure 12-56, in which you specify which of the server's network interfaces provides access to the Internet and which to the intranet.

Figure 12-56

The DirectAccess Server Setup page on Windows Server 2008 R2

3. The *Infrastructure Server Setup* page appears, as shown in Figure 12-57, in which you specify the URL of the network location server.

Figure 12-57

The Infrastructure Server Setup page on Windows Server 2008 R2

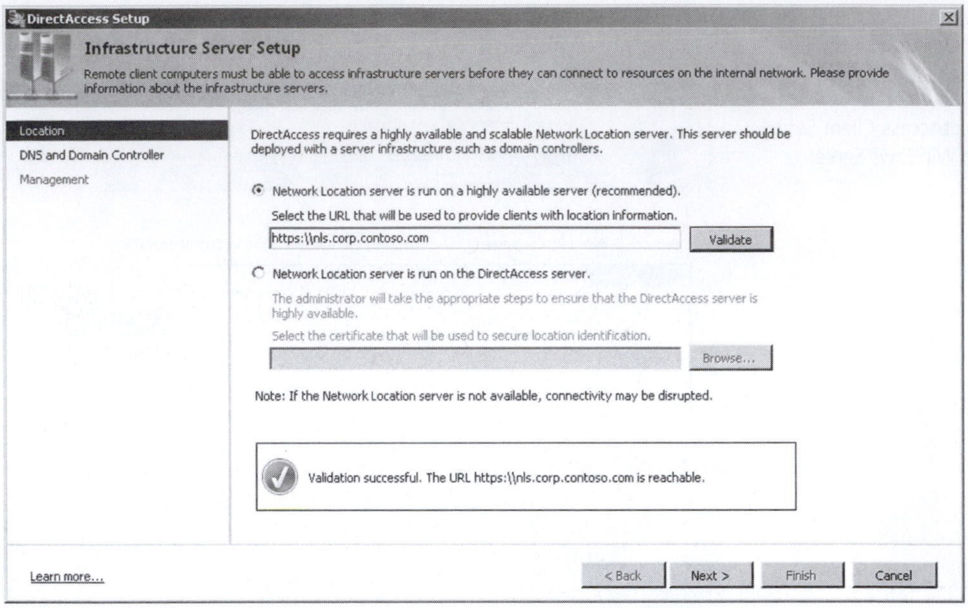

4. The *DirectAccess Application Server Setup* page appears, as shown in Figure 12-58, in which you identify the application servers that require authentication and specify the groups that can access specific applications.

Figure 12-58

The DirectAccess Application Server Setup page on Windows Server 2008 R2

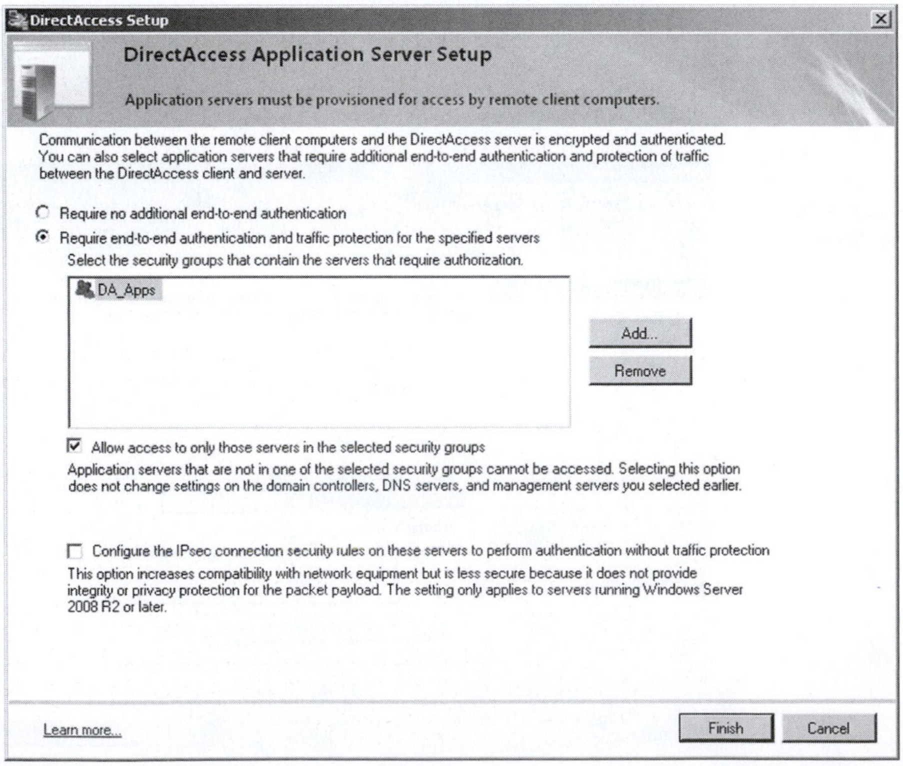

Although the clients do not have to be connected to the intranet as you perform the server setup, you must connect them afterward so they can receive the Group Policy settings that the setup process creates. To force a Group Policy update on a client, you can either restart the system or open a Command Prompt window, type the following command, and press Enter:

```
gpupdate -force
```

SKILL SUMMARY

IN THIS LESSON YOU LEARNED:

- Wired networks typically rely on physical security to protect the privacy of their communications. However, if a wireless network is not properly secured, an intruder in a car parked outside can use a laptop to gain full access to the network's communications.

- The 802.11 standards published by the Institute of Electrical and Electronic Engineers (IEEE) dictate the frequencies, transmission speeds, and ranges of wireless networking products.

- Windows Mobility Center is a shell application that provides a central point of access for many of the configuration settings that mobile computer users need frequently.

- Most laptop computers have the capability to connect an external display device, making it possible for a group of users to view the desktop without having to crowd around a single screen.

- To conserve battery power as much as possible, virtually all laptops include the hardware and firmware elements needed to dynamically adjust the power consumption of individual components.

- Windows 7 includes a dialog box that bundles together the configuration settings that users most often adjust before giving a presentation and make it possible to activate all of the settings with a single switch.

- Windows 7 includes the ability to store copies of network files on the local drive for use when the computer is disconnected.

- Sync Center is an application that functions as a central control panel for all of a Windows 7 computer's synchronization partnerships, including those with network drives and mobile devices.

- BitLocker encrypts all of the files on a volume, including operating system and application files, as well as paging files and temporary files, which can also contain sensitive information, and performs an integrity check before it permits the system to start.

- Windows 7 includes remote access client capabilities that enable users to connect to a network using dial-up or virtual private network (VPN) connections.

- In a virtual private network (VPN) connection, the remote client and the remote access server are both connected to the Internet, using local service providers. The client establishes a connection to the server using the Internet as a network medium and, after authentication, the server grants the client access to the network.

- Windows 7 and Windows Server 2008 R2 include a new remote access solution called DirectAccess, which enables clients to remain connected to their host networks whenever they have access to the Internet.

Knowledge Assessment

Matching

Complete the following exercise by matching the terms with their corresponding definitions.

    a. Implemented as VPN Reconnect
    b. Associated with user accounts
    c. BitLocker key storage
    d. Default VPN protocol in Windows 7
    e. Wireless security protocol
    f. Default VPN authentication protocol in Windows 7
    g. PPP frames carried inside datagrams
    h. Provides encryption and authentication services
    i. VPN protocol
    j. Uses CCMP encryption

_____ **1.** Layer 2 Tunneling Protocol (L2TP)

_____ **2.** EAP-MSCHAPv2

_____ **3.** MOBIKE

_____ **4.** Trusted Platform Module (TPM)

_____ **5.** WPA

_____ **6.** IPsec

_____ **7.** data recovery agent (DRA)

_____ **8.** Advanced Encryption System (AES)

_____ **9.** Internet Key Exchange, Version 2 (IKEv2)

_____ **10.** tunneling

Multiple Choice

Select one or more correct answers for each of the following questions.

1. Which of the following wireless networking standards uses spatial multiplexing to increase bandwidth?
   a. IEEE 802.11b
   b. IEEE 802.11g
   c. IEEE 802.11n
   d. IEEE 802.1X

2. Which of the following wireless security protocols is the most secure?
   a. WPA-TKIP
   b. WEP (128-bit) with 802.1X authentication
   c. WEP (128-bit)
   d. WPA-AES

3. Which of the following is the most secure password-based authentication protocol supported by the VPN client in Windows 7?
   a. EAP (PEAP)
   b. EAP-MSCHAPv2
   c. CHAP
   d. POP

4. Which of the following BitLocker operational modes must you configure using Group Policy? (Choose all correct answers.)
    a. TPM + startup PIN + startup key
    b. TPM + startup key
    c. TPM only
    d. Startup key only

5. Which of the following IPv6/IPv4 transition technologies takes the form of a hardware device?
    a. ISATAP
    b. 6to4
    c. NAT-PT
    d. Teredo

6. What is the main advantage of using DirectAccess over VPN connections?
    a. Users don't have to manually connect to the remote network
    b. DirectAccess uses IPv4 rather than IPv6
    c. DirectAccess supports more operating systems than VPNs
    d. DirectAccess connections are unidirectional

7. Which of the following is not a prerequisite for a DirectAccess server?
    a. Membership in an AD DS domain
    b. Two network interface adapters
    c. Two consecutive, public IPv4 addresses
    d. A NAT connection to the Internet

8. Which of the following tools can you use to import and export power management plans in Windows 7?
    a. Powercfg.exe and Group Policy
    b. The Power Options control panel only
    c. Powercg.exe only
    d. The Power Options control panel and Group Policy

9. Transparent caching saves temporary copies of files based on which of the following criteria?
    a. number of requests for the file
    b. user time limits
    c. file size
    d. network roundtrip latency

10. Which of the following steps in the DirectAccess connection establishment process occurs first?
    a. The client and the DirectAccess server authenticate each other using their computer certificates.
    b. The client attempts to connect to a designated network detection server on the intranet.
    c. The client establishes a connection to the domain controller and performs a standard AD DS user authentication.
    d. The client submits a health certificate to a Network Policy Server (NPS) on the host network.

Review Questions

1. Explain why it is preferable to use open system authentication on a wireless network using WEP, rather than shared secret authentication.
2. Explain how wireless networking products conforming to the IEEE 802.11n specification achieve their increases in transmission speed.

■ Case Scenarios

Scenario 12-1: Evaluating Wireless Security Risks

Mark Lee is a desktop technician at a large law firm. Law firms are among the slowest adopters of new technologies, and Mark's employer is no exception. The organization has, to date, not deployed a wireless network. After bringing up the benefits of wireless networks at a recent meeting with the IT staff, Mark was told that the company will not be deploying a wireless network for several years, if ever.

The lack of an IT-configured wireless network has not entirely stopped their adoption, however. Yesterday, Mark noticed a junior attorney surfing the web with his laptop in the lunchroom, without a network cable. When Mark asked the attorney how he was connected to the network, he confessed that he plugged a consumer WAP into the network port in his office.

Which of the following are potential risks of having a rogue wireless network in the office? (Choose all that apply.)

   a. An attacker with a wireless network card could join their Active Directory domain.

   b. An attacker could access hosts on the internal network from the lobby of the building with a wireless-enabled mobile computer.

   c. An attacker could use a wireless network card to capture traffic between two wired network hosts.

   d. An attacker could use the company's Internet connection from the lobby of the building with a wireless-enabled mobile computer.

   e. An attacker could capture an attorney's e-mail credentials as the attorney downloads his messages across the wireless link.

Scenario 12-2: Establishing a Wireless Networking Policy

After evaluating the risks of a rogue wireless network, Mark Lee decides that he must convince the IT director that the company needs a wireless network security policy even if they do not want to sponsor a wireless network. Which of the following strategies would reduce the risk of a security breach resulting from a rogue wireless network? (Choose all that apply.)

   a. Deploying an IT-managed WAP with WEP encryption and 802.1X authentication.

   b. Publishing instructions for other employees to access the current employee-managed WAP.

   c. Educating internal employees about the risks associated with wireless networks.

   d. Publishing a wireless network security policy forbidding employee-managed WAPs.

   e. Deploying an IT-managed WAP using open network authentication without encryption.

   f. Publishing a wireless network security policy allowing employee-managed WAPs, as long as they have authentication and encryption enabled.

Appendix A

Windows 7 Configuration: Exam 70-680

Objective Domain	Skill Number	Lesson Number
Installing, Upgrading, and Migrating to Windows 7		
Perform a clean installation.	1.1	1, 2
Upgrade to Windows 7 from previous versions of Windows.	1.2	1, 2
Migrate user profiles.	1.3	2
Deploying Windows 7		
Capture a system image.	2.1	3
Prepare a system image for deployment.	2.2	3
Deploy a system image.	2.3	3
Configure a VHD.	2.4	4
Configuring Hardware and Applications		
Configure devices.	3.1	4
Configure application compatibility.	3.2	7
Configure application restrictions.	3.3	7
Configure Internet Explorer.	3.4	7
Configuring Network Connectivity		
Configure IPv4 network settings.	4.1	5
Configure IPv6 network settings.	4.2	5
Configure networking settings.	4.3	5, 12
Configure Windows Firewall.	4.4	10
Configure remote management.	4.5	11
Configuring Access to Resources		
Configure shared resources.	5.1	6
Configure file and folder access.	5.2	6, 10
Configure user account control (UAC).	5.3	9

(continued)

OBJECTIVE DOMAIN	SKILL NUMBER	LESSON NUMBER
Configure authentication and authorization.	5.4	10
Configure BranchCache.	5.5	11
Configuring Mobile Computing		
Configure BitLocker and BitLocker To Go.	6.1	12
Configure DirectAccess.	6.2	12
Configure mobility options.	6.3	12
Configure remote connections.	6.4	12
Monitoring and Maintaining Systems that Run Windows 7		
Configure updates to Windows 7.	7.1	8
Manage disks.	7.2	4
Monitor systems.	7.3	8
Configure performance settings.	7.4	8
Configuring Backup and Recovery		
Configure backup.	8.1	11
Configure system recovery options.	8.2	11
Configure file recovery options.	8.3	11

Windows 7 Configuration, Exam 70-680: Lab to Textbook Mapping

LAB	TEXTBOOK LESSON	EXAM OBJECTIVE COVERED
1. Upgrading to Windows 7	2	1.2
2. Migrating User Profiles	2	1.3
3. Installing Windows 7	1 & 2	1.1
4. Capturing a Reference Image	3	2.1, 2.2
5. Deploying a Captured Image	3	2.3
6. Working with Disks	4	2.4, 7.2
7. Configuring Network Connections	5	4.1, 4.2, 4.3
8. Working with Shares	6	5.1, 5.2
9. Working with Printers	6	3.1, 5.1
10. Configuring Applications	7	3.2, 3.3, 3.4
11. Managing and Monitoring Performance	8	7.1, 7.3, 7.4
12. Working with Workgroups and Domains	9	5.3
13. Configuring Security Settings	10	4.4, 5.4
14. Remote Windows 7 Administration	11	4.5
15. Administering Windows 7	11	5.5, 8.1, 8.2, 8.3
16. Configuring Mobile Options	12	6.1, 6.3
17. Configuring Mobile Connectivity	12	4.3, 6.2
18. Troubleshooting Windows 7	11	N/A

Index

itacademy.microsoftelearning.com

r   my.ncu.edu